THE POLITICS OF CULTURE IN

THE SHADOW OF CAPITAL

POST-CONTEMPORARY INTERVENTIONS

Series Editors: Stanley Fish and Fredric Jameson

The

POLITICS

of CULTURE

in the SHADOW

of CAPITAL

Edited by LISA LOWE

and DAVID LLOYD

Duke University Press

Durham & London

1997

© *1997 Duke University Press*

All rights reserved   Printed in the United
States of America on acid-free paper ∞
Typeset in Sabon 3 with Scala Sans display
by Keystone Typesetting, Inc.
Library of Congress Cataloging-in-Publication
Data appear on the last printed page of
this book.

CONTENTS

ACKNOWLEDGMENTS

This project has been inspired by so many conversations and encounters that it is impossible for us to acknowledge them all. Our learning from friends, colleagues, and students in different locations has been an unceasing source of encouragement. We hope that all those who have in their generosity wittingly or unwittingly assisted over the years will find *The Politics of Culture in the Shadow of Capital* a fitting tribute.

This work emerged from our sympathies with struggles in the United States and worldwide: with the opposition to the war in Iraq, with the decolonizing movements of East Timor, Ireland, and South Africa, with the struggles against racism and state-sanctioned wars against migrants and minorities in Europe and North America, and with those organizing locally and across borders against exploitation and patriarchy. Our hope is that this book will contribute in some way to the survival and legibility of such struggles and of those who have dedicated themselves to them.

The Politics of Culture in the Shadow of Capital has been from the start an intensely collaborative effort. Our first thanks go, of course, to the contributors. The work here is the product of their engagements with one another: their willingness to offer, exchange, and receive critique. So many of the contributors, including ourselves, have shifted, rethought, and revised as a result of being in dialogue with one another and with the project. To the writing of the introduction and the shaping of the book, they have all directly or indirectly contributed. Yet we would also like to acknowledge Dipesh Chakrabarty, Donald Lowe, and Aihwa Ong, who each gave us particularly valuable comments on the introductory essay. We also thank those whose work informed and friendship sustained us throughout the vicissitudes of realizing this project: Sandra Azeredo, Homi Bhabha, Judith Butler, Angela Davis, Ann duCille, Yen Le Espiritu, Takashi Fujitani, Rosemary Marangoly George, Luke Gibbons, David Gutiérrez, Judith Halberstam, Elaine Kim, George Lipsitz, Chandra Talpade Mohanty, Satya Mohanty, Michael Omi, Camillo Penna, Naoki Sakai, José David Saldívar, Rosaura Sanchez, and Lisa Yoneyama.

We have also received material and practical support that made it possible to bring the many contributors together, some needing to travel great distances. A University of California Organized Research

Group in the Humanities Grant permitted us to begin the work in 1992. William Simmons, Dean of Social Sciences at the University of California, Berkeley, and Anthony Newcomb, Dean of Humanities at the University of California, Berkeley, provided the resources for a colloquium in 1994 at which the contributors discussed their work with one another. The University of California Humanities Research Institute at Irvine offered us accommodations and meeting space for that colloquium; we thank the staff at the Institute for their cheerful assistance. We thank also the Departments of Literature and Ethnic Studies at the University of California, San Diego, and the Department of English and Comparative Literature at the University of California, Irvine: their generosity and support gave us a year together in which we could work consistently on the book and on our introduction.

Ken Wissoker has been for us, as ever, an editor without compare: we are grateful for his faith in the project. More than an editor, he has been our friend. Finally, at different moments, we have had indispensable practical help and editorial assistance from Grace Kyungwon Hong, Helen Heran Jun, Eithne Luibheid, and Chandan Reddy. Victor Bascara was the "midwife" whose knowledge and patience was crucial in the last stages of manuscript preparation; Helen Jun compiled the index. We thank them all not only for their labor but for their humor, intelligence, and friendship. Without them, *The Politics of Culture in the Shadow of Capital* might never have been realized.

A different kind of acknowledgment goes to our three children: Sam Pauwels Lloyd, Talia Pauwels Lloyd, and Juliet Lowe Nebolon; their loving presences renew and sustain us. To them and to their futures this book is dedicated.

We thank the publishers for permission to republish the following essays, which appeared previously as follows: Aihwa Ong, "The Gender and Labor Politics of Postmodernity," *Annual Review of Anthropology* 20 (1991): 279–309. Reynaldo Ileto, "Outlines of a Nonlinear Emplotment of Philippine History," in *Reflections on Development in Southeast Asia*, ed. Lim Teck Ghee (Singapore: ASEAN Economic Research Unit, Institute of Southeast Asian Studies, 1988). David Lloyd, "Nationalisms Against the State: Towards a Critique of the Anti-Nationalist Prejudice," in *Gender and Colonialism*, ed. Timothy Foley, Lionel Pilkington, Sean Ryder, and Elizabeth Tilley (Galway, Ireland: Galway University Press, 1995). Lisa Lowe, "Work, Immigration, Gender: Asian 'American' Women," in *Immigrant Acts: On Asian American Cultural Politics* (Durham: Duke University Press, 1996). Chungmoo Choi, "The Discourse of Decolonization and Popular Memory:

South Korea," *positions: east asia cultures critique* 1, no. 1 (spring 1993): 77–102. Arturo Escobar, "Cultural Politics and Biological Diversity: State, Capital, and Social Movements on the Pacific Coast of Colombia," in *Between Resistance and Revolution: Cultural Politics and Social Protest*, ed. Richard G. Fox and Orin Starn, copyright © 1997 by Rutgers, The State University. Reprinted by permission of Rutgers University Press. Jacqueline Urla, "Outlaw Language: Creating Alternative Public Spheres in Basque Free Radio," *Pragmatics* vol. 5, no. 2 (June 1995): 245–261.

LISA LOWE AND DAVID LLOYD

Introduction

The Politics of Culture in the Shadow of Capital is a collection of essays that, in their combination, advance a critical approach to the "international," the "global," or the "transnational" as theoretical frameworks within which intersecting sets of social practices can be grasped. These practices include anticolonial and antiracist struggles, feminist struggles, labor organizing, cultural movements — all of which challenge contemporary neocolonial capitalism as a highly differentiated mode of production. While such practices are ubiquitous, they generally take place in local and heterogeneous sites, and rarely make the claim to be "global" models in scope or ambition. Accordingly, the kind of intervention that *The Politics of Culture* makes has become necessary insofar as neither the postmodern conception of the transnational nor the liberal assumption of the congruence of capitalism, democracy, and freedom are currently adequate to address the ubiquity and variety of alternatives.

We understand the transnational to denote the stage of globalized capitalism characterized by David Harvey, Fredric Jameson, and others as the universal extension of a differentiated mode of production that relies on flexible accumulation and mixed production to incorporate all sectors of the global economy into its logic of commodification.[1] It is the tendency of such understandings of transnationalism to assume a homogenization of global culture that radically reduces possibilities for the creation of alternatives, in confining them either to the domain of commodified culture itself or to spaces that, for reasons of mere historical contingency, have seemed unincorporated into globalization.[2] It will be our contention, to the contrary, that transnational or *neocolonial* capitalism, like colonialist capitalism before it, continues to produce sites of contradiction that are effects of its always uneven expansion but that cannot be subsumed by the logic of commodification itself. We suggest that "culture" obtains a "political" force when a cultural formation comes into contradiction with economic or political logics that try to refunction it for exploitation or domination. Rather than adopting the understanding of culture as one sphere in a set of differentiated spheres and practices, we discuss "culture" as a terrain in which politics, culture, and the economic form an inseparable dynamic. This entails not simply a critique of liberal cultural, political, and legal theories that are the social correlative of capitalist economics, but an affirmative inventory of the survival of alternatives in many locations worldwide. Our interest is not in identifying what lies "outside" capitalism, but in what arises historically, in contestation, and "in difference" to it.

Marxism has always theorized capitalism in relation to its globalizing tendencies and accordingly sought to link struggles internationally; the work collected here is in agreement with the importance of such linking.[3] In this introduction, we seek to rethink the older Marxist notion of internationalism in light of the present conjuncture. The limit of this older notion lies in the difficulty of conceptualizing an international proletarian formation within the current global restructuring of capitalism. Since that formation was principally thought in terms of class antagonism within national capitalist state relations, the fact that transnational capitalism now operates at levels that are at once subnational and supranational interrupts the even formation of a uniform proletariat and demands a more differentiated understanding of what constitutes political processes and activities. The challenge to the privileging of class antagonism as the exclusive site of contradiction requires a critique of Western Marxism's assumption of the universality of capitalist development and of the need to "delink" individual national economies.[4] We are arguing for the equal importance of sites of struggle that do not privilege the nation and are not necessarily defined by class consciousness. This is not a question of integrating oppositional formations such as peasant revolts, feminist struggles, antiracist or anti-imperialist movements into a politics ultimately defined by class struggle; rather, these struggles in themselves occupy significant sites of contradiction that are generated precisely by the differentiating process of advanced globalizing capitalism. We would contend, furthermore, that these oppositional formations are neither novel nor outmoded. On the contrary, the critical displacement of "modern" modes of opposition — particularly state nationalism and Western Marxism — permits us to see how feminist, antiracist, and subaltern struggles, in their continual adaptations and transformations over time, have the potential to rework the conception of politics in the era of transnational capital itself.

In assuming the relative autonomy of different sites of contradiction, we are not only signaling the inadequacy of present theoretical frameworks for the "global," but are also making an intervention as to the location of theory. However enabling at one point, the "center-periphery" model of both economic and cultural relations cannot survive a recognition of the heterogeneity of the contemporary capitalist mode of production. For the automatic assumption that theory emanates from the West and has as its object the untheorized practices of the subaltern, the native, and the non-West, cannot be sustained.[5] To "short-circuit" the notion that theory, like capital, flows or travels in one direction from West to non-West, we have brought together essays that make connections between local sites of production, that focus insistently on situated theories and practices as well as the translations and transformations of imported theories in those sites.[6] The challenge to the unidirectional and hierarchical schematic binary "West/non-West" involves the displacement of concepts and practices of "development" and challenges the uniform applications of Western Marxism in all places. That is, by "Western Marxism" we do not mean only Marxism as it is practiced in the West, but rather the adoption of its developmental terms and teleology in other sites. For this reason, a number of the discussions included here consider the transformation of "Marxist" theories and practices in colonized, postindependence, and neocolonized sites. In this sense, we bring together national Marxist, "third world" feminist, and subaltern projects, and note that one effect of this is to highlight the insufficiency of concepts of political agency that are defined within the modern Western nation-state in terms of specific practices governed by the separation of the spheres of politics, culture, and the economic. We will be arguing for the need to reconceive the "social" — as the terrain in which politics, culture, and the economic are related — in terms radically other than those given by post-Enlightenment rationalizations of Western society. This separation of spheres that constitutes "society" is seen in liberal legal and political philosophy to emerge alongside capitalism as a product of historical development. While Marxism arises as the critique of capitalist exploitation, it has not critiqued the theory of historical development that underlies liberal philosophies.

Liberalism and Western Marxism, along with other emancipatory discourses of modernity, share a foundation in what Walter Benjamin refers to as "historicism," that is, the conception of history as the narrative of the development of modern subjects and cultures. For liberalism, historicist temporality entails the gradual emergence of civil society and the citizen-subject of the state out of the barbaric prehistory of human society; for Marxism, the development of proletarian class consciousness out of the contradictions of capital and labor. Both superordinate one particular understanding of what constitutes the "political" over all other forms of opposition or sociality; in consequence, those other forms are relegated to marginality or temporal anteriority. Modern colonialism involved the extension of historicist logic on a global scale: colonized societies were assigned to the prehistory of the West, and political resistance could only be recognized as such insofar as it was organized through nationalisms that took as their object the capture of the colonial state and the formation of modern institutions and subjects. As Partha Chatterjee and Benedict Anderson, and Frantz Fanon before them, have pointed out, bourgeois nationalism is the form in which colonized societies enter modernity.[7] So saturated is historical narrative with assumptions of development that it has been virtually impossible to write the history of alternative modes.

In considering practices that are not adequately revealed by the developmental temporality of the model of state formation, we turn away from the assumption that the critique of modernity and modern institutions is registered within the temporality of the "postmodern." Rather, the essays in *The Politics of Culture* focus especially on locations at odds with the modern institutions of the state that are produced *simultaneously* with state regulations and the intrusions of capital. These locations refer neither to "postmodernism" per se, with the emphasis on a posterior temporality, nor to the concept of "tradition," with its emphasis on anteriority; rather, the essays are interested in another understanding of the temporality of the breakup of modernity, taking into account the antagonisms to modernity that take place in a variety of locations and that emerge simultaneously with and in relation to modernity itself. In their different ways, subaltern historiography, feminist historiography, and some postcolonial critiques have attempted to intervene in developmental historicism by refusing the tendency of historicism to view its objects as representative instances within a totalized, developmental teleology. The essays in this volume by and large put into relief the relatively autonomous meaning of the singular instance without needing to reinscribe it as a founding moment in an oppositional narrative of emancipation. The critique of temporality implied by the choices made in these essays suggests the reconceptualization of history and historical material. In Benjamin's terms, the critique of "the historical progress of mankind" dislocates the material event "out of the continuum of history." It is just this distinction between the universalizing secular time of historicism and "the time of the gods" that is the subject of Dipesh Chakrabarty's critique of modernity, as he contemplates the modern historian's translation of nonsecular phenomenologies of labor in South Asia. Reynaldo Ileto's essay, in turn, emphasizes that the reconstruction of Philippine "banditry" and popular medical practices of the *curanderos* demand historiographical forms that displace the modern linear narratives of either colonial or nationalist histories. We can understand C. L. R. James's act in bringing the Haitian revolution to bear on African decolonization, discussed in Grant Farred's essay, as retrieving similar moments that Benjamin would regard as "lost for history" and grasping their "retroactive force." George Lipsitz, in his essay, likewise reclaims what Marx called the "unvanquished remnants of the past" in recollecting Black soldiers' antagonisms to U.S. imperial wars in Japan and in the Philippines: the meaning of such moments lies not in their inaugural force within a preordained narrative, but in the possibilities opened by their recovery. José Rabasa understands Zapatismo as the irruption of nonmodern cultural forms into the modern state, the significance of which does not depend on projecting the rebellions as either the culmination of a continuous historical development or the avant-garde of national revolution.

The other impulse of the critique is the excavation and connection of alternative histories and their different temporalities that cannot be contained by the progressive narrative of Western developmentalism. Rather than striving to universalize their instances by way of such a narrative, many of the essays signal the need to shift to other frames that permit a comprehension of the lateral relationships between sites in which alternative practices emerge. *The Politics of Culture* includes essays that document exchanges and collaborations across sites, connecting subjugated practices that cut across the orthodox categories that have organized historical understanding: the people, the nation, the epoch, the state. These connections are documented in Clara Connolly and Pragna Patel's essay on coalitions of Middle Eastern, South Asian, and Irish immigrant women in Britain, and in Homa Hoodfar's study of veiling as a highly differentiated Islamic social practice in which modernity and fundamentalism are negotiated. Forging connections is no less important in the above-mentioned historical retrievals that link U.S. Black soldiers in World War II and Japanese Americans interned in camps on the west coast of the United States, and the Haitian revolution with African anticolonial movements. Likewise, the collection suggests lateral connections that may yet be possible: the work of Dipesh Chakrabarty and José Rabasa explicitly connects subaltern studies in India and subaltern studies in Latin America. Through Connolly and Patel's essay, the interview with Angela Davis, and Lisa Lowe's essay, potential connections emerge between the Black feminist movement in Britain and the political struggles of racialized and immigrant women in the United States. Many of the essays discuss alternative political cultures: Jacqueline Urla considers the construction of an alternative public sphere through Basque youth media in Spain; Arturo Escobar discusses the politics of race and development in the context of

Afro-Columbian environmental movements; Nandi Bhatia and Chung-moo Choi both elaborate the political cultures of anticolonial movements through analyses of people's theater in India and South Korea, respectively.

Evidently, the connections explored here are not predicated on a "cosmopolitanism" and its elitist and universalizing purview but, on the contrary, adamantly emphasize diversely localized projects and struggles. Though in a general sense most of the essays address what might be called the "postcolonial" period, we wish to distinguish the work here from the "postcolonial" concept. That is, we understand the postcolonial, as Chungmoo Choi does in her essay, as marking the decisive defining moment of struggle as independence and what happens after, as prioritizing (even in its deconstruction) Western modernity and non-Western hybridity, and as privileging the capture of the state and the relationship between state formations. In contradistinction, we consider here connections and struggles that are ongoing and simultaneous with, but not less important than, state nationalisms — theories and practices that cross national boundaries that need not be mediated by the state, the form in which the West is instantiated. Such connections provide the ground for rethinking the notion of the "political" in terms distinct from those defined by the state and state formations. Insofar as anticolonial struggles have been directed at the capture of the state and the inhabiting of its political forms, then, as Fanon argues, the articulation of such struggles took place in terms of "rights" and "citizenship," through forms like the "nationalist party," modern media like the press, and by way of national bourgeois capital. Elite nationalism and anticolonialism have sought to absorb subaltern struggles into uniformity with the terms of the political sphere, or, where that proved impossible, to subjugate or marginalize them as "feminine" or "racialized" spaces. We wish to understand these subjugated or ignored struggles not as the detritus of history, but as the work of a still ongoing decolonization, the place of different social imaginaries and formations, actively preserved and invented. This implies, in turn, the need to reconceive the sites and ends of cultural struggle. Owing to the history of colonialism underpinning the current global restructuring of capitalism, the "cultural" in colonized sites, far from being rationalized as a separate sphere as it was with Western capitalist social formations, actually embodies, and is the form of, alternative rationalities. The subordinated culture's difference and incommensurability with the economic and political operations of the colonial power, along with the hybridities, damages, and recalcitrances that are produced by colonization, make spaces for alternative practices, alternative public spheres, unofficial countercultures, and the remaking of official civil society and its divisions.[8] Our discussion of the redefined notion of culture will be taken up in the last section.

NATIONALISM, MARXISM, FEMINISM, AND
THE QUESTION OF ALTERNATIVES

As Arturo Escobar has argued, in the period following World War II the domination by the West through direct colonialisms is transformed into a global project of domination by way of modernization and development.[9] For this period, the state is the principal form demanded of postcolonial nations in order that they can provide the body of institutions through which modernization is imposed. Etienne Balibar argues that, practically speaking, the state is the form through which nations enter the modern world system.[10] But the state form entails more than a pragmatic adjustment to that world system; it implies not only an assimilation to a hierarchized system of global power, but compliance with a normative distribution of social spaces within that state's definitions. The entry of the nation through the medium of the modern state into the global world system requires the massive conversion of populations and their cultural forms into conformity with the post–World War II project of universal modernization. Civil society must be reshaped to produce subjects who might function in terms of modern definitions of social spaces, as the political subject of the state, the economic subject of capitalism, and the cultural subject of the nation, however much the discreteness of these spaces is contradicted by conditions that are lived as racialized and gendered labor stratification, apartheid, and poverty. The state form's importance extends beyond the immediate post–World War II geopolitical system; we would wish to maintain that even in the post-Fordist, postmodern transnational economy, the modern state form and its contradictions persist within the mobility of global capital as the primary set of institutions for regulating resources, investments, and populations. Hence the state becomes the site of contradictions and the object of contestation for political projects such as bourgeois nationalism, Marxism, and feminism.[11] To a large extent, the state defines the terms and stakes of these projects: the continuing extension and redefinition of popular democracy or citizenship and the promotion of national culture; the antagonism to regulation of labor on behalf of national and international capital; the contestation of the legal and social subordination of racialized populations and women within the context of a discourse on "rights." In different ways, bourgeois nationalist, Marxist, and feminist movements confront the limits of state-oriented definitions both in the form of the direct antagonism of the state and in the form of the alternative spheres and practices that emerge in the very formation of modernity itself. The contradictions of modernity are not new, though they may take new forms at any given historical moment; they are embedded in the history of colonization and of global capitalism and have been constitutive in the emergence of contemporary social formations. It will be our contention here that productive rethinkings of the categories of these movements take place through the alternative formations that emerge in the space of contradictions.

Nationalism

The nationalism articulated in Western state formations posits a historical continuity between the emergence of a people and the development of the state that represents its political sovereignty.[12] But even contemporary Western theorists of nations and nationalism, such as Gellner, Hobsbawm, Nairn, and Breuilly, do not fundamentally challenge this assumption. The emergence of the nation-state is largely understood in contemporary history as a Western development and as a more or less organic emergence of European civilizations. Even where contemporary historians are skeptical of the nineteenth-century backward projection of the "spirit of the nation" into primordial origins, and prefer the concept of the "invented tradition" by which the people is constituted retrospectively by the modern political imagination, the territorial boundaries and historical claims to legitimacy of modern European nations are accepted as givens of Western modernity. Correspondingly, the European nation-state remains the template of proper political formations globally despite the singularity, from a genuinely world-historical perspective, of its formation. The historical or temporal dimension of the nation, the development and maturation of civil and political society and the formation of their proper subjects, and the spatial dimension, what Akhil Gupta and James Ferguson call "the isomorphism of place, culture, nation, and state," provide the terms to which the political formations of other societies are required to conform or approximate.[13]

Following such theories of the nation-state and of nationalism as a political force, the emergence of the European nation-state and its political ideology is distinct from the forms of anticolonial or "belated" nationalism. Not all thinkers demarcate European from non-European nationalisms as strictly as Hans Kohn in his seminal distinction of

"Western" from "non-Western" forms, but the tendency to make such distinctions is virtually ubiquitous.[14] What is being marked in this kind of formulation is a certain incommensurability between the cultural forms of non-Western societies and the political forms they have sought or been obliged to adopt in the course of decolonization. From the perspective of Western modernity, this incommensurability is perceived as a lack, and the remedy is generally held to be the state-directed development of a mature civil society with its corresponding ethical civil subjects. This prescription is the political correlative of capitalist economic development as imposed by Western-dominated international organizations. Both prescriptions preclude the emergence of alternatives out of contradictions with equal force and constitute the leading edge of neocolonialism as powerfully in the era of transnational capital as at any previous moment.

Contradiction is virtually constitutive of the practices of anticolonial nationalism. On the one hand, the ends of anticolonial nationalism are defined by the goal of the capture of the state, and its ideology is in large part structured in terms of liberal discourses and for liberal state institutions: it speaks of rights and the citizen, of equality, fraternity, and liberty, makes its claims to self-determination on the basis of enlightenment universality, and asserts the cultural if not economic and military equivalence of its nation-people to that of the imperial power. At the same time, within the terms of an anticolonial struggle, it is rare for a nationalist movement not to draw on conceptions of "tradition," of cultural antimodernity, and indeed, of alternatives to capitalist development in order to mobilize the antagonism of the populace against the colonial power and to mark the differences that transform that populace into a people with a legitimate right to separate and sovereign statehood. In this, nationalism repeats the very distinction between tradition and modernity that colonialism institutes to legitimate domination. In the first place, this demands the transformation of the colonial model that largely assumes that tradition must be reformed by modernization. Instead nationalism invokes tradition in order to assert the antagonism between irreconcilable social and cultural values. For this reason, in fact, the moment of anticolonial struggle is generally very productive of "emancipatory" possibilities far in excess of nationalism's own projects, a point to which we shall return. But the ultimate fixation of anticolonial nationalism on the state form tends to reproduce the articulation of tradition and modernity by which traditional society requires to be modernized — even if the forms of postcolonial modernity are modified to accommodate a fetishized version of tradition through which a distinct people is to be interpellated by the nation-state. State nationalism then seeks to mask the contradictions that reemerge between formal political independence and economic dependence (the contradictions of neocolonialism) and to contain the excess of alternatives released by the decolonizing forces of which it was a part.

We would want, therefore, to distinguish, but not separate out, state-oriented nationalism from a larger and potentially more productive decolonizing process that emerges and persists in the very contradictions of colonialism in all its stages. As a range of anticolonial intellectuals from Fanon to Cabral argue, racialization of the colonized population is fundamental to the dynamics of colonial society, constituting the principal impetus that brings nationalist movements into being.[15] The racialization of all colonized subjects permits what Bipan Chandra analyzes as the nationalist "vertical integration" of the caste- and class-stratified colonial society, and enables the nationalist movement to cut across such distinctions.[16] Bourgeois nationalism tends to reshape its antiracist practices and ideologies around a notion of the nation's capacity to develop and assimilate European cultural and political forms. Popular movements, on the contrary, organize around antagonisms to colonialism that are founded on an understanding of racialized exploitation under colonialism that leads to modes of decolonization aimed at creating new and radically democratic forms of social organization. This latter decolonizing process is what Fanon terms, in his broad sense, "national culture," as opposed to bourgeois nationalism's fetishization of selected and canonized "traditions," which artificially freeze cultural difference, reintroducing or reinforcing lines of ethnic or "tribal" stratification within the new nation. With regard to the new nation's external relations to global capitalism and neocolonial powers, the fixing of popular culture into artificial national forms and the racial stratification of society helps to reproduce the concept of a specific "underdevelopment" that facilitates and legitimates neocolonialist exploitation.

Although nationalism seeks, in the Gramscian sense, to direct popular forces, and thereby to gain hegemony over them, it is in fact constituted within a rich site of intersections among simultaneous social processes and modes of organization, which include not only antiracism but linked practices such as subaltern agitation and women's movements, to which nationalism contributes in often unpredictable ways and by which it is inflected at every moment. In *Feminism and Nationalism in the Third World,* Kumari Jayawardena has documented the conditions within which nationalist struggles can furnish some spaces for feminist practice and politics.[17] In this vein, David

Lloyd's essay examines early twentieth-century Ireland, in which Markievicz conjoined Irish feminism with nationalism by redefining the terms of suffrage and of political citizenship. But these alternative practices have their own histories and trajectories, which are not synchronous with the nationalist project of state formation. Focus on nationalism accordingly not only obscures the ways in which alternative social processes, both within the anticolonial struggle and across the longer duration of what we conceive of as decolonization, work concomitantly with and through nationalism; this focus also renders invisible the fact that such struggle occupies another terrain constituted by its externality to the state and shaped by the rhythms of different temporalities. This is at once a historiographical question and suggestive regarding contemporary contradictions. For example, in his essay in this volume, Reynaldo C. Ileto has shown the ways in which Philippine nationalist historiography tends to repeat imperial histories in relegating alternative social formations to the violent and irrational manifestations of "banditry" or, at best, protonationalist consciousness. When the antagonism between colonialism and nationalism is considered the only legitimate site for the political, it relegates alternatives to the domain "outside of history," and obscures the ongoing constitution of other social formations through contemporary antagonisms. For the antagonism between nationalism and imperialism also unleashed other contradictions than those addressed by decolonizing or nationalist movements specifically. This becomes evident in Nandi Bhatia's essay, which discusses an anti-imperial movement that mobilized class antagonism and came into conflict with elite nationalism as much as with British colonialism. The retrieval of such spaces and struggles that are by definition at odds with state projects and elite nationalism has been the characteristic work of subaltern and feminist historiographies, though we will take up later the different emphases of both projects.

Marxism

Bhatia's essay on Indian People's Theatre underscores one of the primary theses of our introduction: that Marxist theory and practice have been crucial correctives to bourgeois nationalism. For although Marxism has tended to share with nationalism the political frame of the nation-state, it has consistently critiqued forms of bourgeois and cultural nationalism that ignore class difference. The classical Marxist understanding of contradiction asserts that the contradiction between capital and labor takes place within the totality of nationalist capitalist relations, and that the exacerbation of contradiction is part of a progressive development that includes the emergence of proletarian consciousness within that totality. For Western Marxism, the proletarian subject emerges primarily in relation to the goal of the capture of the state: in an earlier form in Leninism, dictatorship of the proletariat, in a later form in Gramsci, the construction of working-class hegemony through institutions Gramsci describes as institutions of the ethical state. Gramsci's refinement of the Leninist position for less autocratic states than czarist Russia suggests that the emergence of working-class hegemony necessitates a detour through "culture" by means of working-class consciousness and concomitant cultural forms. It is further assumed that the territorial basis of this culture is national, and that there is a correspondence between a national popular culture and political hegemony; the state that is to be captured is ultimately the expression of that correspondence. Whereas Gramsci would seem to be the Western theorist of Marxism who, through the discussion of the Southern Question, links analysis of the democratic industrial state with the different issues and conditions that affect colonized regions, what he in fact marks are problems of uneven cultural and political, as well as economic, development. We observe that "third world" Marxisms emerge not only from what Western Marxism would designate as such unevennesses, but from entirely different conditions and social formations. In particular, the condition of these Marxisms is that the forms of state and the forms of culture are incompatible. The work collected in this volume is, in part, exploring the question of "third world" Marxism and the specific conjunctures out of which it emerges.

Our critique of Western Marxism, then, is at one with our critique of the developmental narratives of Western modernity, but does not extend to the materialism that founds Marx's method. Rather, "third world" Marxisms, we would emphasize, already diverge from the classical Western Marxist formulation, having sought to come to terms with the intersection of colonization of largely agrarian societies with capitalist exploitation. The differences of Leninism in Bolshevik Russia or Maoism in revolutionary China are precisely an effect of their analyses of different material and historical conditions. Donald Lowe has argued that while the orientalist construction of the "Asiatic mode of production" within Western Marxism had fixed understandings of "China" and other peasant societies in a static, unchanging concept of "underdevelopment," the "later" Lenin and Mao rethought Marxism for Russia and China not in relation to "underdevelopment" but through the understanding that peasant societies are materially different and contain different historical possibilities for transformation.[18] The rethinking of Marxism by Lenin and Mao for their societies is echoed in the rethinking of Marxism in other contexts. For example, Dipesh Chakrabarty has demonstrated in his study of the Calcutta jute mill workers between 1890 and 1940 that the reproduction of capitalist social relations did not necessarily pass through European-style proletarianization but through cultural forms quite incompatible with that model of development; his essay here offers further reflection on the translation of difference into the terms of Marx's labor theory of value.[19] Aihwa Ong has similarly argued that Malaysian factory women protest capitalist discipline not through Western class consciousness or feminist consciousness but by stopping production on the factory floor through local cultural forms like spirit possession.[20] Both arguments are materialist in their modes of investigation, yet clearly demand a rethinking of classic Marxist formulations. In our critical engagement with Marxist theory, there are two axes of analysis that concern us: one is the emergence of new forms of political subjectivity, the other is the domain of race and culture in relation to the transformation of capitalist social relations; both, of course, are closely related.

Western Marxism assumes that conflicts that fall "outside" the development of class consciousness are politically subordinate, or constitute "false consciousness": antagonisms articulated, for example, around gender or race, are seen as effects of a more fundamental contradiction. According to the same logic, it also assumes the necessity of a globalization of capitalist proletarianization that would privilege the locations of greatest modernization and development in ways that obscure the historical expansion of capital through uneven differentiation of geographies, sectors, and labor forces. Thus far, we agree with the postmodern critiques of Western Marxism that argue that, contrary to its classical formulation by Marx, capitalism has proceeded not through global homogenization but through differentiation of labor markets, material resources, consumer markets, and production operations. But we wish to add that it is not simply that there has not been an even, homogeneous spread of development, but that, in what Bipan Chandra has called the "colonial mode of production," different problems emerge in the encounter between "indigenous" forms of work and cultural practices and the modern capitalist economic modes imposed upon them.[21] Whereas the relations of production of nineteenth-century industrial capitalism were characterized by the management of the urban workers by the urban bourgeoisie, colonialism was built on the racialized split between colonial metropolis and agrarian colony, organizing the agrarian society into a social formation in which a foreign class functioned as the capitalist class. In order to maximize the extraction of surplus, the necessary reproduction of the relations of production in the colonial mode was not limited to the reproduction of class relations, but emphasized also that of hierarchical relations of region, culture, language, and, especially, race. In *Reading Capital,* Louis Althusser and Etienne Balibar extend Marx's original formulation of the relationship between the "mode of production" and the "social formation" by defining a social formation as the complex structure in which more than one mode of production, or set of economic relations, may be combined.[22] Their elaboration suggests not only that the situations of uneven development, colonialist incorporation, and global restructuring and immigration are each characterized by the combination of several simultaneous modes of production, but that each constitutes a specific, historically distinct social formation (that includes economic, political, and ideological levels of articulation). The need to understand the differentiated forms through which capital profits through mixing and combining different modes of production suggests, too, that the complex structures of a new social formation may indeed require interventions and modes of opposition specific to those structures. Whereas Western Marxism assumes to a greater or lesser extent the correspondence of the institutions of civil society to the needs of the reproduction of capitalist social relations, in colonial and neocolonial social formations there arise what we might term "discoordinated" structures of civil society, which in themselves mediate a disjunction between existing cultural practices and the modernizing forces embodied in the rationalizing forms of civil society put in place by the nation-state.

That "discoordination," although it is not always theorized as such, can be understood as requiring us to think the existence of different historical temporalities that are simultaneously active within a given social formation. At the level of political analysis, "third world" or national Marxisms, as in the work of Fanon and Cabral, have always understood the necessity for mobilizing anticolonial resistance around the antagonism between indigenous social forms and the colonial state; class relations themselves in the colonial state are always already predicated upon racialization, and thus the dynamic of nationalist revolution is seen by them to involve race and class inseparably. However, in the formation of postindependence policy, national states with quite various political agendas have tended to contain popular movements, and have by and large attempted to resolve the peculiar contradictions of the "colonial mode of production" by adapting Western modernization models. A number of essays in this volume, such as Maria Josefina Saldaña-Portillo's study of Sandinista agricultural policy and Chakrabarty's discussion of Marxist categories and South Asian work practices, suggest the need to rethink the economic and social strategies of modernization in ways that would not capitulate to the mandate of assimilation to Western development and a Western-dominated world system. What is assumed here is not a notion of "the traditional" versus the Western model of "modernity," but rather the possibility of forms of agency that inhere in the longer duration of social forms that have emerged in resistance and in relation to modern institutions; this leads Saldaña-Portillo, for example, to study the importance of the Nicaraguan rural workers defining themselves as "peasantry" rather than "proletariat." In our last section, we will discuss the larger implications of the contradictions between culture and civil society for the emergence of political alternatives.

It is our intention to intervene in discourses on transnational capitalism whose tendency is to totalize the world system, to view capitalist penetration as complete and pervasive, so that the site of intervention is restricted to commodification; or, more insidiously, with the result that all manifestations of difference appear as just further signs of commodification. To pose the argument about transnationalism at the level of commodification not only obscures the practices of exploitation that lead to antagonism, but also ignores the ways in which transnational capital's exploitation of cultural differentiation produces its own contradictions. Our critique of the assumption of absolute globalization or universal commodification does not lead us to fetishize imaginary spaces that are not yet under the sway of capitalism. Rather, what we focus on is the intersection of commodification and labor exploitation under postmodern transnational modes of production with the historical emergence of social formations in time with but also in antagonism to modernity; these social formations are not residues of the "premodern," but are *differential* formations that mediate the processes through which capital profits through the mixing and combination of exploitative modes. What we are concerned with is the multiplicity of significant contradictions rooted in the longer histories of antagonism and adaptation. All of these are obscured by either a totality governed by globalization of capitalism or the superordination of the proletarian subject.

The work of Aihwa Ong, Swasti Mitter, and Maria Mies, for example, suggests that flexible accumulation depends precisely on capitalism's laying hold of "traditional" social formations that have not been leveled by modernity either in terms of labor relations or the political nation; in these encounters, capitalism "respects" those forms even if for exploitative aims.[23] In these analyses, questions of gender, within the racialized consolidation of social forms into traditions that takes place under colonization, are inseparable from the exploitation of labor. As Dipesh Chakrabarty has argued in his study of the Bengali working class, capitalism under colonialism is not reproduced through the formation of abstract political subjects but rather through the formation of subjects embedded in precapitalist social relations. To the extent that the formation of these subjects belies the homogenization of capitalist social relations according to the Western model, it also contradicts the assumption of a correspondence between the cultural and political domains and their reproduction for economic exploitation. Yet at the same time, the "culture" that emerges from this encounter mediates in complex ways the contradiction between contemporary global capitalist development and the culture whose social relations have an extended history that is always in part determined by encounters with emergent modernity. Accordingly, these encounters do not erase contradiction; neither do they produce the resolution of contradictions. Against theoretical prediction, cultural forms that might seem incompatible with capitalist social relations both permit their reproduction and provide for oppositional modes. In other words, it is neither that capitalist modernity expands and commodifies the "traditional," nor that it simply destroys it, making it necessary for one to look for "pure" sites that have not yet been incorporated in order to find "resistance" (as in the as-yet-undiscovered primitive tribe in the Amazon), but rather that both antagonism and adaptation have been part of the process of the emergence of modernity over time. That is, what we are calling the alternative is not the "other" outside, but the "what-has-been-formed" in the conjunction with and in differentiation from modernity over time. The alternative takes place in the contradictions that emerge when the cultural forms of one mode of production are taken up and exploited by an apparently incommensurable mode of production.

Feminism

There is from the outset a dissymmetry between our discussion of "feminism" and the preceding discussions of nationalism and Marxism: it is less possible to discuss a singular "feminism," since its emergence both inside and outside of national contexts, not only in the West but globally, has given rise to a wide variety of theories and practices. Even in the West, given that versions of modern liberal feminism have sought enfranchisement for female subjects within national political spheres articulated through the concept of "rights," no feminist movement has sought a "capture" of the state in the manner proposed by nationalism or Marxism, and feminist projects must be distinguished as nonanalogous to nationalist and Marxist ones.

To the extent that the dominant strands of Western feminism have been articulated within the terms of liberal modernity, the limits of that feminism have been discussed by Chandra Talpade Mohanty, Angela Davis, Chela Sandoval, and others as being marked by their historical articulation with both imperial projects and state racisms.[24] Indeed, where neither nationalism nor Marxism has fully critiqued the "nationalist subject" or the "class subject," international and antiracist feminisms, as well as Anglo-American feminism, have interrogated the subject of feminism — "woman" — as embodying an implicit universalism that obscures unequal power relations that are the consequence of colonialism and capitalism.[25] Therefore, it will not be our task here to write generally about all feminisms, but to look specifically at women's struggles within the racialized structures of colonial modernity and transnational capitalism. The women's struggles we are foregrounding demand neither a homogeneous subject nor a conception of a fixed social totality; rather, they are practices antagonistic to the distinct modes of subjectivity disciplined by divisions of the modern state — the political, economic, or cultural (and its attendant separation into "public" and "private"). To frame the contemporary situation of women, we begin by situating the historical contradictions of women in their encounter with modernity, contradictions that remain active in and continue to determine the dynamics of transnationalism. By the encounter with modernity, we mean with the racialized and gendered regimes of the colonial state and the modern nation-state, which extend not only to the formation and reproduction of gender in the family and in other social spaces and institutions such as schooling, religion, law, the workplace, and cultural and popular media, but to ideological and epistemological suppositions of the particular and universal, constructions of interiority and exteriority, and evaluations of purity and impurity. While the modern state has in theory offered women emancipation in the economic and political spheres, and even participation in anticolonial nationalist struggles, the regulation and consolidation of national identity has generally led to women's political/juridical exclusion, their educational subordination, economic exploitation, and ideological suppression.[26] Within this history, it is often in the violent contestations over the meaning and place of cultural practices that women's contradictory status in relation to the state becomes evident. At the same time, the subordination of women in contradiction with modernity allows transnational capital access to women's labor as a site of hyperextraction. In turn, the contestatory sites of contradiction within modern national forms can provide the very opportunities and tools for practices that challenge transnational exploitation. This is why we need to understand that new subjects operate not exclusively through the "political" or "economic" categories of nationalism and Marxism, but through the politics of culture as well.

It has been the tendency of nationalism and Marxism to consider gender a secondary formation, which has subordinated women's activism to anticolonial nationalist struggle or proletarian labor struggles, respectively. This tendency has symptomatized the most serious limit of these political projects, that is, the insistence on totality and unity to the exclusion of different axes of determination and struggle, other axes whose intersections may be the sites of the most aggravated contradictions. We've argued that the political subject of modernity has been conceived as either the citizen of the nation or the proletarian class subject. Both forms of political subjectivity depend on a gendered ideology of separate spheres; the political and economic subject is presumed to be male and must be differentiated from realms cast as "feminine": the domestic sphere of the "home," the "spiritual" cultural antecedents of modernity, and labors situated as "reproductive." The counterspheres marked "feminine" are seen as sites of *reproduction* rather than *production,* and in that respect correspond to sites of culture. Along with the antinomy "private" and "public," women have been subject to the construction of "tradition" and "modernity," which perpetually locates "third world women" as the "other" of modernity, the symbol of premodern "tradition" to be "modernized." We contend, to the contrary, that women have always been agents in the dialectical production of the heterogeneous, differentiated forms of modernity itself.[27] Even before the currently gendered international division of labor, women under colonialisms and in so-called developing nations composed the primary labor force exploited in the production of economic modernity.

Extending materialist theory in ways adequate to the present moment requires an understanding of the gendered division of labor that not only interprets the era of transnationalism but allows us to grasp retrospectively the historical occlusion of women's struggle. Feminist historiography sheds light on formerly undocumented and unanalyzed histories of women's contradictory engagement with modernity. As much as feminist historiography that recaptures the agencies of women as makers of history shares some of the impulse of subaltern historiography, its methods and purposes are not identical. Subaltern historiography in general seeks to recover practices from domains that are defined as external to the state or public sphere; consequently, the reference point of subaltern study has continued to be the relation of subaltern struggles and practices to elite nationalist or colonialist formations. In contradistinction, feminist historiography that regards women's activities and gendered social relations as central is concerned with sets of cultural and political practices that cut across all domains of the social and require a different periodization and temporality.[28] Though nationalist narratives have subordinated the ubiquity of women's participation in social struggles to the terms of a national model, it is not a matter now of simply inserting "women" into the nationalist narrative. As Kumkum Sangari and Sudesh Vaid state, "A feminist historiography rethinks historiography as a whole and discards the idea of women as something to be *framed* by a context, in order to be able to think of gender difference as both structuring and structured by the wide set of social relations."[29] Radha Radhakrishnan has put it this way: "feminist historiography secedes from the structure [of nationalist totality] not to set up a different and oppositional form of totality, but to establish a different relation to totality."[30] In a way that nationalism cannot, and Marxism has not yet, this feminism rethinks historical periodization and agency, reconceptualizes the division of social spheres, and ultimately advances a new conception of the political subject itself. Homa Hoodfar's discussion in this volume of the refunctioning of the practice of veiling among Muslim women disrupts the periodization of nationalist historiography; veiling is at one time a symbol of traditional community for Western imperialism, at another a sign of challenge to Western-backed authoritarian regimes, and at another a pragmatic practice permitting entry of women into the labor force. Veiling, as discussed by Hoodfar, also cuts across the spatial demarcations of modernity, politicizing "cultural" practices that might otherwise be thought of as extrapolitical.

Feminist historiography thus reveals that women's practices are only partially grasped when reduced to the horizon of the national state, and that implicitly those practices demand alternatives to the formations prescribed by the modern state, whose emancipatory promise is contradicted by the persistent subordinations. In the transnational era, the "modern" forms in which the nation mediates capital come into contradiction with the "postmodern" forces and movements of the global economy; yet we maintain that even in the postmodern transnational economy, the modern patriarchal state form persists within the mobility of global capital as the primary set of institutions for regulating women's labor and sexuality and for dictating spheres of gendered social practice. Furthermore, the globalization of capitalism reorganizes the operations of production exploiting women precisely in ways permitted by their subordination by national patriarchal states. Patriarchal definitions of gender are continuously reproduced throughout a genealogy of social formations: patriarchy is consistently dominant, though not identically so, under colonial rule, in nationalist regimes, and in postcolonial and neocolonial state formations. There is a perpetual dialectic between "traditional" patriarchy and its "modern" rearticulations, whereby the selective redefinition of the "traditional" woman through which modernity rearticulates patriarchy serves both to intensify the constraints upon and to extract differentiated labor from female subjects. The hyperexploitation of women under transnationalism brings women's cultural practices to the fore as incommensurable with capitalist rationality. Since the 1970s and 1980s, the deindustrialization of the United States and Europe has been accomplished by a shifting of production to Asia and Latin America, particularly making use of female labor in overseas export assembly and manufacturing zones.[31] Aihwa Ong points out in her essay that, contrary to the literature on Fordism that predicted the increasing adoption of mass-assembly production, since the early 1970s subcontracting firms and sweatshops have come to typify industrialization in Asia and Central America. One of the distinct features of global restructuring is capital's ability to profit not through a homogenization of the mode of production, but through the differentiation of specific resources and markets that permits the exploitation of gendered labor within regional and national sites. Part of this differentiation involves transactions between national states and transnational capital, which formalize new capital accumulation and production techniques that exploit by specifically targeting female labor markets. This occurs where women are disciplined by state-instituted traditional patriarchy, whether in Malaysia or Guatemala, or by racialized immigration laws that target female immigrants in particular, such as in California. These conditions, produced by the differentiating mode of transnational capital, counter a center-periphery model of spatial or developmental logic, and hence point to the timeliness, which we will take up later, of conceptualizing linkages between and across varied sites of contradiction. Such linkages recognize the dispersed forms of transnational operations of capital accumulation and exploitation as an opportunity for, rather than a limit on, new political practices.

While it is the understanding of some analysts of transnationalism that global capitalism has penetrated and saturated all social terrains, exhausting the possibilities for challenges or resistance, the situations of women workers suggest that transnational capitalism, like colonial capitalism before it, continues to produce sites of contradiction and the dynamics of its own negation and critique. These contradictions produce new possibilities precisely because they have led to a breakdown and a reformulation of the categories of nation, race, class, and gender, and in doing so have led to a need to reconceptualize the oppositional narratives of nationalism, Marxism, and feminism. The latest shift toward the transnationalization of capital is not exclusively manifested in the "denationalization" of corporate power or the nation-state, but, perhaps more importantly, it is expressed in the reorganization of oppositional interventions against capital that articulate themselves in terms and relations other than the "national" or the "international proletariat" — notably feminist activism among U.S. women of color, cross-border labor organizing, and neocolonized and immigrant women's struggles (see Davis, Lowe, and Connolly and Patel).

In its intensification of exploitation, transnational capitalism has exacerbated the gendered political and economic contradictions that were active in modern state capitalisms; paradoxically, this takes place in part through an erosion of the legal and social regulations that underwrite the ideology of separate spheres. Making use of the structures of patriarchal societies and its modes of gender discipline to maximize its exploitation of "docile" female labor, transnational capital simultaneously undermines the reproduction of patriarchies by moving women from one sphere of gendered social control to another. Yet the reconstitution of patriarchy within the transnational capitalist system, we argue, produces different and more varied practices of resistance to that system, practices that do not turn exclusively on the opposition of abstract labor to capital. Where this "feminized" domain of culture is in contradiction with capitalist production we find a convergence of struggles generated by different axes of domination: capitalism, patriarchy, and the processes of racialization that take place through colonialism and immigration. The specific modes of discipline that apply to women as gendered subjects necessarily give rise to different modes of organization and politicization; for example, *maquiladora* workers in Mexico protesting the factory's regular requirement of "beauty pageants" that rearticulate patriarchal domination of women in the workplace have generated cross-border workers' organizations that have targeted more generally the gendered nature of both U.S. and transnational industry's exploitation of *maquiladora* workers in Mexico and Central America.[32] With the feminization and racialization of work that more and more relies on immigrant women and women in the neocolonized world, different strategies for organizing emerge; for example, the variety of strategies for addressing the international garment industry's abuse of immigrant women workers includes actions in the realms of both national and international law, consumer boycotts, and national and cross-border labor organizing modes.[33] These mixed strategies do not imply the dispersal of struggle, we contend, but they recognize a "new" laboring subject impacted at once by axes of domination previously distinguished within an ideology of separate spheres.

It must be emphasized that the differentiated nature of globalization also produces contradictions that give rise to feminist activism in the site of "culture," precisely because the globalization of capitalism depends on the patriarchal cultural regulation of women, and because transnational capitalism reproduces those cultural regulations in the workplace itself. Maria Mies's discussion of the "housewifization" of women's labor in the transnational economy, for example, demonstrates the ways in which global restructuring is both transgressive of and parasitic on the material culture of gendered "public" and "private" spheres as they have distributed and organized social relations.[34] A culturally practiced division of labor that directed women toward atomized, isolated "domestic" work is extended and rearticulated in what Swasti Mitter has termed a newly "spatialized" gendered division of labor that moves women from "domestic" spaces to the international workspaces of casual, ill-paid, insecure work.[35] As Aihwa Ong argues, the "cultural" formation of women, which often appears to run counter to modernization, becomes a specific resource and mode of "capitalist discipline" for forming workers who will fit into the current needs of transnational capital.[36] By the same token, women's resistance on the level of culture has ramifications for every other sphere of social life. Thus, a number of the essays in this volume focus on cultural struggles, with the understanding that women's labor is not the exclusive site of regulation, exploitation, and control. Clara Connolly and Pragna Patel's essay on the activities of Women Against Fundamentalism in Britain makes evident that women's cultural and religious struggles attack the foundations of state-sanctioned "multicultural" policies that subordinate women and seek to discipline and exploit immigrant communities. Similarly, Homa Hoodfar's essay on veiling practices among Muslim women demonstrates that women's struggles on the terrain of culture and religion powerfully shape women's resistance in the labor force and participation in the political sphere. Tani Barlow's essay on the figure of "woman" in post-Maoist People's Republic of China suggests that the disciplining of women's bodies in culture is central to a state project that seeks to regulate the relationship between China and the larger network of Asian capitalist states.

Transnational capitalism has reconfigured the mode of production in ways that are parasitic on the nation-state and its institutions, but rely on a disempowered citizenry; it continues to exploit labor, but redefines and differentiates who that labor is in terms of gender, race, and nation, and thus seeks to preclude the formation of a univocal international proletarian subject. It seeks to extend universal commodification, but by conditions that so impoverish the mass of the global workforce that unrestricted access to those commodities is limited to a few elites within a few nations. This unevenness in the processes of commodification generates contradictions across the globe: the deindustrialization of the United States and Europe and the shift of manufacturing operations to Asia and Latin America result not only in a relatively diminished base of consumers in relation to the expanded exploitation of labor power, but also in an intensification of the monopolization of resources by some and the immiseration of an ever increasing proportion of the world's population. Furthermore, as the base of consumers fails to expand in keeping with the expansion of the mode of production, the capitalist transformation of culture by way of universal commodification falls short of the exaggerated completion claimed by some theorists of globalization. Therefore, contradictions emerge along the fault lines between the exigencies of capitalist production and the cultural forms directly and indirectly engaged by those disciplines of production.

Within modernity, the sphere of culture is defined by its separation from the economic and political, within the general differentiation of spheres that constitute "society." Against this model, "premodern cultures" are defined as lacking such differentiation or complexity. Several of the essays collected here address orientalist representations of the "primitive": Hoodfar criticizes colonialist understandings of veiling practices among Muslim women; Martin Manalansan problematizes the Eurocentric gay representations of Filipino gay practices as "undeveloped" and "premodern" precisely because they do not seek to enter into a public sphere of visibility. Orientalist definitions of modernity suggest that modern societies "have" culture, while nonmodern societies "are" culture. Against either of these notions — culture specialized as the aesthetic, or culture defined in anthropological terms — we have sought to elaborate a conception of culture as emerging in the economic and political processes of modernization. This is not to say that culture is the space in which capital as commodification reigns; rather, as we have been arguing, it is the space through which both the reproduction of capitalist social relations and antagonism to that reproduction are articulated. If the tendency of transnational capitalism is to commodify everything and therefore to collapse the cultural into the economic, it is precisely where labor, differentiated rather than "abstract," is being commodified that the cultural becomes political again.[37] Insofar as transnational or neocolonial capitalism has shown itself able to proliferate through the seizure of multiple cultural forms, at the same time it brings to light more clearly than earlier capital regimes the volatility of the cultural space as a site of contradictions. To repeat our earlier formulation, culture becomes politically important where a cultural formation comes into contradiction with an economic or political logic that tries to refunction it for exploitation or domination.

One classic instance of such a contradiction between cultural formations and a dominant logic has been analyzed in relation to anticolonial nationalism that seeks to use "traditional" cultural forms in a modernizing project. It is no less true for the political function of culture in postmodern capitalism. As we have seen, under colonialism the correspondence between the modern differentiation of spheres and the reproduction of capitalism did not hold. Postmodern capitalism, in new ways, dispenses with the differentiation of spheres as part of its logic of exploitation; rather than passing by way of a fully articulated civil society, postmodern transnational capitalism exacerbates and intensifies the unevennesses of various national states' transformations of colonial societies. In some cases, it passes by way of state-sponsored modernization, as in some authoritarian states in Asia and Latin America, where it produces the economic forms of capital without the corresponding civil society; the effects of these contradictions have already become manifest in the antagonism between "indigenous" movements and the state, and in liberalizing movements. Where transnational capital comes into contradiction with the autonomy of the nation-state, national struggles against global capitalism, such as in Cuba, China, and Nicaragua, attest to the difficulties and successes of such struggles that often are forced by international pressures into their own forms of state modernization. But where transnational capital grasps hold of forms it might regard as "backward," brutally seizing on existent social forms rather than awaiting their transformation through the nation-state's modernizing projects, it precisely produces conditions for alternative practices that have not been homogenized by economic and political modernity within the postcolonial nation-state.

While it should be clear that we are making use of the Marxist concept of contradiction, we are revising it away from the classical notions of the primary antagonism between capital and labor and the emergence of proletarian consciousness in order to reconceptualize its sites and effects. Multiple sites of contradiction emerge where hetero-geneous social formations that are the differential counterformations of modernity are impacted by and brought into contradiction with postmodern modes of global capitalism. The essays collected here con-sider different sites of contradiction: what they consider are not prin-cipally economically produced contradictions, but contradictions that emerge between capitalist economic formations and the social and cul-tural practices they presume but cannot dictate. These contradictions give rise to cross-race and cross-national projects, feminist movements, anticolonial struggles, and politicized cultural practices.

Linkages between such differentiated movements are of paramount importance. Transnational capitalism no longer needs to operate within the nation as a legal, political, cultural entity, but instead needs the nation as a means of regulating labor, materials, and capital. As we have argued, transnational capitalism exacerbates contradiction and antag-onism between the "local" or regional sites of exploitation and the nation-state. It is the differentiation of the mode of production that permits the exploitation of localities and makes them, rather than the national, the principal nodes of contradiction and therefore the sites of emergent political practices. Indeed, it may be that resistances are more and more articulated through linkings of localities that take place across and below the level of the nation-state, and not by way of a politics that moves at the level of the national or modern institutions. The essays in this volume go some way toward suggesting the contours of the work of aligning local struggles whose very condition it is to be disjoined and differentiated.

Some of the essays in the volume point specifically to black racial solidarities that form against domination and economic exploitation that are global in scope: Escobar outlines the ways Afro-Colombian movements articulate themselves along racial lines in an intervention against the economic and ecological destruction of native communities; Lipsitz writes about Black soldiers in World War II wanting to join the Japanese army in a cross-race, cross-national, anti-imperialist effort; Farred writes of the San Domingan slave revolt as a model for black anticolonial movements in the Caribbean and Africa. Other essays point to feminist practices: Hoodfar discusses the ways in which wom-en's practices of veiling destabilize Western orientalist constructions of Muslim women, while cutting across national patriarchal determina-tions and linking women cross-nationally. Connolly and Patel's essay discusses the linking of South Asian, Irish, and Caribbean immigrant women in Britain within a coalition that is at once antistatist and anti-fundamentalist. Davis reflects on "unlikely coalitions": between the environmental justice movement and U.S. communities of color, between African American women and Asian immigrant laborers, between prisoners in an overdeveloped "prison-industrial complex" and students impacted by the underfunding of schooling. Other essays, like Bhatia's discussion of the Indian People's Theatre, connect anticolonial struggle with a global antifascist one in ways that necessarily refuse the logic of elite nationalism's prioritization of identity. Antiracism, feminism, and anticolonialism must constantly address national economic exploitation and political disenfranchisements, and in doing so deploy countercultural forms and create alternative public spheres. *The Politics of Culture in the Shadow of Capital* emphasizes that the linking of such forms "below" the level of the nation, and across national sites, has had a long and inadequately documented history, the recovery of which is equally if not more important in the present conjuncture.

In this volume, we hope not only to document but to stimulate the pursuit of further possibilities for linking through a differently conceived "politics of culture." In doing so, we argue that returning to political economy as the master narrative and the foundational rationale for "political" transformation, by both left and conservative thinkers, is itself an aftereffect of modernity that would overlook the work of culture, regarding it as universally commodified. To relegate culture to commodification is to replay older arguments about the autonomy of the cultural sphere; neither conception of culture, as commodified or as aesthetic culture, admits culture's imbrication in political and economic relations. The essays here specify instead cultural formations that have emerged, over time, in contradiction to the modern division of spheres and its rationalizing modes; described here, culture involves simultaneously work, pleasure, consumption, spirituality, "aesthetic" production, and reproduction, within an ongoing process of historical transformation in contradiction with colonial and neocolonial capitalism. Culture, understood in this way, constitutes a site in which the reproduction of contemporary capitalist social relations may be continually contested. In such cultural struggles, we find no less a redefinition of "the political," for in contradistinction to abstract modern divisions of society, the political has never been a discrete sphere of practice within the nation-state; these essays demonstrate that "politics" must be grasped instead as always braided within "culture" and cultural practices. The politics of culture exists as the very survival of alternative practices to those of globalized capital, the very survival of alternatives to the incessant violence of the new transnational order with its reconstituted patriarchies and racisms. Violence is manifest wherever capital generates its contradictions. The unimaginable violence of the past years — in Indonesia, Korea, Taiwan, the Philippines, South Africa, Chile, Guatemala, and Nicaragua, to name only a few spaces — is the sign not only of capital's now unrestricted brutality, but also of the insistence of alternatives and the refusal to submit to homogenization. Our moment is not one of fatalistic despair; faces turned toward the past, we do not seek to make whole what has been smashed, but to move athwart the storm into a future in which the debris is more than just a residue: it holds the alternative.

NOTES

1. David Harvey, *The Condition of Postmodernity: An Enquiry into the Origins of Cultural Change* (Oxford: Basil Blackwell, 1990); Fredric Jameson, *Postmodernism, or the Cultural Logic of Late Capitalism* (Durham: Duke University Press, 1992); Masao Miyoshi, "A Borderless World? From Colonialism to Transnationalism and the Decline of the Nation-State," *Critical Inquiry* 19 (summer 1993): 726–751.
2. This is, for example, Jameson's conclusion to *The Geopolitical Aesthetic* (Bloomington: Indiana University Press, 1992). He writes: "those doctrines of reification and commodification which played a secondary role in the traditional or classical Marxian heritage, are now likely to come into their own and become the dominant instruments of analysis and struggle . . . today as never before, we must focus on a reification and a commodification that have become so universalized as to seem well-nigh natural and organic entities and forms" (212).
3. See Karl Marx, *Capital: A Critique of Political Economy,* vol. 1, ed. Friedrich Engels, trans. Samuel Moore and Edward Aveling (London: Lawrence and Wishart, 1954), 702–724, and Karl Marx and Friedrich Engels, *The Communist Manifesto,* intro. A. J. P. Taylor (Harmondsworth: Penguin, 1967), 81–84.
4. Samir Amin, *Delinking,* trans. Michael Wolfers (London: Zed Books, 1990), 7, 28. To the extent that Amin questions the even extension of capitalist development, he offers an alternative to the homogenizing "transnational" model. However, his focus on "delinking" the nation-state from global capitalism does not address adequately the contemporary shift in the mode of production, for the concept of delinking still depends on an understanding of the nation-state as an autonomous regulator of capital and labor flow.
5. See Edward Said, "Traveling Theory," in *The World, the Text and the Critic* (Cambridge, MA: Harvard University Press, 1983); and James Clifford, "Traveling Cultures," in *Cultural Studies,* ed. Lawrence Grossberg, Cary Nelson, and Paula Treichler (New York: Routledge, 1992).
6. See Donna Haraway, "Situated Knowledges," *Feminist Studies* 14, no. 3 (fall 1988): 575–599; Chandra Talpade Mohanty, "Cartographies of Struggle," in *Third World Women and the Politics of Feminism,* ed. Chandra Tal-

pade Mohanty, Ann Russo, and Lourdes Torres (Bloomington: Indiana University Press, 1991); Kumkum Sangari & Sudesh Vaid, introduction to *Recasting Women: Essays in Indian Colonial History* (New Brunswick, NJ: Rutgers University Press, 1990); and Gayatri Chakravorty Spivak, "Can the Subaltern Speak?" in *Marxism and the Interpretation of Culture*, ed. Cary Nelson and Lawrence Grossberg (Urbana: University of Illinois, 1988). Feminist critiques of Western epistemology and imperialism have perhaps gone the furthest in theorizing the importance of location in relation to multiple axes of determination and systemic intersecting oppressions. We acknowledge the importance of these works to our understanding of overdetermined sites of contradiction.

7. Frantz Fanon, *The Wretched of the Earth*, trans. Constance Farrington (New York: Grove Press, 1968); Partha Chatterjee, *Nationalism and the Colonial World* (London: Zed Books, 1986); Benedict Anderson, *Imagined Communities: Reflections on the Origin and Spread of Nationalism* (London: Verso, 1991).

8. The concepts of hybridity, damage, and recalcitrance with respect to Irish culture under British colonialism are elaborated by David Lloyd in "Counterparts: *Dubliners*, Masculinity and Temperance Nationalism," in *Burning Down the House*, ed. Rosemary Marangoly George (Boulder, CO: Westview Press, 1997), and "Regarding Ireland in a Post-colonial Frame," in *Cultural Studies*, ed., Seamus Deane (forthcoming).

9. Arturo Escobar, *Encountering Development* (Princeton: Princeton University Press, 1995).

10. Etienne Balibar, Preface to *Race, Nation, Class: Ambiguous Identities* (London: Verso, 1991).

11. When they emphasize "civil rights," antiracist movements may be said to encounter some of the same kinds of contradictions that face the state-centered projects of bourgeois nationalism and liberal feminism. However, we argue that in relation to decolonization movements worldwide, antiracist anticolonial struggles have produced a profound crisis in the legitimation of the state and in its institutions themselves. As we go on to discuss in the nationalism section, antiracist anticolonialisms have gone beyond the notion of civil rights within the nation-state to a critique of the state form itself. Within the U.S. context, civil rights struggles for racialized peoples always had ramifications beyond enfranchisement within the nation-state; these struggles were met with state violence precisely because mobilizations by racialized peoples not only named the contradiction between the promise of political emancipation and the conditions of racialized segregation and economic exploitation, but they revealed the racial exclusions upon which U.S. liberal capitalism and U.S. neocolonialism are founded. Civil rights struggles in the United States have revealed that the granting of rights does not abolish the economic system that profits from racism; see Melvin L. Oliver and Thomas M. Shapiro, *Black Wealth, White Wealth: A New Perspective on Racial Inequality* (New York: Routledge, 1995); and Cheryl Harris, "Whiteness as Property," *Harvard Law Review* 106, no. 8 (June 1993): 1707–1791. On the extended critique waged

by civil rights struggles, see Angela Davis in this volume; Michael Omi and Howard Winant, *Racial Formation in the United States, from the 1960s to the 1990s* (New York: Routledge, 1994); and Robert Allen, *Black Awakening in Capitalist America: An Analytic History* (Trenton, NJ: Africa World Press, 1990). For a social history of the civil rights movement and organizing tradition, see Charles M. Payne, *I've Got the Light of Freedom: The Organizing Tradition and the Mississippi Freedom Struggle* (Berkeley: University of California Press, 1995). At our present moment, it is an understanding of *race* not as a fixed singular essence, but as the locus in which economic, gender, sex, and race contradictions converge that organizes current struggles for immigrant rights, prisoner's rights, affirmative action, racialized women's labor, and AIDS and HIV patients in communities of color. Both the "successes" and the "failures" of struggles over the past thirty years demonstrate the degree to which *race* remains, after civil rights, the material trace of history, and thus the site of struggle through which contradictions are heightened and brought into relief.

12. This founding equivalence between the history of a people and the history of its political institutions is common to nineteenth-century thinkers as various as Coleridge in England, Fichte in Germany, Michelet and Renan in France, and Mazzini in Italy.

13. Akhil Gupta and James Ferguson, "Beyond 'Culture': Space, Identity, and the Politics of Difference," *Cultural Anthropology* 7, no. 1 (February 1992): 6–22.

14. Cited in Partha Chatterjee, *Nationalist Thought and the Colonial World: A Derivative Discourse?* (Minneapolis: University of Minnesota Press, 1993), 3.

15. Fanon, *The Wretched of the Earth*; Amílcar Cabral, *Unity and Struggle: Speeches and Writings of Amílcar Cabral,* trans. Michael Wolfers (New York: Monthly Review Press, 1979). See also Bipan Chandra, "Colonialism, Stages of Colonialism and the Colonial State," *Journal of Contemporary Asia* 10, no. 3 (1980): 272–285; Anderson, *Imagined Communities*.

16. Bipan Chandra, "Colonialism, Stages of Colonialism and the Colonial State," *Journal of Contemporary Asia* 10, no. 3 (1980): 272–285.

17. Kumari Jayawardena, *Feminism and Nationalism in the Third World* (London: Zed Books, 1986).

18. See Donald Lowe, *The Function of 'China' in Marx, Lenin, and Mao* (Berkeley: University of California Press, 1966).

19. Dipesh Chakrabarty, *Rethinking Working-Class History: Bengal 1890–1940* (Princeton: Princeton University Press, 1989); see also Chakrabarty's "The Time of History and the Times of Gods" in this collection.

20. Aihwa Ong, *Spirits of Resistance and Capitalist Discipline: Factory Women in Malaysia* (Albany: State University of New York Press, 1987).

21. Chandra, "Colonialism, Stages of Colonialism and the Colonial State."

22. Louis Althusser and Etienne Balibar, "On the Basic Concepts of Historical Materialism," in *Reading Capital* (London: Verso, 1968).

23. Aihwa Ong, *Spirits of Resistance and Capitalist Discipline*; Swasti Mitter, *Common Fate, Common Bond: Women in the Global Economy* (London:

Pluto, 1986); Maria Mies, *Patriarchy and Accumulation on a World Scale: Women in the International Division of Labor* (London: Zed Press, 1986).

24. As we have suggested concerning "Western Marxism," it is the case for "Western feminism" that its existence is not limited to the geographical West. See Chandra Talpade Mohanty, "Under Western Eyes: Feminist Scholarship and Colonialist Discourse," in *Third World Women and the Politics of Feminism,* 52. For discussions of white liberal feminism and antiracist feminism in the United States, see Angela Davis, *Women, Race, and Class* (New York: Random House, 1981); and Chela Sandoval, "U.S. Third World Feminism: The Theory and Method of Oppositional Consciousness in the Postmodern World," *Genders* 10 (spring 1991): 1–24.

25. Anglo-American and European feminist interrogations of "woman" include Parveen Adams and Elizabeth Cowie, *The Woman in Question* (Cambridge, MA: MIT Press, 1990); Donna Haraway, *Simians, Cyborgs, and Women* (New York: Routledge, 1991); and Judith Butler, *Bodies That Matter: On the Discursive Limits of Sex* (New York: Routledge, 1993).

26. For a greater elaboration of this argument, see Deniz Kandiyoti, "Identity and Its Discontents," in *Colonial Discourse and Post-Colonial Theory: A Reader,* ed. Patrick Williams and Laura Chrisman (New York: Columbia University Press, 1994).

27. For accounts of women's roles in anticolonial political and labor struggles, see Jayawardena, *Feminism and Nationalism in the Third World*; and Nanneke Redclift and M. Thea Sinclair, eds., *Working Women: International Perspectives on Labour and Gender Ideology* (London: Routledge, 1991). On women's survival within formal and informal economies, see Homa Hoodfar, *Between Marriage and the Market: Intimate Politics and Survival in Cairo* (Berkeley: University of California Press, 1997).

On women's activities in labor struggles in the United States, see for example Ruth Milkman, *Gender at Work: The Dynamics of Job Segregation by Sex during World War II* (Urbana: University of Illinois Press, 1987); Jacqueline Jones, *Labor of Love, Labor of Sorrow: Black Women, Work, and the Family from Slavery to the Present* (New York: Basic Books, 1985); Vicki Ruiz, *Cannery Women, Cannery Lives: Mexican Women, Unionization, and the California Food Processing Industry, 1930–1950* (Albuquerque: University of New Mexico, 1987).

Our consideration of non-Western and antiracist feminism as the site for the convergence of feminist, labor, anticolonial, and antiracist work is sympathetically allied with a variety of feminist projects represented by, for example, Sangari and Vaid, eds., *Recasting Women;* Mohanty, Russo, and Torres, eds., *Third World Women and the Politics of Feminism;* Inderpal Grewal and Caren Kaplan, eds., *Scattered Hegemonies: Postmodernity and Transnational Feminist Practices* (Minneapolis: University of Minnesota, 1994); and M. Jacqui Alexander and Chandra Talpade Mohanty, eds., *Feminist Genealogies, Colonial Legacies, Democratic Futures* (New York: Routledge, 1996).

28. Kapil Kumar's essay "Rural Women in Oudh 1917–1947: Baba Ram

Chandra and the Women's Question" in Sangari and Vaid, *Recasting Women,* is exemplary in this respect. Rather than focusing on the punctual moment of a specific peasant revolt in Oudh, or on the genderless "peasant" subject, the essay not only explores the roles of women in the revolt, but suggests how the refiguration of the cultural forms of womanhood in relation to particular economic and social issues necessitates a rethinking of the nature, temporality, and periodization of the struggle.

29. Sangari and Vaid, *Recasting Women,* 3.

30. Radha Radhakrishnan, "Nationalism, Gender and the Narrative of Identity," in *Nationalisms and Sexualities,* ed. Andrew Parker et al. (New York: Routledge, 1992), 81.

31. Committee for Asian Women, *Many Paths, One Goal: Organizing Women Workers in Asia* (Hong Kong: CAW, 1991); June Nash and Maria Patricia Fernandez-Kelly, eds., *Women in the International Division of Labor* (Albany: State University of New York Press, 1983); Vicki Ruiz and Susan Tiano, eds., *Women on the U.S.-Mexican Border* (Boston: Allen & Unwin, 1987); Paul Ong, Edna Bonacich, and Lucie Cheng, eds., *New Asian Immigration in Los Angeles and Global Restructuring* (Philadelphia: Temple University Press, 1994); Richard P. Appelbaum, "Multiculturalism and Flexibility: Some New Directions in Global Capitalism," in *Mapping Multiculturalism,* ed. Avery Gordon and Christopher Newfield (Minneapolis: University of Minnesota, 1996).

32. See Kyungwon Hong and Mary Tong, "Aguirre v. AUG: A Case Study," in *Multinational Human Resource Management: Cases and Exercises,* ed. P. C. Smith (Tulsa, OK: Dame Publishing Company, forthcoming).

33. See Laura Ho, Catherine Powell, and Leti Volpp, "(Dis)Assembling Rights of Women Workers along the Global Assemblyline: Human Rights and the Garment Industry," *Harvard Civil Rights–Civil Liberties Law Review* 31, no. 2 (summer 1996): 383–414.

34. Mies, *Patriarchy and Accumulation on a World Scale.*

35. Mitter, *Common Fate, Common Bond.*

36. See also Aihwa Ong's study of Malaysian factory women's practices, *Spirits of Resistance and Capitalist Discipline.*

37. Marx theorized that it is the tendency of capital to use "abstract labor," or labor as "use value" unencumbered by specific human qualities. In the *Grundrisse,* Marx describes abstract labor: "as *the* use value which confronts money posited as capital, labour is not this or another labour, but *labour pure and simple,* abstract labour; absolutely indifferent to its particular specificity. . . . but since capital *as such* is indifferent to every particularity of its substance, and exists not only as the totality of the same but also as the abstraction from all its particularities, the labour which confronts it likewise subjectively has the same totality and abstraction in itself" (Karl Marx, *Grundrisse: Foundations of the Critique of Political Economy [rough draft],* trans. Martin Nicolaus [Harmondsworth: Penguin, 1993], 296). However, in most capitalist situations, capital lays hold of labor that is precisely not abstract but differentiated by race, gender, and nationality. In the development of racialized U.S. capitalism, in

colonial capitalism, and now in transnational capitalism, it is through differentiating, rather than homogenizing, labor forces that capital expands and
profits. For further discussion of Marx's concepts of "abstract" and "real"
labor, see Dipesh Chakrabarty's "The Time of History and the Times of Gods"
in this volume; and Lisa Lowe, *Immigrant Acts: On Asian American Cultural
Politics* (Durham: Duke University Press, 1996), chap. 1.

Our argument throughout this introduction, and that of the papers in this
volume, is that within the logic of capital, neither the economic nor the political
subject have ever emerged as pure abstractions. To grasp the implications of
this demands a rethinking of Marxism, right at the core of the labor theory of
value, and prompts a new understanding of the continual production of cultural differences in the history of modernity. Culture is, over and again, the field
on which economic and political contradictions are articulated.

I

CRITIQUE OF MODERNITY

DIPESH CHAKRABARTY

The Time of History and
the Times of Gods

In truth, the historian can never get away from the question of time in history: time sticks to his thinking like soil to a gardener's spade. FERNAND BRAUDEL, *On History*

The vulgar representation of time as a precise and homogeneous continuum has . . . diluted the Marxist concept of history. GIORGIO AGAMBEN, *Infancy and History*

At its core, this essay is about the problems a secular subject like history faces in handling imaginations in which gods, spirits, or the supernatural have agency in the world. My central examples concern the history of work in South Asia. Labor, the activity of producing, is seldom a completely secular activity in India. It often entails, through rituals big and small, the invocation of divine or super-human presence. Secular histories are produced usually by ignoring the signs of these presences. In effect, we have two systems of thought, one in which the world is *ultimately,* that is, in the final analysis, disenchanted, and the other in which the humans are not the only meaningful agents. For the purpose of writing history, the first system, the secular, translates the second into itself. It is the question of this translation — its methods and problems — that interests me here as part of a broader effort to situate the question of subaltern history within a postcolonial critique of modernity and of history itself.

This critique has to issue from within a dilemma that must mark a project such as subaltern studies. The dilemma is this: Writing subaltern history, documenting resistance to oppression and exploitation, must be part of a larger effort to make the world more socially just. To wrench subaltern studies away from the keen sense of social justice that gave rise to the project would be to violate the spirit that gives this project its sense of commitment and intellectual energy. Indeed, it may be said that it would be to violate the history of realist prose in India, for it may be legitimately argued that the administration of justice by modern institutions requires us to imagine the world through the languages of the social sciences, that is, as disenchanted.

I

History's own time is godless, continuous, and, to follow Benjamin, empty and homogeneous. By this I mean that in employing modern historical consciousness (whether in academic writing or outside of it), we think of a world that, in Weber's description, is already disenchanted. Gods, spirits, and other "supernatural" forces can claim no agency in our narratives. Further, this time is empty because it acts as a bottomless sack: any number of events can be put inside it; and it is homogeneous because it is not affected by any particular events: its existence is independent of such events and in a sense it exists prior to them. Events happen in time but time is not affected by them. The time of human history — as any popular book on the evolution of this universe will show — merges, when thought of backwards, into the time of prehistory, of evolutionary and geological changes going back to the beginning of the universe. It is part of nature. This is what allowed J. B. S. Haldane once to write a book with the telltale title *Everything Has a History.*[1] Hence the time of Newtonian science is not different to the time historians automatically assume as providing the ontological justification of their work. Things may move faster or slower in this time: that is simply the problem of velocity and speed. And the time may be cyclical or linear: the weeks belong to cyclical time, the English years go in hundred-year cycles, while the procession of years is a line. And historians may with justification talk about different regions of time: domestic time, work time, the time of the state, and so on. But all these times, whether cyclical or linear, fast or slow, are normally treated not as parts of a system of conventions, a cultural code of representation, but as something more objective, something belonging to "nature" itself. This nature/culture division becomes clear when we look at nineteenth-century uses of archaeology, for instance, in dating histories that provided no easy arrangements of chronology.

It is not that historians and philosophers of history are unaware of such a commonplace as the claim that modern historical consciousness, or for that matter academic history, as genres are of recent origin (as indeed are the imaginations of the modern sciences). Nor have they been slow to acknowledge the changes these genres have undergone since their inception.[2] The naturalism of historical time lies in the belief that *everything* can be historicized. So while the nonnaturalness of history, the discipline, is granted, the assumed universal applicability of its method entails a further assumption: that it is always possible to assign people, places, and objects to a naturally existing, continuous flow of historical time.[3] Thus, irrespective of a society's own understanding of temporality, a historian will always be able to produce a time line for the globe whose structure is like this:

Time   Events in

T1   Area X Area Y Area Z

T2   Area X Area Y Area Z

It does not matter if any of these areas were inhabited by peoples such as the Hawaiians or the Hindus, who (unlike, as some would say, the Chinese or the Arabs) did not have a "sense of chronological history" — as distinct from other forms of memories and understandings of historicity — before European arrival. Contrary to whatever they may have thought and however they may have organized their memories, the historian has the capacity to put them back into a time we all are supposed to have shared, consciously or not. History as a code thus invokes a natural, homogeneous, secular, calendrical time without which the story of human evolution/civilization — a single human history, that is — cannot be told. In other words, the code of the secular calendar that frames historical explanations has this claim built into it: that independent of culture or consciousness, people exist in historical time. That is why it is always possible to discover "history" (say, after European contact) even if you were not aware of its existence in the past. History is supposed to exist in the same way as the earth does, for instance.

I begin with the assumption that, to put it strongly, this time, the basic code of history, is not something that belongs to nature (i.e., is not completely independent of human systems of representation). It stands for a particular formation of the modern subject. This is not to say that this understanding of time is false or that it can be given up at will. But, clearly, the kind of correspondence that exists between our sensory worlds and the Newtonian imagination of the universe, between our experience of secular time and the time of physics, breaks down in many post-Einsteinian constructions. In the Newtonian universe, as in historical imagination, "events" are more or less separable from their descriptions: what is factual is seen as translatable from mathematics into prose or between different languages. Thus an elementary book on Newtonian physics can be written completely in Bengali alphabet and numerals, using a minimum of mathematical signs. But not so with post-Einsteinian physics: language strains wildly when trying to convey in prose the mathematical imagination contained in an expression like "curved space" (for, thinking commonsensically, in what would such a space exist if not in space itself?). In this second case, one might say that the assumption of translatability does not quite hold, that the imagination of Einsteinian physics is best learned through the language of its mathematics — for we are speaking of a universe of events where the events cannot be separated from their descriptions. Modern physics, one might say, took the linguistic turn early in this century. Post-Einsteinian cosmology, as the physicist Paul Davis puts it, makes even mathematical sense only so long as we do not try to take "a God's-eye-view" of the universe (i.e., so long as one does not try to totalize or to view the "whole"). "I have grown used to dealing with the weird and wonderful world of relativity," writes Davis. "The ideas of space-warps, distortions in time and space and multiple universes have become everyday tools in the strange trade of the theoretical physicist. . . . I believe that the reality exposed by modern physics is fundamentally alien to the human mind, and defies all power of direct visualization. . . ."[4]

Historians writing after the so-called linguistic turn may not any longer think that "events" are completely accessible by language, but the more sober among them would strive to avoid absolute lunacy by resorting to weaker versions of this position. As put in the recent book *Telling the Truth about History* by Lynn Hunt and her colleagues, historians, writing in the aftermath of postmodernism, would work toward an ideal of "workable truths," approximations of "facts" that can be agreed to by all even after it is granted that language and representations always form a (thin?) film between us and the world (in the same way we can mostly ignore the insights of Einsteinian or quantum physics in negotiating our everyday movements in practical life). The higher ideal of translatability between different languages — thus Vietnamese history into Bengali — remains something worth striving for even if language always foils the effort. This ideal — a modified Newtonianism — is, in their view, the historians' protection against the sheer madness of postmodernist and cultural relativist talk about "untranslatability," "incommensurability," and all that.[5]

Unlike in the world of the physicist Paul Davis, then, the imagination of "reality" in the discipline of history is dependent on the capacities of "the human mind," its powers of visualization. The use of the definite article is critical here, for this "reality" aspires to achieve a status of transparency with regard to particular human languages, an ideal of objectivity entertained by Newtonian science where translation between different languages is mediated by the higher language of science itself. Thus *pani* in Hindi and *water* in English can both be mediated by H_2O. Needless to say, it is only the higher language that is capable of appreciating, if not expressing, the capacities of "*the* human mind." I would suggest that the idea of a godless, continuous, empty, and homogeneous time that history shares with the other social sciences and modern political philosophy as a basic building block belongs to this model of a higher, overarching language — a structure of generality, an aspiration toward the scientific — which is built into conversations that take the modern historical consciousness for granted.

A proposition of radical untranslatability therefore comes as a problem to the universal categories that sustain the historian's enterprise. But it is also a false problem created by the very nature of the universal itself that aims to function as a supervening general construction mediating between all the particulars on the ground. The secular code of historical and humanist time — that is, a time bereft of gods and spirits — is one such universal. Claims about agency on behalf of the religious, the supernatural, the divine, and the ghostly have to be mediated in terms of this universal. The social scientist–historian assumes that "contexts" explain particular gods: If we could all have the same context, then we would all have the same gods as well. But there is a problem. Whereas the sameness of our "sciences" can be guaranteed all the world over, the sameness of our gods and spirits cannot be proved in quite the same objective manner (notwithstanding the protestations of the well-meaning that all religions speak of the same God). So it could be said that while the "sciences" signify some kind of sameness in our take on the world across cultures, the "gods" signify differences (bracketing for the moment the history of conversion, which I touch on, very briefly, in a later section). Writing about the presence of gods and spirits in the secular language of history or sociology would therefore be like an act of translating into a universal language what belongs to a field of differences.

The history of work in South Asia provides an interesting example of this problem. *Work* and *labor* are words deeply implicated in the production of universal sociologies. *Labor* is one of the key categories in the imagination of capitalism itself. In the same way that we think of capitalism coming into being in all sorts of contexts, we also imagine this modern category *work* or *labor* to emerge in all kinds of histories. This is what makes possible studies in the genre of "history of work in. . . ." In this sense, "labor" or "work" has the same status in my posing of the problem as does H_2O in the relation between *water* and *pani.* Yet the fact is that the modern word *labor,* as every historian of labor in India knows, translates into a general category a whole host of words with divergent and different associations. What complicates the story further is the fact that in a society such as the Indian, human activity (including what one would, sociologically speaking, regard as "labor") is often associated with the presence and agency of gods or spirits in the very process of labor itself. *Hathiyar puja* or the "worship of tools," for example, is a common and familiar festival in many north Indian factories. How do we — and I mean narrators of the pasts of the subaltern classes in India — handle this problem of the presence of the divine or the supernatural in the very history of labor as we render this enchanted world into our disenchanted prose, a rendering required, let us say, in the interest of social justice? And how do we, in doing this, still retain the subaltern (in whose activity gods or spirits present themselves) as the subjects of their histories? I will go over this question by examining the work of three subaltern studies historians who have produced fragments of histories of work in the context of "capitalist transition" in India: Gyan Prakash, Gyan Pandey, and myself. And I hope that my discussion will have something to say about the historian's enterprise in general.

II

Let me begin with an example from my research in labor history. Consider the following description from the 1930s of a particular festival (still quite common in India) that entails the worshiping of machinery by workers:

In some of the jute mills near Calcutta the mechanics often sacrifice goats at this time [autumn]. A separate altar is erected by the mechanics. . . . Various tools and other emblems are placed upon it. . . . Incense is burnt. . . . Towards evening a male goat is thoroughly washed . . . and prepared for a . . . final sacrifice. . . . The animal is decapitated at one stroke . . . [and] the head is deposited in the . . . sacred Ganges. . . .[6]

This particular festival is celebrated in many parts of north India as a public holiday for the working class, the day being named after the engineer god Vishvakarma. How do we read it? To the extent that this day has now become a "public" holiday in India, it has obviously been subjected to a process of bargaining among employers, workers, and the state. One could also argue that, insofar as the ideas of "recreation" and "leisure" belong to a discourse on what makes labor efficient and productive, this "religious" holiday itself belongs to the process through which labor is managed and disciplined and is hence a part of the history of emergence of abstract labor in commodity form (for the very "public" nature of the holiday shows that it has been written into an emergent national, secular calendar of production). We could thus produce a secular narrative that would apply, really, to any working-class "religious" holiday anywhere. Christmas or the Muslim festival Id could be seen in the same light. The difference between Vishvakarma *puja* (worship) and Christmas or Id would then be explained anthropologically, that is, by holding another master code — "culture" or "religion" — constant and universal. The "differences" between "religions" are by definition incapable of bringing the master category "culture" or "religion" into any kind of crisis. We know that these categories are problematic, that not all people have things called "culture" or "religion" in the English senses of these words, but we have to operate as though this limitation was not of any great moment. This was exactly how I treated this episode in my own book. The workers' practices suggesting a belief in gods was no threat to my Marxism or liberalism. Worshiping of machinery — an everyday fact of life in India, from taxis, to scooter-rickshaws, minibuses, and lathe machines — was something I interpreted, as do many of my colleagues in labor history, as an insurance policy against accidents and contingencies. That in the so-called religious imagination as in language, redundancy — the huge and, from a strictly functionalist point of view, unnecessarily elaborate panoply of iconography and rituals — itself proved the poverty of a purely functionalist approach, never deterred my Marxist narrative. (The question of whether or not the workers had a conscious or doctrinal belief in gods and spirits would also be wide of the mark; after all, gods are as real as ideology is, that is to say, after Žižek, they are embedded in practices.[7] More often than not, their presence is collectively invoked by rituals rather than by conscious belief.)

Gyan Prakash's monograph on the history of "bonded" labor in Bihar in colonial India contains an imaginative discussion on *bhut*s (spirits) that are thought to have supernatural power over humans, while not belonging to the pantheon of divinity. Prakash documents how these *bhut*s intercede in the relations of agrarian production in Gaya in the Indian state of Bihar, particularly a special category of *bhut* called *malik devata* (spirits of dead landlords). But Prakash's monograph, at the same time, is part of a conversation in academia, as all good work has to be, for that is the condition of its production. This conversation is also an inherent part of the process through which books and ideas express their commodified character; they all participate in a general economy of exchange made possible through the emergence of abstract, generalizing ideas. It is instructive, therefore, to see how the protocols of that conversation necessarily structure Prakash's explanatory framework and thereby obliterate from view some of the tensions of irreducible plurality I am trying to visualize in the very history of labor itself. Prakash writes:

In such fantastic images, the malik's [landlord's] power was reconstructed. Like Tio, the devil worshipped by the miners in Bolivia, the malik represented subordination of the Bhuinyas [laborers] by landlords. But whereas Tio expressed the alienation of miners from capitalist production, as Michael Taussig so eloquently argues, the malik devata of colonial Gaya echoed the power of the landlords over kamiyas [bonded labor] based on land control.[8]

Now, Prakash is not wrong in any simple sense. His sensitivity to the "logic of ritual practice" is in fact exemplary. It is just that I am reading this passage to understand the conditions for intertextuality that govern its structure and allow a conversation to emerge between Prakash's study, located in colonial Bihar in India, and Taussig's study of labor in the Bolivian tin mines. How do the specific and the general come together in this play of intertextuality, for we are trying to think our way to the art of "holding apart" that which coalesces *within* the process of this "coming together" of disparate histories?

The intertextuality of the passage from Prakash is based on the simultaneous assertion of likeness and dissimilarity between *malik devata* and Tio: witness the contradictory moves made by the two phrases "like Tio" and "whereas Tio." They are similar in that they have similar relationship to "power": they "express" and "echo" it. Their difference, however, is absorbed in a larger theoretic-universal difference between two different kinds of power, capitalist production and "land control." Pressed to the extreme, "power" itself must emerge as a last-ditch universal-sociological category (as indeed happens in texts that look for sociology in Foucault). But this "difference" already belongs to the sphere of the general.

A structure of generality within which specificities and differences are contained is normally the condition for conversation between historians and social scientists working on disparate sites. Paul Veyne's distinction between *specificity* and *singularity* is of relevance here. As Veyne puts it: "History is interested in individualized events . . . but it is not interested in their individuality; it seeks to understand them — that is, to find among them a kind of generality or, more precisely, of specificity. It is the same with natural history; its curiosity is inexhaustible, all the species matter to it and none is superfluous, but it does not propose the enjoyment of their singularity in the manner of the bestiary of the Middle Ages, in which one could read the description of noble, beautiful, strange or cruel animals."[9]

The very conception of the "specific" as it obtains in the discipline of history, in other words, belongs to the structure of a general that necessarily occludes our view of the singular. Of course, nothing exists as a "singular-in-itself." "Singularity" is a matter of viewing. It comes into being when we look on things in such a way as not to see them as "particular" expressions of that which is general. Philosophically, it is a limit-concept, since language itself mostly speaks of the general. Facing the singular might be a question of straining against language itself; it could, for example, involve the consideration of the manner in which the world, after all, remains opaque to the generalities inherent in language. Here, however, I am using a slightly weaker — philosophically speaking, that is — version of the idea. By "singular" I mean that which defies the generalizing impulse of the sociological imagination. To indicate what the struggle to view the singular might entail in the case of writing history, let us begin from a seemingly absurd position and see what happens to our intertextual conversation if we reverse the propositions of Prakash (and Taussig) to claim (a) that the "alienation of [Bolivian] miners from capitalist production" expressed the spirit of Tio, and (b) that "the power of the landlords over [Bihari] kamiyas" "echoed the power" of the *malik devata*. The conversation stalls. Why? Because we do not know what the relationship is between *malik devata* and Tio. They do not belong to structures of generalities, nor is there any guarantee that a relationship could exist between the two without the mediation of the language of social science. Between "capitalist production" and the "power of the landlord," however, the relationship is known, or at least we think we know it, thanks to all the grand narratives of transition from precapital to capital. It is always at least implicit in our sociologies that permeate the very language of social science writing.

The history of weaving in colonial Uttar Pradesh that Gyanendra Pandey examines in *The Construction of Communalism in Colonial North India* offers us another example of this tension between the general secular time of history and the singular times of gods and spirits.[10] Pandey's work deals with the history of a group of north Indian Muslim weavers called the Julahas and constitutes an imaginative radical reexamination of the stereotype of religious fanatics through which the British colonial officials saw them. The Julahas, Pandey shows, faced increasing displacement from their craft as a consequence of colonial economic policies in the late nineteenth and early twentieth centuries, and this had much to do with the history of their culture in this period. Pandey's text, however, displays tensions similar to those that operate in Prakash's. On the one hand there is the figure of the weaver-in-general-during-early-industrialization that underlies his comparativist gestures toward European history. The sentence that opens the chapter on "The Weavers" in E. P. Thompson's *The Making of the English Working Class*—"The history of the weavers in the nineteenth century is haunted by the legend of better days"—and a generalizing quote from Marx act as the framing devices for Pandey's chapter. "[B]ecause of the nature of their occupation," writes Pandey, "weavers everywhere have been commonly dependent on money lenders and other middlemen and vulnerable to the play of the market forces, all the more so in the era of the advance of industrial capitalism"; he adds a few pages later, "The history of the north Indian weavers in the nineteenth century is, in E. P. Thompson's phrase from another context, 'haunted by the legend of better days.' "[11] Further on, he writes in a Thompsonian vein of the weavers' "fight to preserve . . . their economic and social status" and of "their memories and pride" that fueled this fight.[12]

Pandey's own sensitivity and his acute sense of responsibility to the evidence, on the other hand, presents the question of difference, already hinted at in his gesture of assigning the Thompson quote to a "different context," in such a forceful manner that the comparativist stance is rendered positively problematic. The "legend of better days" in Thompson's account is entirely secular. It refers to a golden age made up of stories about "personal and . . . close" relations between "small masters and their men," about "strongly organized trade societies," about relative material prosperity, and about the weavers' "deep attachment to the values of independence."[13] A Wesleyan church in the village community marked if anything a physical distance between the loom and God, and the weavers, as Thompson says, were often critical of the "parish-church pa'son's."[14] God, on the other hand, is ever present in the very phenomenology of weaving in north India, as Pandey explains it, and it is a rather different god from Thompson's. Indeed, as Pandey himself makes clear, work and worship were two inseparable activities to the Julahas, so inseparable in fact that one could ask whether it makes sense to ascribe to them the identity of what only in the secular and overlapping languages of the census, administration, and sociology becomes the name of their "occupation": weaving.

As Pandey explains, his weavers called themselves *nurbaf* or "weavers of light." Drawing on Deepak Mehta's study of "Muslim weavers in two villages of Bara Banki district," Pandey notes "the intimate connection between work and worship in the lives of the weavers, and the centrality of the weavers' major religious text (or *kitab*), the *Mufid-ul-Mominin* in the practice of both." The *Mufid-ul-Mominin*, Pandey adds, "relates how the practice of weaving came into the world at its very beginning" (by a version of the Adam, Hawwa [Eve], and Jabril

[Gabriel] story), and "lists nineteen supplicatory prayers to be uttered in the different stages of weaving."[15] During the initiation of novices, notes Pandey, "all the prayers associated with the loom are recited. . . . 'The male headweaver, in whose household this initiation takes place, reads out all of Adam's questions and Jabril's answers from the *kitab* during the first six days of the month when both the loom and the *karkhana* [workshop or work-loom] are ritually cleaned.' When the loom is passed on from father to son, again, 'the entire conversation between Adam and Jabril is read out once by a holy man.' "[16] To cap it all, this was nothing like an enactment of some "memory" of times past, not a nostalgia, as Thompson sees it, haunted by the "legend of better days." The *Mufid-ul-Mominin* is not a book that has come down to present-day Julahas from a hoary antiquity. Deepak Mehta expressed the view to Pandey that "[it] may well date from the post-Independence period," while Pandey himself is decidedly of the opinion that "it is more than likely that the *Mufid-ul-Mominin* came to occupy this place as *the* 'book' of the weavers fairly recently—not before the late nineteenth or the early twentieth century in any case, for it is only from that time that the name 'Momin' (i.e. the faithful) was claimed as their own by the weavers."[17]

So Pandey's Julahas are both quite like and quite unlike Thompson's weavers, and it is their difference that allows us to raise the question of singularity. Was their god the same as the god of Thompson's Wesleyans? How would one translate into the other? Can we take this translation through some idea of a universal and freely exchangeable god, an icon of our humanism? I cannot answer the question because of my ignorance—I have no intimate knowledge of the Julahas' god—but Richard Eaton's study of Islamic mysticism in the Deccan in India gives us further insight into what I might crudely call nonsecular phenomenologies of labor.[18]

Eaton quotes from seventeenth-, eighteenth-, and early nineteenth-century Sufi manuscripts songs that Muslim women in the Deccan sang while engaged in such "domestic" tasks as spinning, grinding millet, and rocking children to sleep. They all reveal, as Eaton puts it, "the ontological link between God, the Prophet, the *pir* [the Sufi teacher] and [work]."[19] "As the *chakki* [grindstone] turns, so we find God," Eaton quotes an early eighteenth-century song; "it shows its life in turning as we do in breathing." Divinity is brought to presence sometimes through analogy, as in:

The *chakki's* handle resembles *alif*, which means Allah;
And the axle is Muhammad . . .

and sometimes in ways that make the bodily labor of work and worship absolutely inseparable experiences, as is suggested by this song sung at the spinning wheel:

> As you take the cotton, you should do *zikr-i jali* [*zikr*=mention of God].
> As you separate the cotton, you should do *zikr-i qalbi,*
> And as you spool the thread you should do *zikr-i 'aini.*
> *Zikr* should be uttered from the stomach through the chest,
> And threaded through the throat.
> The threads of breath should be counted one by one, oh sister.
> Up to twenty-four thousand.
> Do this day and night,
> And offer it to your *pir* as a gift.[20]

Straining further toward the singularity of this phenomenology of turning the *chakki* would require us to explore the differences between the different kinds of *zikr*s mentioned in this song and to enter imaginatively the "mysticism" (once again, a generalizing name!) that envelops them. But on what grounds do we assume, ahead of any investigation, that this divine presence invoked at every turn of the *chakki* will translate neatly into a secular history of labor so that — transferring the argument back to the context of the tool-worshiping factory workers — the human beings collected in modern industries may indeed appear as the subjects of a metanarrative of Marxism, socialism, or even democracy?

Let me make it very clear that it is not the raging Medusa of cultural relativism rearing her ugly head in my writing at this point. To allow for plurality, signified by the plurality of gods, is to think singularities. To think singularities, however — and this I must make clear since so many scholars these days are so prone to see parochialism, essentialism, or "cultural relativism" in every claim of non-Western difference — is *not* to make a claim against the demonstrable and documentable permeability of cultures and languages. It is in fact to appeal to models of cross-cultural and cross-categorical translations that do not, unlike in sociological or social-scientist thinking, take a universal middle term for granted. The Hindi *pani* may be translated into the English *water* without having to go through the science of H_2O. In this, at least in India but perhaps elsewhere as well, we have something to learn from nonmodern instances of cross-categorical translation. I give an example here of translation of Hindi gods into expressions of Islamic divinity that was performed in an eighteenth-century Bengali religious text called *Shunya-puran.* (The evidence belongs to the "history of conversion" to Islam in Bengal.) This text has a description, well-known to students of Bengali literature, of Islamic wrath falling upon a group of oppressive Brahmins and in the course of this description gives the following account of an exchange of identities between individual Hindu deities and their Islamic counterparts:

Dharma who resided in Baikuntha was grieved to see all this [Brahminic misconduct]. He came to the world as a Muhammadan . . . [and] was called Khoda. . . . Brahma incarnated himself as Muhammad, Visnu as Paigambar and Civa became Adamfa (Adam). Ganesa came as a Gazi, Kartika as a Kazi, Narada became a Sekha and Indra a Moulana. The Risis of heaven became Fakirs. . . . The goddess Chandi incarnated herself as Haya Bibi [the wife of the original man] and Padmavati became Bibi Nur [Nur=light].[21]

Eaton's recent study of Islam in Bengal gives many more such instances. Consider the case of an Arabic-Sanskrit bilingual inscription from a thirteenth-century mosque in coastal Gujarat that Eaton cites in his discussion. The Arabic part of this inscription, dated 1264, "refers to the deity worshipped in the mosque as Allah," while, as Eaton puts it, "the Sanskrit text of the same inscription addresses the supreme god by the names Visvanatha ('lord of the universe'), Sunyarupa ('one whose form is of the void'), and Visvarupa ('having various forms')."[22] Further on, Eaton gives more examples from medieval Bengal of such cross-categorial translation: "The sixteenth-century poet Haji Muhammad identified the Arabic Allah with Gosai (Skt. 'Master'), Saiyid Murtaza identified the Prophet's daughter Fatima with Jagat-janani (Skt. 'Mother of the World'), and Saiyid Sultan identified the God of Adam, Abraham, and Moses with Prabhu (Skt. 'Lord')."[23]

The interesting point, for our purpose and in our language, is how the translations that take place in these passages take barter for their model of exchange rather than that of a generalized exchange of commodities which always needs the mediation of a universal, homogenizing middle term (such as, in Marxism, "abstract labor"). The translations here are based on very local, particular, one-for-one exchanges, guided in part, no doubt, at least in the case of *Shunya-puran*, by the poetic requirements of alliterations, meter, rhetorical conventions, and so on. There are surely rules in these exchanges, but the point is that, even if I cannot decipher them all — and even if they are not all decipherable, that is to say, even if the processes of translation contain a degree of opacity — it can be safely asserted that these rules cannot and would not claim to have the "universal" character of the rules that sustain conversations between social scientists working in disparate sites of the world.

One critical aspect of this mode of translation is that it makes no appeal to any implicit universals or sociologies. Codes are switched locally, without going through a universal set of rules. Which is another way of saying that there are no overarching censoring/limiting/defining systems of thought that neutralize and relegate differences to the margins, nothing like an overarching category of "religion" that is supposed to remain unaffected by differences between the entities it seeks to name and thereby contain. The very obscurity of the translation process would allow the incorporation of that which, strictly speaking, is untranslatable. It is obvious that this nonmodern mode of translation lends itself more easily to fiction, particularly of the nonrealist or magic-realist variety practiced today, than to the secular prose of sociology or history.[24] In these fictive narratives, gods and spirits can indeed be agents. But then what of history? What of its abiding allegiance to secular, continuous, empty, homogeneous time? And what of the project of Marxist-subaltern history in which my work participates?

I want to argue that the question of having to translate difference back into the sociological/secular same poses an ethical challenge to our writing. The following section takes up this point.

III

The ethical challenge is twofold. Mine is not a postmodern argument announcing the death of history and recommending fiction writing as a career for all historians. (For one thing, *I* do not have the talents to do this.) But personal talents apart, there is another reason why the training of the mind in modern historical consciousness is justified even from the point of view of the subaltern, and this has to do with the intermeshing of the logic of secular human sciences with that of bureaucracies. One cannot argue with modern bureaucracies and other instruments of governmentality without recourse to the secular time and narratives of history and sociology. The subaltern classes need this knowledge to fight their battles for social justice. It would therefore be unethical not to make historical consciousness available to everybody, in particular the subaltern classes. When has the International Monetary Fund or the United Nations listened to an argument involving the agency of gods?

Yet at the same time, historicism — the idea that things develop in historical time, that this time is empty and homogeneous, that history is layered and contains what Marx called the "unvanquished remnants of the past," something that Marxists (after Ernst Bloch) have often tried to capture in the expression "simultaneity of the non-simultaneous" — carries with it, precisely because of its openness to certain kinds of

"evolutionism" and its association with the logic of bureaucratic decision making, an inherent modernist elitism that silently lodges itself
into our everyday consciousness.[25]

Historicism, as Heidegger explained in his critique, consists in a very
particular understanding of the question of contemporaneity: the idea
that things from different historical periods can exist in the same time
(the so-called simultaneity of the non-simultaneous) but belong to different worlds. Thus we may have a "medieval" object before us, but it is
relic from a past world that is no longer there. One could, in historicism, look at peasants in the same way: as survivals from a dead
world.[26] This is a fundamental characteristic of historicist thought. It is
what allows us to think that the "agency of the supernatural" is a
problem from the past surviving, for good and understandable historical reasons, in a disenchanted present. So often historians see themselves as either reading the past off something like a palimpsest or
engaged in a work of geologic interpretation. Eaton begins the last
chapter of his meticulously researched book on Bengali Islam with a
sentence that aims to appeal to the trained aesthetic sensibility of all
historians: "Like the strata of a geologic fossil record, place names
covering the surface of a map silently testily to past historical processes."[27] I could launch into an examination here of the thought habits
of most historians, but it is not the self-regarding attitude of historians
that make history, the subject, important in the world outside of academia. History is important as a form of consciousness in modernity.
(Historians may want to see themselves as its arbiters and custodians,
but that is a different question.) Let me explain, therefore, with the help
of an ordinary, casual example, how a certain sense of historical time
works in the everyday speech of public life in modern societies. Consider the following statement in a newspaper article by the cultural
studies specialist Simon During in an issue of the Melbourne daily *Age*
(19 June 1993): "thinking about movies like *Of Mice and Men* and *The
Last of the Mohicans* allows us to see more clearly where contemporary
culture is going."[28] The source for the statement actually does not
matter, for During is not the target of my comments. My remarks
pertain to a certain habit of thought that the statement illustrates. What
I want to discuss is the imagination of historical time that is built into
this use of the word *contemporary*. Clearly, the word speaks a double
gesture, and an implicit acceptance of this gesture between the author
and the reader is the condition that enables the sentence to communicate its point. The gesture is double because it is at the same time a
gesture of both inclusion and exclusion. Obviously, *contemporary* refers to all that belong to a "culture" at a particular point on the (secu-

lar) calendar that the author and the intended reader of this statement inhabit. In that sense everybody is part of the *contemporary*. Yet, surely, it is not being claimed that every element in the culture is moving toward the destination that the author has identified in the films mentioned. What about, for instance, the peasants of Greece, if we could imagine them migrating to the "now" of the speaker? (I mention the Greeks because they constitute one of the largest groups of European immigrants into Australia.) They may inhabit the speaker's "now" and yet may not be going in the direction that *The Last of the Mohicans* suggests.[29] The implicit claim of the speaker is not that these people are not moving, but whatever futures these others may be building for themselves will soon be swamped and overwhelmed by the future the author divines on the basis of his evidence. That is the gesture of exclusion built into this use of the word *contemporary*.

If this sounds like too strong a claim, try the following thought experiment. Suppose we argue that the contemporary is actually plural, so radically plural that it is not possible for any particular aspect or element to claim to represent the whole in any way (even as a possible future). Under these conditions, a statement such as During's would be impossible to make. We would instead have to say that "contemporary culture," being plural and there being equality within plurality, was going many different places at the same time (I have problems with "at the same time," but let's stay with it for the present). Then there would be no way of talking about the cutting edges, the avant-garde, the latest that represents the future, the most modern, and so on. Without such a rhetoric and a vocabulary and the sentiments that go with them, however, many of our everyday political strategies in the scramble for material resources would be impossible to pursue. How would you get government backing, research funding, institutional approval for an idea if you could not claim on its behalf that it represents the more "dynamic" part of the "contemporary," which thus is pictured as something already always split into two, one part rushing headlong into the future, and another passing away into the past, something like the "living dead" in our midst?

A certain kind of historicism, the metanarrative of progress, is thus deeply embedded in our institutional lives however much we may develop, as individual intellectuals, an attitude of incredulity toward such metanarratives. (Lyotard in *The Postmodern Condition* actually concedes this point.)[30] This is why the subaltern classes would need the idea of history and the historicist mode of thinking. And as intellectuals we need tools that help us develop critiques of institutions on their own terms, secular critiques for secular institutions of government. Hence,

Marx's thoughts, still the most effective secular critique of capital, remain indispensable to our engagement with the question of social justice in capitalist societies. But my point is that what is indispensable remains inadequate, for we still have to translate into the time of history and the narrative of "human (secular) labor" — the key to emancipation in European romantic thought to which both Hegel and Marx were heirs — the story of work that incorporates agency on the part of gods and spirits.[31] And historicism will continue to produce an elitism in the very way we imagine the structure of historical time.

There is an additional point I want to make here. It is to acknowledge and learn from the modes of translation that I have called non-modern the barterlike term-for-term exchanges that bypass all the implicit sociologies of our work. Here translation is antisociology and for that reason has no obligation to be secular. Fiction and films are the best modern media for handling it. This is where the past is pure narration no matter who gets to have agency in it. But this option is not open to the historian. The moment we think of the world as disenchanted, we set limits to the ways the past can be narrated. As a practicing historian one has to take these limits seriously. For instance, there are cases of peasant revolts in India where the peasants claimed to have been inspired to rebel by the exhortations of their gods. For a historian, this statement would never do as an explanation, and one would feel obliged to translate the peasants' claim into some kind of context of understandable causes animating the rebellion. I assume that such translation is both inevitable and unavoidable (for we do not write for the peasants). The question is: How do we conduct these translations in such a manner as to make visible all the problems of translating diverse and enchanted worlds into the universal and disenchanted language of sociology? Here let me say what I have learned from Vicente Rafael's and Gayatri Spivak's discussions of the politics of translation.[32] We know that given the plurality of gods, the translation from godly time into the time of secular labor could proceed along a variety of paths. But whatever the nature of the path it took, this translation, to borrow from Spivak's and Rafael's handling of the question, must possess something of the "uncanny" about it. An ambiguity must mark the translation of the tool-worshiping jute worker's labor into the universal category *labor*: it must be "enough like" the secular category *labor* to "make that sense," yet the presence and plurality of gods and spirits in it must also make it "enough unlike to shock."[33] There remains something of a scandal in every translation, and it is only a relationship of intimacy to both languages that makes us aware of the degree of this scandal.

This property of translation—that we become more aware of the complexities involved in the translation process only if we know intimately both of the languages—has been well expressed by Michael Gelven:

> If an English-speaking student . . . sets out to learn German, he first looks up in a lexicon or vocabulary list a few basic German words. At this point, however, these German words are not German at all. They are merely sounds substituted for English meanings. They are, in a very real sense, English words. This means that they take their contextual significance from the . . . totality of the English language. . . . If a novice in German language picked up a copy of Schopenhauer's book and wondered what *Vorstellung* meant in the title, he would probably look the term up in the lexicon, and find such suggestions as "placing before." And although he might think it strange to title a book "The World as Will and Placing Before," he would nevertheless have some idea of the meaning of that remarkable work. But as this novice worked himself through the language, and became familiar with the many uses of the term *Vorstellung* and actually used it himself . . . [h]e might, to his own surprise, realize that although he knew what the term meant, he could not translate the German term back into his own language—an obvious indication that the reference of meaning was no longer English as in his first encounter with it.[34]

Usually, or at least in South Asian studies, the Marxist or secular scholar translating the divine is in the place of the student who knows well only one of the two languages he is working with. It is all the more imperative, therefore, that we read our secular universals in such a way as to keep them always open to their own finitude so that the scandalous aspects of our unavoidable translations, instead of being made inaudible, actually reverberate through what we write in subaltern studies. To recognize the existence of this "scandal" in the very formation of our sociological categories is the first step we can take toward working the universalist and global archives of capital in such a way as to "blast . . . out of the homogeneous course of history," times that produce cracks in the structure of that homogeneity.[35]

IV

This is where, it seems to me, deconstruction helps. In this concluding section I will try to show, by reading Marx with the help of the Derridean notion of the trace, how one may hold one's categories open in translating and producing, out of the pasts of the subaltern classes, what is undeniably a universal history of labor in the capitalist mode of production.[36]

Looking back at my own work on Indian "working-class" history a few years ago, I seem to have only half-thought the problem. I documented a history whose narrative(s) produced several points of friction with the teleologies of "capital." In my study of the jute mill workers of colonial Bengal I tried to show how the production relations in these mills were structured from the inside, as it were, by a whole series of relations that could only be considered precapitalist. The coming of capital and commodity did not appear to lead to the politics of equal rights that Marx saw as internal to these categories. I refer here in particular to the critical distinction Marx draws between *real* and *abstract* labor in explaining the production and the form of the commodity. These distinctions refer to a question in Marx's thought that we now recognize as the question of the politics of difference. The question for Marx was: If human beings are individually different from one another in their capacity to labor, how does capital produce out of this field of difference an abstract, homogeneous measure of labor — which Marx called abstract labor — that makes the generalized production of commodities possible? This is how I then read the distinction between real and abstract labor (with enormous debt to Michel Henry and I. I. Rubin):[37]

Marx places the question of subjectivity right at the heart of his category "capital" when he posits the conflict between "real labour" and "abstract labour" as one of its central contradictions. "Real labour" refers to the labor power of the actual individual, labor power "as it exists in the *personality* of the labourer" — that is, as it exists in the "immediate exclusive individuality" of the individual. Just as personalities differ, similarly the labor power of one individual is different from that of another. "Real labour" refers to the essential heterogeneity of individual capacities. "Abstract" or general labor, on the other hand, refers to the idea of uniform, homogeneous labor that capitalism imposes on this heterogeneity, the notion of a general labor that underlies "exchange value." It is what makes labor measurable and makes possible the generalized exchange of commodities. It expresses itself . . . in capitalist discipline, which has the sole objective of making every individual's concrete labor — by nature heterogeneous — "uniform and homogeneous" through supervision and technology employed in the labor process. . . . Politically, . . . the concept of "abstract labour" is an extension of the bourgeois notion of the "equal rights" of "abstract individuals," whose political life is reflected in the ideals and practice of "citizenship." The politics of "equal rights" is thus precisely the "politics" one can read into the category "capital."[38]

It now seems to me that Marx's category of commodity has a certain built-in openness to "difference" that I did not fully exploit in my exposition. My reading of the term *precapital* remained, in spite of my efforts, hopelessly historicist, and my narrative never quite escaped the (false) question, Why did the Indian working class fail to sustain a long-term sense of class-consciousness?, the metaproblem of "failure" itself arising from the well-known Marxist tradition of positing the working class as a transcultural subject. Besides, it is also clear from the above quote that my reading took the ideas of the "individual" and "personality" as unproblematically given, and read the word *real* (in "real labour") to mean something primordially natural (and therefore not social).

But my larger failure lay in my inability to see that if one read the word *real* not as something that referred to a Rousseauian "natural," that is, the naturally different endowments of different, and ahistorical, individuals, but rather as something that questioned the nature-culture distinction itself, other possibilities open up, among them the one of writing "difference" back into Marx. For the *real* then (in this reading) must refer to different kinds of "social," ones that could include nonhumans — and hence to different orders of temporality as well. It should in principle even allow for the possibility of these temporal horizons being mutually incommensurable. The transition from *real* to *abstract* is thus also a question of transition/translation from many and possibly incommensurable temporalities to the homogeneous time of abstract labor, the transition from *nonhistory* to *history*. Real labor, the category, itself universal, must nevertheless have the capacity to refer to that which cannot be enclosed by the sign *commodity*, even though what remains unenclosed constantly inheres in the sign itself. In other words, by thinking of the commodity itself as constituted by a permanent tension between real and abstract labor, Marx builds, as it were, a memory into this analytical category of what lies on its outside, something that it can never completely capture. The "outside" is constitutive of the category. The gap between real and abstract labor and the force ("factory discipline," in Marx's description) constantly needed to close it is what then introduces the movement of "difference" into the very constitution of the commodity, and thereby eternally defers its achievement of its true/ideal character.

The sign *commodity*, as Marx explains, will always carry as parts of its internal structure certain universal emancipatory narratives. If one overlooked the tension Marx situated at the heart of this category, these narratives could indeed produce the standard teleologies one normally encounters in Marxist historicism: that of citizenship, the juridical subject of Enlightenment thought, the subject of political theory of rights, and so on. I have not sought to deny the practical utility of these narratives in modern political structures. The more interesting problem for the Marxist historian, it seems to me, is the problem of temporality that the category commodity, constituted through the tension and possible noncommensurability between real and abstract labor, invites us to think. If real labor, as we have said, belongs to a world of heterogeneity whose various temporalities — Michael Taussig's work on Bolivian tin miners has already showed that they are not even all "secular" (i.e., bereft of gods and spirits) — cannot be enclosed in the sign *History,* then it can find a place in a historical narrative of capitalist transition (or commodity production) only as a Derridean trace of something that cannot be enclosed, an element that constantly challenges from within capital's and commodity's — and, by implication, History's — claims to unity and universality.[39]

The prefix *pre* in *precapital,* it could be said similarly, is not a reference to what is simply chronologically prior on an ordinal, homogeneous scale of time. *Pre-capitalist* is a hyphenated identity; it speaks of a particular relationship to capital marked by the tension of difference in the horizons of time. The precapitalist, on the basis of this argument, can only be imagined as something that exists within the temporal horizon of capital and is at the same time something that also disrupts the continuity of this time by suggesting another time that is not on the same, secular, homogeneous calendar (which is why what is precapital is not chronologically prior to capital, that is to say, one cannot assign it to a point on the same continuous time line). This is another time that, theoretically, could be entirely immeasurable in terms of the units of the godless, spiritless time of what we call "history," an idea already assumed in the secular concepts of *capital* and *abstract labor.*

Subaltern histories, thus conceived in relationship to the question of difference, will have a split running through them. On the one hand, they are "histories" in that they are constructed within the master code of secular History and use the accepted academic codes of history writing (and thereby perforce subordinate to themselves all other forms of memory). On the other hand, they cannot ever afford to grant this master code its claim of being a mode of thought that comes to all human beings naturally, or even to be treated as something that exists out there in nature itself. Subaltern histories are therefore constructed within a particular kind of historicized memory, one that remembers History itself as a violation, an imperious code that accompanied the civilizing process that the European Enlightenment inaugurated in the eighteenth century as a world-historical task. It is not enough to historicize history, the discipline, for that only uncritically keeps in place the very understanding of time that enables us to historicize in the first place. The point is to ask how this seemingly imperious, all-pervasive code might be deployed or thought so that we have at least a glimpse of its own finitude, a vision of what might constitute an outside to it. To hold history, the discipline, and other forms of memory together so that they can help in the interrogation of each other, to work out the ways these immiscible forms of recalling the past get juxtaposed in our negotiations of modern institutions, to question the narrative strategies in academic history that allow its secular temporality the appearance of successfully assimilating to itself memories that are, strictly speaking, unassimilable — these are the tasks that subaltern histories are suited to accomplish in a country such as India. For to talk about the violent jolt the imagination has to suffer to be transported from a temporality cohabited by nonhumans and humans to one from which the gods are banished is not to express an incurable nostalgia for a long-lost world. Even for the members of the Indian upper classes, in no sense can this experience of traveling across temporalities be described as merely historical.

Of course, the empirical historians who write these histories are not peasants or tribal themselves. They produce History, as distinct from other forms of memory, precisely because they have been transposed and inserted — in our case, by England's work in India — into the global narratives of citizenship and socialism. They write history, that is, only after the social-existence form of their own labor has entered the process of being made abstract in the world market for ideational commodities. The subaltern, then, is not the empirical peasant or tribal in any straightforward sense that a populist program of history writing may want to imagine. The figure of the subaltern is necessarily mediated by problems of representation. In terms of the analysis that I have been trying to develop here, one might say that the subaltern is what fractures from within the very signs that tell of the insertion of the historian (as a speaking subject) into the global narratives of capital; it is that which constantly, from within the narrative, calls into question the various global narratives that aid particular forms of domination. It is what gathers itself under real labor in Marx's critique of capital, the figure of difference that governmentality — in Foucault's sense of the term (i.e., the pursuit of the goals of modern governments) — all over the world has to subjugate and civilize.[40]

There are implications that follow: subaltern histories written with an eye to difference cannot constitute yet another attempt, in the long and universalistic tradition of "socialist" histories, to help erect the subaltern as the subject of modern democracies, that is, to expand the history of the modern in such a way as to make it more representative of society as a whole. This is a laudable objective on its own terms and has undoubted global relevance. But thought does not have to stop at political democracy or the concept of egalitarian distribution of wealth (though the aim of achieving these ends will legitimately fuel many immediate political struggles). Fundamentally, this thought is insensitive to philosophical questions of difference and can acknowledge difference only as a practical problem in a world that is assumed to be same. Subaltern histories will engage philosophically with questions of difference that are elided in the dominant traditions of Marxism. At the same time, however, just as real labor cannot be thought outside of the problematic of abstract labor, subaltern history cannot be thought outside of the global narrative of capital — including the narrative of transition to capitalism — though it is not grounded in this narrative. Stories about how this or that group in Asia, Africa, or Latin America resisted the "penetration" of capitalism do not, in this sense, constitute "subaltern" history, for these narratives are predicated on imagining a space that is external to capital — the chronologically "before" of capital — but that is at the same time a part of the historicist, unitary time frame within which both the "before" and the "after" of capitalist production can unfold. The "outside" I am thinking of is different from what is simply imagined as "before or after capital" in historicist prose. This "outside" I think of, after Derrida, is something attached to the category *capital* itself, something that straddles a border zone of temporality, something that conforms to the temporal code within which "capital" comes into being while violating that code at the same time, something we are able to see only because we can think/theorize capital, but something that also always reminds us that other temporalities, other forms of worlding, coexist and are possible. In this sense, subaltern histories do not refer to a resistance prior and exterior to the narrative space created by capital; they cannot therefore be defined without reference to the category *capital. Subaltern Studies,* as I think of it, can only situate itself theoretically at the juncture where we give up neither Marx nor "difference," for, as I have said, the resistance it speaks of is something that can happen only *within* the time horizon of capital and yet has to be thought of as something that disrupts the unity of that time. Unconcealing the tension between real and abstract labor ensures that capital/commodity has heterogeneities and incommensurabilities inscribed in its core.

The real labor of my mill workers, then — let us say their relationship to their own labor on the day of Vishvakarma *puja* — is obviously a part of the world in which both they and the god Vishvakarma exist in some sense (it would be silly to reduce this existence to a question of conscious belief or of psychology). History cannot represent, except through a process of translation and consequent loss of status and signification for the translated, the temporality of that world. History as a code comes into play as this real labor gets transformed into the homogeneous, disciplined world of abstract labor, of the generalized world of exchange where every exchange will be mediated by the sign *commodity*. Yet, as the story of the Vishvakarma *puja* in the Calcutta mills shows, real labor inheres in the commodity and its secularized biography; its presence, never direct, leaves its effect in the breach that story makes in history's system of representation. As I have already said, the breach cannot be mended by anthropological cobbling, for that only shifts the methodological problems of secular narratives on to another, cognate territory. In developing Marxist histories after the demise of Communist Party "Marxisms," our task is to write and think this breach as we write history (for we cannot avoid writing history). If history is to become a site where pluralities will contend, we need to develop ethics and politics of writing that will show history, this gift of modernity to many peoples, to be constitutionally marked by this breach.

Or, to put it differently, the practice of subaltern history aims to take history, the code, to its limits in order to make its unworking visible.

NOTES

This essay draws on my earlier essay, "Marx after Marxism: History, Subalternity, Difference," published in *positions: east asia cultures critique* and reprinted in Saree Makdisi et al., eds., *Marxism beyond Marxism* (New York: Routledge, 1996). For the revisions, I am grateful to Anne Hardgrove, David Lloyd, Lisa Lowe, and Sumathi Ramaswamy and to criticisms received at a seminar on South Asian Labour organized at the Institute of Social Studies, Amsterdam, by Dr. Prabhu Mahapatra and his colleagues in October 1995.

1. J. B. S. Haldane, *Everything Has a History* (London: Allen and Unwin, 1951).

2. See Peter Burke, *The Renaissance Sense of the Past* (London: Edward Arnold, 1970); E. H. Carr's classic *What Is History?* (New York: Vintage, 1961) is at one level a discussion of how the genre has changed in Carr's own lifetime; R. G. Collingwood's *The Idea of History* (1936, reprint, Oxford: Oxford University Press, 1976) distinguishes "the modern European idea of history" from other historical sensibilities or the lack thereof; Marc Bloch in *The Historian's Craft* (1954, reprint, Manchester: Manchester University Press, 1984) relates the historian's method to the modern "method of doubt"; for Fernand Braudel, *On History,* trans. Sarah Matthews (Chicago: University of Chicago Press,

1980), "history," the discipline, "makes up one single intellectual adventure" in partnership with sociology (69); J. G. A. Pocock's *The Ancient Constitution and the Feudal Law* (1957, reprint, Cambridge: Cambridge University Press, 1990) gives the modern historical method a specific origin in seventeenth-century juridical thought.

3. The only place I have found an explicit critique of this "ahistorical concept of time" with particular reference to Marxist history writing practices is Giorgio Agamben's essay "Time and History: Critique of the Instant and the Continuum," in his *Infancy and History: Essays on the Destruction of Experience,* trans. Liz Heron (London: Verso, 1993), 103–104.

4. Paul Davis and John Gribbon, *The Matter Myth: Beyond Chaos and Complexity* (Harmondsworth: Penguin, 1992), 103–104.

5. Joyce Appleby, Lynn Hunt, and Margaret Jacobs, *Telling the Truth about History* (New York: Norton, 1994).

6. Dipesh Chakrabarty, *Rethinking Working-Class History: Bengal, 1890–1940* (Princeton: Princeton University Press, 1989), 89–90.

7. Slavoj Žižek, *The Sublime Object of Ideology* (London: Verso, 1989), 30–34.

8. Gyan Prakash, *Bonded Histories: Genealogies of Labor Servitude in Colonial India* (Cambridge: Cambridge University Press, 1990), 216.

9. Paul Veyne, *Writing History: Essays on Epistemology,* trans. Mina Moore-Rinvolucri (Middletown, CT: Wesleyan University Press, 1984), 56.

10. Gyanendra Pandey, *The Construction of Communalism in Colonial North India* (Delhi: Oxford University Press, 1992).

11. Ibid., 71, 74; E. P. Thompson, *The Making of the English Working Class* (New York: Vintage, 1963), 297.

12. Pandey, *The Constitution of Communalism,* 99, 102.

13. See Thompson, *The Making of the English Working Class,* 302, 303, 305.

14. Ibid., 305, 323.

15. Pandey, *The Construction of Communalism,* 88, 97–98. See also Deepak Mehta, "The Semiotics of Weaving: A Case Study," *Contributions to Indian Sociology* 26, no. 1 (January–June 1992), 77–113.

16. Pandey, *The Construction of Communalism,* 98–99.

17. Ibid., 97.

18. Richard Maxwell Eaton, *Sufis of Bijapur, 1300–1700: Social Role of Sufis in Medieval India* (Princeton: Princeton University Press, 1978).

19. Ibid., 161.

20. Ibid., 163–164.

21. This translation is by Dinesh Chandra Sen; see his *History of Bengali Language and Literature* (Calcutta: University of Calcutta, 1911), 36–37. See also the discussion of this passage in Sukumar Sen, *Bangala sahityer itihas* (in Bengali), vol. 1 (Calcutta: Ananda Publishers, 1978), 114–116.

22. Richard Maxwell Eaton, *The Rise of Islam and the Bengal Frontier, 1204–1760* (Berkeley: University of California Press, 1993), 275.

23. Ibid., 276.

24. I have in mind recent fictions by Indian authors such as Mukul Kesvan and Shashi Tharoor.

25. Karl Marx, *Grundrisse: Foundations of the Critique of Political Economy,* trans. Martin Nicolaus (Harmondsworth: Penguin, 1974), 105; see also Fredric Jameson's discussion of Bloch in his *Postmodernism, or, the Cultural Logic of Late Capitalism* (Durham: Duke University Press, 1991), 307.

26. See the discussion in Martin Heidegger, *Being and Time,* trans. John Mc-Quarie and Edward Robinson (Oxford: Blackwell, 1985), 430–432, and the gloss in Michael Gelven, *A Commentary on Heidegger's Being and Time* (DeKalb: North Illinois University Press, 1989), 200–221. See also Michael Allen Gillespie, *Hegel, Heidegger and the Ground of History* (Chicago: University of Chicago Press, 1984), 153–169.

27. Eaton, *The Rise of Islam,* 305.

28. Simon During, "Is Literature Dead or Has It Gone to the Movies?" *Age* (Melbourne) (19 June 1993).

29. There is a fine analysis of this "now" in an essay entitled "The Migrant's Time" by Ranajit Guha (unpublished).

30. Jean-François Lyotard, *The Postmodern Condition,* trans. Geoff Bennington and Brian Massumi (Minneapolis: University of Minnesota Press, 1984), 31–37.

31. The idea that "work" or "labor" is a critical medium for expressing the "self" has strong connections with European romantic thought.

32. See Gayatri Chakravorty Spivak, "Politics of Translation," in *Outside in the Teaching Machine* (New York: Routledge, 1993), 182, and the chapter entitled "Untranslatability and the Terms of Reciprocity" in Vicente L. Rafael, *Contracting Colonialism: Translation and Christian Conversion in Tagalog Society under Early Spanish Rule* (Durham: Duke University Press, 1993), 110–135.

33. Spivak, "Politics of Translation," 182.

34. Gelven, *A Commentary,* 41.

35. The phrase is Benjamin's; see Walter Benjamin, "Theses on the Philosophy of History," in *Illuminations,* ed. Hannah Arendt, trans. Harry Zohn (New York: Schocken, 1969), 263.

36. On the idea of the "trace," see the discussion in Drucilla Cornell, *The Philosophy of the Limit* (New York: Routledge, 1992), 72–77.

37. Michel Henry, *Marx: A Philosophy of Human Reality* (Bloomington: Indiana University Press, 1983), and I. I. Rubin, *Essays on Marx's Theory of Value* (Montreal: Black Rose Books, 1975).

38. Chakrabarty, *Rethinking Working-Class History,* 225–26.

39. Michael Taussig, *The Devil and Commodity Fetishism in South America* (Chapel Hill: University of North Carolina Press, 1984).

40. See Michel Foucault, "Governmentality" in *The Foucault Effect: Studies in Governmentality,* ed. Graham Burchell, Colin Gordon, and Peter Miller (London: Wheatsheaf, 1991), 87–104.

AIHWA ONG

The Gender and Labor Politics
of Postmodernity

The literature on export-industrialization and the feminization of industrial work challenges theory to catch up with lived realities. Reports from the new frontiers of industrial labor reveal a widening gap between our analytical constructs and workers' actual experiences. This puzzle arises from our limited theoretical grasp of the ingenuity of capitalist operations and the creativity of workers' responses in the late twentieth century.

Modernization models of capitalist development[1] predicted an increasing adoption of mass-assembly production[2] and the gradual decline of cottage industries in the third world. Yet, since the early 1970s, mixed systems based on free-trade zones, subcontracting firms, and sweatshops have come to typify industrialization in Asia, Central America, and elsewhere. Lipietz[3] argues that the current mix of mass production, subcontracting, and family-type firms represents a new regime of accumulation worldwide. Since the 1973 world recession, new patterns of "flexible accumulation"[4] have come into play as corporations struggle in an increasingly competitive global arena. Flexible labor regimes, based primarily on female and minority workers, are now common in the third world, as well as in poor regions of metropolitan countries.[5]

Another common assumption about industrialization is that "class consciousness" is the most fundamental category by means of which we are to understand workers' experiences. Furthermore, theorists construct workers' engagements with capitalism in terms both of a core-periphery framework and of other binary models such as metropolitan/ex-colonial formations and hegemonic/despotic labor regimes.[6] Thus, the feminization of the transnational industrial force has also raised expectations that a female working-class solidarity in the periphery will grow.[7] However, a closer look at ethnographic cases does not indicate the widespread emergence of class and/or feminist consciousness in developing countries. Instead, the range of engagements with capital that such an examination reveals, and the various forms of consciousness reported in the ethnographies, preclude the application of a single analytical rubric.

In this essay I analyze the links between flexible labor regimes and the distinctive labor worlds found in Asia and Mexico. I discuss easily available studies, of uneven ethnographic and methodological quality, conducted between 1970 and 1990. Rather than a homogeneous spread of Fordist production and "despotic" labor regimes, we find local milieux constituted by the unexpected conjunctures of labor relations and cultural systems, high-tech operations and indigenous values. First, I argue that industrial modes of domination go beyond production relations strictly construed; new techniques operating through the control of social spaces are a distinctive feature of postmodern regimes. Second, workers' struggles and resistances are often not based upon class interests or class solidarity, but comprise individual and even covert acts against various forms of control. The interest defended, or the solidarity built, through such acts is more often linked to kinship and gender than to class. To analyze the complex and shifting relations of domination and subordination (and insubordination), I substitute the concept of "cultural struggle" for class struggle.[8] In his historical study of the English working class, Thompson argues that class is a cultural formation.[9] I suggest that the daily practices of workers in defending themselves against various modes of control are also struggles over cultural meanings, values, and goals. These cultural values are shaped, contested, and defended in different domains of power relations. While such conflicts may not necessarily result in structural transformation, the changes they effect in everyday attitudes and norms — or what Williams calls "structures of feeling"[10] — are part of the dynamics of civil society.

FROM WORLD SYSTEM TO FLEXIBLE ACCUMULATION

In the 1960s, developing economies greatly improved conditions for a new round of investments by foreign capital. Earlier attempts at import-substitution had failed, and the United Nations proposed a new plan building on the export functions already characteristic of ex-colonial countries. In addition to raw materials and crops, developing economies could export goods manufactured in "free-trade zones" (FTZs). To attract foreign capital, tax-free privileges in trade were combined with new incentives such as provision of buildings and utilities by the local government, and ease of profit repatriation. Export-industrialization seemed to complement the "green revolution" sponsored by the World Bank and International Monetary Fund.[11]

This two-pronged strategy for developing poor countries was elegantly simple. The commercializing rural economy would supply and feed the labor released for work in the "free-trade zones." Local governments were enticed by the promise that offshore industrialization would boost foreign earnings, while solving the problems linked to rapid population growth, namely un- and underemployment. Host governments hoped that the large number of rural male migrants, the group thought to have the greatest potential for political unrest, would be absorbed by the new offshore industries. Instead, foreign companies investing in the FTZs sought young single women, thus creating a new female industrial force where none had been envisioned.[12]

By the 1970s, a network of industrial zones scattered throughout Southeast Asia opened up the region to industrial investments by Japanese transnational companies, to be quickly followed by Western corporations. At about the same time, the implementation of the *Maquiladora* (assembly plant) program along the U.S.-Mexican border opened up Mexico to North American firms.

To explain this corporate shift to overseas production scholars relied heavily on Wallerstein's concept of the "modern world-system."[13] He argues that European capitalism historically produced a transnational division of labor ("core, semi-periphery, and periphery") which reflected the degree of capitalist development achieved by each country drawn into global exchange relations. Employing Wallerstein's notion of different labor regimes in the core and periphery,[14] Froebel et al. argued that the key principle of the "new international division of labor" was the search for cheap labor by transnational companies.[15] Corporate activities divided the world economy into "core" metropolitan countries, from which most capital originates, and "peripheral" countries where capital can realize its greatest profits.

In recent years, the world-system model has come under criticism for its static and mechanical formulation. Observers note that a complex global economy has been created by the shifting operations of transnational corporations and their articulation with the ambitions of third world governments.

Instead of exploiting a single global periphery, corporations tap into different labor pools, contributing to varying employment relations in unevenly developed countries and regions.[16] Thus, Marxist geographers maintain that FTZs represent a transitional pattern of capital accumulation characterized by great instability and dynamism: "The geography of capitalism is uneven, to be sure; but it is, above all, inconstant."[17] Following the 1970s world recession, intensified competition in the global arena compelled a new pattern of accumulation marked by flexible strategies. Mixed production systems were located anywhere in the world where optimal production, infrastructural, marketing, and political conditions existed. Such dispersal strategies became a means for the social reorganization of accumulation, pitting capital against capital, and one region of the world against another. Thus the Japanese move into the Pacific Rim area recalls the prewar "Great Co-Prosperity Sphere" strategy whereby Japan sought to make Asia the offshore base of Japanese capitalist expansion.[18] Today, Japan's "globalization" approach uses investment and aid to coordinate what commodities countries in Southeast Asia should produce.[19] American and European capital has also entered the arena, but at a lower level of investment and success. To achieve global dominance, Japanese and Western companies bypassed high production costs, labor militancy, and environmental concerns at home by moving to Southeast Asia or Mexico. Such rapid shifts with respect to labor markets and their attendant maneuvers in new financial markets enhance the flexibility and mobility that allow corporations to exert greater labor control worldwide.[20]

In offshore sites corporations seek a peculiar mix of benefits, including tax breaks, low labor costs, and access to markets—benefits that exist already or can be created. Flexible financial operations characterize each level of transaction. Depending on the host country, FTZ benefits include tax incentives, government services, and such features as "total or partial exemption from laws and decrees of the country concerned;"[21] such advantages are negotiable as economic conditions change. An "inter-enclave, export-import type of transaction" allows transfer pricing (whereby profits are transferred from one site to another), thereby escaping local taxes.[22] This mobility of capital from zone to zone reduces overall costs of production while it strengthens the bargaining position of corporations vis-à-vis local governments competing for foreign investments. Firms choose countries like Singapore where maximization of profit is ensured not only by cheap labor but also by "nonwage" costs of production such as the general business environment, the advantageous infrastructure, efficiency, and the political environment.[23] Access to large consumer markets also facilitates quick turnover of capital.

The most important recent experiment in corporate production is its flexible combination of mass assembly and subcontracting systems, of modern firms and home work as linked units dominated by transnational capital. In Southeast Asia and Mexico, export manufacturing is not confined to FTZs but is increasingly dispersed in subcontracting arrangements that may include part-time work by peasants. In Malaysia, transnational production is carried out mainly in FTZ mass-assembly plants; these highly stratified systems employ hundreds to thousands of workers, about 80 percent of whom are female operators on the shop floor.[24] By contrast, in Hong Kong, the prototypical export-industrial economy, most export production is undertaken by subcontracting family firms, many operating under sweatshop conditions. Despite its high labor costs relative to other Asian enclaves, Hong Kong is favored by global companies precisely for its peculiar mix of family production units, legislation that ensures a disciplined and tractable labor force, "peaceful industrial relations," infrastructure, and flexibility in meeting market conditions.[25] Taiwanese export-industrialization is also based on a majority of small firms and a few FTZ plants.[26] In the Philippines, where wages are among the lowest in Asia, subcontracting reduces the visibility of transnational firms, enabling them to bypass further political and economic costs. For instance, only a quarter of Filipino garment workers are based in FTZs; the bulk of garment manufacturing depends on a four-tiered subcontracting system that relies mainly on village home-sewers.[27] Similarly, Beneria and Roldan report that outside the Mexican *maquiladora* zone, home work by housewives is a part of the low level of the segmented labor market; though hidden behind illegalities and mixed forms of production, it is indirectly controlled by industrial capital.[28]

Corporate reliance on mixed production systems in offshore sites has produced an increasingly heterogeneous workforce — including children, men, and imported labor. Along the U.S.-Mexican border, recent labor shortage has led *maquiladoras* to use child and male labor in jobs initially reserved for young women.[29] In China, special economic zones (SEZs) have spawned home work in villages where women and children in their spare time make electronics gear, toys, and artificial flowers. Even SEZ-based factories illegally employed children as young as ten to work up to fifteen hours a day, at salaries less than half of the $40 paid to workers over sixteen.[30] Such flexible and varied labor arrangements organized by transnational firms have generated a range of heterogeneous workers, no longer strictly defined by space, age, or sex.

In other words, global firms increasingly come to share the labor pools used by service industries that depend on cheap labor. While FTZ jobs have generated out-migration of rural women throughout Asia, low wages and vulnerability to layoff have driven many to moonlight as prostitutes in China, Malaysia, Thailand, the Philippines, and Sri Lanka.[31] This overall rise in demand for female labor from poor countries is linked to increasing demands in richer countries for consumer goods and services. For instance, Filipino women have been imported as maids into Hong Kong and other Southeast Asian countries where local young women have flocked into factories. Female migrants from Thailand and Sri Lanka have also sought employment as maids and sex workers in places like the Gulf Emirates, Japan, and West Germany.[32] As production capital roams the world seeking more flexible conditions of maximization, its labor needs become intertwined with those of transnational service industries, further blurring the traditional boundaries between different occupational, sectoral, and national groups.

Under postmodern capitalism, this proliferation of diverse work situations has produced a range of work experiences and histories. It challenges theories that assume that the form of worker consciousness in any one locale is significantly shaped by structural categories defined as core/periphery, metropolitan/ex-colonial, first world/third world formations.

MODES OF REGULATION

Despotic Regimes?

The study of export-industrialization has contributed to the routine characterization of labor regimes in Asia and Mexico as "despotic" and "paternalistic." This perspective was developed by world-systems theorists concerned with the political consequences of uneven capitalist development worldwide.[33] In Burawoy's formulation, "production politics" varies according to the degree of capitalist development in the core-periphery. He distinguishes between "relations of production" (through which surplus is appropriated and distributed by capital), and "relations in production" (the everyday relations between and among workers and managers).[34] The particular combination of these production relations is determined by core or periphery location. In advanced capitalist societies, "hegemonic" regimes prevail, with managers striking a balance between coercion and consent in regulating labor. In developing countries, where the state is bent on relative surplus extraction through production, labor control is "despotic," involving physical violence and often direct state intervention.[35] In Burawoy's view, core-periphery structural conditions account for differences in the behavior of workers, while the " 'belief systems' people carry around in their heads" (i.e., cultural attitudes) are considered irrelevant factors in the formation of class consciousness.[36] The hegemonic/despotic model thus privileges class as a fundamental dynamic of social change, constructing a working-class Other in conflict with capital, while treating as an afterthought the effects of preexisting aspects of social organization like race, ethnicity, religion, and nationalism.

Besides their reductionist tendencies, the labels "despotic" and "paternalistic" have Orientalist overtones. While Burawoy explains "despotic" relations as the outcome of particular state-capital relations, other writers suggest a singular set of cultural differences forming industrial systems in non-Western societies.[37] This construction implies an Other who cannot benefit from the emancipatory promise of social change.[38] This usage also implies that despotic and paternalistic conduct is not found in advanced capitalist countries. Furthermore, Burawoy's argument that "brutal" forms of domination are found in despotic regimes, while coercion and consent prevail in hegemonic metropolitan systems, discourages more fine-grained analysis of diverse forms of power relations in newly industrializing countries.

Below, I discuss the various forms of control that enforce and induce compliance, as well as call forth resistance, among women workers at Asian and Mexican industrial sites. The disciplinary schemes include power relations in the workplace and in society at large. In addition to the division of labor, new techniques of power operate through controlling a series of spaces—the body, the shop floor, the state, and the public sphere—defining permissible and impermissible cultural forms in society.

State Intervention

Burawoy makes the important point that both competition among capitalists worldwide and the struggle between capital and labor in any country have historically been shaped by the state.[39] He argues that the "colonial/neo-colonial state" facilitates the transfer of surplus to advanced countries, while organizing conditions for production that are attractive to foreign capital. Asianists also stress the role of the state in securing conditions for profitable export-industrialization. They maintain that in the so-called newly industrializing countries (NICs), the outcomes of struggles between the colonial or "authoritarian" state and labor were crucial to the subsequent capitalist expansion. State suppression of workers in traditional industries greatly weakened labor movements before large-scale industrialization was undertaken. Anticommunism was a legitimating formula for authoritarian rule in Hong Kong (1920s), South Korea (1940s–1950s), Taiwan (1940s), and Singapore (1960s). Thus, export-oriented industrialization has often required state intervention to weaken labor movements and ensure industrial peace as conditions for the early success of industrialization in these countries.[40] Modernization theorists argue that by disciplining labor, the state benefits the business climate and labor markets, producing conditions that will eventually permit an equitable income share for the working population.

A reliance on the "authoritarian state" model would imply that the state's primary role is to secure the material conditions for controlling, punishing, and rewarding the industrial labor force. While I do not wish to reify the state, its agencies and agents are crucial in preparing and regulating society for the disruptions of industrial development. Elsewhere, I have argued that capitalist discipline operates through overlapping networks of power relations in the workplace and the political domain, regulating daily practices, norms, and attitudes that give legitimacy to the unequal relations that sustain capitalism.[41] Similarly Harvey and others have maintained that the disciplining of the labor force is an intricate, long-drawn-out process involving a mixture of repression, habituation, co-optation, and cooperation within the workplace and throughout society.[42] Modern nation-states routinely regulate social life, promoting certain norms, practices, and identities, while marginalizing others. In newly industrializing countries, one state function is to redefine the public spaces in which particular struggles between rural and town folk, between males and females, and among classes take place (see below). In many countries, state policies promoting a female industrial force produce challenges for young women as daughters, workers, and citizens.

Kinship and Gender: Claims on Daughters

Ethnographers of Asian workers in export industries have developed tropes emphasizing the junior status of the women, for example, "working daughters" and "factory daughters."[43] Indeed, if we look at the figures for all offshore industries, women tend to comprise the lower-paid half of the total industrial workforce in developing countries. In 1980, over 50 percent of Hong Kong manufacturing workers were female, compared to 46 percent in Singapore (1978), 43 percent in Taiwan (1979), and nearly 40 percent in Korea. They are concentrated in a few industries: textiles, apparel, electronics, and footwear. Most are considered "secondary workers" by policymakers in the sense that they take lower wages than men in comparable work ranks and perhaps consider wage work as an interlude before marriage. Thus branded as a secondary labor force, female workers are subjected to low wages, long hours, frequent overtime, little or no prospects for advancement, and generally uncertain employment. In these industries, foremen, technicians, supervisors, and labor contractors are almost all men, while shop floor operators and home workers are almost all young women. Thus, the "daughter" status at home is reproduced in the workplace, generating tensions between new feelings of personal freedom on the one hand, and the claims of family and society on the other.

For instance, Salaff notes that in the Hong Kong working class, parents viewed daughters as "poor long-term investments," and working daughters saw themselves paying back their natal families for giving them life and nurture before they left home.[44] After marriage, these women helped to pay domestic expenses in return for increased influence in family matters. In a Chinese Taiwan case, Kung observes that women working in FTZs fulfilled and expanded "traditional roles/expectations of daughters."[45] It was a question of repaying parents the cost of bringing up a "useless" daughter — a child lost to the natal family after marriage. Working daughters did not gain power, but because they helped to pay household expenses, mothers praised them for being more "filial" than sons, whose education was often paid for with their sisters' earnings.[46] Both writers view the Chinese family as an exchange system. The daughters' strength expended in wage work repaid the gift of life. In return for their "filial" conduct, Hong Kong daughters received economic support from their families.[47] In Taiwan, working daughters were unwilling to challenge the distribution of domestic power because they viewed their families as their only source of affection and security.[48] Thus, in both Hong Kong and Taiwan, the claims of the Chinese family on its members' labor, having as their ultimate goal ascent of the class ladder, serve to enforce workers' compliance with the demands of industrial employment, while at the same time they diminish class-based solidarity.

Socialist China adopted export-industrialization as part of its "four modernizations" in 1979. Andors did preliminary research at the Shenzhen SEZ, where most of the industries — textiles, electronics, toys, and tourism — were operated by Hong Kong subcontracting firms.[49] Women, mainly single and under thirty-five years old, comprised 70 percent of the workforce. They were recruited by a special labor contracting agency from rural home units that received compensation for releasing them. Although claimed to be among the best-paid workers in China, they were easily exploited by the contracting service and by factories that routinely demanded overtime. Separated from their families, working women did enjoy such new freedoms as living in singles' dormitories, having more buying power, and postponing marriage.

These personal choices, including premarital sex, were already available to working women in Hong Kong and Taiwan, in recognition of their filial contribution to the family economy.[50] Nevertheless, in socialist and capitalist Chinese communities, young working women did not attain social equality with men at home or in society at large.

Southeast Asian cases also indicate that industrial employment produced a break in customary practices that confined unmarried girls to the home. However, bilateral kinship organization and cultural norms exerted fewer claims on daughters than did the patrilineal Chinese system. The influx of factory jobs meant that young women had the opportunity to help households in a declining farm economy, or to escape from unbearable family situations.[51] For the first time, village girls had the chance to go away to work, handle their own money, save for higher education, and choose their own husbands,[52] enjoying greater freedom from family claims than Chinese female workers. Wolf mentions that young girls in Central Java eagerly sought wage work, often against their parents' wishes. Many kept their earnings for themselves and felt a sense of improved status.[53] In Malaysia, the earnings of village daughters helped furnish their parents' houses and improve daily consumption; the women themselves had discretionary income and could save for their weddings.[54]

These changes in the working daughter's status, with its mix of (and tension between) family obligations and growing personal autonomy, must modify sweeping assertions that preexisting East and Southeast Asian "patriarchy"[55] alone is to blame for the construction of unequal industrial relations. Access to wages did gain young Asian women some personal forms of freedom, weakening customary family claims to varying degrees. In the Chinese cases, wage employment has allowed daughters to demonstrate how "filial" they can be, and thus to be considered "worthier" than before. In Southeast Asia, the unprecedented influx of young working women into public spaces produced a social backlash, generating demands for the regulation of female conduct (see below).

The Sexual Division of Labor and Taylorism

Some scholars claim modern industrial organizations in Asian societies are rarely "paternalistic"; any "vestiges of kin relations" are dissolved in the workplace.[56] In contrast, others assert that harsh and personal forms of control are features of peripheral Fordist systems.[57] However, the ethnographies suggest that the labor politics are neither exclusively despotic nor antipaternalistic but involve different disciplinary schemes institutionalized by local capitalist and cultural practices.

In Asia, the division of labor introduced by transnational firms separates managers and workers along lines of nationality, race, gender, and age. Central activities like research and finance are controlled by experts in the metropolitan headquarters, while the low-skilled and labor-intensive production processes employ young, poorly trained women in the offshore sites.[58] For instance, Japanese industries based in Malaysia are headed by male Japanese managers and engineers. Malaysian Chinese and Indian men fill the mid-level professional ranks, while shop floor operators are mainly composed of young Malay women of rural origin.[59] This institutionalization of race, gender, and age inequalities in industrial enterprises is reflected by daily practices. Elson and Pearson argue that the dialectic of gender and capital has the tendency to "intensify, decompose, and recompose" existing gender hierarchies, thereby incorporating gender inequalities in modern work relations.[60] In Hong Kong, subcontracting agents simply rely on parental pressures at home to make the "girls" work for long hours and low wages.[61] In contrast, Malaysia-based Japanese firms absorb Malay notions of male superiority into a "Pan Asian" philosophy that emphasizes the moral authority of the Japanese management, and of the managers, supervisors, and foremen over nubile female operators. Corporate discourse on the "Asian family" defines workers as "children" who should "obey their parents" (i.e., supervisors) in the factory.[62] Thus, despite claims that capitalism has destroyed traditional patriarchy, these examples show that the industrial labor relations articulating with local norms often elaborate and reinvent principles of male and racial superiority.[63]

Such gender- and race-based forms of domination help make "scientific management" (or Taylorism)[64] an even more formidable apparatus for extracting surplus value. The essence of Fordist production, Taylorism is based on "time-motion" techniques that dictate precisely how each task is to be performed in order to obtain the highest level of productivity within a strict time economy.[65] The fragmentation of skills into simple procedures and the stripping away of individual judgment (separation of conception and execution) are intended by the system to treat workers as appendages of the machine.

Factory Regulations: The Gaze and the Body

Foucault reminds us that some forms of modern power cannot be attributed directly to the reproduction of capitalist relations and labor power.[66] He maintains that specific technologies of knowledge and power, associated with institutions like the prison, clinic, and school, produce discursive practices that enforce social regulation through establishing "the norm." In multinational enterprises, Taylorism is complemented by surveillance techniques that operate through the control of space.

Thus, it would be a mistake to think of scientific management as solely a process of technical detail-level control. It specifies exact bodily posture and requires tedious repetition of the same finger, eye, and limb movements, often for hours on end at the assembly line, a form of body discipline especially intolerable to neophyte factory women. In many enterprises, continual surveillance enforced the worker's compliance with the relentless Taylorist procedures.[67] At a Malaysia-based microchip firm, male supervisors pressured female workers assembling thousands of components to achieve 100 percent efficiency; even trips to the locker room were penalized. A Japanese director was pleased to note that the production rate of Malay workers exceeded that of Japanese ones at the corporate home base.[68] In another plant, operators working under the strict eye of foremen were reported to almost double their daily output, especially when their efforts were sweetened by incremental cash allowances.[69]

Other forms of spatial control include the deployment of workers on the shop floor in relative isolation from each other but under the constant surveillance of foremen, an arrangement that induces self-monitoring.[70] Factory women often felt they had few places left to hide; some complained of being spied upon in their locker rooms. Furthermore, even unions were used to watch over workers. A Japanese factory based in Malaysia set up an in-house union to operate as a "grievance procedure system," or, in the words of a union leader, to act "as a watchdog, for both sides."[71]

Foucault notes that knowledge-power ultimately fastens on sex, making the body the ultimate site at which all strategies of control and resistance are registered.[72] Ethnographic findings reveal that disciplinary practices frequently define the industrial presentation and workings of the body. Malay workers felt that the "tight work discipline" extended to regulation of clothing and footwear — policies that bodily constrained them.[73] Japanese corporate policies in Malaysia defined Malay workers as "wards" under the moral custody of factory managers. By focusing on the young women's virginal status, the management capitalized on Malay fears about their daughters' vulnerability.[74] Other techniques of control more closely monitored workers' bodies. In mass-assembly factories from South Korea to Mexico, operators were subjected to humiliating innuendoes about menstruation and were required to request permission to use the toilet.[75] In the Shenzhen SEZ, the normally quiescent workers went on strike in a toy factory after a pregnant woman, prevented from resting, fainted.[76] Controlling the space of the worker's body is related to a wider corporate perception of women's "nature."

While Taylorism as a management policy aims to minimize the possibilities of resistance by reducing workers to tools, disciplinary procedures seek to induce "docile bodies"[77] without resorting to "brutal" forms of control in the workaday life. However, electronics workers from Taiwan to Sri Lanka complain of the detail work that literally wears away at the "instruments of production" — for instance, eyes fitted to microscopes.[78] Indeed, neophyte workers, whose sensibilities were shaped by peasant and/or preindustrial cultures, often challenge the work process for its dehumanizing effects and accompanying forms of social control. Instead of opposing capital as an abstract entity, factory women's daily struggles against corporate policies — over body discipline, pressures for high productivity, and surveillance — aim to push back the varied norms and forms of domination.

A mode of social regulation often ignored in our analysis of labor regimes and their effects on workers is the production of cultural discourses. Although Foucault does not see a necessary connection between discursive practices and the systematic domination of capitalism, Marxists maintain that as part of cultural production, images and discourses have a material basis in the symbolic reproduction of capitalism.[79] There is much evidence that transnational capitalism has produced, along with microchips, discourses that naturalize the subordination of women in industrial enterprises.

Early in their operations, transnational companies explained their preferences for third world female workers by producing a language defining them as "low grade" (meaning unskilled) and "docile." Bureaucrats in developing countries were quick to appeal to biology to woo foreign investments while gaining acceptance at home for the creation of a female industrial force. A Malaysian government brochure promoted "the oriental girl" as blessed with nimble fingers and thus "qualified by nature and inheritance" to contribute to assembly production.[80] Elsewhere, I have discussed how industrial discourses "disassemble" the female worker into eyes and fingers adapted for assembly work, at the same time reassembling other parts of their bodies according to commodified sexual images.[81] Factories also pointed to other "natural" attributes of their female workforce. A Japanese manager claimed that factories prefer "fresh female labor [that,] after some training, is highly efficient."[82] Similarly, a manager in Cuidad Juarez on the Mexican border said he preferred women who were "unspoiled" — that is, young and inexperienced: "Women such as these are easier to shape to our requirements."[83] In Taiwan, factories sought young women from the remote areas said to "have a higher capacity for eating bitterness."[84] This language of essentialism and commodification creates an image of dull-witted work animals that can be trained for hard, tedious work. By implication, such a cultural (or is it a natural?) Other provides justification for the low wages offered.

Corporate practices also promoted a sexual image of third world women workers. American firms in Malaysia and elsewhere in Southeast Asia encouraged extracurricular activities that stress consumerism, dating, and beauty competition. New sexual images, elaborated through makeup classes and newsletters, induce the consumption of commodities (e.g., Clairol toiletries) made available in company stores. Such emphasis on Western images of sex appeal engendered a desire for goods that working women could satisfy only by increasing their commitment to wage work.[85]

Social Regulation: Women in Public Spaces

Throughout industrializing Asia and Mexico, the emergence of large female industrial forces has occasioned negative public commentary on the conduct of female workers. Douglas observes that persons in an interstitial position are often symbolized as dangerous and filthy, since they suggest a poorly articulated social system.[86] As new workers, young women engage in activities that violate traditional boundaries (spatial, economic, social, and political) in public life, forcing a redefinition of the social order. Thus, states attempting to shape a new moral consensus on industrial development have found it necessary to regulate the activities of female workers along clearly marked gender lines, defining what is culturally appropriate and what is not.

In Malaysia, the influx of young rural women into industrial sites was widely considered the cause of moral decadence in Malay Muslim society. While the state promoted female industrial employment, the government-controlled media criticized factory women, citing their Westernized outfits, footloose behavior, and reputation as "microdevils" and "bad women."[87] Islamic revivalists opposing industrial development viewed factory women, many of whom have deferred marriage, as would-be infidels indulging in the pleasures of consumer society. Malay working women were thus perceived as an Other invading (male) public spaces; while they were permitted to work, their social activities had to be curtailed. Religious leaders urged repentance, rejection of consumerism, and the embrace of a new sexual asceticism for young women. Transnational companies that held religious classes in the workplace and monitored the behavior of workers were applauded by the religious authorities. Each vying to be more "Islamic" than the other, the state and revivalist movement competed in enforcing a moral discipline on working women in public life. By controlling female images and regulating their activities, this particular constitution of civil society makes it, like the FTZ, a place where women are free to work, but only under the male authority. Similarly, in West Java, Mather[88] reports that the "Islamic patriarchy" allied itself with factory managers to control the movement of workers between home and workplace. In Buddhist Thailand, rural women were pushed into wage work by cultural notions of a daughter's duty and the crime of ingratitude. While politicians warned that officials should not be "morally fastidious" and prohibit sexual entertainment, working women were accused of moral laxity.[89] These examples show that state encouragement of female industrial employment was paralleled by increased surveillance of their multiple "transgressions" as viewed by dominant groups in society. While the conditions differ in each country, the widespread stigmatization of working women came to define public spheres where female productive activities were deemed necessary but their civil rights were not.

In contrast to the polarities noted above (e.g., virgin/whore, purity/immorality) that were used to regulate working women elsewhere, Chinese society in Taiwan evaluated such women according to a mind/body model.[90] As we have seen, mass-assembly work divided mental from physical labor to an extreme, making workers vulnerable to the Chinese cultural preference for mental over manual labor. Female industrial workers suffered from "damaged" identities,[91] mainly because of the "low" nature of their work. Factory girls complained of being looked down upon by society because of their low-status job, which "does not give a person any face."[92] In complaints to Kung, they were especially bitter about being deprived of higher education (the "penality" of daughters) that would open the route to higher status.[93] Doubly marginalized as daughters and as factory hands, these women were obstructed from attaining the education that would shield them from the social contempt attached to their jobs. Thus, in Taiwanese society, moral regulation marginalized factory women mainly because of their low occupational (class) rank, but also because of their sex.

Along the Mexican border, cross-racial constructions of workers' activities and identities appear to be a major part of social regulation.[94]

In Cuidad Juarez, Fernandez-Kelly reports the development of a "factory harem mentality." Although young women might have used their charms to attract suitors before, they were now encouraged to use sex as a bait and payment for access to jobs.[95] A news article on Nogales notes a popular image of the Border Program as a place of sexual conquest where everyday talk included "innuendos about *maquiladora* managers who fornicate their way down assembly lines or companies that provide stud services as incentives."[96] An American manager in Nogales joked: "Imagine if we could harness sexual energy. When someone here has sex, the news travels . . . like electricity through a printed circuit."[97] Noting that "the only fun [female workers] ever have is love," he said that in the previous month, 10 percent of his workers had been pregnant.[98]

If the dominant discourse portrayed female operators as sexually wanton, implying that they were not such good workers, men were seen as emasculated by *maquila* work. In the early phases, most *maquilas* employed single women, but by 1983, more and more factories had turned to men and children under fourteen years old.[99] In Nogales, American managers dealt with male workers by exploiting their sense of machismo. One said he tried to raise productivity by appealing to "the Mexican's pride" and "need to save face in front of others."[100] In Cuidad Juarez, Lugo also observed the corporate manipulation of machismo to humiliate men who could not keep up with female workers.[101] The factory men's sex talk and word games disclosed their sense of having been socially reduced (and thus becoming more womanlike). By accepting dominant images of male weakness, they unwittingly reproduced the very cultural categories now used to prod them to higher levels of productivity. The larger cultural significance of such corporate discourses is that *maquila* men are socially devalued for working in female-identified jobs.

The race/sex typing of workers becomes most elaborated in situations where female workers participate in manufacturing and in service industries based overseas. In Sri Lanka, the post-1977 development pattern led to the simultaneous growth of FTZ industries, prostitution, and the export of servants and brides.[102] In the process, the control of women shifted from male relatives to "alien male authorities — the factory supervisor, the employment agent, the government bureaucrat, the Western tourist, the Arab employer, or the Japanese farmer [who imports a bride]."[103] Sri Lankans alarmed at this mass entry of daughters into wage labor at home and abroad branded women workers with a sexual stigma.[104] These workers thus join the mobile female labor force epitomized by Filipino women — as imported maids, nurses, mail-order brides, and entertainers in Asia and Europe.[105] Such transnational formation of working relations may allow workers to escape social regulation in their home country temporarily, but it exposes them to other forms of domination abroad. They become migrant workers with few legal rights.

Ethnographies of working women in various locales encourage us to investigate the kinds of power such women are subjected to both at the workplace and in the wider society. In each locale, different modes of industrial and social domination promote certain cultural forms and identities, while undermining or suppressing others. In each case, the particular mix of production systems, state policies, and cultural forces both limit and enable workers' struggles,[106] a topic to which we now turn.

CULTURAL STRUGGLES

The variety of industrial situations linked to flexible accumulation raises anew questions about workers' responses to capitalist transformation. Indigenous experiences of colonialism and capitalism are frequently assessed in terms of the concept of "class consciousness," that is, the degree of recognition of class interests, organized action against capital, and even the goal of structural redistribution of power in society.[107] Although anthropologists have avoided a generic concept of class consciousness in discussing third world experiences, scholars like Mintz would nevertheless consider unions and political parties as minimal evidence of the presence of "proletarians" in the Caribbean.[108] In her important book, Nash seeks in pre-Columbian rituals the class solidarity of Bolivian miners, but she then evaluates their consciousness according to strict Marxist criteria of class identity and union activity.[109] By insisting on a single measure of class agency, we risk diluting the political significance of cultural resistances in encounters with capitalism.

A related tendency is to see the political importance of third world workers in globalist terms. Vincent notes that among the laboring poor in colonial Uganda, the sense of "no-classness" was a condition of their "subaltern" position in transnational capitalism.[110] Comaroff analyzes the religious imagery of worker-peasants in South Africa as "simultaneously unique and yet one instance of a very general class of social movement" that is "part of the second global culture."[111] Thus, anthropologists describe (and celebrate) the varied expressions of class/ethnic/religious consciousness in subaltern groups (i.e., the politically dominated), but often feel compelled to construct these struggles in the universalist terms of emergent collective consciousness.[112] In a cautionary note, Spivak argues that the arena of the subaltern's consciousness is situational and uneven, and the subaltern's subjectivity is locally shaped and delimited.[113]

Feminists influenced by the world-systems model also predict the emergence of solidarity among the transnational female labor force in developing economies.[114] In recent years, such feminist elaboration of a utopian discourse as an alternative to modernist, patriarchal narratives has itself come under criticism.[115] These feminist critics argue that acknowledging the plurality of subject positions and self-representations puts us in a better position to understand different social realities. Without relying on totalizing "first" or "third" world frameworks, a theory about the variable "subject-constitution" of subaltern women must link individual consciousness to the local workings of international capital.[116]

Indeed, the ethnographical evidence on factory women in flexible labor systems indicates that they rarely construct their identities or organize themselves in terms of collective or global interests. Although demonstrations of female workers have been widely reported in Asia and Central America,[117] they tended to be wildcat strikes in individual firms. Union activities, especially in Asian FTZs, are controlled through company unions, or are otherwise severely limited.[118] What we do find are attempts to escape from or live with industrial systems without losing one's sense of human dignity.

Worker consciousness and subject-constitution, I would argue, must be investigated in contexts shaped by the intersection of state agencies, the local workings of capital, and already configured local power/culture realms.[119] Instead of direct labor-capital confrontations, we discover workers' resistances in their oppositional tactics, embodied desires, and alternative interpretations and images. What seems key in their emerging consciousness is an awareness of how their status as daughter/young woman is linked to domination by family, industry, and society. In manipulating, contesting, or rejecting these claims, working women reassess and remake their identities and communities in ways important for social life.

Accommodation and Personal Mobility

At some industrial sites, factory women seemed overwhelmed by the needs of their families, a concern that restrains their capacity to participate in sustained social action. Industrialization in Mexico has generated a heterogeneous female working population variously employed in different labor systems. According to Fernandez-Kelly, workers in

Cuidad Juarez included single women (seventeen to twenty-five years old) as well as older women who have been widowed, divorced, or separated from men. Female-headed households may have dependents (children, fathers, husbands, and boyfriends) who were unemployed or underemployed.[120] Since the border area is a transit point for U.S.-bound, predominantly male migrants, many single women are compelled to seek wage work in the *maquila*. Companies prefer young, single, and childless women; older women with children can find work only in garment factories, where work conditions are worse.[121] Working women often fall back on exchange networks that help them adjust to economic uncertainty as they enter and leave this unstable labor market.[122] Others augment their wages by working as prostitutes or slipping across the border on weekends to work as maids.[123]

Beneria and Roldan note that among home workers in Mexico City, young, single, and married "semi-prole" women routinely labored in and were discharged from various capitalist enterprises.[124] They argue that this flexibility afforded by the informal economy produced subproletarianization among women, in contrast to more regular proletarianization of men.[125] Since capital constantly creates and destroys job opportunities, the work conditions do not foster collective class or even gender consciousness. Although home workers are aware of oppression, "a configuration of ideological, economic and coercive mechanisms support[s] oppressive marital contracts." Women, because of limited resources, "could not renegotiate" their situations.[126] Even in the absence of rebellion, each woman's awareness of her exploitation occasions reassessment of her status.[127]

In Taiwan, female workers unhappy with their jobs are in a better position to escape industrial employment. Kung reports that many feared reprimand, and were either resigned to the job conditions or planning to leave soon.[128] They displayed not the classic type of class consciousness but acute consciousness of having to adjust to a low status.[129] In their view, the company environment fostered manipulative behavior between superiors and inferiors as well as among workers themselves, thus sowing doubts and distrust about dealing effectively with conflicts.[130] As in FTZs based elsewhere, women in Taiwan were reluctant to take leadership roles because of a sense of betraying the interests of the rank and file. The most common expression of discontent was a high rate of turnover, which further undermined community spirit. Besides, contrary to Western feminist expectations, most working daughters did not seek more equal relations at home and would gladly trade their "bitter" independence for the security of the college student who has a family to look after her needs.[131] Thus, although initially family pressures denied daughters higher education and pushed them into factory employment, factory daughters developed a sense of self-direction through seeking better qualifications and jobs. In other words, they hoped eventually to evade production politics (and family claims) not by resisting control at work but by "graduating" from industrial employment altogether.

In mainland China, too, what was initially regarded as an opportunity has come to produce a sense of entrapment. Export-industrialization in Kwantung has increased class differentiation to the extent that few factory women wanted to marry local men because marriage would add to their work burden.[132] Some hoped to achieve upward and geographical mobility by marrying Hong Kong tourists or entering Hong Kong prostitution rings. The potential stigma of being a prostitute seemed to them preferable to the status of a factory worker. Whether family or individually inspired, aspirations for upward mobility both conditioned the women's consciousness of their bitter fate and strengthened their resolve to escape it.[133] For many, the goal was not to stay and challenge the industrial system, but, like their Taiwanese sisters, to use factory jobs as a stepping stone to more lucrative employment elsewhere. Attaining such personal mobility also weakens family control over one's life. A sense of subjective rights began to replace traditional authority over one's fate.

Bodily Truths and Contested Categories

In other cases, workers trapped in industrial enterprises frequently contest hegemonic representations of their situations. Factory women untutored in ideologies are capable of making alternative interpretations based on their own visceral experiences and cultural traditions. By thus challenging dominant discourse, they expand the space of political struggle in their everyday lives.

A few ethnographic accounts provide descriptions of women challenging dominant images of their purported "freedom" as factory workers. In Taiwan, female workers spoke of being shut up all day and wasting the "spring" of their youth, a bitter contrast to pre-factory days when the period before marriage seemed carefree.[134] This sense of imprisonment is also felt by factory women in Malaysia who, released from the custody of their parents and widely accused of "unrestrained" conduct, felt "shackled" in the factory.[135] An operator noted that her coworkers were ignorant of the wider industrial situation, "working as if they were imprisoned . . . like a frog beneath the coconut shell."[136] The theme of entrapment extends to their experience of work discipline. Malay women rejected corporate expressions of welfare concern, claiming that the management treated them as things, not human beings.[137] Many found the relentless drive for higher productivity and disregard for worker fatigue intolerable. They also complained of bodily deprivations (aches and burns, insufficient sleep, skipped menstruation) that registered the grip of industrial discipline. More assertive workers tried to enforce traditional morality, demanding human empathy (*timbang rasa*) and justice from their foremen.[138] They sold their labor but not their right to human consideration.

Workers in Taiwan also contested categories and practices that treat them as extensions of machines. Seeing themselves as "mere assemblers," factory women did not expect their views to count for much. However, in their everyday conversations, they denounced workplace conditions in moral terms. Instead of using the language of class or sexual oppression, they posed questions of "how to be a person."[139] Foremen were described as "mean," "overly strict," "slippery," and "putting on airs."[140] Workers were therefore suspicious of perceived attempts to manipulate their emotions, for example, foremen who chatted up workers, who took "pleasure" in ordering them around, and who made a habit of patting them on the shoulder.[141] The refusal of such gestures echoes a Hong Kong worker who scornfully denounced implicit expectations that to get a slight pay raise one should "pat the horse's rump" (i.e., curry favor).[142] Like their Malaysian counterparts, these women wished to be treated with greater personal consideration, but they feared attempts to prime the pump. They complained that the companies did not allow for the development of human feelings (*kanching*) in the workplace, promoting instead opportunistic and impersonal behavior.[143] According to their cultural expectations, factory work was dehumanizing.

In mainland China, the introduction of capitalist methods of production in Hangzhou silk factories has produced similar policies for controlling female workers. In the discourse of economic reform, management emphasized higher productivity and the gendering of differences between manual labor (defined as women's work) and technical and mental labor (considered men's work). Using terms that echo corporate discourses in Southeast Asia, women were said to have nimble fingers but to lack the intellectual and leadership capabilities of men. Rofel reports that although women workers subscribed to the sexual division of labor, they also used such gender images to subvert new pressures for higher productivity.[144] They routinely cited family and female reasons for taking time off work. Using the same categories management uses has allowed workers to negotiate some work conditions, but they also thereby reproduce aspects of the larger culture, reinforcing the sense that women are inherently less productive than men.[145]

The above examples indicate that dominant images of women workers — as footloose consumers, instruments of production, and the weaker sex — are contested or used by factory women to their own advantage. On the one hand, Malay and Taiwanese women felt factory work deprived them of their youth and of the kinds of pleasures and protection promised by local cultures. On the other, the shock of factory work led them to demand moral consideration and fairness. In different cultural idioms, these neophyte workers expressed a view of industrial work as an assault on the body as well as on the moral value of human beings.[146] By contesting hegemonic categories of human worth, factory women attempted "to seize language for their own purposes," engaging in "symbolic struggles over social position, identity and self-determination."[147] They thus found voices to validate their actual experiences, breaking the flow of meanings imposed on them, and thus directly defining their own lives.

Cultural Resistance: Tactics and Movements

In his notion of "everyday forms of resistance," Scott maintains that the oppositional practices of Malay peasants flourish precisely because they are outside hegemonic relations.[148] This ethnographic observation is itself doubtful,[149] and many would question a theoretical construction of subjects as external to power relations. As Foucault has argued, disciplinary technologies call forth counterstrategies within shifting fields of power.[150] While Foucault emphasizes resistant tactics within discourse, de Certeau identifies nonverbal ruses that proliferate in the interstices of a system of domination.[151] This layer of moral resistance is derived from the basic, practical consciousness of subjects, and though often lacking an articulated awareness of its own, it can disrupt and subvert the established order, as we shall see below.

Reports on *maquila* production politics have been sparse, but despite their difficult employment situation and domestic responsibilities, Mexican workers do challenge industrial discipline. Fernandez-Kelly and Lugo provide accounts of female and male workers manipulating dominant sexual images to their own advantage, earning short-term reprieves or gains in the workplace.[152] Others briefly mention a form of covert resistance called *tortuosidad*, whereby workers worked "at a turtle's pace" in response to speed-up pressures.[153] These scattered acts of resistance, sometimes not even recognized owing to management's view of "lazy" workers, did not collectively challenge the status quo, but they opposed the prevailing hegemonic interests.

My study of Malay factory women in Kuala Langat, Malaysia, indicates a range of resistance tactics that silently negotiated the contours of daily work relations. The Malay feminine ideal constrains young women from directly confronting their social superiors, yet female workers often resorted to isolated nonverbal acts to gain a symbolic and physical space despite contrary factory rules. Tactics to fool the system and lessen work demands included frequent absences from the shop floor, ostensibly to attend to "female" problems or to perform obligatory Islamic prayers.[154] At the workbench, operators sometimes feigned ignorance of the technical details of work, thus frustrating attempts to raise productivity rates. Even more hidden ruses were the destruction of microchips and jamming of machines; in both cases, the management was often unpleasantly surprised and unable to trace the culprits.[155]

Subversion also takes the more startling form of spirit attacks on female workers, events that transfigure normal factory routines. Spirit possession is a complex phenomenon in Malay culture, but its repeated eruptions in modern factories can be partly accounted for in terms of work relations. A worker attacked by a spirit wails, runs about creating havoc, struggles violently, and screams obscenities against restraining supervisors. In some cases, the possessed exclaimed, "I am not to be blamed!" "Go away!" "I will kill you, let me go!" The effect on production was immediate.[156] Other workers soon became infected, creating such a disturbance that a shutdown proved necessary, and the "hysterical women" were sent home.

Possession episodes were the inarticulate expression of individual anguish, transferred to the public sphere. The contortions of afflicted workers spoke of the ills experienced in the social body.[157] Some possession victims reported visions of fearsome old men at the workbench, spirits haunting bathrooms, or devils lurking in the microscopes. These "signs and symptoms"[158] of possession, though complexly motivated, constituted "a cryptic language of protest"[159] and social disease. Their vivid imagery defined the factory premises as a spiritually polluted place. To avoid attacks, young women had to be "spiritually vigilant" against fear and violation.[160] Possession discourse thus contested the management's view of "mass hysteria" as caused by female physical weaknesses. Like other oppositional tactics, spirit attacks are not capable of identifying the common adversary but indirectly expressed the interests of others in a similar predicament.[161] The surreptitious foot-dragging, Luddite tactics, and possession rites count among the "polymorphous maneuvers and mobilities"[162] that, linking a basic sense of moral freedom, aesthetic creation, and practical action, have surprising effects on power relations, while managing to elude repression.

In contrast to Malay factory women, their South Korean counterparts are among the most militant in Asia, confronting a state more repressive of labor than other industrializing countries. The growth of collective consciousness among South Korean female workers is also fostered by their relative social and geographical isolation. The Anglophone literature gives only tantalizing glimpses of the South Korean female workers' movements — "underground" struggles that, while protracted and culturally elaborated, tend not to be accessible to outsiders.

In South Korea, the dramatic performance of the economy has relied heavily on unskilled female labor, paid half the wages of comparable male workers.[163] In 1969, a ban on strikes in foreign-invested firms was followed by the breakup of unions in the mid-1970s, through the New Community Factory Movement. In two large industrial estates, Oh found most factories violated the Labor Standard Act by insisting on overtime and depriving workers of holidays and medical leaves. The work was arduous: textile workers, who routinely worked night shifts, put in an average of 10.5 hours per day but were paid "below sustenance wages."[164] Layoffs were not a bargaining option because of labor shortages. Companies therefore relied on "crude forms of control" by inventing rules requiring twenty-hour work days.[165]

Most female workers were single migrants from remote areas, who were thus cut off from family support. Socially isolated in the industrial estates, most of the female workers were under twenty-five years old, and many were adolescents. They were employed for an average of three years, and many had begun to stay on after marriage.[166] Although most were "working daughters" supplementing family income, about 11 percent were primary income earners in their families. They lived in housing near the industrial zones where they could share stories and common circumstances on a daily basis. This led to the creation of a female class solidarity, further strengthened by women's wide experiences across different industries and by their involvement in labor disputes. Furthermore, the large population and the expanding South Korean economy generated intense job competition between women and men. As a category, men were upgraded to more lucrative jobs, discarding "lower" ones to women. Most female workers desired wages at least equal to those of men, and wages were the main focus of their struggle.[167] These factors refute the suggestion that because of "patriarchal family structures" Korean workers were relatively quiescent.

In fact, labor disputes involving female workers have sharply increased since the mid-1970s, but they have been underreported by the state.[168]

In the late 1970s, when the national economy surpassed the "developing country" level, the Dong-II Textile Company was engaged in a major labor dispute.[169] Women workers rejected representatives of a puppet union led by men.[170] The factory women determined that they could not depend on support from male union organizers, nor could they rely on sympathetic middle-class women to lead them. Female workers began to organize and develop their own leadership. They told Kim that they no longer needed students to awaken their consciousness: The time had come for "real laborers" to take care of themselves.[171] In another context, Christian leaders were advised that they should leave after helping female workers to organize themselves.[172]

Female workers, organized into different groups, have developed a whole repertoire of tactics and images expressing their struggles. In the Dong-II Textile Company strike, women protested "miserable work conditions," poor food, imposed silence among coworkers, and prohibition from going to the toilets.[173] They developed an anticapitalist ideology that focused on "recover[ing] our human rights." At the climax of their struggle against the company union, women on a hunger strike faced off against police by stripping and singing union songs.[174] The women were brutally beaten, and seventy-two were arrested. When the strikers presented their case to the regional union leader, he asked, "What sort of women are you, who prefer the labor movement to marriage?"[175] Because they chose to struggle as workers, women were apparently perceived as acting outside cultural traditions of femininity. Some of the women involved in this labor action were raped.[176]

Thus, while male superiors tried to domesticate female protesters by using traditional forms of male control, the women workers drew on local and imported religious traditions for inspiration. Building resistance out of their daily suffering, workers found in shamanism a vital tradition for interpreting historical tragedies,[177] while Christianity offered new concepts to articulate their oppression and the possibilities for change. Sun argues that the goal of Korean feminist theology was to promote the full humanity of women by struggling to transform a society in which development depended on women's labor but disregarded improving women's status.[178] Working women were said to be suspicious of bourgeois women's assertions that women would be liberated through work, when their work conditions were, "for the most part, exploitative and dehumanizing."[179] Instead of adopting bourgeois feminism, many female workers turned to Christianity. Some reported experiencing God's presence in their lives; their experiences led them to construct a new conception of power based on gender solidarity and human dignity. Sun observes:

[The women workers] cannot afford to see themselves as helpless victims: their survival depends on continued exercise of whatever personal powers they possess. They combine their strengths to survive and often assume responsibility for others in their struggle, sometimes even sacrificing their security — the safety of their bodies. By recognizing that the exercise of their power is an act of resistance, they reject both the dominant group's definition of them as powerless and dispensable, and the ideology of sexism which teaches that women are powerless and easily victimized.[180]

South Korean female workers' struggles culminated in battles that extend beyond the workplace. They led to the emergence of a separate female labor movement in the 1987 mass labor struggle, the largest in Korean history.[181] The conflict began with male workers at the Hyunda plant demanding "democratic labor unions." Women in the Masan FTZ were also inspired to strike; as a result, factory wages were raised from $4 to $7 a day in 1988. To a greater extent than the other cases, these South Korean worker movements have led to social changes, producing a new sense of effectiveness in the female workers and posing questions about their gender identity and cultural community.

CONCLUSION

As I write this, the world speeds ahead. Corporations are retreating from offshore manufacturing in developing countries where growing labor strife and rising wages since 1988, in addition to the declining U.S. dollar, have increased production costs.[182] More and more, Western companies are preferring sites in metropolitan countries where market access is optimal and ever-increasing pools of immigrants and refugees supply the cheap labor.[183] Indeed, such changes in capital-labor engagements underlines the need for theoretical flexibility on our part. I have suggested an alternative to the conventional framing of working-class experiences as a trajectory from the development of class consciousness to class struggle to structural change. Instead, I propose that we conceive of workers' experiences as cultural struggles — that is, workers struggle against new and varied forms of domination, and seek new ways of grappling with social realities. Such cultural resistance and production engender a new sense of self and community, potentially challenging the constitution of civil society.

Williams uses the phrase "structure of feeling" to describe such an emergent and fluid sensibility, a kind of "practical consciousness" derived from actively lived and felt relationships.[184] A structure of feeling does not equate with an articulated formal system (ideology), shaped as it is by "a living and interrelating continuity," together with all its tensions.[185] Above, I described the constitution of such "structures of feeling" in the context of class and other hegemonic forms of domination.

In different ethnographic contexts, institutions like the state, kinship, gender, and religion, as well as industrial enterprises, play important roles in constituting workers' activities and consciousness. Through their complex accommodations and resistances, the female workers under discussion here gained a sense of their particular oppressions and interests, but also achieved some degree of effectiveness and self-worth. Although such structures of feeling do not necessarily have significant political effects, they constitute a change in the everyday attitudes and practices of workers.

In negating hegemonic definitions daily, factory women came to explore new concepts of self, female status, and human worth. While many tactics of resistance were individual, and even covert, other forms of protest in the public sphere compelled a modification or renegotiation of power relations. In Kwantung and in Taiwan, factory daughters developed a sense of personal rights, while in South Korea, female workers learned to be sovereign subjects, acting as self-determining agents of social change. The latter have gone furthest in developing culturally new notions of human worth and individual rights, and in organizing resistance. They rejected traditional constructions of their status and selectively adopted foreign categories to articulate their own goals, as individuals and collectively. They have realized, to a greater extent than many female workers elsewhere, the liberating potential of the new structure of feeling. They achieved the voices to question the place of women in the economy and to demand democratic practices in civil society. In viewing their silences, subterfuges, interpretations, and goals as "cultural struggle," we are merely acknowledging the role of subaltern women in making local histories, in their own ways.

NOTES

Thanks to the following scholars: Allan Pred for guiding me through the geography of capital accumulation; Brackette Williams for her penetrating insights into racial and sexual exploitation; John Gumperz for explicating narrative forms; Scott Guggenheim for his trenchant remarks and refreshing perspective; and Carol Smith for her cautionary comments.

1. In American social sciences, a leading argument is spelled out in William W. Rostow, *Stages of Economic Growth: A Non-Communist Manifesto* (Cambridge: Cambridge University Press, 1960). This model informed anthropological studies like Clifford Geertz's *Peddlers and Princes* (Chicago: University of Chicago Press, 1962).

2. That is, stage and system of capitalist production and accumulation that has been called "Americanism and Fordism." See Antonio Gramsci, *Selections from the Prison Notebooks,* ed. and trans. Quintin Hoare and Geoffrey Nowell Smith (New York: International Publishers, 1917), 279–318.

3. Alain Lipietz, "New Tendencies in the International Division of Labor: Regimes of Accumulation and Modes of Regulation," in *Production, Work, Territory: The Geographical Anatomy of Industrial Capitalism,* ed. A. Scott and M. Stroper (Boston: Allen and Unwin, 1986), 16–39.

4. Lipietz, "New Tendencies"; and David Harvey, *The Condition of Postmodernity* (Oxford: Basil Blackwell, 1990), 141–197.

5. Flexible accumulation strategies also shape labor conditions in sites within advanced capitalist countries. The early 1970s' world recession compelled capitalists in metropolitan countries to restructure production in the face of rising labor costs and increased competition from developing countries. Informal or unregulated economic activities, long associated with third world peasants, emerged in advanced capitalist centers as women, minorities, and immigrants furnished low-wage labor. In the United States, this informalization — decentralized production, unaccounted labor, and earnings — included the assembly of electronics components, garment sweatshops, and home work. See Alejandro Portes, M. Castells, and L. Benton, *The Informal Economy* (Baltimore: Johns Hopkins University Press, 1989); Saskia Sassen-Koob, "Notes on the Incorporation of Third World Women into Wage Labor through Immigration and Off-Shore Production," *International Migration Review* 13 (1984): 1144–1167; and Karen J. Hossfeld, "'Their Logic Against Them': Contradictions in Sex, Race, and Class in the Silicon Valley," in *Women Workers and Global Restructuring,* ed. K. Ward (Ithaca: University ILR Press, 1990), 149–178. This "downgraded" manufacturing sector (see Sassen-Koob, "Notes on the Incorporation") expanded alongside the service industries and depended on the same supplies of native-born and immigrant women. Similarly, in Kyushu, Japan, females increasingly sought employment in electronics and service industries. See K. Fujita, "Women Workers, State Policy, and the International Division of Labor: The Case of Silicon Island in Japan," *Bulletin of Concerned Asian Scholars* 20, no. 3 (1988): 42–53. Thus, flexibilization strategies disregard the traditional boundaries of the global "core-periphery," operating anywhere a peculiar mix of labor and service conditions favors profit maximization. Such radical reorganization of production forms and spaces is sometimes referred to as "postmodern." See Harvey, *The Condition of Postmodernity.*

6. Michael Burawoy, "The Anthropology of Industrial Work," *Annual Review of Anthropology* 8 (1979): 231–266; F. Froebel, J. Heinrichs, and O. Kreye, eds., *The New International Division of Labor* (Cambridge: Cambridge Uni-

versity Press, 1980); and June Nash and Maria Patricia Fernandez-Kelly, eds., *Women, Men and the International Division of Labor* (Albany: State University of New York Press, 1983).

7. This is especially the case in works by feminists. See, for example, K. Young, C. Wolkowitz, and R. McCullagh, eds., *Of Marriage and the Market* (London: CSE Books, 1981); Cynthia Enloe, *Bananas, Beaches, and Bases* (Berkeley: University of California Press, 1989); and Maria Patricia Fernandez-Kelly, *"For We are Sold, I and My People": Women and Industry on Mexico's Frontier* (Albany: State University of New York Press, 1983).

8. I borrow the term *cultural struggle* from Brackette F. Williams, *Stains on My Name, Blood in My Veins: Guyana and the Politics of Cultural Struggle* (Durham: Duke University Press, 1991), 2–29.

9. E. P. Thompson, *The Making of the English Working Class* (New York: Vintage, 1963), 11–12.

10. Raymond Williams, *Marxism and Literature* (Oxford: Oxford University Press, 1977), 128–135.

11. See Walden Bello, D. Kinley, and E. Elinson, *Development Debacle: The World Bank in the Philippines* (San Francisco: Food First Publication, 1982), and the special issue on free-trade zones in Asia, *AMPO: Japan-Asian Quarterly Review* 8.4–9.1–2 (1977).

12. For key studies of female workers in free-trade zones, see Fernandez-Kelly, *"For We Are Sold"*; Lydia Kung, *Factory Women in Taiwan* (Ann Arbor: University of Michigan Research Press, 1983); Linda Y. C. Lim, *Women Workers in Multinational Corporations: The Case of the Electronics Industry in Malaysia and Singapore* (Ann Arbor: University of Michigan Women's Studies Program, Occ. paper no. 9, 1978); Aihwa Ong, *Spirits of Resistance and Capitalist Discipline: Factory Women in Malaysia* (Albany: State University of New York Press, 1987); and Diane L. Wolf, *Factory Daughters: Gender, Household Dynamics, and Rural Industrialization in Java* (Berkeley: University of California Press, 1992).

13. Immanuel Wallerstein, *The Modern World-System*, vol. 1 (New York: Academic Press, 1974).

14. Ibid., 99–106.

15. Froebel, Heinrichs, and Kreye, *The New International Division of Labor.*

16. Lipietz, "New Tendencies in the International Division of Labor," 23.

17. Ibid., 4–5.

18. *AMPO: Japan-Asian Quarterly Review* 8.4–9.1–2 (1977).

19. B. Wysocki Jr., "Guiding Hand: In Asia, Japan Hopes to 'Coordinate' What Nations Produce," *Wall Street Journal,* 20 August 1990, A1, 4.

20. Harvey, *The Condition of Postmodernity,* 147.

21. T. Tsuchiya, "Introduction," *AMPO: Japan-Asian Quarterly Review* 8.4–9.1–2 (1977): 1–32.

22. I. Muto, "The Free Trade Zone and Mystique of Export-Oriented Industrialization," *AMPO: Japan-Asian Quarterly Review* 8.4–9.1–2 (1977): 9–32.

23. Linda Y. C. Lim and E. F. Pang, "Technological Choice and Employment Creation: A Case of Three Multinational Enterprises in Singapore," in *The Pacific Challenge in International Business,* ed. W. C. Kim and P. K. Y. Young (Ann Arbor: University of Michigan Research Press, 1985), 191.

24. A. Ong, *Spirits of Resistance,* 151.

25. Janet Salaff, *Working Daughters of Hong Kong* (Cambridge: Cambridge University Press, 1981).

26. Ping-Chun Hsiung, *Living Rooms as Factories: Class, Gender, and the Satellite Factory System in Taiwan* (Philadelphia: Temple University Press, 1995); and Kung, *Factory Women in Taiwan.*

27. R. Pineda-Ofreneo, "Sub-contracting in Export-Oriented Industries: Impact on Filipino Working Women," in *Development and Displacement: Women in Southeast Asia,* ed. G. Chandler, N. Sullivan, and J. Branson (Clayton, Australia: Monash University Papers on Southeast Asia, no. 18, 1988), 17–40.

28. Lourdes Beneria and Martha Roldan, *The Crossroads of Class and Gender: Industrial Homework, Subcontracting, and Household Dynamics in Mexico City* (Chicago: University of Chicago Press, 1987), 68, 73–74.

29. Alejandro Lugo, "Cultural Production and Reproduction in Ciudad Juarez, Mexico: Tropes at Play among Maquiladora Workers," *Cultural Anthropology* 5, no. 2 (1990): 173–196.

30. D. Lee and R. Brady, "Long Hard Days — At Pennies an Hour," *Business Week,* October 31, 1988, 46–47.

31. When one figures in the expanding tourist trade, the exploitation of cheap female labor is pervasive in developing economies. See, for example, Thanh-Dam Troung, *Sex, Money, and Morality: Prostitution and Tourism in Southeast Asia* (London: Zed Books, 1990).

32. See A. Bandarage, "Women and Capitalist Development in Sri Lanka, 1977–87," *Bulletin of Concerned Asian Scholars* 20 (1988): 57–81; and S. Siriporn, "In Pursuit of an Illusion: Thai Women in Europe," *Southeast Asia Chronicle* 96 (1985): 7–12.

33. Burawoy, "The Anthropology of Industrial Work"; and *The Politics of Production* (London: Verso, 1985), 246.

34. Burawoy, *The Politics of Production,* 13–14.

35. Ibid., 226–235.

36. Burawoy, "The Anthropology of Industrial Work," 263; cf. 103.

37. See, for example, Lipietz, "New Tendencies in the International Division of Labor," 294.

38. Such tendencies of othering third world women as primarily victims of their cultures are also evident in feminist writings on "women and development." See my essay, "Colonialism and Modernity: Feminist Re-presentations of Women in non-Western Societies," *Inscriptions* 3–4 (1988): 79–93.

39. Burawoy, *The Politics of Production,* 246.

40. Hagen Koo, Stephen Haggard, and Frederic Deyo, "Labor and Development Strategy in East Asian NICs," *Items* 40, nos. 3–4 (1986): 64–68.

41. A. Ong, *Spirits of Resistance,* 4–5.

42. Harvey, *The Condition of Postmodernity,* 123. See also E. P. Thompson, "Time, Work Discipline, and Industrial Capitalism," *Past and Present* 38 (1967): 56–97.

43. Wolf, *Factory Daughters.*

44. Salaff, *Working Daughters of Hong Kong,* 35.

45. Kung, *Factory Women in Taiwan,* xiv.

46. Ibid., xv–xvii.

47. Salaff, *Working Daughters of Hong Kong,* 256.

48. Kung, *Factory Women in Taiwan,* 125.

49. Phyllis Andors, "Women and Work in Shenzhen," *Bulletin of Concerned Asian Scholars* 20, no. 3 (1988): 22–41.

50. Salaff, *Working Daughters of Hong Kong,* 266.

51. For an overview of female out-migration in Asia, see J. T. Fawcett, S-E. Khoo, and P. C. Smith, eds., *Women in the Cities of Asia* (Boulder, CO: Westview, 1984).

52. See, for example, A. Ong, *Spirits of Resistance,* 191–192.

53. Wolf, *Factory Daughters.*

54. A. Ong, *Spirits of Resistance,* 125–128.

55. Harvey, *The Condition of Postmodernity,* 294; Lim, *Women Workers in Multinational Corporations.*

56. Salaff, *Working Daughters of Hong Kong,* 3–4.

57. Burawoy, "The Anthropology of Industrial Work"; and Harvey, *The Condition of Postmodernity,* 192, 294.

58. See essays in Nash and Fernandez-Kelly, *Women, Men and the International Division of Labor.* For a historical view of the ways labor is increasingly deskilled in manufacturing, see Harry Braverman, *Labor and Monopoly Capital: The Degradation of Work in the Late Twentieth Century* (New York: Monthly Review Press, 1974), chap. 4.

59. A. Ong, *Spirits of Resistance,* chap. 7.

60. D. Elson and R. Pearson, "The Subordination of Women and the Internationalization of Factory Production," in *Of Marriage and the Market,* ed. K. Young et al. (London: CSE Books, 1981), 144–166.

61. Salaff, *Working Daughters of Hong Kong,* 22–23.

62. A. Ong, *Spirits of Resistance,* 163, 170–178.

63. In her "Subaltern Studies: Deconstructing Historiography," in *Selected Subaltern Studies,* ed. R. Guha and G. C. Spivak (New York: Oxford University Press, 1988), 29, Gayatri Spivak argues that such particular collusion between local forms of "patriarchy" and transnational capitalism have made the "subproletariat" woman "the paradigmatic subject" of the international division of labor. I think we should be cautious about making such a universalizing, though provocative, model of female workers, because what seems at stake for her is to add to the classically designated Marxist (male) proletariat a newly discovered but equally generic "subproletariat" female one. The main theme of my essay is that there is no such overwhelmingly class-determined cross-cultural female figure, but rather a multiplicity of historically situated subjects

at the intersections of particular local-global power structures who by engaging in local struggles define who they are in cultural terms.

64. See F. W. Taylor, *Two Papers on Scientific Management* (London: Routledge and Sons, 1919).

65. Braverman, *Labor and Monopoly Capital*, chap. 4.

66. Michel Foucault, *Discipline and Punish: The Birth of the Prison*, trans. A. Sheridan (New York: Vintage, 1979); and *The History of Sexuality*, Vol. 1, *Introduction*, trans. R. Hurley (New York: Vintage, 1980).

67. A. Ong, *Spirits of Resistance*, 164–167. See also Maria Patricia Fernandez-Kelly and A. Garcia, "Informalization at the Core: Hispanic Women, Home Work, and the Advanced Capitalist State," in *The Informal Economy*, ed. A. Portes, M. Castells, and L. Benton (Baltimore: Johns Hopkins University Press, 1989), 128.

68. A. Ong, *Spirits of Resistance*, 162–163.

69. Ibid., 166.

70. Ibid., chap. 7. See also V. Lin, "Productivity First: Japanese Management Methods in Singapore," *Bulletin of Concerned Asian Scholars* 16, no. 4 (1984): 12–25. It is now very common for capitalist enterprises located anywhere in the world to routinely use electronic surveillance, an even more relentless form of control, in both industrial and office settings.

71. A. Ong, *Spirits of Resistance*, 172–173.

72. Foucault, *The History of Sexuality*, 103.

73. A. Ong, *Spirits of Resistance*, 168.

74. Aihwa Ong, "Japanese Factories, Malay Workers: Class and Sexual Metaphors in Malaysia," in *Power and Difference: Gender in Island Southeast Asia*, ed. J. Atkinson and S. Errington (Stanford: Stanford University Press, 1990), 385–443.

75. Ibid. See also Asian Women's Liberation Newsletter, "Outcries of Poor Workers: Appeal from South Korea," in *Third World—Second Sex*, ed. Miranda Davies (London: Zed Press, 1983): 233–239; and Fernandez-Kelly and Garcia, "Informalization at the Core."

76. Lee and Brady, "Long Hard Days," *Business Week* 46.

77. Foucault, *Discipline and Punish*.

78. See, for instance, Kung, *Factory Women in Taiwan*; and Bandarage, "Women and Capitalist Development."

79. For different Marxist analyses of the material dimensions and effects of cultural production, see R. Williams, *Marxism and Literature*, and Fredric Jameson, "Postmodernism, or the Cultural Logic of Late Capitalism," *New Left Review*, no. 146 (July–August, 1984): 53–92.

80. A. Ong, *Spirits of Resistance*, 152.

81. Aihwa Ong, "Disassembling Gender in an Electronics Age: Review Article," *Feminist Studies* 13 (1987): 609–627.

82. A. Ong, *Spirits of Resistance*, 153.

83. Fernandez-Kelly, "*For We Are Sold*," 117.

84. Kung, *Factory Women in Taiwan*, 63.

85. See Rachel Grossman, "Women's Place in the Integrated Circuit," *Southeast Asia Chronicle* 66 (1979): 2–17.

86. Mary Douglas, *Purity and Danger* (Harmondsworth: Penguin, 1970), 120–124, 142–147. For a brilliant application of Douglas's ideas to symbolic practices associated with urbanization and class formation in Europe, see Peter Stallybass and Allon White, *The Politics and Poetics of Transgression* (Ithaca: Cornell University Press, 1986).

87. A. Ong, "Japanese Factories, Malay Workers."

88. Celia Mather, "Industrialization in the Tangerang Regency of West Java: Women Workers and the Islamic Patriarchy," *Bulletin of Concerned Asian Scholars* 15, no. 2 (1983): 2–17.

89. S. Hanatrakul, "Prostitution in Thailand," in *Development and Displacement,* ed. G. Chandler, N. Sullivan, and J. Branson (Clayton, Australia: Monash University Papers on Southeast Asia, no. 18, 1988), 132–133.

90. For a mainland comparison, see Lisa Rofel, "Hegemony and Productivity: Workers in Post-Mao China," in *Marxism and the Chinese Experience,* ed. A. Dirlik and M. Meisner (Armonk, NY: M. E. Sharpe, 1989), 235–252.

91. See Erving Goffman, *Stigma: Notes on the Management of Spoiled Identity* (New York: Simon & Schuster, 1963).

92. Kung, *Factory Women in Taiwan,* 156–157.

93. Ibid., 158–159.

94. For an overview of labor conditions in Mexican factories, see Vicki L. Ruiz and Susan Tiano, eds., *Women on the U.S.-Mexican Border* (Boston: Allen & Unwin, 1987).

95. Fernandez-Kelly, *"For We Are Sold,"* 129.

96. A. Weisman, "The Other Side of Nogales," *The Arizona Republic, City Magazine* (Tucson), February 1989, 39.

97. Ibid., 31.

98. In 1989, on a brief field trip to Nogales, I visited American factories, shantytowns, and service centers. Factory employees and social workers complained that sexual harassment was a common occurrence in what they called "the maquila culture." At a rape crisis center, volunteers noted that the frequency of rapes of workers and their children was "alarmingly high." Aborted fetuses were sometimes found in maquila toilets. Rapists were found among factory supervisors, household members, and the police, that is, men on whom the factory workers depended for their everyday survival and security. This environment of daily violence appears much more brutal than the situation of female workers in Malaysia, with whose circumstances I am much more familiar. The contrasting experiences of violence highlight the particular historical and cultural conditions whereby different modes of religious, sexual, and labor controls are brought into play in factory settings.

99. J. Kammer and S. Tolan, "Many Plants Look Other Way When Children Apply for Work," *The Arizona Republic,* 17 April 1989, 11.

100. Weisman, "The Other Side of Nogales," 39.

101. Lugo, "Cultural Production and Reproduction."

102. Bandarage, "Women and Capitalist Development."

103. Ibid., 79.

104. Ibid., 69.

105. See also Enloe, *Bananas, Beaches, and Bases.* The importation of prostitutes and brides into regions being opened up for capitalist development, whether in colonial Southeast Asia or in California during the gold rush, is the historical antecedent of contemporary linkages between global factories and women from poor countries.

106. M. Stroper and R. Walker, *The Capitalist Imperative: Territory, Technology, and Industrial Growth* (New York: Basil Blackwell, 1989), 223.

107. For a succinct summary of an attempt to use the classic type of class consciousness for anthropological analysis, see Sydney Mintz, "The Rural Proletariat and the Problem of the Rural Proletarian Consciousness," in *Peasants and Proletarians,* ed. R. Cohen, P. Gutkind, and P. Brazier (New York: Monthly Review Press, 1974), 187–195. Drawing a rigid distinction between "class-in-itself" (in the objective sense) and "class-for-itself" (when it develops collective interests) sometimes prevents the recognition of collective consciousness when the requisite stereotypical "working-class" behavior is absent.

108. Ibid., 193.

109. June Nash, *We Eat the Mines and the Mines Eat Us* (New York: Columbia University Press, 1983).

110. Joan Vincent, *Teso in Transformation* (Berkeley: University of California Press, 1982), 232–262.

111. Jean Comaroff, *Body of Power, Spirit of Resistance* (Chicago: University of Chicago Press, 1986), 254.

112. Many Marxist anthropologists have tended not to consider rituals of solidarity and resistance as sufficient expressions of protest against capitalism, but as merely a "stage" in the development of "authentic" class consciousness, when class-based political action is taken as in some ideal European scenario of working-class struggle, but now on a global level.

113. Spivak, "Subaltern Studies," 16–17.

114. See, for example, Young, Wolkowitz, and McCullagh, *Of Marriage and the Market;* and Enloe, *Bananas, Beaches, and Bases.*

115. Donna Haraway, "Situated Knowledges: The Science Question in Feminism and the Privilege of Partial Perspective," *Feminist Studies* 14, no. 3 (fall 1988): 575–599; Chandra Talpade Mohanty, "Feminist Encounters: Locating the Politics of Experience," *Copyright* 1 (1987): 30–44; and Henrietta Moore, *Feminism and Anthropology* (Minneapolis: University of Minnesota Press, 1988).

116. Spivak, "Subaltern Studies," 29. But having said that, Spivak herself is also very susceptible to the model of universal proletarian predicament and struggle, as mentioned in note 63 above.

117. As reported, for example, in Asian Women's Liberation Newsletter, "Outcries of Poor Workers"; and Ruiz and Tiano, *Women on the U.S.-Mexican Border.* A good documentary is L. Gray, A. Bohlen, and M. P. Fernandez-Kelly,

The Global Assembly Line (16 mm film, 58 min., color), New Day Films, Wayne, NJ, 1987.

118. Lim, *Women Workers in Multinational Corporations.*

119. For a different formulation of this position, see Alan Pred, "In Other Wor(l)ds: Fragmented and Integrated Observations on Gendered Languages, Gendered Spaces, and Local Transformations," *Antipode* 22, no. 1 (1990): 33–52.

120. Fernandez-Kelly, "*For We Are Sold*," 48–50.

121. Ibid., 49–51; see also S. Tiano, "Maquiladoras in Mexico: Integration or Exploitation?" in Ruiz and Tiano, *Women on the U.S.-Mexican Border,* 98.

122. Fernandez-Kelly, "*For We Are Sold*," 153–177.

123. Ibid., 142–150.

124. Beneria and Roldan, *The Crossroads of Class and Gender.*

125. Ibid., 102.

126. Ibid., 160–161.

127. After their factories were destroyed in the 1987 earthquake, garment workers in Mexico City formed the first female workers union, mainly to help members and their families put their lives back together again. Refer to Ruiz and Tiano, *Women on the U.S.-Mexican Border,* for problems in organizing maquila workers.

128. Kung, *Factory Women in Taiwan,* 106–107.

129. Ibid., 163.

130. Ibid., 156–161.

131. Ibid., 166–168.

132. Andors, "Women and Work," 37–38.

133. Not that they always succeed in doing so. Compare such observations with those of English working-class youths depicted in Paul Willis, *Learning to Labor: How Working Class Kids Get Working Class Jobs* (New York: Columbia University Press, 1977), 27.

134. Kung, *Factory Women in Taiwan,* 164–165.

135. A. Ong, "Japanese Factories, Malay Workers," 414–415.

136. A. Ong, *Spirits of Resistance,* 197.

137. Ibid., 167.

138. Ibid., 167, 201–202.

139. Kung, *Factory Women in Taiwan,* 89.

140. Ibid., 94–98.

141. Ibid.

142. Salaff, *Working Daughters of Hong Kong,* 103.

143. Kung, *Factory Women in Taiwan,* 98, 159–161.

144. Rofel, "Hegemony and Productivity."

145. Ibid., 246–248.

146. Again, such responses to capitalist exploitation echo earlier cries of outrage during the early modern eras of industrial capitalism in Europe. See, for example, Friedrich Engels, *The Condition of the Working Class in England,*

trans. W. O. Henderson and W. H. Chaloner (Stanford: Stanford University Press, 1968); and Thompson, *The Making of the English Working Class.* The moral transformation of the capital-owning class is of course theorized in Max Weber, *The Protestant Ethic and the Spirit of Capitalism,* trans. T. Parsons (New York: Charles Scribner & Sons, 1958).

147. Pred, "In Other Wor(l)ds," 46–47.

148. James C. Scott, *Weapons of the Weak* (New Haven: Yale University Press, 1986), 335–336.

149. In *Spirits of Resistance,* I show throughout that Malay peasants, though located in the countryside, are very much within the hegemonic influences of the state and of capital.

150. Foucault, *The History of Sexuality,* 95.

151. Michel de Certeau. "On the Oppositional Practices of Everyday Life," *Social Text* 3 (fall, 1980): 3–43.

152. Fernandez-Kelly, *"For We Are Sold"*; and Lugo, "Cultural Production and Reproduction." In "Their Logic Against Them," Karen Hossfeld identifies a similar tactic among workers in Silicon Valley, California. She reports that female workers exploit the management's racist/sexist logic—such as the "lazy" Chicana or the "China doll" stereotypes—to gain excuses for evading or subverting work rules.

153. D. Pena, *"Tortuosidad:* Shopfloor Struggles of Female Maquiladora Workers," in *Women on the U.S.-Mexican Border,* ed. Vicky Ruiz and Susan Tiano (Boston: Allen & Unwin, 1987), 129–154; and G. Young, "Gender Identification and Working-Class Solidarity among Maquila Workers in Ciudad Juarez: Stereotypes and Realities," in *Women on the U.S.-Mexican Border,* ed. Ruiz and Tiano, 105–127.

154. A. Ong, "Japanese Factories, Malay Workers."

155. A. Ong, *Spirits of Resistance,* 210–213.

156. Aihwa Ong, "The Production of Possession: Spirits and the Multinational Corporation in Malaysia," *American Ethnologist* 15 (1988): 28–42.

157. See Michael Taussig, "Reification and the Consciousness of the Patient," *Social Science and Medicine* 14B (1980): 3–13.

158. Ibid.

159. Nancy Scheper-Hughes gives analytical importance to reading "the cryptic language of protest" in her "The Subversive Body: Illness and the Micropolitics of Resistance," in *Anthropology in the 1990s,* ed. R. Borowski (New York: McGraw Hill, 1991).

160. A. Ong, *Spirits of Resistance,* 207–209.

161. In her introduction to *Dealing with Inequality,* ed. M. Strathern (Cambridge: Cambridge University Press, 1987), Marilyn Strathern argues that the question of agency goes beyond the independent actions of individuals and should focus on the interests "in terms of which they act." Their aims are neither "necessarily . . . independently conceived" (22), nor in my view, necessarily fully conscious.

162. de Certeau, "On the Oppositional Practices of Everyday Life," 8.

163. Soon Hua Sun, "Women, Work, and Theology in Korea," *Journal of Feminist Studies in Religion* 3 (1987): 128.

164. Sun Joo Oh, "The Living Conditions of Female Workers in Korea," *Korea Observer* 24, no. 2 (1983): 192–193.

165. Ibid., 211.

166. Ibid., 191.

167. S. H. Sun, "Women, Work, and Theology in Korea."

168. Soon Kyong Cho, "The Labor Process and Capital Mobility: The Limits of the New International Division of Labor," *Politics & Society* 14, no. 2 (1985): 220.

169. Oh, "The Living Conditions of Female Workers in Korea," 186.

170. Asian Women's Liberation Newsletter, "Outcries of Poor Workers."

171. S. K. Kim, "Women Workers and the Birth of Labor Unions in Masan, Korea" (paper presented at the Annual Meeting of the American Anthropological Association, Phoenix, AZ, December 1988).

172. S. H. Sun, "Women, Work, and Theology in Korea."

173. Asian Women's Liberation Newsletter, "Outcries of Poor Workers."

174. Ibid., 235.

175. Ibid., 237.

176. S. H. Sun, "Women, Work, and Theology in Korea," 133–134.

177. This is a strong tradition in Korean society. See, for instance, S. N. Kim, "Lamentations of the Dead: The Historical Imagery of Violence on Cheju Island, South Korea," *Journal of Ritual Studies* 3, no. 2 (1989): 251–271.

178. S. H. Sun, "Women, Work, and Theology in Korea."

179. Ibid., 129.

180. Ibid., 132.

181. S. K. Kim, "Women Workers and the Birth of Labor Unions."

182. D. J. Yang et al. "Is the Era of Cheap Asian Labor Over?" *Business Week*, 15 May 1989, 44–45.

183. Creating the conditions discussed in Kim, "Women Workers and the Birth of Labor Unions"; and Hossfeld, "Their Logic Against Them."

184. R. Williams, *Marxism and Literature*, 132.

185. Ibid.

REYNALDO C. ILETO

Outlines of a Nonlinear Emplotment
of Philippine History

Most sensitive thinkers today regard the concept of "development" not as universal but as historically conditioned, arising from social, economic, and ideological trends in eighteenth-century Europe. The idea of Progress — the belief that the growth of knowledge, capabilities, and material production makes human existence better — placed science at the summit of knowledge. It gave birth to high imperialism, as the West identified Progress with civilization and set out to dominate the rest of the world. Today, the idea of Progress and the developmental ideology it engendered are under attack. We are aware of how scientific knowledge and technique can bring disaster, how increased material production does not necessarily lead to a better life. The reality of poverty, exploitation of workers, domination of certain groups by others, and destruction of the environment flies in the face of rational planning by technocrats.[1]

Despite the growing awareness of what "development" really means, it remains a formidable task to identify and negate the features of an outlook that has been internalized for decades and continues to shape our thinking. In the Philippines, the developmental outlook is deeply implicated in power relationships within the society as well as between the Philippines and the outside world. It shapes behavior and thought without being fully articulated itself. The concept of development is still understood as a universal "given" — the "given," for example, of any text emanating from the national government and its technocrats. Even the critics of government and the technocratic elite who like to point out distortions and misapplications of policy remain trapped in the very discourse of development. It is as if to become an educated Filipino one had to internalize this central organizing concept of the modern age.

From the moment typical Filipino students begin to learn about themselves, their society, history, and culture through books, the mass media, and the classroom, they become immersed in ideas of development, emergence, linear time, scientific reason, humane pragmatism, governmental ordering, and nation building. They become so caught up in these that they take them to be part of the natural ordering of things. Little do they know that such categories are historical, that they were devised at a certain time in the past by men and women bound by their unique interests and environments. The operations by which some events are highlighted while others are suppressed, the division into arbitrary historical periods, the establishment of chains of cause and effect, the evolutionary ordering of phenomena such as from primitive to advanced, religious to secular — all these are obscured in textbooks and teaching methods. The student is made to learn the facts as they are strung out in some linear fashion, not the relationship of histories to power groups, the silences of the past, or the history of the linear scheme itself.[2]

This essay will, first of all, look into the common structural features that underlie linear Philippine histories of different political persuasions. These texts have dominated the educational scene for at least a decade, and have become part and parcel of the intellectual baggage of the present generation of politicians, radical activists, and technocrats. By interrogating these texts one may begin to understand why it is so difficult for the men and women at the top to escape the "linear developmental" mode of comprehending national problems and prospects. But it is not enough to identify the structure or grammar of modern Philippine history. The second part of this essay looks into the late nineteenth-century context of its irruption, particularly the still unexplored rise of medical power. Finally, the question of what to do with the data that are marginalized in the dominant histories will be discussed. An alternative historical project might consist of retrieving such data and allowing them to challenge the dominant constructs, fomenting what Foucault calls "the insurrection of subjugated knowledges" that were "present but disguised within the body of functionalist and systematizing theory."[3]

LINEAR HISTORY

The late Teodoro Agoncillo, the Philippines' most influential history textbook writer, is famous for his construction of a history that begins after 1872, the year of the executions of three reformist priests, or the year that a "national consciousness" was born.[4] Agoncillo justified this view on the grounds that one cannot hear an authentic Filipino voice prior to 1872 in the mass of Spanish colonial records that have survived. At most there are isolated, regional, and tribal assertions against the colonial order, but hardly one that articulates a common experience and destiny of the Filipino people.

Spanish colonialism is to blame, says Agoncillo. Before the conquest in the sixteenth century the native inhabitants had a sense of belonging to the Malay world; they were literate, prosperous, and united under their respective chiefs. Spanish rule encouraged the docility of the people, the corruption of leaders, their collaboration with the foreigners, and above all a loss of authentic customs and beliefs. Only with nineteenth-century economic development and the consequent rise of a native intelligentsia called the *ilustrado* would things be set straight again.

Agoncillo's textbooks are considered exemplary in the nationalist tradition, but an examination of *all* modern history textbooks will reveal that they contain the following categories and chronological sequence: a Golden Age (pre-Hispanic society), the Fall (i.e., the conquest by Spain in the sixteenth century), the Dark Age (seventeenth and eighteenth centuries), Economic and Social Development (nineteenth century), the Rise of Nationalist Consciousness (post-1872), the Birth of the Nation (1898), and either Suppressed Nationalism or Democratic Tutelage (post-1901, the U.S. Regime). Either 1872 or 1896—the year of the Katipunan revolt against Spain—is the linchpin of several binary oppositions structuring such texts: forward/backward, reason/superstition, enlightenment/enslavement, modern/traditional, religion/progress, and so forth. To put it another way, sometime in the late nineteenth century there is seen to be a breakthrough, a movement forward out of darkness and subjection, toward progress, independence, and the Philippine nation-state.

To understand how deeply rooted this conception of history is we must go back to its *ilustrado* emplotment in the late nineteenth century. The *ilustrados* were the offspring par excellence of the Spanish ordering of society. This began with the *reducción,* the gathering together of scattered settlements into more compact, Hispanicized *pueblo* centers. From the pueblos or towns emerged a native and mestizo elite called the *principalia,* who, educated by the Spanish friars in the convents, began to assimilate the basic elements of a progressivist outlook such as the Judeo-Christian concept of man working out the Divine Plan over time, or the notion of man's perfectibility. Townspeople as a whole, through their familiarity with localized versions of the Old and New Testaments, came to be familiar with the notion of "history" as a series of events with a beginning (the Creation) and an end (the final Judgment). After the Fall from an original state of perfection in the Garden of Eden, history consists of man's strivings for salvation, which ultimately is to be found in the afterlife, in the City of God.[5]

The opening of the countryside to capitalist penetration from the 1820s on, reaching full swing by the 1850s, was followed by the crystallization of new knowledges that were readily accepted by middle- and upper-class Filipinos who were admitted to Spanish-language colleges after the education reforms of the 1860s. Before this period, man's perfectibility was deemed impossible on earth; the Spanish clergy in the colony was determined to keep this perception intact. In the second half of the nineteenth century, however, the educated, *ilustrado* members of the *principalia* elite, increasingly resentful of the archaic dominance of the Church over practically all aspects of *indio* life, were prepared to assimilate late-Enlightenment ideas of secular progress guaranteed by history and biology. Ironically, their exposure to Christian catechism and Church history in the convent schools predisposed them to linear, progressive ideas of history. Despite their attacks on what they saw as Spanish-controlled religiosity that kept the ordinary people in subjection, the *ilustrados* nevertheless retained the Christian constructs of "Fall" and "Recovery" in their emplotment of the Philippine past.

The first native students of Philippine history — Jose Rizal, Gregorio Sanciangco, Isabelo de los Reyes, Ramon Paterno, and Trinidad Pardo de Tavera — saw their generation as the first to be guided by Reason rather than Superstition. As a way of liberating themselves from their colonial consciousness, they studied the ancient alphabets, literature, religion, and other aspects of pre-Hispanic society, and posited a time in the past when the Philippine archipelago was a flourishing civilization that, however, succumbed to the proffered benefits of alliance with the Spanish *conquistadores*. History, hence, begins with a "Fall." As heirs of the humanist tradition, the *ilustrados* further posited a break *in their time* between the "Dark Age" of Spanish colonialism, when religion and ignorance ruled men's minds, and a new age of enlightenment, when the glory of an ancient past would be fused with the progress of nationhood. The future hope was no longer bliss in heaven but a prosperous nation-state that would take its place in the international community.[6]

With *ilustrado* writing, then, Philippine history became intelligible, progressive, linear, and, to some extent, "purposive." The people, or its vanguard intelligentsia, could help push history to its goal by education/reform or revolution. Subsequent histories, both of the liberal and radical varieties, have reproduced this nineteenth-century emplotment. In fact, this has formed the backbone of the dominant state ideology, and intelligentsia-led opposition to it, since the triumph of the First Republic in 1898.

In Ferdinand Marcos's unfinished, multivolume work, *Tadhana: The History of the Filipino People*, fully a quarter of the series is allocated to the pre-Hispanic "roots of Filipino heritage." Marcos identifies the origins of the future Filipino nation in the idealized pre-Spanish *barangay* — a community bound together by kinship ties and loyalty to the paternal leader — whose natural evolution into a state was frustrated by the Spaniards. Another quarter of *Tadhana* discusses Spanish rule, "during which the Filipinos struggled first to assimilate and participate in the Hispanization process, gradually and consciously moving towards the idea of a national community in the reform or propaganda movement." Then in 1872 the "counter-society" is mobilized and begins the move toward the birth of the nation-state in 1898. From 1898 to 1946 (the year in which the United States finally grants political independence) the Marcos history tells of this dream, this destiny — *tadhana* means "fate" or "destiny" — being realized in the face of U.S., Japanese, rightist, leftist, and other threats to it.[7]

Marcos's history departs from Agoncillo's in taking a more positive view of the "Conquista" (the "Fall") and the "Dark Age." It accommodates the research of John Phelan and others that showed that while the native perception of reality was strained by the impositions of colonialism, there was no break or disruption arising from the conversion and relocation of the lowland populace. Spanish missionaries could not have succeeded in their enterprise without building on preexisting notions of curative waters, amulets, spirit worship, family alliances, and the like. The process of Hispanicizing the native elite was as much through the latter's initiative as it was Spain's.[8] Marcos develops this notion of *indio* creativity and assertion into that of the "counter-society" — the substratum of indigenous civilization, taking the form of a primitive yearning for liberty that simmered beneath the surface of Spanish rule.

The "counter-society" in Marcos's history, in the process of revealing itself, of making liberty manifest, gradually transforms itself into a state. Here is the culmination of *ilustrado* efforts to construct a chain of events leading to the modern nation-state. Marcos, in fact, is also the name of a group of intellectuals under the regime's patronage who use the idiom of modern scholarship to essentially fulfill the dreams of their forebears. They see the origins of the state in the pre-Spanish *barangay,* which was gradually transformed during the colonial period into the much larger *pueblo* dominated at the center by the municipal hall and church/convent complex. From this center emerged the *principalia* and *ilustrado* classes, which wrote and subscribed to a history organized from the center's perspective.

To put it another way, if history was continuous and progressive, then the *pueblo* and its fulfillment — the state — would be the very site of progress. Thus there is a disproportioned celebration, in both history books and national festivities, of the founding of the first Philippine republic in 1898, despite its suppression of religiopolitical movements that preceded it and plagued its short-lived existence. The sacred character of the state is evidenced in Marcos's self-consciously Hegelian argument that the state was the "self realization of the Absolute" and that the form of constitutional authoritarianism his regime practiced — in which through him as "world historical" Leader the guiding hand of History/Progress operated — was the only way that the *ilustrado* dream could be realized.[9]

Among the most effective critics of the "statist" construction of history have been those who go by the much misunderstood name Marxist. Two examples will be mentioned here: Renato Constantino, author of a best-selling textbook, *The Philippines: A Past Revisited,* and the National Democratic Front (NDF) whose version of Philippine history is derived from Amado Guerrero's *Philippine Society and Revolution.*[10]

Constantino pointed out, in reply to Agoncillo's dismissal of the "Dark Age" of Spanish rule, that Spanish colonial policy, and even Spanish history and society, from the beginning "had profound effects on the evolving Filipino society and cannot therefore be ignored." His criticism of Agoncillo's "great men" approach was also an attack on Marcos's history at the height of martial rule: "All powerful leaders, and especially tyrants, exerted efforts to insure that the history of their time would be written in their image" (p. 7). In the final analysis, however, "it is the people who make or unmake heroes" (p. 7). The NDF has likewise rejected the "great heroes" approach; leaders or rebels are thrown up by the particular social and economic formations in which they lived. In fact, one of the preoccupations of the NDF (as well as other, competing Marxist groups) has been to identify discrete stages in the Philippine past so that development and its concomitant struggles can be more scientifically plotted.[11]

"There must be no segmentation of the different stages of our history," argues Constantino. Despite the "evolution and disappearance of forms of social life and institutions" (p. 11), there is a continuity in the people's material and subjective growth. Constantino calls revolts and other assertions during colonial rule "the schools of the masses" (p. 10). "From blind responses to foreign oppression, mass actions against the Spaniards and later against the Americans underwent various transformations until they finally became a conscious struggle for national liberation" (p. 10). Note that the endpoint of popular struggles is not state formation but "national liberation" or, as Constantino says elsewhere, "the birth of a *nation.*" Note, too, that revolts are shown to be increasingly self-conscious and secular, evolving in stages as the economy develops. Variations on the theme are found elsewhere. For example, Constantino-inspired Church activists picture religious unrest as developing in stages, from Apolinario de la Cruz's primitive Cofradía movement of 1840–41 to the highest stage in Fr. Gregorio Aglipay's schism from the Roman Catholic Church during the revolution. The former is pictured as a blind groping, the leader Apolinario still encumbered by "Dark Age" superstition, hence its failure.[12]

The problem is that, their sincerity notwithstanding, Constantino and the NDF have failed to extricate themselves from the discourse of the liberal nationalists they condemn. Like Agoncillo and Marcos, they present an image of a pre-Hispanic feudal order bastardized by colonialism and a native culture contaminated by Christianity. What these texts have in common with their liberal rivals is that they proceed from the same construct of Fall-Darkness-Recovery (or Triumph), where there is a necessary development from a point in the past to the present, and everything in between is either taken up in the march forward or simply suppressed. Older ideas of progress can be gleaned in these texts' insistence on consciousness of the "laws of motion" and on "correct" organizational responses to historical opportunities for revolutionary change.

While Constantino and the NDF look upon the masses as the real "makers of history," the masses are not allowed to speak. They exist only to be represented by articulate leaders who are said to have a deeper understanding than "ordinary people" of the causes of oppression, and who begin to emerge in the second half of the nineteenth century. Here we see another intersection of nationalist establishment writing and nationalist/Marxist oppositionist writing. It is a very subtle kind of elitism, because it draws upon the Filipino "commonsense" view that colonialism made the masses passive, that the Spanish clergy preached such virtues as "resignation, passivity and respect for authority." An example cited by both Marcos and the NDF in their handbook for activists is the Spanish use of such texts as the *Pasyon* — indigenous versions of the New Testament story — to make the masses submissive.[13] Naturally, if such writers ignore the popular, creative appropriation of Spanish-Christian texts, it follows that the coming of the intelligentsia is sorely needed.

It is not surprising that such ostensibly diverse texts share a common historical emplotment. The reason most educated Filipinos find the linear-developmental mode a natural one for ordering such phenomena as revolts and the consolidation of state power in the name of nationalism is because this framework puts *them* at the forefront of the development process. Whether as apologists or activists, they are able to recognize themselves in a comfortable way in the past, and they are assured of a primary role in the fulfillment of the end toward which history moves.

PHYSICIANS AND THE STATE

Rizal is rightly regarded as the foremost Filipino nationalist writer and interpreter of history in the late nineteenth century. But the other Rizal is the medical practitioner who devoted much scholarly investigation to the natural sciences. Those who comment on Rizal's medical career avoid such terms as "propagandist" and "interpretation," in deference to the neutral category of science that medicine is perceived to belong to. But if his total intellectual activity is located in the episteme of the period, the writer Rizal surely cannot be divorced from the physician Rizal. Nineteenth-century history and science shared the same basic assumptions: chains of cause and effect, perfectibility of man on earth, triumph over untruth and superstition, biological evolution, and so forth. That Rizal, Paterno, and Pardo de Tavera were medical practitioners who also wrote histories suggests the discursive complicity of the medico scientific outlook in the *ilustrado* construction of Philippine history.

After 1872, parents, with good reason (that is, the execution of the three reformist priests), were reluctant to send their sons to seminaries. The medical profession succeeded the priesthood as the most popular career goal for bright and well-to-do youth. Medicine and its auxiliary discipline, pharmacy, were regarded as having long since broken away from fantasy and superstition to arrive at objective truth about the body and its diseases. The rise of medicine as a distinct discipline depended upon the view that knowledge could be steadily accumulated and perfected, and that science was moving toward the final triumph over death. Filipinos reading their history through this medicoscientific matrix quite naturally were attracted to the emplotment or construct described at the beginning of this paper. Fall–Dark Age–Enlightenment and Progress.

Our alternative reading of the nineteenth-century rise to prominence of the medical profession is based on the actual intersection of medicine, politics, and society during the cholera epidemics that swept the colony from 1820 to 1902. The 1820 epidemic forms a traumatic backdrop to the emergence of science in the nineteenth century. Since Asiatic cholera had not been experienced previously, European doctors were at a loss as to how to respond to the crisis. Official remedies like the distribution of tonics only spread the infection further. Preventive measures proved to be generally useless.

Worse, the 1820 epidemic led to social disorder: antiforeign riots originating in the native districts surrounding Manila resulted in the deaths of many foreigners. Afflicted natives of the lower classes abandoned the *pueblos,* turning in droves to what the French physician Gironiere termed "native sorcerers" occupying the fringes of Spanish centers. The almost total disruption of public order at the height of the epidemic was as much the problem as the disease itself.[14] The experience of the 1820 epidemic as a time of chaos was constantly at the back of the minds of colonial health officials during subsequent visitations. Medical and sanitary practices that were devised in succeeding decades had the additional, if not essential, function of maintaining public order.[15]

Soon after 1820, Spanish health officials were in touch with physicians from British India, thus many of the developments in cholera treatments and quarantine and hospitalization procedures elsewhere were adopted. From hindsight it is easy to smile at the naïveté of the cures and such "mistaken" conceptions as the dreaded *miasma.* But documents of the sanitary and health commissions reveal a genuine reverence toward the advances in knowledge and techniques in the nineteenth century. Battling a killer disease such as cholera with the weapons of science gave the *juntas sanitarias* (sanitary commissions) a rising prestige among the nascent Filipino middle class, a prestige previously enjoyed only by the Church.

The fairly extensive documentation on the 1882 and 1889 epidemics reveals a situation far different from that of 1820.[16] Sanitary commissions were quickly mobilized in each town at the first sign of an outbreak. Initially, parish priests, either Spaniard or native, served as presidents of these commissions, but, increasingly, *gobernadorcillos* (town mayors) were allowed to assume this function. Individuals who showed a lack of enthusiasm and competence were immediately sacked. By and large, local officials, municipal policemen, ranking *principales,* and the Guardia Civil worked remarkably well as a team to enforce state regulations. These consisted principally of the daily monitoring and inspection of houses and public facilities, the daily accounting of infected persons and cholera deaths, strict quarantines, the banning of "dangerous" food items (such as the foul-smelling shrimp paste or *bagoong*), the limiting or outright elimination of death rituals and funeral processions, the evacuation and fumigation (or burning) of infected houses, the prohibition of gatherings, and the patrolling of outlying villages and hamlets that could be the source of pollution or infection.

The reorganization of society and surveillance over ritual practices and individual consciences that accompanied conversion to Christianity in the seventeenth century was repeated in the nineteenth century by the colonial state, which made its presence felt at the household level through the system of door-to-door inspections, the monitoring of casualties, and the bans on visiting the sick and the dead. Furthermore, running parallel with the surveillance and curtailment of population movements during epidemics were similar techniques of dealing with the phenomenon of "banditry." Local sanitary commissions were particularly worried at the threat of contamination offered by unhygienic clusters of peasant dwellings and movements of people to and from them. The *pueblo* elite's energetic response to anticholera programs was a measure of its desire to ward off threats of infection from the lower orders and not much different from its attitude toward "banditry." For example, the Spanish infantry's campaign to eradicate banditry in southern Luzon in 1881 was tantamount to a massive quarantine operation that isolated the "hard working and peaceful" inhabitants of town centers from rough, unsettled, and sometimes murderous elements in the peripheries that posed a threat to the centers. In both operations, that is, epidemic and bandit suppression, Spanish commanders, parish priests, and the *principales* were allies. The saga of progress in health and sanitation is also that of the involvement of the local elites in the deployment of state power under the aegis of disease control.

After the middle of the nineteenth century, the nascent *ilustrado* segment of the *principalia* began to assert itself in the name of scientific medicine. During the 1882 cholera visitation, which rivaled in intensity that of 1820 (34,000 died in Manila alone), the frequent appeal to Manila of provincial governors, parish priests, and municipal officials was "Send a *médico títular* at once!" A *médico títular* was a bona fide graduate of a medical course, a physician, variously called *médico* or *licenciado*. In the mid-1860s the University of Santo Tomas had opened its medical faculty to Filipinos (natives and mestizos), and so by the late 1870s the native physician was becoming a powerful figure in the towns that had one.[17]

Due to the scarcity of physicians in 1882 they had to be rotated. The majority of towns, and even some provinces, had to do without one, relying (officially, that is) on the *vacunadorcillo,* the vaccinator who had been around since the beginning of the century, and the *mediquillo,* a name designating anyone with a smattering of formal training who could prescribe medicines, apply poultices, set broken bones, and the like. There was no strict line separating *mediquillo* and *curandero,* the Spanish name for an herbalist or a healer aided by spiritual powers.

One glaring feature of the rise of "medico power" was the full support it had from the colonial state. The office of the director general for civil administration, for example, regularly consulted with the faculties of the University of Santo Tomas and the College of San Jose. The words and deeds of the medicos were thus framed by the aura, the power, of *Ciencia* and *Medicina Racional,* which in turn were harnessed for state consolidation. In the towns, physicians easily displaced the vaccinators whom they regarded as practitioners of *malas artes* (the evil arts). The post of *vacunador general* was taken over by a *medico titular* in 1889. In some cases, though, power struggles between the two erupted, usually as a result of physicians clumsily attempting to subordinate long-established vaccinators in the towns. The physicians did not really know much more about cholera control than the vaccinator who had the experience of past epidemics to his credit, but an arena of conflict was created by the distinction that had been created between "licensed" and "unlicensed" medical practitioners, with the vaccinator slipping into the latter category.[18]

The physicians inevitably encountered the power of the parish priests, particularly the Spanish friars. The latter, armed with handbooks that encapsulated the missionary experience with tropical disease, had in the past assumed the role of doctors in the *pueblo* centers, dispensing medicines and even performing minor surgery. It was still common for parish priests to head the local sanitary commissions in 1882. With the appearance of the medico, clerical dominance in health matters began to decline. The medicos' struggle against the priests was an uphill one, however. Since medicos, aside from being small in numbers, were generally helpless against the 1882 visitation, priests still ruled the scene as deaths multiplied, preaching that a proper moral condition was still the best weapon against disease. Conflicts arose over the extent to which moral preparation, ritual, and proper dying could coexist with strict quarantine and burial procedures. Physicians might think that priests were obstructionists, while priests might accuse physicians of being more concerned with status and privilege than public service.[19]

The rise of scientific medicine in the context of the epidemics of the 1880s also signaled the delegitimation of the activities of the *mediquillo/curandero.* In keeping order and enforcing public health measures, local police tried to prevent access to curers. The epidemics were also a time of war on illegitimate doctors. To quote an 1889 proposal for reforms in the vaccination service: "hopefully these changes, without added cost to taxpayers, will diminish the numbers of *curanderos* and *mediquillos,* and will advance the public's education in the methods of rational medicine."[20] *Mediquillos,* formerly indispensable in the town centers, were steadily pushed back to the peripheries, their activities increasingly coming to coincide with those of "illicit associations."

There was, needless to say, resistance to disease control measures even in the town centers. Documents of the sanitary commissions complain of stubborn, secretive, apathetic, filthy, undisciplined town dwellers, generally of the poorer class. They are accused of "self-centered indifference" and "passive resistance." Worst of all, as far as the commissions were concerned, was the "irrational" preference of many for *mediquillos* and *curanderos,* resulting in discernible population movements to the fringes of *pueblos* or to nearby hills where these curers continued to practice their art virtually unimpeded.

The 1882 cholera epidemic began to subside, not so much as a result of action by the local sanitary commissions, but in the aftermath of powerful storms that washed out the sources of infection. The onset of natural immunity among the populace was also a factor. The Filipino physicians nevertheless emerged as powerful figures in the community.[21] It quite naturally fell upon them to speak on behalf of the Filipino people during the propaganda or reform movement from 1882 to around 1895. The physicians in the towns, together with the schoolteachers, secretly disseminated the views that their compatriots were publicly advocating in Europe: that *indios* should be recognized as equal to any Spanish citizen; that the people's education and livelihood should be properly attended to by the state.[22] The friar quite easily became the figure of backwardness, the "other" of the rising *médico titular.* When separation from Spain became a reality at the turn of the century, physicians and pharmacists were among the most actively involved in setting up the First Republic and even commanding its army.

MEDICAL PROGRESS/WARFARE

The irony of the story narrated above is that when the United States began to take over the reins of the colonial state at the beginning of this century, the progress of the earlier decades was simply consigned to another "Dark Age." In other words, the whole process described above was repeated, albeit with a different constellation of characters.

American occupation was greeted by a massive cholera epidemic in 1902–1903. Former Secretary of Interior Dean Worcester, in his 1909 book on cholera epidemics, contrasts the backwardness of Spain's response to the 1882 visitation with that of the U.S. government in 1902–1903, which involved the application of modern medicine and public health measures. In fact much, if not all, of the literature on the subject treats the American handling of the 1902–1903 epidemic as a triumph of rationality and science over Filipino superstition and obstinacy, a legacy of Spanish rule. Cholera is regarded as a biological, physical (in short, objective) fact requiring efficient, scientifically proven solutions.[23]

What is concealed in this saga of Western medicine's triumph? When the disease appeared in Manila in March 1902 and spread to the rest of Luzon in subsequent months, it provoked a massive medical, quarantine, and sanitation effort on the part of the newly installed colonial government. To this there were various kinds of resistance on the part of the populace. The burning of infected houses, burial in mass graves and attempted cremations, application of unfamiliar treatments and solutions, to name a few, were met with flight, concealment, and a general "sullenness" of people in some areas. The segregation of infected persons in cholera hospitals was particularly resisted. Quarantine measures were broken whenever possible. *Curanderos* were secretly active, attracting villagers to their mountain redoubts. In the end, the objective presence of a killer disease was justification enough for colonial policies to be pushed through — *by force,* if necessary. U.S. cavalrymen and soldiers were recruited by Worcester to serve as crack officers of his sanitation brigades. The image of the conquering soldier quickly became transformed into that of the crusading sanitation inspector.[24]

In southwestern Luzon, the cholera appeared at the tail end of years of guerrilla resistance to U.S. occupation. In a final attempt to break the resistance, the U.S. Army under General J. Franklin Bell implemented hamleting (reconcentration) and search-and-destroy strategies in late 1901, up to the middle of the following year when cholera began to threaten the region. The rapid spread of cholera was, in fact, greatly facilitated by the movement of U.S. troops as well as the crowding of villagers in the *pueblo* centers, now called "protected zones." Quarantine measures aggravated an already precarious food situation. War, disease, and hunger were inextricably linked in the experience of the southern Tagalogs, yet in accounts such as Worcester's one finds nothing but the saga of cholera suppression, with its concomitant disciplining of the natives and the sanitizing of their habitat.[25]

With the final surrender of most guerrilla officers in May 1902, the discourse of "pacification" quickly gave way to the discourse of "germ warfare." Military surgeons supplanted the strategists and combat troops of the earlier period. As one veteran surgeon wrote, "the sanitary work of combating this disease among an ignorant and suspicious people, impoverished by war, locusts and rinderpest and embittered by conquest was an extremely difficult task, calling for much patience, tact and firmness, the brunt of which fell on the Army."[26] In effect, the epidemic was the scene of another war, a "combat zone" of disputes over power and definitions of illness and treatment, involving U.S. military surgeons, Filipino physicians (veterans of '82 and '89), parish priests, the *principales,* stricken townspeople, and alternative curers at the fringes of the towns.

Why was there a conflict between Filipino/Spanish physicians and their U.S. counterparts, if both were the standard-bearers of progress? Worcester, at the onset of the epidemic, met with the Filipino and Spanish physicians who promised without exception to aid the Board of Health. However, with few exceptions, "they not only failed to give assistance, but in many instances, by neglecting to report cholera cases, by falsely reporting them, and by decrying the sanitary measures deemed necessary by the authorities, added materially to the crushing burdens which rested upon the Board of Health."[27] The Board had to threaten Filipino physicians, heads of families, and other responsible persons with prosecution for concealment of cases.

At one level, the *médicos'* passive resistance may be explained by their threatened loss of influence over the populace occasioned by the advent of U.S. rule. Filipino physicians, in particular, were chafing under the overbearing manners of their American superiors. The only way they could be made to cooperate was when they were given some measure of control themselves. In Manila this came when Filipinos were made heads of auxiliary boards of health. That physicians simply desired what later would be called the "Filipinization" of the bureaucracy — in this case, control over health programs involving their compatriots — is only part of the story. Their conflict with U.S. health authorities appears to have run deeper. The fact that their exemplar, Jose Rizal, had been an associate of the German physician and scientist Rudolf Virchouw has some implications here.

In an investigation of an epidemic in Upper Silesia in 1847, Virchouw traced its origins to heavy rains that had ruined the year's crops, resulting in famine. The winter following had been extremely severe, forcing the poor to huddle together in their homes, cold and hungry. It was then that a typhus epidemic broke out and spread rapidly among the poorer class, eventually attacking the wealthy classes as well. Virchouw's experience led him in 1848 to found a new journal, *Medizinische Reform,* in which he professed that poverty bred disease and that physicians must support reforms that sought to reconstruct society in a manner favorable to the people's health. Epidemics, he said, "resemble great warnings from which a statesman in the grand style can read that a disturbance has taken place in the development of his people." In the control of crowd diseases, social and even political action was necessary.[28] Filipino physicians (Rizal had led the way) were sympathetic to Virchouw's ideas. Their antipathy toward U.S. anticholera efforts is, therefore, not surprising.

U.S. physicians by 1902 almost universally subscribed to the germ theory, or more generally the doctrine of "specific etiology" of disease. Pasteur's writings on the subject appeared at about the same time as Darwin's theory of evolution. At a time when relationships between living beings were being set in a context of a struggle for survival, where one was either friend or foe, the germ theory gave rise to a kind of aggressive warfare against disease-causing microbes, which had to be eliminated from the stricken individual and from the community. Toward the end of the nineteenth century, the notion of disease as, in the final analysis, a lack of harmony between people and their environment, was giving way in the West to the search for the specific germ and the specific weapon against it. In Germany, Emile von Behring regarded Virchouw's ideas as an antiquated expression of the vague nineteenth-century *Naturphilosophie* — a characteristic, incidentally, of some of Rizal's writings.[29]

Accounts of the 1902 cholera epidemic evidence the contrast between Filipino and U.S. views of disease control. U.S. military surgeons were prone to try out all sorts of germ-killing preparations. One of them, called benzozone, soon was in short supply despite the fact that, orally taken, it was found to burn the mouth and stomach linings. Such treatments, experimental in nature, were based on the assumption that some drug ought to be able to attack and destroy the cholera vibrio within the patient. A report from the Santa Mesa cholera hospital admitted that "the definite lines of treatment advocated from time to time have never proved of material service in true cholera." Whether or not it was due to the medicines used, the U.S. method of treatment came to be feared by cholera patients, so much so that force often was used. Significantly, though, when "a few simple medicines" were distributed to the auxiliary boards of health under Filipino direction, the effect on popular attitudes was decidedly positive. These medicines did not cure many cases of cholera, but did of diarrhea, "thus removing a predisposing cause and gratifying the people, as the poorer class firmly believe under these circumstances that they have been cured of true cholera."[30]

Filipino patients encountered U.S. physicians only in hospitals, and we have noted the horror with which confinement was viewed. Filipino physicians, in the cities at least, generally visited their patients in their homes. They treated families with which they presumably had had long-standing relationships. They applied what U.S. physicians termed, with derision, "mixed treatment," which meant the inclusion of some features of what used to be the official treatment throughout most of the nineteenth century — such as, in an 1843 directive, the calming of the patient, since "the moral state has an influence over the physical and predisposes him to disease." The relatively backward and unscientific Filipino *medicos* — as the U.S. surgeons viewed them — thus turned out to be more effective vis-à-vis the populace.[31] It was rather as in 1882, when cholera victims were more attracted to the *mediquillos* and *curanderos* than to the new, Manila-trained physicians! In 1902, the *medicos* were applying old treatments and keeping patients in a familiar and reassuring environment, where their "morale" as well as body would have been attended to. Families were determined to keep it that way even if their doctors had to conceal cases from the government. For the alternative was the hospital and the frightful treatment (whatever it consisted of) rendered by alien physicians. The fear of detention only began to subside when hospital reforms were enacted that placed Filipino *médicos* in contact with native patients.

All this interaction between Filipino and U.S. physicians took place in Manila and a few other larger towns and cities. In the vast majority of cholera-stricken towns the locally run boards of health and the parish priest were the agents of disease control, and they invariably collided with the U.S. military surgeons and other agents of Worcester. The contrast between their enthusiastic implementation of sanitary measures under Spain and their lethargy under U.S. supervision is striking. But the explanation for this is obvious: the revolution was not yet over for most of them; memories of the guerrilla war were not easily cast aside; their traditional dominance over the *pueblo* centers was threatened by a still unfamiliar, colonial ruler. Only the strict surveillance of U.S. Army surgeons from the local garrisons, and the brute fact of accelerating cholera death rates, brought the *principales* around to acquiescing to the colonial solutions. After a long "military" phase, the colonizing process began to shape the people's daily lives and thinking in the inescapable context of surviving cholera.

Whatever Worcester may have claimed, germ warfare methods, including the use of powerful drugs, strict quarantine, and attempted cremation of the dead, all failed for various reasons. In the end, as in 1882, it was the combination of heavy rains and the growing immunity of the populace that caused the epidemic to subside. As a result of this event, however, modern medicine and sanitation are said to have been implanted in the Philippines — a fact that not even nationalist histories deny. What needs to be pointed out in an alternative history is that fine, humanitarian objectives mask other dimensions of colonial health and welfare measures: the "disciplining" of the populace, the supervision and regulation of more and more aspects of life, and the suppression or elimination of what the state perceived as forms of resistance, disorder, and irrationality. The participation of natives in colonial health and sanitation matters implicates them in the process. Not surprisingly, for in the twentieth century control of the reins of the state would pass on to Filipinos whose attitudes toward forms of undiscipline, disorder, irrationality, and deviancy were no different from those of their colonial predecessors'.

BEYOND THE *PUEBLO* CENTER

"The plague as a form, at once real and imaginary, of disorder had as its medical and political correlative discipline. Behind the disciplinary mechanisms can be read the haunting memory of contagions, of the plague, of rebellions, crimes, vagabondage, desertions, people who appear and disappear, live and die in disorder."[32] Foucault's suggestions have a ring of familiarity in the Philippine context. Disease control in 1882 and 1902 are repetitions of other events in which the taming of disorder figures prominently. Historical writing, in giving emphasis to the linkages between *pueblo* centers and the primate city, Manila, and the leading actors of both (*principales,* clergy, bureaucrats), has relegated to the margins the events taking place beyond the control of such centers. Much of recent Philippine social history deals with the expansion of the frontiers, the rise of cash crop agriculture and urban entrepots, the links of the colonial economy to the world capitalist system, and the activities of the increasingly entrepreneurial *principalia*/Chinese mestizo class.[33] After all, these are what the colonial archives tell us most about. But, to cite W. H. Scott, there are "cracks in the parchment curtain," through which we can fleetingly glimpse the unique ways in which Filipinos reacted to Spanish rule. Unfortunately, continues Scott, "these insights do not generally appear in the official histories."[34] Even "nonofficial" histories can be at a loss as to how to situate such insights. For example, Bruce Cruikshank's history of Samar offers us fascinating glimpses of the "other side" of the *pueblo* center, where vagabonds are a "plague," alternative priests beckon the populace, and a pilgrimage site constitutes a powerful focus of popular aspirations. But in the end Cruikshank warns us that all this may give us "a distorted image of the major themes of Samar's history," a history that was largely enacted on the coasts (with settled populations) and that reflects the long impact of Catholicism and economic/commercial development.[35]

Research into the records of the Guardia Civil and provincial courts enables us to reread the nineteenth-century saga of development quite differently. The *pueblo* can be viewed as an *ambiguous* center of Philippine life, coming into play when the foci of investigation are "proper" Catholicism, bureaucratic centralization, the expansion of the export economy, technological advancements, and the activities of the elite. To sustain this series of modern developments, the Spanish state and its local allies had to combat and suppress what were named "banditry" and "illicit associations" inhabiting the fringes of the *pueblo*. I suggest that, instead of aberrations or "problems," these can be read as the suppressed "other," the condition for the possibility, of the *pueblo* center.

One of the suppressed figures of Philippine history is the *tulisan* (bandit, highwayman). In Tagalog literature, he signifies contempt for the law and for settled *pueblo* life. He is often a victim of false accusations by the parish priest or threats from the "big men" of the towns, thus the resort to flight. E. J. Hobsbawm has inspired a whole generation of historians to view the "ideal type" of bandit, based on peasant perceptions, as the embodiment or expression of peasant hopes for liberty and justice. Banditry is regarded as a rural and prepolitical phenomenon; the bandit is a substitute for the peasantry's failure to lift itself from its condition.[36] There is, indeed, a lot of evidence that Robin Hoods existed in the Philippines. What concerns us here is not a Hobsbawm type of analysis that locates the bandit in the evolutionary scheme of peasant protest, but the bandit as the emblem of disorder, of the fundamental discontinuity of any *pueblo*-based history.

The bandit or *tulisan* had, in fact, already been there since the Conquista, as the name given by the establishment to the shadowy rival of the pro-Spanish *datu*, and later *gobernadorcillo*, for control over territory and followers. Isagani Medina suggests that banditry was "a revolt against the policy of the *reducción*." *Reducción*, at one level, is almost synonymous with *conquista*, the religious and civil aspects of friar missionary activities; its second, later, meaning is "the process of resettling or consolidating a community." According to Medina, Filipinos who did not recognize Spanish authority and laws, thus refusing to become part of the *reducción*, fled to the hills and were called *ladrones monteses* (mountain thieves), *tulisanes*, or *taga-labas* (outsiders; or outside of the established *reducción*). One of Medina's conclusions is that banditry was an inchoate form of peasant unrest during the Spanish period and that it developed through the nineteenth century into full-blown peasant movements. His data, however, suggest that banditry was always "already there," a perpetual threat to settled, *pueblo* existence.[37]

The bandit was ubiquitous, yet he remained a hidden and slippery figure. In contrast to the inhabitants of a *pueblo* center, the bandit often lacked a proper Christian name and lineage, or was known by an alias signifying a certain character or physical trait. He was illiterate, yet held in awe by the common folk for his bravery and invulnerability. He robbed and killed the rich, particularly Chinese merchants and native landlords, including the occasional Spanish priest. Unlike *pueblo* people, he usually had no fixed abode, was a "wanderer" by definition; when a base was staked out, it was in distant and isolated barrios or in forests and mountain caves.[38]

It is almost impossible to trace the origins of bandit chiefs and their followers. We only know of their existence because they attacked and even occupied many towns, leaving their marks in official reports. After the middle of the nineteenth century, their presence was intensified as the economy developed and the *principalía* prospered, prompting the organization of the Spanish-commanded elite constabulary force, the Guardia Civil, in the 1860s. In the 1870s and early 1880s a special regiment of the Spanish army under Faustino Villa Abrille tried to flush them out of their hideouts in Luzon and the Visayas. But despite massive arrests and the capture of a few key bandit chiefs, the difficult terrain and the weakness of Spanish control outside of the *pueblos* prevented this "hydra-headed monster" from being stamped out.[39]

The proliferation of archival records dating from the 1870s to the 1890s is a measure of the central government's attempts to eliminate this plague it called "banditry." The police network was periodically reorganized, the keeping of dossiers systematized, and the judicial system streamlined. The character of *pueblo* life itself was shaped by the preoccupation with banditry. Surveillance was practiced down to the village level. Settlements were relocated into more compact units, and ways to control population movements between them were put into practice. Scott points out that a member of the Guardia Civil was allowed "to enter houses situated in populated areas at any hour of the day or night if he believes it useful for the service." The police regulations of the day "amounted to virtual martial law, with no civil rights to redress for military abuses." For bandits were feared. Spanish leaders and local gentry alike imagined an army of them poised to attack not only towns but also at one point Manila itself. In the sugar districts of Negros such groups proliferated in the hills surrounding the canefields, creating the need for extensive police surveillance and military operations. The abaca plantations of Bikol, the districts of Cagayan planted with tobacco, and just about every region where economic development took place all witnessed the same phenomenon.[40]

One common explanation for brigandage is that it is a consequence of capitalism's onslaught upon village society, producing a deprived class that then turned to pillage. True enough, but it should also be pointed out that the terrain of the nineteenth-century brigands was almost always the site of "disorder," "apostasy" or "resistance" in earlier periods, and revolutionary guerrilla warfare at the turn of the century. Instead of seeing banditry as a unique nineteenth-century response to new socioeconomic forces, it can just as readily be regarded as just another, perhaps more visible, embodiment of that shadowy "other side" of the developing *pueblo* and its *principalia.*

The intensity of banditry in the nineteenth century may perhaps be explained by the fact that the Spanish colonial state was determined to become self-supporting or financially independent from Spain and Mexico. Looking to its neighbor, the Netherlands East Indies, for inspiration, it tried to implement a new ethic of efficiency and profit. The Spanish, English, American, French, Chinese, and mestizos were invited to finance the labor-intensive clearing of virgin lands. Sturtevant, following Hobsbawm, sees the coalitions of bandit groups that emerged after 1850 as another sign of the attempt of the "Little Tradition" to "turn back or resist unwelcome change." By depicting "banditry" as a form of resistance to change, Sturtevant subsumes it into another form of linear history through the implication that "change" was inevitable and historically determined, and that more effective forms of resistance to its negative consequences would appear later.

On the contrary, to restate what we said earlier, banditry is the name of the "other" of the developing *pueblo* center. In combating banditry, the state and its native allies were extending the state's authority and legal apparatus beyond the *pueblo* centers. Cruikshank describes how a new system of head tax, the proliferation of bureaus and regulations, and the increase in number of provincial and *pueblo* police, functioned to tie the Samareño people to the administrative centers. *Pueblo* identities were enhanced by the bandit wars. Town dwellers became more conscious of the difference between them and unsettled, threatening "outsiders." Another function of bandit suppression was to enable ranking *principales,* especially *gobernadorcillos,* to gain distinctions and rewards and longer terms of office in the colonial system. Their self-conception as leaders or spokesmen of the townspeople was made possible not only through their cooperation with or opposition to the Spaniards, but through their perceived difference — in terms of behavior, status, appearance, and culture — from bandit leaders.

However banditry is treated in Philippine histories, whether as Robin Hood-ism or a precursor of peasant rebellion, its status remains tied to the "Dark Age" of such histories. There is silence about the wars against bandits that served so much to shape a *pueblo*-based Filipino identity. Instead, it is against the backdrop of friar abuses and the influx of liberal ideas that the *principalia* and the masses are seen to emerge during the 1896 revolution against Spain. But ironies abound in the narrative of the revolution: bandit and nationalist Katipunan chiefs collaborated to terrorize the suburbs of Manila. There was considerable confusion in the eyes of townspeople and Spanish authorities alike as to the identity of the rebels: were they revolutionaries or plain bandits? The mountain redoubts of bandits in the Montalban–San Mateo area, east of Manila, became refuges of the Katipunan. The semieducated Katipunan *supremo,* Andres Bonifacio, was accused by Cavite *principales* of being nothing more than a bandit chief; he himself admitted that if defeated he would turn to banditry.[41] The revolution, it would appear, produced a massive blurring of distinctions and hierarchies.

The Philippine-U.S. war is what really thrusts the issue of banditry into contemporary historical consciousness. During the guerrilla resistance to the U.S. takeover from 1901, the new colonial government controlled the town centers, establishing loyal municipal governments wherever possible. Guerrilla chiefs, who largely originated from the *principalia,* now occupied the site of their archenemies and rivals, the bandit chiefs. U.S. propaganda concentrated on identifying guerrilla resistance with banditry. There was thus a frantic attempt by chiefs like Aguinaldo and Malvar to procure the proper uniforms so as to distinguish soldiers from bandits. The exigencies of war brought the residents of the town centers to the very margins that normally distinguished them from their "other."[42]

Thus, to generations of Filipinos educated in U.S. schools, the Philippine-American war was a brief episode in history, since the greater part of it had become conflated with the familiar theme of town centers establishing order in the countryside. Most official town histories unabashedly subscribe to this framework; the line between anti-U.S. resistance and banditry is never clearly drawn.[43] Not surprisingly, one of the most heated debates in Philippine history in recent decades concerns precisely the status of guerrillas who continued to fight the Americans and their new Filipino allies after 1902: was the most famous among them, General Macario Sakay, a bandit or a patriot? It is a sensitive issue because "bandit" connotes a disregard for life, property, and settled existence, and Sakay's group did fit the bill. A paramount concern even during the height of the revolution was security for the lives and property of residents of the town centers. To that segment of the *principalia* that became attracted to nationalist models and inherited the colonial state, brigands had at least to be domesticated—that is, turned into romantic rebels or patriots—if not avoided in discussions of national unity.

ILLICIT ASSOCIATIONS, DISJOINTED HISTORIES

The theme of banditry as the "other side" of events in the *pueblo* center is repeated in the phenomenon of curers, kings, gods, and goddesses who promised peasants release from the ravages of cholera and other diseases, a life of abundance, and freedom from taxes and the police. Curiously enough, these figures, more or less evenly distributed around the archipelago, multiplied in the 1880s during and after the great cholera epidemic of 1882, at precisely the time the state, gentry, and practitioners of scientific medicine thought they had things under control. These "illicit" figures again made their presence felt, as "antirevolutionaries," during the Republican period of 1898–99, and again—this time as "fanatics"—during the years following the official end of resistance to U.S. occupation.

During roughly the years 1880 to 1897, when the *ilustrados* were making their statements about nationalism and progress, "fanatical" religious movements were proliferating all over the archipelago. Some of them are named: for example, the Pulajan, Dios Dios, Colorum, Santa Iglesia, Baylan, and Tres Cristos. Others are identified in the records by place names, such as the Dapdap affair in Samar, or the names of their leaders, such as the Gabinista in Pampanga and Buhawi in Negros.[44] Conventional Philippine history, in valorizing the saga of the *ilustrados*, has ignored this parallel set of events. Where they are given ample treatment, as in the works of Constantino and Sturtevant, they are subjected to a classificatory scheme that includes categories such as "primitive," "proto-nationalist," "nativist," "fanatical," "religious," "millenarian," and "irrational." The understanding is that such phenomena are transitory in character, bound sooner or later to disappear from the modern scene. The vantage point is rationality, progress, rather than the inner logic of these movements, their plain and simple difference from familiar, "modern," ones.

Spanish officialdom called these movements or communities "illicit associations" (*asociaciones ilícitas*), discovering them around such sites as a mountain regarded as sacred, an efficacious statue of a saint (for example, St. Francis or the Virgin Mary), or a curer residing in an outlying village. Some leaders identified themselves as Christs, Virgin Marys, and other figures of the Bible. They claimed to have the power to deliver people from smallpox, cholera, and lesser ailments through a combination of herbal cures and spiritual powers recognized by their followers. Some of them were the very *mediquillos* displaced by the modern physicians.

These gods, priestesses, and kings attracted mainly illiterate peasants, particularly those who lived in villages beyond the influence of the church/*pueblo* center. Among those who joined were sugarcane workers impoverished by the price crash of the 1880s, debtors, displaced farmers, and tax or labor evaders. Many were survivors of cholera and smallpox epidemics who journeyed to pilgrimage sites in fulfillment of their vows. Some were seekers of spiritual potency, others plain vagabonds. Some associations were dominated or led by women, whose access to curing powers could be greater than men's. The followers came together informally, perhaps to pray, to listen to the leader's homilies, to partake of a meal, to be cured, or to obtain the powers of amulets (*anting anting*).

An illicit association could be a more structured affair: a church, a confraternity (*cofradía*), or an association (*samahan*). These became natural sites of resistance to control by *pueblo* centers and the state. Members generally refused to pay the poll or head tax and thus were called *indocumentado;* in short, they refused to be "processed" by the state. Furthermore, the larger associations transcended not only *pueblo* but provincial boundaries — those lines drawn by the state to bolster the control of populations. A shrine in the Visayan island of Samar, for example, attracted pilgrims from the neighboring islands of Leyte, Bohol, and Cebu. The various associations on Mount Banahaw in southern Luzon periodically drew pilgrims from Tayabas, Batangas, Laguna, and Cavite provinces. The Gabinista in central Luzon, which grew into the Santa Iglesia (Holy Church) movement, had members from the provinces of Pampanga, Bulacan, Nueva Ecija, Tarlac, and even Manila. Alongside the Catholic Church and the *ilustrado* nationalists, "illicit associations" had their own visions of a wider community.

In the late 1880s, the time — in linear history, that is — of the Propaganda Movement, there seems to have been an expectation of a new era, in which all inhabitants of the archipelago would be unified under one or more native kings or queens; in which the poor and dispossessed, in particular, would enjoy an era of knowledge (light), prosperity, and physical well-being. The City of God would become a reality on earth. But first the people would have to experience hardship in nurturing the growth of their associations. In depressed areas such as Negros and central Luzon, followers armed themselves and raided the houses of the rich. To the Guardia Civil and the victimized *principales* nothing distinguished them from bandits. They were, above all, signs of irrationality and disorder surrounding and threatening the *pueblo* centers.

In this essay there is no attempt to enter the world of these "illicit associations," for this would require a detailed elaboration of the complex of Spanish Catholic and Malay cultural elements that shaped their perception of reality. We can, however, reflect on their function in the construction and challenging of developmental history. It is a mistake to regard these social movements as simply reactions to accelerated social and economic changes. They appeared in the 1880s because the Spanish police and concerned *principales* "discovered" them in the process of putting order in the countryside. The language of investigative reports shows a concern that the hold of the center would be contaminated, and ultimately subverted, if these associations were allowed to exist and spread. While a few movements involved the participation of estranged *principales,* most of the followers were of the subaltern class, precipitating conflicts with *principales* or landlords based in the towns. To the *ilustrados,* joining illicit associations was not the proper mode of challenging the colonial order. Thus both native elite and colonial state felt it had to conquer and reform this phenomenon.

What is the function of this type of event in an alternative history that allows it to enter into play with more "traditional" elements? Since the *ilustrado* emplotment of history is a construction along the lines of enlightenment and progress, and not necessarily the true, correct, or proper view, in effect it has the same status as the world of the Tres Cristos and Dios-Dios. The difference is that the *ilustrado* construction has been upheld by current standards of objectivity and truth, while the Tres Cristos and Dios-Dios were marks, precisely, of what had to be excised from history.

Illicit associations, as their name implies, have been cast outside the mainstream of Philippine history, and for understandable reasons. They were marginal, archaic, and undecidable in their orientation to progress and change. True, the Dios Dios in the Visayas and the Colorum in Luzon, among others, called on their followers in 1889 to pray for the spirit of martyred nationalist Fr. Jose Burgos. But the Propaganda Movement had trouble tapping popular movements that had the appearance of the grotesque, exhibiting lopsided combinations of elements borrowed from diverse, often patently "colonial" sources. One king announced that he was married to the Queen of Spain. Others were Jesus Christs, Virgin Marys, or God himself. Still another distributed pamphlets claiming that he was a *médico título*. Bearing all the marks of the "Fall" (none claimed to be a rajah or an ancient god), neither could they be granted recognition as survivals of a lost, pre-Hispanic civilization.

Yet, despite attempts to ignore or marginalize this "dark side" of Philippine history, it appears in the gaps of this history. For an example of ironic reversals we need go no farther than the career of the very archetype of *ilustrado*-ness, Jose Rizal.[45] Here the *principal* and *ilustrado*, the physician and historian, is conflated in popular accounts with Jesus Christ and various Tagalog mythical figures. In 1888 this Filipino reformist based in Madrid was expected by people "in the mountains" to return as the Messiah. When he did return he was hailed as a magical curer. The Spanish courts decided that because Rizal was regarded by the "ignorant classes" as a god-man and redeemer he must be publicly executed. Just the same, his mode of death was a scattering of signs that the *pasyon* and death of Christ were being reenacted. Rizal the Filipino Christ, rather than Rizal the physician and historian, was the rallying point of tens of thousands who joined the Katipunan rebellion in 1897. After his death, he became the source of healing and other powers to peasant leaders far into the twentieth century.

The word *katipunan* means "association." The revolutionary organization's full Tagalog name means "Highest and Most Venerable Association of the Sons and Daughters of the Land." It was, in fact, an illicit association not too different in some respects from the others mentioned above. Historical writing, however, has turned it into an emblem of development. The uprising against Spain that it instigated in 1896 is regarded as a turning point in the struggle for national independence, a state higher than the ineffectual reform movement of earlier decades. The sanitized version of this period of history portrays a working man, Bonifacio, fusing together the ideas of Rizal and the French revolutionists and calling for armed struggle against foreign rule. The Philippine Army and Communist Party find common inspiration in this historical episode.

Yet, *katipunan* also means those illicit associations in the peripheries of the *pueblo* centers whose members, as a measure of their basic ambiguity, switched signs and reemerged as revolutionary fighters. The Colorum, now the Katipunan of San Cristobal, with their saints and magical ropes attacked the Spanish garrison at Tayabas. The Gabinistas were resurrected as the Santa Iglesia of Felipe Salvador. The followers of Buhawi became a Katipunan under Papa (Pope) Isio. In the name of the Katipunan revolution these groups threatened not just the Spanish establishments, but the *principalia* of the *pueblo* centers.

Many members of the *principalia* regarded the Katipunan of Bonifacio not just as a bandit gang, as we have seen, but as a fanatical, illicit association as well. In Cavite province, the heartland of the revolution, Bonifacio was accused of entertaining ambitions to kingship, and ridiculed for, among other things, making the unlettered folk think that the mythical Tagalog king Bernardo Carpio would soon escape from his mountain prison to aid the Katipunan forces. It was all right for the "superstitious" Gabinistas in the 1880s to hold the same expectations of King Bernardo's return, but in the revolutionary era it was anathema for the supreme leader to hold such "Dark Age" views. Bonifacio had to go; indeed, he was executed by fellow revolutionists under orders from a new leader of the revolution, a former town mayor. Aguinaldo put the Katipunan in "proper order" as a liberal nationalist movement seeking to form a republican state that would be recognized by all civilized nations.[46]

Philippine histories conveniently ignore the "Dark Age" aspects of Bonifacio's career. His death is attributed to a variety of causes: personal or factional rivalry, class antagonism, his stubborn commitment to the secret society mode of struggle, and even his hot temper. His death has left a rough patch in the otherwise smooth transition to the next stage of the nationalist struggle. The first Philippine republic of 1898–1901 is universally regarded as the crowning achievement of nationalist efforts from the 1880s on. Advanced state institutions were created, among them a cabinet, a congress, an army, and a school system. Only in recent historical writing, however, has the chaos and disorder of this period come to light. Newly installed officials all over the nation complained to President Aguinaldo of attacks by bandits and fanatics—all of which Aguinaldo labeled "antirevolutionary."[47] Are these to be regarded simply as technical problems faced by a fledgling nation-state?

The fact is, most of these "bandit" groups and "fanatical" associations had participated in the liberation of *pueblo* centers from Spanish control in 1898. But their support for the national revolution was inconsistent, as shown by the mixed results of the government's efforts to tap their energies by incorporating them into the army and awarding military ranks to their leaders. Stories abound of how these men were abused on account of their "illicit" backgrounds. Their followers then turned to violence against Filipino officials and landlords as well as foreign enemies. The controversies involving these groups cannot be discussed here individually. I shall, however, outline below the roots of their differences with the first Philippine republic.

From scattered poems, songs, and interrogation records it is possible to glimpse the mentality that brought disorder to the Republic. With the defeat of Spain a new era or condition of independence was expected to set in. "Independence" or "liberty" was imagined as a kind of paradise on earth, where those, at least, who participated in the unfolding of victory would enjoy prosperity and comfort. There was an expectation of authentic, even Christ-like, leaders staffing the government, individuals with courage and evidence of inner powers, but who also showed compassion and willingness to undergo sacrifices, even to die, for the sake of the whole.[48]

Government was a term with negative connotations, implying the management of people by some superior force, based on superior/subordinate relationships that characterized colonial society. If there had to be "government," this was expected to be based on a covenant between the chosen leader and his followers. These ideas are brought out in an *awit* (song, metrical romance) about the travails of "Mother Country" that circulated in Luzon during the war against the United States.[49] It begins with the parable of the lost sheep. The image of the enclosed space into which the sheep are to be led signifies salvation, unity, and identity. This fenced-in space is conflated later on with images of kingdom, nation, and motherland. In this *awit,* as well as other texts I have collected, the nation and its administrative apparatus are to be built upon closely knit, village-based associations. The nation is to be a voluntary "coming together" of many small clusters of people rather than the forging of a whole. There are to be no taxes, no surveillance, no police, and no forced labor.

"History" takes on a different complexion as well in the imagined new order. The *awit* speaks of a rajah, Matanda (Old man), who is the ancestor of the Tagalog people. In *ilustrado* history, Rajah Matanda is one of those who signify the preconquest civilization. In the *awit,* however, Rajah Matanda is prefigured by Noah, described as "old beloved father." Furthermore, his immediate ancestor is no less than Jesus Christ himself. Unlike *ilustrado* history, the *awit* does not posit a more authentic, pre-Christian past. There is no anxiety about some lost purity of race. *Katoliko* and *Kristiano* are appropriated and made emblems of Filipino identity in the "Holy War" then being waged against the American invaders.

Not all groups and individuals subscribed to the same set of ideals. Challenges to the Republic were not necessarily on the side of the good and the moral. And there were Republican officials who had similar ideals in mind but simply could not put them into action. I am not necessarily outlining better alternatives to the goals of the first Republic and its present-day successor. The point of this discussion is to show that the Republic cannot be abstracted as a stage in the development of political institutions, national consciousness, and the struggle for freedom. Despite the good intentions of most of its leaders, the Republic failed to break out of the structures that preceded it. Differences characterized it from the start. It then reproduced the same instruments of domination and control as its Spanish predecessor. In short, it became caught up in the age-old problem of establishing order in what seemed, to its representatives in the *pueblo* centers and provincial capitals, to be a sea of anarchy.

This rereading of the past can be extended indefinitely. The saga of nationalism and progress as it continues into the U.S. colonial period, the Japanese occupation, the New Society, and the "People Power" revolution can be confronted with suppressed data similar to those presented above. Enough has been said, however, to enable us to return to the original problematic of this paper.

A reflection on "development" has to take into account those things that have stood in opposition to it, those irreducible differences that in the final analysis may be our only way out of the present development bind. In examining historiography, criminality, epidemics, and popular movements, one has only begun to reflect upon those crucial moments when the state, or the historian, or whoever occupies the site of the dominant center performs a cutting operation: remembering/furthering that which it deems meaningful for its concept of development, and forgetting/suppressing the dissonant, disorderly, irrational, archaic, and subversive.

For historians, in particular, such an operation enables the data of the past to be strung together into a trajectory of emergence, growth, complexity, and increasing rationality, and enables great moments and individuals to be celebrated. Such an operation, however, also leaves behind a surplus of data that can be retrieved and restored into play in an alternative history, in which an event, to cite Foucault's reading of Nietzsche, "is not a decision, a treaty, a reign, or a battle, but the reversal of a relationship of forces, the usurpation of power, the appropriation of a vocabulary turned against those who had once used it, a feeble domination that poisons itself as it grows lax, the entry of a masked 'other.' "[50] This history should throw into focus a whole range of phenomena that have been discredited or denied a history. It should have a conception of historical beginnings as lowly, complex, and contingent. It should give equal status to interruptions, repetitions, and reversals, uncovering the subjugations, confrontations, power struggles, and resistances that linear history tends to conceal. It should reveal history for what is has been: a weapon in the struggle for and against domination of all shades. As has been shown here, the subversion of linear history also strikes at the "developmentalism" that presently dominates the core of the state/center's ideology.

NOTES

1. Rather than plowing through the morass of development literature, I have allowed myself to be guided by the following: Alain Birou, Paul-Marc Henry, and John Schlegel, *Toward a Redefinition of Development: Essays and Discussions on the Nature of Development in an International Perspective* (Paris: Development Center, OECD/Pegamon Press, 1977); George Aseniero, "A Reflection on Developmentalism: From Development to Transformation," in *Development as Social Transformation: Reflections on the Global Problematique* (London: Hodder and Stoughton/UN University, 1985), 48–85; P. W. Preston, *Theories of Development* (London: Routledge and Kegan Paul, 1982).

2. On this subject see also Reynald C. Ileto, "Bonifacio, the Text, and the Social Scientist," *Philippine Sociological Review* 32 (1984): 19–29.

3. Michel Foucault, *Power/Knowledge: Selected Interviews and Other Writings, 1972–1977* (New York: Pantheon, 1980), 80–81.

4. This idea was first broached by Teodoro Agoncillo in "A Re-interpretation of Our History under Spain," *Sunday Times Magazine* (Manila), August 1958. Also, Agoncillo, "On the Rewriting of Philippine History," *Historical Bulletin* (Philippine Historical Association) 17 (1973): 178–187. The scheme was applied in his textbook, initially coauthored with Oscar Alfonso; Teodoro Agoncillo and Oscar Alfonso, *History of the Filipino People* (Manila: University of the Philippines, 1960). This textbook has appeared in many editions and is still in use today.

5. Reynaldo C. Ileto, *Pasyon and Revolution: Popular Movements in the Philippines, 1840–1910* (Quezon City: Ateneo University Press, 1979), 18, 38.

6. Reynaldo C. Ileto, "Rizal and the Underside of Philippine History," in *Moral Order and Change: Essays in Southeast Asian Thought,* ed. D. Wyatt and A. Woodside (New Haven: Yale Southeast Asia Studies 24, 1982), 276–278. For an introduction to *ilustrado* historical writing, see John Schumacher S.J., "The Propagandists' Reconstruction of the Philippine Past," in *Perceptions of the Past in Southeast Asia,* ed. A. Reid and D. Marr (Singapore: Heinemann, 1979), 264–280.

7. Ferdinand E. Marcos, *Outline: Tadhana, the History of the Filipino People* (Manila: Marcos Foundation, 1980), sketched the overall design of his new history project.

8. John Phelan, *The Hispanization of the Philippines: Spanish Aims and Filipino Responses, 1565–1700* (Madison: University of Wisconsin Press, 1967).

9. Marcos spoke of his role in history and state construction in "A Sense of National History" (keynote address, annual seminar on history, Philippine Historical Association, 29 November 1976), published in *Historical Bulletin* 26 (1982): 1–15. For an exposition of *Tadhana*'s Hegelian underpinnings, see Jaime Veneracion's review in *Kasaysayan* 1 (Dept. of History, University of the Philippines) (November 1977): 213–216.

10. Renator Constantino's immensely popular *The Philippines: A Past Revisited* (Quezon City) was first published in 1975. I quote liberally from chapter 1, "Towards a People's History." My source for NDF history is their mimeographed *Handbook for the Middle Forces* (undated); chapter 3 is titled "The Historical View of Philippine Society." The work of Amado Guerrero (pseudonym) was originally published in 1970 by the Revolutionary School of Mao Tsetung Thought. Its first chapter is titled "Review of Philippine History."

11. For representative examples see the essays in Temario Rivera et al., eds., *Feudalism and Capitalism in the Philippines* (Quezon City: Foundation for Nationalist Studies, 1982). Also, Ricardo Ferrer, "On the Mode of Production in the Philippines: Some Old-Fashioned Questions"; and Julieta de Lima-Sison, "Jose Maria Sison on the Mode of Production," both in *The New Philippine Review* 1, nos. 1–3 (1984).

12. Examples abound in the magazine *Kalinangan* (Institute of Religion and Culture, Bicutan, Metro Manila). Organizations aligned with the NDF apply the basic historical construct in text written for the respective "sectors" they represent. For example, the Ecumenical Institute for Labor Education and Research has published an illustrated history, *Manggagawa, Noon at Ngayon* (The worker, past and present), Manila, 1982. The Joint Committee for Moro Concerns has its own illustrated history, *Ang Moro* (The Moro), Marawi, 1985.

13. Ferdinand E. Marcos, *An Ideology for Filipinos* (Manila: Marcos Foundation, 1983), 90–91; NDF *Handbook,* 73.

14. Paul de la Gironiere, *Adventures of a Frenchman in the Philippines,* 9th ed. (Manila: Burke-Miailhe, 1972), 3, 9–10 (originally published in French in 1853); Maria Luisa Camagay, "Manila — A City in the Throes of Epidemics," *Historical Bulletin* 26 (1982): 105–108.

15. The changes in government and medical attitudes to disease control after the 1820 epidemic are outlined in fragments of a long treatise by Fernando Gonzales Casas, with the endorsement of the Junta Municipal de Sanidad, 15 January 1822; Philippine National Archives (henceforth, PNA), *Cólera* 74.

16. My main source of information on the 1882 and 1889 epidemics is the bundles in the PNA with the following markings: *Cólera* 1, *Cólera* 4, *Cólera* B-S 86, *Cólera* 101, *Cólera* 121, *Cólera* 6 (B-S 93), and *Cólera* 7 (B-S 90). There are also fragments of information on epidemics in 1843 and 1863. Scattered throughout these bundles are government orders, daily reports of sanitary commissions, and complaints of medicos, vaccinators, and parish priests.

17. For the history of medical education I have relied on Jose P. Bantug, *Bosquejo historico de la medicina Hispano-Filipina* (Unfinished historical sketch of Spanish-Filipino medicine), Madrid, 1952. Part 2 is a history of medical and charitable institutions and public sanitation projects.

18. For a representative text that illustrates these processes, see "Expediente sobre reorganizacion del servicio de vacuna del Archiepelago e instalación de un Ynstituto de vacunación," Manila, 6 May 1889. This document is accompanied by an assessment by the Faculty of Medicine, Real Colegio de San Jose (mss. in PNA, *Cólera* 7). A good example of a dispute between a physician and a vaccinator is that between Medico Titular Don Mariano Felizardo and Vacunador General Don Nemesio Valbuena, Catbalogan, Samar, 1889 (mss. in PNA, *Cólera* 7).

19. A representative example is the case of the parish priest of San Pedro Macati, Fr. Mariano Umali, who headed the local sanitary commission during the 1882 epidemic. Critical of the *médico títular,* he wrote to the governor of Manila that the inhabitants were "reluctant to seek the help of Science, preferring instead the advice of *mediquillos*" (14 September 1882, PNA, *Cólera* 121). A good number of cases were filed against physicians for arrogance, nonperformance of duties, and even sedition. Examples in the PNA: *expediente* against the *médico títular* of Calamianes Don Matias de Arrieta, 1890, in *Expedientes Gubernativos* (henceforth, EG) 1881–97; *expediente* against the *médico títular* of Cavite Don Federico Jayme, 1880, in EG 1859–88; and *expediente* to investigate accusations against Don Lucindo Almeida, *médico títular* of La Union, 1893, in EG 1892–93.

20. "Expediente sobre reorganización." It should be noted that Filipino and Spanish scientists were at the same time conducting research on the efficacy of herbal cures. Much of the analysis of medical power in this paper is indebted to the work of Michel Foucault, *Madness and Civilization: A History of Insanity in the Age of Reason,* trans. Richard Howard (New York: Random House, 1965); and *The Birth of the Clinic: An Archaeology of Medical Perception,* trans. A. M. Sheridan Smith (New York: Vintage, 1973).

21. The local concerns and scientific outlook of medicos in the provinces can be gleaned from their *memorias* or reports to the central government, in the bundle *Memorias Médicas: Varias Provincias,* PNA. The PNA bundles labeled *Médicos Títulares* are a still untapped source of information.

22. A well-known example is Dr. Pio Valenzuela of Polo, Bulacan, who became an advisor to Andres Bonifacio and physician of the Katipunan revolutionary secret society. See the surveillance reports on Medico Don Felipe Zamora in *Sediciones y Rebeliones* (henceforth, SR) vol. 35, and Medico Rianzares of Nagcarlan, SR vol. 17, PNA.

23. Dean C. Worcester, *History of Asiatic Cholera in the Philippines* (Manila: Bureau of Printing, 1909). See also Worcester, *The Philippines Past and Present* (New York: Macmillan, 1914), chap. 16. For a thorough examination of early American attitudes toward medical progress in the Philippines, see R. J. Sullivan, *Exemplar of Americanism: The Philippine Career of Dean C. Worcester* (Ann Arbor: University of Michigan Press, 1991), 105–115.

24. This account of the 1902 cholera visitation is based largely on the following: reports of commanding officers and surgeons of U.S. Army garrisons in the southern Tagalog provinces, in Record Group 395, United States National Archives (henceforth, USNA); Report of the Philippine Commission for 1902; and the circulars and reports collected in Bureau of Insular Affairs file 4981 (USNA).

25. The precise linkages of war, disease, and famine are examined in Reynaldo C. Ileto, "Cholera and the Origins of the American Sanitary Order in the Philippines," in *Imperial Medicine and Indigenous Societies*, ed. D. Arnold (Manchester: Manchester University Press, 1988), 125–148.

26. George de Shon, M.D., "Medical Highlights of the Philippine-American War," *Bulletin of the American Historical Collection* 12 (1984): 69.

27. "Report of the Secretary of the Interior," in *Report of the Philippine Commission* (1903), part 1, 271.

28. Rene Dubos, *Mirage of Health: Utopias, Progress and Biological Change* (New York: Harper, 1959), 146; also, C. E. Rosenberg, "Cholera in Nineteenth-Century Europe: A Tool for Social and Economic Analysis," *Comparative Studies in Society and History* 8 (1966): 453.

29. Dubos, *Mirage of Health*, 151–152. Paul de Kruif, *The Microbe Hunters* (New York: Harcourt Brace, 1926) captures very well the drama and excitement surrounding the quest, mainly by colonial or military surgeons, for the "magic bullet" against microbes.

30. Report of Dr. F. Bourns, Commissioner of Public Health, August 1902, appendix to "Report of the Secretary of Interior."

31. The 1843 directive recommends the following: "drink freely every half hour *taju* (a bean curd preparation) or tea or decoction of Santa Maria flowers, sambon or ginger, adding to these drinks, during the first two hours of the disease, a teaspoonful of Cologne water, bitters or brandy." Sometime after 1895, the ideas of Pasteur, Koch, Klebs, and other "microbe hunters" were introduced to medical students in the Philippines via the work of Enrique Mateo Barcones, *Estudio para un Nosología Filipina* (Towards a scientific classification of Philippine diseases) (Madrid: Asilo de Huerfanos, 1895), but the chaotic half-decade beginning with the revolution of August 1896 must have crippled medical education in Manila.

32. Michel Foucault, *Discipline and Punish: The Birth of the Prison*, trans. A. Sheridan (New York: Vintage, 1979), 198.

33. Representative examples of this genre can be found in Alfred McCoy and Ed de Jesus, eds., *Philippine Social History: Global Trade and Local Transformations* (Quezon City: Ateneo de Manila, 1982).

34. William Henry Scott, *Cracks in the Parchment Curtain* (Quezon City: New Day, 1982), 1.

35. Bruce Cruikshank, *Samar: 1768–1898* (Manila: Historical Conservation Society, 1985), 197.

36. E. J. Hobsbawm, *Primitive Rebels: Studies in Archaic Forms of Social Movement in the 19th and 20th Centuries* (New York: Norton, 1959), chap.

2. Much of this evolutionism is overcome in Hobsbawm's later work, *Bandits* (1969; revised New York: Delacorte, 1981); see chap. 7, "Bandits and Revolution."

37. Isagani Medina, *Cavite before the Revolution, 1571–1896* (Diliman: University of the Philippines, 1994), chap. 3 (based on his 1985 Ph.D. thesis).

38. The generalized picture of banditry in this essay is based on a reading of operations reports and other official transmissions preserved in the Guardia Civil (henceforth, GC) bundles, PNA. The best sources are the catalogued bundles marked GC 1864–98, GC 1870–77, and GC 1889–91, and the uncatalogued bundles numbered GC 27 and GC 57. Other sources of information used are the *Deportados, Expedientes Gubernativos,* and *Varias Provincias* series of bundles, which contain files of individuals captured and sentenced mainly in the wake of Lt. Col. Villa Abrille's campaigns.

39. David Sturtevant, *Popular Uprisings in the Philippines, 1840–1940* (Ithaca: Cornell University Press, 1976), 119.

40. Scott, *Cracks in the Parchment Curtain,* 25–26. One such threat to Manila is investigated in "Expediente gubernativo . . . en averiguación de una cuadrilla de ladrones que merodean por esta capital y sus arrabales" (Official investigation of a bandit gang marauding this capital and its outskirts), January 1882, in EG 1879–1889, PNA. Aside from the works of Medina and Sturtevant cited above, banditry is given chapter-length treatment in Angel Cuesta O.A.R., *History of Negros* (Manila: Historical Conservation Society, 1980), 427–435; and Edilberto C. de Jesus, *The Tobacco Monopoly in the Philippines, 1766–1880* (Quezon City: Ateneo de Manila Press, 1989), 57–70.

41. Ileto, *Pasyon,* 228–229. The best juxtapositions of Katipunan and *tulisanismo* are found in Spanish reports from the August 1896 to March 1897 period, in the *Sediciones y Rebeliones* bundles, PNA. Cuesta, *History of Negros* (436ff.), shows how support for the Katipunan in Negros came solely from groups tagged as bandits.

42. These are conclusions based largely on research on the Philippine Insurgent Records lodged in the Philippine National Library, and record groups 395 and 94, Military Records Division, USNA.

43. Such town histories can be found in the Historical Data Papers lodged in the Filipiniana Division, Philippine National Library.

44. The Tres Cristos, in the Libmanan area of Kabikolan, dates from an earlier period, 1865 (SR vol. 28 [1864–68], PNA). The Gabinista in central Luzon and the *Dios-Dios* that appeared all over the Visayan islands are the most extensively documented in the PNA. But there must have been countless tiny *reuniones ilicitas,* such as the four to five women "fanatics" under one Severino Morales, discovered in the outskirts of Manila in 1887 (EG 1886–89, PNA). For recently published studies: on the Dapdap affair and other Dios Dios phenomena see Cruikshank, *Samar,* chaps. 7–8; on Buhawi see Cuesta, *History of Negros,* 433–435; on the Babaylan and others in the western Visayas see Alfred McCoy, "Baylan: Animist Religion and Philippine Peasant Ideology," in *Moral Order and Change,* ed. D. Wyatt and A. Woodside (New Haven: Yale South-

east Asia Studies, 1982), 373–382; on the Gabinista and Colorum, see Ileto, *Pasyon.*

45. For a fuller account, see Ileto, "Rizal," 307–321.

46. See Ileto, *Pasyon,* 135–144.

47. See ibid., 146ff.; Milagros Guerrero, "Luzon at War: Contradictions in Philippine Society" (Ph.D. diss., University of Michigan, 1977), chap. 4.

48. See Ileto, *Pasyon,* chaps. 3–4.

49. *Awit na Pinagdaanang Buhay ng Islas Filipinas* (Awit of the life experience of the Philippine islands), by "Dimatigtig," 15 July 1900, ms. in Philippine Insurgent Records, box I-19, Philippine National Library.

50. Michel Foucault, "Nietzsche, Genealogy, History," in *Language, Counter-memory, Practice: Selected Essays and Interviews by Michel Foucault,* ed. D. Bouchard (Ithaca: Cornell University Press, 1977), 154.

MARÍA JOSEFINA SALDAÑA-PORTILLO

Developmentalism's Irresistible Seduction — Rural Subjectivity under Sandinista Agricultural Policy

Development emerged in the post–World War II era of national libera-tion struggles as a containment strategy during this period of crisis when colonialism and neocolonialism were being threatened. Develop-ment policy and projects proliferated in an attempt to manage the evident poverty and inequality in the periphery by isolating the causes of these conditions to the periphery, thereby rendering invisible the role of colonialism in instituting these very conditions. National devel-opment was scripted by this new discourse. Developmentalism con-structed third world nations as suspended in a preliminary stage of productivity and an elementary stage in the history of becoming mod-ern, industrialized, capitalist nation-states.[1] It did so by inventing an underdeveloped, underproductive subject to be named, located, stud-ied, theorized, and ultimately policed through development policy and projects. "Development colonized reality, became reality," as Arturo Escobar has succinctly stated. "Development proceeded by creating abnormalities ('the poor,' 'the malnourished,' 'the illiterate,' 'pregnant women,' 'the landless') which it would then treat or reform."[2] Once located and enumerated, these subjects could presumably benefit from development projects imparted from above by governments under the direction of international agencies. This teleology of progress not only provided an alibi for colonialism's role in forging the conditions in which decolonized and decolonizing nations found themselves, it also provided the conditions for continued surveillance of peripheral nations and their citizens. Categories of need abstracted by this dis-course warranted development projects that extended the opportunity for exploitative economic and social relations into every corner of the globe. The promise of development was to bring the benighted subjects of the third world into the epochal history of the modern nation — into full productivity — with the subsequent rights and priv-ileges available to the productive citizen of an international family of nations.[3] From Pinochet to the Zapatistas, this promise of full produc-tivity, this horizon of political evolution, this discourse of development has seduced the Right and the Left in Latin America for over thirty years.

The origins of the discourse of development can be traced back to the ideologically laden early rhetoric of the cold war, to W. W. Rostow's 1960 treatise on modernization, *Stages of Growth: A Non-Communist Manifesto*.[4] However, development as a discursive phenomenon and as a policy field quickly assumed a stubbornly "nonideological" character. James Ferguson, in his case study of livestock development projects in Lesotho, has suggested that international development agencies and state bureaucracies become "antipolitics" machines because they continually reduce poverty and inequality to failures of technological advancement. Developmentalism is not only antipolitical in its refusal to analyze the role of exploitative geopolitical power relations in generating such conditions, it is "nonpolitical" and "nonideological" in that it perceives development as an "*omni-historical* reality." Althusser suggested of ideology in general "that it is endowed with a structure and functioning such as to make it a non-historical reality, i.e. an *omni-historical* reality, in the sense in which that structure and functioning are immutable, present in the same form throughout what we can call history. . . ."[5] It is precisely in this Althusserian sense of ideology that developmentalism takes on an apparently nonideological character. The discourse of development renders development an immutable fact, a value-neutral process taking place throughout history. Development represents itself as an imperative prior to and beyond ideologies of capitalism or Marxism. Hence, it is not surprising that although there have been extensive critiques of particular development models, policies, or projects — by dependency, unequal exchange, and world systems theorists — few, if any, neo-Marxist critics have questioned the imperative *to develop*. Quite the contrary, most of these critical endeavors have been in the service of arriving at an alternative development — a diversified, independent development within equal terms of trade — and not as an alternative *to* development, for which Escobar and Ferguson, among other recent critics, have called.

The Sandinista National Liberation Front (FSLN) explicitly attempted to forge a revolutionary approach to development in Nicaragua. Through this case study of Sandinista agricultural policy, I will attempt to address both the call by neo-Marxists for a model of alternative development and the call by post-Marxists for an alternative to development. The Sandinista case demonstrates the seductive power that the imperative to develop has had on the Left, but it also clearly demonstrates the real, material limits prohibiting countries from simply stepping outside this paradigm.

The FSLN came to power in 1979 after two years of general insurrection in Nicaragua. While party origins date back to the *foquista* guerrilla movements of the 1960s, the party that came to power in 1979 corresponded to the "second generation" of armed movements in Latin America. The FSLN of the late 1970s had successfully brought together the different ideological tendencies that engaged in armed struggle in Nicaragua, divisions similar to those that had destroyed armed struggles in other countries. The party had subsequently abandoned *foquismo* for a policy of national alliance with members of the oligarchy, the bourgeois, the press, and various parties. Most importantly, the FSLN had successfully coordinated its efforts against the dictatorship with the efforts of mass-based social movements: the liberation Church, the women's movement, the student movement, syndicalists, and peasant organizations. The Sandinistas—like the FMLN in El Salvador, the URNG in Guatemala, and the M-19 in Colombia—accomplished something the guerrilla movements of the 1960s had been unable to do: theoretically and practically to move beyond a vanguardism that saw the party as creating a mass movement to a vanguardism that saw the party in a supporting or coordinating role for the mass movement.[6]

Once in power, the Sandinistas were committed to restructuring Nicaragua's dependent economy for the benefit of the country's poor majority, promoting the interests of this mass movement that had brought them to power. The conditions of Nicaragua's insertion into the global market, however, placed certain structural constraints on Sandinista choices in agricultural policy. The devastating U.S. war against the Sandinistas stands as testimony to the ferocity with which these constraints are enforced. But not every choice made by the Sandinistas was predetermined by market, fiscal, and geopolitical constraints. Key decisions in agriculture corresponded to the Sandinistas' faith in the teleology of progress implicit in developmentalism. Sandinista agricultural policy intended to produce a model of revolutionary subject-citizenry in agriculture, a model of subjectivity that would benefit the citizen and the nation. But this model of revolutionary citizenship did not emerge from the material reality in which the peasants found themselves. Consequently, the peasant formation ended up outside a Sandinista vision of revolutionary national development, even though the peasant was at the very center of the revolutionary imagination. The FSLN implemented an agricultural development policy that negatively impacted their peasant base of support in the countryside. By 1985 peasants were filling the ranks of the U.S.-backed counterrevolutionaries, and in 1990 the FSLN lost the presidential and parliamentary elections. My interest in this project is motivated by a very simple question: How is it that the Sandinista revolutionary movement met with resistance from the very people their model of development presumably intended to liberate? In other words, What was this model, and what were the points of confluence and contradiction with peasant consciousness?

The peasantry as a category represents a broad, heterogeneous, diffuse, and in-flux population in Nicaragua. Thus, before proceeding, it is necessary to clarify which sectors of the peasantry I will focus on since clearly agricultural policy affected different sectors of the peasantry differently. Nicaragua has always had a significant percentage of production in the hands of private peasant producers with small- and medium-scale holdings, ranging between fifty and five hundred *manzanas*.[7] Most of these producers hold enough land to necessitate the hiring of workers on a full- or part-time basis, or they rent land in exchange for services. Together they make up 30 percent of Nicaragua's economically active population (EAP) in the countryside. They are the bourgeoisie of the peasantry and were not defined politically by the need for land.[8] Indeed, some of these producers were subject to expropriation in the last two years of agrarian reform.[9] Nevertheless, they were among the intended beneficiaries of credit, pricing, and distribution policies. While they are not the central focus of this study, I will discuss how agricultural policies affected them in contrast to the land-poor peasants.

But even the category of "land-poor peasantry" demands clarification, for it describes a diffuse and in-flux population. Carlos Vilas, a political economist who worked for the Ministry of Planning (MIPLAN) in Nicaragua from 1980 to 1984, reveals the complexity of this category while also reflecting some of the developmentalist biases of early policymakers and analysts. Vilas estimated that by the late 1970s half a million Nicaraguans worked in agricultural production. Of these, roughly 50,000 were agricultural proletariats, that is, agricultural laborers with permanent employment. Another 75,000 were what he termed itinerant proletariats, or laborers without permanent employment who changed jobs every three to four months. These "itinerant proletariats," however, were the recently dispossessed peasantry. They were *minifundistas* who had been forced off their land during the post–World War II cotton and cattle booms but were not reabsorbed in permanent labor positions.[10] However, by the end of the 1970s there still remained 165,000 *minifundistas* — peasants with ten *manzanas* of land or less — who sold their labor during harvest seasons because their holdings were not sufficient for meeting their needs for the entire year. Vilas identifies these *minifundistas* as the semiproletariat.[11] Together with the permanent proletariat, the itinerant proletariat and the *mini-fundistas* made up 68 percent of the rural EAP in Nicaragua.

Vilas's schematization of the rural population illustrates the level of stratification that existed among the poorest of the rural EAP. It also betrays the developmental imperative shared by the administrators at MIPLAN who viewed these sectors of the peasantry as a social formation in transition. Vilas's purpose is to show that the proletarianization in Nicaragua's countryside remained "incomplete" in a dependent agro-export economy, and in doing so he determines sectors of the rural population as "problems" with calculable parameters. However, the peasants in these sectors constitute "incomplete" social formations only insofar as proletarianization constitutes *the* natural developmental outcome for MIPLAN. At the level of consciousness, or of self-identification, such a transformation had not even begun to take place. After all, less than a generation separated many of the itinerant and semiproletariat from land tenure. Invariably, when I interviewed *mini-fundistas*, itinerant laborers, and even most members of the permanent proletariat, they continued to identify themselves as *campesinos* — as peasants. They identified as such not out of ignorance of their "true" economic position, but rather they recognized that their dual positionality facilitated the extraction of higher rates of surplus and profit for the agro-export economy. While the members of all three of these categories had a definite interest in improved labor conditions, their future aspirations were actually tied to a return to a prior, perhaps even mythical state of autonomy as *campeches* (*campeche* is slang in Spanish for *campesino,* which means peasant/farmer). The *minifundistas,* the itinerant proletariats, and even many of the permanent proletariats still identified greater access to land as their overriding interest. Together the itinerant proletariat and the *minifundistas* made up 240,000 people, roughly half of the rural EAP. Their interests and the interests of an agro-export economy were directly at odds, because this economy could neither absorb them as full-time workers nor afford to lose their part-time or seasonal labor. These two groups of the peasantry, the *minifundistas* and the itinerant proletariats, are the central focus of this study in considering the Sandanista's model of revolutionary development.

I conducted the research for this study during the three years I lived in Nicaragua from 1984 to 1987 and on two return research trips in 1988 and 1989. During the three years that I lived in Nicaragua I worked as a part-time research assistant at the Instituto Historico CentroAmericano (IHCA), a center affiliated with the Jesuit Central American University in Managua. While I worked there my area of research was agrarian reform. In conducting my research, I interviewed agricultural policy analysts and technicians in the Ministry of Agriculture (MIDINRA) from several regions in Nicaragua; members of the FSLN-affiliated organization for farmers and ranchers (UNAG); representatives from the FSLN-affiliated agricultural workers' union (ATC); agricultural laborers on state and private farms; beneficiaries of agrarian reform on cooperatives and on private parcels; and small-, medium-, and large-scale private producers who either supported the Sandinistas or actively conspired against them. I also consulted official and unofficial government documents, as well as secondary, background readings. During my research for the Institute I visited several state farms, cooperatives, resettlement communities, private farms, and villages; I also spent extended periods of time (up to two months) on three cooperatives and two state farms on construction and harvest brigades.

It is as difficult for me to write up this research as it was to conduct it, although for very different reasons. Ten years ago every visit I made to a cooperative or state farm was difficult because I never knew if the friends that I laughed and argued with, played cards with, shared lean meals with would still be alive. Perhaps they would be dead — tortured and killed by counterrevolutionaries trained and financed by the United States for daring to imagine a different set of power relations, a different distribution of wealth. Today, it is difficult to write about this research not because I naïvely find it a betrayal to criticize the Sandinista vision of development for which so many people died. Rather, it is because of the growing consensus between conservatives and leftists (in the apparent triumph of neoliberalism), where they are finding it all too easy to blame the failure of socialism to take root in Latin America on the "antidemocratic tendencies" or "dogmatism" of revolutionary groups, or on the structural impossibility of placing controls on markets. As Zora Neale Hurston once wrote, we forget, perhaps, because it is too painful to remember what was once so apparent just a short time ago. The blame for the failure of the Sandinista attempt to institute a different model of development lies first and foremost with the U.S. government. The CIA's recruitment and direct support of the counterrevolutionaries caused nearly $5 billion of damage in eight years to a country with a GNP of less than U.S. $800 million in any given year between 1980 and 1990. However, the credit for the Sandinista successes — most notably the improvements to education, nationalized health care, enforcement of child support payments and domestic violence laws, lasting changes in land tenure, and, of course, the institutionalization of representative democracy — belongs solely to the Nicaraguans. And so I write this essay because I believe in the possibility of these successes and not in the inevitability of failure.

THE LEGACY OF DEPENDENCY IN ESTABLISHING AN AGRICULTURAL STATE SECTOR: 1979–1981

On July 20, 1979, one day after the triumph of the revolution, the new government nationalized the property belonging to Somoza and his associates, as well as the country's entire banking system. The expropriation of Somocista property brought 20 percent of Nicaragua's arable land under state control. From these expropriated lands the new government created the Area of People's Property (APP), or state farms, to be administered by MIDINRA.[12] The Sandinistas envisioned state farms as the most direct path to satisfying the interests of the majority of the peasants. MIDINRA's decision to create state farms rather than redistribute lands suggested that the Ministry intended to "complete" the process of proletarianization through increased employment and improved conditions on state farms. They assumed, to some degree correctly, that the workers on these farms would not only gain a sense of ownership about these farms, but a proprietary identification with the FSLN's vision of centralized, large-scale, industrialized farming. However, there were never enough jobs. The newly established MIPLAN in the *1980 Plan for Economic Reactivation* called for the creation of 50,000 permanent jobs in state agriculture.[13] Although this was a significant number of jobs for the new government to generate, it was by no means enough to absorb the 240,000 *minifundistas* and itinerant proletariats. In fact, it took three years for MIDINRA to attain accurate estimates of these sectors of the peasant population, a delay perhaps symptomatic of the government's persistent and more general misapprehension of the condition of the land-poor peasantry. The measures creating new jobs left 190,000 *minifundistas* and itinerant proletariats in the same precarious economic conditions that they had lived under prior to the revolution. This initial reform did nothing to benefit the majority of *minifundistas* and itinerant proletariats who worked on these farms only seasonally, if at all, and thus they would enjoy neither broadened democratic participation nor improved living conditions in the APP sector.

To the itinerant proletariat and the *minifundistas* who were not guaranteed full-time employment, this limited agrarian reform appeared as a betrayal by the party that had rallied the peasants to its side with the promise of "land to those who work it."[14] Pressure for land from the peasantry had increased during the two decades prior to the revolution given the accelerated dispossession that had taken place with the cotton boom. In one region alone, Leon and Chinandega, peasants launched 240 land takeovers between 1963 and 1973.[15] These were just the most evident forms of resistance to the agro-export economy. There is no way to calculate the less spectacular acts of everyday resistance, such as squatting and production sabotage that went on prior to the insurrection.[16] But as just one example of more hidden forms of resistance, an agricultural laborer on the state farm La Concepcion in Chinandega told me that many of the workers on this farm, prior to the revolution, had channeled part of the foodstuffs and revenues from their private production on parcels they rented from the landlord to the guerrilla ranks.

This rash of takeovers during the 1960s and '70s and the pursuant repression by Somoza's National Guard contributed not only cadres to the ranks of the guerrillas, but moral legitimacy to the FSLN's cause. And during the two years of insurrection, the permanent workers in coordination with the itinerant proletariats and the *minifundistas* took over abandoned farms and organized production cooperatives, providing crucial logistical support for the Sandinistas. Nevertheless, MIDINRA legalized only a chosen few of the cooperatives that had formed during the insurrection, and less than 1 percent of Somocista lands were turned over to these peasants as cooperatives in this initial phase of agrarian reform. In most cases, once in power, the FSLN used its moral (and sometimes military) authority to intervene and disband cooperatives that had formed on the APP lands or on private farms unaffected by the anti-Somicista decree of July 20, 1979.[17]

Certainly the conditions of development that already existed on the confiscated lands favored the state farm structure. Of the 2,000 farms confiscated, half were larger than 500 *manzanas* in area[18] and had belonged to the wealthiest clique of large-scale farmers. They were immense, technologically sophisticated estates representing millions of dollars worth of investment in highly mechanized production practices that "unified" the land holding. Breaking up these coherent units into smaller parcels would not lead to efficient use of the technology on these estates, and this in turn would lead to a sharp decrease in their productivity. Planners in MIDINRA feared, perhaps justifiably, that if they distributed land to the land-poor peasantry, the new recipients of land would stop tending to export production altogether and begin planting basic grains and domestic foodstuffs.[19] Nicaragua in 1979 was a model of the first stage of dependent capitalist development in the periphery: exporting primary goods to the center, while importing most manufactured goods. Trade acted as a substitute for production, where Nicaragua depended entirely on the export of a few primary products (coffee, cotton, beef, sugar) to generate foreign exchange for purchasing almost all capital goods and inputs necessary in the agricultural sector *and* the nascent industrial sector.[20] Thus, maintaining the agro-export sector was essential to the basic reproduction of the national economy, even though this ironically entailed maintaining an inexpensive, seasonal labor force to ensure margins of profitability in a world market.

The technological sophistication of these farms and the policy of proletarianization of these land-poor peasant classes dovetailed with the FSLN's vision of state vanguardism in the economy. MIPLAN's *1980 Plan* established the state as the *eje dynamico* (the dynamic axis) in all economic sectors. Through the direct ownership of some of the means of production, and the nationalization of the financial system and segments of the commercial system, the state would manage the entire economy.[21] The state was to become the center for the accumulation of surplus and would thereby direct its redistribution through investments intended to benefit the various classes more equitably. Where the state did not directly own the means of production, it could direct production and accumulation of surplus through the distribution of foreign and domestic credit, controls over wages, and the control of international commerce.[22] Where the state could not act as direct employer, it could service the permanent rural workers on private farms, and the itinerant proletariats and *minifundistas* through investments in a social wage — education, health care, child care, and credit — rather than through measures involving land distribution.

However, if we consider the implementation of these social wage measures, they often exacerbated the stratification between the permanently employed and the underemployed, land-poor peasantry. The literacy and health brigades of the early 1980s were extensive in their reach. Since these were roving brigades made up of volunteer, urban youths, they were able to extend basic literacy, child immunization, prenatal care, and preventive medical information to the most isolated areas in the countryside. Follow-up measures, however, tended to benefit the already privileged state farm worker. Health clinics, schools, and child care centers were constructed first on the state farms and then in outlying villages. Thus, the social wage was disproportionately distributed to the most economically stable sector of the rural poor, the permanent proletariat. While schools, child care centers, and clinics were also constructed in rural villages, itinerant proletariats were by definition a transient population moving from farm to farm, and the *minifundistas'* tiny plots of land were often located far outside the villages. Also, their precarious economic position meant that they were less likely to spare the labor of their children so that they could attend school. Thus, access to these services did not have as dramatic an impact on their daily lives as it did on the lives of those living on state farms or in the villages. Most often, those living in the villages were the peasants with small and medium-sized holdings who could afford to maintain a house in the village as well as on their farms; after 1983, these centers became the primary targets of counterrevolutionary activity, further limiting their scope.

The Sandinistas hoped that this first economic plan, which resisted radical redistribution of land, would calm any private-sector fears and maintain the delicate balance of forces in the governing junta. The Sandinistas came to power thanks to the alliance of classes and nationalist visions that formed to remove the figureheads of a despotic regime. Clearly, properties classes would not long support a party promoting the rights and welfare of the classes these elites exploited for capital accumulation. Contradictions between classes reemerged quickly to affect the broad-based approval the FSLN enjoyed immediately following July 19. The FSLN, however, initially appealed to national consciousness, foregrounding the principle of unity and insisting that their political and economic platforms for participatory democracy and a mixed economy could incorporate the *patriotic* private producer. Any Sandinista concession to the *minifundistas'* and itinerant proletariats' demands for "democratizing" land tenure at this early stage in the revolution could be interpreted as an indication of more expropriations to come. Such a possibility would lead to decreased investment or outright liquidation by the agro-export sector. And once again, if the *minifundistas* and the itinerant proletariats found themselves in the capacity of reproducing their families through private agricultural production, they would have little reason to sell their family's labor to the private and state sectors during the harvest season.

John Weeks, in "The Mixed Economy in Nicaragua," compellingly argues that it was naïve for the Sandinistas to expect the private sector to participate in this economic model since this sector had been stripped of its political power to direct the economy.[23] Due to the nationalization of financial institutions, government control of exportation and importation, and qualitative increases in permanent workers' rights and wages, the private sector lost its ability to accumulate capital on its own terms: "It is difficult to produce any other example of a country in which private capital remained the dominant form of property, while in the political realm capital had been disenfranchised. . . . The typical outcomes are either a counter-revolution by which propertied interests regain the political power commensurate with their economic importance, or a rapid move by the revolutionary government to confiscation of large-scale property (in part to prevent the former outcome)."[24] Weeks goes on to attribute the rapid decapitalization of large-scale property that followed the revolution's triumph to the bourgeoisie's lack of a nationalist identity that would supersede this sector's historical ties to Washington.[25] However, Weeks's analysis shows a very narrow understanding of affective ties of nationalism. I would argue that the bourgeoisie was committed to a vision of national progress that agreed with liberal, free market modernization theory and was bound to conflict with a revolutionary model of centrally planned development. The bourgeoisie believed that the country's "development" was best left to a few responsible men, meaning themselves, who could reinvest accumulated capital prudently and according to the laws of a competitive international market. The Sandinistas not only eliminated the competitive market, but they displaced the bourgeoisie from their function as the agents of economic change. The bourgeoisie saw Somoza's monopolistic control of the economy as a flaw in an otherwise rational and just system. With the correction of this flaw, the bourgeoisie expected a perfected capitalist development to proceed under their direction. Ultimately the bourgeoisie did not abandon Nicaragua out of a lack of patriotism. They did not abandon Nicaragua at all, but rather invested the money they decapitalized from their farms and industry in the counterrevolutionaries.[26]

The landed elites were more antagonistic to a consolidated state sector in agriculture than they may have been to the redistribution of lands to the itinerant proletariats and *minifundistas,* even with the reduction of the labor force this would have entailed. In my own research I have conducted many interviews with landed elites who are members of the conservative Union of Nicaraguan Agricultural Producers (UPANIC). At some point during these interviews, the representatives invariably charged that the Sandinistas were "worse than Somoza ever was" because of the state's "monopolistic" control of the agricultural economy. During an interview with me in 1986 Rosendo Diaz, then president of UPANIC, displayed questionable sympathy for the plight of the agricultural proletariat and declared, "Before the revolution, the Sandinistas lured the *campesinos* with flowery promises that they would own their own land. Instead MIDINRA has turned the *campesino* into a peon of the state, a slave of the state who is going to do whatever the state says, whenever to do it, and by whatever means it dictates." Whether this was rhetorical posturing on the part of the landed elites or an accurate representation of state control is beside the point. These representatives echoed the positions of counterrevolutionary leaders in Washington, in Miami, and in the Nicaraguan countryside. This right-wing critique by these elites and the counterrevolutionaries made political headway among the dissatisfied *minifundistas* and itinerant proletariats because it asserted, above all else, the autonomy of the peasantry, albeit within the bourgeoisie's framework of private property. In other words, these elites capitalized on the itinerant proletariats' and *minifundistas'* continued identification as *campesinos*; in effect, this right-wing rhetoric positioned the landed elites and the land-poor peasants in a relationship of equivalence vis-à-vis a state that denied an abstracted concept of freedom. These appeals by the elites and counterrevolutionaries spoke to the itinerant proletariats' and *minifundistas'* interest in autonomy over their interests as workers, especially since the FSLN was unable to dramatically improve their status as proletariats.

Consider the impact such a critique would have even among the laborers with secured permanent employment on state farms in the following situation. With relatively few exceptions, MIDINRA did not allow agricultural workers to cultivate small parcels of land on state farms for their personal consumption, whereas previous owners had allowed the workers to do so. The Sandinistas interpreted this practice by private owners as exploitative and paternalistic.[27] Undoubtedly, it was both. Private owners allowed workers to cultivate unused parcels of land to keep the capital costs of reproducing labor to a minimum. Wage laborers employed on private farms provided some of their own foodstuffs by farming these parcels on their own time, which functioned as part of their wage, allowing the employer to pay them less. MIDINRA policymakers associated this practice with "precapitalist" forms of labor that hindered the complete proletarianization of the peasantry. However, MIDINRA officials were wrong to expect the agricultural worker to interpret this practice similarly — strictly as a form of precapitalist labor exploitation and paternalism. Instead, what the *terratenientes* (large- and medium-scale land owners) may have interpreted as their own benevolent patronage, the workers may have interpreted as a hard-earned right ensuring them a minimal level of autonomy and an identification with a subject position other than strictly "worker." In the context of soon-to-be chronic inflation and food shortages, permanent workers on state farms experienced the elimination of this practice as a decline in their material condition and an infringement of their rights. Again, from the Ministry's teleological perspective, this policy was meant to pull the workers further toward their true positionality. But one of the long-standing claims pressed by the ATC leaders at the local, regional, and national levels was the right of state farm workers to use part of the state farms for individual production of basic grains.

Clearly, I have emphasized the Sandinistas' efforts to "complete" proletarianization among the permanent workers, the itinerant proletariats, and the *minifundistas* to underscore their tendencies to redefine these sectors' interests in the state's developmentalist terms. From the FSLN's perspective, the interests of these three groups of peasants and the interests of the nation's development were best served through the combination of their freed labor and the state's capital. While the impetus behind initial agrarian reform policy was to hurry the process of proletarianization, the Sandinistas *did* enact some policies that were intended to reinforce the economic position of small-scale farmers and the *minifundista* segment of the peasantry as such. Two policies were aimed specifically at making them more effective private producers: a policy for the extension of credit and a policy for pricing and marketing basic grains and foodstuffs. To a degree, the enactment of these policies recognized the important role these groups could play as private producers in generating capital. However, they also revealed a paternalistic bias on the part of the state that ultimately undermined the position of the *minifundista* vis-à-vis the richer segments of the peasantry.

Under Somoza's regime, roughly 30,000 producers with small- and medium-scale holdings received 10 percent of the credit extended to rural areas through private banks, while the other 90 percent of rural credit went to landed elites. Under the FSLN, 100,000 *minifundistas* and small-holding peasant producers received 27 percent of the rural credit extended by the nationalized banking system.[28] The amount of credit extended by financial institutions increased by 600 percent during the first credit cycle in 1979–80.[29] Thousands of small-scale farmers and *minifundistas* who had never had access to credit received loans for the production of basic grains and foodstuffs in the first credit cycle.[30] Success of the credit program for the *minifundistas* and small-holdings peasantry depended on their possession of certain entrepreneurial skills: on their ability to invest loans efficiently — that is, to further rationalize production on their lands — and to repay the loans promptly. These "skills" necessary to enhance production on private parcels translated into a knowledge of more sophisticated modes of agricultural production, a basic level of technification of production on farms that could be enhanced by this new capital, access to means of transporting the new inputs and goods that must be purchased in the cities and towns — in short, an ability to combine increased capital, technology (capital goods like irrigation systems, processing plants, or even a tractor), and free labor. Since the small-holdings producers could improve the relationship between technology and wage labor with their increased capital, their surplus production increased; however, the majority of the *minifundistas'* production costs were not in capital goods or wage labor, but family labor.[31] Hence, investment of capital could not increase absolute or relative surplus production on these lands, and most *minifundistas* used the funds to satisfy immediate consumption needs. Consequently, credit extension did not lead to the expected rise in production, and the Sandinistas had to forfeit the majority of loans extended to the *minifundistas,* which led to a growing state deficit. After the first two years, the vast majority of *minifundistas* dropped out of the credit program, leaving the small-holding private producers to benefit the most.[32]

The rural credit program effectively accelerated the stratification among the lower echelons of Nicaragua's peasantry: "That is, the small-holding 'peasantry' [small-holding producers and *minifundistas*] was becoming increasingly divided into two groups: at one pole, producers who employed wage labor and had access to additional land by buying or renting from others [small-holders], and, at the other pole, producers who were forced to sell their labor power and rent and/or sell their land to that first group [*minifundistas*]."[33] A de facto effect of MIDINRA's rural credit program was to further proletarianize the *minifundistas* as they were forced to sell their labor and in some cases their land to the small-holding peasantry who were now able to extend their production due to the heretofore inaccessible credit. For the *minifundistas* the credit program was an intervention by the state that led to further dispossession and loss of the autonomy they associated with the ownership of land. The FSLN resisted distributing lands to the land-poor peasants because they did not want to reinforce the private property relation among this class, or to solidify their identification as peasant farmers, but rather as proletariats in the making. Yet, their policies strengthened the bourgeois position of the small-holding and medium-holding peasants, to the detriment of the land-poor peasants.

The FSLN displaced the mercantile class by setting fixed prices for the purchase of certain basic goods from these producers (rice, beans, sugar, milk, eggs, beef) and by monopolizing the purchase and distribution of these goods.[34] These policies corresponded to the FSLN's vanguardist position in directing agricultural development. MIDINRA wanted to guard the *minifundistas* and small-scale producers against the exploitative practices of these merchants. As I said earlier, the *mini-fundistas* historically had produced the bulk of the rice and beans consumed by the country. While the prices set by the state for these basic foodstuffs initially responded to production costs (they were increased significantly between 1979 and 1984), these prices were ultimately unable to keep pace with the increase in inflation of rural consumer prices. In effect, price controls became another means of extracting absolute surplus from the *minifundistas,* who were unable to lower their production costs by a relative increase in productivity, as many of the small-, medium-, and large-scale peasants were able to do.

To enforce its pricing policies and to eliminate the exploitative merchant class, the state also attempted to displace merchants from the buying and selling of these basic foodstuffs by taking over these functions. Not only was the state unable to reach all the *minifundistas,* dispersed as they were throughout the countryside, but the state was unable to replace all the services offered to the *minifundistas* by the merchants for those they did reach. Again, the Sandinistas' paternalistic thinking led to a narrow interpretation of the merchant-*minifundista* relationship. The relationship between the merchant and the *minifundista* was clearly exploitative, but each merchant serviced a variety of *minifundista* needs (mail service, short-term loans, transportation, information on part-time jobs in other areas, legal and medical advice) that no single state agency could replace even if state agents were able to reach the *minifundista.*[35] Small-holding peasants were far less likely to need these services. Often, merchants came from the peasant communities and were not seen as "outsiders." Most importantly, these merchants offered better prices for their goods than the state provided. Inevitably, a black market for the purchase and sale of basic foodstuffs developed because of the low prices the state paid for the goods.

In 1984 I spent two months on La Virgencita cooperative, eleven miles north of the city of Esteli. This was one of the few production cooperatives awarded during the first period of reform immediately following the triumph of the revolution. These workers were given the land because of the historical commitment they had shown to the FSLN. However, the president of this cooperative regularly lent one of the cooperative's trucks to his cousin, a *minifundista* who farmed nearby, so that he could travel by night and circumvent the state distribution authorities, taking his production directly to the markets in Esteli. Of course, I was left wondering if the cousin might not be marketing some of the cooperative's production as well. Thus, although the merchant-*minifundista* relationship was ultimately an exploitative one, even those peasants most committed to the revolutionary process—

those awarded land early in the process because of their loyalty—
recognized that the state in its role as merchant was becoming equally if
not more exploitative of the *minifundista.*

STAGE TWO: AGRARIAN REFORM 1981–1985

The development policies put forth by MIDINRA in the first two years
of the revolution strengthened the economic position of the permanent
proletariat and the small-holding peasantry. However, for the vast majority of itinerant proletariats and the *minifundistas* these same policies
either had no long-term effect on their economic position or, in fact,
placed them in an even more precarious economic position. Thus, demand for land from these two groups of peasants continued unabated
during the first two years of the revolution. In Masaya, the department
in Nicaragua with the largest concentration of *minifundistas,* thousands of these peasants marched on the regional office of MIDINRA in
February 1980. They demanded that no more lands be returned to
previous owners and that instead they be redistributed among the peasantry.[36] While demands for lands in other regions were not as spectacular, they were chronic. In the name of the itinerant proletariat and the
minifundistas, the ATC consistently petitioned regional MIDINRA of-
fices for the expropriation and redistribution of unproductive farm
lands. No one knew better than the agricultural workers and *minifundistas* in each area which farmers were nonproductive or actively de-
capitalizing. This early agitation by the *minifundistas* and the itinerant
proletariats clearly indicated their dissatisfaction with their precarious
status as agricultural laborers in the government's new development
plans and with the revolutionary government's compromise with the
landed elites.

The 1981 agrarian reform law cites as its raison d'être the FSLN's
historical duty to restore these peasants' right to live off the land with
dignity.[37] Much of the literature on the first agrarian reform law describes it as a political response by the Sandinistas to their social base
among the dispossessed and land-poor peasantry. This was a partial
truth. In the context of the inadequate response of landed elites to
incentives, the primary purpose of the law was to enable the state to use
force where flattery had failed. As early as 1981, it was clear to the
government that this segment of the private sector was not fully reinvesting its profits. MIPLAN's *1981 Plan for Economic Austerity* indicates that, although profits had recuperated faster than salaries, the
private sector, *especially in agriculture,* was in most cases simply main-

taining *post*triumph production levels.[38] Where were these profits going? Already there were signs of decapitalization by some producers.[39] While domestic agricultural production — which was largely in the hands of small- and medium-holding peasants — rebounded, export production lagged behind.[40]

The new law stipulated that land holdings in excess of 500 *manzanas* along the Pacific Coast and 1,000 *manzanas* in the mountainous regions would be subject to expropriation if these lands were abandoned, lying idle, or underutilized. However, productive properties, regardless of their size, would be left untouched.[41] Even after the expropriations of Somocista land, 21.5 percent of land remained in private holdings exceeding 500 *manzanas*. A full fifth of the land, then, remained in the hands of large-scale agro-export producers. This was roughly comparable to the state's holdings.[42] Meanwhile, 165,000 *minifundista* families continued to live off 2.5 percent of the land.[43] And between 25,000 and 35,000 itinerant proletariats owned no land and had no permanent employment. Although the 1981 law stipulated that newly expropriated lands be handed over to the dispossessed and land-poor peasants, allowing for limited private ownership, it emphasized the need for these peasants to organize themselves into production cooperatives in order to receive the land.[44] Therefore, the first agrarian reform law allowed for individual or family ownership of land only if the beneficiaries agreed to join some type of cooperative association (i.e., credit and service cooperatives or dead furrow cooperatives).[45] But even if the peasants were willing to join such cooperatives, priority would be given to peasants with historical ties to the revolutionary struggle. In effect, the only peasants to receive individual plots of land under this law were those with long-standing claims to party loyalty. MIDINRA's enforcement of the new law between 1981 and 1983 demonstrated the agency's absolute reluctance to recognize an autonomous peasant social formation to any significant degree when it came to the *minifundistas* and the itinerant proletariats. Sectors of the FSLN in MIDINRA adhered to a stubbornly Leninist construction of small-scale private property as the petit bourgeois basis for the reproduction of capitalist relations. They could not imagine an alternative outcome to this capitalist developmental narrative and instantiated reform policies equally as rigid in their developmental framework. Ultimately, their credit and social wage policies inadvertently furthered bourgeois class positions of the small- and medium-holding peasants at the expense of the *minifundistas* and itinerant proletariats.

In January 1985, I traveled with a technician from Masaya's local MIDINRA office to visit ten farms owned by *minifundistas*. In the 1984 elections, the FSLN's poorest show of support had come from this department. Several of the men and women on these farms admitted to not having voted at all in the elections, most claiming that they did not vote because they lacked time or were "not political." However, in a region that had been a base for guerrilla actions during the insurrection, these responses from farmers say something in and of themselves. Others admitted that they did not vote because they did not see the point, and one farmer stated, "If you are standing between a person who is hitting you and another who does nothing to help you, you duck." Of those who said they had voted, most said they had voted for the FSLN. However, one woman I spoke to said candidly, "The Sandinistas want us to give them our sons [referring to military recruitment to fight the war], they want us to give them our produce [referring to the low prices on goods]. Well, I don't have to give them my vote." This woman used the verb *regalar*, which I have translated as "to give"; however, in Spanish the words *regular* is used in association with the giving of gifts. Thus, the woman was implying that they gave something precious to the Sandinistas and they were now tired of giving things away without getting anything in return.

Over the course of three years, MIDINRA expropriated 7 percent of the national arable land from the private sector. Private holdings exceeding 500 *manzanas* shrunk from 21 percent of the national total to 14 percent, and large-scale agriculture was reduced by 33 percent. The honeymoon between the state and large-scale agro-export producers was over. However, improved relations between the state and the majority of dispossessed and land-poor peasants did not immediately follow. MIDINRA redistributed these lands almost exclusively to peasants willing to form production cooperatives: 33,000 peasant families received land in cooperative form; in the same three years, only 1,000 peasant families received land in the form of individual ownership.[46] From the perspective of the state, cooperatives appeared to be a compromise between large-scale agro-export production (state or private) and individual peasant production. From the perspective of the itinerant proletariats and the *minifundistas*, however, cooperatives meant either land on the state's terms or no land at all.

Cooperatives appeared to be an ideal form of production to the Sandinistas because, during these four years, it had become increasingly clear that MIDINRA could not absorb any more lands and administer them effectively.[47] Cooperative production, then, could form an adjunct to the APP production. Expropriated properties did not need to be broken up; rather, one or more cooperatives could work as coherent units. As such, they posed less of a threat to export agriculture than individual ownership, since they could increase food production by planting basic grains between the seasons for export goods. Furthermore, cooperative ownership, because it concentrated the new land recipients into units, would also facilitate the extension of technical services by an already overextended MIDINRA. This seemed an ideal way of reinforcing the precarious economic living conditions of the land-poor peasant without reinforcing private property as a formation.

Carmen Deere, in "Agrarian Reform in the Transition," contends that cooperativization under the 1981 agrarian reform law was strictly voluntary and that the state did not prioritize it over private ownership of land.[48] This analysis, however, is somewhat misleading. Deere projects a liberal notion of agency onto the *minifundistas* and the itinerant proletariats that effaces the state's power and the poverty of choices available to these peasants. On the one hand, access to land, to technical services, to social services, and to credit was only assured to those peasants willing to form production cooperatives. On the other hand, as the counterrevolutionaries increased their activities in the northern countryside, these production cooperatives became prime targets of their attacks. Thus, if the *minifundistas* or the itinerant proletariats chose not to join production cooperatives, they "chose" to continue their marginal economic position, while joining cooperatives meant that they risked death at the hands of the counterrevolutionaries. For Deere to presume that the actions of the land-poor peasants were "voluntary" in this context presupposes an equality of choices that simply did not exist. Such a presupposition is naïve indeed, especially when projected onto a revolutionary transition that is negotiating the very issues of equality and freedom within the overdetermined constraints of underdevelopment in the context of a war. Arguably, most sectors of the peasantry had more choices under the Sandinistas than they had ever enjoyed under the Somoza dictatorship (or would have under the neoliberalism of Violeta Chamorro), but the "choice" to join a cooperative was not among them.

The Sandinistas did not use physical force in their efforts at cooperativizing the dispossessed and land-poor peasantry.[49] However, the state's role in the *minifundistas'* and itinerant proletariats' lives was already effectively a coercive one with regard to pricing and purchasing policies. I am not arguing that state-initiated cooperativization among the peasantry could not or should not take place. However, we must recognize that even under optimum conditions, there were likely to be subtle forms of pressure by the state to convince peasants to join cooperatives. After all, unlike the indigenous peasants in Guatemala, the *minifundistas* and itinerant proletariats in the Pacific regions of Nicaragua had no history of communal farming. Thus, the transformation of consciousness required by cooperativization would necessarily be a violent and troubled one at the level of subjectivity. It requires that these dispossessed and land-poor peasants reconstruct their concept of community. It asks that they, *from an extremely precarious economic position,* suspend immediate individual and familial needs not only for the sake of this larger collective community but for the national community that has an investment in the cooperative as a revolutionary experiment and an economic unit of production. It requires the abandonment of a traditional mode of production in favor of a theoretical one. Thus, while MIDINRA may not have used force to cooperativize peasants, the high rates of labor absenteeism and changing membership that plagued many cooperatives indicate that not all cooperative members were committed to the cooperatives they presumably "chose" to join.

To emphasize the necessarily long-term and materially bound nature of this transformation to collective consciousness, I recount an exchange I had with a cooperativized peasant on a return visit to Nicaragua in 1989, while visiting a coffee cooperative outside of El Cua, Matagalpa. This cooperative had been established six years earlier, that is, in 1983, and this man had been a member since it was founded. Most of the members had a history of loyalty to the party. Yet he told me frankly that, due to the scarcity of rural credit in 1989, cooperative members were reinvesting their profits in the farm *for the first time* in the 1989–90 crop cycle. These are the profits they received after selling their coffee and paying themselves their regular salaries. I asked him what they had done with the profits all those years. He said that they had divided them according to how hard each member worked, and each member spent the profits as he or she saw fit. What does this reveal? Savvy financing on the part of these cooperative members? (After all, why invest your own profits when the bank will provide low-interest loans?) A fundamental lack of a sense of ownership? (After all, who could say what would be the outcome of the war and if they would still own their lands after it was over?) A failure to prioritize national needs over personal needs (even though these peasants were presumably committed to the revolutionary project)? I can only speculate. Until 1988, this zone was virtually off-limits to foreigners because of the heavy fighting in the area. Perhaps, with the relaxation of the counterrevolutionary war, these cooperative members were now physically and economically secure enough to reinvest their profits in their farms for the first time. Perhaps the state's inability to provide services facilitated a reorientation of a previously paternalistic relation. In either case, the transformation in consciousness and economic conditions that would make this cooperative a self-sustaining collective had not completely taken place.

Despite these crises, Deere states that "the internal organization of the cooperatives is quite democratic" and that "the cooperatives are totally independent of the Ministry of Agriculture . . . [although] they receive technical assistance from the ministry and credit from the National Development Bank."[50] Once again, this romantic rendition presents the relationship between the state and the peasant as an untroubled exchange between equal partners in an uncontested national development project. In effect, MIDINRA was only able to extend full technical services to 500 prioritized cooperatives. This was 25 percent of the total number of production cooperatives; 75 percent were disenfranchised from most state services.[51] I would not presume that these disenfranchised cooperatives enjoyed a *greater* degree of internal democracy or choice simply because of their autonomy from the state. However, "technical services" on prioritized cooperatives often boiled down to orders from MIDINRA representatives.

Focusing on the cooperatives receiving technical assistance, let us rethink the context of the state-peasant relationship. The state chose 500 cooperatives with the intention of modernizing their production, of intensifying their production through the importation of technology.[52] This explicit intention of increasing technical sophistication and industrialization precluded any serious autonomy for the chosen production cooperatives, since the modernizing effort would require more than a little advice and a few loans. The prioritized cooperatives represented a *national* investment of increasingly scarce resources. In effect, these cooperative members, even more than their proletarian counterparts on state farms, were the critical link in a new schema of national development. They were the agents of transformation. However, these ex-*minifundistas* and agricultural proletariats would need planning, managerial, and technical skills that would take years to acquire in the best of circumstances before they could direct industrialized production. Until the peasants acquired these skills — this *further* transformation in consciousness — a paternalistic relationship on the part of the state as the provider of such skills was only to be expected. In effect, a recurrent problem on cooperatives was the tendency toward state intervention in the cooperatives' internal organization, norms, and decisions.[53]

It is not my intention to present peasants on cooperatives as being completely without agency in their relationship to the state. Rather, the relationship was a dialectical one, fraught with power imbalances that played themselves out in the daily exchange of activity between the peasants and the representatives of MIDINRA. It was this tension between the particular interests of the peasants and the universalized interest of the state that often retooled the state's nationalist vision. For example, in 1986 I visited a group of five prioritized coffee cooperatives an hour outside of the city of Esteli. Three of these neighboring cooperatives had been attacked by counterrevolutionaries a week before, and the counterrevolutionaries had burned down a new coffee processing plant. This was the third in a series of five attacks on these cooperatives that had taken place in the span of three years. At one of the two cooperatives that had not been attacked, I was walking up a hill with one of the zonal MIDINRA's five technical assistants to the cooperatives and a cooperative member. The technical assistant enthusiastically explained to me that this cooperative was the beginning of a project to replace corn production with potatoes and diversify consumption patterns nationally. Not only would this improve nutrition, it would also provide a potential new export product to generate much needed foreign exchange, and it would replenish the soil. When we reached the top of the hill, he looked down onto the cooperative members in the valley who were busy planting, and a look of shock came over his face as he stated in an agitated voice, "I told you to plant potatoes!" Deadpan, the cooperative member answered, "Oh? I thought you said corn." (The cooperative member privately explained to me later that they had taken advantage of the technician's weekend away to advance on the planting.) As quickly as anxiety had overcome the technician, it left him. He shrugged his shoulders and said, "Oh well, no big difference." The technician, from his perspective of resistance to Nicaragua's history of dependent monocultural development, registered the peasants' resistance to MIDINRA's modernizing vision and accommodated it. Fortunately, this technician was much more attuned to the discrepancies between the peasant interests and the national interests than his superiors in Managua. He explained to me that he and the other technicians in this area were sensitive to the top-down structure of much of the technical assistance to cooperatives, and went to great pains to try to accommodate the peasants' opinions on production decisions. The next time I visited these cooperatives, this twenty-one-year-old technician had been killed in an attack by the counterrevolutionaries.

Clearly, cooperativized peasants intervened at all levels of the production process. Some co-ops were more democratically run and autonomous than others. The newly trained MIDINRA representatives brought technical expertise to the project, but the peasants, who in many cases had worked on the farms they now owned, brought an expertise about the specific farms, work relations, and local community. We can assume that the peasantry asserted this expertise whenever possible, given their newly empowered status in the years following the revolution. Nevertheless, modernization through collectivization privileged state power, and peasant participation should always be read in this context. The peasant's participation could only be the result of a negotiation between the state's vision of a national development project, the individual MIDINRA representatives, and the heterogeneous national and local visions of the peasantry.

To assess the overall success or failure of the cooperative movement in Nicaragua would be inappropriate. Success or failure, in terms of productivity and the cooperatives' ability to maintain long-term members, varied tremendously. A cooperative's viability depended on a number of factors: location, number of members per *manzana,* labor discipline, members' identification as owners, the degree of democratic practices within the cooperative, appropriate technical sophistication among members, access to small plots of land on cooperatives for familial production, and, perhaps most importantly, the degree of preexisting group consciousness and ideological commitment to the Sandinista nationalist vision.[54] In northeast Nicaragua, specifically in the departments of Leon and Chinandega, where favorable conditions predominated, productivity on cotton cooperatives surpassed the levels of their state and private competitors.[55] In the mountainous war zone, cooperatives demonstrating a high degree of group consciousness and ideological commitment to the Sandinistas became prime targets for the counterrevolutionary attacks; in this context, it would be incorrect to interpret their subsequent lack of productivity as "failure." Before the institution of the military draft, cooperatives were the prime source of recruits for fighting the escalating war against the counterrevolutionaries.[56] This defense effort negatively impacted production, however. But the overdetermining factor in the fate of *all* the cooperatives was the U.S.-backed counterrevolutionary war. In cases where cooperatives were not directly affected by the aggression—through attacks by the counterrevolutionaries or recruitment by the Sandinista army—they suffered from the overall lack of resources, flexibility, and time caused by the war. Nevertheless, MIDINRA's cooperative program required a peasant subject who had *already undergone a revolutionary enlightenment:* a peasant predisposed to collectivization, committed to a vision of modernization, who placed the needs of national development above the immediate domestic needs of the autonomous family and the community and viewed the state as an ally in this development — and who was willing to die for this nationalist vision.

This implied subject of cooperativization was male. While there are no state figures on the number of female cooperative members, there were very, very few. Although women worked on cooperatives alongside men, they were "represented" in decision making only through their husbands, fathers, or brothers. They were not listed as members on property titles, nor did they have voting power within the collective. Generally, women who were members had been granted membership as a reward for their husband's dying in combat. During the debates and town hall meetings that took place around the drafting of the national constitution in 1985–86, women's representatives in the National Assembly, from cooperatives, from the ATC, and from the FSLN-affiliated national women's organization AMNLAE repeatedly petitioned the party and the National Assembly to make land ownership a constitutional right for women, but to no avail. During the same visit I made to the cooperative outside El Cua in 1989, I asked a group of women what party they were planning to vote for in the upcoming national elections. Quickly, one woman said with feigned indifference, "I'm not voting. Remember, I'm not a member of this cooperative." This was received with affirming laughter and nods from the other women in the group.

Any analysis of cooperativization under the 1981 agrarian reform law must recognize the limited scope of this law. Only 33,000 peasants received land under this reform, and some of these were members of the permanent proletariat who had worked on the private farms before they were expropriated. But even if we assume that all of this land went to the dispossessed or land-poor, this figure represents only one-sixth of the *minifundista* and itinerant proletariat population who were in need.[57] After five years of revolution, only 7 percent of the national arable land had been redistributed to these peasants, a relatively small amount. The vast majority of this population failed to benefit from the 1981 agrarian reform law. In certain cases, land reform created class stratification among the peasantry, in that those benefiting from these reforms, especially on export-oriented cooperatives, would hire the remaining disenfranchised peasants as seasonal and part-time labor.[58] In part, the slow pace of redistribution was due to the *minifundistas'* and itinerant proletariats' resistance to cooperatives, but it also reflected the Sandinista's contradictory reluctance to (a) alienate the private sector, or (b) recognize the potential that small, private holdings might offer not only in terms of economic development but also in terms of political support for the revolutionary process. With the bulk of production still in the hands of large-scale and medium-scale private production or the state, the FSLN moved too cautiously and were largely ineffective in their redistribution efforts.

LAND OWNERSHIP AND NATIONAL IDENTITY: 1985–1986

On my first visit to the office of MIDINRA's Center for the Study and Investigation of Agrarian Reform (CIERA) in January 1985, an investigator, Fredy Quesada, explained to me that the standard of living for the *minifundista* and itinerant proletariat had been drastically reduced over the previous three years. During this conversation, a jeep pulled up outside the window and a man dressed in army fatigues and a white T-shirt got out and entered the office, interrupting our conversation with the agitated pronouncement, "Fredy, the peasants in Boaco and Chontales are becoming counterrevolutionaries." He had just returned from a two-week investigation for CIERA of Nicaragua's central mountainous region, comprised of the departments of Boaco and Chontales. Quesada was not terribly surprised, and answered, "*¡Se puede jugar con la limozna, pero no con el Santo!* [You can fool around with the alms but not with the Saint!]" I asked him to explain what he meant by this, and he responded that the FSLN could afford to make policy mistakes affecting the urban populations because it was unlikely they would move to the mountains and join the counterrevolutionaries; however, the dissatisfied sectors of the peasantry were more likely to join, and they formed a more critical proportion of the country's population. Quesada's analysis reveals that early in the revolutionary process some members of the lower echelons *within* MIDINRA were well aware of the flaws in agricultural and agrarian reform policies. Unfortunately, it took some time for MIDINRA's investigators in the field to convey the severity of the situation in the countryside to Managua policymakers.

As stated earlier, pricing and marketing policies intended to benefit the *minifundistas* and small-holding peasants had failed because of unforeseen difficulties in their implementation. By 1985, the negative impact of these policies on this sector of the peasantry was severe. A comparison of prices for rural and manufactured goods best illustrates the degree of this crisis. While producer prices for rural goods (rice, beans, corn) had increased sevenfold since 1978, the price of a pair of rubber boots had increased 28 times, and the price of a pair of pants had increased 140 times.[59] One reason for the disparity was the lack of domestic industry and the scarcity of foreign exchange. Most of the products used by the *minifundistas* (fertilizers, machetes, wire fencing, rubber boots) were not domestically produced and had to be imported. Thus, with the allocation of scarce foreign exchange to agro-export production and to long-term, capital-intensive state agro-industry, there was little left for the importation or subsidization of the goods necessary for basic food production, the domain of the *minifundista* and the small-holding peasant.[60] Consequently, the costs of these goods skyrocketed, making it impossible to meet production costs without resorting to the black market.

There is another reason for the unequal terms of trade between the countryside and the city. The majority of the original FSLN leadership was forged in the urban underground, from student activists attending the universities along the Pacific Coast. Thus, their analysis emerged from the perspective of the popular urban classes who had provided crucial support for the revolution and had suffered the worst effects of Somocista repression. The Sandinistas were rightly concerned with immediately improving the purchasing power of these classes; however, they did so by artificially suppressing prices of domestic foodstuffs. This policy dovetailed with the classical development dictate that the exploitation of peasant production facilitates urban industrialization. To maintain low wages in the cities around primary industrialization projects *and* the popular support from the urban population, the FSLN subsidized food costs. However, since the Sandinistas were not inclined to resort to violence as a means of coercion, they were unable to force the *minifundistas* to stay on their land or keep the itinerant proletariats in the countryside. The dispossessed and land-poor peasants flocked to the cities, where they could buy staples for less than it cost to produce them, benefit from extended urban state services, and enjoy the large profit margins of petty trading.[61] The impact of migration on basic grains production was palpable. Whereas in 1981 production of beans, rice, and corn was on the rise, by mid-1984 production of these crops was on the steady decline again.[62]

The increase of counterrevolutionary activity in the countryside contributed to migration and decline in productivity; however, agrarian reform, pricing, and marketing policies contributed to the rise in counterrevolutionary activity. Peasants migrating to the cities were not the immediate concern, although it appeared as such to the urbanite. Of greater consequence were those peasants who were not migrating and were thus unable to reproduce themselves from their labor. Where did they go? Estimates on the number of armed counterrevolutionaries operating inside the country at this time fluctuated between 6,000 and 10,000, depending on whether the source was the FSLN or the U.S.

Embassy. However, after the war ended, estimates on the number of counterrevolutionaries and their families in Costa Rica and Honduras in need of relocation ranged from 28,000 to 40,000. Even in 1985 it had become obvious to all but the most idealistic that this was no longer strictly a mercenary force. These counterrevolutionaries were mostly of Nicaraguan peasant extraction. While this is a fraction of the rural EAP, counterrevolutionary operations in the countryside required the tacit complicity of many more. It is impossible to assess the degree of the *minifundistas'* and itinerant proletariats' political commitment to counterrevolutionary ideology — to distinguish coercion and need from fervor. Nevertheless, they were there in numbers. Leon Trotsky, writing about the transition period in the Soviet Union, once declared: "politically, the civil war is the struggle between the proletariat in opposition to the counter-revolutionaries for the conquest of the peasantry."[63] Such a war was taking place in Nicaragua.

MIDINRA's *Work Plan for 1985* reveals the sudden and strategic changes in agrarian reform policy that took place in that year. Official projections for land redistribution for 1985, made in 1984, show that the Ministry intended to continue agrarian reform at the previous sleepy pace. It proposed that 2 percent of the national arable land be expropriated from large-scale production; of this 2 percent, 110,000 *manzanas* would go directly into cooperative production, benefiting 4,000 peasant families, while 10,000 *manzanas* would go to 400 peasant families as private property. The state sector, which had dropped down to 19 percent in 1984, would remain constant.[64] The projections are worth noting as a comparison with the pattern of distribution that actually came to pass. The FSLN faced deteriorating support from the *minifundistas* and the itinerant proletariat nationwide. In the war zones, this deterioration registered as counterrevolutionary activity. Along the Pacific Coast, especially in Masaya, it registered as political apathy.[65] The war forced the FSLN's hand: maintain a contradictory alliance with the agricultural bourgeoisie and a commitment to cooperativization and lose the countryside; or abandon the bourgeois agroexport production and previous positions on the *minifundistas'* and itinerant proletariats' preference for individual ownership, in favor of food production and the hope of winning back these sectors. The fact is, however, given the country's economic conditions, the FSLN had no "choice." The war effort required a subsistence economy.

Jaime Wheelock, the director of MIDINRA, announced in June 1985 that emergency expropriations would take place in Masaya and that expropriated lands would be redistributed in individual holdings.[66] Of the 108,000 *manzanas* actually distributed in that year, 47,000 were given in private holdings to 6,500 dispossessed or land-poor peasant families. The remaining 61,000 *manzanas* were distributed to 5,000 peasants in cooperative holdings. While the balance of land still favored the cooperative sector, a change in policy was evident. In January 1986, the legislature passed a revised agrarian reform law. The new law allowed MIDINRA to expropriate idle or abandoned holdings of under 500 *manzanas* on the Pacific Coast and under 1,000 *manzanas* in the mountainous regions. This did away with the protection of nonproductive medium-holding producers under the 1981 law.[67]

During the next three years, significant reductions in land holdings occurred, not only in the private sector, but in the APP as well.[68] The state no longer had the resources to subsidize inefficient production in any sector. Thirty-three thousand peasants received 550,000 *manzanas* of these lands. While these overall figures are comparable to the figures for 1981–84, the distribution patterns were radically altered. Sixteen thousand *minifundistas* and itinerant proletariats received land in cooperative holdings, while 17,000 of these peasants received land in individual holdings. By the end of 1988, roughly 80,000 peasants had benefited from agrarian reform, capturing 16.5 percent of the total national arable land.

The Sandinistas defeated the counterrevolutionaries militarily in 1989. However, in February 1990 the Sandinistas lost the national elections for the presidency and the legislature to the U.S.-backed conservative coalition, the Union of National Opposition (UNO). A pious perspective, exploiting the benefits of hindsight, would admonish the FSLN for doing too little too late. Certainly, the arrogant delay in responding to the dispossessed and land-poor peasantry's interests undermined Sandinista support among a crucial rural base. This contributed to the decline in food production, which in turn led to a decline in support from an urban base. This negligence on the part of the FSLN had disastrous implications that cannot be ignored. However, the narrative I have recounted here is itself partial. To focus on the Sandinistas' seduction by the paradigm of development in their approach to the peasantry, I have excluded the multifaceted destruction by the U.S.-backed war and minimized the dead to marginal references in this essay. Rather than pious observations, therefore, I will offer more useful ones.

Regardless of the tarnished, strategic motivations behind the 1985 change in agrarian reform policy, this change registered a qualitative transformation in consciousness on the part of the leadership of FSLN, from MIDINRA policymakers in Managua to the technicians in the field. The changes in policy were complicitous with military considerations; nevertheless, a fundamental redefining of the FSLN's national project took place within the span of six years. Given the uneven productivity on APP and cooperative holdings, the Sandinistas were forced to recognize that the most dynamic production of surplus would come from small, private holdings in the hands of the peasantry. Thus, they took a risk in radically redefining their understanding of the *minifundista* and itinerant proletariat economic formation. The dispossessed and land-poor peasantry's desire for individual plots of land was complicitous with the hegemonic construction of private property that predated the revolution. The Sandinistas were adamantly opposed to abetting this "petit bourgeois" consciousness by giving away land in private parcels. Paradoxically, because of the need to maintain agro-export production, the Sandinistas reinforced this bourgeois positionality in the other sectors of the rural population—the medium- and small-holding peasants—with their generous incentive packages. This segment of the rural population benefited enormously during the Sandinista years, whether or not they politically supported the Sandinistas. Unlike the *terratenientes*, these medium- and small-scale producers did not liquidate their farms; they simply were not wealthy enough to move to Miami and reproduce their same standard of living there. Unlike the *minifundistas,* they were in a position to benefit from agricultural incentives and to at least withstand the harmful impact of some policies. By 1986, however, the FSLN fell back from its attempt to impose revolutionary consciousness on the *minifundistas* and itinerant proletariats from above through the cooperative program or state farms. In effect, cooperativization could not bring about revolutionary consciousness because its successful implementation necessitated that a commitment to the revolution, to a particular vision of modernization, and to the national community be in place before the cooperative was even formed. Thus, the *minifundistas* and itinerant proletariats were interpreted as the "prerevolutionary" moment of consciousness in a double sense. As a social formation they were considered to be at a prior stage of development to the higher formation of collective agency implicit in the cooperatives and state farms. Yet, at the same time, the Sandinistas projected an organic predisposition to revolutionary consciousness onto the land-poor peasants. It was then the role of the party to elicit this consciousness from them through their "enlightened" agricultural policy that, after all, corresponded to a "natural" course of development for them anyway.

In the end, the FSLN stopped assuming this paternalistic role and focused on strengthening the *minifundistas* and itinerant proletariats as private producers in the hopes that these sectors would be able to respond to a call for revolutionary transformation from a more secure economic position. CIERA, in a 1986 diagnosis of the Nicaraguan co-operative movement, concludes, "The distribution of land in individual holdings could be preferable for various reasons, in certain situations. Redistribution in this form does not signify an abandonment of the cooperative movement, but rather provides a solid base for future co-operative development."[69] As this passage suggests, of the 17,000 peasant subalterns awarded lands in individual holdings under the third agrarian reform law (1986), 10,000 of them joined some form of cooperative association, either credit and service cooperatives, work cooperatives, or dead furrow cooperatives. This reveals the dialectical nature of the transformation of consciousness that took place. The proclivity toward cooperative associations that was demonstrated by these producers would not necessarily have been as dramatic without the predominance of the cooperative ideology of the previous four years.

In light of these transformations, how do we explain the Sandinista electoral defeat? Behind the agrarian reform policies lay the supposition that ownership of land (in any form) would lead to an identification of the dispossessed and land-poor peasants with the nationalist vision of those implementing the reform. The peasant ownership of land was mediated by the nationalist project. That is to say, the acceptance of land implicated the peasant in a model development for the nation predicated on the transformation — "transcendence" — of his or her subject position. However, these sectors of the rural population were never brought into the decision-making process over this development plan because of the FSLN's basic distrust of these formations. For the first six to seven years of the revolution, the Sandinista national development project was devoutly modernizing — pull the land-poor peasantry into large-scale agro-industry — which may have been progressive in a global context as a response to dependent development, but was regressive in the local context. The *minifundistas,* the itinerant proletariats, and even the cooperativized sectors of the peasantry suffered the negative impacts of Sandinista production policies for many years under this nationalist vision. The increase in land turnovers to private farmers was not accompanied by a parallel increase in participation in development decision making. Receiving land from the government implicated the land-poor peasant in a vision of development, but it did so without granting the peasant any say in the development project. Therefore, when I interviewed peasants who had received private parcels of land after 1987, they were hardly filled with a sense of gratitude. Most were guarded, if not openly hostile, in their attitude toward MIDINRA and the party. There was a common assumption among those I interviewed that they had won the land from a recalcitrant state rather than through "their" revolutionary government, and they felt uncertain about their future relationship to the Sandinistas.

It seems clear that ownership of land was not enough to ensure identification with the FSLN, even on the cooperatives. Meanwhile, the counterrevolution appealed to the conservative elements of peasant consciousness with its emphasis on the church, respect for private property, and, most importantly, autonomy for the producers; or, "no more interventionist state policies that end up hurting more than helping the peasant." This held sway not only with the *minifundistas* and itinerant proletariats, who were in the most precarious economic position, but with members of cooperatives, those who presumably benefited the most from the revolutionary process as the earliest recipients of lands and services. When I visited El Cua, Matagalpa, in the summer of 1989, I interviewed a local UNAG representative and asked him if production on the cooperatives had improved significantly now that the war had ended in that area. "Production is much better," he replied, "now that they [cooperative members] are sleeping at night." I had lived in Nicaragua long enough to know what this meant. "Counterrevolutionaries on *production cooperatives*?" I asked. Amused by my naïveté, he pulled out a list of the twenty-five local cooperatives and pointed to the ten or twelve that had had members in the counterrevolutionary forces.

CONCLUSION

In 1979, Sandinista policymakers correctly assessed Nicaragua's economy as an export-oriented, dependent economy. However, the policy choices made in agriculture by the Sandinistas to remedy this situation reflected a logic of modernization that was implicit in capitalist development. The FSLN's attempt to practice revolutionary socialist development in Nicaragua shared with modernization theory a model of human development that viewed the peasant formation as a precursor to higher levels of political, economic, and social consciousness. Rather than accept these sectors of the peasantry as historically given social formations and basing policy accordingly, the Sandinistas viewed the *minifundista* and itinerant proletariat formations, if not as "backward," then certainly as precursors to the preferred model of economic development. In the Sandinista imaginary of revolutionary development, the peasant subalterns existed in a mythological past tense or future tense, but not in the "real" material sense of the present. Given this, the Sandinistas wrongly assessed the desires and interests of these peasant classes and extended the peasantry two options: cooperativization or proletarianization. These peasants, for the most part, lacked either the interest or possibility to choose either.

Partha Chatterjee has shed some light on the reason for the Sandinista's assumptions about development and the peasantry. In *Nationalist Thought and the Colonial World: A Derivative Discourse?* Chatterjee considers the formation of twentieth-century third world nationalist thought as an explicit response to the organization of the world into "developed" and "underdeveloped" regions. In Chatterjee's analysis, the term *underdevelopment* diagnoses more than an economic condition; it implicitly refers to the epistemic conditions of a country as well. Because the ideology of development colonizes at the level of representation as well as the level of policy, the effects of underdevelopment are not only material, but also social and psychological. Thus, various classes in these countries rally nationalism(s) to remedy their prescribed psychosocial and economic condition of "underdevelopment." Through his analysis of India's struggle for national independence, Chatterjee identifies two prominent strands of third world nationalisms mobilized by third world peoples to subvert the developed/underdeveloped dichotomy. Chatterjee stresses that the two types of nationalism often occur simultaneously, acting at times in consort and at other times antagonistically. *Progressive* bourgeois nationalism, represented in India by Nehru, is eager to displace foreign economic interests but is committed to the project of modernization and asserts the country's ability to "achieve" development in Western terms. *Conservative* mass-based nationalism, represented in India by Gandhi, is eager to displace exploitative imperialist elements *and* their internal allies, but is resistant to modernization and rejects Western development models to greater or lesser degrees. While this abbreviated discussion may oversimplify Chatterjee's position on third world nationalisms, I want to illustrate how he brings out the divisions and tensions in third world nationalisms so often represented in the West as uniform. From Chatterjee's perspective, capitalists and Marxists often share a commitment to a particular mode of development that leads them to similar conclusions and political collusion, though these two groups of nationalists are, in the final analysis, ideologically opposed. For example, capitalists are likely to see recalcitrant mass-based or popular formations, such as the dispossessed or land-poor peasantry, as "backward elements," while Marxists may view them as "precapitalist" or, as in the case of the Sandinistas, as "prerevolutionary," representing an "incomplete" process of proletarianization.[70] It then becomes the mission of classical modernization theory and socialist revolutionary development to complete this process and bring these elements into productive history by effecting a transformation of consciousness from the top down.

The case of the Sandinista nationalist project as exemplified by agricultural policy fits within Chatterjee's analysis of third world nationalisms. While committed to a mass-based liberation movement on the one hand, the FSLN was also committed to a large-scale industrialized agro-export economy as the means of overcoming Nicaragua's economic dependence on the United States. These two visions for the nation — mass-based liberation and further industrialization — did not always coincide. Chatterjee's model of heterogeneous and contradictory nationalist visions occurring in the same geographical space usefully frames the tensions the Sandinistas encountered in their model of revolutionary development in agriculture. In their conceptualization and implementation of agricultural policy, the Sandinistas encountered resistance not only from the landed elites, but often from the social group they intended to benefit, the land-poor peasantry. Chatterjee's theorization extracts us from the ideological gridlock in which capitalist development and revolutionary socialist development are viewed as diametrically opposed phenomena, allowing us to locate the complicity between the two in their commitment to a particular model of human development. In his analysis of India, Chatterjee also helps us to understand how the Sandinistas, as progressive nationalists with obvious Marxist-Leninist theoretical bases, could have enjoyed so much mass-based support among the peasantry at the beginning of the revolution only to have lost this support by as early as 1985. The Sandinistas' resistance to a significant redistribution of land among the peasant classes was due to their belief in a classic developmental paradigm. The FSLN identified the itinerant proletariat and *minifundista* formations with preproletariat or precollective consciousness, and interpreted their desires for land as petit bourgeois aspirations toward private property. The Sandinistas hoped to leapfrog over these formations through an acceleration of proletarianization on state farms or collectivization on cooperatives. Had the Sandinistas been truer to their materialist training in their analysis, then perhaps they would have resisted grafting this ideologically determined developmental narrative onto peasant consciousness and instead based their analysis on the peasants as constituting part of the present tense of the nation.

In the interest of the next revolutionary attempt at improving the quality of life of rural communities, I believe it necessary to critique the paternalistic and narrowly modernistic attitude toward the peasantry so often assumed by revolutionary states under the guise of benevolent efforts toward the development of the peasants into productive members of a nation. This benevolent development can prove deadly to everyone involved. James C. Scott, who studies everyday forms of resistance among the peasantry, has suggested for both conventional and socialist development schemes that "The radical solution [to development] . . . raises as many problems as it solves. Only revolutionary victory and the structural change it brings, they argue, can engender true participation and economic justice. Here the history of socialist revolutions is not encouraging. In most cases such revolutions have brought to power regimes that are, if anything, more successful in extracting resources from their subjects and regimenting their lives." And furthermore: "Under state socialism . . . all the vital decisions about commodity prices, the prices of agricultural inputs, credits, cropping patterns, and — under collectivization — the working day, and the wage, are direct matters of state policy. Conflicts that might have been seen as private sector matters, with the state not directly implicated, become, under state socialism, direct clashes with the state. The peasant meets the state as employer, buyer, supplier, money lender, foreman, paymaster, and tax collector. . . . Though it may occasionally improve his or her welfare, the aim of state socialism is invariably to reduce the autonomy of a strata previously classified as petite bourgeoisie. The loss of autonomy by itself has been a source of ferocious resistance."[71]

I have tried to document the reasons for and methods of resistance among the peasantry to the FSLN's revolutionary development. As Scott suggests, the FSLN's development model intervened in every aspect of the *minifundistas'* and itinerant proletariats' lives without ever granting these sectors of the peasantry the political means for negotiating the terms of this intervention. The land-poor peasantry fell out of the revolutionary government's corporativist loop. Representatives of the pro-Sandinista UNAG saw their job as that of defending the rights of the medium- and small-scale producer, and given how much more powerful these sectors are today than in 1979, they did so quite successfully. The Sandinista ATC, while more sympathetic with the plight of the land-poor peasants, were primarily concerned with labor conditions on state and private farms. In ten years the Sandinistas never established an equivalent organization to represent the rights and interests of the *minifundistas* and itinerant proletariats within the party. Consequently, the dispossessed and land-poor peasants had no way of lobbying the Sandinistas from the inside. Of course, this oversight was symptomatic of the party's fundamental disbelief in the consciousness of these two sectors as viable or rational forms of revolutionary consciousness.

The Sandinistas were working with idealized revolutionary subjects in agriculture. There was "the patriotic private producer," "the state farm worker," and "the cooperative member." The Sandinistas believed that the state, in one way or another, could successfully direct all these idealized citizen-subjects into technified, rationalized production units. The dispossessed and land-poor peasants were outside or prior to this evolutionary chain of rationalized and enlightened consciousness. Nothing illustrates this better than the Sandinistas' failure to create a political organization to directly represent peasant interests to the party. The Sandinistas believed that land in the hands of the land-poor peasants would lead to irrational production. They believed the peasantry would revert to production for consumption with little or no surplus, and that this would lead to a precipitous drop in the production of export crops. Ultimately, they feared that this type of production would escape the control of the state and their national plan of modernization. I am not suggesting that the Sandinistas should have abandoned all efforts at production for export and modernization in favor of some utopian pastoral vision. However, the Sandinistas could have negotiated between their own progressive, vanguard nationalist vision and the peasants' "conservative," but not necessarily antirevolutionary, massed-based nationalist vision of economic development. If the Sandinistas had not considered the peasant formation as regressive, they might have been able to direct political and economic resources toward incorporating this level of peasant production into a revolutionary vision of national development early on in the process. Perhaps then the startling revolutionary vision of the Sandinistas that emerged in 1979 would have been more viable.

NOTES

1. Of course, this is a reformulation of the work of early classical economists such as David Ricardo, Adam Smith, and Jean-Baptiste Say.
2. Arturo Escobar, "Imagining a Post-Development Era? Critical Thought, Development and Social Movements," *Social Text* 31–32 (1992): 25.
3. For a more extensive critique of the ideology of development as an epistemological strategy for managing the crisis of colonialism, see María Josefina Saldaña, "The Discourse of Development and Narratives of Resistance" (Ph.D. diss., Stanford University, 1993). Also, Arturo Escobar, "Power and Visibility: The Invention of the Third World" (Ph.D. diss., University of California, Berke-

ley, 1987). James Ferguson's *The Anti-Politics Machine* (Cambridge: Cambridge University Press, 1990), provides an excellent Foucauldian analysis of the institutionalization of "development" as a strategy for managing poverty in the African nation of Lesotho. Ferguson traces the ways in which international development agencies and local state bureaucracies invent a "traditional peasant class" in Lesotho and then proceed to spin out plan after plan for the modernization of an agricultural people. Meanwhile, these "agricultural people" lost their land to South Africa in the very processes of modernization and colonization in the past century and have functioned as an international proletariat for five generations, providing domestic labor and seasonal labor in the mines for South Africa. Hence, these development agencies and local state bureaucracies appear to be "doing something" about poverty with their projects for improving the productivity of livestock or for the privatization of reduced tribal lands while remaining resolutely "antipolitical" in their ahistorical interpretation of poverty and its possible solutions.

4. W. W. Rostow, *Stages of Growth: A Non-Communist Manifesto* (Cambridge: Cambridge University Press, 1960).

5. Louis Althusser, *Lenin and Philosophy and Other Essays*, trans. Ben Brewster (New York: Monthly Review Press, 1971), 161.

6. Jorge G. Castañeda, *Utopia Unarmed: The Latin American Left after the Cold War* (New York: Vintage, 1993).

7. A *manzana* equals 1.75 acres.

8. These relatively wealthy peasants are not the landed elites. Those owning more than 500 *manzanas* of land — the landed elites or *terratenientes* — made up only 2 percent of the EAP and held 36.2 percent of the arable land in 1978. See Carlos Vilas, *The Sandinista Revolution* (New York: Monthly Review Press, 1986), 66, and Centro de Investigacion y Estudios de la Reforma Agraria (CIERA), *Cifas y Referencias Documentales* (Managua: CIERA, 1989).

9. Vilas, *The Sandinista Revolution*, 66.

10. Between 1952 and 1978, there was a 14 percent decrease in the number of land holdings consisting of 1 to 99.9 *manzanas,* as these lands were taken over by agricultural bourgeoisie. The number of *minifundistas* decreased by half, with the dispossessed either finding permanent employment or, more often, joining the ranks of the underemployed. This peasant displacement took place predominantly along the Pacific Coast, in the departments of Chinandega, Leon, Managua, and Masaya, where cotton production flourished. See Rose J. Spalding, ed., *The Political Economy of Revolutionary Nicaragua* (Boston: Allen and Unwin, 1987), 19– 20.

11. Vilas, *The Sandinista Revolution*, 63–69.

12. While realistically one-fifth of the nation's arable land might have been more than the newly organized government could effectively administer, MIDINRA had expected more. Sandinista leaders shared the popular belief that Somoza and his associates owned half of all the nation's resources. Until October 1979, when investigators finished compiling estimates of Somocista holdings, FSLN leaders in MIDINRA believed the state possessed 60 percent of the

arable land. See Joseph Collins, *What Difference Can a Revolution Make?* (New York: Grove Press, 1986), 39. These estimates showed that the state sector controlled less than 20 percent of the land in cotton and coffee production; less than 10 percent of the land in livestock production; and only had significant control (40 percent) of the land in sugar and rice production. See Forrest D. Colburn, *Post-Revolutionary Nicaragua* (Berkeley: University of California Press, 1986), 42. Clearly, the state sector had considerably less direct control over agricultural production in general and export production in particular than the FSLN had hoped. This miscalculation increased the political clout of an already powerful sector — the landed elites and medium-holding private producers — in the eyes of the FSLN.

13. Ministerio de Planificacion Nacional (MIPLAN), *Programa de Reactivacion Economica en Benefacio del Pueblo* (Managua: MIPLAN, 1980), 17.

14. Collins, *What Difference,* 45.

15. Bill Gibson, "Structural Overview of the Nicaraguan Economy," in *The Political Economy of Revolutionary Nicaragua,* ed. Rose J. Spalding (Boston: Allen and Unwin, 1987), 30.

16. Here I am borrowing from James Scott's concept of "everyday resistance," coined in his analysis of local class relations in the Malaysian village of Sedaka. See James C. Scott, *Weapons of the Weak: Everyday Forms of Peasant Resistance* (New Haven: Yale University Press, 1985).

17. Central American Historical Institute (CAHI), "Agrarian Reform Undergoes Changes in Nicaragua," *Update* 5, no. 4 (1986): 2.

18. David F. Ruccio, "The State and Planning in Nicaragua," in *The Political Economy of Revolutionary Nicaragua,* ed. Rose J. Spalding (Boston: Allen and Unwin, 1987), 67.

19. Collins, *What Difference,* 60.

20. Valpy Fitzgerald, "National Economy in 1985: Transition in Progress," unpublished mimeograph, 1985, 1. Adding to the pressure of maintaining the production of foreign exchange were the immediate costs of reconstructing the agricultural and industrial infrastructure. Material destruction caused by the insurrection was estimated at U.S. $400 million. This figure, not including production losses or losses from decapitalization, equaled more than half of an average year's export earnings under Somoza. See Instituto Historico Centro-Americo (IHCA), "The Nicaraguan Peasantry Gives New Direction to Agrarian Reform," *Envio* 4, no. 51 (1985): 6c.

21. MIPLAN, *Programa de Reactivacion Economica,* 13.

22. Ruccio, "The State," 76.

23. John Weeks, "The Mixed Economy in Nicaragua," in *The Political Economy of Revolutionary Nicaragua,* ed. Rose J. Spalding (Boston: Allen and Unwin, 1987). The state, in fact, provided a cushy incentive package for private producers: 80 to 100 percent financing of working capital for the production of export crops, subsidized inputs, and fixed prices for the purchase of export crops, which were generally declining in value on the world market. Between January 1980 and August 1981, 52 percent of foreign exchange was redistrib-

uted to the private sector for reinvestment (IHCA, "The Right of the Poor to Defend Their Revolution," *Envio* 4, no. 36 [1984]: 19). Nevertheless, the *state* was now mediating all these transactions, and, in effect, large-scale production suffered a decline in political weight vis-à-vis medium- and small-scale agricultural production. For example, under Somoza large-scale agro-production had received 90 percent of all credit extended; with the democratization of credit under the Sandinistas, large-scale producers were receiving only 29 percent of the credit extended by 1985. See Spalding, *The Political Economy,* 114. The increase in credit extended, in cordobas, was artificially maintained through the printing of money, which in turn led to spiraling inflation. Ironically, guaranteed financing of production costs negatively affected the productivity of state and large-scale production. In an economic crisis, private enterprise will use credit as a means of rationalizing production, forcing unprofitable businesses into liquidations, mergers, or bankruptcies. The state financial institutions never performed this regulatory role because of political considerations, hence nonproductivity escaped reprisals. See ibid., 53.

24. Weeks, "Mixed Economy," 49.

25. Ibid., 60.

26. Another problem with Weeks's analysis is his failure to differentiate between sectors of the bourgeoisie. His analysis holds true for large-scale producers (with few exceptions), and some medium-scale producers. However, over the course of ten years, medium- and small-holding peasant producers proved to be the most consistently productive, taking full advantage of the benefits extended by the Sandinistas. Even according to Weeks's construction of nationalist identity, these producers prove to be quite "patriotic."

27. IHCA, "The Nicaraguan Peasantry," 8c.

28. Laura Enriquez and Rose J. Spalding, "Banking Systems and Revolutionary Change," in *The Political Economy of Revolutionary Nicaragua,* ed. Rose J. Spalding (Boston: Allen and Unwin, 1987), 113.

29. Carmen D. Deere and Peter Marchetti, "The Worker-Peasant Alliance in the First Year of the Nicaraguan Agrarian Reform," *Latin American Research Review* 8, no. 3 (1981): 57.

30. Collins, *What Difference,* 56. For a thorough critique of the Sandinista credit policy, see Enriquez and Spalding, "Banking Systems." Also see Collins, *What Difference,* chap. 6.

31. Colburn, *Post-Revolutionary Nicaragua,* 185.

32. By 1985, there were only 66,000 recipients of the rural credit program. Stricter state regulations on credit, fear of indebtedness, inaccessibility of banking facilities, and inability to deal with bank bureaucracy combined to discourage eligible *minifundistas* — and even many small-holding producers — from attaining loans (Enriquez and Spalding, "Banking Systems," 118).

33. Ibid., 73.

34. For a thorough critique of the state's pricing policies, see María Veronica Frenkel, "The Evolution of Food and Agricultural Policies during Economic Crisis and War," in *Nicaragua: Profiles of the Revolutionary Public Sector,* ed.

Michael E. Conroy (Boulder, CO: Westview Press, 1987), 211–213. For a critique of the state's ability to handle the marketing of goods see Alfred H. Saulniers, "State Trading Organization in Expansion," also in Conroy, *Nicaragua*.

35. Frenkel, "The Evolution of Food and Agricultural Policies," 211–212.

36. IHCA, "The Nicaraguan Peasantry," 7c.

37. Consejo de Estado, *1979–1984 Principales Leyes Aprobadas por el Gobierno de Reconstruccion Nacional* (Managua: Consejo de Estado, 1985), 186.

38. MIPLAN, *Programa Economico de Austeridad y Eficiencia* (Managua: MIPLAN, 1981), 121.

39. Collins, *What Difference*, 45.

40. By the 1983–84 crop cycle, domestic production had surpassed its prerevolutionary average of *manzanas* planted; in the same crop cycle, the export sector had not yet recuperated its prerevolutionary average. See Gibson, "Overview," 39. The 1979–83 period was the most favorable for production in Nicaragua because the counterrevolutionary war was not yet fully underway. While we cannot attribute the drop in export production exclusively to ill will, it was clear early on that the large-scale agro-exporters were recalcitrant.

41. Consejo de Estado, *1979–1984*, 187.

42. The only figures that I have been able to find in my research for the evolution of land tenure between 1979 and 1983 are in Collins, *What Difference*, who gives figures for 1980 (271). He cites MIDINRA as his source, but does not give the name of the publication. Collins's figures place state holdings at 18 percent for 1980. Conflicting estimates of state holdings during this period exist in the literature on Nicaragua. However, I will continue to use 20 percent as a rough estimate.

43. Ibid.

44. Consejo de Estado, *1979–1984*, 189.

45. A dead furrow cooperative is a cooperative in which members own a farm collectively, but they divide the farm into individualized plots separated by dead furrows. This allows them to farm individually but to do some of the work collectively, especially work involving large capital goods such as tractors and irrigation systems.

46. IHCA, "The Nicaraguan Peasantry," 11c.

47. One way of gauging APP productivity is to examine its credit history. Between 1981 and 1984, the APP share of agricultural credit grew from 34 percent to 41 percent, even though the share of land under its control decreased from 20 percent to 19.2 percent in that same period. Meanwhile, credit recuperation rates for the APP had only reached 60 percent by 1984. See Enriquez and Spalding, "Banking Systems," 120–121. Continued growth in credit to the APP is partially explained by MIDINRA's continuing investment in capital-intensive, long-term agro-industry. During this period of regional recession, Nicaragua was the only Central American country with growth in investment. See ibid., 138. Several external and internal factors, however, explain the drop in productivity that led to low profits on the APP farms. Nicaragua experienced a general decline in its terms of trade during this period. The country suffered a

severe drought in May 1982, affecting production. State farms became the prime targets of the escalating counterrevolutionary war. Finally, state farms experienced a decline in both the number of hours worked and productivity of labor. In some sectors of agriculture, norms for labor productivity were reduced between 25 and 40 percent. The reduction of labor productivity was not restricted to the working class: professionals and technicians lacked the expertise to effectively do their jobs. See ibid., 77, 137.

48. Carmen D. Deere, "Agrarian Reform in the Transition," in *Transition and Development,* ed. Richard Fagen, Carmen D. Deere, and Jose L. Coraggio (New York: Monthly Review Press, 1986), 127.

49. I exclude the resettled communities in regions I and VI from my discussion of cooperatives because of the extraordinary circumstances surrounding their formation. While these communities were resettled as cooperatives by force, this was strictly a military decision that fell outside the purview of MIDINRA and the agrarian reform law.

50. Deere, "Agrarian Reform," 128.

51. IHCA, "The Nicaraguan Peasantry," 10c.

52. Ibid.

53. CIERA, "Propuesta de Trabajo para un Diagnostico de la Situacion del Mouimiento Coperativo," unpublished mimeograph, 1986, 6.

54. Ibid., 3–7.

55. IHCA, "The Nicaraguan Peasantry," 10c.

56. By 1984, the defense effort required between 70,000 and 100,000 people-in-arms, an effort the permanent army alone could not meet. See Peter Utting, "Domestic Supply and Food Shortages," in *The Political Economy of Revolutionary Nicaragua,* ed. Rose J. Spalding (Boston: Allen and Unwin, 1987), 136. Men and women from cooperatives and state farms were mobilized into battalions to fight the war. If the prospect of possible counterrevolutionary attack did not sufficiently discourage peasants from joining a cooperative, the probability of military recruitment did.

57. In their assessment of the first five years of agrarian reform, the IHCA claims that by the end of 1984, 22 percent, or one-fifth, of the total peasant families had received lands through cooperativization (IHCA, "The Nicaraguan Peasantry," 12c). I believe this is a miscalculation that underestimated demand for land and overestimated Sandinista efficacy in meeting that demand. In their calculations, the IHCA adheres to a rigid definition of peasant identity, maintaining a distinction between the *minifundistas* as "true peasants" and the dispossessed itinerant proletariat as "true proletariat." However, it is necessary to recognize the itinerant proletariat as dispossessed *peasantry* in order to fully comprehend the inordinate pressure for land.

58. CIERA, "Propuesta," 6.

59. Conroy, *Nicaragua,* 211.

60. Collins, *What Difference,* 185, 201.

61. Utting, "Domestic Supply," 134–135.

62. CIERA, *Cifras,* 89, 91, 93.

63. Quoted in CIERA, "Propuesta," coversheet.

64. CAHI, "Agrarian Reform," 4.

65. CAHI, "Masaya Peasants Prompt Land Expropriations," *Update* 4, no. 23 (1985): 3. For a complete analysis of the Masaya situation, see IHCA, "The Nicaraguan Peasantry," 51.

66. CAHI, "Masaya," 1.

67. CAHI, "Reactions to Agrarian Reform Modifications in Nicaragua," *Update* 5, no. 20 (1986): 1–2.

68. Between 1984 and 1988, the percentage of national arable land in holdings exceeding 500 *manzanas* decreased from 13 to 6.4 percent; in holdings between 50 and 500 *manzanas,* from 43 to 26.4 percent; in state holdings, from 19 to 11.4 percent. See CIERA, *Cifras,* 39.

69. CIERA, "Propuesta," 4.

70. See Partha Chatterjee, *Nationalist Thought and the Colonial World: A Derivative Discourse?* (London: Zed Books, 1986).

71. James C. Scott, "Everyday Forms of Resistance," in *Everyday Forms of Peasant Resistance,* ed. Forrest D. Colburn (London: M. E. Sharpe, 1989), 3, 15.

DAVID LLOYD

Nationalisms against the State

In the large and still expanding corpus of theoretical and historical work on nationalism, a singular contradiction is so persistently apparent that it may be regarded as constitutive of the discourse. On the one hand, as writers like Ernest Gellner and Benedict Anderson have amply shown, nationalism is inconceivable except as a product of modernity. For Gellner, that modernity is defined in terms of what can be succinctly termed the new industrial state, and nationalism itself is "inherent in a set of social conditions; and those conditions . . . are the conditions of our time."[1] For Anderson, the "imagined community" of the nation is predicated upon the emergence of print capitalism and concomitant notions of "homogeneous empty time" that furnish the formal space of the novel and the newspaper, cultural forms in which the abstract simultaneity of the nation can be imagined.[2] For John Breuilly, a less well-known but, to my mind, equally valuable analyst of nationalism, the emphasis falls on the politically transformative nature of national mobilization.[3] At the same time, and often in the same works that acknowledge its modernity, nationalism is seen as the vehicle or the stimulus for the resurgence of atavistic or premodern feelings and practices, at best as a nostalgic hankering after irretrievable and probably figmentary modes of sociality, a futile protest against inevitable cultural modernity or economic transnationality. As Eric Hobsbawm puts it, "the characteristic nationalist movements of the late twentieth century are essentially negative, or rather divisive. . . . [They are mostly] rejections of modern modes of political organization, both national and supranational. Time and again they seem to be reactions of weakness and fear, attempts to erect barricades to keep at bay the forces of the modern world. . . ."[4] Where Hobsbawm sees this as characteristic of contemporary nationalisms in the moment of their twilight, Tom Nairn, in a generally more sympathetic account, sees the tension between modernity and premodernity as a permanent structural feature of this "modern Janus."[5]

In the present moment, the disintegration of the former Soviet Union and of Yugoslavia has intensified the bad press that nationalism receives in liberal circles, usually in a simplified form of Hobsbawm's contentions. "Negative" and "divisive," nationalism inevitably gravitates from separatism to "ethnic cleansing," driven by economic insecurity and the resurgence of irrational but immemorial hatreds. Focusing as it may, now, on the undeniably painful events in some parts of Eastern Europe and Central Asia, current Western antinationalism has deeper historical roots and remains ideologically and formally continuous with traditional metropolitan antagonism toward anticolonial movements in the third world. Indeed, emphasis on the *resurgence* of European and Islamic nationalisms in the former second world conveniently replicates the widely held idea that nationalism itself involves a resurgence of atavistic forces that civilization, in the form of the centralized state, has struggled to expunge or contain. The notion of the *return* of intertribal violence, which structures so much of contemporary reportage as it has structured the discourse on newly independent Africa, ignores the role of the state in restructuring and producing ethnic or tribal antagonism, as Frantz Fanon long ago perceived.[6] More importantly, it substantially dehistoricizes nationalism in its multiple varieties and contexts, reducing its complexities to the binary and recurrent form of atavism versus modernity. Currently hegemonic accounts of nationalism in the West are locked into a singular narrative of modernity that is able neither to do historical justice to the complex articulation of nationalist struggles with other social movements or, consequently, to envisage the radical moment in nationalisms that, globally, are not resurgent but continuous, not fixated, but in transformation.[7]

The mutually conditioning relation between nationalism and modernity is generally located in the exigencies of political economy in the fullest understanding of that term. It is not only that nationalisms generally seek to control the deterritorializing flows of capitalist economies, whether externally imposed or internally emergent, but that they seek to do so in large part through the politicization of a population in quite specific ways. Nationalism in this sense is, as Gellner has argued, inseparable from the nation-*state* that constitutes its end: "Not only is our definition of nationalism parasitic on a prior and assumed definition of the state: it also seems to be the case that nationalism emerges only in milieux in which the existence of the state is very much taken for granted."[8] Far from being a defense of traditional modes of social organization, nationalist mobilization, according to such arguments, effects the transformation of traditional "moral economies," to borrow E. P. Thompson's term, into modern political economies regulated by the state.[9] Simultaneously, the effect of this transformation is to produce the modern citizen-subject, the "interchangeable" individual[10] of political economy, and the social institutions — law, schooling, police — that permit the integration of any nation into the world economic system.

For Gellner, the decisive concept is industrialization and the nation-state its unavoidable manifestation.[11] The related term for Nairn is "development," nationalism being seen as the product of an uneven interaction between developed and underdeveloped societies and as the means by which the underdeveloped seek to "make up" the difference and establish economic and political equilibrium.[12] Nationalism is accordingly a transitional vehicle or detour on the way to the cosmopolitanism or socialism that is the proper end of history.

It is as a consequence of nationalism's historically transitional status in such views that its structure is marked by ambivalence, its modernity constantly intertwined with atavism. It is interesting to follow Nairn's argument here: In the absence of the institutions of modernity, the nationalist intelligentsia of a peripheral or underdeveloped region is obliged to mobilize the populace through appeal to cultural or ethnic identity posed as against modernity:

All that there *was* was the people and peculiarities of the region: its inherited *ethnos,* speech, folklore, skin-colour, and so on. Nationalism works through *differentiae* like those because it has to. It is not necessarily democratic in outlook, but it *is* invariably populist. People are what it has to go on: in the archetypal situation of the really poor or "under-developed" territory, it may be more or less all that nationalists have going for them. For kindred reasons, it has to function through highly rhetorical forms, through a sentimental culture sufficiently accessible to the lower strata now being called into battle. This is why a romantic culture quite remote from Enlightenment rationalism always went hand in hand with the spread of nationalism. The new middle-class intelligentsia of nationalism had to invite the masses into history; and the invitation had to be written in a language they understood.[13]

We will momentarily pass over the numerous questions begged by this passage in order to stress that its logic is that the progressive moment of nationalism is achieved *"by a certain sort of regression"*:[14] "In mobilizing its past in order to leap forward across this threshold, a society is like a man who has to call on all his inherited and (up to this point) largely unconscious powers to confront some inescapable challenge."[15] In this light, "the emergence of irrationality in modern history"[16] is virtually predictable, the return of an already partially unleashed repressed.

Nairn's argument is virtually impossible to reconcile with Gellner's equally forceful contention that, in keeping with its relatively recent and historically contingent emergence, "nationalism does not have any very deep roots in the human psyche."[17] This incompatibility highlights certain problematic passages in these "modernist" accounts of nationalism that will force us to rethink their historical foundations. Either argument is consistent with the well-known "romanticism" of nationalism. For it is true that it frequently relies on "invented traditions," cultural phenomena that can scarcely indeed be assumed to have "deep roots" in the psyches of the intellectuals who produce them even where they are derived from popular cultural resources. Nonetheless we can read Nairn's argument as attending to a forceful "atavism effect" in nationalism that testifies to the psychic power of its cultural forms *at some level*. The appearance of a contradiction between these positions derives from the metaphorical slippage by which what is "psychically *deep*" is identified with what is historically anterior. But this is no occasional slippage: it is in fact intrinsic to the general historical form of the argument about modernity within which these accounts of nationalism take shape.

Let us pass to the historiographic critique by way of remarking that in neither of these accounts nor, for example, Hobsbawm's, is adequate attention paid to the psychic impact of domination in the cultural and political dynamic through which the emergence and formation of nationalist movements takes place. Yet if, as is generally acknowledged, and often regretted, what nationalism achieves is a *vertical* integration based on political solidarity against a common enemy rather than a horizontal integration based on class antagonisms, it must equally be acknowledged that such solidarity is not based merely in ideological manipulation of the masses but to some extent at least in the common experience of domination. (I speak here, of course, of insurgent nationalisms rather than those of the metropolitan powers for which vertical integration is achieved in an inverse relation to the exercise of domination.)[18]

The key term here is *racism,* alluded to so fleetingly in Nairn's list of cultural items as "skin-colour," and it is instructive to turn to Fanon's unsurpassed analyses of the dynamic of nationalism and of the relationship between bourgeois intellectuals and the masses in "Racism and Culture" and *The Wretched of the Earth*. For Fanon, the "insufficiency" of the colonized intellectual or migrant worker is not so much the product of the underdevelopment of "his" preindustrial society of origins as of the racism by which its systematic underdevelopment is legitimated and reproduced. The phenomenology of racism, experienced as an absolute limit to the modernizing narrative of assimilation, opens the way to a systematic comprehension of relations of domination.[19] At the same time, it leads to that "plunge into the past" that is, for Fanon, the beginning of nationalism in the emerging intellectual's turn back to "his" own culture to find another reflection, another human image. If that turn to the cultural past is in a strict sense fetishistic, and strictly because it involves the desire for an image of wholeness to set against the mutilating experience of deracination and alienation, it is so not merely on account of the subjective sources of the desire. It is in the first place necessarily fetishistic because of what Fanon terms the "sclerotization" of the colonized culture, the paralysis of a society whose previous, relatively autonomous paths of transformation have been blocked by colonialism. What the dispossessed intellectual turns to is fixed, archival, and available for fetishistic recovery only in part because of the intellectual's own relation to it; in large part, it is because that culture no longer exists except as an object of archaeological recovery. It is, indeed, strictly speaking "fetishistic" in involving the disavowal of the intellectual's cultural mutilation by way of fixation on an apparent prior wholeness. But what this means is not that the colonized people itself is paralyzed in an unchanging prehistory of modernity, but rather that the people has moved on, is elsewhere. Damaged and dominated it may be, denied or unwilling to have access to the modernity of the colonial state, the people, Fanon constantly insists, nonetheless inhabits an irreducibly contemporary space. In this space, and out of the resources of a hybrid, "unevenly developed" culture that is neither traditional nor modern but contemporary, the means of resistance are constantly being invented.[20] It is to the contemporaneity of the people that the trajectory of the committed intellectual, often unwittingly, tends, passing beyond the fetishism that is an inevitable moment of emergent nationalism and yet the specular double of the colonialist's denomination of the colonized as "the people without history." What is at stake is not so much the attempt "to invite the masses into history"[21] as the form in which that is done. What for Fanon distinguishes the "sterile formalism"[22] of bourgeois nationalism from the inventiveness of popular democratic movements is the former's inability to recognize the contemporaneity of the people, its desire to refine them into modernity. For Fanon, that formalism is bound up with the reproduction of European state forms by the new nation state. Indeed, his concluding call to the "Third World" is: "let us not pay tribute to Europe by creating states, institutions, and societies which draw their inspiration from her."[23]

What is common to most Western accounts of nationalism, then, is that, unlike Fanon, they take its "bourgeois" forms at their word, so to speak. That is, even where the tenor of the argument may be generally antagonistic to nationalism as a political form, what remains historiographically of that form is its self-representation as superseding or subordinating other social movements. In this, historians effectively fail to challenge the fundamental philosophy of universal history that underwrites nationalism's inscription in modernity: the particularism of its contents, potentially in contradiction with the universalism of modernity, is subsumed in the *formal* congruence between its own narratives of identity, directed at one people, and the narrative of identity that universal history represents for humanity in general. This potential terminus of nationalism in the cosmopolitanism of nations was certainly not lost on nineteenth-century European nationalists like Giuseppe Mazzini or Thomas Osborne Davis, even if it is more systematically expressed by Ernest Gellner.

Granting, if only implicitly, the assumption that nationalism supersedes or subordinates other modes of social organization — both those that are then termed "protonationalist," like peasant movements, and those that are seen as counternationalist, like feminism or Marxism — historians misunderstand the continuing dynamic by which nationalism is formed in articulation or conjuncture with other social movements. We will return to that dynamic later, pausing here to note the double form in which nationalism's modernity is posed against the modes it supposedly supersedes. There is on the one hand the question of ends: Where the nation-state is assumed as the proper end of historical processes, only one line of development can be seen as the properly historical in history. Accordingly, movements whose struggles chronologically precede or coincide with nationalism, but are not identical or entirely isomorphic with it, can only be seen as *proto*nationalist. In this, Hobsbawm's account of "popular proto-nationalism"[24] accords with works written more or less from within particular nationalist perspectives such as Renato Constantino's *The Past Discovered,* on Philippine history, or Tom Garvin's *The Evolution of Irish Nationalist Politics.* For each, popular movements are absorbed into the historically progressive trajectory of nationalism so that what is significant in them is the set of traits that lend themselves to national ends. Other traits, which may indeed be incompatible with nationalism, such as modes of organization and communication and certain kinds of spiritualism, are relegated to the residual space of historical contingency. Here they constitute the non-sense, the irrepresentable of historiography. On the other hand, this relegation writes such popular movements out of history and into the mythopoeic space of arrested development and fixity vis-à-vis the forward movement of nationalism itself. It is, then, to the resources of this mythopoeic space that national culture is held to recur in its atavistic moments, while its historical modernity finds expression in the state form. The state is both the proper end of historical process and the eternal antagonist of contingency and myth.

As the form and end of history, the nation-state in effect regulates what counts as history and gives the law of historical verisimilitude that decides between the contingent and the significant. This law, and its foundational relation to a universal history predicated on ends and on the supercession of a prior, contingent history, is spelt out in Kant's celebrated essay "Idea of a Universal History on a Cosmo-political Plan": "the very same course of incidents, which taken separately and individually would have seemed perplexed, incoherent, and lawless, yet viewed in their connexion and as the actions of the human *species* and not of independent beings, never fail to discover a steady and continuous though slow development of certain great dispositions of our nature."[25] Universal history on these assumptions, which are curiously Aristotelian in their narratology, breaks down an age-old distinction between history, which is the chronicle of all that is proven possible merely by happening (the contingent), and the poetic, which is the narrative of what seems probable according to ends (the verisimilar). Universal history is, in the strict sense of the Third Critique, *aesthetic* not only in this rotation from the axis of possibility to that of verisimilitude, from metonymy to metaphor, but more fundamentally in its absolute relation to ends, that through which the manifold finds form. The historical judgment of nationalism is accordingly always also an aesthetic one, predicated on the adequacy of any given nationalism to the state form that is the institutional embodiment of the end of humanity. But what that implies is that the negative judgment of nationalism, predicated on those aspects of it that tend toward particularity rather than universality ("negative," "divisive"), must be seen not only in terms of the temporal schema, "atavism versus modernity," that is most apparent, but also in terms of a topology in which the space of the probable is divided from contingency. On the continuum of judgments, from the most negative to the most positive, nationalism is either absorbed by the irrationality of its particularity, and irredeemably antagonistic to the normative universality of the center, or divided between a rational, centripetal core, which finds expression in the state, and an irrational, centrifugal periphery in which there is a constant struggle between destruction and reconstruction. It is clear enough how this topology both articulates a global disposition of power, within which the nationalisms of the center evidently are never in question, and maps onto the temporal schema "atavism/modernity" by which that disposition gains its legitimating self-evidence (verisimilitude). The discourse on nationalism, in other words, is saturated with the entwined logics of development and of core-periphery analysis that are at present globally hegemonic.

Antonio Gramsci's brief but invaluable notes on this relation between the form of dominant history ("the history of the ruling classes") and that of state formation are now well known on account of the impetus they have given to the work of "subaltern historiography" within which some of the most valuable recent critical discussion of nationalism has been conducted.[26] Gramsci still retains, however, the view that the history of the subaltern classes is only contingently "episodic and fragmentary" and will achieve the form of major historiography at the point when those classes, in their turn, capture the state. He is still working within the model of a universal history that regulates the history of individual national blocks. It is rather to Walter Benjamin that we must turn for the theoretical suggestions on which an alternative materialist history of nationalism in its relation to other social movements might be based. In a particularly luminous moment of the "Theses on the Philosophy of History," Benjamin remarks on the relation between what he terms "historicism," which "rightly culminates in universal history"[27] and by which we may understand that narrative of modernity that is always on the side of the victors, and the "conception of progress" that informs social democratic theory and practice.[28] In this end-directed political historicism, Benjamin sees simultaneously the displacement of a more radical socialist tradition of looking always to the past, with a redemptive eye on the succession of defeats and setbacks that litter its passage to the present. Its rallying cry, erased by social democracy, is "Remember Blanqui!"[29]

Those of us who come from "postcolonial" locations are probably all too familiar with the accusation that we are overly obsessed with the past. But in these reflections of Benjamin's, though they can easily be misread, there is no space for the nostalgia of which we may be accused. What he is exploring is the meaning of a materialist historiography that "brushes history against the grain,"[30] its interest in an understanding of social movements whose potential and formative effects have not been exhausted simply because they were not victorious. The "fragmentary and episodic" form of their narratives becomes, in this reading, not a symptom of failure to totalize, but the sign of a possibly intrinsic resistance to totalization: "They have retroactive force and will constantly call in question every victory, past and present, of the rulers."[31] From the perspective of a modernist historiography, these are movements whose lines of force are interrupted, inconsequential, peripheral to the main line of historical development. They are the superseded and overlooked residues of history and, in that sense, do not even offer fruitful sites for atavism to dwell on. For unlike the matter of atavism, which is usually assumed to be in some prehistorical relation to modernity, these residues are history's inassimilable. Their very forms are incommensurable with those of a statist historiography so that it becomes questionable whether their peripheral status derives from their "actual" failure to enter significantly into the course of history or from their incommensurability with its narrative modes.[32] The answer, of course, is both: The recalcitrance of such movements to state formation is bound up with modes of social organization, symbolic and rhetorical styles, or collective ends that are what have to be dissolved and recomposed for the imagination of the nation, in an Andersonian sense, to take place. The imagination of the nation is both the form and the representational limit of history, properly speaking. By the same token, as Benjamin most clearly understood, the recovery of the "subaltern" for materialist history, and therefore not only for the archives but for radical practice, is inseparable from the critique of what he termed "historicism": "The concept of the historical progress of mankind cannot be sundered from the concept of its progression through a homogeneous, empty time. A critique of the concept of such a progression must be the basis of any criticism of the concept of progress itself."[33]

Such a critique, which fundamentally challenges not only the concept but the form of history as/of progress, does not simply dismiss nationalism but rather rearticulates it with those movements it has sought to supersede and which are, in effect, its constitutive antagonists. We will return to some instances of this, and their theoretical consequences, shortly. What this critique at the same time entails is a rethinking of the location and the meaning of the "irrational" in relation both to modernity and to the nation-state. The historicist view of the irrational is, as we have seen, mapped onto a temporal schema: forms marginalized with regard to the state are attached to the prehistory of the nation and become sites attainable only through regression.[34] And it is the temporal axis itself, structured along movements of progress and regress, that materialist history calls into question. In its place is posed a topological model of relations, which is not so much the core-periphery model discussed above as a map of movements and contiguities, conjunctions and incommensurabilities, and the irrational is located in/as those spaces of radical discontinuity with the rationale of a developmental history. We might say that the irrational is located in the topological cusps as that which is unavailable to historical representation. But its relation to historical rationality is akin to that of unsanctioned to sanctioned violence in Benjamin's "Critique of Violence": what the state fears in each is an alternative system of legality or rationality, rather than the unbridled and formless motion of force that has yet to be subordinated.[35] The "irrational" appears as such through the very rationality of the state form whose homogenizing drive connects the apparent particularity of national identities to the greater homogeneity of universal history. At one level, the reason of state needs and accepts the thought of the irrational as its primitive substrate, as that which required to be developed. But what it cannot accept or accommodate is the irrational that its own rationality produces by virtue of the drive to identity and which in consequence persists in irreducible contemporaneity. Benjaminian materialism demands always the contemporaneity of the dead, the subterranean persistence of social forms that make no sense, for the sake of their recalcitrance to the morbid logic of identity.

Now, without doubt, the desire of nationalism is to saturate the field of subject formation so that, for every individual, the idea of nationality, of political citizenship, becomes the central organizing term in relation to which other possible modes of subjectification — class or gender, to cite only the most evident instances — are differentiated and subordinated. Ideological and strategic subordination can take place either in terms of tactical priority — the exigencies of the national struggle demand the temporary suspension of class or feminist concerns — or in terms of the premodern/modern dichotomy — peasant movements, for instance, involve modes of consciousness that predate and therefore hamper nationalist politicization. The fact, however, that hypostasization of national identity as the central term of subjectification does not cease with independence and is no less predominant in great power nationalisms indicates that strategic questions are not the sole determinants of the process of subordination. The logic of both modes of subordination can be derived from the centrality of the state formation that constitutes the end of nationalism. The challenge that both feminism and class politics present to nationalism is commensurate with the resistance that they must ultimately pose, ideologically and practically, to the state.[36] Or, to reverse the terms, the power that nationalism has historically proven to have in containing alternative social movements of whatever kind may be derived from its intimate conjunction with the state. For it is a peculiarity of nationalism that of all modes of potentially counterhegemonic formations none is more thoroughly reinforced or sanctioned by the formations it ostensibly opposes. As we have been seeing, the desire of nationalism for the state is congruent, for all the particularism of national identification, with the universalism of which, indeed, the nation-state is the local representative. The superordination of nationalism is accordingly predicated not on contingent requirements but on its intrinsic logic.

In practice, however, the dream of nationalism is contradicted. This is not a question of the internal contradictions with which nationalism is rife and which need no further elaboration here. It is rather to do with the fact that virtually all nationalist movements emerge in conjunction with other emancipatory movements, a conjunction determined by the intersection of the intensification of social dislocations that any transition to nationalism requires and the proliferation of "modern" emancipatory discourses.[37] Conjunction, however, does not entail entire congruence or subordination in the first instance, so that the history of nationalist movements must be understood in terms of their constant inflection not only by conditions of struggle but by their interaction with allied but differently tending social movements. We may take two instances of such processes here: the Irish independence struggle of 1916–22 and contemporary Marxist nationalism in the Philippines.

The social ferment that preceded the Easter Rising in 1916 and the subsequent Anglo-Irish war of 1919–22 issued from constantly shifting conjunctions among a broad ideological spectrum of social and political movements ranging from the racialist nationalism of Arthur Griffith to the Marxist republican socialism of James Connolly (whose writings remain among the most important essays in anticolonial Marxism). The spectrum includes the pacifist feminism of Hannah Sheehy-Skeffington, the cultural nationalism of the Irish Literary Revival and Language Movement, and the socialist feminism of Constance Markievicz and, in her later years, Maud Gonne. To express things in this fashion, of course, minimizes the extent to which most of the principal figures of the period in fact circulated through all the major movements, and the extent to which at different moments particular groupings took the lead, whether in the socialist-led strike of 1913, in suffragist activism, or in the nationalist uprising and war of independence. Markievicz, who was deeply involved in all three movements, was constantly alert to their intersections. Margaret MacCurtain remarks suggestively on their conjunction: "It is true as Countess Markievicz asserted . . . that three great movements were going on in Ireland in those years, the national movement, the women's movement and the industrial one, yet as each converged on 1916 they moved at their own pace."[38] Moving at different paces, these movements attend to a time determined not by a single end but by their distinct ends, only one of which could be subsumed in the declaration of independence of 1916 and the struggle for autonomous *state* institutions. Each movement has a distinct history and a distinct tempo that may be occluded but is not terminated by the consistent focus of subsequent history, nationalist or revisionist, on political institutions and state apparatuses.[39] But what is striking about their conjunction is its possibility:

among the most radical nationalists were socialist feminists who clearly saw no contradiction between their distinct but articulated affiliations, though different historical conjunctures demanded different emphases. It is equally striking that these radical feminists, as MacCurtain points out,[40] unanimously opposed the compromise Free State that was established in 1922.

Markievicz's own political transitions are illuminating here as they are sketched out unprogrammatically in her letters from prison, written in several periods of incarceration between 1916, when she was arrested and sentenced to death for her leading role in the Rising, and 1923, when she was jailed for her republicanism by the Free State government. Certainly her initial understanding seems to have been that the nationalist struggle required the momentary subordination of the feminist and socialist struggle.[41] In her later writing, however, as the independence struggle progressed, her analysis of the relation between the history of colonialism in Ireland and the mode of the present struggle becomes closely tied to her understanding both of the requirements of socialist practice and those of the feminist struggle. Arguing that the historical endurance of Irish resistance could be attributed to the absence there of a centralized state form, so that British colonialism had never been able to subdue Ireland through seizure of a seat of government or an acknowledged single leader, Markievicz proposes that in domains ranging from language and education to political organization, Ireland's decentralization, though perpetuated by colonialism itself, furnished both the possibility for the kind of decentered guerrilla resistance then in progress and hints toward the kind of social organization that might emerge from the struggle: "There was something that prevented any man or woman ever desiring to conquer all Ireland — a sort of feeling for 'decentralisation' (modern 'soviets'). . . . It's very curious, for in a way it was that that prevented the conquest of Ireland, till the English enemy got rid of every family of note: at the same time it always prevented the Irish getting together under one head for long enough to do more than win a battle. This makes me have such faith in the Republic. The country is now all organised and can do without leaders, but it has learnt that it must act together."[42] Her antagonism to centralization and leadership emerges equally in her relation to the women's movement.[43] Throughout, the very articulation of distinct engagements together maintains all in a mutually critical condition of process, a process that the superordination of one reactionary version of nationalism in the Free State could only arrest.

It would not be difficult to trace comparable conjunctions within the dynamics of the Philippine anticolonial Left since the mid-1960s, complicated perhaps by the emergence of a new Left-influenced student movement and the neocolonial nature of the Philippine state, which has been nominally independent since 1946. At least since the formation of the Communist Party of the Philippines (CPP) and its break with the older PKP (Partida Kumunista ng Pilipinas) in the mid-1960s, leftist opposition has involved a series of shifting coalitions between Marxist and nationalist tendencies, student activism, and longer-standing traditions of peasant and worker organization, guerrilla struggle in the form of the New People's Army (NPA), and cultural work. More recently, movements for socialist democracy have emerged both within the National Democratic Front and outside it, as have feminist groups, including Gabriela within the NDF and Kalayaan, a feminist movement that coordinates across a broad left spectrum. The complexity, both historical and ideological, of the interaction of these tendencies is impossible to elaborate here, and I will focus on the conjunction between the CPP and rural activism, particularly in the domain of cultural politics.

The tradition of rural armed resistance to colonialism in the Philippines has been persistent if not quite continuous at least since the 1840s, in opposition successively to Spanish, U.S., and Japanese colonialism and, since 1946, to neocolonial Philippine regimes. But although the period has seen several strictly nationalist and/or Marxist military struggles, most significantly the nationalist struggle against the Spanish and then U.S. forces from 1896 to 1902, led by the *ilustrado* elite, and the PKP-led campaign in the early 1950s, it is clear that armed movements in the Philippines have never been entirely identifiable with "modernist" political movements. In fact, stemming from a long tradition of what the Spanish first castigated as "banditry," armed resistance has shown a capacity for persistence and survival beyond that of state-oriented movements whose ends have forced them into frontal offensives with superior imperial forces. Despite the "legal murder" by *ilustrado* nationalists of Andres Bonifacio, the peasant leader of the populist Katipunan resistance against the Spanish in 1897, rural resistance against the subsequent U.S. colonization continued through 1910, long after Emilio Aguinaldo, leader of the nationalist Philippine Army, had surrendered in 1901. Traditions of armed resistance continued even after formal "pacification," often in conjunction with the emergent socialist movement in the 1920s and 1930s. Accordingly, rural guerrilla struggle became the core of Philippine resistance to Japanese occupation in the form of the Hukbalahap (People's Army against the Japanese), whose resistance to neocolonialism continued into the postwar period and was only put down with great difficulty and atrocity by the Philippine and U.S. forces. The capacity of the CPP/NPA to mobilize in conjunction with the legacy of such struggles, having learned from the failure of the PKP's "premature" offensive in the 1950s, has been a principal factor in their ability to maintain effective control of large portions of the Philippine countryside and to remain active in others.[44]

Despite relative success in military terms, it is clear that such a conjunction between a Maoist-inspired Marxist nationalist movement, founded by young urban intellectuals, and long-standing if "local" traditions of resistance could not be sustained without continuous mutual modifications of quite fundamental kinds. This process of modification is already reinforced by the neocolonial nature of the Philippines, combined with persisting feudal relations according to CPP analysis. On the one hand, the struggle cannot be defined simply in nationalist, anticolonial terms, since its end is the transformation rather than merely the capture of the state. On the other, the neocolonial nature of the state defines the terrain of struggle as that of the nation, and the kind of vertical as well as centralized integration of oppositional tendencies pursued by nationalism remains requisite. The process of "conscientization" that is fundamental to the politicizing work of the CPP embodies this double requirement: it seeks first to produce a class consciousness in rural workers through the analysis of specific local concerns and second to connect that local analysis to the larger national economic and political system. What this assumes is the necessity of transforming local consciousness into national class consciousness, a process mediated by the pedagogical function of the movement activist. In this process, accordingly, the mobility of the student cadre[45] becomes not merely a practical asset but an expression of the structural relations of a dispersed *national* intellectual class, formed initially in keeping with the exigencies of the *national* state, and a localized proletariat. "Conscientization" in principle occupies the intersection between the spatial and temporal axes of political modernity, transforming the local into the national through the development of a more evolved consciousness.[46]

It is clear, however, that for many if not most activists, the work of politicization involves a complex and reverse transformation of consciousness in the direction of localization rather than higher-level integration. From the learning of ethnic languages to the encounter with local cultural and political practices, the experience may be one that challenges the desire for integration from the center and discovers the relative autonomy of local cultural inventiveness. A model for this transformation of theoretical and practical understanding can in fact be derived from CPP founder Amado Guerrero's innovative "Specific Characteristics of Our People's War," which, though it focuses on guerrilla strategy, has profound implications for all levels and spheres of radical practice in the Philippines. Commencing from Maoist precepts concerning guerrilla warfare, especially the need to maintain centralized control, Guerrero reflects on the peculiarities of guerrilla struggle under the geographical conditions of the mountainous and forested Philippine archipelago, conditions that hamper where they do not obviate continuous communication between central command and local operations. Under such conditions, what must transpire is a reduction in central control and the corresponding relative autonomy of local units, units that frequently may have to operate in isolation for extended periods without the possibility of linking with others or receiving communications from central command.[47] Though Guerrero's emphasis is on geographical conditions and military organization, the essay has rich, perhaps even richer implications for cultural politics, particularly since the geographical conditions, always an obstacle to communication and centralization, produce and are complicated further by cultural differences that are deeply resistant to homogenization: there are at least eighty distinct ethnic groups and languages across the seven thousand or so islands of the archipelago; beyond this frequently noted ethnic diversity, economic conditions and corresponding cultural differentiations are remarkably various. That is to say, it is not merely a question, as for the Spanish missions, of adapting one message to different language groups and local religions, but, further, of a deployment of cultural and social analysis with a view to transformative engagement, one that often involves a transformation of established cultural and political forms in the process.

Nowhere has this been more apparent than in the radical theater movement that has emerged in the Philippines out of the conjoined work of NDF cultural workers and the radical Basic Christian Communities. This has been amply described by scholars and activists,[48] and I wish here only to emphasize two characteristics of the movement. In the first place, though initiated by either seminary-educated priests or university-educated student activists, the interactional principles of radical theater, in many cases formed through the theoretical synthesis of Boal and Brecht, produce a theater that is decentered in its forms and emplotment as well as in its processes. Participation of local people in the enactment of dramas leads not simply to their interpellation into the matrices of established political analysis, but into the local invention of the terms of political and cultural analysis, terms that have in turn the effect of transforming the practice of urban or intellectual activists. In the second place, and in some senses perhaps with more radical effect in the long term, such theater enacts the breakdown of developmental schemata imposed from the center. Just as radical cultural movements, as part of their dynamic, demand that priority be given to local analysis, so also local cultural forms cease to be seen as atavistic survivals of primordial cultures and are rediscovered as functioning resources in their irreducible contemporaneity. The extraordinary syncretism of theatrical productions by the Philippine Educational Theatre Association (PETA), the umbrella group for radical theater movements, indicates the potential for a performance that enacts the contemporaneity of multiple cultural forms in the name of a radical affirmation of difference against homogeneity. Peking Opera combines with Islamic dance forms from Mindanao or traditional martial arts from Luzon and with Brechtian tableaux or Spanish-derived theatrical modes like *zarzuela* and *moro-moro* or similar religious ritual forms. In some respects, the theater movement may be valuably conceived as a contemporary version of what Reynaldo Ileto so movingly describes in *Pasyon and Revolution* as the popular adaptation and transformation of familiar and hegemonically intended Spanish liturgical forms.[49]

Intense resistance to Ileto's work from some quarters, however, is a reminder that what is described above can only be thought of as a tendency rather than some achieved ideal. The resistance is expressed in terms of the antagonism between Marxist-nationalist modes of enlightenment and the primitive superstition of the millenarian movements Ileto describes.[50] Much is legitimately at stake here in terms of the exigencies of political practice, and the conjunctions in play are virtually by definition in process. Nor can it simply be said that the radical theater movement is unambivalently an agent either of conscientization or of more localized and syncretic processes: as a site of conjunction it is evidently also a site of contestations. Among the issues at stake in such a contestation is the relationship within left nationalism between "modernity" and what we may call this "contemporaneity of the nonmodern," of that which has generally been relegated to the domain of the atavistic or irrational.

Two observations follow from these historical examples. The first is that it is the superordination of the state form that puts an end to the processes of articulation and conjuncture that maintain nationalism differentially as an element of broader, more complex, and often internally antagonistic social formations. This can take the form either of the actual attainment of formal independence or, at the ideological level, before or after independence through the effective dominance of state-oriented tendencies within hegemonic groups or parties. The distinction is logical only: in actual practice, the independent state tends to be structured in accord with the ideology of hegemonic elites created by colonialism. Fanon's *Wretched of the Earth* is a relentless analysis of both aspects of this process. The fact that Irish socialist feminists could play leading roles within the nationalist struggle and be entirely opposed to the Free State that resulted is not only logical but may even be quite typical of decolonization processes generally.

The second observation, which follows from the first, is that it is important to recognize that other social movements are not necessarily entirely absorbed or otherwise dissolved in the hegemony of state-oriented nationalisms. On the contrary, they persist as distinct elements of the struggle or as recalcitrant tendencies for the state. But they do so not as particles of the prehistory of nationalism awaiting absorption, but as active constituents of the modern, inflected just as is nationalism by recent history, though with different ends and correspondingly different narratives. And these are continuing narratives: the fetishization of "folk culture" as a fixed and primordial expression of a transcendental people is in fact most often itself an idée fixe of official state culture, deployed in the monumental rituals and ceremonies that perform the identity of citizen and state. Popular culture continues its complex and partially self-transforming, partially subordinated existence in the shadow of the state.[51] Indeed, it is a paradox of nationalism that though it may often summon into being a "people" that is to form and subtend the nation-state, it is always confronted with that people as a potentially disruptive *excess* over the nation and its state.

It would be wrong to see that excess as the index of irrational or atavistic forces escaping the controlling, "repressive-tolerant" vigilance of the modern and rational state. Rather, what is in play is a chiasmatic relation between the designations "rational" and "irrational" through terrains whose specularity is staked out in the continuing contestation between incommensurable modes of subject formation or interpellation. If nationalism calls forth a people for the nation-state, its modes of subjectification still cannot exhaust the identifications available to the individuals thus summoned. Faced with that strictly uncontainable excess, the state designates it irrational, primitive, or criminal. Yet the state in its turn depends on the mobilization, at the individual and the mass levels, of forces we might term "irrational," and it is exactly in proportion to the power of our own intellectual discipline that we fail to acknowledge the perception of the colonized or the subaltern that the state is crazy. As Adorno puts it in *Negative Dialectics:* "After feudalism perished, a precarious form of centralized organization was to tame the diffuse combines of nature so as to protect bourgeois interests. It was bound to become a fetish unto itself; there was no other way it might have integrated the individuals, whose economic need of that form of organization is as great as its incessant rape of them. And where the nation failed to accomplish the union that is the prerequisite of a self-emancipating bourgeois society—in Germany, that is—its concept becomes overvalued and destructive. To take in the *gentes,* the concept of the nation mobilizes additional regressive memories of its archaic root."[52] Adorno's remarks are in part founded in the analysis of fascism, but they recognize fascism as the extreme case of processes that are entirely congruent with the universal requirements of modern state formation. And if fascism recurs in critiques of nationalism as the horizon on which its tendencies are realized, we need to understand that this is in fact not simply because of the force of irrationality it unleashes, but precisely in the profound rationality of its unreason, in the violence of the state that is, in a formalist sense, "typical."

As is well known, the emergence of the modern state is inseparable from a massive restructuring of the modes of interpellation by which individuals are transformed into citizen-subjects who will, as Althusser puts it, "work by themselves,"[53] whether in economic, legal, political, or cultural domains. Althusser's critique of ideology as determined by the category of the subject draws on a psychoanalytic narrative of the formation of the subject through oedipalization and its sublimation in relation to the figure of the father, the Lacanian "Name-of-the-father." The importance of Althusser's intervention in the psychoanalytic understanding of subject formation is in a certain sense belied by his own slippage into positing the ideological as universal and transhistorical. For where both Freudian and Lacanian paradigms can be critiqued for universalizing the decisive moments in their narratives—castration anxiety and the bourgeois family for Freud, the phallus as signifier of differentiation for Lacan—Althusser emphasizes the crucial historical importance of educational apparatuses. The meaning of oedipalization, as a psychic process determined by the specific historical form of the bourgeois family, can only be grasped in relation to its function within educational institutions against which the modern family is differentiated and defined. The pedagogical process replicates and normativizes the protoethical narrative that occurs, or is supposed to occur, at the "private" level of the family. The disciplining of the individual subject, which takes place by way of what that subject learns to desire, paves the way for the socialization of the subject in accord with the ethical maxim of learning to will one's own subordination.

To insist on the historicity of these social forms is not to diminish or rationalize away the psychic hold they exert upon the modern subject. On the contrary, it is to return to Gellner's account of subject formation in nationalism, which is remarkably congruent with Althusser's in its emphasis on education, the psychic force he sublimates into an elegant historical joke:

A man's education is by far his most precious investment, and in effect confers his identity on him. Modern man is not loyal to a monarch or a land or a faith, whatever he may say, but to a culture. And he is, generally speaking, gelded. The Mamluk condition has become universal. No important links bind him to a kin group; nor do they stand between him and a wide, anonymous community of culture.

We are all of us now castrated, and pitifully trustworthy. The state can trust us, all in all, to do our duty, and need not turn us into eunuchs, priests, slaves, or mamluks first.[54]

Gellner luminously brings out here the way in which what Freud first described as "sublimation" involves not only "the dissolution of the oedipus complex" but also the sublimation of the family for the individual, insofar as the *figuration* of the father as superego makes that figure available for transference onto other and generally abstract forms of authority. (By the same token, it is crucial for Lacan that the signifier of difference is the *phallus,* not the anatomical organ, the penis.) But the congruence of his own modernizing narrative with the forms he invokes and sublimates metaphorically prevents him from acknowledging fully their continuing irrational dimension.

This is neither to suggest that castration anxiety or the Oedipus complex are irrationalities that are superseded by access to enlightened culture nor even to claim that the "irrationality" of the state lies in its dependence for interpellation on "regressive" psychic identifications. On the contrary, it is to take seriously the psychoanalytic contention that what occurs in these processes, at every level, is the constitution itself of rationality and irrationality, sense and non-sense. The sense of the state depends on the relegation of other modes of sociality to the domain of non-sense; its rationality requires the production of irrationality as the form of that which *must* exceed its modes of interpellation. Oedipalization, at the level of the individual, constructs obsessively that individual's sense of verisimilitude, but always obsessively precisely because, although it has the form of the truth, the ethical subject can never represent the "whole truth." There is accordingly a link far profounder than Gellner can admit between the Weberian definition of the state as possessing a "monopoly of violence" and his own revision of that to emphasize, rightly, the state's "monopoly of education."[55] The state must expunge, through ideological or repressive state apparatuses, cultural or social forms that are in excess of its own rationality and whose rationale is other to its own. Though this may take the form of outright repression, the mechanisms of the modern state tend in fact toward transformation (rather than transcendence) of alternative forms. Herein lie the secret and function of the fetishism of the state that invokes "traditional" figures precisely to mask difference and excess. To take one signal example, the female figures of the nation, such as Ireland's Kathleen Ni Houlihan, often regarded in Irish cultural analysis as the essence of an irrational and regressive nationalism's devotion to oedipal emotions, is in fact a product of modernity and its insistence on the homogenization of national identity. Based indeed on popular figures, which, in the metonymic manner of popular/nonmodern culture, made no hard and fast distinctions between the actual and the figurative, it reduces them to a metaphor for national identity and a powerful interpellative figure in the nationalist struggle for the state. It refines out of the popular, with its excess and overdetermination, an image around which to form the desire of political subjects. Nor is this a peculiarity of anticolonial nationalisms: quite similar, and even more fraught transformations are evident in the invention of France's Marianne after 1848.[56]

The modern state, then, is always in a profoundly ambivalent relation to the forces of rationality and irrationality at whose interface it is constituted. The displacement of irrationality onto nationalisms is an ideological convenience of a historical moment in which a further effort of homogenizing rationalization is taking place globally in the names of the New World Order or transnational capital. At such a moment, when the violence of militarist and patriarchal states is literally beyond reason, and when that irrationality is conjoined with the profound economic rationality of transnational capitalism, there are sound pragmatic reasons to adhere to nationalism as a minimal defense against homogenization. But if the nationalisms with which we are in solidarity are to be radical or emancipatory, rather than fixed in the repressive apparatuses of state formations, it is their conjunctural relation to other social movements that needs to be emphasized and furthered, at both theoretical and practical levels. The possibility of nationalism against the state lies in the recognition of the excess of the people over the nation and in the understanding that that is, beyond itself, the very logic of nationalism as a political phenomenon.

NOTES

1. Ernest Gellner, *Nations and Nationalism* (Ithaca: Cornell University Press, 1983), 125.

2. Benedict Anderson, *Imagined Communities: Reflections on the Origin and Spread of Nationalism* (London: Verso, 1981).

3. John Breuilly, *Nationalism and the State* (New York: St. Martin's Press, 1982).

4. Eric J. Hobsbawm, *Nations and Nationalism Since 1780: Programme, Myth, Reality* (Cambridge: Cambridge University Press, 1990), 164.

5. Tom Nairn, *The Break-up of Britain: Crisis and Neo-Nationalism* (London: New Left Books, 1977), 331–350.

6. Frantz Fanon, *The Wretched of the Earth,* trans. Constance Farrington (New York: Grove Press, 1963), 94.

7. I have been inspired in writing this by Alok Yadav's valuable essay, "Nationalism and Contemporaneity: Political Economy of a Discourse," *Cultural Critique* 22 (winter 1993–94): 191–229.

8. Gellner, *Nations and Nationalism,* 4. As the title of *Nationalism and the State* would imply, Breuilly's argument concurs by and large with Gellner's assumption here, at least in seeing the state as the decisive term for nationalist movements. See Breuilly, *Nationalism and the State,* esp. 355–359 and 374.

9. E. P. Thompson, "The Moral Economy of the English Crowd in the Eighteenth Century," *Past and Present* 50 (February 1971): 89–90. I have explored the relation between moral economy and the emergence of Irish nationalism in David Lloyd, "Violence and the Constitution of the Novel," in *Anomalous States: Irish Writing and the Post-Colonial Moment* (Durham: Duke University Press, 1993), 141–149.

10. Gellner, *Nations and Nationalism,* 46.

11. Ibid., 53.

12. Nairn, *The Break-up of Britain,* 342–343.

13. Ibid., 340.

14. Ibid., 348.

15. Ibid., 349.

16. Ibid.

17. Gellner, *Nations and Nationalism,* 53.

18. See Bipan Chandra, "Colonialism, Stages of Colonialism and the Colonial State," *Journal of Contemporary Asia* 10, no. 3 (1980): 282, on the focus of the indigenous population as a whole on the state, which makes nationalist movements in the colonial state far easier to organize than other kinds of social movement.

19. Among Western theorists of nationalism, Benedict Anderson is one of the few who clearly grasps this dynamic of nationalism. See Anderson, *Imagined Communities,* chap. 7.

20. The essay "Algeria Unveiled" by Frantz Fanon, in *A Dying Colonialism,* trans. Haakon Chevalier (New York: Grove Press, 1967), analyzes the ironic, performative relation of women in the Front pour la Libération Nationale (FLN) to both modernity and tradition. Lisa Lowe has analyzed such strands in Fanon's thinking in Lowe, *Critical Terrains: British and French Orientalisms* (Ithaca: Cornell University Press, 1991), 190–192. In my reading of Fanon, and

especially in my understanding of the "contemporaneity" rather than the "modernity" of heterogeneous social movements at any given time, I have of course learned greatly from the work of Homi Bhabha. See especially Bhabha, "DissemiNation: Time, Narrative, and the Margins of the Modern Nation," in *Nation and Narration,* ed. Homi Bhabha (London: Routledge, 1990), 291–322.

21. Nairn, *The Break-up of Britain,* 340.

22. Fanon, *Wretched of the Earth,* 204.

23. *Ibid.,* 315.

24. Hobsbawm, *Nations and Nationalism Since 1780,* 46–79.

25. Immanuel Kant, "Idea of a Universal History on a Cosmo-political Plan," in *Works,* vol. 12, trans. Thomas de Quincey (Edinburgh: Adam and Charles Black, 1862), 133.

26. Antonio Gramsci, "Notes on Italian History," in *Selections from the Prison Notebooks,* ed. and trans. Quintin Hoare and Geoffrey Nowell Smith (New York: International Publishers, 1971), 52–55; Ranajit Guha and Gayatri Chakravorty Spivak, eds., *Selected Subaltern Studies* (New York: Oxford University Press, 1988), 35, 37–43. The single most important rethinking of "Third World" nationalism in relation to modernity is Partha Chatterjee's *Nationalist Thought and the Colonial World: A Derivative Discourse?* (Minneapolis: University of Minnesota Press, 1993).

27. Walter Benjamin, "Theses on the Philosophy of History," in *Illuminations,* ed. Hannah Arendt, trans. Harry Zohn (New York: Schocken, 1963), 264.

28. Ibid., 262.

29. Ibid.

30. Ibid., 259.

31. Ibid., 257.

32. This is clearly a fundamental problematic of subaltern historiography: see in particular Ranajit Guha, "The Prose of Counter-Insurgency," in *Selected Subaltern Studies,* ed. Ranajit Guha and Gayatri Chakravorty Spivak, 45–86. Reynaldo C. Ileto's "Outlines of a Nonlinear Emplotment of Philippine History," in this volume, is a valuable combination of new historical research and formal critique that addresses these questions very subtly. I have attempted some analysis of the incompatibilities between agrarian movements and emergent nationalist ideology in nineteenth-century Ireland in Lloyd, "Violence and the Constitution of the Novel," in *Anomalous States.*

33. Benjamin, "Theses on the Philosophy of History," 263.

34. The use of a Freudian vocabulary in this relation, and the implicit congruence thereby established between individual and national history, is unremarkable insofar as Freud himself employs the same metaphors in the inverse direction: national history provides the constant analogy for individual integration and development. See Sigmund Freud, "Some Psychical Consequences of the Anatomical Distinction between the Sexes," in *On Sexuality: Three Essays on the Theory of Sexuality and Other Works,* Pelican Freud Library, vol. 7, ed. Angela Richards, trans. James Strachey (Hammondsworth: Penguin, 1977), 341.

35. Walter Benjamin, "Critique of Violence," in *Reflections: Essays, Aphorisms, Autobiographical Writings,* ed. Peter Demetz, trans. Edmund Jephcott (New York: Harcourt Brace Jovanovich, 1978), 279.

36. The same could be said, mutatis mutandis, for ethnic or minority politics in multicultural states like the United States or diasporic populations in more "mono-ethnic" cultures. The destabilizing figure of Leopold Bloom, the wandering Jew, is for this reason one of the things that makes Joyce's *Ulysses* a great counternationalist text without its becoming a pro-imperialist one.

37. The term *modern* is probably misleading here, since some social movements such as agrarian or peasant movements invoke not, say, the modern discourse of rights but terms that appear traditional (though some social movements, as in the 1798 uprising in Ireland, managed to combine both). The conditions of dislocation, however, produce a transformation of the "traditional" such that it becomes a new cultural form that responds to "modernity" in the narrower sense. Opposition to modernity is, then, no less contemporaneous and cannot simply be relegated to the status of outmoded traditionalism. Reynaldo Ileto's *Pasyon and Revolution: Popular Movements in the Philippines, 1840–1910* (Quezon City: Ateneo de Manila, 1979), is a brilliant analysis of "contemporaneous" adaptations of the traditional for emancipatory purposes in the context of Philippine resistance to both Spanish and American colonialism.

38. Margaret MacCurtain and Donncha O Corrain, eds., *Women in Irish Society: The Historical Dimension* (Westport, CT: Greenwood Press, 1979), 52.

39. For a succinct account of these historiographical categories in Ireland, see Kevin Whelan, "Come All Ye Blinkered Nationalists: A Post-Revisionist Agenda for Irish History," in *Irish Reporter* 2 (2d quarter 1991): 24–26. They are comparable to Guha's distinction between colonialist and nationalist historiography in India (Guha, in *Selected Subaltern Studies,* ed. Guha and Spivak, 37–40). I find it striking that the most innovative new history of Irish nationalism as a movement is emanating now from the biographical and historical studies of feminist historians. See, for example, Margaret Ward, *Maud Gonne: Ireland's Joan of Arch* (London: Pandora, 1990); Diana Norman, *Terrible Beauty: A Life of Constance Markievicz* (Dublin: Poolbeg, 1991); Maria Luddy and Cliona Murphy, eds., *Women Surviving: Studies in Irish Women's History in the 19th and 20th Centuries* (Dublin: Poolbeg, 1990); and MacCurtain and O Corrain, *Women in Irish Society.* For an excellent exploration of relations between the sympathetic critique of nationalism and gendered historiography, which focuses on the Indian context, see R. Radhakrishnan, "Nationalism, Gender, and the Narrative of Identity," in *Nationalisms and Sexualities,* ed. Andrew Parker et al. (New York: Routledge, 1992).

40. MacCurtain and O Corrain, *Women in Irish Society,* 55.

41. Constance Markievicz, *Prison Letters,* with a biographical sketch by Esther Roper and preface by President de Valera (London: Longmans Green, 1934), 12.

42. Ibid., 246–247. For a discussion of similar debates among other Irish

Marxists of the time, like Aodh de Blacam and James Connolly, see Luke Gibbons, "Identity without a Centre: Allegory, History, and Irish Nationalism," in *Cultural Studies* 6, no. 3 (October 1992), 358–375. His thinking on these issues has been of enormous value to me throughout this essay.

43. Markievicz, *Prison Letters*, 191.

44. See Benedict Anderson, "Cacique Democracy in the Philippines: Origins and Dreams," *New Left Review* 169 (May–June 1988): 3–33; Renato Constantino, "Identity and Consciousness: The Philippine Experience," *Journal of Contemporary Asia* 6, no. 1 (1976): 5–29; Norman Lorimer, "Philippine Communism — An Historical Overview," *Journal of Contemporary Asia* 7, no. 4 (1977): 462–485.

45. See Lorimer, "Philippine Communism," 477.

46. See Ileto, "Outlines of a Nonlinear Emplotment of Philippine History," in this volume.

47. Amado Guerrero, "Specific Characteristics of Our People's War," in *Philippine Society and Revolution*, 3d ed. (Manila: International Association of Filipino Patriots, 1979), 179–215.

48. See Priscelina Patajo-Legasto, "Philippine Contemporary Theater, 1946–1985" (Ph.D. diss., University of the Philippines, 1988); Lulu Torres-Reyes, "Anticipating Hegemony: Brecht and the Philippines Today," *Makisa* 1, no. 1 (1st quarter 1989): 18–19; Rosario Cruz Lucero, "Negros Occidental, 1970–1986: The Fall of the Sugar Industry and the Rise of the People's Theater" (Ph.D. diss., University of the Philippines, 1990).

49. Ileto, *Pasyon and Revolution*. PETA's adaptation of "Yesterday, Today and Tomorrow" (Manila, January 1991) is an allegory of the contemporaneity of cultural forms, taking a turn-of-the-century seditious and anti-American *zarzuela* and reinflecting it both by culturally diverse elements of performance and by emphasizing its original thematization of the cyclical or repetitive nature of Philippine resistance to colonialism. One consideration here is the tension between contemporary women's activism and nationalist figurations of the feminine: the role of Inang Bayan, mother of the nation, portrayed as perpetually supplicant, is in constant tension with the foregrounding of women militants in the "chorus," thus mobilizing and unsettling the oedipal elements of nationalism.

50. Domingo Castro de Guzman, "Millenarianism and Revolution: A Critique of Reynaldo C. Ileto's *Pasyon and Revolution*," in *Journal of Social History* (Institute of Social History: Polytechnic University of the Philippines) 3–4 (n.d.): 31–95.

51. The recent revival of Irish music, for long enveloped in the dreary drapery of the church- and state-sanctioned *fleadh ceoil* or cultural festival, is an excellent instance of such "resurgences," determined in part by the encounter with international contemporary music and in part by phenomena such as the encounter between Irish and black young immigrants in the hostile environment of racist Britain, with the consequent interaction of cultural styles.

52. Theodor Adorno, *Negative Dialectics,* trans. E. B. Ashton (New York: Seabury Press, 1973), 339.

53. Louis Althusser, "Ideology and Ideological State Apparatuses: Notes towards an Investigation," in *Lenin and Philosophy and Other Essays,* trans. Ben Brewster (New York: Monthly Review Press, 1971), 181–182.

54. Gellner, *Nations and Nationalism,* 102.

55. Ibid., 34.

56. Gibbons, "Identity without a Centre"; T. J. Clark, *The Absolute Bourgeois: Artists and Politics in France, 1848–1851* (London: Thames and Hudson, 1973).

II

ALTERNATIVES

ARTURO ESCOBAR

Cultural Politics and Biological Diversity: State, Capital, and Social Movements in the Pacific Coast of Colombia

THE CULTURAL POLITICS OF NATURE

The centrality of nature for politics of diverse kinds, from the reaction-ary to the progressive, has become increasingly clear in recent times. The invention and reinvention of nature is, in the words of theorist Donna Haraway, "perhaps the most crucial arena of hope, oppression and contestation for inhabitants of the planet earth of our times."[1] Inherent in this claim is the belief that what counts as nature can no longer be taken for granted. While most of us continue to adhere to an anachronistic ideology of naturalism—the belief in an external and even untouched Nature, preexisting any construction and independent of human history—recent technoscientific advances promise to free us from the shackles of this tradition. From recombinant DNA on, the inroads of technoscience into the molecular fabric of nature have ad-vanced steadily. That life forms can today be patented, the human genome mapped, reproduction conducted under conditions that only yesterday seemed impossible, and crops strengthened with genes bor-rowed from microorganisms—all of these are instances of a profound transformation in the relation between humans and nature. As Paul Rabinow put it in explaining the regime of biosociality that he sees emerging, "nature will be made and remade through technique and will finally become artificial, just as culture becomes natural."[2]

If there is a place on earth where the ideology of naturalism is alive and well, that would be the tropical rainforests. They are instances of "violent nature, resilient life . . . one of the last repositories on earth of that timeless dream [of primeval nature]," as Edward O. Wilson ex-plains to us in his much-cited treatise on biological diversity.[3] Not in vain are the humid forests of the tropics perceived as the most natural form of nature left on earth, inhabited by the most natural people ("indigenous peoples") possessing the most natural knowledge of sav-ing nature ("indigenous knowledge"). As we shall see, however, tropical rainforests worldwide are being ineluctably thrust into the techno-scientific and managerial project of designing nature. In places as diverse as Costa Rica, Thailand, Ivory Coast, Colombia, Malaysia, Cameroon, Brazil, and Ecuador projects of "biodiversity conservation" — most often funded by northern environmental NGOs and the World Bank's Global Environment Facility (GEF) — are incorporating national planners and local communities alike into a complex politics of technoscience that sees in the genes of rainforest species the key to the preservation of these fragile ecosystems. As the basic argument goes, the genes of rainforest species constitute a veritable library of genetic information, a source of wonder drugs and perhaps a cornucopia of foods, all of which could be converted into valuable products by biotechnology. The rainforest would thus be preserved at the same time that sizable profits are made, benefiting local people along the way.

The reason so much attention is given to rainforests today lies in what could be termed "the irruption of the biological" as a central social fact in the global politics of the late twentieth century. After two centuries of systematic destruction of nature and life, and through a dialectical process set in motion by capitalism and modernity, the survival of biological life has emerged as a crucial question in the global landscape of capital and science. Conservation and sustainable development seem to have become inescapable problems for capital, thus forcing it to modify its older reckless logic according to which nature was seen chiefly as an external domain of raw materials to be appropriated at any cost; but the irruption of the biological in the global theater of development, environment, and security concerns is fostering a new look on life itself. As Wilson puts it, "the key to the survival of life as we know it today is the maintenance of biological diversity."[4] The rising discourse of biodiversity is the result of this problematization of the biological. It places tropical rainforest areas in a key position in global biopolitics.

This essay examines the reconversions of nature and culture that are taking place around this discourse. Its geographical focus is the Pacific Coast region of Colombia, a rainforest area of almost legendary biodiversity. In this region, the cultural politics of nature are circumscribed by three main processes that have developed simultaneously after 1990: the radical policies of economic *apertura* (opening to world markets) pursued by the government in recent years, particularly the push toward integrating the country into the Pacific Basin economies; the novel strategies of sustainable development and biodiversity conservation; and growing and increasingly visible forms of black and indigenous mobilization.

I take cultural politics to be the process enacted when social actors shaped by or embodying different cultural meanings and practices come into conflict with each other. The notion of cultural politics assumes that cultural meanings and practices — particularly those theorized as marginal, oppositional, minority, residual, emergent, alternative, dissident, and the like, all of them conceived in relation to a given dominant cultural order — can be the source of processes that must be accepted as political. That this is rarely seen as such is more a reflection of entrenched definitions of political culture than an indication of the social force, political efficacy, or epistemological relevance of cultural politics. A given cultural politics has the potential to redefine existing social relations, political cultures, and knowledge circuits. Culture becomes political when meanings become the source of processes that, implicitly or explicitly, seek to redefine social power. In tropical rainforest areas, this redefinition is mediated by forms of knowledge production and political mobilization intimately related to the construction of ethnic identities. This cultural politics unsettles familiar understandings and practices of nature, as it attempts to wrest away local ecologies of mind and nature from entrenched networks of class, gender, cultural, and ethnic domination.

The first section describes the Pacific Coast region of Colombia as it has become the object of recent interventions by capital and the state in the context of *apertura* and in the name of sustainable development. The second section surveys briefly the discourse of biodiversity as it emerged in the 1990s out of northern NGOs and international organizations, and its particular application in Colombia. The third section analyzes in detail the black movement that has arisen as a response to the developmentalist onslaught and the ways in which this movement engages with biodiversity discussions. The final section elaborates the notion of the cultural politics of nature by imagining a strategy of hybrid natures that would rely on new articulations between the organic and the artificial. It argues that social movement activists and progressive intellectuals concerned with the nature of nature are thrown into a situation of defending local modes of consciousness and practices of nature the success of which might depend on alliances with the advocates of biotechnological applications of biodiversity — that is, with the advocates of the artificial. Like the concept of hybrid cultures, the strategy of hybrid natures is seen as a medium for new representations of third world situations and a possibility for postdevelopment.

Tropical rainforest areas constitute a social space in which the reinvention of nature, the search for alternative social and economic approaches, and the changing modes of capital can be observed. In fact, the interweaving of these three processes can serve as an interpretive framework for investigating the political practices of the various social actors. This interweaving of forces suggests the following questions: First, in what particular ways is the relation between people and nature being transformed? What lessons can this transformation teach us about postmodern theorizations of nature and culture that have been derived mostly in first world contexts? Second, what can be gleaned from struggles and debates in tropical rainforests about alternative socioeconomic designs and the possibility of transcending the imaginary of development?[5] Third, do events in these areas substantiate the claim that capital is entering an "ecological phase,"[6] where modern destructive forms would coexist with postmodern conservationist forms? Finally, what do the socioeconomic and cultural struggles to define tropical rainforests tell us about oppositional politics, dissenting imaginations, and collective action by social groups? In what follows, we will explore the meaning of these questions by drawing on fieldwork in one particular rainforest region of Colombia.

The Pacific Coast region is a vast rainforest area, about 600 miles long and 50 to 100 miles wide, stretching from Panama to Ecuador, and between the westernmost chain of the Andes and the Pacific Ocean. About 60 percent of the region's 900,000 inhabitants live in a few cities and large towns, the rest sparsely settling the areas along the large number of rivers flowing from the Andes toward the ocean. Afro-Colombians, descendants from slaves brought from Africa beginning in the sixteenth century to mine gold, make up most of the population, but there are also about 50,000 indigenous people, particularly Emberas and Waunanas living mostly in the northern Chocó province. Black groups, with which this paper is primarily concerned, have maintained and developed a significantly different set of cultural practices of both Spanish and African origin—such as multiple and shifting economic activities, extended families, matrilineality, unique dance, musical and oral traditions, funerary cults, sorcery, and the like—even if these practices are increasingly hybridized with urban, modern forms due to in- and out-migration and the impact of commodities, media, and development programs from the interior of the country. Although the region has never been isolated from the world markets—"boom-and-bust" cycles of gold, platinum, precious woods, rubber, timber, and (as we shall see shortly) genes have successively tied black communities to the world economy — not until the 1980s has the region been subjected to coordinated policies of development.[7]

What is happening in the Pacific Coast region is in many ways unprecedented: large-scale development plans; opening up of new fronts for capital accumulation, such as African palm plantations and artificial shrimp cultivation; and growing black and indigenous mobilization. Three main actors — state, capital, and social movements — struggle over the definition of the present and future of the region. Behind these three sets of actors lie different cultural and political economies whose genealogies and links to cultural and socioeconomic rationalities have to be elucidated. The investigation of the cultural politics of these actors is important to the extent that the future of the region will largely depend on how the region is defined and represented. Let us then analyze how state, capital, and social movements seek to deploy their discourses and practices in the littoral.

Discourses of the State: *Apertura* and Sustainable Development

Almost every document on the Pacific Coast started until recently with the same image of the littoral as a region forgotten by god and government, its inhabitants living under primitive subsistence conditions, the environment unhealthy, hot and humid as in almost no other part of the world — a sort of "no man's land" where only rugged capitalists, colonists, missionaries, and the occasional anthropologist ventured to work among "blacks and Indians." The region is, indeed, very poor by conventional indicators such as income per capita, literacy rates, and levels of nutritional status; malaria is also rampant, in part because the region, especially its northern part, has one of the highest indices of rain and humidity in the world.

Since the early 1980s, these features are emphasized in such a way as to make development interventions ineluctable and undisputable. The geographical and ecological determinism with which the region is endowed in these representations — backward and diseased, in need of the white hand of government and of capital and technology to free it from the lethargy of centuries — sets it up as an empirical reality to be dealt with through appropriate economic and technical interventions. Almost four centuries after the rest of the country, the region entered the development era with the launching of the Plan for the Integral Development of the Pacific Coast (Plan de Desarrollo Integral para la Costa Pacífica, PLADEICOP) in 1983. The Plan significantly changed the policy of neglect that the government had maintained for centuries toward this region. It was designed and implemented by a regional development corporation, the Autonomous Corporation of the Cauca (cvc), that had been set up in the mid-1950s with World Bank funding and the advice of David Lilienthal of the Tennessee Valley Authority, and was based in Cali. Since its inception, the cvc has been the chief social force shaping the dynamic capitalist development of the fertile Cauca River Valley area in southwestern Colombia.

In keeping with the regional development approach followed by the corporation in the Andean Cauca Valley, the new plan for the Pacific Coast had three basic components: the building of infrastructure (roads, electrification, water supply, etc.); social services (health, education, nutrition, women's income-generating programs); and rural development projects for small farmers in the riverine settlements. The main achievement of the Plan, however, was the creation for the first time in the country's history of an image of the Pacific Coast region as an integrated ecocultural and geographic whole susceptible to systematic and well-concerted development. This "developmentalization" was the most important resignification to which the region has been subjected in the modern period. It placed the region into a new regime of representation in which capital, science, and the institutions of the state provide the signifying categories. PLADEICOP began and then intensified the project of modernity in the littoral by creating the necessary infrastructure for capital to arrive in an ordered way and by initiating the process of expert-based social intervention, so central to modernity, throughout the towns and riverine communities of the littoral. In fact, reversing the conventional development philosophy of seeing economic growth as the driving force for social development and following UNICEF's lead and the basic human needs approach that became trendy in the early 1980s, PLADEICOP attempted to place social programs at the basis of their strategy for "integral development."

Nevertheless, the design and implementation of the basic social services programs were marred by many problems, including the fact that the programs obeyed technocratic blueprints crafted for the extremely different conditions existing in the Andean interior of the country. Despite some attempts to enlist local participation, the programs did not take into account local cultures and conditions. For instance, in the late 1980s and early 1990s, agriculturalists in river communities were offered a package of credit and technical assistance for the cultivation and commercialization of cocoa and coconut. This package mimicked the integrated rural development packages designed more than a decade earlier for Andean peasants. The program overlooked the very different social, ecological, and farming conditions and practices of the local Afro-Colombian families. By introducing practices such as the "farm planning methodology," which called for profit-oriented models of cultivation and accounting, unheard of previously in the region, the program fostered the cultural reconversion necessary for the successful commodification of land, labor, and subsistence agriculture. Indeed, some of the farmers participating in the program seemed to undergo this transformation, while still retaining many of their traditional beliefs and practices concerning the land, nature, the economy, and life in general. The program thus started the process of cultural hybridization of nonmodern and modern forms fostered by development interventions in so many parts of the third world.

Since the late 1980s, the government has been pursuing an overarching policy of integration with the Pacific Basin economies. The Pacific Ocean — rebaptized as "the sea of the xxi century" — is seen as the socioeconomic and, to a lesser extent, cultural space of the future. Within this nascent imaginary, the Pacific Coast littoral occupies an important place as the launching platform for the macroeconomics of the future. As we will see, the discovery of the region's biodiversity is an important component of this imaginary. It coexists contradictorily, however, with the radical policy of economic *apertura* inaugurated by the government after 1990. In the midst of this contradiction, development approaches have taken two directions. On the one hand, there is the dominant intervention, an ambitious plan for "sustainable development," the Plan Pacífico.[8] This plan is even more conventional in its design than PLADEICOP, and its results will be more devastating. It self-consciously promotes capitalist development. As such, it is opposed by black and indigenous communities, who see in the discourse of *apertura* an ominous trend for wresting away from them control of the rich resources of the region. On the other hand, the government has also started a more modest ($9 million as compared with the $250 million allocated to Plan Pacífico for a four-year period) project for the conservation of the region's biological diversity, under the sponsorship of the GEF.[9] We shall return to this project in the next section.

New Forms of Capital in the Pacific Coast Region

Timber and mining have been extractive activities in the Pacific Coast rainforest for decades, although the scale of operations has increased with the use of technologies such as industrial gold mining, a good part of which is fueled by drug money. Timber is harvested by large multinational and Colombian companies and by poor colonists. Deforestation from all sources reaches 600,000 hectares a year by some estimates. In recent years, besides an increase in capital accumulation in these sectors, and in the wake of Pacific Basin integration and *apertura* strategies, investment in the new sectors has increased, such as in African palm plantations for the production of oil, artificial shrimp cultivation, hearts of palm canning, coastal and offshore fishing, shrimp and fish processing and packaging for export, and tourism.

Each of these new forms of investment is producing noticeable cultural, ecological, and social transformations, most visible perhaps in the Tumaco region in the southern part of the littoral, near the border with Ecuador, where African palm oil production and shrimp cultivation have reached sizable levels. Land for African palm plantations has been obtained from black farmers by force or purchase, causing massive displacement from the land and intensive proletarianization. Displaced people now work for meager wages in the plantations or, in the case of women, in shrimp and fish packaging plants in the port city of Tumaco. Colombia is now the fifth largest producer of African palm oil; production has increased sharply especially in the Tumaco area after 1985, mostly in large plantations of several thousand hectares, set up by well-known capitalist groups from Cali. In dollar terms, African palm now represents 3 percent of the GDP in agriculture; it is a significant operation that has transformed the biocultural landscape of the area from small patches of cultivated land by local people in the midst of the forest to the interminable rows of palm trees so characteristic of modern agriculture. The army of workers start their journey from the rivers of adjacent towns to the plantations before daybreak, returning to their homes at the end of the day, day after day, unable any longer to engage in their own farming activities.

The construction of large pools for shrimp cultivation has similarly modified the local cultural and physical landscapes. It has disrupted the fragile balance of river/sea borderline ecosystems, destroying large areas of mangroves and estuaries essential to the reproduction of marine and river life. The destruction is more advanced in neighboring Ecuador, where the farm production of shrimp reaches many times that of Colombia. The shrimp is processed and packaged locally by women under conditions reminiscent of those faced by the women studied by Aihwa Ong in multinational electronics factories in Malaysia.[10] Many of these women previously practiced subsistence agriculture, fishing, or charcoal making and have now joined the ranks of the new proletariat under extremely precarious conditions. In both African palm and shrimp cultivation sectors, these nineteenth-century conditions of work coexist with late twentieth-century technology; African palm production, for example, has benefited greatly from genetic improvement carried out in the larger producer countries, such as Malaysia and Indonesia.[11] Shrimp cultivation is also a highly technologized operation, requiring laboratory preparation of the seed, artificial feeding, and careful monitoring of the conditions of cultivation. Science and capital thus operate as apparatuses of capture[12] that have remade and disciplined the landscape, money, and labor alike in one single, complex operation.

In the past, as anthropological studies suggest, the integration of Afro-Colombians into the capitalist world economy was based on limited boom-and-bust cycles that did not produce enduring transformations in the local cultural fabric and social structures. Local communities were able to resist, utilize, and adapt to the boom-and-bust dynamics without very significant permanent alterations.[13] The scale and form of new capital forces, however, is making long-standing adaptive strategies untenable. Socially, new forms of poverty and inequality are appearing as displaced people move to crowded slums in booming cities like Tumaco, which has doubled its population (now about 100,000) in less than a decade. Politically, a new black elite has appeared that wants to take control of their part of the "development pie," "modernize" black culture and institutions, and finally bring blacks "into the twentieth century." Capitalists foster these changes with some degree of consciousness, forming convenient alliances with the nascent local elites. While they are beginning to fear widespread violence as in other parts of the country, they are not willing to slow down the pace of accumulation.

BIODIVERSITY: NEW IMAGINARY OF NATURE AND CULTURE

Nothing is more inimical to the much-touted conservation of rainforest biodiversity than gold mining, plantation agriculture, uncontrolled timber extraction, and the like. Yet the argument has been made that capital might be entering an "ecological phase" in which capital's modern, reckless logic would coexist with a postmodern, conservationist tendency.[14] The label *green capitalism* is an expression of this change, even if the concrete modes of operation and the mutual articulation and conflict of the two forms of capital — modern and postmodern, let us say — are not well understood yet, and certainly escape the superficial connotations suggested by "green capitalism." The fact is that a powerful discourse emphasizing the preservation of the earth's species, ecosystem, and genetic diversity as one of the most important issues of the times has arisen in recent years, and its credo is rapidly spreading in many quarters. It is by no means an arbitrary event; after two centuries of systematic destruction of nature, the biodiversity discourse responds to what might be called "the irruption of the biological," that is, the survival of biological life as a central problem for the modern order.

The discourse of biodiversity promises to deliver nature from the grip of destructive practices and establish in its stead a conservationist culture. This constitutes a new way of talking about nature deeply mediated by technoscience, and a new interface between nature, capital, and science. The origins of this discourse are very recent indeed; they can be traced to two founding texts, the *Global Biodiversity Strategy*[15] and the Biodiversity Convention signed at the Earth Summit in Rio de Janeiro in 1992. The chief architects of the discourse are easily identifiable: northern environmental NGOs, particularly the Washington, D.C.-based World Resources Institute (WRI) and the Swiss-based World Conservation Union (previously IUCN); the World Bank's GEF, a multibillion-dollar fund with 40 percent of its budget earmarked for biodiversity conservation; and the United Nations Environment Program (UNEP). Dozens of documents, reports, and expert meetings on the scientific, institutional, and programmatic aspects of biodiversity conservation have succeeded in consolidating the discourse and deploying an institutional apparatus devoted to its growing reach and sophistication.

The key to biodiversity conservation, in the view propagated by dominant institutions, resides in finding ways of using rainforest resources that ensure their long-term conservation. These uses must be based on the scientific knowledge of biodiversity, which is acknowledged to be extremely inadequate at present since only a relatively small percentage of the world's species is known to science; appropriate systems of management; and adequate mechanisms of intellectual property rights for the protection of those discoveries that might lead to commercial applications. As the subtitle of *Global Biodiversity Strategy* reads, after modification by one of the world's foremost biodiversity experts, Daniel Janzen: "you've got to know it to use it, and you've got to use it to save it." Biodiversity prospecting — the surveying and screening of nature by taxonomists, botanists, and others with the goal of finding species that might lead to valuable pharmaceutical, agrochemical, food, or other commercial applications — is emerging as a leading practice among those adhering to the "know it–save it–use it" equation. Also known as "gene hunting," since the promise of conservation-*cum*-profits is believed to lie in the genes of the species, biodiversity prospecting is presented as a respectable protocol of saving nature.[16] In various "hot spots" of diversity in the third world, prospecting activities of this sort are underway, involving prospectors such as U.S. and European botanical gardens' staff, pharmaceutical companies, independent biologists, and third world NGOS. Prospecting and biodiversity inventories oftentimes rely, as in Costa Rica, on the labor of parataxonomists and paraecologists, who act as paramedics of nature under the guidance of highly trained biologists belonging to what Janzen calls the "international taxasphere."[17]

The apparatus for biodiversity production encompasses a host of disparate actors — from northern NGOS, international organizations, botanical gardens, universities, and corporations, to newly created national biodiversity institutes in the third world, third world planners and biologists, and local communities and activists — each with their respective interpretive framework of what biodiversity is, should be, or could get to be. These frameworks are mediated by machines of all kinds, from the magnifying lens of the botanist to the computer-processed satellite data fed to Geographical Information Systems (GIS) programming and forecasting. Species, including humans, and machines participate in the making of biodiversity as a historical discourse in what can be seen as another example of the mutual production of technoscience and society.[18] This discursive formation can be theorized as a network with multiple agents and sites where knowledge is produced, contested, utilized, and transformed. We will see shortly how black activists of the Pacific Coast have attempted to insert themselves in this network.

One interesting feature characterizing the biodiversity network is that, despite the dominance of northern discourses and perhaps for the first time in the history of development, a number of third world NGOS have been successful in articulating an oppositional view that is circulating in some of the network sites, thanks in part to new practices and media such as electronic networks and the UN preparatory meetings. Although this is an aspect that cannot be elaborated upon in this essay, it is important to point out that from the perspectives of these NGOS — most of them from South and Southeast Asia, a few in Latin America — the dominant strategy amounts to a form of bioimperialism. GEF projects, for instance, usually come in connection with other conventional initiatives of rainforest utilization and privatization. More importantly, critics argue that biotechnology-based biodiversity conservation will in fact erode biodiversity, given that all biotechnology depends on the creation of uniform market commodities. The history of the genetic manipulation of seeds, for instance, is also the history of its progressive commodification and the loss of seed diversity.[19] Habitat destruction by development projects and monocultures of mines and agriculture are the main sources of biodiversity destruction, not the activities of poor forest peoples. With GEF and biodiversity prospecting, destruction is furthered, not contained; dominant strategies amount to placing the wolf in charge of the sheep.[20]

From a biological standpoint, biodiverse ecosystems are characterized by a multiplicity of interactions and the coevolution of species in such a way that biological disturbances are reduced, biological threats minimized, and multiple outcomes favored. Culturally, third world critics strategically argue, diverse societies in forest areas have favored self-organization, production based on the logic of diversity, and cropping practices that favor diversity, such as multiple cropping, crop rotation, extractive reserves, and multiple outcomes. To the regime of bio-imperialism, critics like Vandana Shiva maintain, should be opposed a notion of biodemocracy predicated on the termination of large-scale development projects, the recognition of community rights, a redefinition of productivity and efficiency to reflect multiple outcome ecosystems, a recognition of the cultural character of biodiversity, and local control of the resources by communities.

Without attempting to analyze the rationality of these claims — and avoiding the trap of assuming a priori any sort of "primitive environmental wisdom" or the existence of a benevolent relation between local culture and sustainability, as many environmentalist are prone to do[21] — it is possible to underscore, from an anthropological point of view, the necessary connection that exists between a system of meanings of nature and concrete practices of nature. This relation is not static. New ecological, cultural, and political orders are continuously being crafted at the local level as communities are brought into the politics of development, capital, and expert knowledge. There is a connection between history, identity, and meanings that regulates local environmental practices. In the rainforests of the world, more often than not the use-meanings in place account for practices of nature that are ostensibly different from those characteristic of Western modernity.

The biodiversity discourse embodies the postmodern form of capital;[22] it effects a resignification of the rainforest (as a reservoir of value at the genetic level), its peoples (as "custodians of nature"), and their knowledge (as traditional knowledge of saving nature). Whether this set of resignifications will necessarily result in new forms of colonization of the biophysical and human landscapes, or contribute to creating new economic and political possibilities for local communities, is still an open question. The answer will depend largely on the extent to which local communities succeed in appropriating and utilizing the new significations for their own ends, linking them to other identities, circuits of knowledge, and political projects. This in turn brings into consideration the strength of local social movements. Will rainforest social movements be able to become significant social actors in the conversations that are shaping rainforest futures? Will they be able to participate in the coproduction of technoscience and society, nature and culture, set into motion by the biodiversity network?

COLLECTIVE ACTION, ETHNIC IDENTITY, AND THE POLITICS OF NATURE

The events of recent years in tropical rainforest areas suggest that what is at stake there goes beyond the politics of resources, the environment, and even representation. At issue is the existence of multiple constructions of nature in all of its complexity, contrasting practices of meanings-use, entire groups with different outlooks on life, the dreams of collectivities. They also make visible power configurations in the making, woven by the development apparatus out of the fabric of capital and technoscience. In short, rainforest events present us with a cultural politics of nature, the lessons of which overflow the rainforests themselves. One of the most salient aspects of this cultural politics is the organized responses emerging from it in the form of social movements.

In Colombia, attempts at black organizing in recent decades have taken place since the early 1970s, mostly in urban areas, inspired by the U.S. black movement. These efforts emphasized the exploitation and resistance of black people since their arrival as slaves in the New World. Studies of the afrogenesis of black people in the country became important in this regard; politically, the strategies of early and most present-day urban black movement organizations have emphasized the pursuit of equality and integration within society at large. Only in recent years, particularly as a result of the emergence of a black movement in the Pacific Coast, has cultural difference become the most important banner of black organizing. Two factors have been most important in this regard: the developmentalist and capitalist onslaught on the region, fostered by the process of *apertura* and the country's integration in the Pacific Rim; and the process of constitutional reform that culminated with the election in 1991 of a National Constituent Assembly and the reform of the 1886 constitution.

Intended to build a multicultural, pluriethnic society — and thus reversing the nineteenth-century project of constructing a homogeneous national identity through race blending and assimilation into mestizo (coded white) culture — the new constitution granted unprecedented rights to indigenous, ethnic, and religious minorities. The reform of the constitution served as a historical conjuncture for a variety of social processes, black and indigenous organizing being the most visible of them. For the black communities of the Pacific Coast, it was a question of unprecedented identity construction under the guise of cultural, political, and socioeconomic demands and proposals. While blacks were unsuccessful in securing their own representatives in the Constituent Assembly, the plight of Pacific Coast blacks was presented in the Assembly by the indigenous representatives. Initially approved by the Assembly as a provisional measure, Transitory Article 55 (A.T. 55), the cultural and territorial rights of the black communities were finally enshrined in the constitution as a law (Ley 70) two years later, in July 1993.

The process of black organizing in the Pacific Coast and other parts of Colombia grew in intensity and complexity from the initial drive to obtain representation in the Constituent Assembly, to the ensuing mobilization to draft and get approved the transitory article into a law during the years 1991–93, to today's complex and conflictual negotiations entailed by the demarcation of the collective territories under Ley 70. By the time Ley 70 came into effect, the conjunctural character of the organizing process fostered by the constitutional reform had been largely superseded, and a widespread and heterogeneous movement had come into place. The fact that the new constitution allocated several seats in the national congress to ethnic and religious minorities motivated the opportunistic appearance of "black leaders" associated with the traditional political parties and the nascent black elite. Despite these difficulties, and despite increasing divisions within the black movement itself, particularly between the northern Chocó organizations and those from the southern part of the littoral, an increasingly articulate movement continued to grow throughout the first half of the decade.[23]

The organizing drive for A.T. 55 and Ley 70 made manifest to the rest of the nation the presence of unsuspectedly vibrant black communities along the rivers of the littoral. The fact that these communities had maintained significantly different cultural practices and social relations also became visible, thus contributing to reverse the long-standing Andean-based representations of the region as a jungle inhabited by indolent people unable to exploit its resources. The rich cultural traditions of the people, the exploding discourse around the region's biodiversity, the government's commitment to its "sustainable development," and the possibility of collective land titling for the local communities became the most important elements for activists in their attempt at launching a well-coordinated, massive campaign for black rights. This determination crystallized in important events such as the Third National Convention of Black Communities, realized in a predominantly black town in the southern tip of the Cauca River Valley in September 1993. At this event, attended by more than three hundred activists from various parts of the country, it was agreed that the goal of the strategy should be "the consolidation of a social movement of black communities of national scope capable of undertaking the reconstruction and affirmation of black cultural identity," a process to be based in turn "on the construction of an autonomous organizing process aimed at struggling for our [black people's] cultural, social, economic, and territorial rights, and for the defense of natural resources and the environment."[24]

The same declaration identified and explained the movement's main principles for political organizing as follows: First, the right to an identity, that is, the right to being black according to the cultural logic and worldview rooted in black experience, in contradistinction to the dominating national culture; this principle also called for the reconstitution of black consciousness itself and the rejection of the dominant discourse of "equality" with its concomitant obliteration of difference. Second, the right to a territory as a space for being and an essential element for the development of culture. Third, the right to political autonomy as a prerequisite for the practice of being, with the possibility of fostering social and economic autonomy. Fourth, the right to construct their own vision of the future, development, and social practice based on customary forms of production and social organization. Fifth, a principle of solidarity with the struggles of black peoples for alternative visions throughout the world.

The approval of these principles as the basis for the articulation of a black movement of national scope was not achieved at the convention because the black organizations of the Chocó refused to endorse them; once Ley 70 was approved, they argued, the direction of the movement could not be dictated only by those who had been prominent in the organizing effort around A.T. 55, but should be expanded to all communities and social actors, presumably the traditional political parties as well. As the only black *departamento* (province) in the nation, the Chocó region had a long history of traditional party activity; this became sharply visible when the time came for electing black representatives to the national congress, for which their candidates predominated. The debate on electoral participation thus acted as a divisive force among the black communities of the southern littoral, the Chocó, and the Atlantic Coast. Confronted with these divisions, the organizations from the south, particularly those gathered around the Organization of Black Communities of Buenaventura—the major city of the entire region, with about 250,000 inhabitants, mostly black—decided to constitute themselves into a Network of Black Communities (Proceso Nacional de Comunidades Negras, PCN), while continuing to push for the creation of a national movement of black communities.[25]

The most distinctive feature of the PCN is the articulation of a political proposal with a primarily ethnocultural character and basis. Their vision is not that of a movement based on a catalogue of "needs" and demands for "development," but a struggle couched in terms of the defense of cultural difference. In this lies the most radical character of the movement. The shift to emphasizing difference was a pivotal decision, as some of the leading activists explain:

We don't know exactly when we started to talk about cultural difference. But at some point we refused to go on building a strategy around a catalogue of "problems" and "needs." The government continues to bet on democracy and difference; we respond by emphasizing cultural autonomy and the right to be who we are and defend our own life project. To recognize the need to be different, to build an identity, are difficult tasks that demand persistent work among our communities, taking their very heterogeneity as a point of departure. However, the fact that we do not have worked out social and economic proposals makes us vulnerable to the current onslaught by capital. This is one of our foremost political tasks at present: to advance in the formulation and implementation of alternative social and economic proposals.[26]

The "persistent work" referred to in this interview has been impressive indeed. As mentioned before, the conceptualization and actual drafting of Ley 70 was the linchpin for the organizing process, particularly in river communities, although much less so in urban areas where organizing the communities has proven to be much more difficult and ineffective. From 1991 to 1993, activists organized information and discussion workshops in a large number of river communities on topics such as the concept of territory, traditional production practices, natural resources, the meaning of development, and the question of black identity. Results of these workshops in the local communities were subsequently taken up to subregional and, finally, national forums where all of the multiple conceptions were discussed. This construction was advanced as a dual process: first, according to "the logic of the river," that is, taking as a point of departure the everyday life and aspirations of the local communities; and second, by engaging in a more thorough conceptual elaboration on identity, territory, development, and political strategy at the regional and national levels. Out of this double process emerged the five principles proposed at the Third National Convention.[27]

The choice of cultural difference as an articulating concept for political strategy was informed by various historical factors, although it was, of course, related to the broader debates propitiated by the constitutional reform. In their reinterpretation of the history of the region, Pacific Coast activists not only moved away from the integrationist perspective, strongly denouncing the myth of racial democracy,[28] they also highlighted the fact that black communities of the littoral have historically favored isolation from the national society and economy, while recognizing that this ethics of isolation and independence is increasingly untenable under today's forceful policies of integration and the inevitable presence of modern media, commodities, and the like. The relationship between territory and culture is of paramount importance in this regard. Activists conceptualize the territory as "a space for the creation of futures, for hope and the continuation of existence." The loss of territory is likened to "a return to the times of slavery."[29] The territory is also an economic conception to the extent that it is linked to natural resources and biodiversity.

The interest in biodiversity stems from this recognition. It provides an opening to the future. It is not a coincidence that several articulate black professionals associated with the movement have decided to participate in the national biodiversity project. While they recognize the risks entailed by this participation, they believe that the discourse of biodiversity presents possibilities they cannot afford to ignore. Biodiversity might also be an important element in the formulation of alternative development strategies. As activists are quick to mention, they know they do not want any form of conventional development, although they are less clear about what they do want.[30] They also recognize that experts (planners, ecologists, anthropologists, biologists, etc.) might be important allies in this regard. This suggests the possibility for a new practice of collaboration between experts and social movement activists. The role of mediation that experts may play between the state and social movements needs to be theorized further.[31] Dissident, oppositional, and solidarity practices need to be imagined by those who are experts in the discourses of modernity.

The notion of "territory" is a new concept in rainforest social struggles. All over Latin America, peasants have engaged in struggles over "land." The right to a territory—as an ecological, productive, and cultural space—is a new political demand. This demand is fostering an important reterritorialization, as Deleuze and Guattari refer to processes of this type[32]—that is, the formation of new territories fueled by novel political perceptions and practices. Social movement activists fulfill this role as well: to make evident both the processes of deterritorialization and reterritorialization effected by the apparatuses of capture of modernity, such as capital, media, and the development apparatus (for example, the centrifugal forces of media on local cultures and the reorganization of the landscape by African palm plantations and shrimp cultivation), and the potential reterritorializations by the mobilized communities. During the organizing for Ley 70, this process took a literal form, that of physically traveling up and down the rivers with local people to identify long-standing patterns of land use, signs of new occupations (e.g., by colonists of the interior), and signaling possibilities for reterritorialization of forest "empty" lands. This was an important movement practice. The collective traveling of the territory was shaped and favored by the fractal character and contours of littoral, rivers, estuaries, forest edges, and patterns of cultivation.

Like territory, the question of identity is at the heart of the movement. Most Pacific Coast activists take identity to be based on a set of cultural practices believed to characterize "black culture": practices such as shifting and diverse economic activities, the importance of oral traditions, the ethics of nonaccumulation, the importance of kindred and extended families, matrilineality, local knowledge of the forest, and the like. However, activists are increasingly drawn to understanding identity as a construction, thus converging in some ways with current scholarly trends. Social movement theorists have underscored that the construction of collective identities is an essential feature of contemporary struggles.[33] Recent work in cultural studies has contributed additional insights regarding ethnic identities. Stuart Hall, for instance, has suggested that the construction of ethnic identities is marked by a certain doubleness.[34] Identity is thought, on the one hand, to be rooted in a shared culture embodied in concrete practices, a collective self of sorts; this conception of identity has played an important role in anticolonial struggles; it involves an imaginative rediscovery whose importance cannot be overestimated, to the extent that it contributes coherence to the experience of fragmentation, dispersal, and oppression. On the other hand, while recognizing continuity and similarity, another conception of identity highlights the difference created by history: it emphasizes becoming rather than being, and involves positioning rather than essence, discontinuity as well as continuity.

The coexistence of difference and sameness constitutes the doubleness of cultural identity today. Identity is thus seen as something that is negotiated in economic, political, and cultural terms. For communities of the African diaspora, cultural identity involves a retelling of the past "by another route":[35] Africa not as ancestral land but as it has become in the New World, mediated by colonialism. This retelling takes place in two other contexts: that of the European and Euro-American presence — a dialogue of power and resistance, recognition of the inevitable and irreversible influence of modernity; and the context of the "New World," where the African and the European are always creolized, where cultural identity is characterized by difference, heterogeneity, and hybridity.

The doubleness of identity can be seen at play in the Pacific Coast black movement. For the activists, the defense of certain cultural practices of the river communities is a strategic question to the extent that they are seen as embodying resistance to capitalism and modernity. Although their arguments are often couched in a culturalist language, they are aware that the intransigent defense of black culture is less desirable than a cautious opening to the future, including a critical engagement with modernity. The challenges they see the movement facing stem from this recognition, challenges that include acknowledging the heterogeneity of the movement(s); addressing the specificities of the movement, particularly the inclusion of gender as an organizing principle for the movement as a whole, without decontextualizing it from the overall cultural and ethnic struggle; consolidating the organizations of river communities, particularly through the creation of local councils for the implementation of territorial law; and reaching black people in urban areas, which has proven difficult until now. One of the most pressing needs, of course, is to articulate alternative socioeconomic proposals, lest they be swept away by green redevelopment in the fashion of Plan Pacífico. The increasing presence of drug money after 1995, particularly in industrial gold mining, is one of the toughest forces impinging upon the movement, given the tremendously deleterious effects it is having on the physical and cultural ecologies. It is, indeed, a problem they feel unable to face without national and international support.

The discourse of biodiversity and the potential for biotechnology-based economic projects appeal to the movement, to the extent that they might present opportunities for improving living standards while avoiding the destruction of nature and local cultures. Unlike the view from the state and the ecodevelopment apparatus, the scope for using natural resources sustainably is seen by the movement from the perspectives of territory and identity. It is, in short, a question of cultural politics. Unfortunately, the bargaining position of the local communities is weak. In addition, black movement organizations have to compete with stronger institutions and organizations for the political space generated around environment and development. Timber extraction, gold mining, shrimp cultivation, hearts of palm canning, and other extractive activities continue apace in some areas even in contravention of Ley 70, oftentimes with the complicity of local authorities and without the movement's being able to put a stop to them. However, social movement organizations have been able to negotiate successfully with the state in several cases involving environmental conflict.[36]

To sum up, the discourses of biodiversity and the dynamics of capital in its ecological phase open up spaces that activists try to seize upon as points of struggle. This dialectic posits a number of paradoxes for the movement, including the contradictory aspects of defending local nature and culture by relying on languages that do not reflect the local experience of nature and culture. The alliance between social movements and the state effected by the biodiversity project is tenuous at best; it is foreseeable that the tension will grow as the project's national staff continue their attempts at tempering the political nature of the project by emphasizing its scientific aspects instead, and as prospecting activities and agreements with private agents start to take place. Community needs and aspirations will not be easily accommodated into these schemes, as the experience with GEF projects in other countries indicates. As we shall see below, however, theoretically there are grounds for envisaging alliances between local communities and technoscience. The political expediency of these alliances should not be hastily dismissed.

THE CULTURAL POLITICS OF HYBRID NATURES

The ways of understanding and relating to nature that have existed in the Pacific Coast region are being transformed by the increased presence of capital, development, and modernity, including the discourses of sustainable development and biodiversity. Programs for small farmers in river communities, for instance, affect conceptions of land and the forest, even if they do not displace completely older systems of meanings-use. Nature starts to be conceived of in terms of "natural resources," an idiom that local people are increasingly adept at using. Even the concept of biodiversity is beginning to circulate locally as a currency of sorts, with ambiguous and imprecise meanings.

What lends tropical rainforest areas specificity in today's politics of nature and culture worldwide is the coexistence — even in stark contrast — of different modes of historical consciousness and practices of nature. Black and indigenous communities, African palm and shrimp production capitalists, and advocates of biodiversity prospecting seem to enact different modes of nature. We may speak of three different regimes for the production of nature — organic, capitalist, and technonature — that can be characterized only briefly in this paper. Broadly speaking, organic nature represents those modes that are not strictly modern; from the perspective of the anthropology of local knowledge, they may be characterized in terms of the relative indissociability of the biophysical, human, and spiritual worlds, vernacular social relations, nonmodern circuits of knowledge, and forms of meanings-use of nature that do not spell the systematic destruction of nature. Capitalized nature, on the contrary, is based on the separation of the human and natural worlds, and capitalist and patriarchal social relations. From the perspective of historical materialism, it appears as produced through the mediation of labor. Technonature, finally, is nature produced by new forms of technoscience, particularly those based on molecular technologies. As argued in poststructuralist and feminist studies of science and technology, it appears as produced more by technoscientific intervention than by labor-based production of value. But meanings, labor, and technoscience are important to all three regimes.

These three regimes for the production of nature, it must be pointed out, do not represent stages in the history of social nature; it is not a linear sequence, since the three regimes coexist and overlap. Although the three of them represent instances of constructed nature — to the extent that nature never exists for humans outside of history — the respective practices of construction are relatively distinct. The terms *organic, capitalized,* and *technonature* are used to convey particular intensities and practices of meanings-use. More important, the three regimes produce each other symbolically and materially; they represent relational elements in the forms of nature's production. Moreover, the dominant capitalist nature necessarily invents its own forms of organic (for instance, ecotourism and a large part of environmentalism, which are forms of capitalist organicity) and technonatures; most biodiversity prospecting applications today could be thought of as capitalist technonature. It is important to emphasize that within organic nature the rainforest is not an external resource but an integral part of social and cultural life. In this resides its difference, to the extent that capitalist forms of the organic cannot reconstitute this integral relationship.

One could then posit the hypothesis that today's landscapes of nature and culture are characterized by hybrid natures. Hybrid natures would take a special form in tropical rainforest areas, where popular groups and social movements would seek to defend through novel practices organic nature against the ravages of capitalist nature, with technonature — biotechnology-based conservation and use of resources — as a possible ally. The feasibility of this strategy raises many important intellectual and political questions. For instance, what sort of collective practices — by cultural activists, scientists, ecologists, feminists, planners, prospectors — could foster hybrid natures that contribute to the affirmation of local cultures and postdevelopment? How could local activists position themselves effectively in the network of biodiversity production. How could anthropologists and others contribute to invent new ways of talking about nature that are appropriate to the new tools for conceiving of and producing nature now in place?

The obstacles to this strategy of hybrid natures are immense, and here is not the place to discuss them. Activists in the Pacific Coast, in their attempt to reconfigure traditions and infuse them with an operational measure of diversity, seem to be aware of the need to take traditions into new directions, some of which will perhaps be unrecognizable or even undesirable from today's vantage point. But this might be the only way in which, out of their limited power and with the odds stacked against them, Afro-Colombians might retain a degree of autonomy in a world where not only traditions but also many of the markers of modernity seem to be increasingly weakened. At the margins of the "Black Atlantic,"[37] they make us aware of the recombinant aspects of nature and culture from a place in which organicity and artificiality might not be mortal enemies, and where the unbounding of culture and ethnicity might not spell the end of local communities rich in diverse traditions.

In places like the Pacific Coast of Colombia, struggles for cultural difference are also struggles for biological diversity. What kinds of nature will it be possible to design and protect under these conditions? Is it possible to construct a cultural politics of biodiversity that does not deepen the colonization of natural and cultural landscapes characteristic of modernity? Perhaps in the tropical rainforests of the world we might have the chance to weave together sociosphere, biosphere, and machinosphere in novel "ecosophical" practices.[38] By envisaging other forms of being modern, we might be able to renew our solidarity with what until now we have called nature.

Placed at the juncture of different historical and epistemic regimes — the hybridization of which constitutes a unique form of postmodernity — struggles in the world's rainforests might have exemplary stories about what "nature" has been, is, and might get to be in the future. Here may lie one of the deepest meanings of dissent: the creation of life possibilities and modes of existence through new concepts and practices, particularly those that most people might find unthinkable or impracticable. If it is true that the task of philosophy is the creation of concepts — a construction of life possibilities through novel practices of thought, imagination, and understanding[39] — and that this task today entails a recasting of the resistance to capitalism, then activists in the world's rainforests might be keeping alive the dream of other peoples and lands of the future. Utopian? Perhaps. But let us keep in mind that "utopia designates the conjunction of philosophy with the present. . . . It is with utopia that philosophy becomes political, carrying to its extreme the critique of its era."[40] Some of these utopias of nature and culture can be read in the dissenting practices of black activists of the Pacific Coast of Colombia.

NOTES

This essay is based on fieldwork carried out from January to December of 1993. The research was conducted by a small research team coordinated by Alvaro Pedrosa and myself, including two researchers from the Pacific Coast. The group project was funded by grants from the Division of Arts and Humanities of the Rockefeller Foundation, the Social Science Research Council, and the Heinz Endowment. I am grateful to them for their support. I also thank Alvaro Pedrosa (Universidad del Calle, Cali); Libia Grueso and Carlos Rosero (Organización de Comunidades Negras de Buenaventura); Tracey Tsugawa, Jesús Alberto Grueso, and Betty Ruth Lozano (members of the research team); and the participants at the Harry Guggenheim Conference in Ecuador — particularly Sonia E. Alvarez, Orin Starn, and Faye Ginsburg — for their concern and support when I was hospitalized in Quito. I also thank my Quito friends Beatriz Andrade and Susana Wappenstein in this regard.

1. Donna Haraway, *Simians, Cyborgs, and Women: The Reinvention of Nature* (New York: Routledge, 1991), 1.

2. Paul Rabinow, "Artificiality and Enlightenment: From Sociobiology to Biosociality," in *Incorporations*, ed. J. Crary and S. Kwinter (New York: Zone Books, 1992), 141.

3. Edward O. Wilson, *The Diversity of Life* (New York: Norton, 1992), 1, 7.

4. Ibid., 15.

5. Arturo Escobar, *Encountering Development: The Making and Unmaking of the Third World* (Princeton: Princeton University Press, 1995).

6. Martin O'Connor, "On the Misadventures of Capitalist Nature," *Capitalism, Nature, Socialism* 4, no. 4 (1993): 7–34.

7. Norman Whitten, *Black Frontiersmen: Afro-Hispanic Culture of Ecuador and Colombia* (Prospect Heights, IL: Waveland Press, 1986); Nina Sánchez de Friedemann, *Críele Críele Son* (Bogotá: Planeta, 1989).

8. Departamento Nacional de Planeación de Colombia, *Plan Pacífico: Una Estrategia de Desarrollo Sostenible para la Costa Pacífico de Colombia* (Bogotá: DNP, 1992).

9. Global Environment Facility/United Nations Development Program, *Conservación de la Biodiversidad del Chocó Biogeográfico: Proyecto Biopacífico* (Bogotá: DNP/Biopacífico, 1993).

10. Aihwa Ong, *Spirits of Resistance and Capitalist Discipline* (Albany: State University of New York Press, 1987).

11. Arturo Escobar, "Viejas y nuevas formas de capital y los dilemas de la biodiversidad." In *Pacífico: Desarrollo o Diversidad?* ed. A. Escobar and A. Pedrosa (Bogotá: CEREC/ECOFONDO), 109–131.

12. Gilles Deleuze and Félix Guattari, *A Thousand Plateaus,* trans. Brian Massumi (Minneapolis: University of Minnesota Press, 1987).

13. Whitten, *Black Frontiersmen;* Jaime Arocha, "La Ensenada de Tumaco: Invisibilidad, Incertidumbre e Innovación," *América Negra* 1 (1991): 87–112.

14. O'Connor, "On The Misadventures of Capitalist Nature."

15. World Resources Institute, World Conservation Union, United Nations Environment Program, *Global Biodiversity Strategy* (Washington, D.C: WRI/IUNC/UNEP, 1991).

16. World Resources Institute, *Biodiversity Prospecting* (Oxford: Oxford University Press, 1993).

17. Daniel Janzen and H. Hallwachs, *All Taxa Biodiversity Inventory* (Philadelphia: University of Philadelphia Press, 1993); Daniel Janzen, H. Hallwachas, J. Jiménez, and R. Gómez, "The Role of the Parataxonomists, Inventory Managers and Taxonomists in Costa Rica's National Biodiversity Inventory," in *Biodiversity Prospecting,* by World Resources Institute (Oxford: Oxford University Press, 1993).

18. Haraway, *Simians, Cyborgs, and Women.*

19. Jack Kloppenburg, *First the Seed: The Political Economy of Plant Biotechnology, 1492–2000* (Cambridge: Cambridge University Press, 1988).

20. Vandana Shiva, *Monocultures of the Mind: Perspectives on Biodiversity and Biotechnology* (London: Zed Books, 1993); Vandana Shiva, ed., *Close to Home: Women Reconnect Ecology, Health, and Development Worldwide* (London: Zed Books, 1994); Christine von Weizsacker, "Competing Notions of Biodiversity," in *Global Ecology,* ed. W. Sachs (London: Zed Books, 1993), 117–131.

21. Kay Milton, ed., *Environmentalism: The View from Anthropology* (London: Routledge, 1993); Mark Hobart, ed., *An Anthropological Critique of Development* (London: Routledge, 1993); Gudrun Dahl, ed., *Green Arguments for Local Subsistance* (Stockholm: Stockholm University Press, 1993).

22. Arturo Escobar, "Constructing Nature: Elements for a Poststructuralist Political Ecology." In *Liberation Ecologies,* ed. R. Peet and M. Watts (London: Routledge, 1996), 46–68.

23. This brief account of the black movement is based on my own research with Alvaro Pedrosa. See Arturo Escobar and Alvaro Pedrosa, eds., *Pacífico:*

Desarrollo o Diversided? Estado, Capital y Movimientos Sociales en el Pacíf-
ico Colombiano (Bogotá: CEREC/ECOFONDO, 1996); and on the work of two
of the main activists of the movement in the southern part of the littoral, Libia
Grueso and Carlos Rosero, "El Proceso Organizativo de Communidades Negras en el Pacífico Sur Colombiano," unpublished manuscript 1995; L. Grueso,
C. Rosero, and A. Escobar, "The Politics of Nature and the Black Movement of
the Pacific Coast of Colombia," in *Cultures of Politics/Politics of Cultures:*
Revisioning Latin American Social Movements, ed. Sonia E. Alvarez, Evelina
Dagnino, and Arturo Escobar (Boulder, CO: Westview Press, forthcoming). I
should point out that this account refers mostly to the experience of the black
movement in the southern Pacific Coast, especially that led by the Organization of Black Communities of Buenaventura, to whom Grueso and Rosero
belong.
24. Declaration of the Tercera Asamblea de Comunidades Negras, Puerto
Tejada, September 1993.
25. Grueso and Rosero, "El Proceso Organizativo de Communidades Negras
en el Pacífico Sur Colombiano."
26. Interview with Libia Grueso, Carlos Rosero, Leyla Arroyo, and other
members of the Organización de Comunidades Negras de Buenaventura,
3 January 1994. Included in Escobar and Pedrosa, eds., *Pacífico: Desarrollo o*
Diversidad?
27. A word about the activists of the movement is in order. In the southern
part of the Coast, the most important leaders are social science professionals
who grew up along the rivers and traveled to cities like Cali, Bogotá, or Po-
payán for university training. These leaders are very articulate, and, despite dis-
agreements, their political vision is impressively clear. The presence of women
in the higher echelons of groups like the Organization of Black Communities of
Buenventura, and in the movement as a whole, is extremely important. But the
strength of the movement lies in a relatively large cadre of activists in the littoral
itself, only a few of whom have received university training. Often, the pace
of activities is dictated by young activists involved with the various aspects of
the growing cultural politics, such as local radio stations, dance and theater
groups, local newsletters, and the preparation of workshops for the discussion
of Ley 70. This impressive, although still fragile, process of organizing is yet to
be chronicled adequately.
28. See also Peter Wade, *Blackness and Race Mixture: The Dynamics of Ra-*
cial Identity in Colombia (Baltimore: Johns Hopkins University Press, 1993).
29. Encuentro de Comunidades de Buenaventura held in Puerto Merizalde,
November 1991. This meeting was attended by 1,600 people.
30. The difficulty of formulating alternative proposals is a worldwide phenomenon. Once the failure of development became evident, and after its radical
deconstruction as a discourse of domination, there are few clues for re/con-
structing regimes of representation and practice. The increasingly widespread
call for "alternative development" is a recognition of this fact (see Escobar,
Encountering Development).

31. Nancy Fraser, *Unruly Practices* (Minneapolis: University of Minnesota Press, 1989).

32. Deluze and Guattari, *A Thousand Plateaus.*

33. See Arturo Escobar and Sonia E. Alvarez, eds., *The Making of Social Movements in Latin America: Identity, Strategy, and Democracy* (Boulder, CO: Westview Press, 1992), for a review of the literature.

34. Stuart Hall, "Cultural Identity and Diaspora," in *Identity, Community, Culture, Difference,* ed. J. Rutherford (London: Lawrence & Wishart, 1990), 392–403.

35. Ibid., 399.

36. Libia Grueso, "Diagnósticos, Propuestas y Perspectivas de la Región del Chocó Biogeográfico en Relación con la Conservación y Uso Sostenido de la Biodiversidad," report presented to the Proyecto Biopacífico, Bogotá, 1995.

37. Paul Gilroy, *The Black Atlantic* (Cambridge, MA: Harvard University Press, 1993).

38. Gilles Deluze and Félix Guattari, *Qué es la Filosofía?* (Barcelona: Anagrama, 1993).

39. Ibid.

40. Ibid., 101.

GRANT FARRED

First Stop, Port-au-Prince: Mapping Postcolonial Africa through Toussaint L'Ouverture and His Black Jacobins

> I once met a Haitian intellectual who told the story about how astonished people were in Haiti to discover that *Black Jacobins* was written first by a black man, secondly by a West Indian. Because of course it had come back to them through London, through Paris. . . . STUART HALL[1]

Stuart Hall's anecdote reveals at once the geographical and historical marginality to which the Caribbean, and especially Haiti, have been assigned vis-à-vis metropolitan intellectual centers. But equally it signals the critical importance of acts of historical recovery in intervening in the disabling logic of "center-periphery" models and in establishing the importance of alternative circuits of theoretical reflection. C. L. R. James's *The Black Jacobins,* to which Hall refers and with which this essay will be concerned, was itself an exemplary act of rethinking relations between the history of the center and the periphery and of establishing the importance of nonmetropolitan models for contemporary anticolonial struggle. James's project was to retrieve the history of the San Domingan revolution as one that had profound lessons for the African and Caribbean anticolonial movements of his moment. For, whatever the failings of the leadership of the San Domingan revolt and of subsequent Haitian regimes, the slaves who revolted made anti- and decolonizing movements a substantial ideological bequest. They provided those in a new "revolutionary situation," leaders and rank and file alike, with the "plans" that were invaluable for those undertaking their own programs of radical social reorganization. In addition to recuperating this legacy, James lent the event a sharp critical edge. Prior to the publication of *The Black Jacobins,*[2] the history of Haiti was obscure, even to those in and from the Caribbean—as Stuart Hall reminds us in his interview with James. The Haitian political lineage, which stretched from Toussaint and Dessalines to the Duvaliers, was unknown before the Trinidadian journeyed to Paris to research this momentous event in postcolonial history. James's work attempted to counteract the silences about Toussaint and Dessalines and the (thousands of) slaves who became soldiers, military leaders, and statesmen. *The Black Jacobins* writes the history of the San Domingan revolution to insist on its status as an anticolonial movement — as a beacon of and for (qualified) anticolonial achievement. James's text maps the theoretical, geographical, and historical axes of the San Domingan revolution. *The Black Jacobins* outlines a theory that engaged the conflicts and nuanced overlapping between Marxism and Pan-Africanism; it charts the relationship between peripheral modes of struggle across the expanse of vast geographical space and historical moment. Most importantly, James's work on the trade routes of anticolonial resistance, from Europe to the Caribbean to Africa, made revolutionary Haiti available as an instance and example that could be still active in the present. And, as a model and despite its flaws, Haiti helped to inspire a whole continent to decolonizing projects.

The Black Jacobins is of a piece with James's lifelong work in anticolonialist struggles in Britain, the United States, and Africa. Born and raised in Tunapuna, some eight miles from Port-of-Spain, James was continually engaged in struggles around race, ideology, Marxism, philosophy, class, and cultural politics not only in his native Caribbean, but also in Britain and the United States, where he spent, over a period of decades, some twenty years. James's capacity for conducting his politics on a global scale is of course nowhere more manifest than in the anticolonial campaigns he waged against British, French, and U.S. imperialism in the Caribbean, Latin America, and Africa. Anti-imperialism was a consistent feature of James's life, as evident in his commitment to the 1930s anticolonial campaigns as it was in his 1980s support for Polish workers and the Solidarity movement. The "Russian army," James said at a 1981 rally for the Polish struggle in London, "cannot go anywhere when it will have at its back Solidarity in Poland today and Solidarities tomorrow."[3]

In this respect, James was not untypical. One of the outstanding features of Trinidadian political activists born around the end of the nineteenth and the beginning of the early twentieth century is their commitment to global rather than local struggles. The inveterate internationalism that marks Trinidadians of that generation takes on a range of expressions, sometimes in personages with unlikely professions. Mostly, however, these activists have identifiably political pursuits. The talented prewar cricketer Learie Constantine, at different times James's sporting adversary and political ally, exemplifies the more unusual profile.[4] A sportsperson who later became a lawyer and took up permanent residence in England, Constantine supported campaigns around the world. He worked tirelessly for his island's independence, he supported attempts to secure national sovereignty for other peoples engaged in anticolonial struggles, and he immersed himself in the battles waged by the working-class community of Nelson in northern England, whom he represented at cricket. Another Trinidadian, George Padmore, born Malcolm Nurse, stands as one of the most prominent black intellectuals to ever join the Communist Party. The son of Hubert Alphonso Nurse, a dissident schoolteacher who converted to Islam from the Church of England after reading Edward Blyden's *Christianity, Islam and the Negro Race,* Padmore, a childhood friend of James's, left the Caribbean and journeyed to the Soviet Union after his stint as student and activist at Howard University in the United States.

In Moscow, Padmore was appointed head of the Comintern's African and Pan-African Affairs Department. Padmore broke with the Soviet Union in the early 1930s because of the Comintern's sudden about-face on antiracism and anticolonialism at the moment that the country committed itself to an antifascist relationship with Britain and France. Expeditiously, the Politburo quickly acquired a sympathetic understanding for the colonial practices of their new European allies. This change in Soviet policy affected Padmore directly because it required him to soft-pedal on the major colonial powers and to critique Germany's, Italy's, and Japan's colonial ambitions. Though this particular brief could not apply to Japan, the two European nations did have designs on Africa: Abyssinia was the target of Mussolini's aggression and South West Africa's (Namibia's) occupation was the result of Germany's foray into the continent. In comparison to Britain and France, however, these antagonists were minor players on the African scene. Padmore resigned in disgust at the expedience of the Soviet Union's policies and returned to the West to continue his work against colonialism in association with James. One of the highlights of this Trinidadian's career was his appointment to a post in Kwame Nkrumah's first government in the newly independent Ghana.

But the most important feature of James's own globalism, which distinguishes him from these compatriots, is his belief in the capacity of the working classes the world over to effect revolution and social reconstruction. His enduring internationalism, as hinted at in his domino-theory reading of Solidarity's battle, has a remarkable origin: the San Domingan revolution of the late eighteenth century. For the rest of his life, the Trinidadian-born intellectual retained an unwavering faith in global revolution that was borne out, sustained, and amplified by the research he did in the 1930s on San Domingo. The struggle of the slaves that transformed San Domingo into the independent black state of Haiti became for James the model for conducting the struggle against twentieth-century European colonialism. James would return to the centrality of this struggle against French colonialism repeatedly over the years, whether it was directly mentioned in conversations about the Cuban Revolution or obliquely referred to in a speech supporting Solidarity.[5]

James's book on the subject, *The Black Jacobins: Toussaint L'Ouverture and the San Domingo Revolution,* should be read as the reappropriation and re-presentation of a crucial moment in the history of black people throughout not only the diaspora, but the entire world.[6] *The Black Jacobins* is a dramatic articulation of the successful San Domingan slave rebellion. The slaves' victorious campaign against late eighteenth- and early nineteenth-century French colonialism also becomes, however, a striking prefiguration of the struggle that was yet to be conducted against colonialism in sub-Saharan Africa and the Caribbean — a struggle that took place almost a hundred and fifty years later. Published in 1938, *The Black Jacobins* is a reinterpretation of the late eighteenth-century San Domingo slave uprising. In this text James posits the slaves as a radical community that parallels the revolutionary Parisian masses of the 1789 French Revolution. In his account of the San Domingan revolution, the Trinidadian native explores the means by which a revolutionary ideology originating in Europe transports and transforms itself while crossing the Atlantic Ocean. James is interested, as it were, in the means, the shape and form, by which revolution travels from the streets of Paris to the insurrectionary plantations of the French colony in the Caribbean. In the process of transplanting a revolutionary ideology, the San Domingan slaves forge oppositional practices that are distinct from but evocative of metropolitan upheavals; all these activities take place in a context that is apparently discrete from that of the colonial capital. James, ever alert to the differences between the two contexts, investigates the ways in which the French revolutionary impulse is taken to new heights in a location, San Domingo, with its huge slave population, remote and ostensibly so unsuited for dramatic sociopolitical restructuring. According to James, the San Domingan slaves quickly comprehended the upheaval in Europe and rapidly recast the French Revolution to fit their own particular needs: "They [the slaves] had heard of the revolution and had construed it in their own image: the white slaves in France had risen, and had killed their masters, and were now enjoying the fruits of the earth. It was gravely inaccurate in fact, but they had caught the spirit of the thing. Liberty, Equality, Fraternity. Before the end of 1789 there were risings in Guadeloupe and Martinique. As early as October, in Fort Dauphin, one of the future centres of the San Domingo insurrection, the slaves were stirring and holding mass meetings in the forest at night."[7]

Central to the project of *The Black Jacobins* is Toussaint L'Ouverture, *the* Black Jacobin himself. A slave entrusted with the responsibility of running a plantation household, L'Ouverture was an extraordinary product of an extraordinary moment: "Toussaint did not make the revolution. It was the revolution that made Toussaint."[8] James identifies in the ex-slave Toussaint, as he calls him, the apogee of the revolutionary doctrines that underpinned the French Revolution: "The blacks were taking their part in the destruction of European feudalism begun by the French Revolution, and liberty and equality, the slogans of the revolution, meant far more to them than to any Frenchman. That was why, in the hour of danger, Toussaint, uninstructed as he was, could find the language and accent of Diderot, Rousseau, and Raynal, of Mirabeau, Robespierre and Danton."[9] By locating the revolt of the San Domingo slaves within the historical framework of the "destruction of . . . feudalism begun by the French Revolution," James adroitly forges close ideological links between the metropolis and the colonial periphery. The revolutionary struggle that the slaves in the faraway Caribbean are conducting is being waged in the spirit with which the French peasants eradicated feudalism. Toussaint's troops are extending that battle to a distant site, but the enemy is a common one, the French aristocracy and their functionaries: "The workers and peasants of France could not have been expected to take any interest in the colonial question in normal times, any more than one can expect similar interest from British or French workers today. But now they were roused. They were striking at royalty, tyranny, reaction and oppression of all types, and with these they included slavery. . . . Henceforth the Paris masses were for abolition, and their black brothers in San Domingo, for the first time, had passionate allies in France."[10] The newly "roused" revolutionary classes in France, now armed with the insight that they were not the only victims of "royalty" and "tyranny," transformed their conception of the revolution into a critique of their country's colonialism — and of the racism implicated in that policy. It was this revolutionary recognition, achieved in the midst of the struggle against the feudal state and its repressive apparatus, that motivated the "Paris masses" to rally against the enslavement of "their black brothers in San Domingo." Embattled in the alleys of Paris, the "workers and peasants," that new social group Foucault would later call "*la plèbe*, the common people of Paris,"[11] claimed "their black brothers" as Caribbean comrades engaged in the same struggle. The Parisian revolutionaries extended their political horizons beyond the local battles and critiqued their society's construction of race. In making this ideological break, the Paris masses became "passionate allies" of the San Domingo slaves.

The Black Jacobins reconstructs the events of 1789 in France as an international phenomenon that redrew the revolutionary paradigm of the eighteenth century as one that was racially diverse and that incorporated a number of subjugated constituencies, including the San Domingan slaves and *la plèbe*. The striking achievement of *The Black Jacobins* is to comprehend the French Revolution at the point where it is forced to confront questions of race and colonialism. Its salient feature is accordingly that it spans a vast geographical range, moving seamlessly between Port-au-Prince and Paris, demonstrating that the French Revolution was not an insurrectionary experience limited to Europe. We are introduced to discrete moments and different sites, one historically familiar, even overdetermined, the other new, previously nominal, out of which James produces a narrative that is apparently out of historical joint. James, however, makes clear to us that we are in the throes of the same revolution. Geographical distance, *The Black Jacobins* insists, is no real obstacle in a situation such as this where the slave community and the French masses share an ideology. The San Domingan slaves are exceptional, however, in that they exceed even the French peasants and the fledgling Parisian proletariat in terms of bravery and commitment to the basic tenets of the Revolution. "[L]iberty and equality, the slogans of the revolution," James points out, "meant far more to them than to any Frenchman" because they stood to gain considerably more from a victory over slavery and colonialism. "Liberty and equality" meant so much to the San Domingan slaves that in 1804, when Haiti became an independent state, they constitutionally enshrined these rights for all their citizens, an achievement the slaveholding United States of America would not be able to claim for decades.

While the San Domingan slaves believe more fervently in "liberty and equality" than their French counterparts, it is their leader who demonstrates in his political correspondence with Paris how the periphery is really immersed in the historical unfolding of the metropolitan history. Toussaint, "uninstructed as he was," captured in his missives to the capital the very "language and accent" of the philosophes, those militant intellectuals who gave shape to the democratic energies of the disenfranchised French masses. This barely literate son of slaves, who customarily dictated his letters to secretaries over and over again until he was satisfied with them, was able to emulate and give expression to Rousseau's and Danton's egalitarian visions. In recognizing how located he was within their ideological orbit, the French philosophers became for Toussaint comrades who provided him with the theoretical underpinning to articulate the experiences and the liberatory visions of his people. Diderot and Robespierre and Toussaint belonged to the same intellectual fraternity. While the Frenchmen provided the ideological guidelines, it was the ex-slave who took the Revolution's democratic impulses to their most radical end. Toussaint saw himself and the Haitian slaves as fellow members of a movement, fully enfranchised and empowered by the Declaration of the Rights of Man and equally dedicated to the liberation of those subjected to centuries of aristocratic rule. "The San Domingo representatives realized at last what they had done," James writes; "they had tied the fortunes of San Domingo to the assembly of a people in revolution and thenceforth the history of liberty in France and of slave emancipation in San Domingo is one and indivisible."[12]

The "indivisib[ility]" that is established between the political contestations in France and the drive toward emancipation in San Domingo emblematized for James the successful construction of a radical international working class. The French peasants and proletariat and the San Domingo slaves formed a unique late eighteenth-century political community. It was an alliance that spanned continents, rendered racial differences temporarily insignificant, and forged ideological unity so that metropolitan revolution and peripheral emancipation-via-revolution were incorporated within the same political project. It was also, however, the very closeness of the ideological, cultural, economic, and political ties that bound the periphery to the metropole that disabled Toussaint. Opposed to slavery and direct colonial domination, he nonetheless continued to act within a metropolitan French paradigm at a moment that called for a more thorough process of intellectual as well as political decolonization. He could challenge, refine, and extend the European revolution, but finally he could not break with the terms in which it was framed when the historical moment demanded. To attempt to produce ideological suture rather than recognize the ultimate incommensurability of metropolitan and anticolonial practices was Toussaint's predominant and fatal tendency. He tried to reconcile the competing factions — black slaves, a racist and ambitious mulatto class, and a reactionary white settler grouping — when he might have focused on protecting the interests of the newly freed slaves. Santiago Cólas has argued, in an essay on the strategies by which resistance travels in Latin America, that in a "revolutionary situation in which the new leaders [are] often planless, they must learn the language of and take their cues from the mass of the population."[13] Embattled and without a "plan" in a historically unprecedented situation of decolonization, Toussaint was unable to "learn the language and take cues from" the black slaves. He looked instead to Europe, where the masses spoke — in some crucial respects — a foreign ideological language and where they had a plan inapplicable to the historical newness of his situation. In any case, "learning the language and taking their cue from the mass of the population" is a lesson for which neither Toussaint nor his successor Dessalines had much aptitude. Rather than drawing inspiration from the masses, Haiti became (like many other postcolonial nations) a place where the aspirations of the general populace were to be expressly — and often violently — denied.

Toussaint's inadequate response to the San Domingan crisis should, however, be read in terms of his complex subjectivity and his unprecedented political conjuncture. Illiterate but educated in the ways of French parliamentary politics and social etiquette, he knew how to become a French subject, how to assume the language and democratic behavior of Europe; he could even act as a French statesman in his negotiations with Bonaparte's representatives. But from that position, Toussaint could not formulate the terms by which to grasp the processes of decolonization that were emerging around him. He quickly grasped the radical import of "Liberty, Equality, Fraternity," but he did not know that the desire of the slaves for decolonization was entering into ideological territory beyond even that revolutionary battle cry. Toussaint understood how the Paris masses and the San Domingo slaves were the same, but he could not conceptualize their differences. He understood only some of the revolutionary impulses of his people and could envisage only in part the processes that were underway: he could comprehend insurrection but not civil war, liberation but not nationhood, colonialism but not neocolonialism. Located as he was at the genesis of black postcolonial history, he could not grasp the enormity of the task he was undertaking. But the consequences of his failure have been of such magnitude, as I discuss briefly later, that Haiti has still not corrected them almost two hundred years later. Toussaint's failure to conceptualize and give bureaucratic shape to a postcolonial Haiti can be attributed in part to his unwarranted belief in the tenets of revolutionary France. The ex-slave could easily turn commander-in-chief and act appropriately in that capacity, as he did in a November 1797 correspondence with the French government. Responding to a French threat to invade and reenslave, Toussaint wrote curtly: "*But if, to re-establish slavery in Santo Domingo, this was done, then I declare to you it would be an attempt impossible: we have known how to face dangers to obtain our liberty, we shall know how to brave death to maintain it*" (Toussaint's emphasis).[14] Forthright as Toussaint is being, he is still operating within the wrong paradigm: he is concerned with "liberty" when he should be addressing the question of an independent Haitian state. He is too much a product of 1789 to recognize that his political allegiance should be a more singular one: to the new citizens of Haiti and not the former colonial rulers in Europe. Toussaint did not understand that he would have to break entirely with France, that he could no longer position himself as subservient, as he did in that same letter: "It is to the solicitude of the French government that I have confided my children."[15] In the act of establishing himself paternally, Toussaint served only to infantalize himself (and his fellow citizens) and to undermine the project of decolonization that emerged so powerfully and unprecedentedly from the overthrow of the slave-holding San Domingan society. (It is, of course, the very discourse of infantalization that Toussaint initiated that has shaped the antidemocratic tendencies of the Haitian ruling class.) Toussaint equated liberation from slavery with the continuation of colonial status, locating himself as a high-ranking bureaucrat when he should have turned to the business of postcolonial leadership. Toussaint was convinced that "San Domingo would decay without the benefits of the French connection."[16] His limitations, much as his radicalness, marked him as a man too deeply embedded in the ethos of the French Revolution; he did not know where liberty from European slavery ended and postcolonial nationhood began. Comparing Toussaint to his chief lieutenant and (brutal) successor Dessalines, James eloquently explains the dissimilarity between the two leaders. At the core of the difference between the two men, James shows us, was their different relationship to the metropole: "If Dessalines could see so clearly and so simply, it was because the ties that bound this uneducated soldier to French civilisation were of the slenderest. He saw what was under his nose because he saw no further. Toussaint's failure was the failure of the enlightenment, not of darkness."[17] Besides, he was producing anti- and postcolonial models at a historical conjuncture that was unique. Dessalines was Toussaint's heir and could benefit from his predecessor's successes as well as his failures; he could mark himself off from the French Revolution only because Toussaint had positioned Haiti in relation to it in the course of a crucial historical event.

As a phenomenon of its time, however, the French Revolution was clearly a complete historical novelty. There were no other contemporaneous instances of such efforts to construct an international, nonracial proletariat. Yet this is precisely what permitted James to use the historical instance of a collaboration between an embryonic metropolitan proletariat and a non-European revolutionary class to signify beyond its confines: *The Black Jacobins* projected into and onto a restive sub-Saharan Africa. On a continent displaying the first signs of its readiness to embark upon a revolutionary campaign against the European imperialists, James found instructive the anticolonial guidelines that the San Domingan slaves had sketched out. Toussaint and the slaves represented for the anticolonial movement of James's day the possibility of political liberation. The determinedness of the San Domingan's historical mission provided intellectuals such as James and Padmore with an ideological focus at a moment when there were several competing schools of thought in the African liberation movement. James and Padmore, for instance, disagreed publicly in the pages of the *New Leader* about the role blacks (and the black intelligentsia) should play in the Abyssinian crisis. Padmore advised caution and collaboration with the white European Left, while James, although not unmindful of the need for European support, struck a more strident and militant tone. James attacked Padmore in the journal's May 1936 issue: "It is on the future of Africa that the author, himself a man of African descent, is grievously disappointing. He heads one section, 'Will Britain Betray Her Trust?' as if he were some missionary or Labour politician." He then went on to make his real point: "Africans must win their own freedom. Nobody will win it for them."[18]

Within James's own ideological trajectory, *The Black Jacobins* marks a phase when he was both a Trotskyist and a Pan-Africanist. James was an anticolonial intellectual negotiating the varying demands of each of these political tendencies. The text represents an intellectual juncture where James reoriented and expanded his conceptualization of a radical political community. *The Black Jacobins* represents a moment when James engaged, to imbue a phrase from Cedric Robinson with a moderated meaning, with the "doctrinaire constructions of the anti-Stalinist Left and Engels and Marx themselves."[19] Written in the declining years of the Third International (which had started with the Russian Revolution), James's work on the San Domingan revolution reveals both how steeped he was in the ideology of the Trotskyist movement[20] and how close he was to breaking from it. Unlike the Second International, which favored a policy of gradual social change through parliamentary democracy, the Third International advocated the Lenin-Trotsky line of the global revolution headed by the proletariat. The radical ideological parameters of the Third International were politically synchronized with the conditions in which the alliance between *la plèbe* and the San Domingan slaves had been constructed. Implicitly included within the imaginary of the Third International, though never explored as creatively by any Marxist historian of the period other than James, was the potential for alignment of political forces in the metropolis and on the periphery. Such an international solidarity of working-class forces was eminently possible in the technologically advanced mid-twentieth century. Undergirding *The Black Jacobins* is James's suggestion that if the colonized Africans' struggle for liberation and independence matched or exceeded the achievements of the San Domingan slaves, then the relationship with the metropolitan laboring classes would be even more dramatically altered than in Toussaint's conception of sociopolitical reorganization. Toussaint's belief in "Complete liberty for all, to be attained and held by their own strength" addressed itself to his fellows in both Haiti and France.[21] "Complete liberty," in Toussaint's terms, meant the reconciliation of the exploitative white settlers, disgruntled and untrustworthy mulattoes, and ex-slaves in the new Haitian nation as well as the strengthening of economic, cultural, and political ties between France and Haiti in the post-1789 era. Of course, Toussaint badly misread that situation. But his cosmopolitan black twentieth-century heirs and their leftist allies shared with Toussaint the commitment to expelling European colonizers and asserting their national independence, as well as reconfiguring the internal political structures of the metropolitan powers. In fact, for Padmore, James, and Nkrumah, no liberty would have been "complete" without the achievement of a sovereign state and a European revolution. For the International African Service Bureau (IASB), headquartered in England, the anticolonial campaign was a global one, stretching from Africa to the Caribbean to Asia; for this organization, the struggle against colonialism was as much a struggle against European capitalism.[22] To use one of James's own phrases, which served as the title of a book he wrote in that period, the "world revolution" seemed a real possibility.

However, at a moment when the metropolitan working masses and the colonized peoples were subjugated by the same class, bourgeois capitalists (the constituency that had replaced the European aristocracy as the hegemonic grouping), the two communities were positioned significantly differently in relation to the dominant class. In the late 1930s a substantial section of the European masses was implicated in, if not always endorsing, fascism (fascism, of course, was the movement that would ultimately draw the colonies into World War II). But even that segment of the white European working class that did not subscribe to fascism was too economically devastated to be global in its understanding of its materially depressed conditions. The participation of colonials in the war, we are well aware, played no small role in reconstituting the metropolis-periphery relationship. For one thing, black triumph in battle over white troops dispelled the myth of racial supremacy, a founding tenet of the colonial enterprise. However, while the European masses were struggling to survive the hardships of the Depression, the subjugated peoples on the now vastly expanded periphery, no less affected by the economic collapse, were showing the first signs of concerted anticolonial resistance. Nowhere was this tendency for defiance more evident than in Abyssinia, where this people in the Horn of Africa, despite the reactionary leadership of Haile Selassie, demonstrated their opposition to the shackles of European domination.[23]

The Black Jacobins was conceived in the mid-1930s as an extended commentary on the Italian invasion of Abyssinia, a project that grew from James's 1935 founding of the International African Friends of Ethiopia. James was assisted in this venture by, among others, Padmore, Jomo Kenyatta, I. T. A. Wallace Johnson, Amy Ashwood Garvey (Marcus Garvey's ex-wife), and T. Ras Makonnen. A year later, James gave the crisis his full scholarly attention in his essay "Abyssinia and the Imperialists."[24] Through his analysis of events in San Domingo, James was able to identify — from the signal historical vantage point he had himself created — the underlying political forces and energies that spurred oppressed indigenous populations to achieve national independence. Toussaint and his people symbolized the determination of oppressed peoples to throw off the yoke of colonialism, furnishing a historical event that James transformed into a metaphor for the resistance movement then unfolding vigorously in Abyssinia, present-day Ethiopia, and more mutedly in the rest of the African continent. The struggle for sub-Saharan African liberation would find full and often violent expression in the aftermath of World War II. It is through his work on Abyssinia and San Domingo that James came to recognize the limitations of the Third International, an insight that precipitated his break with this position in Marxist thinking. Although he was fully committed to the world revolution, *The Black Jacobins* registers James's impending rupture with the Third International because he did not see it as an ideological position capable of accounting fully for the anti-imperialist struggles the African peoples were about to engage in. The ideological undergirdings of these battles for liberation and national sovereignty would be, for reasons Anna Grimshaw points out, unrecognizable to European Marxists.

"First of all," Grimshaw argues in her introduction to *The C. L. R. James Reader*, James "cast doubt on the assumption that the revolution would take place first in Europe, in the advanced capitalist countries, and that this would act as a model and a catalyst for later upheaval in the underdeveloped world. Secondly, there were clear indications that the lack of specially trained leaders, a vanguard, did not hold back the movement of the San Domingo revolution."[25] By displacing Europe as the revolutionary hub, undermining the role of the vanguard, and thereby invalidating the leadership responsibilities of the "Party," *The Black Jacobins* establishes the slaves as fully developed political agents. The Third International's main limitation, in James's view, was its inability to accommodate the unique agency of the San Domingan slaves, a class that fought a successful revolutionary struggle without adhering to the fundamental principles of Trotsky's Marxism. Toussaint and the slaves demonstrated that revolutions on the periphery could be conducted in forms, and by exercising strategies, that in significant ways contradicted the theories of European political thinkers and their constituencies. *The Black Jacobins* establishes the periphery as a distinct political force capable of engaging dialectically with the metropolis. Simultaneously, however, the metropolis was equally capable of exercising a singular agency and influence in peripheral locations.

The Black Jacobins recovers the San Domingo revolt as a peculiarly radical event. In its terms, the great failure of the French Revolution was that it was bourgeois. The French Revolution simply facilitated the transfer of hegemony from the aristocracy to the merchant class, an experience only repeated after an extended period in the newly sovereign Haiti. There, the bourgeoisie was, and continues to be, a ruling bloc determined as much by color as by class. The bourgeois class was composed mainly of light-skinned mulattoes, a sociopolitical grouping who wanted to extend their few privileges, such as limited property ownership and the opportunity for minimal upward mobility in the military ranks, under the colonial regime. A deeply prejudiced and racist class, the mulattoes resented the black slaves and the authority they gained from the Revolution and they sought to undermine and, where possible, invalidate those achievements. The consequences of the San Domingan slave rebellion, where former slaves assumed power in a new postcolonial state, was considered instructive by leaders of the revolutions in Latin America, a movement that lasted from 1812 until 1830. Latin revolutionaries took pains to prevent freed slaves—a constituency crucial to their insurrectionary activities but a threat to their postrevolutionary ambitions—from achieving a status similar to that of Haitian ex-slaves within newly independent Latin societies. Haiti became a negative postcolonial example for Latin America—a democracy that released unbridled political energies, causing the eruption of unwanted class conflicts.[26] Class tension, and its attendant violence, is a postrevolutionary feature that has proven intrinsic to Haitian life—as it has in many other postcolonial societies. This ongoing conflict has been described by Cedric Robinson in terms lyrically evocative of the French Revolution. The centuries-old struggle between Haiti's different social constituencies, Robinson writes in *Black Marxism,* has resulted in the "destruction of Democracy by Property in fear of Poverty."[27]

The crucial difference between San Domingo and France, however, is that in the ex-French colony the interregnum — the moment between the transfer of power from the old ruling class, the French colonial functionaries, to the new one, the liberated slaves — was sufficiently extended by the slaves themselves so that they were able to complete a more revolutionary transformation. Toussaint and the slaves accomplished, if only momentarily, a radical reorganization of the social order that was premised upon the very terms of the bourgeois revolution — liberty, equality, and fraternity — which they thought they were merely emulating. From where the slaves stood in relation to the history they were making, liberty and equality resonated with the prospect of a very different social reality from the only one they had known. Although the slaves were soon subject to the same political expediency and repressive excesses in Port-au-Prince as their comrades in Paris, the promise of liberty and equality sustained a revolution on the periphery where it had merely facilitated the transfer of power from one class to another in Europe. Toussaint's historically determined inability to grasp what had been achieved in terms that might have given expression to the specificity and difference of the Haitian revolution did not preclude that revolution from becoming exemplary for James at a later moment. The freed slaves of San Domingo, who had abandoned Toussaint's position in favor of Dessalines's, recognized "at last that without independence they could not maintain their liberty, and liberty was far more concrete for former slaves than the elusive forms of political democracy in France."[28] It was the commitment to "independence," born of the slaves' ability to reconceptualize political goals, that made the Haitian revolution such a crucial event in anticolonial black history for James and his IASB colleagues. The slaves demonstrated an ideological flexibility and increased political ambition as they altered their position from a struggle for emancipation from slavery to freedom from European domination to national black sovereignty.

As a Marxist and a Pan-Africanist, James grappled in *The Black Jacobins* with the discrete demands of the two ideologies (the class-based analysis of the former versus the race-based one of the latter) and the extent to which imperial oppression entangled the two categories. In his research on Toussaint and the slaves, James constantly had to weigh the significance of race against that of class in the designs of empire, setting up a dialectic between the two ideologies that he returned to again and again. Although *The Black Jacobins* identifies James as Marxist first, Pan-Africanist second, the text is marked by a skillful negotiation between the two historical forces of class and race. Therefore, although James's pronouncements are securely grounded in Marxism, they are also adroitly qualified. "The race question is subsidiary to the class question in politics," he writes, "and to think of imperialism in terms of race is disastrous. But to neglect the racial factor as merely incidental is an error only less grave than to make it fundamental."[29] The ideological hierarchy is in place for James, the "race question is subsidiary to the class question," but the impact of the former is such that it can never be left out of any political consideration. The "class question" may be the "fundamental" one, but its importance is always already predicated upon its relationship to "race." The "black" in the title of the San Domingan text is therefore particularly significant. "Black" establishes the San Domingan upheaval as parallel to, and implicated in, the "white" Jacobin revolution.

James reconceptualizes what was previously considered a historical oxymoron and sets it up as a revolutionary precedent. The "black" "Jacobins" represents a creative, not uneasy, union of James's dual ideological commitment. James's deep investment in the revolutionary potentialities of both Marxism and Pan-Africanism finds an ideological reconciliation in the title *The Black Jacobins* and within the workings of the text itself. James's class-race hierarchy is shown to be a fluid political arrangement that is maintained, with considerable ideological effort, within *The Black Jacobins*. The ideological "tension" (if we might call it that), between the title and the content emblematizes James's effort to locate himself in relation to the demands of Marxism and an emergent Pan-Africanism. It was an ideological tussle that James could never resolve, but his Marxism, if anything, became more sensitive to the notion of "context" and the particularities of each site of struggle, and his Pan-Africanism was always qualified by the recognition that those communities designated "black" were never homogeneous. San Domingo had taught him that rather rudely. This "black" Caribbean community was composed of slaves, freed blacks, and mulattoes and was fractured not only along the lines of class but also of caste. In Haiti, as I have already mentioned, the history of violent class and caste antagonisms predates the revolution. An independent Haiti continues to be ravaged by these divisions long after the euphoric days of that turn-of-the-nineteenth-century revolution. The recent coup led by Raoul Cédras after the Port-au-Prince parish priest Jean Bertrand Aristide won a democratic election makes that point amply. A black working-class leader was unacceptable to the Haitian military and the mulatto elite, to say nothing of the Roman Catholic Church establishment, who asked Aristide to resign following his return to power. Blacks continue to be the most oppressed and impoverished constituency. A poor, often homeless majority, blacks have long found themselves unprotected against the excesses of the mulattoes. Democracy has proven to be, at best, an uneven experience for black Haitians living in a society where one class/caste has controlled the economy, the civil sector, the military, and the infamous security forces. The urgent ideological issues James engaged in writing *The Black Jacobins* are today the most urgent questions confronting Haiti, a social arrangement in which class conflict and caste privilege continue to dominate. As a critique of repressive forces and a model for how social reorganization can have a truly revolutionary impact, James's reworked race-class paradigm has perhaps even greater applicability in Haiti now than when he studied it in the mid-1930s.

Despite his often uneasy grappling with and inability to adequately "resolve" the race/class question, James was still able to produce creative theoretical conceptualizations of the problem. Out of the different contexts, metropolitan France and peripheral San Domingo, and conflicting political categories, Marxism and Pan-Africanism, James was able to produce an incisive socioeconomic critique. *The Black Jacobins* makes clear how race or class, both, or various combinations of the two can be used to mobilize human beings. Based on Marxism, Pan-Africanism, or a hybrid of these ideologies, people take actions capable of reconfiguring their society, such as the San Domingo slaves had done and Africans across the continent were poised to do just months before the Second World War broke out.

As James learned through his work with George Padmore, who headed the IASB, the emergent tendencies for independence in Abyssinia belonged to the same drive for independence that had characterized the San Domingo slaves' revolution. The bureau was an organization that James helped Padmore establish and it included in its ranks the future leaders of sovereign African states, among whom Kwame Nkrumah and Kenyatta were most notable. *The Black Jacobins* performed the vital political task of mapping a trajectory of independence that Padmore, Nkrumah, and Kenyatta could use as a handbook for their nationalist campaigns. James, however, was providing more than a battle plan or a theoretical outline for the leadership of the IASB and their growing constituency, though he was doing that particularly well. By recovering the San Domingo insurrection as an epic moment of anticolonial struggle, *The Black Jacobins* imagined the possibility of a successful revolution in Africa and the Caribbean in the face of massive repression by the European colonial powers. Researching the history of the San Domingo revolution as it had never been done before, James reconstructed the achievement of the national Haitian state as a triumph of the colonized peoples over their European rulers. In recreating Toussaint's victory, James established the independent Haiti as a precedent for Ghana and Kenya and Trinidad. At a juncture where colonialist discourse premised itself upon the inability of the colonized to rule themselves, James created through Toussaint a critique of that discourse: Haiti represented an enabling moment in the history of resistance to colonialism because it culminated in the establishment of the postcolonial state. Toussaint and the slaves, therefore, became symbols for African liberation and nationalism.[30]

The Black Jacobins recuperated a legacy of successful black revolution and made it available to colonized peoples engaged in the task of overthrowing European imperialism. The San Domingo uprising's historical limitations may have diminished its force as a model for twentieth-century revolution and may have rendered it, in practice, inimitable to the fledgling nationalist movements in the Caribbean and Africa. But Toussaint's struggle served ideological functions beyond the immediate question of the success of Haiti as a postcolonial state, so that it could, in different ways, be inspirational in Port-of-Spain and Nairobi. Above all else, Toussaint and the San Domingan slaves provided a sense of historical possibility, an example of successful political resistance, and an application and adaptation of Marxism for Padmore and his colleagues at the IASB.

Without displacing historical accountability or rationalizing their tyranny, we can reflect, with a mixture of wry irony and historical bitterness, on whether or not the Duvaliers, "Papa Doc" and "Baby Doc," and Raoul Cédras are simply the heirs of Dessalines and, to a lesser extent, Toussaint. Unlike the brutally despotic Dessalines, who was quite willing to massacre his foes, Toussaint was too much a product of the Enlightenment. He acted like a postrevolutionary French statesman rather than a postcolonial leader, dispensing his hard-won political capital unwisely. As I have said, he sought to mollify the mulattoes, humor Bonapartist France, and guarantee the native white oligarchy a secure place within an independent Haitian society. In the process Toussaint alienated himself from the black masses, the very constituency that had effected the massive social upheaval that brought him to power. "Toussaint's failure," as James so grandly put it, "was the failure of enlightenment, not of darkness."[31] For all that Toussaint himself was not positioned to grasp that the Enlightenment was an "incomplete project" that the Haitian revolution already pushed beyond, the paradox remains that the very challenges of his people's condition might have furnished ample grounds for recognizing its limitations. Instead, however, the processes of democratic decolonization were interrupted at the point where the leader of the revolution, unable to think beyond the formulations of a European Enlightenment, ceased "to take his cues from the mass of the population." Not until James wrote *The Black Jacobins* were the historical and political lessons of Haiti deciphered and recirculated for use in the anticolonial struggle.

Communicating that lesson remained intrinsic to James's critical commitment to the anticolonial movement and decolonizing projects, a commitment marked by his insistence on the capacity of colonized peoples to define their own struggles. James's position, informed by his historical research, often led him into conflict with postcolonial leaders. As is all too well known, none of the leaders of independent Haiti between Toussaint and President Aristide bothered to learn the lesson of democracy, deploying at best its rhetoric and often not even that. All of these men, however, have proven themselves masters of the art of autocracy. In this way, of course, Haitian leaders have set the pattern for the leaders of many subsequent postcolonial nations. Nkrumah, Kenyatta, and Nyerere bore an often striking resemblance to Toussaint, Dessalines, and "Papa Doc" Duvalier. The elder statesman of this group, Nkrumah set the antidemocratic tone for sub-Saharan postcolonial Africa. In 1963, five years after Ghana achieved independence, Nkrumah dismissed his chief justice because he did not agree with a decision the judge had made in an important case. Writing in *Nkrumah and the Ghana Revolution,* a work that starts out as a history of the West African country's struggle for independence, James quickly goes on to rebuke his ex-IASB colleague severely for his unconstitutional and therefore undemocratic act. A "head of state does not," James insists, "dismiss his Chief Justice after he has given a major decision on a matter in which the whole country is interested. *The very structure, juridical, political and moral, of the state is at one stroke destroyed, and there is automatically place on the agenda for a violent restoration of some sort of legal connection between government and population.* By this single act, Nkrumah prepared the population of Ghana for the morals of the Mafia" (James's emphasis).[32] In this sharp admonishment of Nkrumah, James captured a sense of the impending crises that postcolonial African populations would face: dictatorial statesmen, fragile, imperfectly functioning organs of the democratic state, and, most important, an ongoing struggle to make their leadership fully accountable. The episode with the Ghanaian chief justice was merely a preview of things to come. Post-Uhuru Kenyatta would rule equally imperially in Kenya, welcoming multinational enterprises and establishing what amounted to a one-party state. Nyerere, despite his best efforts to create and sustain an African socialist revolution in Tanzania, would continue his experiment long after it had failed. The disastrous consequences of his policies had a devastating impact on the Tanzanian people. All too disturbingly, the route to sub-Saharan African postcolonialism resembles Toussaint and Dessalines's road to Port-au-Prince.

The cruelest Haitian paradox, then, is not that its role as the nation that birthed the black postcolonial movement is forgotten. Nor is it that the country that was one of the wealthiest of the Caribbean, its resources struggled over by Britain, France, and Spain, is currently the poorest in its hemisphere. Rather, it is that the very model for resistance that Toussaint and the slaves developed almost two hundred years ago continues to offer unread lessons to contemporary postcolonial societies in Haiti, Ghana, Kenya, Jamaica, and even in the newly post-apartheid South Africa, where many black people wonder if Nelson Mandela's government, currently so enamored of international capital, is any more committed to them than Nkrumah was to the "population of Ghana."

NOTES

1. This quotation is taken from an interview with C. L. R. James conducted by Stuart Hall on the occasion of James's eightieth birthday. The interview was produced by Mike Dibb for BBC's Channel Four network and is published in *Rethinking C. L. R. James,* ed. Grant Farred (Cambridge, MA: Basil Blackwell Publishers, 1996).

2. In only one of the reviews of the first publication of *The Black Jacobins* (London: Purnell & Sons, 1938) have I been able to find any commentary on this analogy between the Haitian insurrection and the broader project of the International African Service Bureau. In the very last paragraph of *The Keys* review, "K. A." writes: "This period in West Indian history provides many invaluable lessons in de-imperialization, and demonstrates the arguments in favour of such a step. . . . But still the clearest warnings are the lessons in revolution, for to the end we are faced with many of the symptoms that exist today, and the writer strikes many parallels in today's imperial world, leaving the reader to draw the moral" (*The Keys* 6, no. 2 [1938]).

3. C. L. R. James, "C. L. R. James on Poland," *Cultural Correspondence* (winter 1983): 19.

4. For a fuller description of the James Constantine relationship, cricketing and political, see James's *Beyond a Boundary* (New York: Pantheon, 1983).

5. James's 1981 Solidarity speech is remarkable for yet another "anticolonial" reason: it stands as a rare moment in his political career in which he pronounces on South Africa. "South Africa," he says: "They carry on a lot of games there . . . I believe that when the people move they will move as a solid body of people who are taking hold of their country again" (James, "C. L. R. James on Poland," 19). The South African struggles represents one of the inexplicable silences in James's life. It is unclear why he did not comment on it more frequently since he evidently kept abreast of developments there.

6. See Robin D. G. Kelley's introduction to the 1995 reissue of James's 1938 work, *A History of Negro Revolt* (Chicago: Charles H. Kerr, 1995), for an excellent reading of the impact *The Black Jacobins* had on the black diaspora.

7. C. L. R. James, *The Black Jacobins: Toussaint L'Ouverture and the San Domingo Revolution*, 2d ed., rev. (New York: Vintage Books, 1989), 81.

8. Ibid., x.

9. Ibid., 22.

10. Ibid., 120.

11. Michel Foucault, "On Popular Justice: A Discussion with Maoists," in *Power/Knowledge: Selected Interviews & Other Writings 1972–1977*, ed. Colin Gordon, trans. Colin Gordon, Leo Marshall, John Mepham, and Kate Soper (New York: Pantheon Books, 1980), 3.

12. James, *The Black Jacobins*, 60.

13. Santiago Cólas, "Silence and Dialectics: Speculations on C. L. R. James and Latin America," in *Rethinking C. L. R. James* (131–164), ed. Farred.

14. James, *The Black Jacobins*, 197.

15. Ibid., 196.

16. Ibid., 290.

17. Ibid., 288.

18. C. L. R. James, " 'Civilising' the 'Blacks,' " *New Leader* (29 May 1936): 5.

19. Cedric Robinson, *Black Marxism: The Making of the Black Radical Tradition* (London: Zed Books, 1982), 382. Robinson provides a compelling description of this stage of James's ideological career, arguing that this was the point at which *The Black Jacobins*'s author would "leap beyond the doctrinaire constructions of the anti-Stalinist left. . . ." Robinson goes on to say that the "force of the Black radical tradition merged with the exigencies of Black masses in a movement to form a new theory and a new ideology in James's writings." *Black Marxism* is a convincing study, proffering an incisive account of James's intellectual trajectory (especially so in terms of the 1930s); Robinson attends adroitly to the issue of race that James took up so richly, and for the first time at such considerable length, in his narrative of Toussaint. It was a theoretical dilemma, the impact of race on class and vice versa, with which James grappled for a considerable portion of his political career. (It is an issue engaged at some length later in this essay.) I am not sure that I agree with the implications of Robinson's phrasing — for him the moment represents a "leap," whereas I think it stands as an indicator of a more gradual process — but that is a small matter, one of tone and not substance.

20. In Britain James was a leading member of the Independent Labour Party, a labor-based organization with a decidedly Trotskyist bent; James was sent to the United States by the British Trotskyists to work in their movement here and he quickly became the chief ideologue for the Socialist Workers Party, collaborating with the likes of Raya Dunayevskaya, Grace Lee Boggs, James Boggs, and Martin Glaberman during the fifteen years he spent here in his first visit to this country.

21. James, *The Black Jacobins*, 106.

22. The IASB (International African Service Bureau) was founded in London by George Padmore, primarily in response to the invasion of Ethiopia by Mussolini. It provided the groundwork for ways of thinking about the shape of the future postcolonial world; Kwame Nkrumah and James were among the figures who assisted Padmore.

23. See George Padmore, *The Life and Struggles of Negro Toilers* (London: The RILU Magazine for the International Trade Union Committee of Negro Workers, 1931), for Padmore's critique of the Abyssinian oligarchy; see also Jon R. Edwards, "Slavery, the Slave Trade and the Economic Reorganization of Ethiopia," *African Economic History* 11 (1982): 3–14.

24. The essay has recently been reprinted in Anna Grimshaw, ed., *The C. L. R. James Reader* (Cambridge, MA: Blackwell Publishers, 1992).

25. Ibid., 7.

26. The disturbing manner in which the Haitian revolution impacted its Latin American counterparts is an insight I owe to a discussion with Santiago Cólas. Haiti's influence on the structure of postrevolutionary Latin American society is part of a larger project on the region's relations to postcolonial studies which Cólas is currently researching.

27. Robinson, *Black Marxism*, 349.

28. James, *The Black Jacobins*, 357.

29. James, *Beyond a Boundary*, 283.

30. It is interesting to note that in the 1938 reception of *The Black Jacobins*, reviewers often gestured toward the connections between James's critique of late eighteenth-century colonialism and contemporary colonial conditions without ever investigating these links more fully. The review in *The Keys*, cited in n. 2, is representative in this regard. See also Edward Said's discussion of James in *Culture and Imperialism* (New York: Knopf, 1993), 245–261.

31. James, *The Black Jacobins*, 288.

32. C. L. R. James, *Nkrumah and the Ghana Revolution* (London: Allison & Busby, 1977), 12.

HOMA HOODFAR

The Veil in Their Minds and on Our Heads:
Veiling Practices and Muslim Women

Muslim women, and particularly Middle Eastern and North African women, for the past two centuries have been one of the most enduring subjects of discussion in the Western media. I can also assert without hesitation that the issue of the veil and the oppression of Muslim women has been the most frequent topic of conversation and discussion I have been engaged in, often reluctantly, during some twenty years of my life in the Western world (mostly in the UK and Canada). Whenever I meet a person of white/European descent, I regularly find that as soon as he or she ascertains that I am Muslim/Middle Eastern/Iranian, the veil very quickly emerges as the prominent topic of conversation. This scenario occurs everywhere: in trains, at the grocery store, at the launderette, on the university campus, at parties. The range of knowledge of these eager conversants varies: some honestly confess total ignorance of Islam and Islamic culture or Middle Eastern societies; others base their claims and opinions on their experiences in colonial armies in the Middle East, or on their travels through the Middle East to India during the 1960s; still others cite as reference films or novels. What I find remarkable is that, despite their admitted ignorance on the subject, almost all people I have met are, with considerable confidence, adamant that women have a particularly tough time in Muslim cultures. Occasionally Western non-Muslim women will tell me they are thankful that they were not born in a Muslim culture. Sometimes they go so far as to say that they are happy that I am living in their society rather than my own, since obviously my ways are more like theirs, and since now, having been exposed to Western ways, I could never return to the harem!

For years I went through much pain and frustration, trying to convey that many assumptions about Muslim women were false and based on the racism and biases of the colonial powers, yet without defending or denying the patriarchal barriers that Muslim women (like women in many other countries, including Western societies) face. I took pains to give examples of how Western biases against non-Western cultures abound. In research, for example, social scientists often fail to compare like with like. The situation of poor illiterate peasant women of the South is implicitly or explicitly compared with the experiences of educated upper-middle-class women of Western societies.[1] Failing to adequately contextualize non-Western societies, many researchers simply assume that what is good for Western middle-class women should be good for all other women.[2] It is frustrating that, in the majority of cases, while my conversants listen to me, they do not hear, and at the end of the conversation they reiterate their earlier views as if our discussion were irrelevant. In more recent years, they treat me as an Islamic apologist, which silences me in new ways that often preclude argument.

I had assumed that my experiences were unique and were the result of my moving in milieux that had little contact with or knowledge about Muslim communities and cultures. However, through my recent research on the integration of Muslim women in educational institutions and the labor market in Canada, which has brought me into contact with many young Muslim women, I have come to realize that these reactions on the part of the dominant group are much more prevalent than I had thought. Moreover, the Muslim community, and in particular veiled women, suffer the psychological and socioeconomic consequences of these views. This situation has created a high level of anger and frustration in response to the deliberate racism toward Muslims in Canada and the unwillingness, despite ample examples, to let go of old colonial images of passive Muslim women. The assumption that *veil* equals *ignorance* and *oppression* means that young Muslim women have to invest a considerable amount of energy to establish themselves as thinking, rational, literate students/individuals, both in their classrooms and outside.

In this essay, I draw on historical sources, my research data on young Muslim women in Canada, as well as my own experience as a nonveiled Muslim woman of Iranian descent. I argue that the veil, which since the nineteenth century has symbolized for the West the inferiority of Muslim cultures, remains a powerful symbol both for the West and for Muslim societies. While for Westerners its meaning has been static and unchanging, in Muslim cultures the veil's functions and social significance have varied tremendously, particularly during times of rapid social change. Veiling is a lived experience full of contradictions and multiple meanings. While it has clearly been a mechanism in the service of patriarchy, a means of regulating and controlling women's lives, women have used the same social institution to free themselves from the bonds of patriarchy. Muslim women, like all other women, are social actors, employing, reforming, and changing existing social institutions, often creatively, to their own ends. The static colonial image of the oppressed veiled Muslim woman thus often contrasts sharply with the lived experience of veiling. To deny this is also to deny Muslim women their agency.

The continuation of misconceptions and misinterpretations about the veil and veiled women has several consequences, not just for Muslim women but also for occidental women. The mostly man-made images of oriental Muslim women continue to be a mechanism by which Western dominant cultures re-create and perpetuate beliefs about their superiority. The persistence of colonial and racist responses to their societies has meant that Muslim communities and societies must continually struggle to protect their cultural and political identities, a situation that makes it harder for many Muslim women, who share the frustration of their community and society, to question the merits and uses of the veil within their own communities. Moreover, the negative images of Muslim women are continually presented as a reminder to European and North American women of their relative good fortune and as an implied warning to curb their "excessive" demands for social and legal equality. Yet all too often Western feminists uncritically participate in the dominant androcentric approaches to other cultures and fail to see how such participation is ultimately in the service of patriarchy.[3] Significantly, Western feminists' failure to critically interrogate colonial, racist, and androcentric constructs of women of non-Western cultures forces Muslim women to choose between fighting sexism or racism. As Muslim feminists have often asked, must racism be used to fight sexism?

To illustrate the persistence of the social and ideological construction of the veil in colonial practices and discourses and its contrast to the lived experience of veiling, I first briefly review a history of the veil and its representation in the West. Then, by examining some of the consequences of both compulsory de-veiling and re-veiling in Iran, I demonstrate the costs to Iranian women of generalized and unsubstantiated assumptions that the veil is inherently oppressive and hence that its removal is automatically liberating. I then discuss some of my findings on the representation of the veil and its usage in the context of Canadian society and its consequences for young Muslim women in their communities and in their interaction with other women, particularly feminists. I point out how the androcentric images and stereotypes of occidental and oriental women inhibit women's learning about and from each other and weakens our challenge to both patriarchy and Western imperialism.

The practice of veiling and seclusion of women is pre-Islamic and originates in non-Arab Middle Eastern and Mediterranean societies.[4] The first reference to veiling is in an Assyrian legal text that dates from the thirteenth century B.C., which restricted the practice to respectable women and forbade prostitutes from veiling.[5] Historically, veiling, especially when accompanied by seclusion, was a sign of status and was practiced by the elite in the ancient Greco-Roman, pre-Islamic Iranian, and Byzantine empires. Muslims adopted the veil and seclusion from conquered peoples, and today it is widely recognized, by Muslims and non-Muslims, as an Islamic phenomenon that is presumably sanctioned by the Qur'an. Contrary to this belief, veiling is nowhere specifically recommended or even discussed in the Qur'an.[6] At the heart of the Qur'anic position on the question of the veil is the interpretation of two verses (Surah al-Nur, verses 30–31) that recommend women to cover their bosoms and jewelry; this has come to mean that women should cover themselves. Another verse recommends to the wives of the Prophet to wrap their cloak tightly around their bodies, so as to be recognized and not be bothered or molested in public (Surah al-Ahzab, verse 59). Modern commentators have rationalized that since the behavior of the wives of the Prophet is to be emulated, then all women should adopt this form of dress.[7] In any case, it was not until the reign of the Safavids (1501–1722) in Iran and the Ottoman Empire (1357–1924), which extended to most of the area that today is known as the Middle East and North Africa, that the veil emerged as a widespread symbol of status among the Muslim ruling class and urban elite. Significantly, it is only since the nineteenth century, after the veil was promoted by the colonials as a prominent symbol of Muslim societies, that Muslims have justified it in the name of Islam, and not by reference to cultural practices.[8]

Although the boundaries of veiling and seclusion have been blurred in many debates, and particularly in Western writing, the two phenomena are separate, and their consequences for Muslim women are vastly different. Seclusion, or what is sometimes known as *purdah,* is the idea that women should be protected, especially from males who are not relatives; thus they are often kept at home where their contact with the public is minimized. Seclusion may or may not be combined with the veiling that covers the whole body.

It has been argued that seclusion developed among Mediterranean and Middle Eastern societies because they prefer endogamous marriages; consequently they tend to develop social institutions that lend themselves to more control of young people, particularly women.[9] The argument is made even more strongly for Muslim women because they inherit wealth and remain in control of their wealth after marriage. Although a daughter's inherited share is equal to half that of a son, it is also established, by religion, that a father does not have the power to disinherit his daughters. It is an irony of history that the more economic rights women have had, the more their sexuality has been subject to control through the development of complex social institutions.[10] Nonetheless, outside the well-to-do social elites, seclusion was rarely practiced to any considerable degree, since women's economic as well as reproductive labor was essential for the survival of their households. In reality, the majority of social classes, particularly in rural settings, practiced segregation and sexual division of labor rather than seclusion. The exertion of these controls often created an obstacle but did not erase Muslim women's control of their wealth (if they had any), which they managed.[11]

However, as the socioeconomic conditions changed and factory production and trade became the major sources of wealth and capital, elite women lost ground to their male counterparts. The ideology of seclusion prevented their easy access to the rapidly changing market and to information, thus limiting their economic possibilities. Consequently their socioeconomic position vis-à-vis their husbands deteriorated. Moreover, the informal social institutions, class alliances, and kin networks that had protected women to some extent were breaking down very rapidly. In the twentieth century, this context is an important, though often neglected, reason for women of the upper classes in the Middle East to become more radically involved in the women's movement. In Egypt, where the socioeconomic changes were most rapid, the women's movement developed into an organized and effective political force that other political groups could not afford to ignore.[12] As for women in other social groups, the "modern" and "traditional" ideologies of domesticity often excluded women from better-paying jobs in the public sector, particularly if this involved traveling outside their neighborhoods and being in contact with unrelated males. Moreover, the early modern governments that sponsored the training of many citizens in fields such as commercial and international law, engineering, and commerce, following the European model, closed these options to women until a much later date, thereby reproducing and occasionally intensifying the gap already existing between men's and women's economic opportunities.[13]

The veil refers to the clothing that covers and conceals the body from head to ankle, with the exception of the face, hands, and feet. Incidentally, this is also a very accurate description of the traditional male clothing of much of the Arab world, although in different historical periods authorities have tried, with varying degrees of success, to make the clothing more gender specific.[14] The most drastic difference between male and female clothing worn among the Arab urban elite was created with the Westernization and colonization of Muslim societies in the Middle East and North Africa. Men, particularly, began to emulate European ways of dress much sooner and on a larger scale than women did.

Although in Western literature the veil and veiling are often presented as a unified and static practice that has not changed for more than a thousand years, the veil has been varied and subject to changing fashion throughout past and present history. Moreover, like other articles of clothing, the veil may be worn for multiple reasons. It may be worn to beautify the wearer,[15] much as Western women wear makeup; to demonstrate respect for conventional values;[16] or to hide the wearer's identity.[17] In recent times, the most frequent type of veiling in most cities is a long, loosely fitted dress of any color combination, worn with a scarf wrapped (in various fashions) on the head so as to cover all the hair. Nonetheless, the imaginary veil that comes to the minds of most Westerners is an awkward black cloak that covers the whole body, including the face, and is designed to prevent women's mobility.[18] Throughout history, however, apart from the elite, women's labor was necessary to the functioning of the household and the economy, and so they wore clothing that would not hamper their movement. Even a casual survey of clothing among most rural and urban areas in the Middle East and other Muslim cultures would indicate that these women's costumes, though all are considered Islamic, cover the body to different degrees.[19] The tendency of Western scholars and the colonial powers to present a unidimensional Islam and a seamless society of Muslims has prevented them from exploring the socioeconomic significance of the existing variations that were readily available, sometimes in their own drawings and paintings. Similarly, scholarly study of Islamic beliefs and culture focused on Islamic texts and use of Islamic dialogues, while overlooking the variations in the way Islam was practiced in different Islamic cultures and by different classes.

Although clothing fulfills a basic need of human beings in most climates, it is also a significant social institution through which important ideological and nonverbal communication takes place. Clothing, in most aspects, is designed to indicate not only gender and stage of life cycle, but also to identify social group and geographic area.[20] Moreover, in the Middle East, veiling has been intertwined with Islamic ethics, making it an even more complex institution. According to Muslims, women should cover their hair and body when they are in the presence of adult men who are not close relatives; thus when women put on or take off their veil, they are defining who may or may not be considered kin.[21] Furthermore, since veiling defines sexuality, by observing or neglecting the veil, women may define who is a man and who is not.[22] For instance, high-status women may not observe the veil in the presence of low-status men.

In the popular urban culture of Iran, in situations of conflict between men and women who are outside the family group, a very effective threat that women have is to drop their veil and thus indicate that they do not consider the contester to be a man.[23] This is an irrevocable insult and causes men to be wary of getting into arguments with women. Similarly, by threatening to drop the veil and put on male clothing, women have at times manipulated men to comply with their wishes. One such example can be drawn from the Tobacco Movement of the late nineteenth century in Iran. In a meeting on devising resistance strategies against the tobacco monopoly and concessions given to Britain by the Iranian government, men expressed reluctance to engage in radical political action. Observing the men's hesitation, women nationalists who were participating in the meeting (from the women's section of the mosque) raised their voices and threatened that if the men failed to protect their country for the women and children, then the women had no alternative but to drop their veil and go to war themselves.[24] Thus, the men were obliged to consider more radical forms of action.

THE MAKING OF THE VEIL IN THEIR MINDS

It was in the late eighteenth and early nineteenth century that the West's overwhelming preoccupation with the veil in Muslim cultures emerged. Travel accounts and observations from commentators prior to this time show little interest in Muslim women or the veil. The sexual segregation among all sects (Muslims, Christians, and Jews) in Mediterranean and Middle Eastern cultures was established knowledge and prior to the nineteenth century rarely attracted much attention from European travelers. Some pre-nineteenth-century accounts did report on oriental and Muslim women's lack of morality and shamelessness based on their revealing clothes and their free mobility.[25] Others observed and commented on the extent of women's power within the domestic domain, an aspect totally overlooked in the latter part of the nineteenth century.[26]

The representation of the Muslim orient by the Christian occident went through a fundamental change as the Ottoman Empire's power diminished and the Muslim orient fell deeper and deeper under European domination. The appearance and circulation of the earliest version of A Thousand and One Nights[27] in the West coincided with the Turkish defeat.[28] By the nineteenth century the focus of representation of the Muslim orient had changed from the male barbarian, constructed over centuries during the Crusades, to the "uncivilized" ignorant male whose masculinity relies on the mistreatment of women, primarily as sex slaves. In this manner images of Muslim women were used as a major building block for the construction of the orient's new imagery, an imagery that has been intrinsically linked to the hegemony of Western imperialism, particularly that of France and Britain.[29]

Scholars of Muslim societies, including feminists, have recently begun to trace the entrenchment of the Western image of the oppressed Muslim woman.[30] This informal knowledge about Muslim women seeped into numerous travel books and occasionally into historical and anthropological accounts of the region.[31] In a century and a half, 1800 to 1950, an estimated sixty thousand books were published in the West on the Arab orient alone.[32] The primary mission of these writings was to depict the colonized Arabs/Muslims as inferior/backward and urgently in need of progress offered to them by the colonial superiors. It is in this political context that the veil and the Muslim harem, as the world of women, emerged as a source of fascination, fantasy, and frustration for Western writers. Harems were supposed to be places where Muslim men imprisoned their wives, who had nothing to do except beautify themselves and cater to their husbands' huge sexual appetite.[33] It is ironic that the word harem, which etymologically derives from a root that connotes sacred and shrine, has come to represent such a negative notion in the Western world.[34] Women are invariably depicted as prisoners, frequently half-naked and unveiled and at times sitting at windows with bars, with little hope of ever being free.[35] How these mostly male writers, painters, and photographers have found access to these presumably closed women's quarters/prisons is a question that has been raised only recently.[36]

Western representations of the harem were inspired not only by the fantasies of A Thousand and One Nights, but also by the colonizers' mission of subjugation of the colonized, to the exclusion of the reality of the harems and the way women experienced them. Of little interest to Western readers was the fact that during the nineteenth century in most Middle Eastern societies over 85 percent of the population lived in rural areas, where women worked on the land and in the homes, with lives very different from the well-to-do urban elites (who, in any case, were a very small minority). When Western commentators of the nineteenth century came across a situation that contradicted their stereotype of the power structure in Muslim households, they simply dismissed it as exceptional.[37]

It is important to bear in mind that the transformation in the representation of Muslim women during the nineteenth century did not occur in isolation from other changes taking place in the imperial land, as Mabro has pointed out.[38] During the same period, the ideology of femininity and what later came to be known as the Victorian morality was developing in Britain, and variations on this theme were coming into existence in other areas of the Western world.[39] Yet Western writers zealously described the oppression of Turkish and Muslim women, with little regard for the fact that many of these criticisms applied equally to their own society. Both Muslim oriental and Christian occidental women were thought to be in need of male protection and intellectually and biologically destined for the domestic domain. Moreover, in both the orient and occident women were expected to obey and honor their husbands. In his book *Sketches of Persia*,[40] Sir John Malcolm reports a dialogue between himself and Meerza Aboo Talib in which he compares the unfavorable position of Persian women relative to European women. Aboo Talib makes the point that "we consider that loving and obeying their husbands, giving proper attention to their children, and their domestic duties, are the best occupations for females."[41] Malcolm then replies that this made the women slaves to their husbands' pleasure and housework. That is, of course, quite correct, but, as Mabro has pointed out, Aboo Talib's comment on Persian women was an equally correct description of women's duty in most European societies, including Britain, at the time.[42]

Neither did Western women traveler-writers draw parallels between the oppression of women in their own society and that of women in the orient. For instance, European women of the nineteenth century were hardly freer than their oriental counterparts in terms of mobility and traveling, a situation of which many European female expatriates repeatedly complained.[43] Mobile Shaman, in her book *Through Algeria*, lamented that women were not able to travel unless accompanied by men.[44] Western women travelers often wrote about the boredom of oriental women's lives. It often escaped them that in many cases it was precisely the boredom and the limitation of domestic life that had been the major motivating force behind many Western women's travels to the orient, an option no doubt open only to very few.[45] Similarly, while Western writers of the nineteenth century wrote about the troubled situation of women in polygamous marriages and the double standard applied to men and women, they totally ignored the plight of "mistresses" in their own societies and the vast number of illegitimate children, who not only had no right to economic support but as "bastards" were also condemned to carry the stigma of the sin of their father for the rest of their life. Clearly, societies in the Muslim orient and the Christian occident both practiced a double standard as it applied to men and women. Both systems of patriarchy were developed to cater to men's whims and to perpetuate their privileges. But the social institutions and ethos of the orient and occident that have developed in order to ensure male prerogatives were/are different. The Western world embraced a monogamous ideology, overlooking the bleak life of a huge group of women and their illegitimate children. In the orient, at the cost of legitimization of polygynous marriages and institutionalizing the double standard, women and their children received at least a limited degree of protection and social legitimacy. Although the occident demonstrated little interest in the oriental images of the European world, numerous nineteenth-century documents indicate that oriental writers were conscious of the contradiction between the presentation of a civilized façade and the hideous and cruel reality of the Western world for many women and children.[46]

Women in Qajar Iran were astonished by the clothing of Western women and the discomfort that women must feel in the heavy, tight garments; they felt that Western societies were unkind to their women by attempting to change the shape of their bodies, forcing them into horrendous corsets.[47] A scenario quoted in Mabro has aptly captured the way oriental and occidental women viewed each other: "When Lady Mary Montague was pressed by the women in a Turkish bath to take off her clothes and join them, she undid her blouse to show them her corset. This led them to believe that she was imprisoned in a machine which could only be opened by her husband. Both groups of women could see each other as prisoners and of course they were right."[48]

As the domination by Europe over the orient increased, it shattered Islamic societies' self-confidence as peoples and civilizations. Many, in their attempt to restore their nations' lost glory and independence, sought to Westernize their society by emulating Western ways and customs, including the clothing. The modernizers' call for women's formal education was often linked with unveiling, as though the veil per se would prevent women from studying or intellectual activities. The reformers proposed a combination of unveiling and education in one package, which at least partly stemmed from their belief that the veil had become in the West a symbol of their society's "backwardness." In many Muslim societies, particularly among urban elites, patriarchal rulers had often enforced (and in some cases still do) the veil to curtail women's mobility and independence. The reformers' criticisms were mostly directed at the seclusion in the name of the veil, for clearly, seclusion and public education were incompatible. Nonetheless, given the connections between the veil and Islamic ethics in Muslim cultures, the reformers and modernizers made a strategic mistake in combining unveiling with formal education. Conservative forces, particularly some of the religious authorities, seized the opportunity to legitimize their opposition to the proposed changes in the name of religion and galvanized public resistance. Though education is recommended by Islam equally for males and female, in fact the public is largely opposed to unveiling.[49]

Despite much opposition from religious and conservative forces, many elite reformists in the Middle East (both males and females) pressed for de-veiling. In Egypt, where feminist and women's organizations had emerged as important political forces vocally criticizing colonial power, it was the women activists who initiated and publicly removed the veil during a demonstration in Cairo in 1923.[50] Egypt thus became the first Islamic country to de-veil without state intervention, a situation that provoked heated debates in Egypt and the rest of the Arab and Muslim world. Recent assessment of de-veiling has dismissed the importance of this historical event on the grounds that veiling only affected upper-class women. But, as I have argued elsewhere, "although Egyptian women of low-income classes never veiled their faces and wore more dresses which did not prevent movement, they nevertheless regarded the upper-class veil as an ideal. It was not ideology which prevented them from taking 'the veil,' rather it was the lack of economic possibilities."[51] The de-veiling movement among upper-class Egyptian women questioned not only the ideology of the veil but also the seclusion of women in the name of the veil and Islam.

In other countries, such as Iran and Turkey, it was left to the state to outlaw the veil. Although the rhetoric of de-veiling was to liberate women so they could contribute to build a new modern nation, in reality women and their interests counted little. Rather, they had become the battlefield and the booty of the harsh and sometimes bloody struggle between the secularists and modernists on one side, and the religious authorities on the other. The modernist states, eager to alienate and defeat the religious authorities, who historically had shared the state's power and who generally opposed the trend toward secularization,[52] outlawed the veil and enlisted the police forces to compel de-veiling without considering the consequences of this action for women, particularly those outside the elite and middle classes of large urban centers. Ataturk (1923–38), who represented the secularist, nationalist movement in Turkey, outlawed the veil and in fact all traditional clothing including the fez; the Turks were to wear European-style clothing in a march toward modernity. Iran followed suit and introduced clothing reform, albeit a milder version, but the stress was put on de-veiling. Feminists and women activists in Iran were less organized than their counterparts in Egypt and Turkey. Debates on women's issues and the necessity of education were primarily championed by men and placed in the context of the modernization of Iran to regain its lost glory.[53] In these discussions, women were primarily viewed as the mothers of the nation, who had to be educated in order to bring up educated and intelligent children, particularly sons. The veil was often singled out as the primary obstacle to women's education.

THE VEIL ON OUR HEADS: IRAN, A CASE STUDY

De-veiling, particularly without any other legal and socioeconomic adjustments, can at best be a dubious measure of women's "liberation" and freedom of movement, and it can have many short- and long-term consequences. To illustrate this point, here I review the experiences of my own grandmother and her friends during the de-veiling movement in the 1930s, and then compare this with some of the trends that have developed with the introduction and strict enforcement of compulsory veiling under the current Islamic Republic of Iran.

In 1936, the shah's father, as part of his plan to modernize Iran, decided to outlaw the veil. The government passed a law that made it illegal for women to be in the street wearing the veil (or, as Iranians refer to it, the *chador,* which literally means *tent* and consists of a long cape-type clothing that covers from head to ankle but normally does not cover the face) or any other kind of head covering except a European hat.[54] The police had strict orders to pull off and tear up any scarf or *chador* worn in public. This had grievous consequences for the majority of women, who were socialized to see the veil and veiling as legitimate and the only acceptable way of dressing. Nonetheless, it is important to note the impact of the compulsory de-veiling for rural and urban women, younger and older women, as well as women of different classes. As the state had little presence in the countryside and since most rural women dressed in their traditional clothing, the law had only a limited impact in the countryside. The women who were urban modern elites welcomed the change and took advantage of some of the educational and employment opportunities that the modern state offered them. Women of the more conservative and religious social groups experienced some inconvenience in the early years of compulsory de-veiling, but they had the means to employ others to run their outdoor errands. However, it was the urban lower middle classes and low-income social groups who bore the brunt of the problem. It is an example of these social groups that I present here.

Contrary to the assumptions and images prevalent in the West, women generally were not kept in the harems. Most women of modest means who lived in urban households often did the shopping and established neighborly and community networks, which, in the absence of any economic and social support by the state, were a vital means of support during hard times. Many young unmarried women, including some of my aunts, went to carpet weaving workshops, an equivalent activity in many ways to attending school. Attending these workshops gave the young women legitimate reason to move about the city and socialize with women outside their circle of kin and immediate neighbors. Learning to weave carpets in this traditional urban culture was however, fundamentally different from the crocheting and embroidery engaged in by Victorian ladies: carpet weaving was a readily marketable skill which enabled them to earn some independent income, however small, should they have need.

The introduction of the de-veiling law came at a time of rapid social change created by a national economy in turmoil. In search of employment, thousands of men, especially those with no assets or capital, had migrated to Tehran and other large cities, often leaving their families behind in the care of their wives or mothers, since among the poor, nuclear families were the prevalent form of household. Those men who did not migrate had to spend longer hours at their jobs, usually away from home, while leaving more household responsibilities to their wife. My grandmother, a mother of seven children, lived in Hamedan, an ancient city in the central part of Iran. By the time of de-veiling, her husband, whose modest income was insufficient to cover the day-today expenses of his family, had migrated to Tehran in the hope of finding a better job, and she carried sole responsibility for the public and private affairs of her household. According to her, this was by no means an exceptional situation but was in fact common for many women. Evidently this commonality encouraged closer ties between the women, who went about their affairs together and spent much time in each other's company.

Because the women would not go out in public without a head covering, the de-veiling law and its harsh enforcement compelled them to stay home and beg favors from their male relatives and friends' husbands and sons for the performance of the public tasks they normally carried out themselves. My grandmother bitterly recounted her first memory of the day a policeman chased her to take off her scarf, which she had put on as a compromise to the *chador*.[55] She ran as the policeman ordered her to stop; he followed her, and as she approached the gate of her house he pulled off her scarf. She thought the policeman had deliberately allowed her to reach her home decently, because policemen had mothers and sisters who faced the same problem: neither they nor their male kin wanted them to go out "naked." For many women it was such an embarrassing situation that they just stayed home. Many independent women became dependent on men, while those who did not have a male present in the household suffered most because they had to beg favors from their neighbors. "How could we go out with nothing on?" my grandmother asked us every time she talked about her experiences. Young women of modest income stopped going to the carpet weaving workshops. Households with sufficient means would sometimes set up a carpet frame at home if their daughters were skilled enough to weave without supervision. Gradually, however, the carpet traders started to provide the wool, the loom, and other necessary raw materials to the households with lesser means and, knowing that women had no other option, paid them even smaller wages than when they went to the workshops. Moreover, this meant that women lost the option of socializing with those outside their immediate kin and neighbors, thus young women were subject to stricter control by their family.[56] Worse yet, male relatives began to assume the role of selling completed carpets or dealing with the male carpet traders, which meant women lost control over their wages, however small they were.

Apart from the economic impact, de-veiling had a very negative impact on the public, social, and leisure activities of urban women of modest means. For instance, historically, among urban Shi'ites, women frequently attended the mosque for prayer, other religious ceremonies, or simply for some peace and quiet or socializing with other women. They would periodically organize and pay a collective visit to the various shrines across town. The legitimacy of this social institution was so strong that even the strictest husbands and fathers would not oppose women's participation in these visits, although they might ask an older woman to accompany the younger ones. My grandmother, and women of her milieu, regretfully talked about how they missed being able to organize these visits for a long time, almost until World War II broke out. She often asserted that men raised few objections to these limitations, and said, "Why would they, since men always want to keep their women at home?"

One of the most pleasant and widespread female social institutions was the weekly visit to the public bath, of which there were only a few in the town. Consequently, the public bath was a vehicle for socialization outside the kin and neighbor network. Women would go at sunrise and return at noon, spending much time sharing news, complaining about misfortune, asking advice for dealing with business, family, and health problems, as well as finding suitors for their marriageable sons, daughters, kin, and neighbors. At midday, they would often have drinks and sweets. Such a ritualized bath was especially sanctioned within Muslim religious practices, which require men and women to bathe after sexual intercourse; bathing is also essential for women after menstruation before they resume the daily prayers. A long absence from the public bath would alarm the neighbors of a possible lapse in the religious practices of the absentee. Therefore they had to develop a strategy that would allow them to attend to their weekly ablutions without offending modesty by "going naked" in the street, as the de-veiling law would require them to do.

The strategies they developed varied from bribing the police officers to disappear from their route, to the less favored option of warming up enough water to bathe and rinse at home. Due to the cold climate in Hamedan, and the limited heating facilities available, this option was not practical during the many cold winter months.[57] One neighbor had heard of women getting into big bags and then being carried to the public bath.[58] So, women of the neighborhood organized to make some bags out of canvas. The women who were visiting the public bath would get into the bags, and their husbands, sons, or brothers would carry them in the bags over their shoulder, or in a donkey- or horse-driven cart to the public bath, where the attendant, advised in advance, would come and collect them. At lunch time the women would climb back in the bags and the men would return to carry them home.[59]

Although this strategy demonstrates how far people will go to defy imposed and senseless worldviews and gender roles envisaged by the state, it is also clear that in the process women have lost much of their traditional independence for the extremely dubious goal of wearing European outfits. One can effectively argue that such outfits, in the existing social context, contributed to the exclusion of women of popular classes and pushed them toward seclusion, rather than laying the ground for their liberation. The de-veiling law caused many moderate families to resist allowing their daughters to attend school because of the social implication of not wearing a scarf in public. Furthermore, as illustrated above, women became even more dependent on men since they now had to ask for men's collaboration in order to perform activities they had previously performed independently. This gave men a degree of control over women they had never before possessed. It also reinforced the idea that households without adult men were odd and abnormal. Moreover, not all men collaborated. As my grandmother observed, many men used this opportunity to deny their wives the weekly money with which women would pay their public bath fare and the occasional treat to consume with women friends. Yet other men used the opportunity to gain complete control over their household shopping, denying women any say in financial matters.

Wearing the *chador* remained illegal, although the government eventually relaxed the enforcement of the de-veiling law. In the official state ideology, the veil remained a symbol of backwardness, despite the fact that the majority of women, particularly those from low and moderate income groups and the women of the traditional middle classes[60] in the urban centers, continued to observe various degrees of *hijab* (covering). The government, through its discriminatory policies, effectively denied veiled women access to employment in the government sector, which is the single most important national employer, particularly of women. The practice of excluding veiled women hit them particularly hard as they had few other options for employment. Historically, the traditional bazaar sector rarely employed female workers, and while the modern private sector employed some blue-collar workers who wore the traditional *chador*, rarely did they extend this policy to white-collar jobs.[61] A blunt indication of this discrimination was clear in the policies covering the use of social facilities such as clubs for civil servants provided by most government agencies or even private hotels and some restaurants, which denied service to women who observed the *hijab*.

This undemocratic exclusion was a major source of veiled women's frustration. To demonstrate but a small aspect of the problem for women who observed the *hijab*, I give two examples from among my own acquaintances. In 1975 my father was paid a visit by an old family friend and her daughter to seek his advice. The family was deeply religious but very open-minded, and the mother was determined that her daughters should finish their schooling and seek employment before they marry. She argued that there is no contradiction between being a good Muslim and being educated and employed with an independent income of one's own. After much argument, the father agreed that if the oldest daughter, who had graduated from high school, could find a job in the government sector, he would not object to her working. Since, as a veiled woman, she had little chance of even obtaining an application, she asked an unveiled friend to go to the Ministry of Finance and fill out the application form. With the help of neighbors, the mother managed to arrange an interview for her. The dilemma was that, should she appear at the interview with *chador* or scarf on her head, she would never get the job and all their efforts would be wasted. It was finally agreed that she would wear a wig and a very modest dress and leave for the interview from a relative's house so that the neighbors would not see her. After a great deal of trouble, she finally was offered a position and convinced her father not to object to her wearing a scarf while at work. Thus she would leave her house wearing the *chador* and remove it, leaving just a scarf on her hair, before she arrived at work. To her colleagues, she explained that because she lived in a very traditional neighborhood, it would shame her family if she left the house without a *chador*.

A similar example can be drawn from the experience of a veiled woman I met at university in Iran. She came from a religious family with very modest means. She had struggled against a marriage arranged by her family, and managed to come to university always wearing her *chador*. She graduated with outstanding results from the Department of Economics and taught herself a good functional knowledge of English. She hoped, with her qualifications, to find a good job and help her family, who had accommodated her nontraditional views. To satisfy the modesty required by her own and her family's Islamic beliefs, and the need to be mobile and work, she designed for herself some loosely cut, but very smart, long dresses that included a hood or a scarf. But her attempt to find a job was fruitless, though she was often congratulated on her abilities. Knowing that she was losing her optimism, I asked her to come and apply for an opening at the Irano-Swedish company where I worked temporarily as assistant to the personnel manager. When she visited the office, the secretary refused to give her an application form until I intervened. Later, my boss inquired about her and called me to his office. To my amazement, he said that it did not matter what her qualifications were, the company would never employ a veiled woman. I asked why, since the company had Armenians, Jews, Baha'is, and Muslims, including some very observant male Muslims, we could not also employ a practicing female Muslim, especially since we needed her skills. He dismissed this point, saying it was not the same thing; he then told the secretary not to give application forms to veiled women, as it would be a waste of paper. My friend, who had become quite disappointed, found a primary teaching job at an Islamic school at only an eighth of my salary, though we had similar credentials.

A few years prior to the Iranian revolution, a tendency toward questioning the relevance of Eurocentric gender roles as the model for Iranian society gained much ground among university students. During the early stages of the revolution this was manifested in street demonstrations, where many women, a considerable number of whom belonged to the nonveiled middle classes, put on the veil and symbolically rejected the state-sponsored gender ideology. Then, in 1980, after the downfall of the shah and the establishment of the Islamic Republic, the Islamic regime introduced compulsory veiling, using police and paramilitary police to enforce the new rule. Despite the popularity of the regime, it faced stiff resistance from women (including some veiled women) on the grounds that such a law compromised their democratic rights.[62] The resistance led to some modification and a delay in the imposition of compulsory veiling. After more than a decade of compulsory veiling, however, the regime still is facing resistance and defiance on the part of women, despite its liberal use of public flogging, imprisonment, and monetary fines as measures of enforcement of the veil. The fact is that both rejection of the shah's Eurocentric vision and the resistance to the compulsory veil represents women's active resistance to the imposed gender role envisaged for women by the state.

The Islamic regime has no more interest in the fate of women per se than did the shah's modernist state. Women paid heavily, and their democratic rights and individual freedom once again were challenged. The Islamic regime, partly in celebration of its victory over the modernist state of the shah and partly as a means for realizing its vision of "Islamic" Iran, not only introduced a strict dress code for women but also revoked many half-hearted reforms in the Iranian Personal Law, which had provided women with a limited measure of protection in their marriage.[63] The annulment meant wider legal recognition of temporary marriage, polygyny, and men's right to divorce at will. Return to the *shariah* (Muslim law) also meant women were prevented from becoming judges. The new gender vision was also used to exclude women from some fields of study in the universities. These new, unexpected changes created such hardship, insecurity, and disillusionment for many women, regardless of whether they had religious or secular tendencies, that they became politically active to try to improve their lot. However, strategies that women with religious and Islamic tendencies have adopted are very different from those of secular women's groups.

The impact of compulsory veiling has been varied. There is no doubt that many educated middle-class women, who were actually or potentially active in the labor market, either left their jobs (and a considerable number left the country) voluntarily or were excluded by the regime's policies. However, these women were replaced by women of other social groups and not by men. Labor market statistics indicate that, contrary to the general expectation of scholars, the general public, and the Islamic state itself, the rate of female employment in the formal sector has continued to increase in the 1980s even during the economic slump and increased general unemployment.[64] Similarly, the participation of women in all levels of education, from adult literacy to university level, has continued to increase.[65]

Significantly, whether women believe and adhere to the veiling ideology or not, they have remained active in the political arena, working from within and outside the state to improve the socioeconomic position of women. Iranian women's achievements in changing and redefining the state vision of women's rights in "Islam" in just over one and a half decades have been considerable. For instance, the present family protection law, which Muslim women activists lobbied for and Ayatollah Khomeini signed in 1987, offers women more actual protection than had been afforded by the shah's Family Code, introduced in 1969, since it entitles the wife to half the wealth accumulated during the marriage.[66] More recently, the Iranian parliament approved a law that entitles women to wages for housework, forcing the husbands to pay the entire sum in the event of divorce.[67]

Although, as in most other societies, the situation of Iranian women is far from ideal or even reasonable, nonetheless the lack of interest or acknowledgment of Muslim women activists' achievements on the part of scholars and feminist activists from Europe and North America is remarkable. Such disregard, in a context where the "excesses" of the Islamic regime toward women continue to make headlines and Muslim women and religious revivalism in the Muslim world continue to be matters of wide interest, is an indicator of the persistence of orientalist and colonial attitudes toward Muslim cultures.[68] Whenever unfolding events confirm Western stereotypes about Muslim women, researchers and journalists rush to spread the news of Muslim women's oppression. For instance, upon the announcement of compulsory veiling, Kate Millett, whose celebrated work *Sexual Politics* indicates her lack of commitment to and understanding of issues of race, ethnicity, and class (although she made use of Marxist writings on development of gender hierarchy), went to Iran supposedly in support of her Iranian sisters. In 1982 she published a book, *Going to Iran,* about her experiences there.[69] Given the atmosphere of anti-imperialism and anger toward the American government's covert and overt policies in Iran and the Middle East, her widely publicized trip to Iran was effectively used to associate those who were organizing resistance to the compulsory veil with imperialist and pro-colonial elements. In this way her unwise and unwanted support and presence helped to weaken Iranian women's resistance. According to her book, Millett's intention in going to Iran, which is presented as a moment of great personal sacrifice, was not to understand why Iranian women for the first time had participated in such massive numbers in a revolution whose scale was unprecedented, nor was it to listen and find out what the majority of Iranian women wanted as women from this revolution. Rather, according to her own account, it was to lecture to her Iranian sisters on feminism and women's rights, as though her political ideas, life expectations, and experiences were universally applicable. This is symptomatic of ethnocentrism (if we don't call it racism) and the lingering, implicit or explicit assumption that the only way to "liberation" is to follow Western women's models and strategies for change; consequently, the views of third world women, and particularly Muslim women, are entirely ignored.[70]

VEILED WOMEN IN THE WESTERN CONTEXT

The veiling and re-veiling movement in European and North American societies has to be understood in the context not only of continuing colonial images but also of thriving new forms of overt and covert chauvinism and racism against Islam and Muslims, particularly in these post–cold war times. Often, uncritical participation of feminists/activists from the core cultures of Western Europe and North America in these oppressive practices has created a particularly awkward relationship between them and feminists/activists from Muslim minorities both in the West and elsewhere.[71] This context has important implications for Muslim women, who, like all other women of visible minorities, experience racism in all areas of their public life and interaction with the wider society, including with feminists and feminist institutions. Muslim women, faced with this unpleasant reality, feel they have to choose between fighting racism and fighting sexism. Their strategies have to take account of at least three interdependent and important dimensions: first, racism; second, how to accommodate and adapt their own cultural values and social institutions to those of the core and dominant cultures that are themselves changing very rapidly; and finally, how to devise ways of (formally and informally) resisting and challenging patriarchy within both their own community and that of the wider society without weakening their struggle against racism. In my ongoing research on young Muslim women in Montreal, I was impressed by how the persistence of the images of oppressed and victimized Muslim women, particularly veiled women, creates barriers for them, the majority of whom were brought up in Canada and feel a part of Canadian society.[72] Consequently, many now do not even try to establish rapport with non-Muslim Québecoise and Anglo women. A college student, angered by my comment that "when all is said and done, women in Canada share many obstacles and must learn to share experiences and develop, if not common, at least complementary strategies," explained to me:

it is a waste of time and emotion. They [white Canadian women] neither want to understand nor can feel like a friend towards a Muslim. Whenever I try to point out their mistaken ideas, for instance by saying that Islam has given women the right to control their wealth, they act as if I am making these up just to make Islam look good, but if I complain about some of the practices of Muslim cultures in the name of Islam they are more than ready to jump on the bandwagon and lecture about the treatment of women in Islam. I wouldn't mind if at least they would bother to read about it and support their claims with some documentation or references. They are so sure of themselves and the superiority of their God that they don't think they need to be sure of their information! I cannot stand them any more.

Another veiled woman explained the reasons for her frustration in the following manner:

I wouldn't mind if only the young students who know nothing except what they watch on television demonstrated negative attitudes to Islam, but sometimes our teachers are worse. For instance, I have always been a very good student, but always when I have a new teacher and I talk or participate in the class discussion the teachers invariably make comments about how they did not expect me to be intelligent and articulate. That I am unlike Muslim women. . . . What they really mean is that I do not fit their stereotype of a veiled woman, since they could hardly know more Muslim women than I do and I cannot say there is a distinctive model that Muslim women all fit into. Muslim women come from varieties of cultures, races, and historical backgrounds. They would consider me unsophisticated and criticize me if I told them that they did not act like a Canadian woman, because Canada, though small in terms of population, is socially and culturally very diverse.

Some Western feminists have such strong opinions about the veil that they are often incapable of seeing the women who wear them, much less their reasons for doing so. Writing in the student newspaper, one McGill student said that she could not decide whether it is harder to cope with the sexism and patriarchy of the Muslim community, or to tolerate the patronizing and often unkind behavior of white feminists. She then reported that her feminist housemate had asked her to leave the house and look for other accommodations because she couldn't stand the sight of the veil and because she was concerned about what her feminist friends would think of her living with a veiled woman, totally disregarding the fact that, though veiled, she was nonetheless an activist and a feminist.[73]

The stereotypes of Muslim women are so deep-rooted and strong that even those who are very conscious and critical of not only blatant racism but of its more subtle manifestations in everyday life do not successfully avoid them. To the Western feminist eye, the image of the veiled woman obscures all else. One of my colleagues and I were discussing a veiled student who is a very active and articulate feminist. I made a comment about how intelligent and imaginative she was. While he admiringly agreed with me, he added (and I quote from my notes): "She is a bundle of contradictions. She first came to see me with her scarf tightly wrapped around her head . . . and appeared to me so lost that I wondered whether she would be capable of tackling the heavy course she had taken with me. . . . She, with her feminist ideas, and critical views on orientalism, and love of learning, never failed to amaze me every time she expressed her views. She does not at all act like a veiled woman." As a "bundle of contradictions" only because she wears the veil, consisting of a neat scarf, while otherwise dressed like most other students, she has to overcome significant credibility barriers. The fact that, at the age of nineteen, without language proficiency or contacts in Montreal, she came to Canada to start her university studies at McGill has not encouraged her associates to question their own assumption about "veiled women." Neither has anyone wondered why Muslim women, if by virtue of their religion they are so oppressed and deprived of basic rights, are permitted by their religious parents to travel and live alone in the Western world.

I had thought that part of the problem was that the veil has become such an important symbol of women's oppression that most people have difficulty reducing it to simply an article of clothing. However, I discovered that the reality is much more complicated than the veil's being simply a visible marker. For instance, a Québecoise who had converted to Islam and observed the veil for the past four years said she had no evidence that wearing the veil was a hindrance to a woman's professional and educational achievements in Canada.[74] In support of her claim she told me of her recent experience at work:

When I was interviewed for my last job, in passing I said that I was a Muslim and since I wear the veil I thought they made note of it. . . . I was offered the job and I was working for almost nine months before I realized nobody seemed to be aware that I was a Muslim. One day, when I was complaining about the heat, one of my colleagues suggested that I take off my scarf. To which I answered that as a practicing Muslim I did not want to do that. At first he did not believe me, and when I insisted and asked him and others who had joined our conversation if they had seen me at all without the scarf, they replied, no, but that they had thought I was following a fashion!

She then added that while she is very religious and believes that religion should be an important and central aspect of any society, the reality is that Canada is a secular society and that for the most part people care little about what religious beliefs one has.

While her claim was confirmed to varying degrees by a number of other white Canadian veiled women, converts to Islam, my own experience, and that of other nonwhite, non-Anglo/French Canadian veiled women is markedly different. Here is a recent experience. Last year, my visit to a hairdresser ended in disastrously short hair. I was not accustomed to such short hair and for a couple of weeks I wore a scarf loosely on my head. While lecturing in my classes I observed much fidgeting and whispered discussions but could not determine the reason. Finally, after two weeks, a student approached me to ask if I had taken up the veil. Quite surprised, I said no and asked what caused her to ask such a question. She said it was because I was wearing a scarf; since I was always saying positive things about Islam[75] they thought I had joined "them." "Them?" I asked. She said, "Yes, the veiled women." Perplexed, I realized that what I discuss in lectures is not evaluated on the merits of my argument and evidence alone, but also on the basis of the listener's assumption about my culture and background.[76] My colorful scarf, however loosely and decoratively worn, appears to my students as the veil, while the more complete veil of a practicing but culturally and biologically "white" Muslim who had worn the veil every day to work is seen as fashion! The main conclusion that I draw from these incidents is that the veil by itself is not so significant, after all; rather, it is who wears the veil that matters. The veil of the visible minorities is used to confirm the outsider and marginal status of the wearer. Such incidents have made me realize why many young Muslim women are so angry and have decided against intermingling with Anglo/Québecoise women. After all, if I, as a professor in a position of authority in the classroom, cannot escape the reminder of being the "other," how could the young Muslim students escape it?

Many Muslim women who are outraged by the continuous construction of Islam as a lesser religion and the portrait of Muslims as "less developed" and "uncivilized" feel a strong need for the Muslim community to assert its presence as part of the fabric of Canadian society. Since the veil, in Canadian society, is the most significant visible symbol of Muslim identity, many Muslim women have taken up the veil not only from personal conviction but to assert the identity and existence of a confident Muslim community and to demand fuller social and political recognition.

In the context of Western societies, the veil can also play a very important role of mediation and adaptation, an aspect that, at least partly due to colonial images of the veil, has been totally overlooked by Western feminists. The veil allows Muslim women to participate in public life and the wider community without compromising their own cultural and religious values.[77] Young Canadian Muslim women, particularly those who are first-generation immigrants to Canada, have sometimes seen the wearing of the veil as affording them an opportunity to separate Islam from some of their own culture's patriarchal values and cultural practices that have been enforced and legitimated in the name of religion. Aware of the social and economic consequences of wearing the veil in the Western world, taking it up is viewed by many Muslims as an important symbol of signifying a woman's commitment to her faith. Thus many veiled women are allowed far more liberty in questioning the Islamic foundation of many patriarchal customs perpetuated in the name of Islam. For instance, several veiled women in my sample had successfully resisted arranged marriages by establishing that Islam had given Muslim women the right to choose their own partners. In the process, not only did they secure their parents' and their communities' respect, but they also created an awareness and a model of resistance for other young women of their community.

Wearing the veil has helped many Muslim women in their effort to defuse their parents' and communities' resistance against young women going away to university, particularly when they had to leave home and live on their own in a different town. Some of the veiled women had argued successfully that Islam requires parents not to discriminate against their children and educate both male and female children equally; hence, if their brothers could go and live on their own to go to university, they should be given the same opportunities.[78] The women in the study attributed much of their success to their wearing of the veil, since it indicated to the parents that these young women were not about to lose their cultural values and become "white Canadian";[79] rather, they were adopting essential and positive aspects of their Canadian and host society to blend with their own cultural values of origin.[80]

Many Muslim women have become conscious of carrying a much larger burden of establishing their community's identity and moral values than their male counterparts, the great majority of whom wear Western clothes entirely and do not stand out as members of their community. Yet frequently, when Muslim women criticize some of the cultural practices of their own community and the double standards often legitimized in the name of Islam, they are accused by other elements in their community of behaving like Canadians and not like Muslims. Many women eager to challenge their family's and community's attitude toward women have found that wearing the veil often means they are given a voice to articulate their views and be heard in a way that nonveiled Muslims are not. Their critics cannot easily dismiss them as lost to the faith. However, in wearing the veil they often find that they are silenced and disarmed by the equally negative images of Muslim and Middle Eastern women held by white Anglo/Québecoise women, images that restrict the lives of both groups of women.[81]

CONCLUSION

In this paper I have tried to demonstrate how the persistence of colonial images of Muslim women, with their ethnocentric and racist biases, has formed a major obstacle to understanding the social significance of the veil from the point of view of the women who live it. By reviewing the state-sponsored de-veiling movement in the 1930s in Iran and its consequences for women of low-income urban strata, and the reemergence of veiling during the anti-shah movement as an indication of rejection of state Eurocentric gender ideology, I argued that veiling is a complex, dynamic, and changing cultural practice, invested with different and contradictory meanings for veiled and nonveiled women as well as men. Moreover, by looking at the reintroduction of compulsory veiling in the Islamic Republic of Iran under Khomeini and the voluntary veiling of Muslim women in Canada, I argued that while veiling has been used and enforced by the state and by men as means of regulating and controlling women's lives, women have used the same institution to loosen the bonds of patriarchy imposed on them.

Both de-veiling, as organized by the Egyptian feminist movement in the 1920s, and the current resistance to compulsory veiling in Iran are indications of defiance of patriarchy. But veiling, viewed as a lived experience, can also be a site of resistance, as in the case of the anti-shah movement in Iran. Similarly, many Muslim women in Canada used the veil and reference to Islam to resist cultural practices such as arranged marriages or to continue their education away from home without alienating their parents and communities. Many veiled Muslim women employ the veil as an instrument of mediation between Muslim minority cultures and host cultures. Paradoxically, Western responses to Muslim women, filtered through an orientalist and colonialist frame, effectively *limit* Muslim women's creative resistance to the regulation of their bodies and their lives.

The assumption that veiling is solely a static practice symbolizing the oppressive nature of patriarchy in Muslim societies has prevented social scientists and Western feminists from examining Muslim women's own accounts of their lives, hence perpetuating the racist stereotypes that are ultimately in the service of patriarchy in both societies. On the one hand, these mostly man-made images of the oriental Muslim women are used to tame women's demand for equality in the Western world by subtly reminding them how much better off they are than their Muslim counterparts. On the other hand, these oriental and negative stereotypes are mechanisms by which Western-dominant culture re-creates and perpetuates beliefs about its superiority and dominance. White North American feminists, by adopting a racist construction of the veil and taking part in daily racist incidents, force Muslim women to choose between fighting racism and fighting sexism. The question is, why should we be forced to choose?

NOTES

An early version of this paper was published in *Feminist Research Resource* 22, nos. 3–4 (1993), and I benefited greatly from Melani Randall's skillful editorial effort. I wish also to thank Sherene Razack for incisive comments, as well as the participants in the Other Circuits Seminar (University of California at Irvine, 14–17 July 1994), organized by Lisa Lowe and David Lloyd. I would also like to acknowledge Patricia Lynn Kelly for her careful reading and our numerous discussions on the subject.

1. See M. Lazreg, "Feminism and Difference: The Perils of Writing as a Woman on Women in Algeria," *Feminist Studies* 14, no. 1 (1988): 81–107.

2. Judy Mabro, *Veiled Half-Truths: Western Travellers' Perceptions of Middle Eastern Women* (London: I. B. Tauris, 1991); Rana Kabbani, *Europe's Myths of the Orient* (Bloomington: Indiana University Press, 1986); Malek Alloula, *The Colonial Harem* (Minneapolis: University of Minnesota Press, 1986).

3. Sherene Razack, "What Is to Be Gained by Looking White People in the Eye? Culture, Race, and Gender in Cases of Sexual Violence," *Signs* 19, no. 4 (1994): 894–923.

4. Guity Nashat, "Women in the Ancient Middle East," in *Restoring Women to History* (Bloomington, IN: Organization of American History, 1988); Nikki R. Keddie and Lois Beck, *Women in the Muslim World* (Cambridge, MA: Harvard University Press, 1978).

5. Nikki R. Keddie and Beth Baron, *Women in Middle Eastern History: Shifting Boundaries in Sex and Gender* (New Haven: Yale University Press, 1991), 3.

6. Fatima Mernissi, *The Veil and the Male Elite: A Feminist Interpretation of Women's Rights in Islam* (New York: Addison-Wesley, 1991).

7. Jamal A. Bedawi, *The Muslim Woman's Dress According to the Qur'an and the Sunnah* (London: Ta-Ha Publishers, n.d.).

8. John Esposito, *Islam: The Straight Path* (New York: Oxford University Press, 1988). Of course, this is not to say that there have not been other historical attempts to control women's dress and clothing, rather that these attempts have not been in the name of Islam. See, for example, Leila Ahmed, *Women and Gender in Islam: Historical Roots of a Modern Debate* (New Haven: Yale University Press, 1992).

9. Germaine Tillon, *The Republic of Cousin: Women's Oppression in Mediterranean Society* (London: Al Saqi Books, 1983). The French edition was published in 1966.

10. The situation of Nambudiri Brahmin women, through whom the family property passes from one generation to the next and who are carefully secluded, provides a good example. See the discussion in Mary Douglas, *Purity and Danger: An Analysis of Concepts of Pollution and Taboo* (Harmondsworth: Penguin, 1970), 140–158.

11. Much of the property that women held, such as gold and agricultural land, could be managed from within the household. This was a widespread practice among both males and females of the elites during the Ottoman period.

12. Soha Abdel Kader, *Egyptian Women in Changing Society 1899–1987* (Boulder, CO: Lynn Reinner Publishers, 1988); Kumari Jayawardena, *Feminism and Nationalism in the Third World* (London: Zed Press, 1986); Homa

Hoodfar, "A Background to the Feminist Movement in Egypt," *Bulletin of Simone de Beauvoir Institute* 9, no. 2 (1989): 18–23.

13. For more discussion see Judith E. Tucker, *Women in Nineteenth-Century Egypt* (Cambridge: Cambridge University Press, 1986).

14. For instance, a law in 1293 forbade women to wear *imams*, a style of head covering, and other masculine clothing. See Ahmed, *Women and Gender in Islam*.

15. Unni Wikan, *Behind the Veil in Arabia* (Chicago: University of Chicago Press, 1982).

16. Homa Hoodfar, "Return to the Veil: Personal Strategy and Public Participation in Egypt," in *Working Women: International Perspectives on Labour and Gender Ideology*, ed. Nanneke Redclift and M. Thea Sinclair (London: Routledge, 1991); Leila Abu-Lughod, *Veiled Sentiments: Honour and Poetry in a Bedouin Society* (Berkeley: University of California Press, 1986).

17. Elizabeth Warnock Fernea, *Guests of the Sheikh* (New York: Doubleday, 1965).

18. In 1991 I conducted an informal survey among my Western acquaintances and students; they invariably described the veil as an all-enveloping black robe; some added that it is designed to prevent or hamper women's mobility.

19. See Andrea Rugh, *Reveal and Conceal: Dress in Contemporary Egypt* (Syracuse, NY: Syracuse University Press, 1986).

20. See ibid., and Abu-Lughod, *Veiled Sentiments*.

21. Arlene Elowe MacLeod, *Accommodating Protest: Working Women and the New Veiling in Cairo* (New York: Columbia University Press, 1991).

22. C. M. Pastner, "Englishmen in Arabia: Encounters with Middle Eastern Women," *Signs* 4, no. 2 (1978): 309–323.

23. Hoodfar, "Return to the Veil."

24. Nikki R. Keddie, *Religion and Rebellion in Iran: Tobacco Protest of 1891–92* (London: Frank Cass, 1966).

25. Mohammed Tavakoli-Targhi, "The Exotic Europeans and the Reconstruction of Femininity in Iran," paper presented at Middle East Studies Association of America, 25th annual meeting, Georgetown University, Washington, DC, 23–26 November 1991.

26. James Atkinson, *Customs and Manners of Women of Persia and Their Domestic Superstitions* (New York: Burt Franklin, 1832); Tucker, *Women in Nineteenth-Century Egypt*.

27. Also known as *The Arabian Nights,* this work is a collection of folk fairy tales orally narrated as entertainment, usually for children, at family gatherings and sometimes in coffee/tea houses; it has come to represent the Middle Eastern worldview in the West.

28. Kabbanni, *Europe's Myths of the Orient,* 138.

29. Edward Said, *Orientalism* (London: Routledge and Kegan Paul, 1978); Edward Said, *Culture and Imperialism* (New York: Knopf, 1993); Kabbani, *Europe's Myths of the Orient*; Alloula, *The Colonial Harem*.

30. Kabbani, *Europe's Myths of the Orient*; Alloula, *The Colonial Harem*;

Mabro, *Veiled Half-Truths;* Leila Ahmed, "Feminism and Feminist Movement in the Middle East," *Women's Studies International Forum* 5, no. 2 (1982): 153–168.

31. Kabbani, *Europe's Myths of the Orient;* Mabro, *Veiled Half-Truths.* By no means is this process limited to Muslim and Middle Eastern societies; rather, the process of making the lesser others exotic or primitive is a common thread in the history of all colonized societies.

32. Laura Nader, "Orientalism, Occidentalism and the Control of Women," *Cultural Dynamics* 2, no. 3 (1989): 323–355. This figure is conservative; it does not include articles and other shorter references to the Arab world, nor does it take into account works on the non-Arab orient.

33. Recent research indicates that the harem is imagined to be not a brothel, but a private sex house for the husband or master where women are kept to perform sexual services. Often when it happens that I go somewhere with my husband accompanied by a number of women friends this image is evoked, and people comment that my husband is traveling with his harem.

34. Kabbani, *Europe's Myths of the Orient.*

35. Alloula, *The Colonial Harem.*

36. Kabbani, *Europe's Myths of the Orient;* Mabro, *Veiled Half-Truths.*

37. For instance, when M. Michaud in 1830 entered a peasant home and heard the wife shouting at her husband in rage, he was very surprised and considered the woman an exception to the rule because the Qur'an says women should be obedient (Mabro, *Veiled Half-Truths,* 14). See also Tucker, *Women in Nineteenth-Century Egypt.*

38. Mabro, *Veiled Half-Truths.*

39. Mary Poovey, *Uneven Developments: The Ideological Work of Gender in Mid-Victorian England* (London: Virago Press, 1989); I. Pinchbeck, *Women Workers and the Industrial Revolution, 1750–1850* (1930; reprint, London: Virago Press, 1981).

40. John Malcolm, *Sketches of Persia from the Journals of a Traveler in the East* (London: J. Murray, 1949).

41. Quoted in Mabro, *Veiled Half-Truths,* 26.

42. Ibid.

43. See, for example, Isabelle Eberhardt, *The Passionate Nomad: The Diary of Isabelle Eberhardt,* ed. and introduction by Rana Kabbani (London: Virago, 1987).

44. Mabro, *Veiled Half-Truths,* 11.

45. The nineteenth-century literature on European women contains ample examples of women's frustration at being limited to domestic activities (see Poovey, *Uneven Developments*). Those who desired to do otherwise were treated as deviant and often suffered severe depression, as was the case with Charlotte Brontë and Florence Nightingale.

46. Here I paraphrase a comment by the oriental rajah, a character in the novel *One of Our Conquerors* (1891) by George Meredith, on a visit to London (quoted in Mabro, *Veiled Half-Truths,* 17).

47. Tavakoli-Targhi, "The Exotic Europeans."

48. Mabro, *Veiled Half-Truths,* 23.

49. For instance, the walls of all adult literacy classes in Iran after the Islamic revolution are decorated by posters reiterating the Prophet's comments such as that Muslim *men and women* are to go to China (which was then the furthest center of intellectual activities) in search of knowledge.

50. Ahmed, "Feminism and Feminist Movement in the Middle East."

51. Hoodfar, "A Background to the Feminist Movement in Egypt," 21.

52. A major reason for the religious authorities' resistance was that it would deprive them of their centuries-long uncontested monopoly over education.

53. For a summary of the debate, see Eliz Sanasarian, *The Women's Rights Movement in Iran* (New York: Praeger, 1982).

54. Until the fall of the shah in 1979, the anniversary of the day of introduction of this law was celebrated as Women's Liberation Day in Iran.

55. Suratgar, who had been traveling in Iran at the time, also writes that she observed policemen shredding headgear that women wore. See Olive Hepburn Suratgar, *I Sing in the Wilderness: An Intimate Account of Persia and Persians* (London: Edward Stanford, 1951).

56. Moreover, this new form of organization created an expectation that all women in the household had to work on the carpet, making their workload much greater.

57. Most traditional houses in Iran did not include a bathtub in those days.

58. In fact, they had heard of this strategy from a woman whose husband was a policeman, who had learned about it at work. The rank-and-file police officers, who were primarily from the popular classes, opposed the practice, but failing to impose the law would mean the loss of a lucrative job in hard economic times.

59. For some similar stories see Badr ol-Moluk Bamdad, *From Darkness into Light: Women's Emancipation in Iran,* trans. and ed. F. R. C. Bagley (Smithtown, NY: Exposition Press, 1977).

60. The middle classes in Iran are divided into two broad categories. One category includes those who are "modern" in outlook; until 1979 they were mostly associated with the government sector, but with the change of regime they are now primarily in professional occupations; sometimes this group is referred to as "Westernized." The second category includes social groups such as bazaar traders and producers and religious leaders who adhere to the traditional Islamic/Iranian worldview and value system and primarily support the cultural worldview of the Islamic Republic.

61. Moreover, the situation was aggravated by the fact that many traditional families, including those who disapproved of the state, would only accept employment in the government sector for their daughters/wives because it was thought that there was less sexual harassment in this milieu.

62. In 1981 I interviewed Muslim women activists; some of them argued that the compulsory veiling law was un-Islamic because only God should judge Muslims, and that there was no precedent of officially punishing women if they

did not adhere to the Islamic dress code. This position was especially supported by the Mujahedin-khalq, a major Islamic opposition political organization.

63. The advantage of these reforms was mostly in their message, which indicated that ideologically the state did not approve of polygamy and divorce at the whim of the husband, rather than in its utilitarian benefits, since it had so many social and legal loopholes that almost any husband could ignore it.

64. Val Moghadam, "Women, Work, and Ideology in the Islamic Republic," *International Journal of Middle Eastern Studies* 20 (1988): 221–243; Val Moghadam, *Modernizing Women: Gender and Social Change in the Middle East* (Boulder, CO: Lynne Rienner Publishers, 1993).

65. Golnar Mehran, "The Creation of the New Muslim Woman: Female Education in the Islamic Republic of Iran," *Convergence* 24, no. 4 (1991): 42–53; Golnar Mehran, "Ideology and Education in the Islamic Republic of Iran," *Compare* 20 (1990): 53–65.

66. Very shortly after the success of the revolution, Ayatollah Khomeini canceled the shah's Family Law on the grounds that it was judged to be un-Islamic. See Azar Tabari and Nahid Yeganeh, *In the Shadows of Islam: The Women's Movement in Iran* (London: Zed Press, 1982); Ziba Mir-Hosseini, *Marriage on Trial: A Study of Islamic Law* (London: I. B. Tauris, 1992).

67. See "Iran Panel Backs Divorce Payments," *New York Times* 14 December 1992.

68. Said, *Orientalism;* Said, *Culture and Imperialism.*

69. Kate Millett, *Going to Iran* (New York: Coward, McCann and Geoghegan, 1982).

70. Chandra Talpade Mohanty, "Under Western Eyes: Feminist Scholarship and Colonial Discourses," in *Third World Women and the Politics of Feminism,* ed. Chandra Talpade Mohanty, Ann Russo, and Lourdes Torres (Bloomington: Indiana University Press, 1991), 51–80; Lazreg, "Feminism and Difference."

71. Awkwardness and strained relationships exist between Western feminists/activists and all minorities, see bell hooks, *Ain't I a Woman?* (Boston: South End Press, 1981); bell hooks, *Talking Back: Thinking Feminist, Thinking Black* (Boston: South End Press, 1989); Mohanty, "Under Western Eyes." However, here I confine myself to the example of Muslim minorities in Canada.

72. Based on participant observation and in-depth interviews, my current research examines young Muslim women's methods of and responses to integration in Canadian society. To date, ninety-two interviews have been completed.

73. Afra Jalabi, "Veiled Oppression and Pointed Fingers," *McGill Daily* 28 September 1992, 3 (special issue on "Culture Fest").

74. However, she did say that she had problems with her family, who, as Catholics, were very upset that she had become a Muslim and a veiled woman.

75. For example, I had pointed out in class that Islam had given women the right to control their own property. On another occasion, in a discussion of postmodern anthropology, I remarked (referring to Kabbani's *Europe's Myths of the Orient* and Alloula's *The Colonial Harem*) that the representation of the

Muslim "harem" says at least as much about the gender relations of the colonizers as it does of the colonized nations.

76. For more discussion of teaching as a minority woman, see Homa Hoodfar, "Feminist Anthropology and Critical Pedagogy: The Anthropology of Classrooms' Excluded Voices," *Canadian Journal of Education* 17, no. 3 (1992): 303–320.

77. Homa Hoodfar, "Veiling as an Accommodating Strategy: Muslim Women in Canada," in preparation.

78. Several of these women had come up with this understanding from their own reading and interpretations of Islamic texts. They were aware that their interpretations were somewhat novel, but they believed they had remained true to the spirit of Islam, something that in their view some of the traditional religious leaders had overlooked by not distinguishing between tradition and Islam.

79. Many minority parents, while they value accommodation and adaption of their culture to that of the host, are preoccupied with the possible prospect of their children's denying their own culture in favor of the dominant culture.

80. This is not to say that they do not have to compromise in the process, but rather to point out that the process of adaptation can be less stressful and more harmonious through strategies that stem from within a community.

81. Nader, "Orientalism, Occidentalism and the Control of Women."

JACQUELINE URLA

Outlaw Language: Creating Alternative Public Spheres in Basque Free Radio

Recent rethinking of Habermas's *Structural Transformation of the Public Sphere* by Negt and Kluge and feminist and social historians Nancy Fraser, Joan Landes, and Geoff Eley,[1] among others, has led to the persuasive argument that the bourgeois public sphere has, from its inception, been built upon powerful mechanisms of exclusion. The idealized image of a democratic theater of free and equal participation in debate, they claim, has always been a fiction predicated on the mandatory silencing of entire social groups, vital social issues, and indeed, "of any difference that cannot be assimilated, rationalized, and subsumed."[2] This is especially clear in the case of those citizens who do not or will not speak the language of civil society. The linguistic terrorism performed with a vengeance during the French Revolution and more recently reenacted in Official English initiatives in the United States reveal to us how deeply monolingualism has been ingrained in liberal conceptions of Liberté, Égalité, and Fraternité. But perhaps silencing is not the best way to describe the fate of linguistic minorities or other marginalized groups. For, as Miriam Hansen notes,[3] what the more recent work on public spheres suggests is that "the" public sphere has never been as uniform or as totalizing as it represents itself to be. Proliferating in the interstices of the bourgeois public — in salons, coffeehouses, book clubs, working-class and subaltern forms of popular culture — are numerous counterpublics that give the lie to the presumed homogeneity of the imaginary public. Spurred in part by ethnic nationalist movements of the nineteenth and twentieth centuries, speakers and writers of "barbarous" tongues and "illegitimate patois" can be seen as one among the many counterpublics who avail themselves of any number of "media" — from novels to oral poetry, from song and regional presses to, more recently, various forms of electronic media — to give expression to other kinds of social experience and perspectives on who the public is, what its interests might be, and what its voice sounds like.

This essay examines the contemporary formation of one such counterpublic in the small towns and cities of the southern Basque country. Here, in the years since Franco's death, one finds among Basque radical nationalist youth a self-conscious attempt to make use of intentionally marginal or "outlaw" publicity—street graffiti, zines, low-power free radio—as well as a lively rock music scene, to give voice to their minoritized language and their not-so-polite critiques of the state, consumer capitalism, police repression, and a host of other social concerns. The alternative media and expressive culture of radical youth can be seen as creating a public sphere in the sense of a discursive matrix within which social experience is articulated, negotiated, and contested.[4] However, as I hope to show, the sphere they have created differs significantly from the kind of public typically imagined within minority language revitalization and/or ethnic nationalist movements. The latter typically are bourgeois and universalistic in nature; the nation or linguistic community is imagined in the singular and envisioned primarily as a reading and writing public. Furthermore, in the Basque nationalist movement, as in many other linguistic minority movements, language politics tend to be oriented toward normalization, expanding literacy, and gaining legitimacy within the terms of state hegemonic language hierarchies. The past century has seen ethnic minority intellectuals form their own language academies and literary and scientific societies and mobilize the tools of linguistic analysis, orthographic reform, mapping, and even the census in order to document the "truth" of their language and to reform the language according to notions of what constitutes a "modern" or "rational" language.[5] The kind of practical exigencies and urgency minority linguists and planners feel to transform their language into what Bourdieu calls a "langue autorisé,"[6] to demonstrate its equivalence to other "world" languages, leads them to a concern with boundary drawing, purifying, and standardizing more commonly associated with the language ideology of the dominant public sphere.

Scholars have tended to focus on these normalizing processes, yet if we look to other arenas like the marginalized publicity of radical youth, we find a very different picture. What follows is an exploration of the public sphere of radical free radio, its distinctive ideology of radical democratic communication, and how these are reflected in a variety of linguistic strategies. Existing on the margins of legality, ephemeral, and often nomadic in both a geographic and temporal sense, free radios provide a sound track for minority languages, values, and cultural expression by pirating the airwaves, appearing and disappearing on the FM dial. The public constructed by radical youth is perhaps better described as a partial public, a segment of a plural, rather than singular, counterpublic sphere.[7] Second, it is decidedly oppositional, challenging both the Spanish state and the Basque regional government's control over the terms of public discourse and the exclusions that control entails. Third, while one of the aims of free radio stations is to open new avenues for the circulation of Basque, programmers embrace a more hybrid, playful, and antinormative set of language practices than do language activists in other areas of language revitalization. Looking beyond formal language politics, beyond the academies and literacy programs, to the particular modes of address and other linguistic forms used in these kinds of experiments in local media, I suggest, reveals a more heterogeneous conception of publics and language than our studies of minority language movements might otherwise convey.

THE MINI fm BOOM

In a particularly poignant passage from *A Dying Colonialism,* Frantz Fanon paints a vivid portrait of the radio as an instrument of revolutionary consciousness. Crowded together in front of the radio dial, straining to hear through the static the French army used to jam the transmissions, peasants, not-yet-Algerians, heard more than fragmentary accounts of battles, writes Fanon; tuning in to the Voice of Algeria they were witness to and participants in the rebirth of themselves as citizens of the new nation of Algerians.

Besides fueling anticolonialist sentiment in France, Fanon's text established a link between radio and insurgency that was to inspire many of the originators of the free radio movement that emerged a decade later in Western Europe. Sometimes called illegal, rebel, or pirate radio, free radio began in Italy as an underground movement of the autonomous Left in the wake of May '68 and spread quickly among a variety of oppositional groups, young people, and ethnic and linguistic minorities.[8] Anarchic and ephemeral by nature, free radio captured the attention of intellectuals on the Left like Félix Guattari, who, inspired by the work of Fanon and Bertolt Brecht (1964) saw in the free radio movement the makings of "a molecular revolution capable of triggering a profound social transformation from below."[9]

Free radio came somewhat late to the Basque provinces of northern Spain. The first stations appeared in the early 1980s and by 1987–88, at the height of the movement, there were about fifty stations in operation.[10] The passage of new telecommunication legislation, known as the LOT (Ley de Ordenación de Telecomunicaciones), in 1988, with the attendant tightening of controls over the airwaves, has been a major contributing factor in the closing of many stations. But they are by no means all defunct. At a meeting of the free radios of the Basque country, held in January 1994, there were representatives from sixteen stations, some of which have been in existence for ten years. While it is undeniable that the movement has waned significantly, new stations continue to be created while others are renovating their studios and have managed to become permanent fixtures in town life.

The appearance of free radio is directly related to the radical youth movement of the 1980s. In the expansive years after the statue of autonomy was passed in 1979, youth, disenchanted with party politics, began to form youth assemblies (*gazte asanbladak*) in many towns across the southern Basque provinces. Drawing on the political philosophy of the autonomous left movement of Italy and France, youth assemblies meld a radical democratic assembly structure with an eclectic blend of nationalist, anarchist, left, and green politics. Antiauthoritarian and bound to no party discipline, their activities call attention to the problems of youth: problems of unemployment (hovering between 50 and 60 percent among people under twenty-five), alienation, lack of housing, compulsory military service, drugs, and repressive Catholic morality. In concert with youth elsewhere in Europe, Basque youth assemblies have been very active in the *okupa* (squatter's) movement. They have occupied abandoned buildings demanding the right to have a youth center (*gaztetxe*) where they could have meetings, socialize, listen to music, and organize concerts or other kinds of events outside the framework of political parties. In some cases, depending on the political climate of the town hall, youth houses were established easily, and in others, as in the case of the *gaztetxe* of Bilbo, the squatters were engaged in a long-drawn-out and violent battle with the police and conservative town council that was ultimately unsuccessful. Youth assemblies and youth houses in many ways draw upon and gain strength from social institutions already well established in Basque social life. Local bars, for example, have long been critical public spaces facilitating a healthy tradition of Basque associational culture.[11] Typically, radical youth will have one or two bars that they frequent on a daily basis. Most often run by individuals sympathetic to the nationalist Left, these bars, not unlike gay bars in the United States, function as gathering places and community bulletin boards. The walls are plastered with pictures of political prisoners, posters announcing upcoming demonstrations, and sign-up sheets for various activities. Here the owners will play the kind of music youth like to hear and generally tolerate their sitting for hours playing cards, hanging out without ordering much. In some respects, then, bars have served informally as spaces for youth to find one another and interact. But the idea behind the *gaztetxe* movement was that something more than a hangout was needed. As one woman explained to me, young people like herself needed an alternative to the bar, a place where individuals could read, organize talks, and do something other than drink alcohol without having music blaring in their ears. Bars were good for meeting friends and organizing concerts, she felt, but they ultimately were in the business of making money by selling drinks. They could not provide the kind of environment for some of the things she was interested in, like film screenings, talks on sexuality, holistic medicine, and creative writing. It is just the desire for alternative public space that lay behind the creation of Likiniano, a bookstore/coffeehouse in Bilbo, which describes itself in the following way: "Likiniano is a cultural project of a group of young people located within the orbit of the antiauthoritarian and assemblarian left. The almost quixotic aim is to break with the stupefying commercial culture they have accustomed us to accept. Likiniano is not a store. It is the result of a rethinking of what our centers of debate and traditional culture could be."[12] Free radio, like the media experiments of autonomous collectives elsewhere in Europe, needs to be understood as part of this larger effort by youth to create spaces for alternative modes of communication and cultural life.[13] Many stations, in fact, were begun by youth assemblies and operated out of the youth houses. And there is considerable overlap in the ethos and individuals who work and frequent the stations, *gaztetxes,* squatters' communities, and radical bars. Free radios, for example, place the schedule of programs on the bulletin boards of the bars youth go to, sell buttons and tee shirts there, and will typically have a *kutxa,* or collection box for donations for the radio on the counter. Free radios perform an interesting role vis-à-vis these alternative spaces. For the stations are themselves sites of cultural production and a technology that makes it possible to take the ideals, communicative practices, aesthetic forms, and cultural values of radical youth and broadcast them beyond the spatial limits of any specific site.

In contrast to large, well-financed, regional Basque radio stations that have emerged since autonomy, free radios are unlicensed, low-cost, low-tech initiatives with a broadcast range of no more than a few miles. Being low-tech is not just a function of inadequate money; low-tech is a part of free radio's political commitment to democratizing access to media, making it as cheap and easy as possible to set up and sustain. Similarly, having a narrow broadcasting range corresponds to free radio's attempt to use radio to create an egalitarian communicative sphere. As Kogawa, an activist in the Japanese free radio movement, explains, "the service area should be relatively small, because free radio does not *broadcast* (scatter) information but *communicates* (co-unites) messages to a concrete audience."[14] Because they are local creations and locally controlled, each one bears the imprint and reflects the interests of those who create and run the station. Those, and only those, people who participate in the radio manage the station's daily affairs and finances and determine what will go on the air. Programmers have virtually complete control over the content of their shows. All policy decisions regarding content or language are made by the general assembly. For example, the use of sexist language came up often as a problem in my discussions with women radio programmers. But instead of writing a language code or policy, it was their feeling that the best way to address this problem was to raise the issue at general assembly and to raise awareness among members about the way this kind of language use reinforced gender hierarchies. What unites free radios is a fierce commitment to freedom of expression, economic independence, and democratic control by assembly. In this respect, free radios are quite different in practice and in their ideology from the British offshore pirate radio stations that were so important to the development of Afro-Caribbean music and cultural styles.[15] In contrast to the pirates, which were largely commercial music stations, free radios are vehemently noncommercial and refuse advertising of any sort. Part of what distinguishes free radios is a notion that freedom of expression requires freedom from any form of economic control. Most stations, therefore, prefer to raise money for operations directly from local residents through weekly or monthly raffles or by running a bar (*txosna*) during the annual fiestas. This produces, of course, a very precarious hand-to-mouth existence. Many stations have been able to supplement their income by squeezing subsidies from local town halls by formally declaring themselves a cultural group that runs workshops in radio production. It is common knowledge that the stations also broadcast without a license, which is technically illegal. Tolerance for the free radios seems to vary widely: some are constantly being shut down and harassed by the police, while others operate much more freely and openly, with financial support or at least tacit acceptance from local officials. Depending on the prevailing political winds, some free radios will be very open about the station's location, leaving their doors unlocked and inviting anyone to come and participate, while others have to be more secretive, fearing the loss of their leases or possible shutdowns by angry neighbors and landlords.

Free from state regulation on the one hand and the tyranny of the Top 40 on the other, Basque free radios take on the identity of unruly "provocateurs" (*zirikatzaile*). This is reflected in the names they adopt, which range from the incendiary to the irreverent: for example, one station calls itself Molotoff Radio, after the favored weapon of urban guerrilla warfare; another calls itself Zirika (Pesky thorn). Others have chosen more nonsensical or humorous names, like Monkey Radio or Kaka Flash. In the words of Jakoba Rekondo, one of the newscasters in the free radio of Usurbil, "we didn't want to make just another normal radio with lots of music and so on. For that, you can listen to a commercial station and get better quality anyway. We saw our radio as a way of contributing to the movement, *la movida.*"

Being part of the movement for free radios means first and foremost, in their words, "giving voice to those without voice" and providing what they call "counterinformation." In practical terms this entails opening the airwaves to all the *herriko taldeak,* that is, local cultural and grassroots organizations — feminists, ecologists, amnesty groups for Basque political prisoners, Basque language schools, mountaineering clubs, and literary groups — to take part in the station. Currently, for example, free radios are, together with political comic-zines like *Napartheid,* an important forum for one of the largest youth movements today, the *insumisos,* that is, youth who are refusing to comply with the mandatory military service requirement. Free radios see their function in large part as one of community bulletin boards, providing a public forum for otherwise marginalized political and cultural perspectives that previously have had to rely on demonstrations, graffiti, and posters in the street as their primary media of public expression.

Sustained by and firmly rooted in an array of oppositional social movements, sympathetic to, but independent of, the Basque nationalist left political parties, free radios constitute an alternative public sphere that challenges the exclusions of the liberal bourgeois media, both Spanish and Basque. Curiously enough, tension surrounding these exclusions is becoming more, not less, heightened in the autonomous Basque provinces. There is no doubt that the transition to a democratic regime in Spain brought about a tremendous expansion of the media and a lessening in censorship codes. Radical, leftist, and nationalist organizations were legalized, and a flood of newspapers, magazines, and other publications emerged onto the streets. Among the more notable developments was the creation of the Basque Radio and Television Network, Euskal Irrati Telebista (EITB), which includes a regional Basque-language station and two television channels, one in Basque and one in Spanish, both of which are controlled by the Basque Autonomous Community's regional government.[16] Furthermore, under the new statute of autonomy, many nongovernmental Basque-language publications and cultural organizations were able to apply to the Basque government's Ministry of Education and Culture and receive at least partial funding to produce Basque-language publications that would not otherwise be economically sustainable. An increasingly acrimonious struggle has erupted in the past several years as the Basque government, controlled by a coalition of the Spanish Socialist Party (PSOE) and center-right-wing Basque Nationalist Party (PNV), has begun to cut back on its support of nongovernmental cultural workers and their publications.

At the center of the struggle have been two daily newspapers: *Egin,* representing the perspective of the radical nationalist Left and many of the autonomous social movements, and *Egunkaria,* the first all-Basque-language newspaper. Both papers have been the subject of a boycott on the part of the Basque government, which refuses to place any official announcements — which represent handsome sums of money — in either of these papers. That newspapers are at the vortex of this struggle is not accidental. Dailies are, as Benedict Anderson has argued,[17] emblematic of the imagined community. The retraction of the government's official announcements not only cripples the papers by taking away a major source of revenue, it also functions as a metastatement that the newspapers, and the publics they represent — that of the radical nationalist Left and progressive NGOs on the one hand (*Egin*), and the radical Basque language movement on the other (*Egunkaria*) — violate the conservative government's terms of belonging in the sphere of rational political speech. The reasons for this are complex and different for each paper. What both papers share is a vision of the nation and its imaginary readers that incorporates all seven of the Basque provinces in both Spain and France. Other factors clearly intervene: *Egin*'s recognition of Euskadi ta Askatasuna's (ETA's) actions as armed struggle rather than terrorism, and *Egunkaria*'s monolingualism run contrary to Basque government policies regarding antistate violence and official bilingualism. In the case of *Egin,* the dispute appears irresolvable, whereas *Egunkaria* appears to be reaching some accord. But the overall chilling effect of the boycott has mobilized many smaller local publications and media. Under the banner *Adierazpen Askatasuna* (Freedom of expression), and *Gu ere Herria Gara* (We, too, are the People), free radios have joined with writers, intellectuals, and artists throughout the southern Basque country in protest against what they perceive to be an attempt to exert ideological control over public discourse.

The latter slogan, "We, too, are the People," is a particularly clear indication of the ongoing contestation in the Basque country over who will get to speak as a public citizen, and whose concerns or interest come to be regarded as matters of the commonweal. Free radios, together with other grassroots organizations and Basque language and cultural revitalization groups, understand themselves to be serving the cultural interests of "the people" (*herria*). *Herria* is a semantically dense and highly resonant term in Basque nationalist discourse; as a noun, it can mean, "the town," "the people," or "the nation," and, when used as an adjective, as in *herriko* or *herrikoia,* it may mean "popular," "public," and even "patriotic."[18] Free radios claim to be the voice of "the People" the *herria,* that has been left outside the imagined community of the middle-class Basque media. And what is left out in their view is not only the perspectives of oppositional groups, but also the perspective and participation of local communities in defining public knowledge.

At stake for free radios and other experiments in local or community-based Basque-language media is something more than *access* to the public sphere. Especially important in the eyes of free radio activists is not just finding a public space in which to express themselves, but getting members of the community, especially teenagers, to become *producers* rather than simply *consumers* of public knowledge. If, under consumer capitalism, mass-mediated forms of publicity construct the public as viewers or spectators,[19] free radio imagines the public as *participant.* In interviews I had with programmers, they would often describe the free radio as trying to be an open mike, where anyone "from the street," as they say, can come and express their opinion. The ideology of communication in free radios, according to Guattari, is to maintain a system of direct feedback between the station and the community. This can happen in a number of ways; free radios encourage people to participate in creating the news by phoning in a piece of information that, in some cases, they will broadcast directly on the air. Listener call-ins are encouraged during many programs, especially when there are demonstrations or confrontations with the police, the station will try to get reports from participants who are on location. In contrast to the mainstream media, individuals can speak publicly on free radio, but they do so not as designated representatives, experts, journalists, or official spokespersons. There is a kind of counter-authority attached to free radio's defiant nonprofessionalism. People who speak the reality of the street, who speak as the common man or common woman, appear to be valorized and endowed with an authority that comes precisely from their marginality to any institutional authority. Such individuals are seen as possessing more authentic knowledge based on lived experience, and to contribute new perspectives and fresh truths via their direct plain speech.[20] More than just an alternative news outlet, free radios imagine themselves almost as a Habermasian ideal sphere of open communication: a communal space where local residents, especially youth, can speak *as citizens* and engage in defining public knowledge and public culture.

This brings us directly to the question of language ideology and practice. How are these ideological commitments expressed in the linguistic practices of free radio? The political ideology and organizational structure of free radios seem to be fairly consistent from one station to the next. However, the variation in sociolinguistic makeup of communities across the southern Basque country makes generalization about language use impossible. Some stations based in predominantly Castilian-speaking towns—Hala Bedi in Gazteiz (Alava), Eguzki in Iruña (Navarre), and Zintzilik in Renteria (Gipuzkoa)—operate almost entirely in Castilian, while others based in areas with high numbers of Basque-speaking youth use much more Basque in their programming. The analysis that follows is based on observations of two radio stations in the province of Gipuzkoa: Molotoff, located in the town of Hernani (population 20,000), and Paotxa, located in Usurbil, seven kilometers away (population 5,000). Paotxa operated entirely in Basque; Molotoff had approximately 80 percent of its programming in Basque, and the rest was identified as "bilingual" or Castilian.

Language policy is probably one of the most controversial issues among Basque free radios. During my research at Molotoff in the spring of 1994, the Station's general assembly had reached an impasse over whether the station should adopt a Basque-only language policy. Some members closely connected to the language activist organization, Basque in the Basqueland, had proposed this, arguing that the station had a moral responsibility to assist in the struggle to normalize the use of Basque in public life and that, without such a policy, Basque would continue in its minoritized status within the station and in Hernani as a whole. For others, this policy went against the ideology of the station, which is to be open to all youth, regardless of their native language. Furthermore, it was argued that a formal language policy went against the station's commitment to freedom of expression and autonomy from any kind of political doctrines, including that of language revivalists. Few stations, in fact, have opted for a Basque-only broadcasting policy; those that do operate in Basque tend to be in towns where Basque speakers are in the vast majority. Nevertheless, there is a clear solidarity between free radios in the Basque country and the language revival movement. This is signaled by the fact that virtually all the free radios adopt Basque names (Txantxangorri, Tximua, Eguzki), even if many of their programs are in Spanish or bilingual. This kind of emblematic or titular Basque identity is actually one of the distinguishing features of membership in many grassroots organizations in the radical or *abertzale* Left. Basque functions as a sign of alterity and oppositionality to the Spanish state and its institutions. At Molotoff, for example, there are several programs in Castilian whose programmers do not know Basque. Yet a conscious decision has been made to have all *kuñas* (program call signs) and station identifications (e.g., "You're listening to the voice of Molotoff Irratia") be in Basque (Euskera). Commonly used in mainstream radio broadcasting, the introduction of these devices domesticates the anarchic pleasure Guattari celebrated in free radio's uncontrolled, free-form broadcasting aesthetic by giving a sense of order and pacing within and between programs. It is significant that while the station could not agree to a language policy for all the programs, the code choice of call signs and station identifications did become a subject of explicit debate in the general assembly of Molotoff. While individuals are believed to be entitled to complete freedom within the context of their programs, call signs occupy a special status as the voice of the station as a whole. Interjected into programs, the use of Basque call signs together with station identifications work as framing devices for the ensuing talk, establishing for the radio and its audience symbolic membership in a Basque-speaking (*euskaldun*) public, even if, later, Castilian is used inside the program and certainly is frequently used in joking and other off-the-record comments.

In keeping with their anti-institutional and oppositional politics, free radio broadcasters interject a great deal of slang and colloquialisms that mark themselves as closer to what they see as "the language of the street." One of the more interesting places to look for this is, again, in the prerecorded opening and closing of programs. At Usurbil's Paotxa radio, for example, in the opening to the community news program announcers use Basque informal modes of address — "*Aizak, hi!*" (for males) and "*Aizan, hi!*" (for women), roughly translatable as "Hey you!" — to address each other and, by extension, the listening audience. In Gipuzkoa, these informal second-person pronouns and the allocutive verb forms associated with them are typically found most frequently among native speakers in rural areas, where it is most commonly used among siblings and same-sex peer groups and for addressing animals on the farm. The use of *hitanoa* or *hika,* as it is called, indexes directness and a familiarity associated with intimate friends of equal status. Opposite-sex siblings will use *hika* with one another, but men and women, especially married couples, generally maintain the more formal, respectful *zuka* pronouns with one another.[21] *Hika* may also index lower status; children, for example, may be addressed frequently as "*Hi*" by adults, but the reverse would elicit a reprimand, especially if the adult is not a member of the family. These forms have been lost in many, especially urban areas, and are not generally known by nonnative Basque speakers. However, recently *hitanoa* has enjoyed somewhat of a renewed interest among some politicized *euskaldun* (Basque-speaking) writers, intellectuals, and youth interested in maintaining this distinctive aspect of spoken Basque. In Usurbil, for example, I found that some radical *euskaldun* youth, particularly males, make a point of using *hitanoa* in most of their everyday interactions with each other and with women in their *cuadrilla* (friendship circle). They will also occasionally use *hika* with storekeepers, teachers, the mayor, the priest, or other individuals who would normally be addressed more formally. Strategic use of *hika* pronouns in these circumstances, I would argue, is one among several ways that some radical *euskaldun* youth express their rejection of the traditional status hierarchies that have dominated Basque society, including much of nationalist political culture.[22] When Paotxa newscasters use these salutations, *aizak* and *aizan,* to introduce the local news, they construct the communicative sphere as an imagined community of "horizontal comradeship"[23] that is in keeping with free radio's vision of radical democracy. This is accentuated by the fact that, at Paotxa, as at most free radios, announcers almost never identified themselves by name: there was none of the cult of personality of named deejays found on commercial and some pirate stations. Everyone is nameless and in some sense equivalent in status. Extending the sphere of intimacy to the town as a whole, of course, might just as easily be perceived not as an expression of solidarity, but as a kind of rude speech. Such a reading probably wouldn't bother most radio programmers, since they often deliberately pepper their broadcasts with humorous, rude, sometimes scatological expressions. Either way, it sets free radio apart from mainstream broadcast etiquette and differentiates it markedly from the language movement's emphasis on creating a formal standard Basque — on making Basque a language of science, technology, and high culture.[24]

As part of their commitment to the language revival, most free radio stations will broadcast Basque language classes. But the overall goal of the station's language use is not didactic. Language play seems to be more valued than imparting normative or standard Basque. Parody and humor are valued traits in both programming and language use. Here again, we see some of the best examples of this in the introductions and titles of programs. For example, a program on Molotoff Radio ironically called *Spanish Only?* is put on by the local Basque language activist group, Basque in the Basqueland, and generally features debates, interviews, and announcements of various Basque-language cultural events. The program, however, begins with a short dialogue that parodies non-Basque speakers. Especially interesting is the way it pokes fun at people who consider themselves Basque patriots, the *abertzale,* doing their part for the language struggle, but sprinkling a few Basque words into their Spanish. In the following dialogue, Basque words inserted into the Spanish are in italics.

Spanish Only?

(Sounds of lightning and thunder crashing in the background)

Woman: Pues, chico, yo ya hago algo; le he puesto a la tienda el nombre de *Garazi.*

 (Hey, guy, I'm at least doing my part; I named my store *Garazi.*)

Young man: Yo al perro ya le digo *etorri,* y al niño *ixo.*

 (Now I say *etorri* [come] to my dog, and *ixo* [hush] to my baby.)

Male "grunge" voice: Ba, yo paso del *euskera!*

 (Bah, I'm through with Basque!)

Young man: Pero, si esa lengua ya no tiene futuro, no?

 (But that language doesn't have a future, does it?)

All together: Erderaz eta Kitto? EZZZZZZZ!

 (Spanish Only? Nooooooo!)

Such ridicule of the *abertzale* is uncommon in the public discourse of the language movement, which has generally tended to use a strategy of welcoming and encouraging people to use Basque in whatever form they can. By juxtaposing the well-meaning but Spanish-speaking patriot with the *pasota,* those who reject Basque altogether, the programmers of this show bring into the public domain what activists often complain about in private. From their perspective, this way of "speaking Basque" is really no better than no Basque at all. Indeed, it might be worse, for using a few Basque words to speak to children or to call a dog trivializes the goal activists have of creating a living Basque language and Basque-speaking culture.

One final example involves the parodic spellings of Spanish words. The most common form this takes is the use of the Basque letters *k* and *tx* in otherwise Castilian words. These letters are found in Basque orthography, but not in Castilian. They appear in Spanish phrases like *ke txorrada* for *que chorrada* (what a foolish or stupid thing) or *la martxa* for *la marcha* (the rhythm, the movement). I also found them appearing often in the titles of punk music programs, such as *El Moko Ke Kamina* (The traveling boogar) and *Koktel de Mokos* (Boogar cocktail). These kinds of orthographic mixings and the kind of Beavis and Butthead humor they engender are found throughout radical Basque youth culture: my examples appear in free radio program schedules, but they also occur in comics, graffiti, and the lyrics and album covers of Basque music groups associated with the Basque radical rock movement (*rok radikal basko*), all of which are self-identified as oppositional. In the case of one program title, *Mierkoles Merkatu* (Wednesday market), the use of the letter *k* makes it ambiguous as to whether we should classify this phrase as colloquial Basque or local Spanish. Such usages play on misrecognition, blurred language boundaries, and a feigned illiteracy in Spanish.

These examples of "bad Spanish" are very much in keeping with free radio activists' rude language ideology. In their deliberate "misspelling" of Spanish words, radical youth are turning what was once a source of stigma for many native rural Basques — that is, the inability to read and write standard Castilian — into a way of mocking Castilian. Recent work on "junk Spanish" by Jane Hill offers an elegant analysis of how joking imitations do their symbolic work.[25] Expanding on the work of Bakhtin and Spitzer, Hill argues that absurd or parodic imitations perform a dual function of both distancing the speaker from the voice he or she is imitating, and denigrating the source of that voice, making the source, whether women, Hispanics, or working-class people, appear ridiculous or contemptible. Hill takes as her case the joking imitations of minority group speech forms by majority-language speakers to show that linguistic play can have very serious metalinguistic messages. The linguistic practices of radical Basque youth give us an example of this same semiotic principle in reverse. The impossible spellings of Spanish by radical youth perform a kind of ironic reversal in which it is the language of the dominant group, Castilian, that is pragmatically lowered.[26] Within radical youth culture, these parodic hybrid spellings create a kind of symbolic allegiance with Basque oppositionality, which allows youth to use Spanish while simultaneously distancing themselves from any associations it has with state hegemony.

ALTERNATIVE PUBLIC SPHERES

In short, Basque free radios create an alternative form of public culture that differs significantly in its language ideology and modes of resistance from the institutionalized sectors of the Basque language movement. Free radios may see part of their mission as that of "exporting" Basque to the wider community, transgressing the existing geography of the language, but they care little for norms and diplomas. In contrast to the conservative codifying concerns of the academicians and planners who dominate the language movement or the bureaucrats of the Ministry of Culture and Tourism, free radio tolerates and at times embraces a mongrel and hybridized "Basque" language and culture. Subversive humor, parody, rude speech, and occasional inventive code mixing are valued skills and markers of participation in this alternative public sphere. It is important not to exaggerate here: Basque free radios are not as linguistically anarchic as Guattari might have liked them to be. Radical Basque youth have not gone the way, for example, of Latino performance artists, rappers, and radio programmers in the United States who deliberately seek to blur the boundaries with their artful uses of Spanglish.[27] Unlike diasporic minorities, Basque youth have more of an investment in retaining the boundary between Basque and Spanish even in their irreverent speech.

The fact that youth have turned to radio as a medium of oppositional cultural expression speaks to an awareness of the centrality of media in shaping cultural life. Free radio, like other forms of alternative media, operates on the philosophy that one must take what is dominant in a culture to change it quickly. One of the changes youth are attempting to make is to put their language and ideas into motion. In doing so, free radio uses the media not to disperse information to people — the consumer model of mainstream broadcast media — but to draw them in to local communicative networks. To borrow from Guattari, free radio's motion is centripetal, hoping to foster in those who listen a sense of involvement in local events and local culture.[28] This is quite different from the strategy of language standardization, which offers up a single translocal language with which to communicate across towns. As a form of activism, the logic of free radio is bottom-up rather than top-down. It works by poaching on the airwaves, rather than by direct confrontation. For Guattari, free radios were to be extensions of the conversations people have in the street, in the cafe, around the dinner table. This is especially clear in the news reports, called *informatiboa* or *albisteak*. At Paotxa radio, for example, programmers attempted to give priority to topics that they believed interested residents. In this way free radio news broke with the formulaic categories of news found in mainstream media: local, national, international, sports, and weather. Even when radio announcers were repeating news reported in the papers, they were encouraged to annotate the reports with their own opinions and perspectives. They also introduced into their news reports a section on town gossip and rumors: who was getting married when, what they were going to wear, whether they were going to have it videotaped, and so on. This was done very tongue-in-cheek of course, but programmers claim that of all the shows, the gossip section was the most popular. They also announced on the radio the recent deaths of town residents. One of Paotxa's programmers explained the reason for this: "the first thing our mothers do when they get the paper is read the death notices. They used to be posted on the wall of the church. We are just taking that custom and putting it on the radio. We are taking what people actually talk about in town, in the street, and making that our definition of news."

The public sphere of free radio is thus framed as emphatically local. But we have to ask, What does *local* mean in this context? If we look at the programming as a whole, these "local" expressions of Basque radical youth culture draw upon and are enriched by a wide array of extranational cultural images, narratives, and modes of representation. In the past couple of years, African American culture and politics were everywhere to be found in the form of rap music, Public Enemy clothing, Malcolm X insignia, and "Fight the Power" slogans, which were written on the program tapes members of Molotoff Radio gave to me. Radical youth appropriate these images and slogans into symbols of Basque oppositionality, inserting them into local narratives, debates, and modes of representation.[29] A quick scan of public cultures today shows us that such complex cultural brews are increasingly common in the urban neighborhoods of London, Paris, and Berlin, forcing us to rethink and redefine not only "the spatial, territorial, and geopolitical parameters of the public sphere," but also the counterpublics, like free radio, that emerge in its orbit. As Miriam Hansen has pointed out: "The restructuring and expansion of the communications industries on a transnational, global scale more than ever highlights the quotation marks around the terms of national culture and national identity. Indeed, the accelerated process of transnationalization makes it difficult to ground a concept of the public in any territorial entity, be it local, regional, or national."[30]

This is *not* to say, of course that free radios are not tied to specific places and specific times. They are. Free radios are linked to identifiable social networks of radical youth in urban and semiurban areas; they come out of particular social settings, bars, and youth houses, and are linked to contestations for particular public spaces. In this sense, the alternative public sphere they create does have a location that we need to address to make sense of their linguistic strategies.[31] It *is* to say, however, that these "local" expressions of Basque radical youth culture are constituted through a kind of cultural bricolage that is facilitated by transnational flows of media, commodities, images, and people. This is nowhere more apparent than in the musical programming, which juxtaposes folk with thrash, funkadelic with *txalaparta* (a wooden percussive instrument), Tex-Mex with Basque accordion music. Through these juxtapositions, radical youth affirm connections to resistance struggles and marginalized groups elsewhere in ways that challenge the bounded and unified representations of Basque language and identity found in nationalist treatises or the census map.

Precisely because they have a history of marginalization, minority language groups have had the burden of establishing their difference from and equivalence to dominant languages. As a result, in certain domains activists have shunned hybrid cultural and linguistic forms as threatening to the integrity of their language.[32] This is not the prevailing attitude of all spheres of minority language production. Free radio works by a different logic, creating a space that is simultaneously syncretic, local, and transnational. Free radios open up new spaces at the same time that they address the spatiality of linguistic domination that relegates the minority language to the sphere of private talk. They aim to take the Basque language out of the private domain and into the street, and to take, as they say, the reality of the street, into the public domain. Their efforts evoke Lizzie Borden's film *Born in Flames,* where radio is seized as a means of taking another kind of delegitimated talk, in this case the talk of feminists, and putting it into the streets. Radio is conceptualized in both cases as an instrument of back talk/talking back.[33] In many ways, the imaginary space of free radios is heterogeneous in contrast to the unitary space of the nationalism. It is also profoundly urban in the sense that Salman Rushdie gives to this term in his *Satanic Verses.* For Rushdie, what distinguishes the urban experience is not skyscrapers or concrete streets, but the simultaneous copresence of multiple realities. Free radios are urban not because they exist only in cities; in some cases, such as Usurbil, the town has no more than five thousand inhabitants. These low-powered, ephemeral stations with their radical philosophy of democratic communication are urban in the sense that they try, in whatever imperfect ways, to place the heterogeneity of Basque society on the airwaves. These representations, too, deserve our attention as part of the ongoing construction of minority languages and their publics.

NOTES

I would like to thank the many members of Molotoff Irratia in Hernani and Paotxa in Usurbil who welcomed me to their stations and gave generously of their time. I owe a special debt to Jakoba Rekondo, who first brought free radio to my attention and has provided guidance, prodding, and support throughout this project. Thanks also to Jokin Eizagirre, Olatz Mikeleiz, Ana

Altuna, Javier Esparza, and Gorka Palazios for their invaluable help in Euskadi. This article grew out of a two-year seminar on language ideology held at the Center for Transcultural Studies in Chicago. I thank the Center and all the participants, in particular Kathryn Woolard and Susan Gal, for the hard questions, insights, and intellectual inspiration that has guided so much of my work.

1. Oskar Negt and Alexander Kluge, *The Public Sphere and Experience,* trans. Peter Labanyi, Jamie Daniel, and Assenka Oksiloff (Minneapolis: University of Minnesota Press, 1993); Nancy Fraser, "Rethinking the Public Sphere: A Contribution to the Critique of Actually Existing Democracy," in *The Phantom Public Sphere,* ed. Bruce Robbins (Minneapolis: University of Minnesota Press, 1993), 1–32; Joan Landes, *Women and the Public Sphere in the Age of the French Revolution* (Ithaca: Cornell University Press, 1988); Geoff Eley, "Nations, Publics, and Political Cultures: Placing Habermas in the Nineteenth Century," in *Habermas and the Public Sphere,* ed. Craig Calhoun (Cambridge, MA: MIT Press, 1992).

2. Miriam Hansen, "Unstable Mixtures, Dilated Spheres: Negt and Kluge's *The Public Sphere and Experience,* Twenty Years Later," *Public Culture* 5, no. 2 (1993): 198.

3. See ibid.

4. See Miriam Hansen, "Early Cinema, Late Cinema: Permutations of the Public Sphere," *Screen* 34, no. 3 (1993): 197–210.

5. See Jacqueline Urla, "Cultural Politics in an Age of Statistics: Numbers, Nations and the Making of Basque Identity," *American Ethnologist* 20, no. 4 (1993): 818–843.

6. See Pierre Bourdieu, *Language and Symbolic Power,* ed. John B. Thompson, trans. Gino Raymond and Matthew Adamson (Cambridge, MA: Harvard University Press, 1991).

7. For example, see Hansen, "Unstable Mixtures," 209.

8. For general overviews of the alternative radio movement in Western Europe and how it compares to pirate and community radio projects, see Richard Barbrook, "A New Way of Talking: Community Radio in 1980s Britain," *Science as Culture* 1, no. 1 (1987): 81–129; Lluís Bassets, ed., *De las ondas rojas a las radios libres: Textos para la historia de la radio* (Barcelona: Editorial Gustavo Gili, 1981); Philip Crookes and Patrick Vittet-Philippe, *Local Radio and Regional Development in Europe* (Manchester, England: European Institute for the Media, 1986). Peter Lewis, "Community Radio: The Montreal Conference and After," *Media, Culture, and Society* 6 (1984): 137–150; and Thomas McCain and G. Ferrel Lowe, "Localism in Western European Radio Broadcasting: Untangling the Wireless," *Journal of Communication* 40, no. 1 (winter 1990): 86–101.

9. See Félix Guattari, "Millions and Millions of Potential Alices," in *Molecular Revolution,* trans. Rosemary Sheed (London: Penguin, 1984), 236–241. *Molecular* and *molar* are terms Guattari uses to contrast different ways of organizing social movements. Molecular collectives are composed of independent

autonomous individuals, whereas molar collectives are homogenized and one-dimensional. One might find these to be useful ways of contrasting publics as well.

10. Sabino Ormazabal, *El movimiento juvenil vasca* (unpublished manuscript), reports that a group of Basque nationalist youth had visited the infamous Radio Alice in Italy and set up their own clandestine radio station in San Sebastian (Guipuzcoa) as early as 1978. Other accounts record 1984 as the creation of the first free radio independent of any direct political affiliation. How the history of this movement is written depends in part on one's definition of free radio. For some free radio activists, affiliation with any political party disqualifies the station as a free radio.

11. For example, see Sharryn Kasmir, "The Myth of Mondragón: Cooperatives, Politics, and Working Class Life in a Basque Town" (Ph.D. diss., City University of New York, 1993).

12. Paul Asensio, "En la parra estan colgaus," *Egin* (Espaloian) 30 April 1993, 10.

13. See Tetsuo Kogawa, "Free Radio in Japan," in *Cultures in Contention,* ed. Douglas Kahn and Diane Neumaier (Seattle: Real Comet Press, 1985), 116–121.

14. Ibid., 117.

15. See Barbrook, "A New Way of Talking"; Paul Gilroy, *There Ain't No Black in the Union Jack: The Cultural Politics of Race and Nation* (Chicago: University of Chicago Press, 1987).

16. The Basque Autonomous Community, Comunidad Autónoma Vasca, is an administrative unit within the Spanish state created by the passage of the Statute of Autonomy of 1979. It comprises the three provinces of Alava, Guipuzcoa, and Vizcaya. The fourth Spanish Basque province, Navarre, was established under separate jurisdiction with its own Foral government. Three other Basque provinces are located within the territory of the French state.

17. See Benedict Anderson, *Imagined Communities* (London: Verso, 1991).

18. See Gorka Aulestia, *Basque-English Dictionary* (Reno: University of Nevada Press, 1989).

19. See Benjamin Lee, "Going Public," *Public Culture* 5, no. 2 (1993): 165–178; Kogawa, "Free Radio."

20. Free radio's commitment to "free speech," explains Guattari, "basically represents a danger to all traditional systems of social representation; it questions a certain conception of the delegate, of the deputy, the official spokesperson, the leader, the journalist. . . . It is as if, in an immense permanent meeting — that stretched as large as the limits of hearing would permit — someone, anyone, even the most indecisive of the lot, the one with the most shakey voice, found himself with the means to take the floor whenever he wanted. From that moment, we can begin to hope that some new truths [and] the basis for new forms of expression will emerge" (Félix Guattari, "Las radios libres populares," in *De las ondas rojas a las radios libres,* ed. Lluís Bassets [Barcelona: Editorial Gustavo Gili, 1981], 233–234).

21. *Zuka* was also described to me as being sweeter (*goxoa*) than *hika*. It is the preferred form to use with infants, for example, while parents may switch to using *hika* when the child gets older.

22. Another example of the appropriation of *hika* modes of address in radical political culture is found in the use of *Aizan!* as the name of a radical Basque feminist organization. However, I should emphasize that my claims to an affinity between *hitanoa* and radical *euskaldun* youth culture are still speculative and not meant to suggest that this association is present at all times and in all contexts. In considering what the use of *hika* may connote in any particular setting, it must also be remembered that knowledge of *hika* forms marks a certain degree of fluency or native control of Basque, since it is not commonly taught in Basque language classes and few nonnative speakers ever learn this form of speech. Further study of the uses of *hika* among activists might help us to understand not only how politicized Basques strategically use their knowledge of linguistic forms as ways of constructing social relations (in this case, along egalitarian lines), but also how these displays of linguistic competence may be a way of staking claims to greater Basque authenticity.

23. Anderson, *Imagined Communities.*

24. It should be emphasized that use of *hitanoa* varies widely from community to community. Very little *hitanoa,* for example, was used at Molotoff Radio, only seven kilometers from Paotxa. Besides considering how this form constructs the listening public, we might also think about how free radio changes the way speakers view *hitanoa*. It is possible that using *hitanoa* in oppositional radio, making it a part of the hip transnational music and culture of radical youth, may also have an effect on the connotations of *hitanoa*, shaking loose its associations with rural life and giving this form of speech a new urban feel.

25. See Jane Hill, "Hasta la vista, baby: Anglo-Spanish in the American Southwest," *Critique of Anthropology* 13, no. 2 (1993): 145–176.

26. Keith Basso's study of joking imitations of "the Whiteman" by Apache speakers is another good example of how subaltern groups may use parody to construct, at least temporarily, a symbolic order in which they are culturally superior to and different from dominant groups. See Keith Basso, *Portraits of the Whiteman: Linguistic Play and Cultural Symbols among the Western Apache* (Cambridge: Cambridge University Press, 1979).

27. See Coco Fusco and Guillermo Gómez-Peña, "New World Radio," in *Radio Rethink: Art, Sound and Transmission,* ed. Daina Augaitis and Dan Lander (Banff, Canada: Walter Phillips Gallery, 1994), 223–244.

28. See Guattari, quoted in Kogawa, "Free Radio."

29. The appropriation of African American rap music and cultural style by European ethnic and linguistic minorities is not uncommon. For a fascinating parallel case among Franco-Maghribi youth, see Joan Gross, David McMurray, and Ted Swedenburg, "Rai, Rap and Ramadan Nights: Franco-Maghribi Cultural Identities," *Middle East Reports* 22, no. 5 (September–October 1992): 11–16.

30. Hansen, "Unstable Mixtures," 183.

31. I want to thank William Hanks for making this point in his comments to an earlier version of this paper.

32. See Alexandra Jaffe, "Obligation, Error, and Authenticity: Competing Cultural Principles in the Teaching of Corsican," *Journal of Linguistic Anthropology* 3, no. 1 (1993): 99–114.

33. See bell hooks, "Talking Back," in *Out There: Marginalization and Contemporary Cultures,* ed. R. Ferguson, M. Gever, T. Minh-ha, and C. West (Cambridge, MA: MIT Press, 1990).

"UNLIKELY COALITIONS"

Angela Davis: Reflections on Race, Class, and Gender in the USA

JULY 1, 1995

LL: Please begin by considering the social, political, and economic shifts that have taken place in the United States during the period of the 1960s to the 1990s. I would like to invite you to characterize what, in your opinion, has shifted and what has not. In other words, we no longer have the FBI and police assaults on Black Panther chapters all over the country; but we do have Mumia Abu-Jamal on death row in Pennsylvania. We no longer have Jim Crow segregation, but we have another kind of segregation: we have a Supreme Court ruling that it is unconstitutional to have "racial preferences" for affirmative action. I wonder if you could put this current moment in the 1990s into a dialectical relation with the 1960s.

AD: There are many ways to talk about the relationship between the '60s and the '90s. The social movements of the '60s — the civil rights movement, various movements of Native Americans, Chicanos/ Latinos, Asian Americans, the women's movement, the student movement — did bring about significant, if not radical, transformations. Much of what we can call progressive change, particularly in the area of race, can be attributed to struggles waged by those movements. However, at the same time, a new terrain was established, which at times appears to contradict the meaning of the movements of the '60s. Did we work so hard in order to guarantee entrance of a conservative Black man, who opposes affirmative action and women's reproductive rights, into the Supreme Court? Rather than simply despair that things are taking a reactionary turn, I think it is important to acknowledge the extent to which the Black movement allowed for the emergence of a much more powerful Black middle class and the breakup of an apparent political consensus. There are similar middle-class formations among other racial ethnic groups. So the question today is not so much how to reverse these developments to re-find ourselves, based on a kind of nostalgic longing for what used to be, but rather, to think about the extent to which movements for racial and gender equality can no longer be *simply* based on questions of desegregation. A different kind of "political," a different kind of politics, really, has to inform this movement. I don't know. Does that make any sense?

LL: It makes a great deal of sense. When Stuart Hall talks about the convergence of the different contradictions of race, class, and gender, he suggests that the material conditions of a given historical moment make a certain contradiction rise to the surface. Could you speak about the conditions of our current moment in relation to these contradictions, addressing the ways that capitalism utilizes racism and sexism? Has the conjunction of race, class, and gender shifted in our contemporary period?

AD: Well, one of the strongest factors that has brought about the current set of transformations is deindustrialization. And the increased mobility of capital. And what I would say initially is that the collapse of an international socialist community — for good reasons, one can point out — which has led to the assumption that capitalism is the only future alternative makes it increasingly difficult to draw connections between the deteriorating conditions in communities of color and the restructuring of global capitalism, for example, the focus on crime as the most serious social problem, and the rise of the punishment industry. Another example is the related criminalization of single mothers of color through the ideological representation of the "welfare queen" as the reproducer of poverty. So the connection between the globalization of capital and these developments — which began with the Reagan-Bush administration, but have reached their peak recently — aren't generally made.

LL: Are you saying that because of global restructuring, the proletarianization of women of color in the United States is simultaneous with the exploitation of women in the so-called third world? In other words, that both exploitations are specific to the global restructuring of capitalism?

AD: Absolutely. But at the same time, what I'm trying to get at is the way in which these developments are actually represented within social movements, for example, within the Black community, the increased focus on young Black males, which is important, but dangerous at the same time. Important because of the fact that Black youth, young Black men, certainly are very much at risk since a quarter of them are under the direct jurisdiction of the criminal justice system, either in prison, on parole, or on probation. But at the same time, the demonization and criminalization of young Black women is often totally neglected. What is also neglected is the fact that the increase in the incarcerated population of women is about twice that of the increase in the rate of incarceration of men.

Consider the recent movement spearheaded by Reverend Ben Chavis and Minister Farrakhan of the Nation of Islam, which calls upon Black men to reassert their primacy within Black families and communities. A Washington demonstration of "a million Black men" in the fall of 1995 is predicated on the fact that women will stay at home in support of "their men." Certainly, in this period of increased mobility of capital, there is a gendered assault on young Black men—jobs that used to be available have migrated to other parts of the world. However, to assume that saving Black communities is equivalent to saving Black men harks back to a dangerous, unreflective masculinist nationalism that informed Black movements earlier on. There are productive ways in which a gender analysis can specifically identify ways in which men are disproportionately affected by deindustrialization. Moreover, during this period, if Black men choose to organize as men, questions such as male support of women's reproductive rights and of lesbians' right to adopt and male opposition to violence against women should be emphasized. Rather than male primacy in families and communities, gender equality in private as well as public spheres needs to be foregrounded.

LL: From your vantage point now, when you think about the breakup and the transformations of Black liberation struggles in the '60s, what is your understanding of the relationship between the external assault from the FBI, the police, and the state and the internal difference and conflict about priorities, about methods?

AD: In a sense, the external assaults worked hand in hand with the internal contradictions. We know that J. Edgar Hoover identified the Black Panther Party as the greatest threat to the internal security of the country, and that the FBI orchestrated assaults from one end of the country to the other, in collaboration with local police departments. This has been documented. What has not been taken as seriously are the internal struggles within radical Black and Latino organizations. It was the inability to address questions of gender and sexuality that also led inevitably to the demise of many organizations. Many elder activists, as well as people who had not yet been born during the era, mourn the passing of the Black Panther Party, and nostalgically look back to that period as one in which questions of who and what constituted the enemy were crystal clear. The recent film by Melvyn Van Peebles represents the Black Panther Party in that kind of nostalgic and romantic way. If you look at Elaine

Brown's book, which has been abundantly criticized — for good reasons, in part — she does reveal the extent to which the BPP and many of its fraternal organizations were very much informed by masculinist notions of what it meant to engage in struggle. These notions of struggle depended on the subordination of women, both ideologically and in practice. The women were responsible for a vastly disproportionate amount of work in a struggle constructed as one for the freedom of "the Black man." This kind of critique has to continue. A number of recent Ph.D dissertations look at women's roles in organizations like the Young Lords, the Black Panther Party, the Brown Berets, and the American Indian movement. Tracy Matthews, who was in the history department at the University of Michigan, has written her dissertation on women in the Black Panther Party. Hopefully there will be a nice collection of books coming out in the next few years, which will begin to demystify the images of radical organizations of people of color in the late '60s and early '70s, for the sake of young people who desire to do activist work in the contemporary period.

LL: Can I ask a little more about a different kind of contradiction? In *Racial Formation in the United States,* Michael Omi and Howard Winant argue that during the period of civil rights struggles, civil rights legislation was in a way the state's attempt to appropriate and co-opt certain parts of the broader, wider variety of social movements pressuring for more change on race.[1] Would you agree with this analysis?

AD: During the civil rights era, the primary struggles were for legal transformation. It was important at the time to break down the legal barriers, to change the laws, to challenge the juridical status of people of color. Parenthetically, one of the real weaknesses of the civil rights movement was its paradigmatic black-white focus on race. But Omi and Winant point out correctly that social movements addressed issues that went beyond the legal construction of race. Beyond voting rights and desegregation, issues of education, health care, police repression, issues of jobs, etc. were raised. Organizations like SNCC [Student Nonviolent Coordinating Committee] that were rooted in voter registration and desegregation struggles initially focused on those issues, but then went on to address questions that emerged from the urban northern Black communities as well.

LL: They don't argue, of course, that there was total co-optation. But rather that civil rights legislation was the response of the state to activist social movements, some of which could have called for much more radical change.

AD: Absolutely.

LL: In a way, it goes along with what you were pointing out earlier, that Clarence Thomas is where he is because of affirmative action and the contradictions of liberalism. Yet, despite such contradictions, we must still insist on the concept of rights, and humanity, and fight to keep in place the legislation that is now under attack.

AD: Yes, but the assumption that the state is the primary guardian of the victories that were won by the civil rights movement has led to a great deal of chaos, and an inability to conceptualize where social movements can go from here. At the same time, many of the leaders of the civil rights movement now occupy putative positions of power within the state structure. Look, for example, at Ron Dellums, who was initially associated with the Black Panther Party in Oakland, California. As a matter of fact, he was elected to Congress based on his militant and radical positions. For the past twenty-five years, he's had to negotiate very different kinds of positions. His work within Congress has been very important. But the constituencies which were activist constituencies became electoral constituencies. With the election of Clinton, which ended the Republican Reagan-Bush era, there was the assumption that now, yes, the state will fulfill the goal that was set for it during the transformative period of the civil rights struggle. And that, as a matter of fact, the reliance on the new administration led to the absorption of oppositional organizations—and sometimes almost entire movements—into state structures.

LL: With the priority, would you say, on enfranchisement and assimilation into the state, as opposed to working for a larger transformation?

AD: That is true, and it is a rather complicated process. In many instances people truly believe that they will be able to bring about radical transformations from and within new positions of state power. The work that I am doing on prisons is a case in point. Many people whose connection with prison issues comes from their earlier involvement in oppositional struggles — who were involved in and in some instances were initiators of the prisoner rights movement — are now working within correctional bureaucracies. Here in San Francisco, the current sheriff and assistant sheriff have a long history of involvement in progressive movements. The assistant sheriff spent many years in prison during the '60s and early '70s and was associated with George Jackson and the internal prisoner movement. He was one of the founders of the California Prisoners Union. Now he inhabits the very positions which were once occupied by his adversaries. Under his leadership people have been hired to work within the jail structures who are former prisoners (such as myself and Johnny Spain, once of the San Quentin Six) and who were once visible as militant activists (such as Harry Edwards, who organized the protests at the 1968 Mexico City Olympics). The assumption, of course, is that these individuals will press for transformation. However, under such conditions transformation is conceptualized very differently. The formulation of radical prison work as leading toward the reduction of prison populations and the abolition of jails and prisons as the primary means of addressing social problems such as crime, unemployment, undereducation, etc. recedes and is replaced with the goal of creating better, more progressive jails and prisons. I am not suggesting that we should not use whatever political arenas are available to us. However, once one becomes integrated into state structures, it becomes increasingly difficult to think about ways of developing radical oppositional practices.

LL: You have always been a voice for feminist concerns within Black liberation struggles, yet it has been difficult for Marxist antiracist work to find a "home" in feminism as it has existed in the U.S. women's movement. In *Women, Race, and Class,* but also in your lectures "Facing Our Common Foe" and "We Do Not Consent," you argue that racism and classism affect the construction of political agendas even and especially in the white women's movement regarding race and reproductive rights.[2] I wonder if you could discuss the struggles within U.S. feminism in the last decade. You argue eloquently that historically rape has been defined as rape of the white woman's body, who is the property of elite white men, which obscures the possibility of thinking of Black women's bodies as victims of rape, or victims of assault, and subordinates the issue of Black women's health. Has the antiracist critique successfully changed white feminism?

AD: From one vantage point, those critiques have been very successful. Which isn't to say that hegemonic white feminism, in the sense in which Chela Sandoval uses the term, has really substantively changed. But it is no longer possible to ignore issues of race. Even those who only pay lip service to race analysis understand this. Twenty-five years ago, dominant feminism began to evolve as if women of color did not exist. As a result, vast numbers of women of color who were interested in women's issues did not associate themselves with early feminist approaches. Toni Morrison, who is very much associated with Black feminists today, wrote an article in the early 1970s in the *New York Times Magazine* in which she argued that feminism belonged to white women and had no relevance for

Black women. The most interesting developments in feminism, I think, over the past couple of decades have occurred within the theories and practices of women of color. U.S. feminism would not be what it is today, U.S. feminisms would not be what they are today, if it hadn't been for the interventions by women of color. So I think that's a very positive sign. At the same time, within communities of color, feminism has become a much more powerful force and has had an impact on all kinds of issues, on the way issues are constructed, the way campaigns are developed. The critique has to continue, though; I'm not suggesting that the work has been done. It's a lot more complicated today. Women of color who refer to themselves as feminists still find that it is not easy to identify as a feminist. For one, feminism is often considered obsolete. There are a number of new works that have been published by young feminists, both feminists of color and white feminists, that, in order to dissociate themselves from traditional feminism, tend to revert to prefeminist ideas.

LL: I would like to ask you to situate yourself in women of color discourse. Many people would locate women of color critique in the antiracist critique of white feminism: Cherríe Moraga, Gloria Anzaldúa, or Audre Lorde would be key figures in this nexus. Or alternatively, others would locate it in the Black feminist critique of male-dominated cultural nationalism. But I understand the genealogy of your work and practice as articulating a feminist antiracist critique within the Marxist critique of capitalism. Yours is a most important synthesis that really advances women of color critique. Please share your thoughts about women of color as a political project and as a research project.

AD: Well, I don't know if we can talk about women of color politics in a monolithic way.

LL: It's perhaps even difficult to understand it as a social movement. In a way it's a critique that has various locations.

AD: There've been really interesting developments over the past fifteen years or so, since most people date the development of women of color as a new political subject from 1981, when *This Bridge Called My Back* was published.[3] Women of color conceptualized as a political project, to borrow Chandra Mohanty's notion, is extremely important. You might also use Omi and Winant's notion and argue that it is possible to think about women of color as a different kind of racial formation. And the work that you, Lisa, have done on women of color emphasizes the fact that it is a provisional identity that allows the move beyond identity politics articulated in the traditional way. The fact that race is placed at the forefront of women of color politics is important, because it also challenges the influence of nationalism on identity politics. Women of color formations are compelled to address intersectionality and the mutual and complex interactions of race, class, gender, and sexuality. That is what is so exciting about the possibilities of women of color research and organizing strategies. For the last four years or so I have been working with the Research Cluster for the Study of Women of Color in Collaboration and Conflict. Many students and faculty involved locate their work within a progressive scholarly and activist tradition that seeks to bring about structural and ideological change. The Women of Color Resource Center here in the San Francisco Bay Area attempts to forge stronger ties between researchers and grassroots organizers. Asian Immigrant Women's Advocates (AIWA) is one of the groups associated with the Women of Color Resource Center. This organization traces its genealogy back to the Third World Women's Alliance founded in 1970. This means that what we call women of color work predates 1981, the year in which *This Bridge Called My Back* was published, which is usually evoked as the originating moment of women of color consciousness. During the earlier era, the anti-imperialist character of third world women's work inflected it with a strong anticapitalist kind of critique. The influence of Marxism is still very much visible in, for example, the Combahee River Collective manifesto. While it is important to affirm the momentous cultural work initiated with the publication of *This Bridge,* the earlier, more explicitly anticapitalist traditions should not be erased.

LL: And those connections are like a history that needs still to be written.

AD: Yes. What we call women of color work or U.S. third world women's work can be traced back to the civil rights era. During the 1964 campaign spearheaded by SNCC in Mississippi, Georgia, and Alabama, there was an emergent antimasculinist critique, directed against the obstinately male leadership. This critique crystallized in an internal organization of Black women, which later established itself as an autonomous organization, the Black Women's Alliance. While cross-racial coalitions were not as self-conscious as they tend to be today, the political projects to which Puerto Rican women (antisterilization work, for example) and Asian American women (Vietnam solidarity work, for example) were drawn, were also embraced by the Black Women's Alliance, which later reconceptualized itself as a Third World Women's Alliance. Some of the same women associated with those efforts in the late '60s — like Elizabeth Martinez, Linda Burnham, Fran Beal — continue to be active through organizations like the Women of Color Resource Center. Around the same time, numerous lesbians of color organizations emerged. In fact, the term *lesbian of color* acquired currency before *women of color* entered into our political vocabulary. In other words, although we refer to "women of color" as a new political subject, there is a rich, unexplored history of women of color political projects. We shouldn't assume that women of color work has been going on for only a decade or so.

LL: Or that it's a reaction against . . .

AD: . . . what we used to call white middle feminism. NOW was founded in 1964. We can also trace the emergence of a radical women of color feminism back to the same year.

LL: Would you speak a bit about your recent book project on women and the blues? I'm wondering if you could comment on the question of cultural forms as alternative spaces, or popular culture as an informal site for the transmission of oppositional strategies and popular wisdom about survival.

AD: The fact that historical modes of transmitting culture are not mechanically determined by economic relations does not mean that all modes are equally possible regardless of a group's class position. I have been interested in the history of gender consciousness in Black communities since the research I did around *Women, Race and Class.* Much of the material I utilized in that work — even that which specifically addressed issues of working-class women's consciousness — was produced by women and men who can be defined as members of the Black intelligentsia. My own interest in popular culture is related to an attempt to expand that original project on gender consciousness in Black communities, focusing on the blues as a site for reflecting on Black working-class feminist consciousness and on the transmission of that consciousness. In this book, which is called *Blues Legacies and Black Feminisms,* I try to present blues performances as an alternative site for recovering historical forms of working-class women's consciousness.

LL: In your autobiography you wrote, "the forces that have made my life what it is are the very same forces that have shaped and misshaped the lives of millions of my people. I'm convinced that my response to these forces has been unexceptional as well, that my political involvement, ultimately as a member of the Communist Party, has been a natural logical way to defend our embattled humanity."[4] I wonder if you could talk about your formation in Marxism and what Marxism has meant to you.

AD: From where I stood — which was a very different location from that of the vast numbers of people who followed my trial — I did not feel that my life experiences were exceptional enough to merit inscription in an autobiography. Besides, I was very young. So I had to think about that project as a "political" autobiography. At the time I didn't realize that I had conceptualized it in the tradition of the Black autobiographical genre that could be said to go back to the slave narrative. That didn't occur to me until long after I had written it. It's difficult to identify a single development that led me to Marxism. I grew up in a family which had numerous ties to individuals in the Communist Party. Although my mother never joined the Communist Party, she worked in organizations with Black communists who were organizing in Birmingham, which, because of the steel mills, had become an industrial center in the '30s. She was an officer in the NAACP and in the Southern Negro Youth Congress, which had been established by communists. Because of my mother's connection with communists, we were often followed by the FBI during the McCarthy era. By the age of six, I was already aware of the extent to which the government would pursue people who had different ideas of what kind of social order should prevail in this country. While I was attending a progressive high school in New York, I read the *Communist Manifesto* for the first time. I was fortunate enough to have a history teacher who openly espoused Marxism and encouraged us to think critically about the class interests represented by dominant historiography. At the same time I was active in a communist youth organization and for many months picketed Woolworth's every Saturday because of their policies of segregation in the South. I guess you might say that I learned very early to take for granted the insightfulness of Marxist literature and also to draw connections between theory and practice.

As an undergraduate, my interest in Marxism was further stimulated by professors like Herbert Marcuse. As a French major, I became very interested in the way Marxism was integrated into existentialist philosophy — and by Sartre's political activism. Working with Marcuse, I began to study the philosophical history of Marxism and read Kant, Hegel, as well as Marx. As a young activist in high school, I already considered myself a Marxist. By the time I finished college, I was even more convinced that Marxist analyses could help me make sense of a world which seemed to be so saturated with racism and class exploitation. I guess I had the good fortune to sort of grow into Marxism or grow up with Marxism, rather than having to later work to replace dominant modes of thought with a critical Marxist approach. I should probably point out that the high school I attended, Elizabeth Irwin High School, was rather exceptional. It was actually cooperatively owned by teachers, many of whom had been blacklisted as a result of their political involvements during the McCarthy era.

LL: How important is it, do you think, for students and young people who want to be activists to read Marx and to have a rich education in Marxist theory?

AD: I think it's extremely important. However, many students today encounter Marx's ideas not so much by reading the original works, but rather through their reception in contemporary theoretical literature and in popular culture. Many students might be familiar with Marx the political economist, but are entirely unfamiliar with the early philosophical writings. While I would not make the kind of argument that conservatives present regarding the need to return to the basic — to the "classical" texts in the Western intellectual tradition — I do think that a closer familiarity with Marx's writings might help students to assess critically our contemporary conditions.

LL: Moving into a discussion of the university, pedagogy, and the role of intellectuals of color, I wonder if I could ask you about how you think of your role as an educator and your role in the formation of intellectuals of color.

AD: I grew up in a household of teachers. Both my mother and father were teachers. Although my own decision to go into education came much later, I learned very early to value education and its liberatory potential. In the Black community in which I was reared, teachers were among the most respected members of the community and were expected to provide leadership — perhaps in even more fundamental ways than ministers, who are often considered the community's natural leaders. Education and liberation were always bound together. I was persuaded very early in my life that liberation was not possible without education. This is one of the reasons I always felt drawn to the radical potential of education and why I am particularly interested in working not only with students of color, but with white students as well who make this connection.

LL: Who and what were your influences in this regard?

AD: Studying with both Adorno and Marcuse allowed me to think early on about the relationship between theory and practice, between intellectual work and activist work. Adorno tended to dismiss intellectual work that was connected with political activism. He argued that the revolution had failed, not so much because of problems presenting themselves in the practical implementation of revolutionary theory, but rather because the theory itself was flawed, perhaps even fundamentally flawed. He therefore insisted that the only sure way to move along a revolutionary continuum was to effect, for the present, a retreat into theory. No revolutionary transformation was possible, he said, until we could figure out what went wrong in the theory. At the time student activism was on the rise in Germany. I studied in Frankfurt from 1965 to 1967, which was a period during which the German Socialist Student Organization gained in membership and influence. Because many of the student leaders were directly inspired by the history of the Frankfurt School — and some young professors affiliated with the Frankfurt School like Oscar Negt were actively involved in the SDS (Sozialitische Deutsche Studentenverbund) — we were able to critically engage with Adorno's ideas. Interestingly enough, many of Horkheimer's and Adorno's ideas were mobilized in challenging this advocacy of theory as the only possible mode of practice. I was involved, in fact, in the production of a pirate edition of *Dialectic of Enlightenment,* which Adorno and Horkheimer were not yet willing to republish. We typed the text on stencils, mimeographed it, and sold it for the cost of its production. A similar edition of Lukacs's *History and Class Consciousness* was also produced.

Marcuse, of course, called for a very different relationship between intellectual work and political practice. There is a story I like to tell about Marcuse's involvement in UCSD campus politics, which certainly informed my ideas on the role of the teacher and on the need to maintain always a creative tension between theory and praxis. Back in the late '60s, the emergent Black student organization, in alliance with the Chicano student organization, decided to campaign to create a new college at UCSD, which we wanted to name the Lumumba-Zapata College. We envisioned it as a college which would admit one-third Chicano students, one-third Black students, and one-third working-class white students. We had it all worked out! Or at least we thought we did. At one point in a rather protracted campaign, we decided to occupy the registrar's office. I said I would ask Herbert about his possible participation in the takeover. I explained to him that we would have to break a window in order to gain entrance. In other words, we risked being charged with breaking and entering and trespassing. If he were the first person to enter the building, we were less likely to be arrested and/or expelled from the university. Without a moment's hesitation, Herbert agreed: "Of course I'll do it." There was no question in his mind. At that time he was about seventy-five years old. He was the first person to walk into the registrar's office. Our work acquired a legitimacy that would have been impossible without his participation. In the classroom and through his writings and lectures, Marcuse defended the radical activism of the late '60s. The emergence of an international student movement, the social movements of people of color, the rise of feminist activism brought a new, more optimistic dimension to Marcuse's ideas. The seduction of the "one-dimensional society" could be resisted. He not only theorized these developments, but actively participated in mobilizations both in the United States and Europe. Working so closely with him during that period, I learned that while teaching and agitation were very different practices, students need to be assured that politics and intellectual life are not two entirely separate modes of existence. I learned that I did not have to leave political activism behind in order to be an effective teacher. Of course, this insight got me fired from my first job at UCLA and during my first year there spies recorded every comment I made in class which might have political undertones. I was first fired for my membership in the Communist Party. The second time I was fired it was because of my off-campus activities in support of political prisoners.

LL: Please speak about your teaching, how you encourage students to do projects that are both activist and intellectual. What sort of role do you take in shaping these projects? Perhaps you could describe the Women of Color Research Cluster at UC–Santa Cruz.

AD: Many of the students who work with me are involved in very interesting projects on social movement history, cultures of resistance, applying new historiographical approaches. One student is attempting to rethink Black women's involvement in the labor movement. Another is attempting to develop new ways of theorizing Puerto Rican migration, foregrounding questions of gender and sexuality. My students are doing very interesting work, work that can potentially make a difference.

The Women of Color Research Cluster at UC–Santa Cruz was formed four years ago. It was the brainchild of Margaret Daniels, a History of Consciousness graduate student who is doing her dissertation on women of color film festivals. She examines these film and video festivals as an important site for the construction of women of color as a political subject. Maria Ochoa, also a History of Consciousness student, worked closely with her. Thanks to their leadership, an impressive number of graduate students, faculty, staff, and some undergraduates came together under the auspices of the cluster, funded by the Center for Cultural Studies. A major project undertaken by the Cluster was the editing of a special issue of *Inscriptions*, the journal of the Center for Cultural Studies.[5] I should point out that the full name of the group is the Research Cluster for the Study of Women of Color in Collaboration and Conflict. Its emergence represented a desire to explore not only the possibilities of cross-racial coalition and alliance, but also to think about the inevitable tensions and conflicts among women of color. We took note of the important role Black and Korean women were playing in the effort to negotiate a relationship between these communities that had become especially difficult in the aftermath of the 1992 Los Angeles uprising.

Other projects we have developed include writing groups for students, a lecture series involving cross-racial conversations, colloquia, meetings with the Women of Color Resource Center in Oakland. When I was chosen to hold the UC Presidential Chair, it meant that the Women of Color Cluster would receive more substantial funding. A significant aspect of my proposal — which was the basis for my selection — was a curriculum development project that would be directed by the Cluster. Over the next period we will develop a number of courses to satisfy the Ethnic Studies requirement at UC–Santa Cruz. These courses will be collaboratively taught by graduate students and tenured faculty. The Cluster will not only collaboratively develop these courses, but there will also be focused deliberations on pedagogical questions.

LL: You mention the focus on women of color "in collaboration and conflict." Moving outside of the university in order to think more broadly about the forging of the alliances across groups, what are the difficulties and the opportunities for Black, Chicana-Latina, and Native and Asian American women working together? What are the specific issues for each group that need to be addressed in order for coalition to take place? What sorts of things keep coming up?

AD: This work is very difficult. Coalition building has never been easy. But I think it might be more productive to move away from constructions of women of color as a coalition. The assumption behind coalition building is that disparate groups or individuals come together with their own separate — and often racially based — agendas, which have to be negotiated and compromised in order for the group to come together. Coalitions also have an ephemeral and ad hoc character. I am not suggesting that the concept *women of color* is not here to stay, but I do think that it might be a very difficult political project. First of all, not all "women of color" choose to embrace this identity. In fact, an Asian American woman who might prefer to call herself Chinese American might be equally reluctant to identify as a woman of color. But that's all right. There is no hard and fast requirement in the sense that a woman of African descent has little choice but to identify as Black. However, those who do involve themselves in women of color projects need to make strong commitments — to borrow Jacqui Alexander's formulation — "to become fluent in each other's stories."

This is not to say that significant women of color work has not taken place within coalitional formations. There is, for example, the Women of Color Coalition on Reproductive Health that has brought together representatives from four different health organizations: the Asian Women's Health Organization, the Latina Women's Health Project, the Black Women's Health Project, and the Native American Women's Health Organization. This coalition played an important role at the UN Conference on Reproductive Rights which took place in Cairo the year before the women's conference and NGO forum in Beijing. However, it has been beset with serious problems that afflict many coalitional forms which emanate from the difficulties of compromise and agenda negotiation. Women of color work also takes place within caucus and task force formations that often develop within predominantly white organizations such as the National Women's Studies Association and the National Coalition Against Domestic Violence. It is interesting that women of color formations emerged within both of these organizations in 1981 — a pivotal year for women of color. Early on, women of color groups also organized within a number of lesbian groups.

The groups I find most interesting, however, are those that consider "women of color" a point of departure rather than a level of organizing which rises out of and breaks down into a series of racially specific agendas: in other words, those organizations that challenge the census-category approach to "women of color." Which means that women of color work can foreground race at a time when dominant discourse attempts to erase it, yet at the same time avoid the pitfalls of essentialism. I referred earlier to the Women of Color Resource Center. This organization develops projects which bring grassroots organizers and scholars together. It also sponsors projects like AIWA — Asian Immigrant Women's Advocates — which in turn appeals to all women of color (and white women as well) to support campaigns like the Jessica McClintock boycott. I have also referred to the Women of Color Research Cluster, which does not establish its agenda by considering so-called priority issues.

A woman of color formation might decide to work around immigration issues. This political commitment is not based on the specific histories of racialized communities or its constituent members, but rather constructs an agenda agreed upon by all who are a part of it. In my opinion, the most exciting potential of women of color formations resides in the possibility of politicizing this identity — basing the identity on politics rather than the politics on identity.

LL: You have written about visiting Egypt, and the complications of being both a Black woman activist and yet also a "representative" from the United States, a dominant first world power.[6] Taking up these complications, I wonder if you could comment about the importance, the possibilities, and the difficulties of work between radical U.S. women and women in the third world.

AD: Women's organizations have been engaged in international solidarity work at least since the previous century, since the beginning of this century. I think it's important to acknowledge this internationalism. Some of this work was supported by the former socialist countries — the former Soviet Union, the German Democratic Republic, where the NGO Women's International Democratic Federation was located. Women for Racial and Economic Equality, a U.S.-based organization, has ties with women's organizations all over the third world. I am suggesting that there are precedents for the kind of organizing across borders that women are presently attempting to do. However, during the earlier period, women's organizations tended to be rather confined to specific agendas: peace, for example, which was certainly important. But now the possibilities are vaster, considering the globalization of capital and the circuits that have been opened up by migrating corporations. In other words, it is even more important today to do transnational organizing — around labor issues, sexual trafficking, and violence against women. While there is not enough time to make specific reference to all the current international struggles U.S. women are and need to be connected with, I would like to mention the need to strengthen women of color work in opposition to the economic embargo of Cuba. Cuban women are hurt most by the blockade and are on the front lines of opposition. Alice Walker and I are presently trying to organize a campaign to "Boycott the Blockade." In general, considering the impact of NAFTA, the need for networking and international organizing among women trade unionists in Canada, the United States, and Mexico is especially great. Considering the global assembly line — and the extent to which immigrant women working within the United States may work for the same corporations that are exploiting women in Asia, in Canada, in Mexico — organizing possibilities are vast.

LL: Yes. Can I ask you about immigration, since we touched on that? How do you think the influx of Asians and Latin Americans into the United States, particularly since 1965, has changed communities of color and race relations in the United States? Is the current policing of immigration and immigrant communities an index of similar, yet different, contradictions than those that operated in the 1960s?

AD: Well, it's no longer possible to talk about issues of race in exclusively black and white terms. While large communities of color that are not Black — Native American, Asian, Latina/o — have parallel histories of racism, oppression, and militant resistance, civil rights discourse established terms that were largely based on a certain construction of Black history that excluded women, gays and lesbians, and other marginalized groups. Especially since questions of immigration are moving to the fore, it is no longer possible to confine race discourse and antiracist activism to a simple black-white binary. New issues, new problems, new contradictions have emerged and old ones have been uncovered. Many veteran activists bemoan the fact that there are so many tensions and contradictions within and among communities of color and that it can no longer be assumed that a person who is not white will necessarily assume progressive positions on racial issues — on affirmative action, for example. They bemoan the fact that you cannot expect a person of color by virtue of her/his racial location to speak out against racism, regardless of the group targeted. This has become especially apparent in the failure of significant numbers of Black organizations to actively mobilize against Proposition 187 in California and similar measures in other states. I am afraid that the impact of anti-immigrant rhetoric on Black communities is inhibiting the development of a political awareness of the radical potential of Latin American and Asian immigrant workers. It used to be the case that within the more progressive sectors of the trade union movement, Black workers were acknowledged as a radical and militant force. Today, if there is any hope for the labor movement, it will come, in my opinion, from the new forms of organizing immigrant workers are developing.

LL: Asian women and Latinas in the garment and electronics industries.

AD: Yes. Absolutely. What is really exciting are the new forms of organizing that aren't contained within single trade unions, nor are they focused on narrow trade union issues. It's been virtually impossible within the labor movement over the decades to address issues that aren't traditional union issues. Like wages, benefits, workplace — these are extremely important. But there are also issues that go beyond the workplace that affect workers as well.

LL: Child care, language.

AD: Yes. Environmental issues, as well. I'm thinking about the work that's being done in Los Angeles immigrant communities, a project that is a multiunion effort with a community base. Considering these new forms of resistance, there are ways to think about these changes in an optimistic way.

LL: Yes. I really agree. Even though there's been an intensification of the exploitation of women of color and third world women, it has also generated new methods and strategies for addressing that exploitation.

Regarding different organizing strategies for the new kinds of populations of workers and the specificities of labor exploitation under new capitalist modes like "mixed production" and "flexible accumulation," perhaps we can get back to the initial discussion of the shifts over the past thirty years. We know that conditions have worsened particularly for the women in communities of color. What kinds of activist projects are possible now? In these times, how do we measure what significant change means?

The Southwest Network for Environmental and Economic Justice is really interesting to me, the group under which AIWA along with La Fuerza Unida organized the Levi Strauss boycott. It seems that the issues of the environment, health, and toxic waste dumping are places where labor concerns and racialized community concerns come together.

AD: Exactly. The environmental justice movement is a relatively new and very promising organizing strategy in communities of color. New strategies are also suggested by the workers centers in Chinatown that link work against exploitative sweatshop conditions with campaigns against domestic violence and simultaneously make appeals for multiracial solidarity. We will have come a long way if we succeed in convincing a significant number of Black women's organizations, for example, to support Asian immigrant women's labor and community struggles. This would be yet another form of women of color consciousness that is politically rather than racially grounded and at the same time anchored in a more complex antiracist consciousness.

LL: There's a project in San Diego called Beyond Borders that has a support committee for *maquiladora* workers in Baja, California,

Mexico, and Central America. They document working conditions and occupational health and safety violations in the *maquilas,* publicize the attacks on workers' rights to organize, and promote cross-border worker organizing by connecting U.S. trade unionists with their counterparts in Mexico. Interestingly enough, a number of the women who work in this group are Asian American.

AD: This kind of cross-racial, cross-border organizing needs to be encouraged in many different contexts.

LL: You've done considerable work with women in prisons, political prisoners, and prisoners' rights. Could you say a bit about your different projects with prisoners?

AD: My work with prisoners — both research and organizing work — has been one of the most consistent themes of my political life. It seems that the struggle to free political prisoners is unending. The campaign to free Mumia Abu-Jamal is a case in point. With respect to women prisoners, I am presently working on a project with Kumkum Bhavnani, who teaches sociology at UC–Santa Barbara and has a similar political history. We have interviewed women prisoners in an attempt to add new voices to the debate around prisons and to suggest that abolitionist strategies need to be taken seriously. In general, we need more activist projects against the proliferation of prisons, against what Mike Davis calls the "prison-industrial complex."[7] Our earlier discussion of labor is relevant here, too. There is a dangerous privatization trend within the correctional industry, which not only involves the privatization of entire state correctional systems and some sectors of the federal system, but the increasing reliance on prison labor by private corporations as well. The state of California can boast of the largest prison system in the country — and one of the largest in the world. The Department of Corrections in California has established a joint venture system, which invites corporations to establish their shops on prison grounds. The advertising scheme represents prisoners as a cheap labor force that does not require employers to respect minimum wage provisions or provide health benefits. The advertisement points out that prison workers never ask for paid vacations or have transportation or baby-sitting problems. This means that prisoners are considered cheap labor in the same sense that immigrants within the United States and third world workers abroad are treated as the most profitable labor pools. Rather than crossing national borders, corporations simply go behind prison walls.

LL: Perhaps that's the "Made in the USA" label.

AD: Yes, that's the "Made in the USA" label at 50 cents an hour with no benefits. Prisoners have been unsuccessfully trying to organize labor unions for decades. Perhaps we need to think about organizing that will bring together prisoners, prisoners' rights groups, immigrant worker organizations, and some of the traditional labor unions. In other words, there *is* a place for coalitions. While I find identity-based coalitions problematic, I do concur with Bernice Reagon when she says that coalition work must be central in late twentieth-century political organizing. However, I think that we should focus on the creation of unpredictable or unlikely coalitions grounded in political projects. Not only prisoners, immigrant workers, and labor unions, but also prisoners and students, for example. This might be the most effective way to contest the shifting of the funding base for education into prison construction and maintenance. One of the other coalitions that should be encouraged is between welfare rights and gay and lesbian organizations. Both welfare mothers and gays and lesbians are directly targeted by conservative emphasis on "family values."

LL: Such a coalition could include legal and undocumented immigrants, too, if it were organized around the proposed Personal Responsibility Act, which bars not only undocumented immigrants but legal permanent residents from receiving federal benefits.

AD: That's right. We might also think about coalition work that would bring together legal and undocumented immigrant youth, on the one hand, and young African American and Latino American youth, on the other, who are all targeted by a devious criminalization process that replaces a legitimate need for jobs, education, and health care with a very effective demonization of these groups. And it is certainly time to revive the demand for a reconsideration of the eight-hour workday. A shorter workday could help provide jobs for undocumented immigrants as well as the vast unemployed sectors among youth in communities of color. If the new cultural arenas that have developed over the past decade are utilized, young activists might be able to create a powerful campaign.

NOTES

1. Michael Omi and Howard Winant, *Racial Formation in the United States, from the 1960s to the 1990s* (New York: Routledge, 1994).
2. Angela Y. Davis, *Women, Race and Class* (New York: Random House, 1981), chaps. 11 and 12. "Facing Our Common Foe: Women and the Struggle against Racism" and "We Do Not Consent: Violence against Women in a Racist

Society" in Angela Y. Davis, *Women, Culture, and Politics* (New York: Random House, 1989).

3. Cherríe Moraga and Gloria Anzaldúa, eds., *This Bridge Called My Back: Writings by Radical Women of Color* (New York: Kitchen Table Press, 1981).

4. Angela Y. Davis, *An Autobiography* (New York: Random House, 1974).

5. Maria Ochoa and Teresia Teaiwa, eds., "Enunciating Our Terms: Women of Color in Collaboration and Conflict," *Inscriptions* 7 (1994).

6. Angela Y. Davis, "Women in Egypt: A Personal View," in *Women, Culture, and Politics*.

7. Mike Davis, "A Prison-Industrial Complex: Hell-Factories in the Field," *The Nation* 260, no. 7 (1995): 229–234.

GEORGE LIPSITZ

"Frantic to Join . . . the Japanese Army": The Asia Pacific War in the Lives of African American Soldiers and Civilians

In his celebrated autobiography, Malcolm X explains how he escaped the draft in 1943 during World War II. At a time when "the only three things in the world that scared me" were "jail, a job, and the Army," the Harlem street hustler devised a plan to fool his foes. Aware that military intelligence units stationed "black spies in civilian clothes" in African American neighborhoods to watch for subversive activity, Malcolm (then named Malcolm Little) started "noising around" Harlem bars and street corners ten days before his scheduled preinduction physical exam. He let it be known that he was "frantic to join . . . the Japanese Army."

Just in case the military found his dramatic displays of disloyalty insufficient, Malcolm informed a psychiatrist at his physical exam that he was eager to enter the military. "I want to get sent down South," he asserted. "Organize them nigger soldiers, you dig? Steal us some guns, and kill crackers!" Not surprisingly, the Selective Service judged Malcolm Little mentally disqualified for military service, sending him home with a 4-F deferment on October 25, 1943.[1]

The distinguished historian John Hope Franklin secured a similar result for himself by very different means. Swept up in the patriotic fervor that followed the bombing of Pearl Harbor, Franklin genuinely *was* frantic to join . . . the U.S. Navy. He saw an advertisement indicating that the Navy needed skilled office workers who could type, take shorthand, and run business machines. At that point in his life, Franklin had six years of experience at secretarial work, had won three gold medals in typing, had taken an accounting course in high school, knew shorthand, and had a Ph.D. in history from Harvard University. The Navy recruiter told him that he was lacking one credential: color; that they could not hire him because he was Black.

Franklin then directed his efforts toward securing a position with the Department of War, then assembling a staff of historians. But here again, color mattered. The department hired several white historians who had not obtained advanced degrees, but never responded in any way to Franklin's application. When he went for his preinduction physical exam, a white doctor refused to let Franklin enter his office and made him wait for a blood test on a bench at the end of a hall near the fire escape until Franklin's protests got him admitted to the physician's office.[2]

Years later, Franklin recalled that these experiences changed his attitude toward the war. They convinced him that "the United States, however much it was devoted to protecting the freedoms and rights of Europeans, had no respect for me, no interest in my well-being, and not even a desire to utilize my services." Franklin came to the conclusion that "the United States did not need me and did not deserve me. Consequently, I spent the remainder of the war years successfully and with malice aforethought outwitting my draft board and the entire Selective Service establishment."[3] Instead of serving in the military, Franklin devoted his time to teaching, scholarship, and activism aimed at undermining the system of white supremacy.

Although they started out with very different intentions, Malcolm X and John Hope Franklin both ended up avoiding military service during World War II. Their actions were hardly typical; an overwhelming majority of Americans, and even an overwhelming majority of African Americans, who were eligible for the draft accepted induction and served effectively. Black draft resisters accounted for less than 5 percent of the 12,343 conscientious objection cases processed by the Justice Department, and more than one million Black men and women served in the armed forces during the war.[4] But the conflicts with the selective service system experienced by Malcolm X and John Hope Franklin bring into sharp relief the potentially explosive racial contradictions facing the United States during the war.

Franklin and Malcolm X expressed more than individual ingenuity and personal pique in their resistance to the draft. They articulated and acted upon a suspicion about the relationship between World War II and white supremacy widely held in their community: about the shortcomings of democracy in the United States, about the racialized nature of the war, about the potential power of nonwhite nations around the globe, and about the viability and desirability of covert and overt resistance to racism.

Although they expressed a decidedly minority view about the draft itself in their own communities during the war, they touched on shared social perceptions that gained majority approval in the postwar period. The emergence of Malcolm X in the postwar period as a Black nationalist leader who connected antiracist struggles in the United States with anti-imperialist efforts around the globe, Martin Luther King Jr.'s role as the leading opponent of the U.S. war in Vietnam as well as the leader of civil rights and poor peoples movements, and the actions of a generation of young people in the 1960s who used the research of scholars including John Hope Franklin to fashion their own understanding of their obligations to the nation at home and abroad all testify to the generative nature of wartime tensions and conflict.

Most important, the strategic maneuvering that Franklin and Malcolm X deployed in their struggles with the selective service system highlights the volatile instabilities sedimented within seemingly stable narratives of nation and race. Malcolm X initially presented himself as an admirer of enemies of the United States and as an active agent of subversion simply so he could stay on the streets and pursue his own pleasures as a petty criminal. Yet, his eventual imprisonment for crimes committed on the streets led him to a religious conversion and political awakening that made him an actual opponent of U.S. foreign policy, turning his wartime charade into an important part of his life's work. John Hope Franklin initially approached the government as a super-patriot eager to enlist in the U.S. war effort, but the racism directed at him by the government led him to evade military service and embark on a lifetime of oppositional intellectual work and activism.

By feigning a desire to join the Japanese Army and by announcing his interest in shooting southern segregationists, Malcolm X drew upon ideas and practices with deep roots in his own life and in the politics of his community. His threat to join the Japanese Army in particular carried weight because it played on the paranoia of white supremacy by posing the possibility of a transnational alliance among people of color. In the process, it brought to the surface the inescapably racist realities behind the seemingly color-blind national narrative of the United States and its aims in the war.[5] The element of internationalism that informed Malcolm X's efforts to evade the draft had deep roots in his individual history and in the collective consciousness of African Americans.

Historically, the prospect of escape to Indian territory, Canada, or Mexico and the assistance offered by European abolitionists made slaves and free Blacks sensitive to international realities in the antebellum period. Robin D. G. Kelley's research on Black communists in Alabama in the 1930s indicates that charges of being instigated by "outside agitators" influenced by Russia had little effect on the descendants of slaves who had been freed from bondage in part by an invading army from the north.[6] But the Japanese were not just any outsiders to African Americans in the 1940s: they were people of color with their own independent nation, a force capable of challenging Euro-

American imperialism on its own terms, and possible allies against the oppressive power of white supremacy.

Paul Gilroy and others have written eloquently about a "Black Atlantic" — about the importance of Africa and Europe as influences on the Black freedom struggle in North America, but there has been a "Black Pacific" as well. Images of Asia and experiences with Asians and Asian Americans have played an important role in enabling Black people to complicate the simple black-white binaries that do so much to shape the contours of economic, cultural, and social life in the United States.[7] In addition, it is not just elite intellectuals who have had an international imagination; working people whose labor in a global capitalist economy brought them into contact with other cultures have often inflected their own organizations and institutions with international imagery and identification.

The African American encounter with Japan has been especially fraught with contradictions. In their zeal to identify with a "nonwhite" nation whose successes might rebuke Eurocentric claims about white supremacy, Blacks have often overlooked, condoned, and even embraced elements of Japanese fascism and imperialism. Within the United States, Japanese agents sometimes succeeded in promoting the crudest kinds of racial essentialism and male chauvinism among Black nationalist groups. But, as Laura Mulvey argues, "It cannot be easy to move from oppression and its mythologies to resistance in history; a detour through a no-man's land or threshold area of counter-myth and symbolisation is necessary."[8] The African American engagement with the existence of Japan has provided precisely that kind of detour through a symbolic terrain sufficiently complex to allow an oppressed racial minority in North America to think of itself instead as part of a global majority of nonwhite peoples. In addition, as Malcolm X's performance at his preinduction physical demonstrated, imaginary alliances and identifications with Japan could also create maneuvering room for dealing with immediate and pressing practical problems.

African American affinities with Asia have emanated from strategic needs, from the utility of enlisting allies, learning from families of resemblance, and escaping the categories of black and white as they have developed historically in North America. These affinities do not evidence any innate or essential characteristics attributable to race or skin color; on the contrary, they demonstrate the distinctly social and historical nature of racial formation. Neither rooted in biology nor inherited from history, racial identity is a culturally constructed entity always in flux. During World War II, the racialized nature of the Pacific War, the racist ideals of Nazi Germany, the enduring legacy of white supremacy, segregation, colonialism, and conquest in the United States, as well as antiracist activism at home and abroad generated contradictions and conflicts that radically refigured race relations in the United States and around the world.

Contradictions between domestic racism and the imperial ambitions of the United States came into sharp relief as early as 1899 during the Filipino insurrection against occupying U.S. troops in the aftermath of what North Americans call the Spanish-American war. African American soldiers from the 24th Infantry regiment could not help but notice that white Americans used many of the same epithets to describe Filipinos as they used to describe them, including "niggers," "black devils," and "gugus."[9] One Black enlisted man in the regiment felt that the rebellion he was sent to suppress emanated from the fact that "The Filipinos resent being treated as inferior," which he believed "set an example to the American Negro" that should be emulated. Similarly, the regiment's Sergeant Major John Calloway informed a Filipino friend that he was "constantly haunted by the feeling of how wrong morally . . . Americans are in the present affair with you."[10]

Filipinos fighting under the command of Emilio Aguinaldo made appeals to Black troops on the basis of "racial" solidarity, offering posts as commissioned officers in the rebel army to those who switched sides. Most remained loyal to the U.S. cause, but Corporal David Fagen deserted the 24th Infantry's I Company on November 17, 1899, to become an officer in the guerrilla army. He married a Filipina and served the insurrectionists with distinction, engaging U.S. units effectively and escaping time after time. Fearing that his example might encourage others to follow suit, U.S. officers offered extensive rewards and expended enormous energy in efforts to capture or kill Fagen. On December 5, 1901, U.S. officials announced that a native hunter had produced "a slightly decomposed head of a negro" and personal effects that indicated the skull belonged to Fagen. Although this may have been a ruse on Fagen's part to cease further searches for him, the gradually weakening position of the rebels made further resistance impossible, and one way or the other, Fagen disappeared from the combat theater. But his example loomed large in the minds of military and diplomatic officials, especially when contemplating military activity against nonwhite populations.[11]

Just as some Black soldiers from the 24th Infantry regiment viewed the Filipino independence struggle as a battle with special relevance to their own fight against white supremacy, individuals and groups in

Japan took an interest in Marcus Garvey's Universal Negro Improvement Association around the time of World War I. Charles Zampty, a native of Trinidad and a leader of the Garvey movement in Detroit for more than fifty years, originally learned about the UNIA by reading Garvey's newspaper, *Negro World,* which he obtained from Japanese sailors in Panama while he worked at the Panama Canal.[12] As early as 1918 Garvey warned that "the next war will be between the Negroes and the whites unless our demands for justice are recognized," adding, "with Japan to fight with us, we can win such a war."[13]

Other African American intellectuals also looked to Japan for inspiration. Shortly after the war between Russia and Japan, Booker T. Washington pointed to Japanese nationalism as a model for African American development.[14] W. E. B. Du Bois included the "yellow-brown East" among the "darker world" poised to resist "white Europe" in his novel *Dark Princess: A Romance,* where Du Bois fantasized about an alliance linking an Asian Indian princess, a Japanese nobleman, and an African American intellectual.[15] At a more grassroots level, Black community groups and newspapers opposed efforts to send Japanese American children in San Francisco to segregated schools because of their own experiences with segregation, and they pointed repeatedly to the ways in which opposition to immigration from Japan manifested the racist prejudices of white Americans.[16]

Malcolm X's Garveyite father and West Indian mother encouraged him to be internationalist in his thinking, to look to Africa, to the Caribbean, and beyond, to render the hegemonic white supremacy of North America relative, contingent, and provisional. This tradition affected Malcolm X directly, but it also shaped the broader contours of relations between African Americans and people of Asian origin. In 1921, members of Garvey's UNIA and Japanese immigrants in Seattle joined forces in an attempt to create a Colored People's Union open to all people "except the whites or Teutonic races."[17] In New York, a young Vietnamese merchant seaman regularly attended UNIA meetings and became friends with Garvey himself in the early 1920s. Years later he would apply the lessons he learned about nationalism from Garvey when he took on the identity Ho Chi Minh and led his country's resistance against Japanese, French, and U.S. control.[18]

Forty members of the Garvey movement in Detroit converted to Islam between 1920 and 1923, largely as a result of the efforts of an Ahmadiyah mission from India. Elijah Muhammad, then Elijah Poole, associated with Garveyites in Detroit during the 1930s before founding the Nation of Islam, which Malcolm Little would later join while in prison during the late 1940s. The Nation of Islam went beyond Garvey's pan-Africanism to include (at least symbolically) all "Asiatic" (nonwhite) people in the same religion.[19]

During the 1930s, a Japanese national using the names Naka Nakane and Satokata Takahishi (sometimes spelled Satokata Takahashi) organized African Americans, Filipinos, West Indians, and East Indians into self-help groups, including the Society for the Development of Our Own, the Ethiopian Intelligence Sons and Daughters of Science, and the Onward Movement of America.[20] Born in Japan in 1875, Nakane married an English woman and migrated to Canada. He presented himself as a major in the Japanese Army and a member of a secret fraternal order known as the Black Dragon Society. Nakane promised financial aid and military assistance to African Americans in Detroit if they joined in "a war against the white race."[21]

Deported in 1934, Nakane moved to Canada and continued to run Development of Our Own through his new wife, an African American woman, Pearl Sherrod. When he tried to reenter the United States in 1939, federal officials indicted him for illegal entry and attempting to bribe an immigration officer. The FBI charged in 1939 that Nakane had been an influential presence within the Nation of Islam, that he spoke as a guest at NOI temples in Chicago and Detroit, and that his thinking played a major role in shaping Elijah Muhammad's attitudes toward the Japanese government. As proof, the FBI offered a copy of a speech that they claimed had been "saved" by an agent since 1933, in which Muhammad predicted that "the Japanese will slaughter the white man."[22]

The Pacific Movement of the Eastern World, founded in Chicago and St. Louis in 1932, advocated the unification of nonwhite people under the leadership of the Empire of Japan. Led by Ashima Takis, who also used the names Policarpio Manansala, Mimo de Guzman, and Itake Koo (among other pseudonyms), the group expressed its ideology of racial unity in the colors of its banners: black, yellow, and brown.[23] The PMEW implied that it had the backing of the Japanese government in offering free transportation, land, houses, farm animals, and crop seed to the first three million American Blacks willing to repatriate to Africa.[24] Although Marcus Garvey warned his followers against the PMEW, Takis frequently represented himself as an ally and even agent of the Garvey movement, and his group enjoyed considerable allegiance among Garveyites in the Midwest, especially in Gary, Indiana, and East St. Louis, Illinois.[25] Madame M. L. T. De Mena of the UNIA defied Garvey's prohibitions and arranged speaking engagements for Takis and Chinese associate Moy Liang before Black nationalist audiences.[26] "The Japanese are colored people, like you," Takis told African American audiences, adding pointedly, "the white governments do not give the negro any consideration."[27] In 1940, Takis told one African American group that war would soon break out between the United States and Japan, and that they would receive rifles from Japan to help them mount an insurrection in the Midwest while Japanese troops attacked the West Coast.[28] In the 1930s, the leader of the Peace Movement of Ethiopia, Mittie Maud Lena Gordon, had asked newly elected President Franklin Roosevelt to help finance Black repatriation to Africa. After the Japanese attack on Pearl Harbor, Gordon described December 7, 1941, as the day when "one billion black people struck for freedom."[29]

Thus, Malcolm X's presentation of himself in 1943 as pro-Japanese and anti-white-supremacist picked up on elements of his own personal history as well as on significant currents of thought and action among Black nationalists. He also exploited well-founded fears among government officials. Some recognized that the pathology of white supremacy posed special problems for the nation as it sought to fashion national unity in a war against German and Japanese fascism. White racism in the United States undermined arguments behind U.S. participation in the war and made it harder to distinguish the Allies from the Axis powers. Racial segregation in industry and in the army kept qualified fighters and factory workers from positions in which they were sorely needed, while the racialized nature of the war in Asia threatened to open up old wounds on the home front. Most important, asking African American, Asian American, Mexican American, and Native American soldiers to fight for freedoms overseas that they did not enjoy themselves at home presented powerful political, ideological, and logistical problems. But other government officials worried more about conspiratorial collaboration between African Americans and agents of the Japanese government.

As far back as the 1920s, the Department of Justice and agents from military intelligence had expressed fears of a Japanese-Black alliance. One report alleged, "The Japanese Associations subscribe to radical negro literature. In California a negro organization, formed in September, 1920, issued resolutions declaring that negros would not, in case of the exclusion of Japanese, take their place; a prominent negro was liberally paid to spread propaganda for the Japanese; and various negro religious and social bodies were approached in many ways." The report continued, claiming, "It is the determined purpose of Japan to amalgamate the entire colored races of the world against the Nordic or white race, with Japan at the head of the coalition, for the purpose of wrestling away the supremacy of the white race and placing such supremacy in the colored peoples under the dominion of Japan."[30]

Similar fears haunted policymakers during World War II. Secretary of War Henry L. Stimson attributed Black demands for equality during the conflict to agitation by Japanese agents and communists. Stimson recognized no legitimate grievances among African Americans, but instead interpreted their demands for jobs in industry and positions in combat as evidence of Japanese-initiated efforts to interfere with mobilization for national defense. In the same vein, the Department of State warned against Japanese infiltration of Black protest groups like A. Philip Randolph's March on Washington Movement as part of an effort "to direct the Negro Minority in a subversive effort against the United States."[31]

Southern journalist and racial "moderate" Virginius Dabney feared African American identification with the Japanese war effort because, "like the natives of Malaya and Burma, the American Negroes are sometimes imbued with the notion that a victory for the yellow race over the white race might also be a victory for them."[32] These predictions could become self-fulfilling prophesies; by showing how frightened they were by the prospect of alliances between African Americans and people of color elsewhere in the world, anxious whites called attention to a potential resource for Black freedom struggles that would eventually come to full flower in the 1960s in the form of opposition to the Vietnam War by the Student Nonviolent Coordinating Committee and the Southern Christian Leadership Conference, and expressions of solidarity with anti-imperialist struggles in Asia, Africa, and Latin America by more radical groups.

Even though extensive surveillance and infiltration of Japanese American and African American organizations by intelligence agents conclusively found little reason to fear any significant systematic disloyalty or subversion, once the war started government officials moved swiftly and decisively against Black nationalist draft resisters and organizations suspected of sympathy with Japanese war aims. F. H. Hammurabi, leader of World Wide Friends of Africa (also known as the House of Knowledge), was indicted in 1942 for delivering speeches praising Japan and for showing his audiences films of the Japanese attack on Pearl Harbor.[33]

Federal agents placed Ashima Takis under surveillance because of the PMEW's efforts to persuade Black nationalists in New York to ready "the dark-skinned races for armed uprisings should Japanese forces invade United States soil."[34] He received a three-year prison sentence for cashing a fraudulent money order some years earlier, and served as a star witness in a federal prosecution of St. Louis area members of the PMEW.[35] Followers reported that Takis spoke German, French, and Spanish, that his English was perfect in private conversation but heavily accented in public speeches, and that he enjoyed success as a faith healer in Black neighborhoods.[36] Robert A. Hill describes Takis as a Japanese who masqueraded as a Filipino under the pseudonym Policarpio Manansala, while Ernest V. Allen represents him as a Filipino who sometimes masqueraded as a Japanese national under the pseudonym Ashima Takis and sometimes used the Filipino aliases Mimo de Guzman and Policarpio Manansala.

Prosecutors also brought charges of sedition and inciting draft resistance against leaders of the Peace Movement of Ethiopia and the Nation of Islam. Federal agents arrested Elijah Muhammad in May 1942, and a federal judge sentenced him to a five-year prison term at the Federal Correction Institute in Milan, Michigan. FBI agents raided the Chicago Temple of the NOI in September 1942, tearing "the place apart trying to find weapons hidden there since they believed we were connected with the Japanese," one suspect later recalled. The agents found no weapons or documents linking the group to the Japanese government, but those arrested all served three years in prison for draft evasion.[37]

Although he later joined the NOI, where he fashioned an impassioned and precise critique of the connections linking U.S. imperialism overseas and anti-black racism at home, we have no reason to doubt the representation Malcolm X provides in his autobiography that in 1943 his conscious motivations entailed little more than a desire to avoid "jail, a job, and the Army."[38] But he could not have failed to notice that the war against Japan gave him leverage that he would not have had otherwise. In that respect, his vision corresponded to that of millions of other African Americans.

Immediately after the Japanese attack on Pearl Harbor, Robert L. Vann, editor and publisher of one of the nation's most important Black newspapers, the *Pittsburgh Courier,* called on the president and Congress "to declare war on Japan and against racial prejudice in our country."[39] This campaign for "double victory" had actually started before the war commenced, when A. Philip Randolph used the threat of a mass march on Washington in June 1941 to extract Executive Order 8802 from President Roosevelt, mandating fair hiring in defense industries. James Boggs, then a Black auto worker in Detroit, later recalled, "Negroes did not give credit for this order to Roosevelt and the American government. Far from it. Recognizing that America and its allies had their backs to the wall in their struggle with Hitler and Tojo,

Negroes said that Hitler and Tojo, by creating the war which made the Americans give them jobs in the industry, had done more for them in four years than Uncle Sam had done in 300 years."[40]

Yet, even in the midst of a war against a common enemy, white Americans held onto their historic hatreds and prejudices. At the Packard Main factory in Detroit, white war workers protesting desegregation of the assembly line announced that it would be preferable to lose the war than have to "work beside a nigger on the assembly line."[41] John L. De Witt of the 4th Army Western Defense Command in San Francisco complained to the Army's chief of classification when badly needed reinforcements he had requested turned out to be African American soldiers. "You're filling too many colored troops up on the West Coast," De Witt warned. "There will be a great deal of public reaction out here due to the Jap situation. They feel they've got enough black skinned people around them as it is, Filipinos and Japanese. . . . I'd rather have a white regiment."[42]

Black workers had to wage unrelenting struggles to secure and keep high-paying posts in defense industries on the home front, while African American military personnel served under white officers in a largely segregated military whose high command did its best to keep Black troops out of combat so that they could not claim the fruits of victory over fascism.[43] On the other hand, to promote enthusiasm for the war among African Americans, the military also publicized the heroism of individual Black combatants like Dorie Miller, a steward on the battleship *West Virginia,* which was among those vessels attacked at Pearl Harbor on December 7, 1941. According to the Navy, Miller was stationed on the bridge of the *West Virginia* near its commanding officer at the time of the enemy attack. He reportedly dragged the ship's wounded captain from an exposed spot on the bridge, and then manned a machine gun, shooting down two enemy planes, despite never having been formerly trained on the weapon. Twelve weeks after the incident, the Navy bowed to pressure from African American organizations and identified Miller, awarding him the Navy Cross.[44] Skeptics have subsequently raised doubts about whether Miller could have actually accomplished the feats for which he was decorated, but his fame made his fate an issue among African Americans regardless. They noted that, consistent with Navy policy at the time, he received no transfer to a combat position, but remained limited to serving food and drink to white officers on the escort carrier *Liscombe Bay,* where he died when that ship sank on November 24, 1943.[45]

Black soldiers sought positions in combat, but found themselves relegated to roles as garrison troops at Efate in the New Hebrides, at

Guadalcanal in the southern Solomons, and at Banika in the Russels group. But Black soldiers from the First Battalion of the 24th Infantry regiment (which had been David Fagen's unit in the Philippines) and members of the all-Black Ninety-third Division eventually served with white soldiers in combat in March 1945 on Bougainville.[46] More than a million Black men and women served in the armed forces during the war, more than half of them serving overseas in Europe or the Pacific.

Despite clear evidence of African American loyalty to the Allied effort, counterintelligence officers made Black people special targets of surveillance, investigation, and harassment. Naval intelligence officials in Hawaii ranked "Negroes" second only to "Japanese" people as primary suspects of subversion.[47] The FBI issued a wildly inflated estimate of more than 100,000 African American members of pro-Japanese organizations (perhaps counting those who escaped the draft in the way that Malcolm X did).[48] Yet, while mass subversion by Blacks was largely a figment of J. Edgar Hoover's always active imagination, the racialized nature of U.S. policy and propaganda in relation to the Japanese did elicit strong responses from African Americans.

In *Lonely Crusade,* a postwar roman à clef based on his own wartime experiences as an African American assembly line worker, Chester Himes narrates the complicated relationship between Japan and his lead character, Lee Gordon. When Navy training exercises make him think for a moment that a Japanese invasion is in progress, Gordon exults, "They're here! Oh, God-dammit, they're coming! Come on, you little bad bastards! Come on and take this city." Himes's narration explains, "In his excitement he expressed a secret admiration for Japan that had been slowly mounting in him over the months of his futile search for work. It was as if he reached the conviction that if Americans did not want him the Japanese did. He wanted them to come so he could join them and lead them on to victory; even though he himself knew that this was only the wishful yearning of the disinherited."[49]

The Office of War Information conducted a confidential survey of African Americans in 1942. Eighteen percent of the respondents indicated that they expected their own personal conditions to improve if Japan invaded the United States; 31 percent reported that their circumstances would remain the same; 26 percent had no opinion or refused to answer.[50] The OWI concluded that only 25 percent of African Americans supported the war effort wholeheartedly and that 15 percent had "pro-Japanese inclinations," yet a careful study of letters to the editor and editorials in the Black press also determined that most African Americans neither supported nor condemned Japan.[51]

Detroit journalist Gordon Hancock accused white government officials of "colorphobia" in their close surveillance of Japanese expansion in the Far East while virtually ignoring what Hancock saw as the manifestly greater dangers posed by German actions in Europe.[52] Chester Himes worked his reaction to the Japanese internment into another mid-1940s novel, *If He Hollers Let Him Go,* by having his narrator, Bob Jones, identify the roots of rage against white supremacy: "maybe it wasn't until I'd seen them send the Japanese away that I'd noticed it. Little Riki Oyana singing 'God Bless America' and going to Santa Anita with his parents the next day. It was taking a man up by the roots and locking him up without a chance. Without a trial. Without a charge. Without even giving him a chance to say one word. It was thinking about if they ever did that to me, Robert Jones, Mrs. Jones's dark son, that started me to getting scared."[53]

Gloster Current, NAACP director of branches, noted how these countersubversive measures taken against Japanese Americans raised special concern in the Black community. When the government announced its plans to incarcerate more than 110,000 law-abiding Japanese Americans, Current observed, "many a Negro throughout the country felt a sense of apprehension always experienced in the face of oppression: Today *them,* tomorrow *us.* For once the precedent had been established of dealing with persons on the basis of race or creed, none of us could consider ourselves safe from future 'security' measures."[54] This sense of interethnic solidarity among aggrieved racial groups was one of the main products of the World War II experience and one of its most important enduring legacies in the postwar period.

Before the war, African Americans and Japanese Americans lived in close proximity to one another in many western cities. On Jackson Street in Seattle, Japanese restaurants and black barber shops catered to customers from both races as well as to customers of Filipino, Chinese, and Mexican ancestry. White-owned hotels, restaurants, and motion picture theaters denied service to Black customers, but Japanese American entrepreneurs welcomed them.[55] In Los Angeles, African Americans and Japanese Americans shared several areas of the city, notably the neighborhood bounded by Silver Lake, Sunset, and Alvarado, the section near Vermont, Fountain, and Lucille, and the streets near Arlington, Jefferson, and Western. People in these neighborhoods shared experiences with discrimination as well; because of the "subversive" and "heterogeneous" nature of their communities, the Home Owners Loan Corporation secret city survey files designated the property of homeowners in each of these districts as undesirable for federal loan support.[56]

Less than a week after the attack on Pearl Harbor, Seattle's Black-owned and -edited newspaper, *Northwest Enterprise,* opposed plans to evacuate Japanese Americans from the West Coast. "Don't lose your head and commit crimes in the name of patriotism," a front-page editorial cautioned. Addressing African American readers in terms they well understood, the newspaper reminded them, "the same mob spirit which would single them [Japanese Americans] out for slaughter has trailed you through the forest to string you up at some crossroad."[57]

Personal relationships between Japanese Americans and members of other racialized groups motivated some responses to the internment at the individual level. Authorities at the Manzanar Relocation Center in 1944 discovered that one of the "Japanese Americans" incarcerated in their camp was actually Mexican American. Ralph Lazo decided to present himself as a Japanese American at the time of the internment in order to stay with his high school friends. "My Japanese-American friends at Belmont High School were ordered to evacuate the West Coast, so I decided to go with them," Lazo explained. "Who can say I haven't got Japanese blood in me? Who knows what kind of blood runs in their veins?" When embarrassed relocation officials ordered his release from Manzanar, Lazo enlisted in the army.[58] One African American in Seattle drove a Japanese family to the train scheduled to take them to a relocation center, and stood by them until it was time to get on board. An interpreter overheard the Black man tell a Japanese woman in the group, "You know that if there's ever anything I can do for you, whether it be something big or something small, I'm here to do it."[59]

In the San Francisco Bay Area, the chair of the Alameda County branch of the NAACP's Legal Committee wrote to the organization's national spokesperson, Walter White, in July 1942 to protest the "inhumane treatment of Japanese evacuees, and the simultaneously eased restrictions against white enemy aliens."[60] Frank Crosswaith of the Negro Labor Committee criticized the Supreme Court's decision to uphold curfews on Japanese Americans on the West Coast as evidence of "the spread of Hitler's despicable doctrine of racism."[61] When New York's usually liberal mayor Fiorello La Guardia objected to the placement of relocated Japanese Americans in that city in 1944, Roy Wilkins, editor of the NAACP's *The Crisis,* joined George Schuyler, then assistant editor of the *Pittsburgh Courier,* Fred Hoshiyama of the Japanese American Citizens League, and socialist Norman Thomas in addressing a mass protest rally. While Cheryl Greenberg is absolutely correct in arguing that the NAACP responded too timidly and too parochially to the internment — the organization opportunistically attempted to take advantage of the internment by seeking to secure positions for Blacks as replacement workers for Japanese American farm-hands in California's agricultural fields — she also demonstrates that the organization did more than most other civil rights or ethnic groups in defending Japanese Americans. Especially in California, the NAACP offered aid to returned evacuees and supplied them with extensive legal assistance.[62]

In 1945, Charles Jackson condemned attacks in California against Japanese Americans returning from the internment camps in an editorial in *The Militant,* the organ of the Socialist Workers Party. Jackson urged his fellow Blacks to "go to bat for a Japanese-American just as quickly as we would for another Negro. These people are obviously being denied their full citizenship rights just as we are. They are pictured in the capitalist press as toothsome, 'brown-bellied bastards,' and are described by the capitalist commentators as 'half-man and half beast.' This vicious type of prejudice indoctrination is familiar to every Negro."[63]

The kind of interethnic identification between people with similar but not identical experiences with racism that characterizes Jackson's response to the assaults on Japanese Americans played an important part in reconfiguring racial politics during World War II. Members of racialized "minority" groups frequently found themselves compared to one another. For example, military officials and political leaders in California favored a plan to move urban Japanese Americans to farm-work in rural areas because they hoped that such a move would prevent the influx of "a lot of Negroes and Mexicans" into the farming regions.[64] At the Poston internment camp, a staff person complained that many of the facility's officials knew little about Japanese Americans but "almost automatically transferred attitudes held about Negroes to the evacuees."[65]

When deployed in combat and support roles, African American service personnel often confronted a fear characteristic of colonial officials everywhere: that contact between native peoples and armed troops of their own race might "contaminate" the population. For example, when large numbers of Black U.S. troops arrived in Trinidad, British colonial officials on that island protested that the "self-assurance" of the troops would spread to the islanders and make them uncontrollable. The U.S. Department of State agreed with the British officials and consequently ordered the troops replaced by Puerto Ricans, who spoke mostly Spanish and consequently constituted less of a threat to the black Anglophone population.[66]

The Puerto Rican presence in Hawaii seemed to play a different role in race relations there. Thirty thousand African American sailors, soldiers, and war workers came to Hawaii during the war, and they discovered that according to the standards of the Hawaii census, people of African origin were classified as Puerto Rican — and therefore "Caucasian" — to distinguish them from native and Asian inhabitants of the islands.[67] Thus, by moving to Hawaii, Blacks could become white. In addition, native Hawaiians often displayed sympathy for Blacks in unexpected ways. One bus driver tried to help African Americans defeat their white tormentors when racial fights broke out on his vehicle. He kept the rear doors closed if Blacks were winning, and then opened the doors to let them slip away when the fights ended. As a Black war worker recalled, "There was what you would call an empathy from the local people as to what the black people had endured. They sort of, I guess, sympathized with us to a degree."[68]

Nonetheless, service in Hawaii hardly insulated Blacks from white racism. During the war, brothels in Honolulu's Hotel Street district refused admission to African Americans or Hawaiians of color because white servicemen and war workers from the mainland objected to their presence.[69] Constantly warned against associating with Black men, local women sometimes viewed the African American presence on their islands with fear. One Chinese Hawaiian wrote, "I am very scared of these Negro soldiers here in Honolulu. They make my skin shrivel and my self afraid to go near them."[70]

Communities of color found their fates intertwined during the war; it was not possible for them to isolate themselves from one another. When large numbers of African American workers from the South moved to war production centers on the West Coast, city officials, realtors, and military authorities saw to it that they found housing in the sections of Seattle, San Francisco, and Los Angeles that had been left vacant by the Japanese internment rather than in white neighborhoods.[71] At the same time, some Mexican Americans felt more vulnerable to racist attacks after the Japanese relocation. "In Los Angeles, where fantasy is a way of life," argued liberal journalist Carey McWilliams, "it was a foregone conclusion that the Mexicans would be substituted as the major scapegoat group once the Japanese were removed."[72] After mobs of white sailors attacked Mexican American youths wearing zoot suits in June 1943, the *Los Angeles Times* printed a caricature of Japanese premier Tojo riding on horseback and wearing a zoot suit.[73]

A 1942 Gallup Poll discovered that "American" respondents held slightly more favorable opinions of Mexicans than they did of Japanese people, but Los Angeles County Sheriff's Department Lieutenant Edward Duran Ayers demonstrated the opposite. He made use of many popular stereotypes and slurs in grand jury testimony, where he paradoxically contrasted "violence-prone" Mexicans with "law-abiding" Chinese and Japanese populations, of course not explaining why 110,000 law-abiding Japanese Americans had been shipped off to internment camps. Even more contradictorily, Ayers "explained" the propensity toward violence that he discerned among Mexicans as a result of the "oriental" background of their pre-Columbian ancestors, which left them with the "oriental" characteristic of "total disregard for human life."[74]

While racialized groups retained their separate (and sometimes antagonistic) interests and identities, pan-ethnic antiracist coalitions emerged on occasion in support of Japanese Americans as well. Representatives of African American, Filipino, and Korean community groups met with delegates from sixteen federal, state, and local agencies at the Palace Hotel in San Francisco in January 1945 to establish the Pacific Coast Fair Play Committee. They agreed that "any attempt to make capital for their own racial groups at the expense of the Japanese would be sawing off the limbs on which they themselves sat."[75] Sometimes, identification could come from a perception of common problems. In the novel *Lonely Crusade*, Chester Himes has his Black protagonist learn about the ways in which Black, Mexican, and Asian American residents share similar experiences with white racism when he reads a newspaper that reports on "a white woman in a shipyard" who "accused a Negro worker of raping her," on a group of white sailors who "had stripped a Mexican lad of his zoot suit on Main Street before a host of male and female onlookers," and about a "Chinese girl" who had been "mistaken for Japanese" and "slapped on a crowded streetcar by a white mother whose son had been killed in the Pacific."[76]

By the end of the war, race had become a decidedly visible and clearly contested element in all areas of American life. The humiliation and indignity imposed on the Japanese during their incarceration left lasting scars, demonstrating once again how state policy marked Asian Americans as permanently foreign in a manner quite dissimilar to every other immigrant group.[77] Japanese Americans not only lost years of their lives and millions of dollars in property that went mostly to whites during the war, but they suffered a systematic assault on their culture by incarceration and surveillance policies aimed at wiping out the key conduits of Japanese culture in America.[78] In addition, a wave of violent attacks against Japanese American persons and property swept the West Coast toward the end of World War II, and the leniency shown to the perpetrators by law enforcement officials and juries portended permanent second-class status for Americans of Japanese ancestry.[79]

Yet Japanese Americans also secured some victories in the postwar period. In 1948, California voters rejected efforts to institutionalize and extend the state's anti-Japanese Alien Land Law by an overwhelming vote of 59 percent against and only 41 percent in favor. The 1952 McCarran-Walter Immigration Act reversed the ban on nonwhites becoming naturalized citizens that had been on the books since 1790, even though the national origins quotas in the act still displayed strong prejudice against immigrants from Asia. Large-scale migration by African Americans and Mexican Americans seeking work in war industries changed the composition of the region's nonwhite population during the war. California's Black population increased from 124,000 to 462,000 during the war; the Black population of Seattle quadrupled between 1941 and 1945 as African Americans replaced Japanese Americans as the city's largest minority group.[80] In some ways, increased hatred against Blacks and Mexicans eased some of the pressures against Japanese Americans. For example, Roger Daniels points out that the same voters who rejected the 1948 Alien Land Law referendum in California also voted overwhelmingly against a Fair Employment Practices measure aimed mainly at prohibiting job discrimination against African American and Mexican American workers.[81]

For African Americans, the Pacific war helped produce a new militancy. Struggles to secure high-paying jobs in defense industries and positions on the front lines in combat led logically to postwar activism that ranged from massive campaigns for voting rights in the South and access to jobs and housing in the North. A. Philip Randolph organized resistance to the draft among African Americans in the postwar period until President Truman capitulated and ordered the desegregation of the military in 1948. But the war did more than incubate a certain amount of militancy; it taught lasting lessons about the inescapably racialized nature of power and politics in the United States.

In a postwar rumination, James Baldwin recalled that "The treatment accorded the Negro during the Second World War marks, for me, a turning point in the Negro's relation to America. To put it briefly, and somewhat too simply, a certain hope died, a certain respect for white Americans faded."[82] John Hope Franklin felt some of those same feelings. "Obviously I was pleased with the outcome of the war," he later recalled, "but I was not pleased with certain policies pursued by our government. I wish that the government could have been less hypocritical, and more honest about its war aims. I wish that it could have won—and I believe it could have—without the blatant racism that poisoned the entire effort; without its concentration camps for our Japanese citizens, which smacked too much of Hitlerism; and without the use of the atomic bomb. . . ."[83] In a book published immediately after the surrender of Japan, Walter White observed, "World War II has given to the Negro a sense of kinship with other colored—and also oppressed—peoples of the world. Where he has not thought or informed himself on the racial angles of colonial policy and master-race theories, he senses that the struggle of the Negro in the United States is part and parcel of the struggle against imperialism and exploitation in India, China, Burma, South Africa, the Philippines, Malaya, the West Indies, and South America."[84]

Malcolm X certainly embraced that sense of anti-imperialism and internationalism after he converted to Islam in a Massachusetts prison in the late 1940s. When the Korean War broke out he wrote a letter from prison (that he knew would be read by that institution's censors as well as by outside intelligence agents) explaining, "I have always been a Communist. I have tried to enlist in the Japanese Army last war, now they will never draft or accept me in the U.S. Army."[85] Paroled in 1953, he secured employment moving truck frames and cleaning up after welders at the Gar Wood factory. FBI agents visited him at work demanding to know why he had not registered for the draft. He pretended that he did not know that ex-convicts had to register, and the FBI apparently believed him. His draft board in Plymouth, Michigan, denied his request for status as a conscientious objector, but judged him "disqualified for military service" because of an alleged "asocial personality with paranoid trends."[86]

Black encounters with Asia became increasingly important between 1940 and 1975, as the United States went to war in Japan, the Philippines, Korea, China, Vietnam, Laos, and Cambodia. These U.S. wars in Asia have played an important role in reconfiguring race relations in North America. They have augmented racist tendencies to conflate Asian Americans with the nation's external enemies, as evidenced most clearly by hate crimes against people of Asian origin in the wake of the war in Vietnam and the emergence of economic competition between Asian and North American industries.[87] But U.S. wars in Asia have also repeatedly raised the kinds of contradictions faced by communities of color during World War II. For example, Gerald Horne and Mary L. Dudziak have shown how the Supreme Court's 1954 decision in *Brown v. Board of Education* responded in part to the imperatives of the cold war and the ways in which desegregation made it difficult for the

United States to present itself as the defender of freedom to emerging nations in Asia, Africa, and Latin America.[88]

In addition, U.S. wars in Asia and their costs to communities of color generated new critiques of their nation's domestic and foreign policies. Amiri Baraka argues that the Korean conflict created many of the preconditions for the modern-day civil rights movement, and indeed many Korean War veterans, including James Foreman and Bobby Seale, played prominent roles in African American protest groups during the 1950s and 1960s.[89] Ivory Perry, a prominent community activist in St. Louis, always credited his service at Camp Gifu, Japan, and in combat in Korea as the crucible for his own subsequent activism. For Perry, meeting Japanese and Korean citizens who seemed to him refreshingly nonracist compared to the white Americans he had known helped him see that white supremacy was a primarily historical national phenomenon and not human nature. In addition, the contrast between the freedoms he was sent overseas to defend and the freedoms he could not realize at home made him more determined than ever to bring about changes in his own country. As he remembers thinking on his return to the United States from the war, "I shouldn't have been in Korea in the first place because those Korean people they haven't ever did anything to Ivory Perry. I'm over there trying to kill them for something that I don't know what I'm shooting for. I said my fight is here in America."[90]

When Muhammad Ali (whose conversion to Islam involved the direct intervention and assistance of Malcolm X) refused to fight in the Vietnam War because "I ain't got no quarrel with them Viet Cong," his celebrated case not only established that anti-imperialist and internationalist thinking had a broad base of support among African Americans, it also played a major role in publicizing, legitimating, and proselytizing for an antiwar movement that was interracial in many significant ways.[91] As Edward Escobar, Carlos Muñoz, and George Mariscal have shown, the Chicano Moratorium in Los Angeles in 1970 demonstrated mass opposition to the war among Mexican Americans, but it also played a crucial role in building the Chicano movement itself.[92] Antiwar protest among Chicanos held particular significance because it required them to oppose the official positions of important institutions in the community, including the Catholic Church, trade unions, and veterans groups.[93]

Just as U.S. wars in Asia brought to the surface the racial contradictions facing African Americans and Mexican Americans, antiracist movements among Blacks and Chicanos also helped Asian Americans address their unresolved grievances in respect to white supremacy in the United States. During the Vietnam War, militant Asian American political and cultural groups emerged as important participants in interethnic "third world" coalitions. African American examples played an important role in guiding these groups. Rie Aoyama, a Japanese American activist from Seattle, explains, "We had no role models for finding identity. We followed what blacks did. Within the whole Asian American identity, part of the black identity came with it. Usually when you say Asian American, you are going to have some aspect of black experience too."[94] Nancy Matsuda similarly attributes her politicization to her recognition while in high school of the parallels between Asian Americans and Blacks: "I realized how blacks were an oppressed people, and I saw how Asians were oppressed too. So for me, it was a complete turn around from wanting to be associated with the whites to wanting to be associated with the blacks, or just a minority."[95] In 1968, Toru Sakahara, a Japanese American attorney and community leader in Seattle, organized a discussion group that brought representatives of the Black Panther Party in dialogue with members of the Japanese American Citizens League and Jackson Street business owners whose property had been damaged during a civil insurrection in that city.[96]

Thus, we can see that the racialized nature of the Pacific war has had enduring consequences for race relations in the United States. It exacerbated the antagonisms and alienations of race, while at the same time instigating unexpected alliances and affinities across communities of color. Yet it is important to understand that fights between men of different races often involved competition for power over women or over access to them. The prophetic currents of African American and interethnic antiracist activity during World War II addressed important issues about race, nation, and class, but they did precious little to promote an understanding, analysis, or strategy about the ways in which hierarchies of gender initiated, legitimated, and sustained social inequalities and injustices.

The Black nationalist organizations that identified with Japan and other "nonwhite" nations during the 1920s and 1930s also advocated a rather consistent subordination of women to men. In some of these groups women did attain visibility as organizers and activists: government agents shadowed Mittie Maud Lena Gordon because of her work as head of the Peace Movement of Ethiopia, and they put Madame M. L. T. De Mena under surveillance because of her public association with Ashima Takis. Pearl Sherrod took over Nakane's newspaper column in local papers after he was deported and served as nominal leader of the society for the Development of Our Own. Nakane himself spoke out forthrightly for women's rights, condemning the "peculiar ideas prevailing among a certain group of men, that the women should not hold any office in an organization, nor even have a voice at the meetings."[97] Counseling respect between men and women, Nakane reminded his followers that a woman held the post of international supervisor in his organization. That woman, however, did most of her speaking to white audiences that Nakane refused to address. In addition, he demonstrated his "respect" for women by having an affair with a young female follower while Pearl Sherrod Takahishi ran his organization for him. This development led Sherrod to report her husband to the Immigration and Naturalization Service when he tried to return to the United States in 1939.[98]

The white servicemen who attacked Mexican American youths in Los Angeles in the 1943 "zoot suit riots" justified their actions as a defense of white women against the predatory attentions of nonwhite "hoodlums." At the same time, many Mexican American youths saw the zoot suiters as heroic defenders of Mexican women from advances by white men. In an article about the riots for the NAACP journal *The Crisis*, Chester Himes compared the sailors to storm troopers, dismissing them as uniformed Klansmen. But he portrayed the riots as primarily a fight about access to women. Condemning the "inexplicable" and "incomprehensible" ego that allows "southern white men" to believe that they are entitled to sex "with any dark skinned woman on earth," Himes explained that Mexican American and Black youths objected to white men dating women of their races because "they, the mexican and negro boys, cannot go out in Hollywood and pick up white girls."[99]

Himes analyzed the ways the war in the Pacific emboldened white men about approaching women of color. He recounted an incident that he witnessed on a streetcar when three white sailors on leave from the "Pacific skirmishes" began talking loudly about "how they had whipped the Japs." Himes noted sarcastically, "It seems always to give a white man a wonderful feeling when he whips a Jap." One sailor boasted about his prowess in combat, and then bragged, "Boy, did those native gals go fuh us." Looking around the streetcar, one of them announced that a white man could get any woman he wanted, in a clear attempt to intimidate two "Mexican" youths in the company of an attractive girl. Himes complained that African American and Mexican American men could not protest remarks like these made to their wives and sweethearts by white men, and even worse, that unescorted Black women would "get a purely commercial proposition from every third unescorted white man or group of white men."[100] Although he fashioned a sensitive and perceptive critique of how official sanction for the attacks on zoot suiters replicated the rule by riot that dominated the lives of Blacks in the South, Himes never identified the role played by gender in constructing racial identities, or the ways in which desires for equality based on equal male privileges over women undermined the egalitarian principles and hopes that he saluted elsewhere.

Part of the prejudice directed at Black soldiers originated from white servicemen who warned the women they met about the dangers of being molested and raped by Black men. A Japanese American woman in Hawaii noticed how her views had been channeled in that direction one day after she shared an uneventful bus ride with four African American servicemen. Surprised that they had not accosted her, she wrote to a friend, "Gee, I was very frightened. . . . Funny isn't it how I am about them. One would be that way after hearing lots of nasty things about them."[101] On the home front and overseas, battles between Black and white war workers, service personnel, and civilians stemmed from struggles over sex: over rumors of rape, competition for dates, and symbolic and real violations of the privileges of white masculinity.[102]

In his important analysis of government distribution of "pinup" photos among U.S. servicemen during World War II, Robert Westbrook shows how the maintenance of white male prerogatives and privileges involved much more than the regressive thinking or selfish behavior of individuals.[103] Westbrook makes a persuasive case that the entire war effort had to be presented as a defense of middle-class male norms in order to solve some difficult ideological problems raised by the government's need for popular sacrifice. Westbrook explains that liberal capitalist states have difficulty providing compelling reasons for their citizens to go to war. Based on promises of protecting private property and personal happiness, how can the liberal capitalist state ask its subjects to surrender property, happiness, liberty, and life in the name of public goals?

In the United States during World War II, the answer came from couching public obligations as private interests, by stressing military service as the defense of families, children, lovers, friends, and an amorphously defined but clearly commodity-driven "American Way of Life." Just as wartime advertisers' promises about the postwar period featured full refrigerators rather than the four freedoms, just as Hollywood films presented soldiers sacrificing themselves for apple pie, the Brooklyn Dodgers, and the girl they left behind rather than for the fight against fascism, the U.S. government chose to supply its fighting men with pictures of Betty Grable in a swimsuit as an icon of the private world of personal pleasure that would be restored to them when the war was won. Grable's identity as a blonde, white, wholesome, middle-class, and married beauty made her an appropriate icon for fitting the war effort firmly within the conventions, history, aspirations, and imagery of middle-class European American life and culture.[104] Consequently, when white men engaged in racist violence against soldiers and civilians of color, they acted on an understanding of their privileges and prerogatives that the government and other important institutions in their society had encouraged.

After World War II, American economic expansion and military engagement in Asia led to a new stage of racial formation. The same propagandists who deployed alarmist images of violated white women as the reason to resist "yellow feet" on U.S. soil during the war, now fashioned fables of romantic love between white U.S. servicemen and Asian women as allegories of empire.[105] In his perceptive analysis of race as the "political unconscious" of U.S. cinema, Nick Browne shows how World War II occasioned a displacement of some of the U.S. film industry's traditional images of African Americans onto Asia. In films including *The Teahouse of the August Moon* (1956) and *Sayonara* (1957), the American presence in Asia becomes naturalized by a grid of sexual relations in which white males have general access to all women, white women are prohibited from sex with nonwhite men, nonwhite men have access to nonwhite women only, and nonwhite women submit to both nonwhite and white men. Consequently, in Browne's formulation, the social world created by the complicated intersections of race, gender, nation, and class attendant to the U.S. presence in Asia relies on a unified "gender-racial-economic system built as much on what it prohibits as what it permits."[106] This use of gendered imagery to make unequal social relations seem natural and therefore necessary endures today as a particularly poisonous legacy of the Asia Pacific war, especially at a time when so much of the project of transnational capital depends on the low-wage labor of exploited Asian women workers.

During World War II, African Americans used Asia as a source of inspiration and emulation, as a site whose racial signifiers complicated the binary black-white divisions of the United States. They exposed the inescapably internationalist past and present of U.S. race relations, and they forged intercultural communications and contacts to allow for the emergence of antiracist coalitions and consciousness. Liberal narratives about multiculturalism and cultural pluralism to the contrary, race relations in the United States have always involved more than one outcast group at a time acting in an atomized fashion against a homogeneous "white" center. Interethnic identifications and alliances have been powerful weapons against white supremacy. All racist identities are relational; communities of color are mutually constitutive of one another, not just competitive and/or cooperative.

The history of interethnic antiracist coalitions among even ostensibly essentialist and separatist Black nationalist groups points toward potentially effective strategies for the present. Yet to abstract race from the other social relations in which it is embedded would be to seriously misread the nature of racial formation and the social construction of identities. As Susan Jeffords argues, "the complex intersections between all of the manifestations of dominance in patriarchal structures will vary according to historical moments and location, and must be specified in each situation in order to be adequately understood and challenged."[107]

In our own time, when rapid mobility across the globe of capital, commodities, images, ideas, products, and people creates fundamentally new anxieties about identities connected to nation, race, class, and gender, the enduring relevance of transnational interracial identifications and alliances prefigured during World War II should be manifestly evident. Race is as important as ever; people are dying every day all around the world because of national narratives with racist preconditions. But at a time when women make up so much of the emerging low-wage world workforce, when patriarchal narratives continue to command the allegiance of killers for so many causes, it is also evident that the same imagination and ingenuity that allowed for unlikely coalitions across continents in the past on the issue of race must now also include a fully theorized understanding of gender as it intersects with identities based on narratives of nation, race, and class.

NOTES

I thank Takashi Fujitani, Jonathan Holloway, Robin D. G. Kelley, Lisa Lowe, George Mariscal, Suzanne Smith, Penny Von Eschen, Geoff White, and Lisa Yoneyama for their excellent and helpful comments on earlier drafts of this piece. This essay will also appear in *Perilous Memories: The Politics of Remembering Asia-Pacific War(s)*, ed. T. Fujitani, Geoffrey White, and Lisa Yoneyama, forthcoming.

1. Malcolm X and Alex Haley, *The Autobiography of Malcolm X* (New York: Grove Press, 1965), 104–105, 106. Robin D. G. Kelley's adroit analysis of this incident in his splendid and indispensable book *Race Rebels* directed my attention to the significance of Malcolm's story; see Robin D. G. Kelley, *Race Rebels: Culture, Politics, and the Black Working Class* (New York: Free Press, 1994),

171. FBI surveillance file on Malcolm X, 30 November 1954, quoted in Ferruccio Gambino, "Malcolm X, Laborer: From the Wilderness of the American Empire to Cultural Self-Identification," paper presented at the Colloque 1984 de L'Association Française d'Etudes Americaines Dourdan (25–27 May 1984, unpublished manuscript in the author's possession), 17.

2. John Hope Franklin, "Their War and Mine," *Journal of American History* (September 1990): 576–577.

3. Ibid., 578.

4. Brenda Gayle Plummer, *Rising Wind: Black Americans and U.S. Foreign Affairs, 1935–1960* (Chapel Hill: University of North Carolina Press, 1996), 74–75. Plummer's comprehensive, persuasive, and fascinating book makes a major contribution to rethinking the roles of race and nation in the U.S. past and present.

5. On the African American trickster tradition, see George P. Rawick, *From Sundown to Sunup* (Westport, CT: Greenwood, 1972), 98. For the definitive analysis of the racialized nature of the Pacific war see John Dower, *War without Mercy: Race and Power in the Pacific War* (New York: Pantheon, 1986).

6. Robin D. G. Kelley, *Hammer and Hoe* (Chapel Hill: University of North Carolina Press, 1991).

7. Paul Gilroy, *The Black Atlantic* (Cambridge, MA: Harvard University Press, 1993); Joseph E. Holloway, ed., *Africanisms in American Culture* (Bloomington: Indiana University Press, 1991); George Lipsitz, *Dangerous Crossroads* (New York: Verso, 1994).

8. Laura Mulvey, "Myth, Narrative, and Historical Experience," *History Workshop*, no. 23 (spring 1987): 11.

9. Michael C. Robinson and Frank N. Schubert, "David Fagen: An Afro-American Rebel in the Philippines, 1899–1901," *Pacific Historical Review* 64, no. 1 (February 1975): 71.

10. Ibid., 72.

11. Ibid., 81–82.

12. Tony Martin, *The Pan-African Connection: From Slavery to Garvey and Beyond* (Dover, MA: Majority Press, 1983), 64.

13. Quoted in Ernest V. Allen, "When Japan Was 'Champion of the Darker Races': Satokata Takahishi and the Flowering of Black Messianic Nationalism," *The Black Scholar* 24, no. 1 (1995): 29.

14. Ibid.

15. Michiko Hase, "Race, Status, and Culture in Trans-Pacific Perspective: African American Professionals in Japan," paper presented at the American Studies Association meetings, Nashville, Tennessee, 28 October 1994, 9–10 (manuscript in author's possession); W. E. B. Du Bois, *Dark Princess* (Jackson: Banner Books, University Press of Mississippi, 1995). See also Gilroy, *Black Atlantic*.

16. David J. Hellwig, "Afro-American Reactions to the Japanese and the Anti-Japanese Movement, 1906–1924," *Phylon* 37, no. 1 (1977): 94–96.

17. Quintard Taylor, "Blacks and Asians in a White City: Japanese Americans

and African Americans in Seattle, 1890–1940," *Western Historical Quarterly* 23, no. 4 (November 1991): 426.

18. Karl Evanzz, *The Judas Factor: The Plot to Kill Malcolm X* (New York: Thunder's Mouth, 1992), 22.

19. E. U. Essien-Udom, *Black Nationalism: A Search for Identity in America* (Chicago: University of Chicago Press, 1962), 44–45, 74–75; Tony Martin, *Race First: The Ideological and Organizational Struggles of Marcus Garvey and the Universal Negro Improvement Association* (Westport, CT: Greenwood Press, 1976), 74–77; Humphrey J. Fischer, *Ahmadiyah* (Oxford: Oxford University Press, 1963); Gambino, "Malcolm X, Laborer," 25–26.

20. Dominic J. Capeci Jr., *Race Relations in Wartime Detroit: The Sojourner Truth Housing Controversy of 1942* (Philadelphia: Temple University Press, 1984), 53; Evanzz, *The Judas Factor,* 24, 138; Dower, *War without Mercy,* 174.

21. Capeci, *Race Relations in Wartime Detroit,* 53.

22. The record of the FBI in counterintelligence is such that any document they release should be met with suspicion. Yet, even if fabricated, this document at the very least shows the anxiety felt at high levels of government about the possibility of African Americans feeling allegiance to Japan because it was a nonwhite country. Evanzz, *The Judas Factor,* 138.

23. Ernest Allen Jr., "Waiting for Tojo: The Pro-Japan Vigil of Black Missourians," *Gateway Heritage* 15, no. 2 (fall 1994): 19, 26.

24. Robert A. Hill, ed., *The Marcus Garvey and UNIA Papers* (Berkeley: University of California Press, 1983), 596; Bob Kumamoto, "The Search for Spies: American Counterintelligence and the Japanese American Community, 1931–1942," *Amerasia Journal* 6, no. 2 (1979): 50.

25. Hill, *The Marcus Garvey and UNIA Papers,* 506–507.

26. Allen, "When Japan Was 'Champion of the Darker Races,'" 37.

27. Hill, *The Marcus Garvey and UNIA Papers,* 506.

28. Ibid., 507.

29. Allen, "When Japan Was 'Champion of the Darker Races,'" 25.

30. Gary Y. Okihiro, *Cane Fires: The Anti-Japanese Movement in Hawaii, 1865–1945* (Philadelphia: Temple University Press, 1991), 116–117.

31. Kumamoto, "The Search for Spies," 54.

32. Stimson and Dabney quoted in Dower, *War without Mercy,* 173–174.

33. Allen, "When Japan Was 'Champion of the Darker Races,'" 37.

34. Capeci, *Race Relations in Wartime Detroit,* 54.

35. Allen, "Waiting for Tojo," 27, 28.

36. Ibid., 19.

37. Essien-Udom, *Black Nationalism,* 48–49, 67.

38. Malcolm X and Haley, *The Autobiography of Malcolm X,* 107.

39. Beth Bailey and David Farber, *The First Strange Place: Race and Sex in World War II Hawaii* (Baltimore: Johns Hopkins University Press, 1992), 133.

40. James Boggs, *The American Revolution: Pages from a Negro Worker's Notebook* (New York: Monthly Review Press, 1963), 79. I thank Suzanne Smith for calling my attention to this quote.

41. Walter White and Thurgood Marshall, *What Caused the Detroit Riot? An Analysis by Walter White and Thurgood Marshall* (New York: National Association for the Advancement of Colored People, 1943), 15.

42. Roger Daniels, *Concentration Camps USA: Japanese Americans and World War II* (New York: Holt, Rinehart, and Winston, 1971), 36.

43. George Lipsitz, *Rainbow at Midnight: Labor and Culture in the 1940s* (Urbana: University of Illinois Press, 1994), 73–83; Bernard C. Nalty, *Strength for the Fight: A History of Black Americans in the Military* (New York: Free Press, 1986), 143–203.

44. Dennis Denmark Nelson, "The Integration of the Negro into the United States Navy, 1776–1947" (master's thesis, Howard University, 1948), 28–29; Otto Lindenmeyer, *Black & Brave: The Black Soldier in America* (New York: McGraw-Hill (1970), 88; Robert Ewell Greene, *Black Defenders of America, 1775–1973* (Chicago: Johnson Publishing, 1974), 202.

45. Nalty, *Strength for the Fight,* 186.

46. Ibid., 166, 169.

47. Bailey and Farber, *The First Strange Place,* 159.

48. Cheryl Greenberg, "Black and Jewish Responses to Japanese Internment," *Journal of American Ethnic History* 14, no. 2 (winter 1995): 22.

49. Chester B. Himes, *Lonely Crusade* (New York: Thunder's Mouth Press, 1986), 46.

50. Allen, "When Japan Was 'Champion of the Darker Races,' " 37.

51. Dower, *War without Mercy,* 174.

52. Capeci, *Race Relations in Wartime Detroit,* 53.

53. Chester B. Himes, *If He Hollers Let Him Go* (New York: Thunder's Mouth Press, 1986), 3.

54. Greenberg, "Black and Jewish Responses to Japanese Internment," 19–20.

55. Taylor, "Blacks and Asians in a White City," 408, 413.

56. Records of the Federal Home Loan Bank, Board of the Home Owners Loan Corporation, records group 195, Los Angeles City survey file, box 74, areas D-50, D-33, D-30.

57. Taylor, "Blacks and Asians in a White City," 425.

58. Beatrice Griffith, *American Me* (Cambridge, MA: Houghton Mifflin, 1948), 321.

59. Taylor, "Blacks and Asians in a White City," 424.

60. Greenberg, "Black and Jewish Responses to Japanese Internment," 15.

61. Ibid., 18.

62. Ibid., 16, 18, 19.

63. Charles Jackson, "Plight of Japanese Americans," *Militant* 10 March 1945, reprinted in *Fighting Racism in World War II,* ed. C. L. R. James et al. (New York: Monad Press, 1980), 342.

64. Daniels, *Concentration Camps USA,* 59.

65. Ibid., 105.

66. Nalty, *Strength for the Fight,* 167.

67. Bailey and Farber, *The First Strange Place,* 139.

68. Ibid., 161.

69. Ibid., 103.

70. Ibid., 162.

71. Daniels, *Concentration Camps USA,* 163.

72. Quoted in Mauricio Mazon, *The Zoot-Suit Riots: The Psychology of Symbolic Annihilation* (Austin: University of Texas Press, 1984), 19.

73. Ibid., 52. On the "zoot suit riots," see Lipsitz, *Rainbow at Midnight,* 83–86.

74. Mazon, *The Zoot-Suit Riots.*

75. Daniels, *Concentration Camps USA,* 158.

76. Himes, *Lonely Crusade,* 207.

77. I thank Lisa Lowe for reminding me of the ways in which anti-Asian racism entails this rendering of Asian Americans as "permanently foreign."

78. Kumamoto, "The Search for Spies," 66–68.

79. Daniels, *Concentration Camps USA,* 159, 168.

80. Ibid., 162; Taylor, "Blacks and Asians in a White City," 428.

81. Daniels, *Concentration Camps USA,* 170. See also Kevin Allen Leonard, " 'Is That What We Fought For?' Japanese Americans and Racism in California: The Impact of World War II," *Western Historical Quarterly* 21, no. 4 (November 1990): 480.

82. From James Baldwin, *The Fire Next Time* (New York: Dial, 1963), 63.

83. Franklin, "Their War and Mine," 579.

84. Quoted in Dower, *War without Mercy,* 177–178.

85. Gambino, "Malcolm X, Laborer," 18.

86. Ibid., 19.

87. Yen Le Espiritu, *Asian American Panethnicity* (Philadelphia: Temple University Press, 1992).

88. Gerald Horne, *The Fire This Time: The Watts Uprising and the 1960s* (Charlottesville: University of Virginia Press, 1995); Mary L. Dudziak, "Desegregation as Cold War Imperative," in *Critical Race Theory,* ed. Richard Delgado (Philadelphia: Temple University Press, 1995), 110–121.

89. Amiri Baraka [LeRoi Jones], *Blues People* (New York: Random House, 1963).

90. George Lipsitz, *A Life in the Struggle: Ivory Perry and the Culture of Opposition* (Philadelphia: Temple University Press, 1995), 63.

91. Thomas R. Hietala, "Muhammad Ali and the Age of Bare Knuckle Politics," in *Muhammad Ali: The People's Champ,* ed. Elliott J. Gorn (Urbana: University of Illinois Press, 1995), 138; John Hope Franklin, *From Slavery to Freedom: A History of Negro Americans,* 4th ed. (New York: Knopf, 1974), 474.

92. Edward Escobar, "The Dialectics of Repression: The Los Angeles Police Department and the Chicano Movement, 1968–1971," *Journal of American History* 74, no. 4 (March 1993): 1483–1504; Carlos Muñoz, *Youth, Identity, Power: The Chicano Movement* (London: Verso, 1989).

93. George Mariscal, " 'Chale Con La Draft': Chicano Antiwar Writings," *Viet Nam Generation* 6, nos. 3–4 (1995): 130.

94. Yasuko I. Takezawa, *Breaking the Silence: Redress and Japanese American Ethnicity* (Ithaca: Cornell University Press, 1995), 147.

95. Ibid., 148–149. See also David Gutierrez, *Walls and Mirrors* (Berkeley: University of California Press, 1995), for a discussion of how the Chicano movement grew from a similar desire to identify with Blacks rather than with whites.

96. Quintard Taylor, *The Forging of a Black Community: Seattle's Central District from 1870 through the Civil Rights Era* (Seattle: University of Washington Press, 1994), 225–226.

97. Allen, "When Japan Was 'Champion of the Darker Races,'" 33, 25, 37.

98. Ibid., 33, 36.

99. Chester B. Himes, "Zoot Riots Are Race Riots," *The Crisis* (July 1943): 200.

100. Ibid., 200, 201.

101. Bailey and Farber, *The First Strange Place*, 162.

102. Lipsitz, *Rainbow at Midnight*, 81–86.

103. Robert B. Westbrook, "'I Want a Girl Just Like the Girl That Married Harry James': American Women and the Problem of Political Obligation in World War II," *American Quarterly* 24, no. 4 (December 1990): 587–614.

104. Ibid.

105. See Nick Browne's very significant "Race: The Political Unconscious of American Film," *East-West Journal* 6, no. 1 (1992): 9.

106. Ibid.

107. Susan Jeffords, *The Remasculinization of America: Gender and the Vietnam War* (Bloomington: Indiana University Press, 1989), 180.

LISA LOWE

Work, Immigration, Gender:
New Subjects of Cultural Politics

Hello, my name is Fu Lee. I am 41 years old, married, and I have a 9-year old daughter. I have been living in Oakland Chinatown since I left Hong Kong 12 years ago. . . .

My eyes hurt from straining under poor lighting; my throat hurt because of the chemical fumes from the fabric dye. Sometimes, I would wear surgical masks so I don't have to breathe in all the dust from the fabric. My back never stopped hurting from bending over the sewing machine all day. Our boss was like a dictator. He was always pushing us to work faster. There was a sign in the shop that said, "No loud talking. You cannot go to the bathroom." When we did talk loudly or laugh during work, he would throw empty boxes at us and tell us to go back to work. When there was a rush order, we had to eat lunch at our work station.

Last year, my employer closed his shop and left us holding bad paychecks. We found out that he had filed for bankruptcy and had no intentions of paying us our meager wages. The twelve Chinese seamstresses including myself were so mad. After working so hard under such horrendous working conditions, we should at least get our pay.

With the help of Asian Immigrant Women Advocates, we began searching for ways to get our pay. . . .[1]

Mrs. Fu Lee's testimony at a community hearing initiated by Asian Immigrant Women Advocates (AIWA) in Oakland, California, describes the conditions of many Asian immigrant women working in the San Francisco Bay Area garment industry: low-waged or unpaid labor, forced increases in productivity through long workdays or speedups, repetitive manual labor, occupational hazards and environmental toxins, and no union or collective bargaining protections. Before the Lucky Sewing Co. closed shop and left the sewing women with bad paychecks, Mrs. Lee and the other seamstresses were to have been paid $5 a dress; the subcontractor was paid $10 a dress, yet each dress was sold by Jessica McClintock, Inc. for $175. In the San Francisco Bay Area garment industry, women sew clothing that their meager wages, when they receive them, will not permit them to buy as commodities. The women work under physical conditions that are unsafe, unhealthy, and fatiguing. Furthermore, the policy of paying the worker by piece exploits the immigrant women in ways that extend beyond the extraction of surplus value from hourly low-waged factory labor. The incentive to complete as many pieces as possible makes certain that the sewing woman will work overtime without compensation and will intensify her productivity even if it results in exhaustion or personal injury. Because many are non-English- or little-English-speaking women and consider their employment options limited, because eight out of ten Chinatown immigrant families with multiple wage earners say they would "barely get by" if there were but one breadwinner in the family, these women are forced to accept the payment conditions dictated by the employer.[2]

Mrs. Lee, in collaboration with AIWA and the other women workers, has produced an important testimony that at once connects her life as a Chinese immigrant woman with her struggle as a worker who desires economic justice. Struggles for empowerment are often exclusively understood within the frameworks of legal, political, and economic institutions; the subjectivity of Mrs. Lee can be comprehended in relation to systemic oppression and systemic change. Yet an important link in this relation is the production of individual and collective subjectivities through cultural forms and practices. In this sense, Mrs. Lee's testimony is compelling not only for the facts it relates, but also for the way it poses relations between those facts. The narrative progression charts a movement from being an aggrieved seamstress to forging a collective campaign for back pay; it inspires identification that has helped to build community solidarity around the immigrant garment workers. In addition, Mrs. Lee's testimony conveys the manner in which the factory extracted surplus value not only through her "labor" as an abstract form, but from using and manipulating her body itself: from her eyes that strained under poor lighting, her throat that hurt because of the chemical fumes from the fabric dye, and her back that ached from being bent over the sewing machine all day. Where Mrs. Lee's narrative evokes her conscious, embodied relation to work, it also refuses the isolation of each part as separate sites to be instrumentally exploited; her narrative integrates the sites of bodily exploitation as constitutive parts of the value of her labor, as well as of the process in which she becomes a "political" subject. Furthermore, as the narrative moves from her description of embodied exploitation to the decision to take collective political action, it alludes to her experiences as a woman, as a mother, as a Chinese immigrant, and as a worker, also refusing the atomization of the conditions that issue from patriarchal subordination, racialized immigration, segregation, and labor exploitation. Mrs. Lee's narrative does not reduce her political identity or actions to one cause or origin; instead it brings together the dimensions of her material and political subjectivity and, in that process, illuminates the intersecting axes of exploitation she inhabits and the differentiating operations of contemporary capital that exploit precisely through the selection and reproduction of racially, culturally, gendered-specific labor power.

Forms of individual and collective narrative are not merely representations disconnected from "real" political life; neither are these expressions "transparent" records of histories of struggle. Rather, these forms — life stories, oral histories, histories of community, literature — are crucial media that connect subjects to social relations. To consider testimony and testimonial as constituting a "genre" of cultural production is significant for Asian immigrant women, for it extends the scope of what constitutes legitimate knowledges to include other forms and practices that traditionally have been excluded from both empirical and aesthetic modes of evaluation. Yet as Chandra Talpade Mohanty has observed of third world women's narratives, they are in themselves "not evidence of decentering hegemonic histories and subjectivities. It is the way in which they are read, understood, and located institutionally which is of paramount importance. After all, the point is not just 'to record' one's history of struggle, or consciousness, but how they are recorded; the way we read, receive, and disseminate such imaginative records is immensely significant."[3] "The way we read, receive, and disseminate" Mrs. Lee's testimony may be, in one context, to cite it as evidence in a hearing to protest the abuse of Asian immigrant garment industry workers; in this context, Mrs. Lee's testimony contributed to AIWA's campaign that succeeded in establishing Jessica McClintock's responsibility for the subcontractor. In another, and not mutually exclusive, context, the way we read Mrs. Lee's testimony may be to place it in relation to other cultural forms that make use of different techniques of narration. Such a reading need not level the differences between evidential forms that gain meaning on the horizon of the "empirical" and literary or art forms that are more commonly interpreted on the horizon of the "aesthetic." The aim is not to "aestheticize" the testimonial text, but rather to displace the categorizing drive of disciplinary formations that would delimit the transgressive force of articulations within regulative epistemological or evaluative boundaries. This mode of reading and reception seeks to situate different cultural forms in relation to shared social and historical processes, and to make active the dialectic that necessarily exists between those forms because of their common imbrication in those processes. It is to understand

Asian American cultural production critically and broadly, and to interpret the interconnections between testimony, personal narrative, oral history, literature, film, visual arts, and other cultural forms, as sites through which subject, community, and struggle are signified and mediated. While specifying the differences between forms, this understanding of cultural production troubles both the strictly empirical foundations of social science and the universalizing tendencies of aesthetic discourse. In this mode, we can read testimony as more than a neopositivist "truth," as a complex mediating genre that selects, conveys, and connects "facts" in particular ways, without reducing social contradiction or compartmentalizing the individual as a site of resolution. Likewise, we can read literary texts like the novel not merely as the aesthetic framing of a "private" transcendence, but as a form that may narrate the dissolution or impossibility of the "private" domain in the context of the material conditions of work, geography, gender, and race. In this sense, cultural forms of many kinds are important media in the formation of oppositional narratives and crucial to the imagination and rearticulation of new forms of political subjectivity, collectivity, and practice.

This notion of cultural production as a site for the formation of new political subjects serves to focus the next section, in which I discuss the current construction of Asian immigrant women's work within the context of what we might term the "racialized feminization of labor" in the global restructuring of capitalism. The location of Asian immigrant women's work — at the intersection of processes of immigration, racialization, labor exploitation, and patriarchal gender relations — marks that work as irreducible to the concept of "abstract labor" and distinguishes the subjectivity it constitutes as unassimilable to an abstract political identity or to a singular narrative of emancipation implied by that identity. Hence, it is often in cultural forms and practices, broadly defined, that we find the most powerful articulation of this complex subjectivity, and through those forms and practices that an alternative "politicization" of that subject is mediated. Furthermore, the focus on women's work within the global economy as a material site in which several axes of domination intersect provides the means for linking Asian immigrant and Asian American women with other immigrant and racialized women. Asian immigrant and Asian American women are not simply the most recent formation within the genealogy of Asian American racialization; they, along with women working in the "third world," are the "new" workforce within the global reorganization of capitalism. In this sense, the active affiliations of Asian immigrant and Asian American women are informed by, yet go beyond, Asian American cultural identity as it has emerged within the confines of the U.S. nation. They are linked to an emergent political formation, organizing across race, class, and national boundaries, that includes other racialized and immigrant groups, as well as women working in, and immigrating from, the neocolonized world.

From roughly 1850 to World War II, Asian immigration was the site for the eruptions and resolutions of the contradictions between the national economy and the political state, and from World War II onward, the locus of the contradictions between the nation-state and the global economy. Hence, Asian immigrant women's work must be understood within the history of U.S. immigration policies and the attempts to incorporate immigrants into the developing economy, on the one hand, and within the global expansion of U.S. capitalism through colonialism and global restructuring, on the other. Elsewhere I have argued that, in the first period, the contradiction between the economic need for inexpensive, tractable labor and the political need to constitute a homogeneous nation was "resolved" through the series of legal exclusions, disenfranchisements, and restricted enfranchisements of Asian immigrants that simultaneously "racialized" these groups as "nonwhites" and consolidated immigrants of diverse European descent as "white."[4] Because of the history in which economic forces and exigencies have been mediated through the legal apparatus that racializes and genders immigrant subjects, for Asian immigrants and Asian Americans, class struggles have always intersected with and been articulated through race and gender determinations. In the latter period, the capital imperative has come into greater contradiction with the political imperative of the U.S. nation-state, with capitalism requiring an economic internationalism in order to increase labor and capital, and the state needing to be politically coherent and hegemonic in world affairs in order to determine the conditions of that internationalism. The expansion that led to U.S. colonialism and war in the Philippines, Korea, and Vietnam violently displaced immigrants from those nations; the aftermath of the repressed history of U.S. imperialism in Asia now materializes in the "return" of Asian immigrants to the imperial center.[5] Both the racialized gendered character of Asian immigrant labor within the emergence of U.S. capitalism and U.S. colonial modes of development and exploitation in Asia provide the basis for understanding that U.S. capital has historically accumulated and profited through the differentiation of labor, rather than through its homogenization; in the global expansion of the capitalist mode, the racial and gendered character of labor has been further exaggerated, refined, and built into the regime itself.

Since the 1980s, the globalization of capitalism has shifted many manufacturing operations to Asia and Latin America and has reorganized a mode of production that at one time employed a U.S. male labor force, white and black, in industrial manufacturing, and formerly employed white working-class and racialized women in assembly, blue- and pink-collar, and service work. In the search for ever cheaper, more "flexible," labor pools, this reorganization also produces a greater "pull" for new Asian and Latino immigrants, especially for Asian and Latina women, to fill the insecure assembly and service sector jobs in the United States that have emerged largely as a result of restructuring and "reengineering." Just as the displacement of U.S. workers as well as increased immigration to the United States are an index of global capitalist restructuring, so, too, has restructuring exacerbated both anti-immigrant nativism and the state's "need" to legislate "undocumented aliens" and "permanent resident aliens" who have entered since 1965. Thus, the proletarianization of Asian and Latina immigrant women is a current instance of the contradiction between the globalization of the economy and the political needs of the nation-state; it takes place in conjunction with a gendered international division of labor that makes use of third world and racialized immigrant women as a more "flexible," "casual," "docile" workforce. Transnational industry's use of Asian and Latina women's labor — in Asia, Latin America, and the United States — is the contemporary site where the contradictions of the national and the international converge in an overdetermination of neocolonial capitalism, anti-immigrant racism, and patriarchal gender stratification.

In this sense, the global restructuring of the capitalist mode of production can be understood to constitute a new social formation, one whose domain has extended beyond the nation-state to global markets and international circuits of exchange. In *Reading Capital,* Louis Althusser and Etienne Balibar extend Marx's original formulation of the relationship between the "mode of production" and the "social formation," by defining a social formation as the complex structure in which more than one mode of production, or set of economic relations, may be combined.[6] Their elaboration suggests not only that the situations of uneven development, colonialist incorporation, and global restructuring and immigration are each characterized by the combination of several simultaneous modes of production, but that each constitutes a specific, historically distinct social formation, which includes economic, political, and ideological levels of articulation. The need to understand the differentiated forms through which capital profits through mixing and combining different modes of production suggests, too, that the complex structures of a new social formation may indeed require interventions and modes of opposition specific to those structures. One of the distinct features of the global restructuring of capital is its ability to profit not through homogenization, but through the differentiation of specific resources and markets that permits the exploitation of gendered and racialized labor within regional and national sites. Part of this differentiation involves transactions between national and international sites that formalize new capital accumulation and production techniques specifically targeting female labor markets. This occurs where women are disciplined by state-instituted traditional patriarchy, whether in Malaysia or Guatemala, or by racialized immigration laws that target female immigrants in particular, such as in California. The global racialized feminization of women's labor is a new social formation characterized by the exploitation of women both in export-oriented production zones in Asia and Latin America, *and* near the center of the market in the Silicon Valley electronics industry, in the Los Angeles manufacturing district, and in the San Francisco Bay Area garment industry.

While some analysts of transnationalism argue that global capitalism has reached a near-universal extension and has incorporated all sectors into its logic of commodification, the situations of Asian and Latina women workers suggest that transnational capitalism, like nation-state capitalism and colonial capitalism before it, continues to produce sites of contradiction and the dynamics of its own negation and critique.[7] For in the complex encounters between transnational capital and women within patriarchal gender structures, the very processes that produce a racialized feminized proletariat both displace traditional and national patriarchies and their defining regulations of gender, space, and work, and racialize the women in relation to other racialized groups. These displacements produce new possibilities precisely because they have led to a breakdown and a reformulation of the categories of nation, race, class, and gender, and in doing so have prompted a reconceptualization of the oppositional narratives of nationalism, Marxism, and feminism. The shift toward the transnationalization of capital is not exclusively manifested in the "denationalization" of corporate power or the nation-state, but, perhaps more importantly, it is expressed in the reorganization of oppositional interventions against capital that articulate themselves in terms and relations other than the singular "national," "class," or "female" subject. Asian, Asian immigrant, and Asian American women occupy some of the sites of contradiction in the current international division of labor, and their agencies are critical to U.S. women of color activism, cross-border labor organizing, and third world and immigrant women's struggles.

Although Asian immigrant women have been in the United States since the nineteenth century, the greater numbers of Asian women immigrated after the mid-twentieth century, and the specific recruitment of women as a labor force has intensified since the Immigration and Nationality Act of 1965.[8] Since that time, along with African American and Mexican American women, Asian immigrant women have constituted an important low-paid workforce within the United States, "occupationally ghettoized" in menial, domestic, and reproductive labor, textile and garment industries, hotel and restaurant work, and a current mix of mass production, subcontracting, and family-type firms. Because of their material, gender, and racial differentiation from the abstract citizen proposed by the U.S. political sphere, they remain at a distance from its nationalist narratives. Immigration laws help to produce a racially segmented and gender-stratified labor force for capital's needs, inasmuch as such laws seek to resolve these inequalities by deferring them in the promise of equality on the political terrain of representation. While the official narratives of immigrant inclusion propose to assimilate immigrants as citizens, the conditions of Asian immigrant women in the United States directly contradict these promises of incorporation, equal opportunity, and equal representation. Asian "American" women, even as citizens, continue to be located at the cultural, racial, and political boundaries of the nation. Indeed, I use quotation marks here to signal the ambivalent identification that both U.S.-born Asian and Asian immigrant women have to the nationalist construction "American." For Asian immigrant women, the American contract of citizenship is quite evidently contradictory; if it proposes the state as the unified body in which all subjects are granted equal membership, it simultaneously asks that differences — of race, class, gender, and locality — be subordinated in order to qualify for membership in that democratic body.

At the same time, as a group formed through the intersecting processes of racialization, class exploitation, and gender subordination, Asian immigrant women are also differentially situated in relation to the political narratives of social movements organized around single forms of domination: for example, the liberal feminist critique of patriarchy, the trade union analysis of capitalism from the standpoint of class exploitation, and the critique of racism and internal colonialism from the standpoint of racialized minority subjects. From the early post–World War II years through the 1960s, political economy in the United States was dominated by the notion of development, and in that period, opposition to exploitation was often articulated in terms of class issues.[9] The late 1960s marked, however, the beginning of a period in which the articulation of opposition became increasingly mediated by analyses of other forms of domination, not only capitalism and imperialism, but also patriarchy and racism.[10] Emerging out of this earlier moment in the capitalist mode of production, U.S. oppositional social movements of the 1970s — feminist, labor, civil rights, and ethnonationalist — produced narratives of political development for the subjects resisting domination within this earlier mode. According to these narratives, the "woman," "worker," and "racial or ethnic minority" subjects were said to develop from a prehegemonic pre-class-identified position to that of politicized participants who could "grasp" their exploitation in relation to their function within patriarchy, capitalism, and racism. Asian immigrant and Asian "American" women, like other racialized women, have a different political formation than that prescribed by *either* narratives of liberal capitalist development and citizenship or the narratives proposed by these oppositional movements of the 1970s. The isolation of one axis of power, such as the exploitation of labor under capitalism, masks the historical processes through which capitalism has emerged in conjunction with, and is made more efficient by, other systems of discrimination and subordination: patriarchy, racism, and colonialism.[11] The Asian "American" woman and the racialized woman are materially in excess of the subject "woman" posited by feminist discourse, or the "proletariat" described by Marxism, or the "racial or ethnic" subject projected by civil rights and ethnonationalist movements. This excess and differential places Asian American and other racialized women in critical, and dialectical, relationships to the subjects of feminism, Marxism, and ethnic nationalisms. In this sense, Asian immigrant and Asian American women may be said to constitute the dialectical sublation of these earlier models of political subjectivity.

The particular location of racialized working women at an intersection where the contradictions of racism, patriarchy, and capitalism converge produces a subject that cannot be determined along a single axis of power or by a single apparatus on the one hand, or contained within a single narrative of oppositional political formation on the other. If Marxism proposes that the classical contradiction exists between capital and labor — a contradiction that permits the accumulation of surplus value through the exploitation of labor at the same time that it produces the class struggles that mark the points of crisis and vulnerability within capitalism — then the current situation of racialized working women makes apparent that we must always speak of more than one contradiction. We may speak, on the one hand, of a racial contradiction by which the state claims to be a democratic body in which all subjects are granted membership, while racial, ethnic, and immigrant subjects continue to be disenfranchised and excluded from political participation in that state. Or we may speak, on the other, of various sites of gender contradiction: one in which the concept of abstract labor in political economy (that work is equivalent to pay) conflicts with unwaged female domestic labor in the home and inadequate pay for women in the "public" workplace;[12] another in which a contradiction exists between the discourse of formal legal equality and the conditions in many countries in which a woman's choice to conceive or bear a child is an action that may be contested by husband, father, or state. Furthermore, within the trajectory of liberal feminism, relative gains of some women in corporate, political, or professional domains accentuates the contradictory persistence of barriers to, and what Evelyn Nakano Glenn has called "occupational ghettoization" of, poor women of color. Throughout lived social relations, it is apparent that labor is gendered, sexuality is racialized, and race is class-associated. A multiplicity of social contradictions with different origins converge at different sites within any social formation — the family, education, religion, communications media, sites of capitalist production — and each is uneven and incommensurable, with certain contradictions taking priority over others in response to the material conditions of a given historical moment. Singular narratives of consciousness aim at developing a subject position from which totalization becomes possible, whereas the cultural productions of racialized women seek to articulate multiple, nonequivalent, but linked determinations without assuming their containment within the horizon of an absolute totality and its presumption of a singular subject. U.S. women of color have located themselves in relationship to intersecting dominations, and these locations have been powerfully translated into critical practices. From the 1980s, work by Audre Lorde, Cherríe Moraga, and the collective Asian Women United of California, for example, exemplify "situated" nontotalizing perspectives on conjoined dominations, as well as the emergence of politicized critiques of those conjunctions.[13]

The necessary alliances between racialized and third world women within, outside, and across the borders of the United States grow out of the contemporary conditions of global capitalism under which immigrant women working in the garment industries of Los Angeles are virtually part of the same labor force as those employed in Asia or Latin America. The sweatshops of the garment industry located in San Francisco and Los Angeles, for example, employ immigrant women from Mexico, El Salvador, Guatemala, Hong Kong, South Korea, Thailand, and the Philippines, while in these countries of origin, U.S. transnational corporations are also conducting garment assembly work.[14] Women migrate from countries of origin formerly colonized by the United States, or currently neocolonized by U.S. corporate capital, and come to labor here as racialized women of color. In this sense, despite the obstacles of national, cultural, and linguistic differences, there are material continuities between the conditions of Chicanas and Latinas working in the United States and the women working in *maquiladoras* and low-cost manufacturing zones in Latin America, and Asian women working both within the United States and in Asian zones of assembly and manufacturing.

Thus, recent immigrant communities constitute the most evident sites for racialized women in the United States to intersect with women in the neocolonized world whose experiences are doubly determined by exploitation that traverses national boundaries. The important ongoing work of organizations like AIWA in the San Francisco Bay Area, in which second- and third-generation Asian American women work for the empowerment of immigrant Asian women workers in the garment, hotel, and electronics industries, and the Garment Workers' Justice Center in Los Angeles and La Mujer Obrera in El Paso, suggests some ways of thinking about the mutual processes of politicization that occur between racialized immigrant women in the United States and women in the third world. Groups like the Asian Law Caucus and the Coalition for Immigrant and Refugee Rights and Services have ongoing projects advocating for immigrants' rights.[15] AIWA is an innovative example of cross-generational women of different national origins, classes, and language backgrounds organizing in ways that address the particular conditions of Asian immigrant women workers.[16] While AIWA organizes Asian immigrant women around the more traditional labor issue of workers' rights — as in the successful campaign to pressure garment manufacturer Jessica McClintock, Inc. — AIWA also focuses on bringing Asian American and Asian immigrant women together as members of Asian communities, and addresses issues that are of concern "outside" of the workplace, such as child care, health care, language, and literacy. In addition, it should be emphasized that AIWA does not organize itself in a traditional hierarchy that would place "organizers" above "workers" or Asian American women above immigrant women; the reciprocally transformative relationship between Asian American organizers and Asian immigrant working women is expressly encouraged by AIWA's structure.[17] Miriam Ching Louie writes: "The challenge to AIWA organizers is to use the classes (in English) so that workers can reflect on their own lives, determine what is fair, visualize alternatives to oppressive conditions, and practice demanding their rights. . . . Organizers must also transform themselves in the process."[18]

Whereas AIWA works with Asian immigrant and Asian American women, other projects create and maintain solidarity across racial and ethnic groups and across national boundaries: groups like the Border Workers Regional Support Committee (CAFOR) and the Coalition for Justice in the Maquiladoras (CJM) have helped Mexican *maquiladora* workers organize against U.S.- and Japanese-owned parent companies. The Support Committee for the Maquiladora Workers in San Diego organizes activists, a number of whom are Asian immigrant women, to assist in documenting the exploitative, unsafe working conditions of the *maquiladoras* and to provide various support services for the mostly female Mexican workers.[19] Recently, the Support Committee assisted in retrieving the back wages for workers formerly employed at Exportadora de Mano de Obra in Tijuana, Mexico, through building pressures at a variety of sites, including bringing a suit in U.S. courts against the parent company, National O-Ring, a division of American United Global Corporation. One hundred and eighty workers had lost their wages when National O-Ring suddenly closed the Exportadora plant in Tijuana, an act precipitated by the women workers having brought charges of sexual harassment against the company president. "Solidarity among workers should cross the border as easily as companies move production," says Mary Tong, director of the Support Committee for Maquiladora Workers. Labor organizing projects are changing both in response to the modes of global restructuring and to the changes in immigration and immigrant communities over the past two decades; new strategies aim to take on the difficult work of forging understanding and political solidarity between women and men across racial and national boundaries.

The work of Asian "American," Asian immigrant, and other racialized women organizing across national boundaries, formations, and displacements entails processes of learning, translation, and transformations of perspective. Chandra Mohanty has written about the movements *between* cultures, languages, and complex configurations of meanings and power: "Experience must be historically interpreted and theorized if it is to become the basis of feminist solidarity and struggle, and it is at this moment that an understanding of the politics of location proves crucial."[20] Asian American cultural forms, containing a repertoire of counterhistory, memory, and resources for different narratives of new subjects and practices, are a medium for this critical historical interpretation. Rather than dictating that subjects be constituted through identification with the liberal citizen-formation of

American national culture, Asian American cultural forms offer the possibility of subjects and practices constituted through dialectics of difference and disidentification. Rather than vertical determination by the state, these forms are suggestive of horizontal relations between subjects across national boundaries. As subjects occupying the contradictions of "the national-within-the-international," the location of Asian immigrant women is nonetheless the U.S. nation-state. Therefore, Asian immigrant women must struggle to understand not only the process of racialization within the U.S. national frame, but also the different processes of other immigrant women who may already be a proletarianized, gendered labor force in their "home" countries but within specifically nationally stratified sets of social relations there: the agencies of women in sites as different as South Korea, Sri Lanka, and Egypt are determined by their specific national histories of colonialism, decolonization, nationalist struggles, postindependence capitalist development, and multinational incursions.[21] Asian immigrant and Asian "American" women, as always, must be vigilant with regard to the dangers of universalizing nationalist notions of "womanhood" or struggle. The attention to "difference" vividly evoked by Audre Lorde's 1979 speech, "The Master's Tools" — "community must not mean a shedding of our differences . . . [but] learning how to take our differences and make them strengths"[22] — is still, and all the more, crucial for Asian immigrant and Asian "American" women in the global instance of our contemporary moment.

Mah was too busy even to look up when I offered her lunch. She said she didn't have an appetite, so I put the aluminum packet of food on the water pipe, where it'd stay warm, and her thermos on the already-filled communal eating table.

She wanted to teach me to do zippers so I could sew another dozen for her at home. . . .

Back home, I started with the darts. I sewed the facing to the interfacing, the front to the back; then I had trouble with the zipper. I wasn't used to the slick gabardine fabric; my seams didn't match up, and the needle kept sliding over to the metal teeth. I undid the seam and tried again. This time the needle hit the metal zipper tab and jammed. I gave up afraid I might break the needle. Mah broke a needle once and its tip flew up and lodged so close to her eye that Luday and Soon-ping had to walk her over to Chinese hospital.[23]

Fae Myenne Ng's novel *Bone* (1993), like Mrs. Lee's testimony with which we began, portrays Chinatown sewing women who provide labor for a transnational consumer market in which they do not participate, and who bring home work and solicit the help of children and relatives, making the "private" domestic space of the immigrant home an additional site of labor. The lives of the Leong family in Ng's novel are legibly imprinted by conditions of Mah's work as a sewing woman: from the central motif of the sewing machine in all their lives, to the vulnerability of the immigrant home to capitalist penetration, to the tense contrast between the father Leon's difficulty staying steadily employed and Mah's "overemployment." The marriage of Leon and Mah mediates the changes in Chinatown's immigrant community, gender, and work, as sweatshops first made use of Chinese male labor during the garment industry's growth in the 1920s to 1940s, then turned increasingly to female labor after the 1946 modification of the Magnuson Act permitted Chinese wives and children to enter as nonquota immigrants and the Immigration Act of 1965 abolished Asian national origin quotas.[24] Finally, the family relations in *Bone* allegorize the conditions of immigrant life within the contradictions of the liberal nation-state as capitalism extends globally: the immigrant's lack of the civil rights promised to citizens of the nation permits the "private" space of the immigrant home to become a workplace that prioritizes the relations of production over Chinese family relations. In contradistinction to the traditional novel whose progressive narrative reconciliation of the individual to the social order symbolically figures the "private" domain as the resolution of struggles and conflicts in the nation, *Bone* "digresses" backward in time, narrating instead the erosion of the "private" sphere under the material pressures of racialized and gendered relations of production in a transnationally divided social space. From the breakdowns in communication between the parents to the various "flights" of the three daughters (emotional, mortal, and physical), the novel allegorizes how the affective, cultural ties in the Leong family bear the weight of immigration laws, geographical segregation, and global flows of exchange.

In associating a literary text like *Bone* with Mrs. Lee's testimony, I emphasize that a relation exists between these literary and evidential forms of narrative owing to their dialectical relationship to common historical and social processes. Both forms emerge in relation to a shift in the mode of production that expands by means of a deepened racialization, gendering, and fracturing of the labor force. Both elaborate the contradictions of this shift — in which the global "pulls" that bring immigrant women to work near the market's center also increase the regulation and segregation of those women by national laws and capital — but neither form seeks to resolve those contradictions in the development of a singular identity. Indeed, both Lee's testimony and

Ng's novel suggest that the exploitation of immigrant seamstresses depends exactly on the cultural, racial, and gendered qualities of the workforce, rather than on the reduction of their work as interchangeable "abstract labor" without characteristics; furthermore, as immigrant women, it is precisely those characteristics that are the material trace of their historical disenfranchisement from the political realm and that differentiate the seamstresses from the concept of the "abstract citizen."[25] Therefore, in both immigrant narratives, opposition to garment industry exploitation is redressed neither through notions of the national citizen nor through strict identification with the proletarian-class subject of traditional trade unions. In other words, both Lee's testimony and Ng's novel refuse the separation of the economic, the political, and the cultural spheres dictated by the modern state, and neither narrative resolves in the formations of abstract subjects predicated on the modern separation of spheres. Rather, immigrant opposition articulates itself in forms and practices that integrate yet move beyond the political formations dictated by the modern institutions separating the political and economic spheres; the immigrant testimony and novel are cultural forms through which new "political" subjects and practices are narrated, and through which new "political" actions are mediated. In their common interruption of the modern separation of spheres and the political formations dictated by that separation, these cultural forms produce conceptions of collectivity that do not depend on privileging a singular subject as the representative of the group, conceptions of collectivity that do not prescribe a singular narrative of emancipation. Engagement with these cultural forms is not regulated by notions of identity or by modes of identification; a dialectic that presupposes differentiation and that crosses differences is always present as part of the process of engagement.

This dialectic of difference marks these texts as belonging to a new mode of cultural practice that corresponds to the new social formation of globalized capitalism. The contradictions of Asian American formation emerged in relation to the modern nation-state's attempt to resolve the contradictions between its economic and political imperatives through laws that excluded Asian immigrant laborers as "non-white aliens ineligible to citizenship" from the nineteenth to the mid-twentieth century. In that period, Asians entered along the economic axis, while the state simultaneously excluded Asians along racial and citizenship lines, and thus distanced Asian Americans, even as citizens, from membership in the national culture. While official U.S. cultural narratives aimed at reconciling the citizen to the modern nation-state, the material differentiation of Asian immigrants through racialization provided the conditions for Asian American cultural nationalism to emerge in the 1970s in contradiction to that official culture; Asian American cultural nationalism is contestatory in the field of culture to the degree that culture operates in and for the modern state. Insofar as this notion of culture as an institution of the modern state remains in force, even today in its complex imbrication with "postmodern" global extensions and distortions, Asian American cultural nationalism as an oppositional mode continues to have significance in relation to both residual and recast modes of the "modern." For transnational capital is "parasitic" on institutions and social relations of the modern nation-state, deploying its repressive and ideological apparatuses, manipulating the narratives of the liberal citizen-subject, as well as rearticulating modern forms of gender, temporality, and spatialization. This is nowhere clearer than in the contradiction within which global expansion precipitates the proliferation of anti-immigrant legislation, combining refortified policing of borders with ideological appeals to the racial basis of citizenship. Hence, Asian American cultural nationalism that emerged in opposition to racial exclusion continues to address these modern institutions within transnational capitalism. Yet at the same time, the current global restructuring—that moves well beyond the nation-state and entails the differentiation of labor forces internationally—constitutes a shift in the mode of production that now necessitates alternative forms of cultural practice that integrate yet move beyond those of cultural nationalism.

Elsewhere I have discussed such alternative forms of cultural practice, ranging from Christine Choy, Dai Sil Kim-Gibson, and Elaine Kim's "Sa-I-Gu," a video documentary of Korean immigrant women after the 1992 Los Angeles crisis, to Monique Truy-Dung Truong's Vietnamese American epistolary short fiction "Kelly," to Mrs. Fu Lee's testimony against the garment industry's abuse of Chinese immigrant women.[26] Each engages with the dominant forces and formations that determine racialized immigrant women—in the city, the classroom, and the workplace—and simultaneously alter, shift, and mark possible resistances to those forces by representing not only cultural difference, but the convergence of differences, thereby producing new spaces and alternative formations. Culture in and for the modern state is not in itself "political," but the contradictions through which immigration brings national institutions into crisis produces immigrant cultures as oppositional and contestatory, and these contradictions critically politicized in cultural forms and practices can be utilized in the formation of alternative social practices.

These alternative forms of cultural practices are the loci of the cultural-, racial-, and gender-specific qualities of the "class" formations of transnational capitalism. Since transnational capitalism does not work through the homogenization of the mode of production, but operates through and because of the differentiations of cultural-, racial-, and gender-specific forms and operations of work, its "class subjects" are not homogeneous. As corporations attempt to remain competitive in the global arena, the new patterns of flexible accumulation and mixed production that have emerged preserve and reproduce these specific differentiated forms of work. Immigration has intensified according to these new patterns of accumulation and production, and is now more than ever the site of the contradictions between the national state and the global economy. Just as these new patterns allow capital to exploit discrete sectors of the labor force in distinct ways and according to different means, the "class subject" of transnationalism cannot be politically and ideologically unified in any simple way, but may come together according to a process based on strategic alliances between different sectors, not on their abstract identity.[27] This shift in the mode of production must also shift our understanding of the terrain of politics itself: away from an exclusive focus on the abstract unified subject's relationship to the state or to capital, and toward those institutions, spaces, borders, and processes that are the interstitial sites of the social formation in which the national intersects with the international. The law, workplaces, schooling, community organizations, family, sexual life, churches, and popular culture are some of the sites that not only govern this intersection and the reproduction of racialized and gendered social relations along that intersection, but mediate the interruption and reorganization of those social relations as well. These are the regulating sites through which "immigrants" are "naturalized" into "citizens" or through which "immigrants" are disciplined as "aliens" and "foreigners," but these are also the sites profoundly transformed by immigration and altered by the immigrant cultures and practices that emerge in contradiction to these regulating sites. In these sites, "immigrant acts" perform the dialectical unification across difference and critically generate the new subjects of cultural politics.

NOTES

1. From Asian Immigrant Women's Advocates, *Immigrant Women Speak Out on Garment Industry Abuse: A Community Hearing Initiated by Asian Immigrant Women Advocates* (Oakland, CA: AIWA, 1 May 1993), 5. Mrs. Fu Lee is one of twelve women who were not paid by a sweatshop contracted by man-

ufacturer Jessica McClintock, Inc. AIWA organized a long-term campaign that secured pay for these women and revealed garment industry abuse of immigrant women workers.

2. See Chalsa Loo, *Chinatown: Most Time, Hard Time* (New York: Praeger, 1991).

3. Chandra Talpade Mohanty, "Cartographies of Struggle: Third World Women and the Politics of Feminism," in *Third World Women and the Politics of Feminism,* ed. Chandra Talpade Mohanty, Ann Russo, and Lourdes Torres (Bloomington: Indiana University Press), 34.

4. Lisa Lowe, *Immigrant Acts: On Asian American Cultural Politics* (Durham: Duke University Press, 1996).

5. See, for example, Helen Heran Jun, "Contingent Nationalisms in Korean and Korean American Women's Oppositional Struggles," and Min-Jung Kim, "Moment of Danger: Continuities, Discontinuities between Korean Nationalism and Korean American Nationalism," both in *positions: east asia cultures critique* 5, no. 2 (fall 1997).

6. Louis Althusser and Etienne Balibar, "On the Basic Concepts of Historical Materialism," in *Reading Capital* (London: Verso, 1979).

7. On transnationalism and the capitalist mode of production, see, for example, David Harvey, *The Condition of Postmodernity* (Oxford: Basil Blackwell, 1990); Fredric Jameson, *The Geopolitical Aesthetic: Cinema and Space in the World System* (Bloomington: Indiana University Press, 1992). For analyses of third world and racialized women's work in the global economy, see Aihwa Ong, *Spirits of Resistance and Capitalist Discipline: Factory Women in Malaysia* (Albany: State University of New York Press, 1987), and "The Gender and Labor Politics of Postmodernity," in this volume; Swasti Mitter, *Common Fate, Common Bond: Women in the Global Economy* (London: Pluto, 1986); Maria Mies, *Patriarchy and Accumulation on a World Scale: Women in the International Division of Labor* (London: Zed Press, 1986).

8. Sucheta Mazumdar, "General Introduction: A Woman-Centered Perspective on Asian American History," in *Making Waves,* ed. Asian Women United of California (Boston: Beacon Press, 1989).

9. See Arturo Escobar, "Imagining a Post-Development Era? Critical Thought, Development and Social Movements," *Social Text* 31–32 (1992): 20–56.

9. See Nancy Hartsock, "The Feminist Standpoint: Toward a Specifically Feminist Historical Materialism," in *Money, Sex, and Power* (Boston: Northeastern University Press, 1985); Catherine Mackinnon, "Feminism, Marxism, Method, and the State: An Agenda for Theory," *Signs* 7 (1982): 515–544; Robert Blauner, *Racial Oppression in America* (New York: Harper, 1972); Mario Barrera, *Race and Class in the Southwest* (Notre Dame: University of Notre Dame Press, 1979); Rodolfo Acuna, *Occupied America: A History of Chicanos* (New York: Harper, 1981).

11. Theorists such as Chela Sandoval, Angela Davis, and Evelyn Nakano Glenn have articulated critiques of single-axis political organization by suggesting that an exclusive gender politics may obscure class hierarchy and racializa-

tion, while an exclusive class politics may ignore gender stratification, racialization, and homophobia. Chela Sandoval, "U.S. Third World Feminism: The Theory and Method of Oppositional Consciousness in the Postmodern World," *Genders* 10 (spring 1991): 1–24; Angela Davis, *Women, Race, and Class* (New York: Random House, 1981); Evelyn Nakano Glenn, "Racial Ethnic Women's Labor: The Intersection of Race, Gender, and Class Oppression," *Review of Radical Political Economics* 17, no. 3 (1983): 86–109. Moreover, the critique established by many women of color has consistently argued against both the hierarchization of oppressions as well as the false unification of women of color as impediments to theorizing and organizing movements for social change.

12. Evelyn Nakano Glenn, Mary Romero, and Patricia Hill Collins have pointed out that for racialized women the analytic categories of "private" and "public" spheres privilege white middle-class women and occlude the work of women of color, whose "double day" often includes unwaged domestic labor in their own "home" and waged domestic labor in someone else's home; for these women, their "public" sphere is another woman's "private" sphere. See Glenn, "Racial Ethnic Women's Labor"; Mary Romero, *Maid in the U.S.A.* (New York: Routledge, 1992); Patricia Hill Collins, *Black Feminist Thought* (Boston: Unwin Hyman, 1990).

13. See Audre Lorde, "The Master's Tools Will Never Dismantle the Master's House," in *This Bridge Called My Back: Writings by Radical Women of Color,* ed. Cherríe Moraga and Gloria Anzaldúa (Watertown: Persephone Press, 1981); Asian Women United of California, *Making Waves: An Anthology of Writings by and about Asian American Women* (New York: Beacon, 1989). These women of color cultural texts propose new subjects and new political formations. Whereas the normative notion of the subject of liberal society assumes an individual "oedipalized" by family relations and the state, these texts suggest that racialized women are differently formed and articulated, defined by a "disidentification" with the national citizen-subject formation, and constituted through lateral movements across distances and disjunctions. On the subject "women of color," see Norma Alarcón, "The Theoretical Subject(s) of 'This Bridge Called My Back' and Anglo-American Feminism," in *Making Face, Making Soul/Haciendo Caras: Creative and Critical Perspectives by Women of Color,* ed. Gloria Anzaldúa (San Francisco: Aunt Lute, 1990). See also Donna Haraway, "Situated Knowledges," *Feminist Studies* 14, no. 3 (fall 1988): 575–599.

14. For discussions of the global garment and electronics industries and the use of women's labor for assembly, see Committee for Asian Women, *Many Paths, One Goal: Organizing Women Workers in Asia* (Hong Kong: CAW, 1991); June Nash and Maria Patricia Fernandez-Kelly, eds., *Women in the International Division of Labor* (Albany: State University of New York Press, 1983); Maria Patricia Fernandez-Kelly, *"For We Are Sold, I and My People": Women and Industry on Mexico's Frontier* (Albany: State University of New York Press, 1983); Edna Bonacich, "Asians in the Los Angeles Garment Industry," in *New Asian Immigration in Los Angeles and Global Restructuring*

(Philadelphia: Temple University Press, 1994); Richard P. Appelbaum, "Multi-culturalism and Flexibility: Some New Directions in Global Capitalism," in *Mapping Multiculturalism,* ed. Avery Gordon and Christopher Newfield (Min-neapolis: University of Minnesota, 1996); and Laura Ho, Catherine Powell, and Leti Volpp, "(Dis)Assembling Workers' Rights along the Global Assembly-line: Human Rights and the Garment Industry," *Harvard Civil Rights–Civil Liberties Law Review* 31, no. 2 (summer 1996): 383–414.

15. Asian Law Caucus, 468 Bush Street, 3rd floor, San Francisco, CA 94108; Coalition for Immigrant and Refugee Rights and Services, 995 Market Street, 11th floor, San Francisco, CA 94103.

16. Asian Immigrant Women's Advocates (AIWA), 310 8th Street, Suite 301, Oakland, CA 94607.

17. See Lydia Lowe, "Paving the Way: Chinese Immigrant Workers and Com-munity-Based Labor Organizing in Boston," *Amerasia Journal* 18, no. 1 (1992): 39–48; Glenn Omatsu, "The 'Four Prisons' and the Movements of Liberation: Asian American Activism from the 1960s to the 1990s," in *State of Asian America: Activism and Resistance in the 1990s,* ed. Karin Aguilar-San Juan (Boston: South End Press, 1994).

18. Miriam Ching Louie, "Immigrant Asian Women in Bay Area Garment Sweatshops: 'After Sewing, Laundry, Cleaning and Cooking, I Have No Breath to Sing,'" *Amerasia Journal* 18 (1992): 14. For other discussions of Asian women's labor in the garment industry, see Chalsa Loo and Paul Ong, "Slaying Demons with a Sewing Needle: Feminist Issues for Chinatown's Women" in *Chinatown: Most Time, Hard Time,* by Chalsa Loo (New York: Praeger, 1991); and Diane Yen-Mei Wong and Dennis Hayashi, "Behind Unmarked Doors: Developments in the Garment Industry," in *Making Waves: An Anthology of Writings by and about Asian American Women,* ed. Asian Women United of California (New York: Beacon, 1989). See also *Through Strength and Struggle,* a video documentary that tells the story of Chinese immigrant women workers and the P & L and Beverly Rose Sportwear shutdowns, by Chinese Progressive Association Workers Center, 164 Lincoln Street, 2nd floor, Boston, MA 02111.

19. Support Committee for Maquiladora Workers, 3909 Center Street, Suite 210, San Diego, CA 92103; see Kyungwon Hong and Mary Tong, "Aguirre v. AUG: A Case Study," in *Multinational Human Resource Management: Cases and Exercises,* ed. P. C. Smith (Tulsa, OK: Dame Publishing, forthcoming).

20. Chandra Talpade Mohanty, "Feminist Encounters: Locating the Politics of Experience," in *Destabilizing Theory,* ed. Michelle Barrett and Anne Phillips (Stanford: Stanford University Press, 1992).

21. See, for example, Kumari Jayawardena's *Feminism and Nationalism in the Third World* (London: Zed Press, 1986), a social history of women's work and women's activities in feminist, nationalist, and labor movements in Turkey, Egypt, India, Sri Lanka, Indonesia, the Philippines, China, Korea, Vietnam, and Japan. For analyses of segmented labor and occupational segregation of wo-men within different national locations, see Nanneke Redclift and M. Thea Sinclair, eds., *Working Women: International Perspectives on Labour and Gen-*

der Ideology (London: Routledge, 1991). Chandra Talpade Mohanty, Ann Russo, and Lordes Torres, eds., *Third World Women and the Politics of Feminism* (Bloomington: Indiana University Press, 1991), contains important accounts of different "third world" feminisms in the context of the specific upheavals of decolonization, national liberation struggles, and transnational capitalism. On the cultural dimensions of women's positions within transnationalism, see Inderpal Grewal and Caren Kaplan, eds., *Scattered Hegemonies: Postmodernity and Transnational Feminist Practices* (Minneapolis: University of Minnesota, 1994).

22. Lorde, "The Master's Tools."

23. Fae Myenne Ng, *Bone* (New York: Hyperion, 1993), 178–179.

24. For a study of San Francisco Chinatown, see Victor G. Nee and Brett de Bary Nee, *Longtime Californ': A Documentary Study of an American Chinatown* (New York: Pantheon, 1972).

25. Lowe, *Immigrant Acts*, 24–28.

26. Lowe, *Immigrant Acts*.

27. Antonio Gramsci conceived "hegemony" in these terms; see "Notes on Italian History," in *Selections from the Prison Notebooks*, ed. and trans. Quintin Hoare and Geoffrey Nowell Smith (New York: International Publishers, 1971); Stuart Hall, "Gramsci's Relevance for the Study of Race and Ethnicity," *Journal of Communications Inquiry* 10 (summer 1986): 5–27.

CLARA CONNOLLY AND PRAGNA PATEL

Women Who Walk on Water: Working across "Race" in Women Against Fundamentalism

Women Against Fundamentalism (WAF) is a feminist organization set up by women active in the South Asian, Jewish, Irish, and Iranian communities in Britain. Its founding moment was the *fatwa* against Salman Rushdie in 1989, but it has gone on to raise issues relating to the oppressive aspects of religiopolitical movements in all the major religions represented in Britain. By fundamentalism, WAF does not mean religious observance, which we see as a matter of individual choice, but rather modern political movements that use religion as a basis for their attempt to win or consolidate power and extend social control. Fundamentalism appears in different and changing forms in religions throughout the world, sometimes as a state project, some-times in opposition to the state. But at the heart of all fundamentalist agendas is the control of women's minds and bodies. All religious fun-damentalists support the patriarchal family as a central agent of con-trol. They view women as embodying the morals and traditional values of the family and the whole community. Resisting fundamentalism means taking up issues such as reproductive rights, safeguarding and extending abortion rights, resisting enforced sterilization, and fighting violence against women. WAF does not confine the term *fundamental-ism* to one religion, and certainly not to only British minority religions. In fact, our main political target is the privileged connection between Christianity and the state in Britain, and the divisive effects of this on all communities living here. At the same time, we challenge the assump-tion that minorities in Britain exist as unified, internally homogeneous groups. This view assumes that women's voices are represented by the community and denies them an independent voice. WAF rejects the politics of what has come to be known in Britain as "multiculturalism" that delivers women's futures into the hands of fundamentalist "com-munity leaders" by seeing these as representatives of the community as a whole.[1]

The present essay is a weaving of two very different voices repre-sented in WAF. It is a celebration of our difference and of our ability to collaborate across difference on a political project that combines our separate social and political formulations in the deepest and most complex way. We have chosen to write the first section as individuals, to complement the analysis in the second section which grows from our joint work.

RUSHDIE THE RELUCTANT CATALYST

Pragna:

Southall Black Sisters (SBS) is an autonomous black feminist group based in the predominantly South Asian (Punjabi) community of West London.[2] The group was set up in 1979 by African Caribbean and South Asian women. I joined in 1982, having just finished a bachelor's degree in sociology and English literature, anxious to find a political home that reflected both the struggles against forced arranged marriage that many women faced within the family, and the struggles against racism, fought out largely in the school playground where other non-Asian children and teachers reminded us of our marginal positions within British society. SBS was a site in which we could put a politicized, theoretical understanding of gender, class, race, and socialism into practice. Above all, it was a place to develop a political consciousness with other black men and women who were proud and confident.

However, when I first started working with SBS, I had little idea of how difficult yet vital simultaneous engagement in struggles against racism and sexism would be. More recently, this struggle has become even more complex as political religious identities have replaced the secular and more radical political identities around which the struggle against racism had been waged. The Rushdie affair in 1989 became the catalyst that forced many of us to reexamine the nature of our struggles, the nature of the British state, and the relationship between the state and minority communities. Much of the antiracist struggle has been collapsed into defenses of "culture" and "community," while feminism has been forced to challenge the growth of religious fundamentalisms and the foundation of communalism on the subordination of women.

The Rushdie affair marked a watershed as we began to understand more clearly the significance of struggles with other Asian women across the caste and religious divides. The *fatwa* issued against Rushdie struck a note of horror and foreboding among many of us in SBS as we came to a realization that we too were in the business of dissenting and exposing the ways in which women are denied freedom of movement, expression, and ultimately self-determination as a result of patriarchal control experienced within the family, community, and wider society. If Rushdie could be silenced by religious fundamentalists, then so too could women. We began to witness fundamentalist and traditional forces reconceptualizing identity around religion, strengthening communal divisions that already existed within our communities. And this maintenance of religious and communal identity rests on the control of women, a control facilitated by liberal, "multicultural" policies that have lent succor to the new reactionary forces.

Another watershed, not unrelated, was the destruction of the Babri-Masjid, a sixteenth-century mosque in northern India, by right-wing Hindu fundamentalists and communalists. For the first time, those of us who were Hindu in Britain were forced to reexamine our Hindu background and remind ourselves that we were part of the Hindu diaspora, many of whom lent active support to the Hindu communalist forces in India. For once, we were part of a majority that was constructing Muslims as the "enemy other," destroying the fragile foundations upon which secular democracy is built in India. The recognition that one may belong at one and the same time to an oppressed minority (in Britain) and an oppressive majority (Indian-Hindu diaspora) was echoed in the work we were doing at SBS, where from the outset we have had to work against the oversimplified construction of our identities and struggles that presumes a fixed dichotomy between a black minority and a white majority. This oversimplification has led to an abrogation of responsibility by many within progressive left movements for the gross abuses of human rights that are taking place in the name of nationalism and religion in our communities and countries of origin. Although the term *black* is a useful means of political mobilization, it has tended to obscure rather than reveal the contradictions that arise in trying to knit together and practice a politics of resistance based on gender, class, and race oppression.

The founding members of SBS faced much hostility and opposition to their existence. The hostility emanated not only from the more traditional, religious, male-dominated groups but also from left-wing, progressive men with whom the women had fought side by side in a number of crucial antiracist uprisings in Southall from 1976 to 1981. In fact, all the early members of SBS had come out of this antiracist activity. Having been politicized within that tradition, they nevertheless felt compelled to strike out for autonomy because the antiracist movement had failed to address the specific issues faced by black women. SBS challenged the broad antiracist movement to recognize the oppression of women and challenged the hegemony that antiracist political groups had over discourses on the nature of black struggle in Britain.

Black women were making themselves heard, but it was ten years or so before SBS moved from the doubly marginalized position to which it was relegated by traditional forms of community and by the racist state to the center that it now occupies, having achieved a measure of success in battles fought to include black women in the antiracist and feminist political agendas.

Very early on, the group grappled with the issue of sexuality and became a forum in which some black women felt comfortable about exploring and asserting their lesbian sexuality for the first time. The group was plural and secular, with members coming from many different ethnic and religious backgrounds. Individually, some members saw themselves as socialist feminists, others as radical/separatist feminists, others still as political lesbian feminists. Now the composition of the group is mainly Asian, and most of us see ourselves as socialist feminists. Nevertheless, in terms of the political outlook, we have tried to hold onto the plural and secular vision forged by the founding members.

The early struggles reflected a variety of issues that touched the lives of black women: protests against the racist and sexist practice of virginity tests carried out by immigration officials on Asian women coming into the country for the purpose of marriage (the assumption being that all Asian women are virgins before marriage); defense campaigns against police harassment and criminalization of black youths; defending the right of black women to join unions; and fighting homelessness and racist attacks. Eventually, SBS was to secure funding from the now defunct Greater London Council (GLC). The GLC in those days was a radical organization espousing the cause of many disadvantaged sections of society in an attempt to create a popular culture around causes such as antiracism. SBS, along with hundreds of other black groups, benefited directly. Yet the policies that funded us were also flawed to the extent that there was an absence of a critical understanding of the heterogeneous nature of black communities; this led to the funding of all manner of black groups, even those that had little or no commitment to equal opportunities. Among these were even very reactionary communalist and religious organizations within the Asian community, some of whom have now come into their own with the rise of religious fundamentalism.

Since SBS is composed mostly of Asian women, it has been particularly active in campaigning to expose the patriarchal structures of the family in connection with domestic violence, a pressing issue in the context of the Asian community. Political struggles by men and women in Asian and African Caribbean communities have taken parallel and diverging courses over the past two decades, sometimes in alliance, owing to similar experiences of state denigration and brutality.[3] Nevertheless, it may be worth noting the differences in the content and direction of the course taken by SBS and other South Asian feminist groups from that taken by our activist African Caribbean sisters. African Caribbean women have been active in highlighting the ways in which racism has historically disrupted their family structures, leading to an acute sense of alienation experienced by the male youth in particular; much of their political activism has focused around educational underachievement and the criminalization of the youth. In contrast, Asian feminists have needed to vigilantly criticize the family as the structure through which "community leaders" and the British state discipline and regulate the lives of women. The differences in our political agendas are not surprising, indeed are a product of racist, colonial rule whereby family and community structures were broken or reinforced in ways that complied with the changing demands of capitalism. Historically, for many African Caribbean communities, the family and religion may have served as strong sites of resistance against racism, particularly when racism has attempted to undermine African Caribbean families as a means of domination and social control. Unmarried African Caribbean women have headed the family for decades if not centuries, unlike their Asian counterparts in Britain for whom single parenthood is still a relatively new but growing phenomenon. While acknowledging the threat of racism by the state, the police, law, and education, in the various Asian communities we have no option but to recognize the traditional, patriarchal extended family structure to the extent that it has been vital not only for economic survival, but also for capital accumulation. Recently, of course, Asian family structures and traditions have been reinvented and reproduced with renewed vigor by the growing ascendency of fundamentalist and orthodox religious forces. Therefore, for many Asian women, the family poses an immediate threat to autonomy, and we are only too painfully aware that the struggle for equality in the wider society is inextricably linked to the need to win personal freedom at home.

The contradictions faced by the founding members in trying to battle racial and sexual oppression have in fact been present throughout our history, posing major challenges not only to wider feminist thinking but also to the thinking of antiracist and left movements as a whole. As black women we have had to grapple with the tensions that arise in recognizing the state as both oppressor and protector. This has led to a contradiction in which we make different demands in the contexts of various struggles. In campaigns against domestic violence, we have made demands for the right of women to leave oppressive family environments and for the state to criminalize domestic violence, dismantling the notion of the family as a sacred and private space. At the same time, we have also needed to demand that the state recognize the right to family unity in immigration cases where racist laws and policies separate and even criminalize members of minority families. The state for us has never been a monolithic entity somewhere "out there" to be resisted. Within the dominant antiracist discourse, for example, the family is constructed as a "haven" against the worst excesses of state intrusion and harassment. While we would not deny the "bulwark" role played by the family in the face of divisive policies and attacks from the state and racists, one cannot escape the manner in which the construction of the homogeneous nature of "the black family" hides other power relations among different caste, class, ethnic, and gender groups, and especially between men and women.[4]

In the 1980s, certain conceptual tools were available to black feminists in the British context, and SBS developed an understanding of black women's oppression that advanced a notion of "triple" oppression, that is, that black women suffer due to their race, class, and gender positions. As we have developed, this has become an unsatisfactory way of understanding our position. Our day-to-day work of assisting women to achieve some form of independence in their lives has given us an insight into the specific ways in which race, class, and gender intersect: class may be an important factor in the forms through which women are subordinated within racialized communities; racism practiced in the larger society against immigrants can exacerbate the sexism within their communities. We have therefore moved away from a mechanistic understanding of how race, class, and gender intersect in black women's lives to one that allows us to unravel the complexities of our positions, one that permits us to act out in terms of those complexities in order to achieve empowerment and autonomy.

Our struggles have necessarily arisen from the routine experiences of the many women who come to our center with stories of violence, persecution, and imprisonment experienced at the hands of their husbands and families and/or the state. Many of our campaigns have focused around Asian women's experiences of violence, forced arranged marriages, sexual abuse, and other restrictions. One of the early campaigns in 1981 that marked a turning point in our history involved the murder of an Asian mother, Mrs. Dhillon, who, along with three of her five daughters, was burned to death by her husband. The crime sparked off protests by SBS that were met by total community silence, in marked contrast to the protests on another occasion, when white policemen were responsible for the death of a black woman, that led to major race uprisings. No one in the community wanted to speak out against these horrific deaths. SBS's protest became the first major challenge by Asian women in Southall to the notion of community unity and to the institution of the family. In 1984, we responded to the death of another Asian woman, Krishna Sharma, who appeared to have hung herself after years of suffering violence at the hands of her husband. This time SBS was much more organized, picketing the Coroner's Court in an effort to pressure it to take account of her entire troubled marital history. When the court refused to properly investigate the circumstances surrounding her death, we organized a spontaneous demonstration outside the house of her husband. In doing so we broke many taboos within the community as well as orthodoxies within the antiracist movement. By campaigning publicly, we subverted the twin notions of honor and shame (*izzat* and *sharam*) which demand from women silence and obedience for the sake of preserving their family name. The women's movement in India regularly organizes such events to shame the perpetrators of such violence rather than allow the women to become victims or carry the burden of shame and dishonor; our demonstrations borrowed heavily from Indian feminist strategies. We faced accusations from many progressive black men and women who charged that we were fueling racist stereotypes, particularly disseminated in the media, about the "pathological" nature of the black family. We refused to back down on the grounds that to keep silent about domestic violence for the sake of preserving the mythical notion of a united black community meant to tacitly support and collude in our own oppression as women. Many of the demonstrators in fact were women who had fled violent homes in Southall and were living in battered women's shelters, but who returned to lead a spirited attack against the values of the community, culture, and religion that sanctioned violence against women.

In the Krishna Sharma campaign, we demanded and received the support of many white feminists, although not without some struggle. Initially, white feminists feared being seen as racist if they were involved in activities that criticized Asian men and the Asian community. We argued that, on the contrary, apart from supporting Asian women on an issue of concern to all women, their participation was vital both to breaking down racist stereotypes and to forging antiracist feminism in this country. The ghettoization of black and white feminism had to be dissolved to allow for genuine alliances to emerge; we believed that we could work for all women, but without losing the specificity of the concrete struggles of different women. Until recently, joint actions among feminists in Britain have been hampered by racial and political divisions. Women Against Fundamentalism affirms that it is possible to bridge race, class, national, and community differences by building alliances around common projects rather than demanding racial identity.

The recent campaign organized around Kiranjit Ahluwalia, an Asian woman who had been jailed for life for killing her violent husband, brought about an effective alliance between black women and white radical feminists who have a long history of fighting male violence in this country. The campaign had two main aims: to free Kiranjit and to highlight the failures of a criminal justice system that incarcerates battered women without taking into account their experiences of domestic violence. The campaign illustrated the need for and the possibilities of alliances across racial divides. We brought attention to the specificity of her experiences as an Asian woman, yet avoided stereotyping the issue as an "Asian" concern only; ultimately our demands were ones that benefit all women.

When the Rushdie affair exploded, SBS immediately identified with his predicament. We felt there was an analogy between the ways in which culture, religion, and tradition have served to reinforce patriarchal domination in our communities and the censoring of what was perceived as Rushdie's criticism of Muslim cultural forms. Aware that his censorship would result in a censorship of feminist activity within our communities, we decided we had no choice but to defend him and the feminist secular spaces that we had created. While there was a deathly silence from all other black political activists, there was little or no dissension in SBS about whether to defend him. Rather than British racists, it was within our communities that young Asian men and some women supported the *fatwa*. They were angered by his so-called denigration of Islam and sought to make him responsible for the media's racist constructions of Islam and Muslims generally.

With women from the local women's section of the Labour Party, we organized a meeting on the rise of religious fundamentalism and its effects on women around the world in countries such as Pakistan, Ireland, and India. At the end of the meeting we issued a statement in support of Rushdie but also made overt political connections with our own struggles as black women defending the right to speak for ourselves.[5] The meeting was well attended by local women and feminists from around London and outside. By the end, we organized another meeting of women from different religious and racial backgrounds in central London, with the aim of examining the role of fundamentalist movements in all religions and its impact on women in particular.

Through these connections, feminists from a number of different political traditions came together to form Women Against Fundamentalism.

In WAF, the analysis of the British state and multicultural politics in particular has continued to strengthen the coalition that has been formed, allowing us to move beyond mere solidarity and slogans to formulate a common agenda for defeating fundamentalism and for advocating a secular and plural society in which the rights of all minority collectivities and women are supported. Organizing with women from a variety of racial and religious backgrounds provides the ground from which to understand the ways religion has circumscribed all our lives and impinged on our autonomy. But the challenges lay in developing ways of resisting racism and religious fundamentalism simultaneously. We confronted this difficulty in the campaign around Rabia Janjua, an Asian woman from Pakistan who fled charges of *zina* (unlawful sex), which carried the penalty of public flogging and long-term imprisonment in that country. She married a British citizen, also of Pakistani origin, and escaped to Britain with him, but in Britain she faced violence and abuse from her husband and was forced to leave him, taking her two young children. Her actions led to her husband's reporting her to the Home Office as an illegal immigrant, and she found herself facing removal to Pakistan. SBS initiated a campaign, later sponsored by WAF, to force the state to allow her to stay in Britain. In the course of the campaign, we confronted the ways immigration laws in Britain discriminate against migrant women by trapping them in violent marriages. Migrant women's choices are severely circumscribed by their not being able to claim public housing and other benefits available to battered women in the wider society. Their options are limited to remaining in the marriage, thus risking physical harm, or leaving and facing deportation by the state. At the same time, we sought to highlight the degrading nature of *zina* laws in Pakistan and demanded that gender persecution be recognized as a legitimate grounds for seeking refugee status in Britain.[6]

Clara:

The first time I met Southall Black Sisters was at the founding meeting of Voices for Rushdie at the Red Rose Club in North London, in May 1989. Gita Sahgal and I were cochairing, she from SBS and I from *Feminist Review*. Present also were representatives from Turkish and Iranian opposition groups, from the Labour Party Black Sections, the socialist movement, and women's groups from a number of minority ethnic communities, mainly Asian, Irish, and Turkish. Of us all, SBS provided the most coherent focus of opposition to an antiracist orthodoxy that was nervous of supporting Rushdie in a climate of anti-Islamic hostility and therefore content to leave his support in the hands of the liberal intelligentsia. Inspired by SBS's defiance, we drafted a press statement: "We reject the attempt to present the controversy surrounding [*The Satanic Verses*] as a crude 'Eastern v. Western' conflict. . . . No culture or society has a monopoly on the values of pluralism and the right to dissent. Indeed, all over the world, people from many different backgrounds and in many different cultures are involved in struggles for those values and rights. We see our campaign to defend Rushdie and against both racism and fundamentalism as an intrinsic part of those struggles. . . ."[7]

That was the crux of our position: solidarity with dissident movements all over the postcolonial world. We did not see how the antiracist work that some of us engaged in — focused on the British state and its immigration laws in particular — could be compromised by a clear stand against religious fundamentalism, even when expressed by the targets of that racism. We were uncomfortable with the mournful pleasures of identity politics, which stressed and celebrated difference at the expense of alliance; we came together across national and "race" lines under the label of *dissidents*. It was no coincidence that there were so many who had the experience of being in opposition to our "home" governments; what we had in common was the experience of double exile — in our own countries and within British society.

Voices for Rushdie pursued a short and lively existence. For example, we organized a press conference at the House of Commons, spoke at the annual conferences of the Labour Party and the socialist movement, and hosted an "Unholy Night" in solidarity with Rushdie, with blasphemous readings from around the world and from Britain's minority communities — defined not only by ethnicity, but also by political and sexual orientation. An instinctive identification with the persona of Rushdie, however, could not sustain for long a coalition with such a diversity of organizational traditions. What was not possible for Voices was possible for the women within it, most of whom were also members of Women Against Fundamentalism, a movement founded out of the same moment, but with a clearer long-term agenda.

What made the Rushdie affair such an important catalyst for me? Novelists in trouble were a familiar phenomenon where I came from, particularly those who mix religion and sex. I grew up in the Republic of Ireland while it was still in the awesome grip of the Catholic Church. The Church's power is now being challenged, but then it was the central institution in defining the parameters of civil and social life and of national identity.[8] The virtual identity of the state with the Catholic Church meant that Catholic doctrine on issues of morality, sexuality, and gender profoundly informed every domain of women's lives. Contraception, abortion, and divorce were banned. The marriage bar still existed for the working women in many areas of the public sector, and since it was assumed that marriage was concomitant with motherhood, permanent and full-time posts were virtually unavailable to married women. Furthermore, as a socialist, I felt despair that a mass civil rights movement in Northern Ireland, which might have led to radical social change, seemed to have metamorphosed into an armed nationalist struggle that had the aim of joining an Irish state based on fundamentalist Catholicism.[9]

Arriving in Britain, I involved myself in socialist and feminist activity, but the only Irish group I felt able to join was the Irish Women's Abortion Support Group (IWASG), a network that supports women coming clandestinely to Britain for abortions. (Later, there were other Irish women's conferences and networks.) The stories told by the women who stayed with me on the night before their clinic appointment suggested that Ireland was changing, but not that much. At the same time, the implacable hostility of the Irish community press in Britain to the activities of IWASG betrayed a form of identity politics that could tolerate only uncritically positive images of minority cultures and communities and that could not recognize conflicts of interest within them. But until I met the women in WAF, I did not have the language to articulate such doubts with political confidence. I had always been happy to denounce the Irish state, but publicly to criticize aspects of Irish community life in Britain raised different and more contradictory issues. Irish women had not managed to articulate a distinctive "take" on *national* identity.[10] Only recently is work being developed by women in Ireland on this issue;[11] it would have been even more difficult to do so in a context in which Irish identity is a minority one, threatened by the mainstream.

Homi Bhabha, also a member of Voices, has commented on how Rushdie's questioning of national identity invigorates the project of forging alternative social identities and practices: "Salman Rushdie sees the emergence of doubt, questioning and even confusion as being part of the cultural 'excess' that facilitates the formation of new social identities that do not appeal to a pure and settled past, or to a unicultural present, in order to authenticate themselves."[12] Crucial here is the question of how those emerging social identities find not just aesthetic but political expression. How does a doubter become a dissenter? Irish women who inhabited the very edge of community without wishing to step "outside" felt such doubt and confusion throughout the eighties, but could rarely find a political forum in which to express it. For doubt may produce only silence, for fear of even worse: that its expression may lead to total ostracism from those for whom one feels an anxious, but real, sense of kinship. By the early 1990s, Irish women organized separately in Britain in two main ways. For instance, groups like Women Against Imperialism or those in defense of women Republican prisoners might give women the approval of a powerful minority of male peers in the community who had the same agenda but were a different constituency. Alternatively, women could organize around gender-specific issues such as access to abortion and lesbianism, but would be ignored if not completely disowned by "community." In neither case were our existence or our separate spaces directly threatened, and we were grateful for small mercies.

The situation for Asian women was different — at least for those who, like SBS and others campaigning around the issue of domestic violence, directly challenged orthodox forms of community organization. Their separate spaces were being threatened, either by incorporation by religious groups or by being shut down.[13] Though their slogans spoke from a history and a location far removed from mine, I recognized them instantly as expressing our shared understanding of the implications for women's autonomy of cultures deeply influenced by religion. This was true for other women who joined — Irish, Jewish, Iranian — despite our recognition of the different forms of racialization that affected us. The outcome of our common work was a politically focused critique of multiculturalism, as practiced in Britain, which we believed locked "communities" in a position of subordination within mainstream society and locked women in a position of subordination within "community." Our political focus was the British state, in particular the privileged position of the established Church, which distorts and stunts the growth of a genuinely pluralist secular society in which it is possible to negotiate across a range of religious and cultural positions.

THE MUDDLE OF MULTICULTURALISM

Multiculturalism has a long history, and we were not the first to express dissatisfaction with it. "The concept of culture, in the distinctly modern sense of a common life, had become, by the thirties and forties, part of a language of controlled re-construction — in the terrain of empire as in Britain itself — according to the dictates of liberal reason. . . . a similar logic was at work in Britain and the Empire, namely the aim of trans-forming (and enabling) subjects and not merely of repressing them."[14] Talal Asad's description of the origins of multiculturalism has the ad-vantage of pointing up two important features: its liberal aspect, which appears all the more progressive in the face of right-wing opposition to it; and the interconnections between state projects for managing class relations at home and for managing race relations, first overseas and, since the 1960s, in Britain itself.

As with other cultural projects, the multicultural project has not been without its tensions, but establishment consensus has largely held on, at least until the Rushdie affair. The main source of tension has been the balance to be maintained between the common elements of a na-tional culture and the degree of "difference" that will be tolerated. Since the Rushdie affair, the pendulum has swung back in favor of em-phasizing elements "in common," by which is meant the dominant cul-ture; the effect on education, for example, has been a renewed emphasis on Britain's "Christian heritage," which has allowed fundamentalist Christian evangelists a disturbing amount of influence over the educa-tional curriculum. That is the focus of WAF's most recent campaign.

While the swings and roundabouts of establishment thinking about the nature of multiculturalism are of concern to WAF on account of their political effects, they do not affect our central critique. We would therefore like to highlight an example of multiculturalism at its best and most progressive, in order to highlight the flaws we see in the project as a whole.

The Swann Report, presented to Parliament in the mid-1980s, was a comprehensive attempt to address the issue of racial disadvantage and inequality in education. Although there were some references to racism, the solution to inequality that the report proposed fitted squarely within the established consensual ideal of tolerance for difference within a pluralist society. Swann's vision of a pluralist society is one that is "socially cohesive and culturally diverse."[15] Its sense of delicate balance admirably expresses the social democratic aspirations of the British postwar period, drawing to its close at the end of the 1970s. Alas, it was out of date even as it was being written: the Thatcher regime was busy dismantling the elements of such social cohesion as had existed. There was no real attempt to implement the report's recommendations.

Swann's view of British society was that it consisted, first, of a ho-mogeneous white population (with some concessions toward regional variation) united by a confidently held common core of moral values, enshrined in a democratically endorsed legal framework. Second, in relation to and difference from that population, a group of (internally homogeneous) ethnic minority communities was intent on maintaining their identity within the framework of a legal system that protected their rights. The relationship — mutual tolerance of difference — between majority and minorities would be mediated by respect for the law and democratic values.

But such an understanding of British society is inadequate on several counts. There was no uncontested core of values then, nor is there now. Queen, Church, and Commons notwithstanding, mainstream British society was riven by conflict, of which the miners' strike of the year before the report's publication was only the most dramatic symptom. The black communities were simultaneously engaged in bitter struggle against the legal framework that was supposed to protect them, in particular against the immigration laws and the policing of inner-city areas. Any injunction to "celebrate diversity" rang hollow in a climate of acute anxiety about immigration, fed by the repressive policies of successive governments that had framed those immigration laws and promoted "law and order" as a means of dealing with the symptoms of urban decay. At the same time, as is more clearly evident now in the aftermath of the Rushdie affair, the ethnic minority communities were divided between and among themselves. A strong dose of moral exhortation was simply not enough to paper over these cracks.

An oppositional version of pluralism would accept the *absence* of social cohesion as its foundation. Rather than depending on the dominant values of existing society — which justify inequality — it would attempt to forge a new consensus around the work of creating the society of the future. And it would have to reassess the meaning of *community*, a pivotal term for multiculturalism.

The discourse of "community" has a long and respectable history of managing deep conflicts in British society. It has the critical advantage of suggesting positive values, no matter who uses the term. Raymond Williams, himself the most eloquent exponent of working-class community values, remarked on one occasion that no one cites the term negatively.[16] But even here, the notion of community has a double and contradictory valence. Initially designating the more or less homogeneous and historically evolved communities that compose the nation as ethnically British and racially white, the term has come to be used more often of racialized and minority immigrant populations. In this shift, the prior meaning is less visible but no less powerful in its effects. In a climate of deepening anxiety about "race," it functions as one of a set of code words for relations with and between various waves of settlers and their families. The word *community* now has an altered territorial meaning (usually, but not always, an inner-city slum) and a cultural one: for mainstream multiculturalists, it denotes a range of views (from sympathetic to bewildered) toward a way of life different from "ours." From the inside, it defines a resistance to assimilation and a resource against the hostility of the host society: Sivanandan's celebration of "communities of resistance" is the best-known use of the term among black writers in Britain.[17] What "insider" and "outsider" definitions share is the sense of a kinship network — families in streets — which is usually seen as natural rather than constructed, a "given" rather than a process. It has a meaning opposed to *nation,* being at the same time smaller than the national unit (and disruptive of it) and larger, including supranational links and structures.

If the predominant meaning of *community* is "kinship" networks, it follows that women are at its heart, but as mothers, wives, and daughters, that is, solely in relation to others within it. Women *as individuals* are excluded from community in a number of ways. First, by multiculturalism, which constructs a relationship between a homogeneous white "society" and a series of inwardly homogeneous "communities." Men, women, and children who "belong" are assumed to have the same interests, whatever their class, gender, or political differences. And those interests are usually represented to the state, central and local, by self-appointed male community leaders, often drawn from the more conservative sections.

Second, women are excluded by patriarchal community structures: religious, political, and social; that is to say, women are addressed by such organizations only in their capacity as mothers, wives, and daughters within the family. The punishment for speaking out as *women* can be severe, as Julia Bard has illustrated in her story of the orthodox Jewish woman driven out of her community for the crime of separately approaching the state, that is, involving police and social workers in the defense of her children against sexual abuse.[18] This process is compounded by women's organizations, when we relate to "community" only through our relations with men and children, and do not address the interests of women as a distinct category. Or alternatively, when, organized in black or ethnic minority women's groups, we make a virtue of the pain of exclusion, rather than confronting it directly and insisting on our right to speak from within. Only by standing outside these options can we contribute to the creation of a "consenting community," containing a rich variety of political and social identities within it.

Religion is one of the most powerful ways of regulating women's relation to community and, in some cases, of policing its boundaries. The rise of fundamentalism among the major religions, which has as one of its concerns the redefinition of "community" and the clarification of its boundaries, is a serious threat to women's autonomy. The less rigid the boundaries, and the more fluid the notion of community, the better it is for women's opportunities for personal autonomy and control over our lives. The concept of personal autonomy, with its emphasis on individualism, is sometimes represented as a threat to communal or class solidarity. This is certainly a more sympathetic argument when the group being defended is under threat from war or racism. But a double standard seems to operate here: the autonomy of (heterosexual) men is seldom seen as threatening the community, so why should *women's* autonomy be so represented? Is it because women are "different," but not equal?

Multicultural policies are all-pervasive within the welfare and legal system. The consequences have been devastating not only for women but also for the fight against racism, insofar as such policies have little or nothing to do with challenging the power and privilege of the dominant community that maintain and reproduce racial oppression. In the experience of WAF and SBS, we have to deal with many cases where multicultural policies have resulted in women's fighting long and hard to win and defend gains they made with respect to their rights in matrimonial, property, and child custody matters as well as their right to control their minds and bodies. In the name of tolerance for "cultural differences" the rights of women are dismissed, and many Asian women seeking support to escape domestic violence, for instance, are often told by state agencies that it is not an acceptable method of marital resolution in their communities. They are denied protection and are delivered back to their families and communities. We quote some recent examples.

In 1991, an Asian man charged with intent to cause grievous bodily harm to his wife was given a lenient noncustodial sentence by the judge on the grounds that he was an immigrant. On passing sentence, the judge commented that had he been white, he would have dealt with him much more severely. The judge acknowledged the criminal offence but offered to "tolerate" it as it was committed in a different cultural context: a view that reinforces the patriarchal control of women in Asian communities as well as racist perceptions about the "barbaric" nature of Asian families. Moreover, the judgment delineates the limits and boundaries of civil rights for Asian women, who are deemed not to be in need of state protection.

In another case, a woman of Muslim origin had been made to endure a protracted and painful battle to retain custody of her daughter following a breakdown in her marriage due to her husband's violence and her refusal to conform as a traditional Muslim wife. She had been unable to marry her boyfriend, also of Muslim origin, due to her ex-husband's refusal to grant her a divorce. This forced her into cohabitation with her boyfriend, which in turn led to a community outcry. She was denounced as adulterous and treated as an outcast by sections of her community. Inside the courts, however, the battle over the question of custody of her daughter took an unexpected turn as the judge failed to base a final decision on a recommendation made by a court welfare officer that the child's interests were best served by remaining with her mother, who was the prime carer. Instead, the judge allowed himself to be swayed by the husband's arguments that in child custody and matrimonial/family matters, the Muslim community is guided by *sharia*, or personal laws. Utilizing Muslim theologians, the husband argued that according to *sharia* laws, his wife is an adulteress and transgressor, ostracized by the entire community, and should in such circumstances obey the dictates of *sharia* laws by returning her child to him. He also argued that the ostracism faced by the mother will affect his daughter's well-being and moral and religious upbringing. Such arguments clouded the court's notion of justice and equality for the woman and, more importantly, for the young child, whose fate now depends on the outcome of theological debates on the position of women in Islam, rather than on rights enshrined in civil law.

These cases send some alarming signals about the future development and implementation of secular civil law in relation to women in minority communities in Britain. In the first case, the judge acknowledged the criminal offense but offered to exercise his tolerance in sentencing, basing his decision on the misguided perception that (male) immigrants have a difficult job adjusting to the demands of the dominant society. In the second case, again in classic multicultural, noninterventionist style, the judge appears to be allowing community/personal law as defined by Muslim theologians and community leaders to supersede the civil rights of the woman, and indeed those of future generations of minority women, reinforcing the view that they must be governed by the rule of their community leaders. The assumption is that community/personal laws are uniformly and rigidly interpreted by all members of the community and that the self-appointed conservative/religious leadership is legitimate and widely accepted. The consequence is that in legal discourses, women are excluded from the construction of the minority community, an exclusion that not only denies the actual lived reality of women but also refuses women the right to construct their own identity according to their personal beliefs and experiences. Instead, the actions and views of women are rendered deviant and illegitimate, while those of the community leaderships are accepted as "authentic." The ultimate danger of such rulings lies in the construction of minority women as the property of their families and communities. Such constructions will in turn feed into a wider social and political culture that marginalizes many minority women and disenfranchises them from their citizenship rights. In this way, a boundary is established between one's belonging to the community and one's right to membership in civil society.

State-regulated multiculturalism is ultimately limited and unworkable, even as it pretends to offer an ideologically enlightened, democratic model by which British society can manage relations between the state and minority communities. For it is ultimately based on essentialist constructions of culture/religion that tend to homogenize both minority and majority communities. While the model may have some use in spreading the message of tolerance, it does not permit diversity or dissent within the constructions of identity it proposes. The state, in tandem with the power brokers of minority communities, accepts as "authentic" interpretations of identity that are more often than not imagined and mythologized as the way life exists "back home" in countries of origin. "Back home," if it ever was home in the first place, is perceived as fixed and unchanging. Connections between fundamentalist projects in the Indian subcontinent and the diaspora have combined with the increased alienation of minorities in a racist "new world order" to justify the need to preserve "authentic" identities by fundamentalists in minority communities. At the same time, however, preserving authenticity becomes a means to maintain power and control over resources and institutions. Deploying the discourse of tolerance and equality, the state in fact permits the community's spokesmen to trade the autonomy and rights of individual women for some degree of communal autonomy. Communal autonomy in the main means control over the family and so over women and children and over matters to do with the religious and cultural life of minority communities.

More generally, such a critique of multiculturalism points to the wider failures of secular democracy in Britain. Far from being tolerant, the modern British state in fact practices a form of secularism that is intolerant of minority communities even where it appears to permit and maintain their cultural autonomy. Despite the common claim that Church and State are separate in practice if not in principle, the British state can perhaps be more appropriately termed a Christian secular state, given the way in which notions of racial and religious superiority continue to underpin its relations with minorities. The question then is how to reappropriate the term *secularism* and prevent this fundamental principle of democracy from being transformed into a mere front or guise by which the dominant community in Britain, through all its various political, social, and cultural institutions, exercises economic and political power over minority communities via policies that range from direct exploitation and discrimination to appeasement. This is the vital question that WAF is attempting to confront — in recognizing that the control of women's minds and bodies is the price that is being paid to shore up the uneasy harmony of multicultural Britain.

WAF's focus on multiculturalism has translated into support for specific struggles waged by women from different collectivities and, more importantly, in developing a common long-term agenda for resistance. Within WAF, women from Irish, Jewish, and Asian backgrounds, for example, have been able to share experiences of struggle from their respective communities. Our analysis of multiculturalism has led to support for runaway Asian women who are hunted down by networks of men keen to preserve communal and fundamentalist identities, Jewish families who have been harassed for daring to break ranks within their communities by speaking out about child sexual abuse, Irish women seeking rights to information on abortion and contraception, and African women who are struggling for recognition of female genital mutilation as an abuse of women's human rights. In the last case, we were able to organize a joint demonstration with African women's groups against a local authority (Brent) that attempted to legitimize female genital mutilation as a cultural and religious practice that ought to be respected and tolerated.

While struggles may be led by women who experience firsthand the brunt of attacks on their autonomy, support is readily forthcoming from women of other ethnic and cultural backgrounds. This in turn feeds into a political and theoretical framework that is capable of reconceptualizing notions of community, identity, culture, racism, and religion and of articulating a common political program of joint action. Nira Yuval-Davis describes how coalition politics should work: "We should see all feminist (and other forms of democratic) politics as a form of coalition politics in which differences among women would be recognized and given a voice, without fixating the boundaries of this coalition in terms of 'who' we are but in terms of what we want to achieve." She goes on to say that, unlike identity politics, "there is no attempt to assimilate the women who come from different backgrounds. Differences in ethnicity and points of view — and the resulting different agendas — are recognized and respected. But what is celebrated is the common political stance of WAF members, as advocating 'the third way' against fundamentalism and against racism."[19]

WAF has tried to tread the thorny and awkward multicultural terrain, offering support and solidarity to women across the racial and ethnic divides and recognizing the threats posed by religious fundamentalism to all women. Solidarity, however, is dependent on our understanding of the nature of the British state and its connections, historical and contemporaneous, to the structures of oppression that reinforce the oppression of women globally. As a coalition of antiracist black and white feminists, we have come a long way in working across race from the Krishna Sharma days, when the struggle to have a united women's front/alliance to fight domestic violence was particularly acute and difficult. Then the need for alliances was vital because we were operating in a climate in which the fight against racism was celebrated over the silencing of other modes of oppression, and feminism was a series of separate and exclusive groups that undermined the possibilities of joint action across ethnic and racial groupings. Ten years later, the possibility of organizing as a coalition of feminists has become a reality because of the central place given by feminists within WAF to the need to critique the British state, challenging new and old forms of racism and the secularizing of religions into new forms of "fundamentalism."

NOTES

The title of this essay borrows from a Southall Black Sisters song, an ironic echo of the 1984 miners' slogan, "Arthur Scargill walks on water." Arthur Scargill was the left-wing leader of the miners' union, the National Union of Miners.
1. This summary of WAF principles is adapted from the founding statement published in the journal *Women Against Fundamentalism,* available from WAF, 129 Seven Sisters Road, London N7.
2. In Britain of the 1980s, *black* designated African, African Caribbean, and Asian peoples and was used in ways not dissimilar to the term *people of color* in the United States. The term *black* was adopted by SBS to express the politics of the group and to reflect the commonality of struggles and experiences, especially around racism and colonialism. At the time, it was more readily acceptable than it now is to radical Asians as a unifying term denoting the fight against racism. Much of the early thinking of SBS borrowed from the wider black left traditions of struggle, particularly from the United States.
3. Owing to the differences between Asian and African Caribbean women's concerns, there have been difficulties in forging stable coalitions. In the early 1980s, SBS was to join the national black feminist forum, Organization of Women of African/Caribbean and Asian Descent (OWAAD). Many members attended the first national black feminist conference, which promoted an agenda that directly opposed the white feminist movement and that was critical of a

notion of "sisterhood" that failed to address racism and the needs of black women. The conference, however, was rife with conflict about the exact meaning of the term *black feminism*. It was difficult to sustain a broad united front, as there were many political views and perspectives, the main fault lines occurring around the issues of sexuality and Afro-Asian unity. The differences were insurmountable and led to the demise of the national forum.

4. See Southall Black Sisters, ed., *Against the Grain: A Celebration of Struggle and Survival* (Southall: Southall Black Sisters, 1990), for an account of the history and work of SBS.

5. See Gita Sahgal, "Fundamentalism and the Multi-Culturalist Fallacy," in *Against the Grain,* ed. Southall Black Sisters (Southall: Southall Black Sisters, 1990), for a complete version of the statement.

6. See Pragna Patel, "Alert for Action — Women Living under Muslim Laws, Dossiers 1–6," *Feminist Review* 37 (spring 1991): 95–102, for a detailed account of this case.

7. Printed in *Guardian,* 26 May 1989.

8. For a lively account of recent dramatic events in the Republic of Ireland, see Ailbhe Smyth, "States of Change: Reflections on Ireland in Several Uncertain Parts," *Feminist Review* 50 (summer 1995), special issue, *The Irish Issue, the British Question,* 24–43.

9. See Clara Connolly, "Communalism: Obstacle to Social Change," in *Women: A Cultural Review* 2, no. 3 (winter 1991): 214–219, for a partial account of my experience of Northern Ireland.

10. Nira Yuval-Davis and Floya Anthias, *Women–Nation–State* (London: Macmillan 1989).

11. See, for example, Eavan Boland, *A Kind of Scar: The Woman Poet in a National Tradition,* Lip pamphlet (Dublin: Attic Press, 1989).

12. Homi Bhabha, "Down among the Writers," *New Statesmen and Society* (28 July 1989), 39.

13. Gita Sahgal names such sites of autonomy "secular spaces": see "Secular Spaces: The Experience of Asian Women Organizing," in *Refusing Holy Orders,* ed. Gita Sahgal and Nira Yuval-Davis (London: Virago, 1991).

14. Talal Asad, *The Genealogy of Religion* (Baltimore: Johns Hopkins University Press, 1993), 252.

15. Swann Committee, *Education for All,* report of the Committee of Enquiry into the Education of Children from Ethnic Minority Groups (London: HMSO, 1985).

16. Raymond Williams, *Politics and Letters* (London: Verso, 1979), 119–120.

17. A. Sivanandan, "All That Melts into Air is Solid," *Race and Class* 31, no. 3 (January–March 1990): 24–29.

18. Julia Bard, "The Outsiders," *Guardian* 28 August 1991.

19. Nira Yuval-Davis, "Women and Empowerment," in *Feminism and Psychology* (Boulder, CO: Sage, 1994).

IV

WORLD CULTURE AND PRACTICE

JOSÉ RABASA

Of Zapatismo: Reflections on the Folkloric and the Impossible in a Subaltern Insurrection

Usted se está equivocando demasiado con la decisión que ha tomado en contra de nosotros, usted cree que matando los Zapatistas de Chiapas o matando al subcomandante Marcos puede acabar con esta lucha. No señor Zedillo, la lucha Zapatista está en todo México, Zapata no ha muerto, vive y vivirá siempre. [You are equivocating too much with the decision you have taken against us. You believe that killing the Zapatistas of Chiapas or killing Subcomandante Marcos can end this struggle. No, Mr. Zedillo, the Zapatista struggle is in all of Mexico. Zapata is not dead; he is alive and will live forever.] COMITÉ CLANDESTINO REVOLUCIONARIO INDÍGENA[1]

In seeking to learn to speak to (rather than listen to or speak for) the historically muted subject of the subaltern woman, the postcolonial intellectual *systematically* "unlearns" privilege. GAYATRI CHAKRAVORTY SPIVAK[2]

"Todos somos indios." La consigna es inobjetable en la medida en que asume el orgullo (novedad histórica) por un componente básico de la nacionalidad. Pero qué decir de "Todos somos Marcos"? La frase parece en exceso retórica, fruto de la pasión militarista, del frenesí romántico o de la escenografía mesiánica. ["We are all Indians." The slogan of the demonstrations is unobjectionable insofar as it expresses pride (a historical novelty) for a basic component of nationality. But what can we say about "We are all Marcos"? This phrase seems to be too rhetorical, the fruit of militaristic passion, of a romantic frenzy or of a messianic scenography.] CARLOS MONSIVÁIS[3]

One of the urgent tasks in the study of subaltern insurrections is to find ways of understanding the compatibility of modern and nonmodern cultural and political practices.[4] Although the "Carta a Zedillo" by the Comité Clandestino Revolucionario Indígena, Comandancia General (Clandestine Indigenous Revolutionary Committee, General Command, CCRI-CG), reached me in Ann Arbor, through the Internet, that most modern — perhaps postmodern — form of communication, it manifests a *folkloric* understanding of revolutionary agency ("Zapata no ha muerto, vive y vivirá para siempre [Zapata is not dead; he is alive and will live forever]") and a willingness to taunt the *impossible* by asserting a communicable Indian discourse beyond its immediate, local situation (an effort to internationalize the Zapatista call for democracy, liberty, and justice). Another communiqué from the CCRI-CG, printed in *La Jornada,* 16 April 1995, further illustrates a folkloric Zapatismo with a millenarian evocation of Votán Zapata: "Votán Zapata es el uno que camina en el corazón de todos y cada uno de los hombres y mujeres verdaderos. Todos nosotros somos uno en Votán Zapata y el es uno en todos nosotros [Votán Zapata is the one that walks in the heart of all and each of the true men and women. We are all one in Votán Zapata and he is one in all of us]." Votán, "guardian and heart of the people," a pre-Columbian Tzeltal and Tzotzil god, also names the third day of the twenty-day period and is the night lord of the third *trecena* (thirteen twenty-day periods) of the Tonalamatl ("count of the days," the Mesoamerican divinatory calendar), and merges with Emiliano Zapata within a poignant view of the power inherent in the multitude as one and the one as the multitude. This communiqué commemorates the betrayal and death of Zapata on 10 April 1919. A communiqué from 1993, also communicating Zapata's death, places Votán Zapata within a 501-year period of resistance ("Votán Zapata, tímido fuego que en nuestra muerte vivió 501 años [Votán Zapata, timid fire that in our death has lived 501 years]") and elaborates in more detail on the one/multitude nature of Votán Zapata:

Es y no es todo en nosotros . . . Caminando está . . . Votán Zapata, guardián y corazón del pueblo. Amo de la noche . . . Señor de la montaña . . . Nosotros . . . Votán, guardian y corazón del pueblo. Uno y muchos es. Ninguno y todos. Estado viene. Votán Votán, guardian y corazón. [Is and is not everything in us . . . He is walking . . . Votán Zapata, guardian and heart of the people. Master of the night . . . Lord of the mountains . . . Us . . . Votán Zapata, guardian and heart of the people. None and all . . . As being is coming . . . Votán Zapata, guardian and heart of the people.][5]

According to Eduard Seler, Votán may very well correspond not only to Tepevollotl of the Nahuas and Pitas-Xoo of the Zapotecs, but also to the bat god of the Cakchiqueles.[6]

Of all the communiqués, this is the one that appears to have struck a vital chord among the radicalized youth, whose preference for rock and roll has very little in common with the oral traditions and music choices of the young Indians comprising the Ejército Zapatista de la Liberación Nacional (Zapatista Army of National Liberation EZLN). The impact of this communiqué can perhaps be attested by the prominence given to Votán and the archetypical resonance of the ubiquitous ski masks in articles published in *La Guillotina,* a student publication from UNAM (Universidad Nacional Autónoma de México).[7] By the way, the motto

of *La Guillotina* is "¡Exigid lo imposible! [Demand the impossible!]."
In reflecting on Zapatismo, we ought to avoid reductive readings of
folklore and retain the impossible as a utopian horizon of alternative
rationalities to those dominant in the West. This reflection informs our
critique of the ideological constraints that have kept intellectual discourse from giving serious consideration to hybrid cultural and political practices that combine modern and nonmodern forms.

The Zapatista rebellion in Chiapas makes full use of the new technologies that circulate local news in global contexts — their political
and physical survival depends on this flow of information. The Zapatistas, furthermore, deploy the new modes of communication along
with consensus politics based on ancestral communalism, just as the indigenous peoples of Chiapas use Western medicine along with *naguales*
(animal soul companions) and shamans.[8] Gary Gossen argues that shamans and *naguales* have as much to do with the spiritual health of the
self as of the community: "Once afflicted [by a disequilibrium of the
causal forces that determine fate], the only traditional way to remedy
one's condition is to hire a shaman to intervene on one's behalf by
performing rituals whose primary goal is to restore equilibrium to the
several individual spirits that influence the body's well being. In practice, however, the shaman also addresses the matter of restoring harmony and equilibrium to one's social relations."[9] The factors that determine individual destinies are "predetermined but also, secondarily,
subject to the agency of and will of others, both human and supernatural."[10] Indian beliefs in co-essences, according to Gossen, should
be understood as "a fluid language of social analysis and social integration."[11] They complement Western medicine: Whereas antibiotics cure
the individual, shamans also have the task of situating the individual in
the cosmos and guiding him or her through the surrounding social
reality. These possibilities of using modern science and technology
without being forced to disavow one's knowledge is a new historical
configuration. It can be argued that the three Ladinos who immersed
themselves in the Selva Lacandona ten years ago were able to tap into
Indians' long history of rebellion only as a result of *learning to talk to*
the community and subjecting themselves to its authority.[12] With a few
modifications (not only *women* subalterns or *female* privilege), the
epigraph from Gayatri Spivak applies to the three anonymous Ladinos
(for all the speaking Marcos does) who unlearned privilege in the formation of the EZLN.

Carlos Monsiváis's comments on the slogans shouted in *yesterday*'s
march in Mexico City would seem to reiterate the uniqueness of this
new historical configuration. Monsiváis goes on to make the distinc-

tion between those who might very well have conflicting vocation and those who identify themselves with Marcos in the sense of "if you condemn Marcos for wanting a better world, a more just Mexico, you might as well condemn me and all of us who want the same." Given the circumstances of the offensive by the army (the witch hunts, the tortures), it is understandable (strategically correct) to call for peace, but to place all the emphasis on sharing the condemnation (and ultimately the martyrdom) is to ignore the military nature of the EZLN. In the "Todos somos Marcos," we ought to also hear a will to resist and fight back. For there is, if not a messianic, an eschatological note in the Zapatista call for justice that goes well beyond a "more just Mexico." Monsiváis's remarks, though clearly sympathetic with the cause, manifest the *impossibility of* the EZLN's subaltern narrative: impossibility in the sense of their incompatibility with "modern" narratives. If this issue of the impossibility of subaltern narratives clearly removes us from the urgency of the immediate events in Chiapas, it also helps us focus on the philosophical significance of the indigenous discursive modalities of the EZLN.

To clear the ground for a serious consideration of the subaltern discourse of the Zapatistas, this essay draws a critique of Gramsci's blindness to the folkloric (I owe this posing of the question to David Lloyd) and addresses recent scholarship that has begun to supersede this interpretative limitation. This theoretical reexamination seeks to understand how the EZLN can constitute itself as a vanguard that is precisely grounded in its self-conscious subalternity, that is, as an instance of the counterhegemony of the diverse. On the basis of a new ethics, politics, and epistemology of subaltern studies, the second part of this essay moves on to examine the discourse on subalternity that Marcos and the CCRI-CG have elaborated since their revolt on 1 January 1995. It examines how their communiqués have been interpreted from several perspectives that range from condemnations of the violence and illegality of the Zapatistas to understandings of the EZLN in terms of a history of guerrilla warfare in Mexico since the 1960s.[13] These articles and books have tended to be written either as a privileging of Marcos over the indigenous communities (it was Marcos's ethnographic acumen that enabled the mobilization of the Indians) or as an unmasking of the Zapatistas that reveals their links to Bishop Samuel Ruiz, Marcos's appropriation of the Indian "voices" in the communiqués from the CCRI-CG, and the absence of a "real" army. The critique of these readings enables us, however, to elucidate the subaltern nature of the EZLN and a narrative of the impossible in the communiqués. The apparent impossibility of the project has as much to do with the denial of a credible Indian-led insurgency as with a hegemonic consensus among Mexican intellectuals that revolution was not an option anymore in Latin America, leaving reform as the only viable political process. As for the government's delegation in the negotiations, Mayor Rolando has put it succinctly: "Es imposible que el gobierno comprenda lo que estamos pidiendo [It is impossible for the government to understand what we are asking]."[14] As we will see in this essay, the Zapatistas attribute the incapacity of the government—as well as of intellectuals—to address their demands to a mixture of moral ineptness (cannot understand what dignity means), racism (cannot dialogue with Indians on an equal basis), and intellectual torpidity (cannot understand the terms of a new communist revolution). The peace talks are proving to be hard lessons for the government on how to speak to subalterns.

It is generally accepted that 1989 marked a radical break in the history of the Left. The fall of the Berlin wall is often taken as marking the "demise" of socialism.[15] The sight of jubilant East Germans gawking at the commodities of the West made manifest the failure to institute a socialist ethic within socialist societies of Eastern Europe. Indeed, these masses soon became a dangerous Other as Western intellectuals and the press perceived them as lacking a democratic worldview. Rather than celebrating a "triumph" of democracy or passing judgment, we ought to read the events of 1989 as manifesting a distance between the ends of the socialist state and the desires of civil society. The closest parallel event in the Americas was the Sandinistas' defeat in the 1990 elections in Nicaragua. What we witness in these events is a failure of the Left to *represent* the interests of the people.[16] This crisis in political representation had an aesthetic antecedent in socialist realism as early as the 1930s in the Soviet Union. Instead of posing the will to represent as a generally misguided project of the West, subaltern studies would ultimately foreground, as John Beverley has put it, "the inadequacy of the models of intellectual and political protagonist that correspond to the period of liberation struggle in the sixties in which many of us were formed."[17]

As we reflect on Zapatismo we must go beyond representation or even performance, which is ultimately a modality of the former. There is much to gain if we view the insurrection in terms of Antonio Negri's concept of constituent subjectivities: "Constituent power against constituted power, constituent power as singular subjectivity, as productivity and cooperation, that asks how to be situated in society—how to develop its own creativity."[18] In one of his most recent communiqués Subcomandante Marcos establishes a connection with labor movements in Italy that suggests a connection with Negri. Under the figure of his literary interlocutor Durito (the Little Hard One), a scarab, Marcos conveys his solidarity with the Fiat workers in Turin by giving to their cause the pay he received for a contribution to a collection of essays. I will return to this communiqué later on, but for now I would like to give as an example of Negri's concept of emergent subjectivities, in addition to the "Todos somos Marcos" slogan in Monsiváis's letter, the massive demonstration on May 1, where the unemployed, street children, housewives, alternative unions, small businessmen, and radicalized high school students marched together. Chiapas turns out to be a metonym for the nation: beyond the Zapatista's local struggle, the EZLN demands a national debate over the meaning and future of democracy in Mexico. A recent communiqué from the CCRI-CG, moreover, suggests the basis for a new internationalism: "Llamamos a todos, a legales y a clandestinos, armados y pacíficos, civiles y militares, a todos los que luchan, en todas las formas, en todos los niveles y en todas partes por la democracia, la libertad y la justicia en el mundo [We call on all, legal and clandestine, armed and pacifist, civilian and military, on all who struggle, by all means, on every level and everywhere for democracy, liberty and justice in the world]."[19] As we will see later on, the political program of the Zapatistas calls for the multiple engagement of democratic groups, for the creation of a political space where different positions may confront each other rather than a pluralistic centrist position.

There is no doubt that the discourse of power has devised forms of representation with a capacity to objectify, know, and control sociocultural and geopolitical domains on a global scale.[20] A Foucauldian perspective would map sites of power as well as of resistance. The task of a specifically Latin American subaltern studies project, confronted with a phenomenon like the Zapatistas, would not limit itself, however, to an affirmation of resistance, a documentation of fluid identities and social fragmentation, or a study of emergent citizenships and new political movements.[21] As I will point out later on, the study of new social movements and patterns of resistant subalternity must devise an epistemology that curtails the appropriation of its findings by dominant discourse. Although subaltern studies has much to learn from, in fact, has built on postmodern theories, the project cannot limit itself to understandings of power that ignore oppositions such as dominant classes vis-à-vis dominated subjects or the colonizer vis-à-vis the colonized. These oppositions tend to be dismissed as instances of Western binary thinking. But these oppositions — as in the case of subalternity — are not stable but relational. For if subalternity partakes of hegemony and consensus, it is no less urgent to examine how subaltern subjects are constituted through dominance and coercion. War, in this regard, would not be an exceptional state of affairs, but the course of the world. Consensus would then be the result of a discursive violence that has been interiorized.

Less concerned with identifying and studying "subalterns" as positive entities, the project as I envision it would call for an analysis of the mechanisms that produce subalternity as well as the formulation of political and cultural practices that would end it. But before dwelling on issues pertaining to the ethics, politics, and epistemologies of subaltern studies, I will draw a critique of Gramsci's blindness to the folkloric.

Antonio Gramsci first used the term *subaltern* in his *Notes on Italian History*. His writings also inaugurated the concept of hegemony as a new mode of understanding ideology. Although readings of Gramsci have a long history in Latin America (including Laclau's early work, *Politics and Ideology*),[22] they have tended not to be critical of his finally elitist conception of Culture or his conception of the corresponding counterhegemonic blocs.[23] Gramsci's notion of the folkloric, which he opposes to the modern conception of the historical emergence of national Culture, needs to be critiqued to make space to comprehend the dynamics of subaltern movements. What is at stake in this critique is the compatibility of modern and nonmodern forms of culture and politics and not the celebration of some sort of pristine indigenous community. We must keep in mind, nonetheless, that the possibility of critiquing the ideology of progress is a recent phenomenon not readily available to Gramsci.

For Gramsci, notions of popular culture and indigenous knowledge were incompatible with his understanding of a Culture that could be established as a counterhegemony. As Gramsci put it in "The Modern Prince," one must study elements of popular psychology "in order to transform them, by educating them, into a modern mentality."[24] His understanding of cultural politics unavoidably privileged Western conceptions of knowledge, art, and ethics — evidently, of History. The elaboration of a counterhegemonic culture signified an alternative modernity that would transform premodern subjects. In "On education," Gramsci wrote: "The first, primary grade should not last longer than three or four years, and in addition to imparting the first 'instrumental' notions of schooling — reading, writing, sums, geography, history — ought in particular to deal with an aspect of education which is now neglected — i.e. with 'rights' and 'duties,' with the first notions of the

State and society as primordial elements of a new conception of the world which challenges the conceptions that are imparted by the various traditional social environments, i.e. the conceptions which can be termed folkloristic."[25] The "folkloristic" would reduce all forms of knowledge not bound by Western criteria of truth to superstition at worst and to unexamined "common sense" at best. "Common sense," in this regard, would parallel what semioticians call natural signs, that is, an uncritical understanding of the world where the signifier bypasses the signified and is thus identified with its referents. The history of philosophy, in itself, would be a chronicle of the institutionalization of "common sense": "Every philosophical current leaves behind a sedimentation of 'common sense': this is the document of its historical effectiveness."[26] For Gramsci, "common sense" continually transforms itself as it incorporates scientific ideas and philosophical opinions into everyday life: " 'Common sense' is the folklore of philosophy, and is always half way between folklore properly speaking and the philosophy, science, and economics of the specialists."[27] This understanding of "common sense" as the folklore of philosophy enables us to turn this concept against Gramsci by pointing out that the reduction of what he terms "traditional social environments" to folklore is in itself a manifestation of philosophical folklore. I term this critical gesture a form of *enlightened de-enlightenment*.

Although "common sense" and folklore were clearly inferior forms of knowledge in Gramsci's assessment, their role in rebellions and insurrections — especially of the peasant — cannot be ignored. If he was critical of voluntarism, of instinct (and called for a transformation of peasants' mentality by modernity), subaltern insurgencies would call for a theoretical reflection rather than a dismissal on grounds of insufficient consciousness — lacking plans in advance or not following a theoretical line. Theory, then, should hold a dialectical relation with movements of revolt that fall out of the schema of historico-philosophical outlooks. The task of subaltern studies, as defined in this essay, would be to conceptualize multiple possibilities of creative political action rather than requiring a more "mature" political type of formation. Subaltern studies, therefore, would not pretend to have a privileged access to subalterns; rather, it would define intellectual work as one more intervention in insurgent movements. In developing practices the intellectual would grow parallel to the emergent social actors and their interventions in everyday life.

We may now consider Gramsci's position and the prominence subaltern studies gives to negation in the context of Gautam Bhadra's analysis of the 1857 rebellion in India.[28] Bhadra concludes his study with a brief allusion to fragmentary leadership in peasant insurrections: "Yet this episodic and fragmentary narrative points to the existence in 1857 of what Gramsci has called 'multiple elements of conscious leadership' at the popular level."[29] Bhadra's account works against dismissals of the indigenous leaders' role in the insurrection as "minor incidents" by academic historians like S. N. Sen in *Eighteen Fifty-Seven*,[30] or their mockery as "mushroom dignities" by soldier historians like R. H. W. Dunlop in *Service and Adventure with the Khakee Ressalah or, Meerut Volunteer Horse, during the Mutinies of 1857–58*.[31] In Bhadra's account, the indigenous leaders played an integral role in the popular insurrection. The four leaders shared ordinariness and had learned to use the logic of insurrection in the practice of everyday life: "The consciousness with which they all fought had been 'formed through everyday experience'; it was an 'elementary historical acquisition.'" Bhadra's analysis of this rebellion differs in the tone and details of the insurrection from Gramsci's historical examples: "It was the perception and day-to-day experience of the authority of the alien state in his immediate surroundings that determined the rebel's action."[32] Though one could argue that the situation of Sardinia and the Italian south in general was one of internal colonialism, Gramsci's counterhegemonic state and project of modernity would reinscribe the south within a narrative that posits historical development. In the case of the British Empire the colonial situation foreclosed a connection, and the consciousness of the rebels was one of insurgency against a colonial power — not against a landed aristocracy, as in the case of what Gramsci conceptualizes as a progressive peasantry, that is, one that does not align itself with the local landlords against the urban leadership of both south and north. In this regard, the work of the Indian subalternists falls within a postcolonial subject position that is fully aware of the colonial impulses that accompany the project of modernity.

This transformation of historiography, however, still believes that the task of tertiary discourse is to recover the place in history *for* subalterns. Its task is to prove that the insurgent can rely on the historian's performance and not that the performance of the insurgent itself can recover his or her place in history. This faith in the historian has less felicitous consequences.

It is not just that positivistic knowledge of subalterns as objects of study runs the risk of providing information to the same institutions that have as their end the control and thus perpetuation of subalternity. Beyond the misuse of empirical knowledge we must question the epistemology that first emerges in the modern period and that we readily identify with the emergence of objectivity and subjectivity in Descartes. This split of the subject and object of knowledge implies a series of forms of disciplining subjectivity. From this perspective the issue would no longer be one of misuse of knowledge, but of the power embedded in the epistemological apparatus itself. The problem would now reside in the production of the subaltern as an object of knowledge, rather than in claiming that subaltern studies will produce a more accurate representation. Subaltern studies cannot continue to practice a Cartesian epistemology where the subject refines his or her cognitive apparatuses to gain a more objective perspective. This modern project would aim to formulate a form of life, a horizon of communication where knowledge would no longer distort its object. But this epistemological end takes for granted a commensurable position that the gaps in resistance texts call into question.[33] It presumes that the form of life of the subaltern can be contained within the objectification of the intellectual. Moreover, it obviates the conflict between Western epistemology (as theory of what we can know and what counts as knowledge) and forms of life with different truth values.

We should instead elaborate inventories of forms of discourse/power that produce subalternity. In this regard, theories of colonial discourse would provide a way to gain access to forms of writing violence in colonialist discourses that informed and gained consolidation in the modernist projects to subject the world to European powers. It is crucial that we retain modernity(ies), European power(s), colonialist discourse(s) in the plural to avoid reifying Reason. The compatibility of the modern projects to subject the world to European powers. It is crucan understanding of reason that does not presuppose a reduction of nonmodern forms of life to the irrational (to locate them in an anterior historical moment — hence, as ineffectual practices). Reason as devised by Kant and Hegel is but one of the possible understandings of modernity. It is only by inventing alternatives to Reason that subaltern studies will devise a counterhegemony that will not generate subalternity in turn. Gramsci's understanding of Culture cannot avoid the need to constitute an intellectual vanguard. If the critique of vanguardism figures prominently in the historiography of the South Asian Subaltern Group, it is a political principle for the Zapatistas. I see this possibility of nonvanguardist meshings of autonomous political movements as the utopian (nevertheless real) horizon of subaltern studies: If Gramscian counterhegemony aspires to state control of truth criteria, the circulation of knowledge, and the consumption of cultural capital, the task of subaltern studies, as I understand its utopian impulse, would not consist of a new administration of capital (cultural or otherwise) but a dissolution of capital's hegemony — not reform, but revolution.

In a key moment in her critique of the South Asian Subaltern Group, Gayatri Spivak suggests an internationalization of historiography that would include "the political economy of the independent peasant movement in Mexico."[34] Spivak's recommendation entails a political economy of the Zapatistas that would avoid (neo)colonialist impulses to situate contemporary communal societies within a developmentalist narrative, and thus to constitute them as incompatible with other forms of property, in fact, as irremediably bound to disappear. This is not the place to elaborate this project in any detail.[35] John Womack documents the astuteness of the Zapatistas in forming an independent movement during the Marxist Revolution of 1910 that was sufficiently powerful to define agrarian policy up to Salinas's recent reforms of Article 27 of the Mexican constitution. And it is not a coincidence that in the armed insurrection of 1 January 1994, the EZLN identified itself with the political theory as well as the military strategies of Zapata without excluding the whole pantheon of national heroes as forebears. One of the last communiqués by the CCRI-CG mocks the identification — unmasking — of EZLN with the Fuerzas de Liberación Nacional (National Liberation Forces):

Al nombre de "Fuerzas de Liberacion Nacional" entre los antecedentes del EZLN, el gobierno debe agregar el de todas las organizaciones guerrilleras de los años 70s y 80s, a Arturo Gámiz, a Lucio Cabañas, a Genaro Vázquez Rojas, a Emiliano Zapata, a Francisco Villa, a Vicente Guerrero, a José María Morelos y Pavón, a Miguel Hidalgo y Costilla, a Benito Juárez y a muchos otros que ya borraron de los libros de historia porque un pueblo con memoria es un pueblo rebelde. [To the name of the "National Liberation Forces" as an antecedent of the EZLN, the government should add the names of the guerrillas from the '70s and '80s, Arturo Gámiz, Lucio Cabañas, Genaro Vázquez Rojas, Emiliano Zapata, Francisco Villa, Vicente Guerrero, José María Morelos y Pavón, Miguel Hidalgo y Costilla, Benito Juárez, and many others that have been erased from history books because a people with a memory is a rebel people.][36]

Womack's and the Zapatistas' narratives are tragic, because they mark not an end of history, but rather a continuation in struggle. Francis Barker has recently argued (against the *bovine* history of the New Historicists) that all history is tragic, but "In contrast to the fetishized memorialization of a dead past, it will certainly have to be a history of the present, shot through with the knowledge and the poetry of that critical part of the present which is the dangerous past."[37] The Zapatistas' injunction "un pueblo con memoria es un pueblo rebelde [a people with a memory is a rebel people]" suggests an open-ended, tragic understanding of Indian insurgency's histories. Womack's concluding comment in the epilogue also suggests a historical narrative without closure: "A foreign visitor winced at seeing them. In this village, he thought, children still learn respect for elders, duty to kin, honor in work and play, curious lessons to carry into a world about to fly a man to the moon, deliberately capable of nuclear war, already guilty of genocide. But being Anenecuilcans, he decided, they would probably stand the strain."[38]

The EZLN stands as a testimony of the endurance of the Anenecuilcans, of indigenous Mexico in general, and, in particular, of Emiliano Zapata's legacy. In the epigraph from the CCRI-CG, the Zapatistas remind Zedillo that this endurance, which should not be seen as a form of essentialism, depends on a living history: "No Señor Zedillo, la lucha Zapatista está en todo México, Zapata no ha muerto, vive y vivirá siempre [No, Mr. Zedillo, Zapata is in all Mexico. Zapata is not dead; he is alive and will live forever]." Zapata did not revolt against the leaders of the Mexican Revolution for a better grant of land, but for what already belonged to the Anenecuilcans. Central to the Zapatistas of Anenecuilco were titles that the community had preserved since the colonial period, titles for land that was legally theirs. In this respect their claims are like those of all Native Americans, for whom land redistribution would imply legitimating the usurpation of what was theirs from the start. As Womack points out: "The land titles Zapata's uncle passed on to him in September 1909 were almost sacred documents. It was no mere bundle of legal claims that Zapata took charge of, but the collected testimony to the honor of all Anenecuilco chiefs before him, the accumulated trust of all past generations in the pueblo. This was his responsibility. And when a year and a half later he decided to commit the village to revolution, he buried the titles under the floor of its church."[39] Contrary to Gramsci's claim that subalterns, in their struggles, "have left no reliable document," the Anenecuilcans have passed from generation to generation a record of their historical rights. If the Anenecuilcans contradict the lack of documents, Gramsci would be partially right when he asserts that subalterns "have not achieved any consciousness of the class 'for itself.' "[40] But this judgment implies that Indian insurgency would embody a legitimate political consciousness only when inscribed in terms of Western history. There was a utopian element in Zapata's revolt precisely in that it did not understand itself in terms of a Western telos but as an ever-present possibility of reclaiming its communal lands. Moreover, Zapata also saw very clearly the need to intervene in — and certainly not be absorbed by — national politics to achieve local ends. The Plan de Ayala testifies to his lucidity.[41]

Although Zapata and the EZLN exemplify indigenous insurgency, the subaltern, as the "Founding Statement" of the Latin American Subaltern Studies Group puts it, should be understood as a migrating subject that includes "an array of the masses — peasants, proletarians, the informal and formal sectors, the sub- and underemployed, vendors, those outside or at the margin of the money economy, lumpens and ex-lumpens of all sorts, children, the growing numbers of the homeless. . . ."[42] Colonial documents on indigenous rebellions without fail give prominence to the leadership of women and make mention of blacks, mulattoes, and mestizos joining ranks with Indians; in the case of the Zapatistas, they find support among urban lumpenproletarians who wear the ubiquitous ski mask at rock concerts or in the recent demonstrations as a symbol of solidarity. Marcos's characterization of the *México de abajo,* from below (vis-à-vis the Mexico of the penthouse, the middle floor, and the basement), vividly portrays subaltern rage: "El México de abajo tiene vocación de lucha, es solidario, es banda, es barrio, es palomilla, es raza, es cuate, es huelga, es marcha y mitín, es toma tierras, es cierre de carreteras, es 'no les creo!' es 'no me dejo,' es ¡órale!' "[43] This popular language cannot be translated without distortion.[44] For instance, *banda* or *palomilla* would call for "gang," but Marcos emphasizes a vocation for solidarity. The "no les creo [I don't believe you]," "no me dejo [I will not take it]" sums up the "¡órale!" which something like "enough" would hardly do justice to. Elsewhere I have traced this same *México de abajo* in the context of a 1692 rebellion in Mexico City.[45] There, as in the case of the demonstrators, there is a solidarity with the Indians: "Todos somos indios," "Todos somos Marcos." One can hear the "¡órale!"

The state-sponsored ideology of *mestizaje* after the 1910 Revolution theoretically should have extended bonds of solidarity with Indians, but its historical effect was to promote a systematic denial of Indian roots — though the pre-Columbian past was idealized — and a program of acculturation that aimed to destroy indigenous languages and cultures. Only "mestizos" were deemed by the state to be authentic Mexicans. In this regard the "Todos somos Indios" would seem to augur (at least on a symbolic plane) the possibility of a radical change in the structures of feeling where the plurality of the Indian peoples of Mexico would be recognized and respected. This emergent sensibility would ultimately depend on the indigenous leadership and its capacity to negotiate on its own with the government. In this regard the porosity among Indian groups in rural Mexico and the corresponding responses from urban subalterns would differ from subalterns in India, who seem to be less mobile, communicative, and communicable. This difference, however, has as much to do with a long history of insurrections in Mexico where Indians occupied the same urban and rural spaces with the *castas* (racial mixtures that colonial documents laboriously break up ad infinitum — namely, beyond mestizos and mulattoes, documents identify *zambaigos* [Indian and Chinese], *lobos* [Indian and African], *pardos* [mestizo and African], *castizos* [mestizo and Spaniard], and so on). These classifications clearly have a very different meaning than the caste system in India, and a very different history. Not only is there a memory continuum (obviously with different interpretations in time, as in any other culture) in the remembrance of past Indian insurrections, but also of the *México de abajo*.

We should heed, nevertheless, the CCRI-CG's constant insistence on the Indian leadership of the EZLN in the face of the government's and the press's accusations of manipulation by "profesionales de la violencia [professionals of violence]": "Lo reiteramos, el EZLN es una organización de mexicanos, mayoritariamente indígena, dirigida por un comité colegiado de las distintas etnias de Chiapas y no tiene, en su composición absolutamente a ningún miembro no indígena [We reiterate it, the EZLN is an organization of Mexicans, with an Indian majority, directed by a committee that gathers all the different ethnic groups of Chiapas and does not have, in its composition, one single member that is not an Indian]."[46]

This statement suggests that nationalism as a mode of relating communities without erasing their linguistic and cultural specificities should be taken seriously as a subaltern political program that should not be "folklorized." If the specificity of the Zapatistas and the history of Mexico should not be erased through a reading that draws parallelisms with rebellions in India and elsewhere in Southeast Asia, the rhetorics of counterinsurgency that Ranajit Guha has identified[47] are nonetheless germane to the Mexican government's policies that have attempted to contain Marcos and infantilize the Zapatistas. For instance, some sectors of the press in the days that followed the rebellion dismissed the first communiqués that listed NAFTA as one of the motivations for the rebellion. How could Indians understand NAFTA without foreign advisors? This same press has consistently condemned the insurgency as illegal violence.[48] A recent collection of articles condemning the violence, proscribing the utopian impulse, suggesting that international drug dealers financed the EZLN, blaming liberation theology and the bishop of San Cristobal de Las Casas, Samuel Ruiz, for the violence, and unmasking the manipulation of the Indians by Marcos has been published with the title *La guerra de las ideas* (The war of ideas). The title gives the impression that its contributors are the only ones who carry out a legitimate "war of ideas." The question is against whom, for at least some of the articles — even though they do not fully sympathize with the taking up of arms by the EZLN — suggest that they are also waging a "war of ideas" against the government. But the editor of the book never seems to consider the violent nature and implications of the moral superiority he ascribes to the contributors to the volume. What do you do to outlaws? What about the communiqués of Marcos and the CCRI-CG that call for dialogue and carry out war by other means, as Clausewitz would put it? In spite of the communiqués' mastery of media, some quarters of the press still disparage their *literary* quality. Most of the contributors chose to ignore that NAFTA was the culmination — the icing on the cake — of neoliberal policies that Salinas had been implementing during his *sexenio*.

Of particular relevance to Chiapas was Salinas's reform of Article 27 of the constitution that had "guaranteed that villages had the right to hold property as corporations, that the pueblo was a legitimate institution in the new order [of the 1910 Mexican Revolution]."[49] Marcos underscored this point several times in the February 1995 interviews held with Blanche Petrich and Elio Henríquez for *La Jornada:*

Esas reformas cancelaron toda posibilidad legal de tener tierra, que era lo que finalmente los mantenía como grupo paramilitar de autodefensa. Luego llegó el fraude electoral del '88 y ahí los compañeros vieron que tampoco el voto servía porque no se respetaba lo que era evidente. Estos dos fueron los detonantes, pero a mi se me hace que lo que más radicalizó a los compañeros fue la reforma al artículo 27, esa fue la puerta que se les cerró a los indígenas para sobrevivir de manera legal y pacífica. Por eso se alzaron en armas, para que se les oyera, porque ya estaban cansados de pagar una cuota de sangre tan alta. [Those reforms canceled all legal possibilities of their holding land. And that possibility is what had kept them functioning as paramilitary self-defense groups. Then came the electoral fraud of 1988. The compañeros saw that voting didn't matter either because there was no respect for basic things. These were the two detonators, but in my view it was the reform of Article 27 that most radicalized the compañeros. That reform closed the door on the indigenous people's strategies for surviving legally and peacefully. That's why they rose up in arms, so that they would be heard.][50]

The Zapatista uprising in January presented itself as a response to the sellout of the country to transnational corporations. As El Sup (the nickname often given to Marcos, mocking Superman as in *superclinton*) has put it, the Indians in Chiapas are among the last few patriots that are willing to fight for the country. In the interview Marcos cites the CCRI-CG's motivation for taking arms: "Porque nosotros, lo que no estamos de acuerdo es que nuestro país se venda al extranjero. Como quiera, morir de hambre pasa, pero lo que no pasa es que en este país mande otro que no sea mexicano [We disagree with selling our country to foreigners. Although we can live with starvation, we cannot accept that this country be ruled by someone that is not a Mexican]."[51] This nationalist statement has very little to do with the state-sponsored nationalism of the PRI — a nationalism that, by the way, also informs the tourist industry that has confined indigenous cultures to curio shops, museums, and archaeological sites.

As in the case of Bhadra's rebels, the Zapatista leadership has a clear understanding of the national situation based on a historical experience. Unlike Bhadra's individualized rebels, the Zapatista contingent includes, besides Marcos, a number of leaders *sin cara* (faceless) and *sin nombre* (nameless) — with the noms de guerre of Comandantes Tacho, David, and Trinidad and Mayor Rolando — who have, nevertheless, gained visibility and a voice in interviews they have held with the press. It is important to note that the CCRI-CG has kept Marcos from participating in the recent peace negotiations with the government. This subordination of Marcos has as much to do with safeguarding him as with keeping in check his protagonist tendencies. The representatives in the round of talks of April and May 1995 were once more infantilized, and in the discussions in July there seems to have been a breakdown with regard to the Zapatista demands for respect for their dignity. Tacho deplores but also mocks the ineptness of the representatives from the government:

También nos dijeron que están estudiando mucho que es la dignidad, que están consultando y haciendo estudios de la dignidad. Que lo que más podían entender era que la dignidad era el servicio a los demás. Y nos pidieron que nosotros les dijéramos que entendemos por dignidad. Les respondimos que sigan con la investigación. A nosotros nos da risa y nos reímos frente a ellos. [They also told us that they were studying very much what is dignity, that they are doing research and studies on dignity. What could understand more was that dignity was service to others. And they asked us to tell them what dignity means to us. We answered them that they should go on with their research. It makes us laugh, and we laughed in their faces.][52]

The collective memory of five hundred years of oppression enables the Zapatista leadership to link local demands to a national agenda. When blamed for wasting time in the negotiations with such issues as respect for dignity, the Zapatista delegation, according to Tacho, responded that "nosotros no somos los culpables, todos los indígenas de México llevamos cinco siglos con la pobreza, el desprecio y con la marginación [we told them that we were not to be blamed because all the Indians of Mexico have lived for the last five hundred years in poverty, disdain, and marginalization]."[53]

The emergence of the Zapatista movement with an Indian feminine leadership also signals a recentering of rationality and the nation in and on Indian terms. Marcos is subordinated to the CCRI-CG, which in turn arrived at the decision of going to war after the committee of each community consulted its members: "los Comités pasaron a preguntar a cada hombre, a cada mujer, a cada niño si ya era tiempo de hacer la guerra o no [the committees went on to ask each man, each woman, each child if it was time to go to war or not]."[54] When queried why women and children participated in the revolutionary organization, Ramona, who is described as a small comandante, responded: "Porque las mujeres también están viviendo en una situación más difícil, porque las mujeres son ellas que están más explotadas, oprimidas fuertemente todavía. ¿Por qué? Porque las mujeres desde hace tantos años, pos desde hace 500 años, no tiene sus derechos de hablar, de participar en una asamblea [Because women are also living in a difficult situation, because women are the most exploited ones, still strongly oppressed. Why? Because women for many years, indeed for the last 500 years, have not had the freedom to speak, to participate in an assembly]."[55] Because of a severe illness, Ramona has been replaced at the table of negotiations by Comandante Trinidad, who is in her sixties and has been described thus: "con el rostro parcialmente cubierto por un palia- cate rojo y una larga cabellera entrecana y lacia [with her face partially covered with a red bandanna and long graying and straight hair]."[56] Trinidad has demanded a special table to discuss women's issues and denounced the response of the government that mocked her by asking why they should not also have "a mesa de jóvenes, de niños o de ancianos [a table of youth, of children, or of the elderly]."[57] If the indigenous leadership has gained prominence in the past few months, the indigenous leaders since the earliest interviews have underscored the subordinate role of Marcos. For instance, in the very early interview of 7–9 February 1995, a member of the CCRI-CG states that Marcos is a spokesperson and a military strategist, but not the political theorist: "Pues Marcos es como subcomandante. Marcos tiene la facilidad del castilla. Nosotros todavía fallan un chingo. . . . [El manda en lo militar.] Nosotros, pues, más la cuestión política, organizativa [Well, Marcos is like a subcomandante. Marcos has the facility of the *castilla*. We still make a *chingo* of mistakes. . . . (He leads the military aspect.) We are in charge of the political and organizational questions]." Because of their flawed Spanish, Marcos functions as a spokesperson, and at least in this interview the *chingo* of mistakes of the Indians' *castilla* are not corrected. Marcos at first, undoubtedly, was indispensable for placing the Zapatistas on a national and international front.

While in one set of texts or statements, Marcos and the CCRI-CG develop a lively rhetoric, often irreverent and mocking of the government, and a critique of the political economy as well as the ideological warfare conducted by the government, in another set, they underscore how the political positions and decisions to go to war were made after consensus was reached in every indigenous community. Marcos's pen might very well be involved in some of the CCRI-CG texts, but it is only in bad faith that some members of the national and international press have ascribed authorship to him. So much ink has flowed trying to unmask Marcos, that is, to peg an identity and a proper name on El Sup. At a time when most Mexican intellectuals were willing to believe that revolution, Marxism, and guerrillas were dead, and that the Left in Latin America could only be reformist, the emergence of the Zapatistas had to be explained away. The theories that informed these views were either wrong or the EZLN was an anomaly if not a historical aberration that tried to exhume Marx and the rest. Thus, Jorge Castañeda reduces the Zapatistas to an "armed reformism."[58] It does not occur to Castañeda that the EZLN might at once be reformist (seek specific democratic transformations) and revolutionary (express a sense of injustice that calls for a radical new time). In a letter responding to Zedillo's inaugural speech, Marcos underscored the revolutionary character of the Zapatistas:

Usted ya no es usted. Es ahora la personificación de un sistema injusto, antidemocrático y criminal. Nosotros, los "ilegales," los "transgresores de la ley," los "profesionales de la violencia," los "sin nombre," somos ahora y desde siempre la esperanza de todos. No es nada personal, señor Zedillo. Simplemente ocurre que nosotros nos hemos propuesto cambiar el mundo, y el sistema político que usted representa es el principal estorbo para lograrlo. [You are not yourself anymore. You are now the personification of an unjust system, antidemocratic and criminal. We, the "illegal," the "transgressors of the law," the "professionals of violence," the "nameless," are now and have always been the hope of all. It is nothing personal, Mr. Zedillo. It is simply that we have proposed ourselves to change the world, and the political system that you represent is the main obstacle to achieving it.][59]

The end of changing the world presupposes the destruction of the PRI and the state apparatuses that support it. It does not mean, however, that the EZLN aspires to take over the state. It remains a revolutionary movement, but the strategy that informs it is not any longer inspired by the Cuban Revolution.

When the press reduces the EZLN to the personal history of Marcos-the-militant-in-previous-armed-movements-in-Mexico, it ends up re-inscribing the Zapatistas as a variation and advancement of the guerrillas in Guatemala, the FSLN in Nicaragua, and the last instance in a series of armed movements in Mexico. Marcos inevitably assumes the image of a caudillo, a role he has contested, but the press insists on it: "Marcos es el caudillo — aunque él lo niega — de un levantamiento armado en el país del surrealismo [Marcos is the caudillo — even if he denies it — of an uprising in the country of surrealism]."[60] This is seemingly an empathetic version of the unmasking — with an exoticizing turn: "el país del surrealismo." But the rhetoric of counterinsurgency can be traced in the reference to Marcos as caudillo. In the ranks of those who seek to unmask Marcos to discredit him figures prominently Alma Guillermoprieto's article in the *New York Review of Books*. Her article (though signed on 2 February 1995) appeared in a suspicious moment that inevitably (regardless of her intentions) would come into play with a "Political Update" from the Chase Bank that called for the extermination of the Zapatistas ("The national government will need to eliminate the Zapatista to demonstrate their effective control of the national territory and of security policy")[61] and the apparent compliance to this demand by the Mexican government that revealed the "true" identity of Marcos, printed "his" photograph, and placed an order for his arrest and that of the other leaders of the EZLN. Marcos emerges as a professional of violence who manipulates the Indians, and, perhaps, more in tune with the Chase Bank memorandum, the EZLN as hardly a military force. The government justified its decision to send the army into Zapatista territories because arms caches had been found in the states of Veracruz and Mexico.

Critics of Marcos who attempt to identify him manifest a will to control the meaning of texts by means of the construction of their authors. Poststructuralist concepts of the author-function as developed by Foucault[62] offer another way of reading the "author*ity*" in the communiqués by Marcos and the CCRI-CG. Instead of insisting on who the real Marcos is, one should understand the particular author-function he as well as the CCRI-CG occupy and produce. The communiqués by the CCRI-CG are ascribed to a collective body and as such manifest the values and position of the indigenous community. They derive their authority and legitimacy inasmuch as they are the expression of a collective body that by definition is subaltern: For dominant discourse,

Indians, as long as they speak and think as Indians, cannot write or formulate a coherent political program. Beyond the obvious racism, this dismissal of indigenous intellectuality entails structural determinants that date back to the early colonization of the Americas—the subjection of native knowledges as superstitious or idolatrous. Indians had to abandon indigenous forms of life in order to make sense. In this regard, the CCRI-CG manifest an instance of writing the impossible in its affirmation that the EZLN is an Indian-led insurgency.

Their call for justice has ancestral roots that cannot be reduced to an immediate program of reforms. The Zapatistas call for justice is in the realm of the incalculable, as defined by Derrida: "the law is the element of calculation and it is just that there be law. But justice is incalculable. It requires us to calculate with the incalculable."[63] Tacho's demand for respect for dignity conveys this call for justice as incalculable. What could make amends for the oppression of indigenous peoples over the past five hundred years? But equally radical are CCRI-CG calls for a broad national and international front to struggle for the transition to a radical democracy, which, perhaps, is nowhere better defined than in Durito's text—the one I mentioned earlier on in this essay, whose pay went to the Fiat workers in Turin.

Marcos refutes the characterization of the EZLN as an armed reformist movement: "cualquier intento de 'reforma' o de 'equilibrio' de esta deformación es imposible DESDE DENTRO DEL SISTEMA DE PARTIDO DE ESTADO. . . . ES NECESARIA UNA REVOLUCION, una nueva revolución [any attempt at 'reform' or 'equilibrium' of this deformation is impossible FROM WITHIN THE STATE PARTY SYSTEM. . . . A REVOLUTION IS NECESSARY, a new revolution]" (Marcos's emphasis).[64] Durito reminds us that this call for revolution actually went back to a communiqué from 20 January 1994, where Marcos had first spoken of "un espacio democrático de resolución de la confrontación entre diversas propuestas políticas [a democratic space for the confrontation of diverse political proposals]." Durito criticizes Marcos's obscure and indigestible style and goes on to clarify what should be understood by revolution. It is "una concepción incluyente, antivanguardista y colectiva [an inclusive, antivanguardist, and collective conception]" that is no longer a problem "de LA organización, EL método, y de EL caudillo (ojo con las mayúsculas) [of THE organization, THE method, and THE caudillo (beware the capitals)]" but a task that pertains to all those who see the revolution as necessary and possible and for its realization everyone is important (Marcos's emphasis).[65] The end of the revolution would not be anymore "la conquista del Poder o la implantación (por vías pacíficas o violentas) de un nuevo sistema social, sino de algo anterior a una y otra cosa. Se trata de construir la antesala del mundo nuevo, un espacio donde, con igualdad de derechos y obligaciones, las distintas fuerzas políticas se 'disputen' el apoyo de la mayoría de la sociedad [the conquest of Power or the implantation (by means of peaceful or violent means) of a new social system, but of something anterior to one and the other thing. It is a question of building the antechamber of a new world, a space where, with equal rights and obligations, the different political forces would 'dispute' the support of society's majority]."[66]

This proposition contains striking parallelisms with Negri's understanding of communism and the constituent power of the multitude: "We may conceive the multitude as minoritarian or subaltern, or more accurately as exploited, but the multitude is always already central to the dynamics of social production; it is always already in a position of power. The power it is endowed with, however, is a power qualitatively different from the power of the State."[67] These calls for revolution do not have in common an alternative socialist state, but a political space that is not bound by the logic of capitalism and socialism as alternative administrations of capita.[68] Both Negri and the Zapatistas call for the formation of strong subjectivities that would resist any transfer of power to a transcendental institution, that is, to any form of political mediation that resides outside the processes of the masses. It could be argued that this commonality could be traced back to a shared affinity with the Zapatismo of the Plan de Ayala. Nevertheless, the connections between the EZLN and the Italian labor movement bear the auspices of a new internationalism that would no longer be grounded in a party or follow the program of a socialist model.

Within the long memory of indigenous oppression, grief, mourning, and rebellion, socialism is but one particular political form, one of the many regimes of laws that have been available from the West. Marcos is but one of the many Western interlocutors that have advocated justice for the Indians. We must here recall Bartolomé de Las Casas, the bishop after whom the town of San Cristobal is named, who, at the end of his long life of struggle against the injustices committed against the Indians, called for a restoration of all sovereignty to the indigenous leaders and condemned the colonial enterprise in its entirety. Las Casas's radicalism extended to threatening Philip II with excommunication[69] and calling for a restitution of all stolen goods and sovereignty to the Indians. Because the colonial enterprise was wrong, the Indians had the right to make war against the Spaniards and uproot them from their territories: "La octava [conclusión] que las gentes naturales de todas partes y de qualquiera dellas donde havemos entrado en las Indias tienen derecho adquirido de hazernos guerra justissima y raernos de la haz de la tierra y este derecho les durara hasta el dia del juyzio [The eighth (conclusion is) that the native people of these parts and of every one where we have entered in the Indies have the right to make a most just war against us and to erase us from the face of the earth, and they hold this right until doomsday]."[70]

One might very well wonder if this position is even within the realm of the impossible today. Indian histories have kept a record of both those institutions of the West that have sought to restore justice as well as those that have oppressed them. This is not the first indigenous rebellion in Mexican history, and one of the tasks of subaltern studies would be to call for a recuperation of the communities' memories of earlier Indian insurgencies and an understanding of how they were subjected to dominant forms of the nation-state. This *knowledge* (not of positivistic data but of the discursive devices that subject Indian cultures and a parallel indigenous awareness that their histories are figures of the impossible) would spare us the banal characterization of the Zapatistas as the first postmodern or, for that matter, postcommunist revolutionary movement. It is precisely in terms of this long history that one can define the subaltern subject position of the CCRI-CG, of the Zapatista insurgency in general, and of Marcos himself as exterior to the logic of capitalism or socialism.

One of the tasks of subaltern studies would consist of writing histories of Indian insurgencies in Mexico that would not be interpreted according to supposedly more advanced or developed political movements. These histories would practice what Guha calls writing in reverse, that is, against the grain of the documents that first recorded rebellions, but also against the counterinsurgent histories that sought to explain and contain insurrection. This would include tertiary histories that would privilege the wars of independence, the revolution or Marxist theory as providing categories to evaluate earlier movements as ineffectual. The Zapatistas respond to the specific conditions of postmodernity (globalization, transnationalism, the "demise" of socialism, neoliberalism, and so on). And if their response is determined by these political and economic conditions, the EZLN should not be reduced to a postmodern phenomenon: Zapatismo is and is not (post)modern; as I pointed out at the beginning of this paper, subaltern movements should be seen as cultural forms where the modern and nonmodern are compatible. Indeed, the EZLN manifests, in its interpretation of the sources of their oppression and counterinsurgent modes of containment, a lucidity that has been from the start a part of Indian resistance to colonialism. It also entails, at least implicitly in the Zapatista denunciation of paternalism, a critique of Gramsci's "folklorization" of popular culture. Subaltern studies would, therefore, also make it its business to draw an inventory of modes of colonial discourse, of forms of writing violence, that have sedimented in "commonsense" developmentalist tropes.[71]

In addressing the subject positions of Marcos (and the CCRI-CG by extension) we must keep in mind that "he" is a series of communiqués, interviews, and speeches that have been recorded on video, and not some sort of coherent and consistent self behind the statements he utters. And let's also not forget that these multiple subject positions have little to do with a celebration of a postmodern fragmented self. Furthermore, Marcos's and the CCRI-CG's understanding of history, and their role within it, is profoundly tragic and eschatological (though not teleological). It is worth recalling here Walter Benjamin's distinction between progress and *jetztzeit*, "the 'time of the now' which is shot through with the chips of Messianic time."[72] The Zapatistas, like Benjamin, would confront "mythical violence," the violence of the storm (progress) that keeps the angel from redeeming the past ("awaken the dead, and make whole what has been smashed"),[73] with "divine violence," a revolutionary violence conceived as "the highest manifestation of unalloyed violence."[74] Marcos's and the CCRI-CG's communiqués evoke a history in which the enemy has always been victorious, but they also formulate a discourse on violence that grounds its purity in the impossibility (paradoxically, also the condition of possibility) of its demands. Though the Zapatistas are a military force, the power of their violence resides in the new world they call forth — a sense of justice, democracy, and liberty that the government *cannot* understand because it calls for its demise. Marcos's multiple subject positions fulfill tactical and strategic functions within his discourse. Within one communiqué he might very well open his text with a poem by Paul Éluard (a gesture that situates his voice within a long-standing Marxist aesthetic), move on to evoke millenarian indigenous narratives (thus asserting that the EZLN struggle for justice has ancestral roots), elaborate a critique of the political economy of Mexico in terms of the four main social classes (the social scientist here complements the intellectual and the "anthropologist"), include multiple voices in the critique where the "social scientist" gains force from popular speech (IMF data are made palatable by satire, humor, evocations of the populace — the "¡órale!" cited above). I could go on and on and draw an exhaustive map of the author-functions in Marcos's communiqués, but there is a danger that in doing so we might reiterate the same closures that author-criticism imposes on texts. An inventory of Marcos's subject position, hence author-functions, runs the risk of neutralizing his discourse.

There are other ways of reading these subject positions. Foucault in "What Is an Author?" poses the question, "What difference does it make who is speaking?"[75] I would answer that in the case of Marcos the question is neither rhetorical nor academic. If one conceives of Marcos as a *revolutionary* in the context of a consensus that Marxism, revolution, communism, and so on are dead, where guerrilla warfare or utopian thinking cannot be *imagined* outside the Cuban model, and revolution is considered unthinkable in a situation that supposedly enables other forms of expression, then it does matter who is speaking. Hence the urgency to elaborate an ethics of reading subalternity. Cheryl Walker's critique of the generally accepted notion among poststructuralist critics of the "death of the author" is pertinent to Marcos, the author of revolutionary discourse.[76] Walker points out that questioning the death of the author would not necessarily mean returning to some sort of (patriarchal) author criticism that would posit an individual as the origin of a text; yet, Walker argues, "writing is not [as Barthes and, to a lesser extent, Foucault would have us believe] 'the destruction of every voice' but *the proliferation of possibilities of hearing*" (Walker's emphasis).[77] Marcos's subaltern position resides in an exteriority to the logic of socialism and capitalism that haunts his articulation of an Indian-led insurgency. The positive response by the demonstrators in Mexico City manifests not only the efficacy of the subject positions he deploys in his communiqués, but a "proliferation of possibilities of hearing."

As an intellectual, Marcos no longer defines his task as one of representation. He does not speak for the Zapatistas (he is one more Zapatista and, as an intellectual, a subordinate), nor does he portray them.[78] This does not mean that Marcos has not functioned as a spokesperson nor that he has not literarily recreated guerrilla life in the Selva Lacandona or provided explanations of how Power operates today. But these "mirrors," as he calls them (we must keep in mind that the numerous communiqués from the CCRI-CG as well as the interviews of the indigenous leadership have also produced mirrors), of who the Zapatistas are, what they want, and who oppresses them must give way to a "crystal ball," which he understands as the production of revolutionary spaces that systematically would undermine the constitution of a vanguard.

Marcos's understanding of the role of the intellectual from within an illegal army can be extended to others working through legal channels.

Intellectual work would run parallel to emergent social movements rather than articulate for them a political program. Thereby, intellectual work would operate on one of the multiple spaces of intervention. If as an intellectual Marcos might define the ends of the Zapatista insurrection, its realization would ultimately depend on the constituent power of the multitude: "En suma no estamos proponiendo una revolución ortodoxa, sino algo mucho más difícil: una revolución que haga posible la revolución . . . [To sum up, we are not proposing an orthodox revolution, but something much more difficult: a revolution that will make the revolution possible . . .]."[79] The ellipses are his, and suggest that this open-ended closing of the communiqué must be completed with the political creativity of the different groups struggling for democracy, liberty, and justice — to repeat once more the Zapatistas' three main demands, demands that define the need to retain the impossible alive in the face of forms of "writing violence" that have systematically infantilized subalterns.

The notion of *writing violence* paradoxically points to the constitution of forms of life that follow a different logic as violent, that is, as devoid of Reason. It also refers to objects of representation, that is, massacres, tortures, rapes, and other forms of material terror. There is an aesthetic, an epistemology, and an ethics of colonial violence. The aesthetic of colonial violence has at hand a whole series of epic topoi that have circulated in Western literature at least since Homer and still are used in denigratory representations of third world peoples.[80] A colonialist ethics informs the laws and regulations that different colonial and neocolonial enterprises have formulated to control voyages of exploration, justify wars of aggression, and rationalize permanent occupations of territories. Clear instances of epistemic violence have been the colonialists' subjections of indigenous knowledges as irrational, superstitious, and idolatrous. In the Zapatista communiqués we have seen how Marcos and indigenous leaders like Tacho, Trinidad, and David have responded to colonialist forms of writing violence by seeing through them, by laughing at counterinsurgent rhetorical moves, and by denouncing the cynical duplicity of the state.

Such is the predicament of postcolonial intellectuals practicing subaltern studies. The specific categories of aesthetic, ethical, and epistemological forms of colonial violence comprise a culture of conquest that still informs the history of the present, of what Foucault has defined as the ontohistory of what makes us subjects.[81] In our case it is the history of what makes of intellectuals oppressive subjects. This ontohistory, as I have suggested above, would consist of an *enlightened de-enlightenment*. Subaltern studies would thus first have the task of elaborating an inventory of the colonial legacy of modernity, before even beginning to conceptualize "elsewheres" to dominant Western rationalities (to borrow Donna Haraway's utopian phrase).[82] Historical narratives are hardly "insignificant" events in the cultural identities of people. As the Zapatistas put it, "un pueblo con memoria es un pueblo rebelde [a people with a memory is a rebel people]." Also consider Rigoberta Menchú's Quiche community's refusal to accept a Ladino version of the conquest and colonization.[83] Clearly, it is not *inconsequential* for her community to "turn the clocks back" and claim a clear understanding of colonialism — a subalternist reading of the ruses of developmentalist ideologies. Both Menchú's *testimonio* and the communiqués of the EZLN are forms of subaltern discourse that should not be confused with what subaltern studies produces in elite intellectual centers.

Subaltern politics and revolutionary interventions are obviously not dependent on nor inspired by academic theory. In the case of Marcos, however, there is a likelihood that he has read Gramsci and, perhaps, elaborated a critique of Gramsci's blindness toward the folkloric. In his interview with Blanche Petrich and Elio Henríquez, Marcos, furthermore, evokes Zapatismo as he critiques the vanguardism of the Cuban-inspired *foquismo* prevalent in the 1970s guerrilla: "nuestra tutoría militar viene de Villa, principalmente Zapata, y de lo que no debió hacerse de las guerrillas de los setenta, es decir, empezar con un movimiento militar localizado y esperar a que las bases se fueran sumando paulatinamente o iluminadas por ese foco guerrillero [our military instruction comes from Villa, principally from Zapata. It also comes by way of negative example from what was done by the guerrillas of the 1970s. They started with a local military movement and expected that the base would slowly join in or that they would be enlightened by this guerrilla *foco*]."[84]

In the manner of a coda, I would like to underscore that my approach to issues pertaining to the *folkloric* and the *impossible* clearly does not presume the transparency for which Spivak criticizes Foucault and Deleuze in their claim that they "know far better than [the intellectual] and they certainly say it very well."[85] The impossibility of speaking and the eminent folklorization that has haunted the discourse of Zapatistas at every stage of their dialogue with the government — exchanges that could very well be understood as colonial encounters caught in a struggle to the death — do not manifest subalterns who "know far better" and "say it well," but a clear understanding that the possibility of their call for justice, liberty, and democracy resides paradoxically in the impossibility of being understood. The point of departure is not that "subalterns speak very well," but that they "cannot speak" and "choose not to learn how" — indeed, they demand that the discourse of power "learn how to speak to them." This position is, perhaps, nowhere better exemplified than in Comandante Trinidad, who, at a session with the government, chose to address the official representatives in Tojolobal and then asked them in Spanish if all was clear.[86] Rather than seeing Trinidad's intervention as a symbolic statement about the difficulties of negotiating in another language, we ought to see it as an allegory of the inevitable subalternization of Indian discourse. Obviously, her denunciation of the oppressive situation of women and children living under the military occupation of the Selva cannot be a mere question of translation, but at a more elemental level must be seen as criticism of deep-seated colonialist attitudes that cannot accept that an old Indian woman could have anything to say and would be able to say it. This allegory of the impossibility of communication implies that the Subject of the West is not only dying but that its demise will come only as a result of specific struggles that make manifest its colonialist (read sexist, classist, racist) worldview that remains concealed in its claims to universality. In discussing Zapatismo, I have brought into play and critiqued theoretical points derived from Gramsci, Foucault, and Spivak. My point has not been to understand Zapatismo in light of these thinkers, but to sustain a dialogue in which Zapatismo ultimately provides a critique of the discourses we produce as privileged intellectuals.

NOTES

Early versions of this paper were read at the symposium Private Culture/Public Policy, organized by Norma Alarcón, at the University of California Humanist Research Institute, 8–12 June 1994; and the colloquium Other Circuits, organized by David Lloyd and Lisa Lowe, at the University of California Humanities Research Institute, 13–16 July 1994. I benefited greatly from the comments on those occasions. Santiago Colás read an early version and provided useful comments and criticisms. David Lloyd and Lisa Lowe went well beyond their editorial task to provide suggestions and encouragement that proved invaluable in writing the final version of this essay. I am, however, solely responsible for any errors of fact or judgment. Unless otherwise specified, translations from the Spanish are my own.

1. Comité Clandestino Revolucionario Indígena, Comandancia General del EZLN, "Carta a Zedillo." Chiapas, Mexico, 10 February 1995. Marcos, one of

the three non-Indians within the Zapatista ranks, bears the title of subcomandante in contradistinction to the higher-ranking Indian comandantes. From the beginning of the rebellion on 4 January 1994 — the same day the North American Free Trade Agreement (NAFTA) was implemented — Marcos has expressed his subordination to CCRI-CG, composed of Tzotzil, Tzeltal, Chol, Tojolabal, Mam, and Zoque Indians, who are in turn obliged to consult their own communities.

2. Gayatri Chakravorty Spivak, "Can the Subaltern Speak?" in *Marxism and the Interpretation of Culture,* ed. Cary Nelson and Lawrence Grossberg (Urbana: University of Illinois Press, 1988), 295. Emphasis in original.

3. Carlos Monsiváis, quoted in *La Jornada,* 17 February 1995.

4. For a sustained formulation of strategies and methods to understand, interpret, and grasp the politics of popular movements from the perspective of the masses themselves, see Reynaldo Clemeña Ileto, *Pasyon and Revolution: Popular Movements in the Philippines, 1840–1910* (Quezon City: Ateneo de Manila Press, 1979). Although the subject of this essay is a contemporary insurrection and not a historical event, Ileto's assessment of the failure to understand popular movements applies to the letter: "Social scientists unable to view society in other than equilibrium terms are bound to conclude that these movements are aberrations or the handiwork of crazed minds, alienated individuals, or external agitators. On the other hand, many scholars sympathetic to these movements tend to fit them into a tight, evolutionary framework that leads to a disparagement all together of cultural values and traditions as just a lot of baggage from our feudal and colonial past" (13).

5. *EZLN: Documentos y comunicados, 1 de enero/8 de agosto de 1994,* prologue by Antonio García de Léon and chronicles by Carlos Monsiváis and Elena Poniatowska (Mexico City: Editorial Era, 1994), 10 April, 1994, 212. Ellipses in original.

6. Eduard Seler, "Wall Paintings of Mitla: A Mexican Picture Writing in Fresco," in *Eduard Seler: Collected Works in Mesoamerican Linguistics and Archaeology,* vol. 1, trans. Charles P. Bowditch (Culver City, CA: Labyrinthos, 1990–1993), 295.

7. See articles in *La Guillotina* 30 (March–April 1995).

8. Gary Gossen, "From Olmecs to Zapatistas: A Once and Future History of Souls," *American Anthropologist* 96 (1994): 566.

9. Ibid.

10. Ibid.

11. Ibid., 567.

12. Camú Urzúa and Tótoro Taulis have written a detailed history of the movement since the early 1980s in *EZLN, el ejercito que salio de la silva* (México: Grupo Editorial Planeta, 1994). Their history establishes both a connection to earlier guerrilla movements as well as differentiates the nature of the Zapatistas precisely in terms of the subordination of the Ladinos to the recommendations of the Indian committees. John Ross has written a most detailed and empathetic chronicle of the early days of the insurrection: *Rebellion from the*

Roots: Indian Uprising in Chiapas (Monroe, ME: Common Courage Press, 1995). For an analysis of the socioeconomic causes of the insurrection, see George A. Collier with Elizabeth Lowery Quaratiello, *Basta! Land and the Zapatista Rebellion in Chiapas* (Oakland, CA: Institute for Food and Development Policy, 1994). This present essay seeks to examine the political discourse of Zapatismo. The sources for this reflection are the communiqués by Marcos and the CCRI-CG, as well as the invaluable reports from the Selva Lacandona of journalists for *La Jornada:* Hermann Bellinghausen, Elio Henríquez, Epigmenio Ibarra, and Blanche Petrich, to mention the most prominent and indefatigable.

13. See Alma Guillermoprieto, "The Shadow War," *New York Review of Books* 42, no. 4 (1995): 34–43; César Romero, *Marcos: ¿Un profesional de la esperanza?* (Mexico City: Editorial Planeta, 1994); Raúl Trejo Delarbre, ed., *Chiapas: La Guerra de las Ideas* (Mexico City: Editorial Diana, 1994).

14. Quoted in *La Jornada,* 16 May 1995.

15. For a testimonial on the significance of Berlin 1989 and an argument for the relevance of Marx and communism, see Emmanuel Terray, *Le Troisème Jour du Communisme* (Arles: Actes Sud, 1992). This book in many ways anticipates Jacques Derrida's assessment of the relevance of Marx's concept of revolution and critique, and his call for a new internationalism, in *Specters of Marx: The State of the Debt, the Work of Mourning, and the New International,* trans. Peggy Kamuf (New York: Routledge, 1995).

16. María Josefina Saldaña-Portillo's contribution to this volume provides a lucid analysis of why the Sandinistas faced resistance to their program of land reform by the same people it was supposed to benefit.

17. John Beverley and José Oviedo, eds., *The Postmodernism Debate in Latin America,* special issue, *boundary 2* 20, no. 3 (1993). The Latin American Subaltern Studies Group has been faulted for inviting a new wave of cultural imperialism (in this case of Indian origin but through the U.S. academy) and for ignoring the long tradition of oppositional writing in Latin America. Both observations harbor a misconception about the project. My own response is that the South Asian Group's work on the category of the subaltern provides an exceptional corpus of texts without parallel elsewhere in the world. In the end, because of the debates within both groups and the temporal and geographic differences, what is of interest in this new circuit of theory are the possible conversations, debates, and shared investigations among scholars working with similar problematics and colonial legacies in different parts of the world.

18. Antonio Negri and Michael Hardt, *Labor of Dionysus: Communism as Critique of the Capitalist and Socialist State-Form* (Minneapolis: University of Minnesota Press, 1994), 310.

19. Quoted in *La Jornada,* 11 June 1995.

20. See Ranajit Guha and Gayatri Chakravorty Spivak, eds., *Selected Subaltern Studies* (New York: Oxford University Press, 1988).

21. For definitions of the project of a Latin American Subaltern Studies Group, see "Founding Statement/Latin American Subaltern Studies Group" in

The Postmodernism Debate in Latin America, ed. Beverley and Oviedo; José Rabasa and Javier Sanjinés, "Introduction: The Politics of Subaltern Studies," in *Subaltern Studies in the Americas,* ed. Robert Carr, José Rabasa, and Javier Sanjinés, special issue of *Dispositio/n* 46 (1994): v–xi.

22. Ernesto Laclau, *Politics and Ideology in Marxist Theory* (London: New Left Books, 1977).

23. My critique of Gramsci has many affinities with David Lloyd's critique of Gramsci's view that the history of subaltern groups is episodic and fragmentary. See David Lloyd, *Anomalous States: Irish Writing and the Post-Colonial Moment* (Durham: Duke University Press, 1993), 127 and passim.

24. Antonio Gramsci, *Selections from the Prison Notebooks,* ed. and trans. Quintin Hoare and Geoffrey Nowell Smith (New York: International Publishers, 1971), 197.

25. Ibid., 30.

26. This passage from *Gli intellectuali e l'organizzazione della cultura* is quoted in n. 5 in Gramsci, *Selections from the Prison Notebooks,* 326.

27. Ibid., 326.

28. On the centrality of negation in subaltern studies, see Ranajit Guha's *Elementary Forms of Peasant Insurgency* (Delhi: Oxford University Press, 1983), 19–76. Guha finds in the following passages by Gramsci a starting point for an understanding of negation in subaltern insurgencies: "Not only does the people have no precise consciousness of its own historical identity, it is not even conscious of the historical identity or the exact limits of its adversary. The lower classes, historically on the defensive, can only achieve self-awareness via a series of negations, via their consciousness of the identity and class limits of their enemy; but it is precisely this process which has not yet come to the surface, at least not nationally" (273). Guha's chapter "Negation" goes on to document modalities and instances of actual negations in the history of Indian peasant insurgencies. But Guha, from the concluding remarks, seems to suggest an incompatibility of nonmodern social formations with modern political concepts, that is, with "advanced ideas of democracy" (76). As we will see, in the Zapatistas we find a *negation* of this teleology that privileges supposedly more developed political forms in the interpretation of subaltern identities. Reynaldo Ileto, as I have pointed out above, presents a lucid argument for approaching popular movements in their own terms.

29. Gautam Bhadra, "Four Rebels of Eighteen-Fifty-Seven," in *Selected Subaltern Studies,* ed. Ranajit Guha and Gayatri Chakravorty Spivak (New York: Oxford University Press, 1988), 173–174.

30. S. N. Sen, *Eighteen-Fifty-Seven,* foreword by Maulana Abul Kalam Azad (Delhi: Publications Division, Ministry of Information and Broadcasting, Government of India, 1957).

31. R. H. W. Dunlop, *Service and Adventure with the Khakee Ressalah or, Meerut Volunteer Horse, during the Mutinies of 1857–58* (London: R. Bentley, 1858).

32. Bhadra, "Four Rebels of Eighteen-Fifty-Seven," 175.

33. See Doris Sommer, "Resisting the Heat: Menchú, Morrison, and Incompetent Readers," in *Cultures of U.S. Imperialism,* ed. Amy Kaplan and Donald E. Pease (Durham: Duke University Press, 1993), 407–432.

34. Gayatri Chakravorty Spivak, "Subaltern Studies: Deconstructing Historiography," in *In Other Worlds: Essays in Cultural Politics* (New York: Routledge, 1988), 211.

35. See John Womack, *Zapata and the Mexican Revolution* (Harmondsworth: Penguin, 1972), which is Spivak's source. For other studies of the Zapatistas of 1910 and their legacy, see Alan Knight, *The Mexican Revolution,* 2 vols. (Cambridge: Cambridge University Press, 1986); Guillermo De la Pena, *A Legacy of Promises: Agriculture, Politics and Ritual in the Morelos Highlands of Mexico* (Austin: University of Texas Press, 1981); and Arturo Warman, "*We Came to Object": The Peasants of Morelos and the National State,* trans. Stephen K. Ault (Baltimore: Johns Hopkins University Press, 1980). More recently, Brunk has attributed the "failure" of Zapata to his dependence on urban intellectuals. See Samuel Brunk, "Zapata and the City Boys: In Search of a Piece of the Revolution," *Hispanic American Historical Review* 73, no. 1 (1993): 33–65. On the other hand, this emphasis on the role of "education" has been undermined by Martin in a study of the use of historical authenticity in a movement to defend communal land in Buena Vista, Morelos, Mexico. See JoAnn Martin, "Contesting Authenticity: Battles over the Representation of History in Morelos, Mexico," *Ethnohistory* 40, no. 3 (summer 1993): 438–465. Both of these articles antecede the Zapatista uprising in Chiapas, but Martin's piece is particularly relevant to the EZLN in the emphasis it places on the future, on contemporary movements, rather than on events in the past (447).

36. Quoted in *La Jornada,* 9 February 1995.

37. Francis Barker, *The Culture of Violence: Essays on Tragedy and History* (Chicago: University of Chicago Press, 1993), 233.

38. Womack, *Zapata and the Mexican Revolution,* 526.

39. Ibid., 509.

40. Gramsci, *Selections,* 196.

41. Although the main ideas as well as the political motivation are Zapata's, the composition of the Plan de Ayala involved other leaders, and the actual writing of the document is attributed to a schoolteacher named Otilio Montaño. Points one to five of the Plan denounce President Francisco I. Madero's negotiations with *hacendados* (large landholders) and *cientificos* (intellectuals) from the dictatorship of Porfirio Díaz. The remaining ten points call for a reappropriation of lands that had been taken from communities (*pueblos*) and citizens (*ciudadanos*) who held the corresponding titles, justify the expropriation of latifundia, define the terms to compensate widows and children of fallen combatants, and establish criteria for a democratic postrevolutionary society.

42. "Founding Statement/Latin American Subaltern Studies Group," in Beverley and Oviedo, *The Postmodernism Debate in Latin America,* 121.

43. Quoted in *La Jornada,* 22 September 1994.

44. See Rabasa and Sanjinés, "Introduction: The Politics of Subaltern Studies," v–xi; and José Rabasa, "Pre-Columbian Pasts and Indian Presents in Mexican History," in *Subaltern Studies in the Americas*, ed. Robert Carr, José Rabasa, and Javier Sanjines, special issue of *Dispositio/n* 46 (1994): 245–270.

45. See Rabasa, "Pre-Columbian Pasts and Indian Presents in Mexican History."

46. Quoted in *La Jornada*, 9 February 1995.

47. See Guha, *Elementary Forms of Peasant Insurgency*; and Guha and Spivak, *Selected Subaltern Studies*.

48. The press repeats what I suggest is a constant form of counterinsurgency that Lloyd has defined as follows: "Of course from the perspective of dominant history, the subaltern must be represented as violence. 'Must' in two senses: that which cannot be assimilated to the state can be understood only as outside the law, disruptive and discontinuous, unavailable for narration; secondly, the history of the state requires a substrate which is counter to its laws of civility and which it represents as outrageous and violent, in order that the history of domination and criminalization appear as a legitimate process of civilization and the triumph of law" (Lloyd, *Anomalous States*, 127).

49. Womack, *Zapata and the Mexican Revolution*, 375.

50. Quoted in *La Jornada*, 5–7 February 1995.

51. Ibid.

52. Quoted in *La Jornada*, 10 June 1995.

53. Ibid.

54. Ibid.

55. Ibid.

56. Quoted in *La Jornada*, 13 May 1995.

57. Ibid.

58. Jorge G. Castañeda, *Sopresas te de la vida: México 1994* (Mexico City: Aguilar, 1994), 44–45.

59. Quoted in *La Jornada*, 7 December 1994.

60. Romero, *Marcos: ¿Un profesional de la esperanza?*, 23.

61. Quoted in Ken Silverstein and Alexander Cockburn, "The Killers and the Killing," *The Nation* 260, no. 9 (1995): 306.

62. Michel Foucault, "What Is an Author?" in *The Foucault Reader*, ed. Paul Rabinow (New York: Pantheon, 1984), 101–120.

63. Quoted in Gayatri Chakravorty Spivak, "Supplementing Marx," in *Whither Marxism?: Global Crises in International Perspective*, ed. Bernd Magnus and Stephen Cullenberg (New York: Routledge, 1995), 111.

64. Quoted in *La Jornada*, 11 June 1995.

65. Ibid.

66. Ibid.

67. Negri and Hardt, *Labor of Dionysus*, 307.

68. See Spivak, "Supplementing Marx," 115.

69. See Helen-Rand Parish and Harold E. Weidman, *Las Casas en México: Historia y obra desconocidas* (Mexico City: Fondo de Cultura Económica, 1992).

70. Bartolomé de Las Casas, *El Tratado de las "Doce Dudas,"* in *Obras Completas* vol. 11, no. 2, ed. J. B. Lassegue (Madrid: Editorial Alianza, 1992), 218.

71. For a critique of developmentalist discourse as the imaginary of our time, see Arturo Escobar, "Imagining a Post-Development Era? Critical Thought, Development and Social Movements," *Social Text* 31–32 (1992): 20–56.

72. Walter Benjamin, "Theses on the Philosophy of History," in *Illuminations,* ed. Hannah Arendt, trans. Harry Zohn (New York: Schocken, 1969), 263.

73. Ibid., 257.

74. Walter Benjamin, "Critique of Violence," in *Reflections,* trans. Edmund Jephcott (New York: Schocken Books, 1986), 300.

75. Foucault, "What Is an Author?", 120.

76. I have found Cheryl Walker's critique useful for reading Garcilaso de la Vega's positioning as an Indian writing in a context where there was no place for an Indian author in late sixteenth-century Spain. See Cheryl Walker, "Feminist Criticism and the Author," *Critical Inquiry* 16 (spring 1990): 551–571. See also José Rabasa, "'Porque soy indio': Subjectivity in *La Florida del Inca,*" *Poetics Today* 16, no. 1 (1995): 79–108.

77. Walker, "Feminist Criticism and the Author," 568.

78. See Spivak, "Can the Subaltern Speak?", 276 and passim.

79. Quoted in *La Jornada,* 11 June 1995.

80. See José Rabasa, "Aesthetics of Colonial Violence: The Massacre of Acoma in Gaspar de Villagrá's *Historia de la nueva México,*" *College Literature* 20, no. 3 (1993): 96–114.

81. See Michel Foucault, "What Is Enlightenment?", in *The Foucault Reader,* ed. Paul Rabinow (New York: Pantheon, 1984), 32–50.

82. Donna Haraway, "The Promises of Monsters: A Regenerative Politics for Inappropriate/d Others," in *Cultural Studies,* ed. Lawrence Grossberg, Cary Nelson, and Paula Treichler (New York: Routledge, 1992), 295–337.

83. Rigoberta Menchú with Elisabeth Burgos-Debray, *Me llamo Rigoberto Menchú y así me nació la consciencia* (Mexico City: Siglo XXI, 1983).

84. Quoted in *La Jornada,* 5–7 February 1994.

85. Quoted in Spivak, "Can the Subaltern Speak?", 274.

86. See Ramón Vera Herrera, "Relojes japoneses," *Ojarasca* 44 (1995): 20–25.

NANDI BHATIA

Staging Resistance:

The Indian People's Theatre Association

If the theatre loses its mass audience, it loses its life, its meaning, its raison d'être. To alienate the theatre from the masses is to alienate oneself still further from the social activity of men, and end in an intellectual madhouse. UTPAL DUTT[1]

In 1942, a group of progressive writers who recognized the potential of popular theater as an effective weapon in the fight for national liberation from British imperialism and fascism, and in the struggles of peasants, workers, and other oppressed classes formed a group called the Indian People's Theatre Association (IPTA). The primary aim of the IPTA, as its organizers identified it in the "All Indian People's Theatre Conference Draft Resolution," was to mobilize "a people's theatre movement throughout the whole of India as the means of revitalizing the stage and the traditional arts and making them at once the expression and organiser of our people's struggle for freedom, cultural progress and economic justice."[2] Accordingly, they described the IPTA as neither "a movement which is imposed from above but one which has its roots deep down in the cultural awakening of the masses of India, nor . . . a movement which discards our rich cultural heritage, but one which seeks to revive the lost in that heritage by interpreting, adopting and integrating it with the most significant facts of the people's lives and aspirations in the people's epoch."[3] What began in 1942 as an organization in Bombay and Calcutta expanded by 1945 into a nationwide movement organized around three divisions: the song and dance division, the drama division, and the film division.

My objective in this article is to examine the ways in which the drama division of the IPTA participated in the political process before independence in 1947 and in the postindependence years. Through an innovative and experimental drama that derived its inspiration and ideas partly from Western and Chinese practices but was rooted in India's own cultural and social practices, the IPTA challenged existing hegemonic structures, both colonial and those intrinsic to Indian society. For example, the Little Theatre Groups in England, the 1930s Works Progress Administration (WPA) theater project in the United States, the Soviet theaters, and the strolling players in China who staged antifascist plays to protest Japanese exploitation[4] exerted immense influence on the IPTA. Inspired by these cultural challenges abroad, IPTA members turned to theater as a political weapon amidst the political turmoil at home, created by the war in Europe, increasing repression from British imperialism, and deepening nationalist sentiments manifested in the Quit India movement of 1942.

To seek the "widest possible mass basis for its activities," the IPTA turned to indigenous popular traditions of different regions such as the *jatra* of Bengal, *tamasha* of Maharashtra, and *burrakatha* of Andhra Pradesh.[5] Given the linguistic, cultural, and geographical diversity of the Indian subcontinent, choices about language, theatrical space, and stylistic devices were important, involving, as they did, questions of viewership and audience. For instance, an audience in a working-class district in Bombay might appreciate a play in Marathi instead of English, or a peasant audience in a Bengal village might need to see a play about the famine in a familiar dialect and surroundings. Linguistic and cultural diversity among a group of people can cause what Immanuel Wallerstein refers to as a "problem of cohesion." According to Wallerstein, however, "[to] the extent that the 'national sentiment' develops, these threats [of internal chaos and colonial consolidation] are lessened."[6] To intervene collectively in counterhegemonic schemes, a "national sentiment" that overcomes this lack of cohesion has to be generated. By presenting the same plays in a range of different languages, IPTA organizers attempted to overcome the "lack of cohesion" among a heterogeneous populace. This was done in the interest of establishing links among the "people" through the people's identification with day-to-day struggles.

Performing for "mass" audience in villages, towns, and working-class districts required open-air presentations. Hence most of the IPTA plays were performed in outdoor theaters such as the Kamgar Maidan in Bombay, where, according to IPTA reports, up to 20,000 people could view a play instead of the limited capacity provided by an enclosed theater. Similarly, stylistic considerations constituted an important feature of IPTA productions. In Calcutta, for example, *Nabanna*, a play about the Bengal famine, was performed on a revolving stage to achieve the desired realistic effects about the lives of starving Bengali peasants for a citified audience. Outside Calcutta, the same play had to be performed on makeshift stages, and much of the realism was derived from its use of the peasants' dialect, details about village life, and the use of local traditions combined with the *jatra* songs and props.[7] The IPTA thus inaugurated a theater of collective resistance and liberation, yet heterogeneous in its constitution, which varied according to the geographical, linguistic, and cultural differences of a diverse populace. This paper will attempt to understand the ways in which the IPTA theorized questions of language, space, geography, culture, and ethnography in light of their broader agenda of dramatizing and disseminating messages regarding contemporaneous issues of fascism, imperialist oppression, and exploitation of socially disadvantaged groups.

Because of its affiliation with "popular" drama, canonical assumptions of "proper" literary and aesthetic values, and its association with the Communist Party of India, which, on account of its antifascist support for the allied powers, was branded by the nationalist bourgeoisie as a party of traitors, the IPTA has remained largely unacknowledged in the dominant discourse of Indian cultural history. To undertake a study of the IPTA, therefore, is important especially because it provides an alternative understanding of the complex events that transpired in nationalist politics both on the eve of independence and after.[8]

An adequate understanding of the IPTA requires us to situate it against the backdrop of historical developments in Indian society during the 1940s and 1950s. Intending to mobilize plays "to propagate anti-fascist ideology and espouse the cause of world democracy," the IPTA emerged as a sister organization of the Progressive Writers' Union, which was formed in 1936.[9] Its organizing group consisted of men and women from diverse backgrounds, including lawyers, professors, students, musicians, journalists, playwrights, farmers, trade union leaders, and workers groups. Some of the most talented figures from the world of theater participated in the IPTA: Balraj Sahni, Shombu Mitra, Bijon Bhattacharyara, Anna Bhau Sathe, and Khwaja Ahmed Abbas, to name only a few. Female IPTA members who were organizers, artists, playwrights, directors, and even protagonists of plays made women's issues an important aspect of the IPTA program. Among these were Sheila Bhatia, Rasheed Jahan, Binata Roy, Uma Chakravarthy, Sarojini Naidu (1879–1949), Kamaladevi Chattopadhyay (1903–1989), and Siddiqua Begum Sevharvi.[10] In Lucknow, Rasheed Jahan staged plays that she and her companions had written or translated. Kondapalli Koteswaramma (b. 1925) wrote poems for children about the lives of peasants and artisans. Moturi Udayam (b. 1924) composed and acted in burrakathas.[11]

The first people's theater was set up in Bangalore in April 1941 but stalled because of severe police repression. Anil de Silva, who was instrumental in organizing the theater in Bangalore, came to Bombay, where she initiated a people's theater in 1942. This became the Indian People's Theatre Association and Bombay became its headquarters. In Bengal, the movement consolidated due to the efforts of the Anti-

Fascist Writers Association and the Youth Cultural Institute, which collectively presented plays on contemporary sociopolitical issues. By 1944, the IPTA expanded into a movement that included a Central Cultural Troupe, which organized dances and ballets on political issues, and provincial and regional units in Malabar, Andhra Pradesh, United Provinces, Assam, Punjab, and Delhi. Until its demise around 1960, the IPTA presented hundreds of plays on a range of topics such as the Japanese aggression in Southeast Asia, Hitler and Mussolini, war and fascism, the Bengal Famine of 1943, the cholera epidemic of 1944, the problems of food, landlordism, debt, and workers' exploitation, and the partition of 1947.[12]

ROAR CHINA, FOUR COMRADES, AND NABANNA

The IPTA's earliest attempts to intervene in the political process came through its presentation in 1942, the year of the launching of the Quit India movement, of two one-act antifascist plays: *Roar China* and *Four Comrades*.[13] Adapted from the Russian play of that name and modified according to the Indian context of 1942, *Roar China* deals with the persecution of the Chinese by the Western imperialists and the subsequent anti-imperialist revolutionary feelings in a small village of fishermen and boatmen in China.[14] Finding the theme of imperialism applicable to the situation of British imperialism in India, the IPTA, in 1942, produced a portion of the drama in English, shifting the context to India. Written jointly by IPTA members, *Four Comrades* dramatizes an incident in the battle of Singapore. The incident recounts the fight that four labor agitators — two Chinese, a Malay, and an Indian — wage against Japanese aggressors. Upon being released from jail on the eve of the Japanese invasion, the four comrades immediately take up arms against the assailants.

Set in the context of war and imperialism, the two plays purport to explain the phenomenon of fascism and its hazards to the marginalized masses in India. A note at the beginning of *Roar China* and *Four Comrades*, says: "These two anti-fascist plays should always have a simple explanation given to the worker and peasant audience before their performance. This explanation can be given by one of the actors, and should give the audience a clear short background of each play, and the political events which brought this about. This is very important, otherwise the full significance of the play will be lost. At the end, perhaps, there can be a few words said to them which will link up the play with India and what it means to us to have a Fascist invader in this country."[15]

As they seek to intervene in the polarized views between Congress nationalists who declined to participate in the war at all costs and the leftist intelligentsia who felt that imperialism would end only if fascism ended, the two plays take on a political significance for handling the situation at home. In 1942, Congress nationalists refused to support the British in their battle against the Axis powers and passed the Quit India resolution, calling for "mass struggle on non-violent lines on the widest possible scale."[16] Within the colonial context, Congress leaders visualized immediate freedom from the British as a more pressing need than averting the threat of fascist forces, which, in their view, only peripherally affected India. The communists found this policy of the Congress limited in its vision. They saw the war as a conflict between imperialist and fascist powers for a redivision of the colonies and hence urged action against fascist Japan and Germany before action against the British. These fears seemed hardly unfounded in 1942. In December 1941, the Japanese had driven through Southeast Asia, seized Singapore, Burma, and Malaya, and threatened to attack India on the eastern frontier. But since Japan's attack on India also meant an end to colonial rule, the Congress reacted differently to the situation. Gandhi, who foresaw a Japanese victory in 1942, reasoned that "if India were freed her first step would possibly be to negotiate with Japan . . . India has no enmity towards Japan."[17]

Both *Roar China* and *Four Comrades* point to the fitting connections between fascism and imperialism and urge the necessity of viewing the situation in India within the global developments of 1942. In *Four Comrades* the connection is invoked in the climactic moment of the play, when Ratan, the Indian comrade, refuses the Japanese officer's offer of freedom in exchange for doing propaganda work in favor of the Japanese in India. "You are an Indian and we have no quarrel with Indians," the official tells Ratan. To which Ratan replies: "The Japs coming to free India! That would be a good joke. Ha. Ha. Just as you freed Manchuria and Korea and China — No, we Indians are not such fools as to exchange our present bondage for a worse slavery."[18] Upon this retort the Japanese soldier kills Ratan. Ratan's death at the hands of the Japanese criticizes the hopes expressed by Gandhi about the possibility of negotiation with the Japanese. The story of *Four Comrades* is thus more than an attack on fascism. Implicit in the play is an attack on the Congress leadership for trivializing the consequences that fascism could have on the Indian populace, especially when Japan posed a real threat on the eastern frontier. The link between fascism and imperialism is drawn to encourage "the people" to view their oppression within the context of global politics. It is conveyed through Ratan's assurance to the Chinese comrade, Chin: "We are not narrow nationalists. We must do what is best for the workers of the world, for the defeat of Fascism is of urgent importance. Without that there is no hope for the toiling masses."[19]

The IPTA's opposition to Congress policies is also manifested through the two plays' attack on Gandhi's recommended strategy of "non-violence" during the Quit India movement. It is conveyed through the actions of the four comrades who counter the Japanese in an armed struggle and die fighting for freedom. The revolutionary action that the comrades undertake may be construed as a message to the masses about the ineffectiveness of nonviolence and the necessity of adopting the revolutionary path of the four comrades. The attack on nonviolence becomes more overtly visible in the prologue of *Roar China*. Within the context of Chinese retaliation, the play discusses the limits of nonviolence:

But there is a limit to non-violence and peace
When the waves of tyranny and justice rise high
The oppressed, the hungry, the poor, the workers,
The peasants — all take arms to resist it.[20]

Ostensibly, the commentaries provided at the beginning and end of the plays are attempts to reconstruct the history of the freedom struggle and the relationship between fascism and imperialism from the viewpoint of members of the Left who had been branded as traitors because of their support for the British against fascism. As such, they also provide access to the contemporaneous international developments and the ramifications of these developments for India to audiences who may have been denied access to the world events in 1942. A description of the connections between fascism abroad and imperialism at home was particularly instructive for those who by this time, in Shahid Amin's words, treated "Gandhi as Mahatma" and his message of nonviolent protest as the words of a saint.[21] The commentary also has another function: since it is separated from the play's action, it creates the potential for a direct participation of the audience through discussion. As *Four Comrades* progresses, the audience is given the time and the opportunity to think through the situation and place the rest of the play within the perspective of the commentary. The last scene, in which Ratan is shot by the Japanese soldier, seeks to inspire the collective participation of the audience as Ratan's individual resistance changes to collective resistance through echoing sounds of his last words: "I will live again. I will be reborn in the spirit of every Indian who will take up arms against you. . . . I will be everywhere you go in India — in Calcutta and in Bombay, in Madras and in Karachi. You will not escape me (*Japs start running*). I shall not die!"[22] While the specific geographical markers that Ratan uses invite the audience to see themselves as Ratan, their voices echoing his words reiterate his sentiment. Presented initially in English, *Roar China* and *Four Comrades* were soon translated into a dozen provincial languages and presented in the different regions of the country by the IPTA's provincial squads. The translations of the plays into different languages suggest a collective political agenda on the part of IPTA members: to ensure the widest possible participation of "the people" in the political process.

The next major IPTA play that followed *Roar China* and *Four Comrades* was Bijon Bhattacharyara's *Nabanna,* about the Bengal famine of 1943. Under Shombhu Mitra's direction, the Bengal IPTA squad performed the play in many parts of the country as part of a festival called the Voice of Bengal. The purpose of the festival was to collect money for the relief of famine victims in rural Bengal. The play became the IPTA's major success and helped in the collection of *lakhs* (hundreds of thousands) of rupees. *Nabanna* presents the intensity of the famine through the starving family of a Bengali peasant, Pradhan Samaddar. The range of disasters that the family goes through are emblematic of the state of the Bengali peasantry during the famine. But *Nabanna* is more than a play about famine. It is also an attempt on the IPTA's part to expose the sordid reality that the famine was not a natural disaster but a man-made calamity. Ironically, far from there being a shortage of food, the per capita availability of the food supply was 9 percent more in 1943 than in 1941, which was not a year of famine. The famine was actually a result of international political developments. The war in Europe had led to inflated prices and shortages of rice and salt. Even though the war economy in England was being run most efficiently, the British government made practically no attempt in its Indian colony to check a rampant black market. Inflation and shortages led to profiteering, black-marketing, and hoarding of food. Rising prices and shortages of food, as a large number of Allied troops arrived on Indian soil, created a fear that the country's food supply was being depleted to feed the army.[23] Burma's fall to the Japanese, on the other hand, cut off rice imports into Bengal, thus aggravating the food crisis. *Nabanna* implicates a combination of the war in Europe and imperialist policies at home as being ultimately detrimental to the economically marginalized groups. These phenomena are conveyed through the play's central character, Pradhan, who, as his family is devastated, reflects on the reasons for the famine. To find answers, his family, along with other peasants from the village, moves to Calcutta.

The peasants' movement from the village to the city is emblematic of the famine victims' realization of the significance of collective mobilization. Their choice to collectively relocate to Calcutta shows an attempt to understand the politics of the famine. In Calcutta, where they are reduced to the worst possible state of poverty despite the surplus of food, they learn that the famine, caused by international politics, could have been averted. Although the peasants return to their village hungry and desolate, their return is a hopeful one, a hope inspired by a new awareness of their basic human rights. The title of the play, which translates as *New Harvest,* is symbolic of the new crop that will be generated through this reawakening of the peasants' consciousness.

THE POPULAR AND THE REALISTIC

Nabanna's challenge to imperialism also occurs in the play's violation of the conventions of "high" realism presented in the "well-made" play that dominated the metropolitan theater in India in the early decades of the twentieth century.[24] This disruption occurs through the episodic structure of the play, which prevents the action from being resolved at the end, frustrating an interpretive closure. *Nabanna* moves in quick succession from one episode to another to depict the lives of the suffering peasants. These range "from the woes of the peasants in their village homes to the hoarder's den, from relief kitchen to charitable dispensary, from the wedding feast to the beggars scrounging for food near the dustbin, from the child dying of malnutrition to the village-wife being approached by the city tout."[25] By converting the stage into a platform on which the spectators are shown various aspects of the famine through sharply contrasting images of opulence and poverty, presented, for instance, through the juxtaposition of the sumptuous wedding feast with the sad plight of the beggars, such an episodic structure violates the rules of realism. In so doing, *Nabanna* purports to evoke "recognition" from the audience as the operative and critical political response. Juxtaposed in this way, such contrasting images serve to draw the audience's empathetic attention to the economic unevenness generated by colonial policies. The episodes also shift the focus from the life of the individual peasant Pradhan and his family, and provide spectators with a multifaceted view of the ramifications of the famine so that spectators recognize these familiar instances of life and intervene in the existing problems.

The possibility of popular accessibility to the IPTA productions was facilitated, in part, by IPTA's concept of a traveling theater. The "chronicles and documents" of the IPTA reveal that its provincial squads emerged out of the closed halls of city theaters to stage plays five or six times a day under open skies, in public parks, on street corners, in village and city courtyards. Travels to remote areas, villages, and working-class settlements brought directors, producers, and playwrights into direct contact with their audiences. Close interaction provided direct access to the "lived experience" of people and raised the directors' awareness of the ways in which hegemonic structures affected the masses. This experience provided IPTA's organizers with fresh insights into ways of connecting their productions with their viewers' subjectivities, contributing to the project of a "people's theatre."

What IPTA directors learned during their travels was that the stories of imperialism and exploitation should be taken from the "lived experience" of "the people." According to James Clifford, ethnographic stories "simultaneously describe real cultural events and make additional . . . ideological statements."[26] Dramatizing the stories of "the people" provided patterns or associations that pointed to coherent additional meanings. The meanings would be provided in two ways: by virtue of the spectators' familiarity with a story, so that they could recognize them and understand the processes that caused oppression, and through identification with the popular traditions of specific regions. While the familiarity of a story had the ability to elicit audience participation in the political process, the knowledge of the intimate cultural details was useful for directors to engage in addressing the problems of a particular region. For example, in Punjab, a mainly agricultural region, the IPTA invoked the relationship between war and poverty through themes related to the food crisis during the war period: the impact of black-marketing and the hoarding of crops by capitalists. The realistic themes pertaining to the contemporary political struggles were interspersed with folk devices such as songs and dances, puppets, clowns, and mimes, which were adjusted according to cultural specificity. According to the 1944 reports provided by the Punjab IPTA, the plays performed in Punjab on issues of national unity and antifascism emerged from discussions with workers and peasants and took into account the local histories, legends, religious beliefs, and traditions. The songs, dances, and puppetry were not only entertaining but also served, by virtue of their familiarity to the people, to capture their attention.

In the industrialized cities of Bangalore and Bombay, on the other hand, where workers' exploitation was rampant in mills and factories, stories about millworkers functioned as an effective theme. Hence, in these places the IPTA presented *Dada* (*Brother,* 1942), about the lives of the Bombay millworkers and their exploitation. Written by T. K. Salmarkar, a millworker, and produced by Prabhakar Gupta, the play was presented on the occasion of May Day, 1942. Written at a time of rising capitalist production in the wake of the World War II, it was filled with "[t]opical illusions to Prohibition, War, Congress Ministries, [and the] Trade Union Movement."[27] The war had created a demand for the production of automobiles, ships, and aircraft and brought for Indian businessmen and traders the opportunity to make quick profits. Between 1939 and 1941, the capitalist bourgeoisie, for whom the war brought gains, kept labor unrest in check by paying workers a substantial dearness allowance and supplying basic goods at subsidized prices.[28] Critically aware of the superficiality and spuriousness of the situation, the playwright attempted to warn the six hundred millworkers who watched the play that their interests were being co-opted for the immediate gains of big business on the one hand and workers' exploitation on the other. As the play climaxed with a scene portraying a workers' rally on May Day, it evoked the collective participation of workers through the popular workers' song, "Nakarepe danka laga hai/Tu Sustra ko apne Sambal. [Bugles are sounding, shoulder your arms]."[29] What took place was the participation of audience and actors alike through a song that was familiar to the audience. As actors and audience joined in a collective spirit to sing this song, a comradeship against oppressive structures was forged.

The open-endedness of the dramas further enabled "popular" participation on a large scale. The IPTA bulletin of 1943 reports workers' participation as actors, as scriptwriters, and as creators of stories they felt needed to be staged. According to the 1944 report of the Punjab IPTA, most of the plays presented in Punjab villages and the districts of Amritsar, Jullunder, and Lahore emerged from this process. For instance, T. K. Sarmalkar's *Dhani* (*Land,* 1942), depicting conflict between a peasant and his landlord, involved peasants as actors in the play. To write a play, two or more people would sit together and devise a rough outline for a plot based on a contemporary problem. Then someone would write its dialogue. The play would be discussed further and alterations made, sometimes even after the first performance to prepare for the second one. Such strategies involving collective authorship, acting, production, and direction of plays suggest a collective political undertaking through a "popular" theater. Through these formalistic alterations and innovations, which shifted from "high" realism to a "popular" social realism, the IPTA took the plays beyond the confines of the profit-oriented commercial theater in cities to its target audience — "the people" — and made their struggles open for intervention. For example, *Nabanna,* the play on the famine of 1943, was performed in villages to peasant audiences, to Kisan Sabhas, and to the workers in different parts of North India, including Punjab, Maharashtra, and Gujarat.

The interweaving of the popular and the political through socially realistic plays had important ramifications for women. The IPTA's close interactions with the "people" forced open the problems of women and their oppression in factories, where women constituted a large part of the workforce. The IPTA members participated in exposing the questions of female oppression both by composing plays about women as well as catering to large female audiences. Ali Sardar Jaffri's *Yeh Kis Kaa Khoon Hai? (Whose Blood Is This?,* 1943), a play about peasants' and workers' resistance in Chittagong to the first Japanese bombing, staged its last performance for an audience of *beedi* workers, most of whom were women.[30] According to the Bombay provincial report of 1944, the audience responded with great enthusiasm to the song at the end that invoked the workers freedom:

> Woh jang hai jang-Azadi
> woh duniya, woh aam hii kyaa
> jisme — dushman taraaj na ho
> woh duniyaa kyaa hogii
> jis duniyaa me — swaraaj naa ho
> aazaadii kyaa
> jisme — mazdoor leo raaj na ho
>
> [That war is a war of freedom
> What is that world
> in which the enemy is not confronted
> What must be that world
> where there were no freedom
> What is that freedom
> in which the workers don't rule. —

So charismatic were the IPTA productions that some of the women in the audience took off their ornaments to donate for a humanitarian cause. At another show in Bombay, workers who were given free tickets offered to pay after the performance. An index of popular response is also provided by Balwant Gargi, a firsthand witness to a production of *Nabanna* in Punjab:

> The lights went down. From the middle of the audience a man suddenly rose to his feet, gave three beats on a drum and made his way towards the stage.

Three men and two women seated in the audience bustled and shoved to follow him. They howled like beggars, "We are hungry! We come from Bengal, the land of plenty, the land of hunger. We are hungry!"

The audience buzzed, annoyed. Who are these people? What were they doing? Why were they causing a disturbance? What did they want?

The broken voices merged into a song as the six mounted the stage. They formed themselves into a group and sang, their eyes burning. All the suffering of famine and poverty was expressed in their voices and strained faces.

Their movements, gestures, expressions and speech had no theatricality; it was as real as the street scenes we experience daily. These faces were familiar to us in the poor quarters of Lahore. . . . they mirrored Indian life, the poverty and suffering under the heel of a foreign power.

Women in the audience sobbed; the eyes of the men misted; two college girls who had wrinkled their noses at the players now wiped their tears. . . . People and players, the two halves of the theatre, kept apart for so long, joined and became one whole.[31]

The enthusiasm that the IPTA generated, the attacks it launched on exploitative structures, and the expectations it aroused are indicative of the initiation of a process that could help "the people" conceptualize the turning upside down of their world. And the participation of "the people" as spectators, as actors, as storytellers, and as donors of money became a seal of their approval of executing collective action. Their attendance and applause were testimony that the events on stage, the acting out of history, had gone beyond the stage itself to the hundreds of "people" to whom the IPTA had intended to take its message.

The formalistic struggle undertaken by IPTA playwrights is part of the larger struggle of India's relation with the British Empire, which exercised its hegemony, among other things (the educational institution, for example, of which Gauri Viswanathan has provided a detailed study), through the imposition of its own dramatic traditions.[32] British rule in India had gradually led to the exclusion of the native popular traditions.[33] Colonial rule generated a cultural hierarchy that drew categorical distinctions of "high" and "low" culture based not on aesthetic decisions but on colonial politics. While the rulers accorded a "high" and privileged status to their own theatrical traditions, especially the drama of Shakespeare, which became canonized as embodying "proper" literary values, indigenous popular traditions such as the *jatras* were relegated to an inferior status.[34] As early as the eighteenth century, British authorities followed a conscious policy of excluding Indians from the European playhouses where plays were performed for the *sahibs* and *memsahibs*. The Calcutta Theatre, supported by Warren

Hastings, governor-general of India, with a repertoire of *The Beaux Strategem*, *The School for Scandal*, *Richard III*, and *Hamlet*, and the Chowringhee Theatre were so exclusive "that even the ushers and doorkeepers were English."[35] The doors were opened to certain classes of Indians only after 1813, when the aristocrat Dwarkanath Tagore was allowed entry into a British theater. Even the plays that were performed there included selections from British and European drama. Popular Indian drama was excluded from British theaters, for fear of the latter being contaminated by the former. To this end, the rulers denounced Indian theatrical traditions and theories, thereby encouraging the natives to follow the "superior" dramatic traditions of the West.

Gradually, British theater became the dominant theater, and the plays performed in these theaters were associated with "high" culture.[36] The "high" naturalism and realism, also imported from the West, became the normative dramatic practices at the beginning of the twentieth century. Well into the twentieth century, the indigenous metropolitan theaters that developed parallel to the Western theater, were imitative of and focused primarily on the naturalistic/high realist conventions of European drama. The IPTA's inception of a popular theater that used traditional popular devices, that was audience-oriented rather than text-oriented, that moved into a space within the reach of "the people," unlike the exclusive commercial theaters of the metropolis, and that increased the use of one-act plays instead of the conventional full-length dramas posed a cultural challenge to colonial and internal hegemonic structures.

DEPENDENCY ON AND APPROPRIATION OF WESTERN DRAMA

The IPTA's resistance to colonial drama did not, however, mean that the Indian and European theatrical traditions were sealed off from each other. The British rulers' attempts to co-opt the Indian bourgeoisie from time to time (even though it was done to make British control stronger) had led to the circulation of British and European drama and an increasing awareness of Western dramatic theories and conventions. These included the use of box sets, footlights, and proscenium stages.[37] Through British clubs and playhouses also filtered Shakespeare and other Western classics, which subsequently flowed into Indian artistic and intellectual life and were gradually disseminated among the public. Such circulation subjected Anglo-European forms to open scrutiny by IPTA organizers, some of whom were well-exposed to them. IPTA artists usefully appropriated these theories for their own needs. For instance, when IPTA directors revived the folk tradition of *jatra,* they learned to cut the performances from many hours to a three-hour show and tone down the overwhelming presence of songs and dances that constituted the original *jatra* performances. This editing was especially useful for those who had to work in factories the following morning and for that reason could not spare the time needed to watch a traditional performance.

European plays were adapted and presented on numerous occasions and tailored according to what IPTA perceived as the demands of the audience. For example, Ibsen's antiestablishment play, *Enemy of the People,* was produced sometime between 1949 and 1952 (the exact date is not available) by Bohurupee of West Bengal and presented to an urban audience in Calcutta as well as to peasants in villages. But instead of following the realistic convention of an Ibsen play, the directors used experimental techniques in this production: actors were asked to extemporize according to the mood of the audience; there was no written script and no sets. According to the producers, the extemporizing was a success: "We invited the audience to imagine that we were sitting in a cosy drawing room, or walking on a road, by pantomime and certain symbols. The audience did believe, first laughingly, then deeply as the story takes a turn."[38]

Since the IPTA was affiliated with the antifascist Progressive Writers' Union in Europe, its members were also aware of the progressive theaters abroad such as The Living Theatre experiments and the Group Theatre of the 1930s in the United States, the popular agitprop theaters in Germany during the 1920s and 1930s, Workers' Theatres in Britain, and the Soviet Shock Troupes in Russia, which had propagated the ideas of socialist reconstruction after the Bolshevik Revolution of 1917. The IPTA adapted plays and formalistic devices from these theaters and shaped them according to the Indian cultural context. For instance, from the Group Theatre in the United States, IPTA directors borrowed Clifford Odets's *Waiting for Lefty,* a realistic play about a taxi driver union's strike in New York. Produced in 1953 by Mulk Raj Anand in Bombay, the play showed capitalist exploitation of workers and the way to counter that exploitation by calling for a revolution, as workers do at the end of *Lefty.* In attempting to create a national identity through drama, the IPTA did not dismiss Western dramatic practices but selectively appropriated them to advance its counter-hegemonic agenda. Progressive plays such as *Waiting for Lefty* served another function: they exposed the corruption rampant in "Western systems," in this way rupturing the falsely perpetuated ideas about the "superior West."

Some scholars, such as Bannerji, find IPTA's Western orientation elitist and see an inherent contradiction in the ideology of the organizers that, they posit, impeded IPTA's eventual success.[39] However, we need to consider the larger context that gave rise to these contradictions and ironies, from which the IPTA sought to impart an "Indian" character to the movement. The IPTA's use of European theories and dramatic practices to counter colonialism may be attributed to the existing historical reality of the Indian stage. A number of playwrights, directors, and producers who sponsored the IPTA (which included intellectuals such as Mulk Raj Anand, K. A. Abbas, and Anil De Silva, the daughter of a Ceylon minister, among others) belonged to the metropolis. Their interaction with the colonizers through British education and participation in British plays had trained them in European theories and practices. For example, Utpal Dutt, a member of the Bengal IPTA from 1950 to 1951, worked in Geoffrey Kendal's Shakespeareana Company after the Kendals came to India in 1947. Dutt professes to have learned all the lessons of the repertory theater from Kendal. Therefore, these playwrights assimilated Anglo-European techniques in their plays.

More important, however, was the British India government's censorship policy on dramatic practices, which played an important role in expediting the IPTA's use of Western plays and practices. Following the passage of the Dramatic Performances Censorship Act in 1876, which empowered government authorities to "prohibit dramatic performances which . . . [were] seditious or obscene, or otherwise prejudicial to the public interests," the colonial government imposed repressive restrictions on the publication and performance of plays that seemed subversive enough to generate anticolonial sentiments.[40] The IPTA angered the government with a number of its dramatic productions and felt the heavy hand of censorship through police atrocities and disruptions of performances and official scrutiny of plays prior to performance.[41] To escape censorship, playwrights sometimes borrowed from European dramas so as to camouflage their messages and propagate their anti-imperial ideas in covert ways.

Censorship of drama continued after independence. The new government that took over the country after 1947 was no less autocratic in this regard, and IPTA productions were constantly crushed by the hands of censors. Until the demise of the IPTA around 1960, severe government repression continued through the censorship laws that had been passed by the British government. Following independence, the Indian government revised the laws, empowering the police to raid places of performance, arrest actors, remove stage property, and confiscate manuscripts of plays. In most cases, the IPTA squads were required to submit playscripts before their performance. An example is the text of a notice served by the commissioner of police in Calcutta to the Bengal branch of IPTA in 1952: "In accordance with the provision laid down under Section 7 of the Dramatic Performance Act, 1876, you are hereby requested to furnish this office by 18th February, 1953, at the latest with the printed or manuscript copies of the dramas mentioned in the statement enclosed. . . . The dramas are required by this office for review so as to ascertain the character of the same." The notice also threatened that failure to submit the dramas would "be treated as violation of the provisions of the Dramatic Performance Act and legal action . . . taken . . . as contemplated under Section 176 of the Indian Penal Code."[42] In the same year in Punjab, police authorities banned the staging of socially significant plays. In Lucknow, four IPTA members, including Razia Sajjad Zaheer and Babulal Verma, were prosecuted for staging a drama without permission. In Cochin, the government banned the drama *You Made Me a Communist*.[43] Censorship also continued through disruption of performances, beating up of actors, even lynching. Continuing censorship resulted in the banning of a number of popular *jatra* plays in Bengal and *powadas* and *tamashas* in Bombay. In 1955 *Haripada Master* was banned in Murshidabad in Uttar Pradesh. For the all-India cultural festival organized in Assam in 1955, the IPTA was required to submit the scripts of the plays "for censor under the Dramatic Performances Act of 1876."[44] In the wake of heavy censorship, the European plays were useful in camouflaging the IPTA's intended messages of social protest. A 1953 list of the plays of the Bengal IPTA that were banned includes only Indian plays written by progressive writers: Sarat Chandra Chattopadhyaya's *Mahesh*, Rabindranath Tagore's *Gora* and *Bisarjan*, and Dinabandhu Mitra's *Nildarpan*.[45] Using plays such as those of Shakespeare and Ibsen may have been useful, since their content was apparently free from the danger of censorship in India. This continued use of a socially committed theater grounded the IPTA in acts of resistance to colonial and neocolonial structures.

INDEPENDENCE AND AFTER

After 1947, the year of India's independence from British rule and also the time that unleashed the most bloody violence in Indian history through the partition of the subcontinent, the IPTA started losing its mass character. The exact date of the association's demise is hard to determine because "a number of splinter groups claiming their origin from the IPTA were gradually formed on the fringe of the theatre movement."[46] It is clear, however, that the IPTA's eighth National Conference, held in Delhi during December 1957, was its last.

Some scholars attribute the IPTA's demise to its strict adherence to the Communist Party line, which after 1948 aligned with the Congress government in the development of a national culture and for the maintenance of world peace. Malini Bhattacharya finds a parallel development in the propagation of social harmony and world peace taken up by the IPTA. She contends that "this is precisely the point where in spite of its broad call to cultural workers and writers irrespective of caste, creed and religion . . . [the IPTA] began to lose its mass character. . . . It seems to me that it was this non-intervention and not too much interference which split up the theatre movement."[47] The IPTA, however, did not adopt a policy of total "non-intervention" after 1947. Nor can its "non-intervention" in government policies be construed as the sole reason that fractured the IPTA. Several other factors contributed to the association's ultimate demise: the partition in 1947, heavier government control through censorship, lack of government patronage to IPTA, and an ideological split among IPTA members.

The postwar years were marked by increased corruption and black-marketing. This in turn raised problems of inflation and poverty because of a sharp increase in prices aggravated by a major food crisis.[48] As India prepared for independence in 1947, it felt the cruelest impact of imperialist policies in the partition of the subcontinent into India and Pakistan. The partition was accompanied by extreme human misery, bloodshed, and loss of lives and property on both sides of the Indo-Pakistan border. The violence of colonialism that ultimately resulted in the violence of partition uprooted many IPTA organizers and members. One such example is Balraj Sahni, an active IPTA member who was in the Rawalpindi district of Punjab (now in Pakistan) on the eve of the subcontinental division. The "wholesale genocide" of partition, he wrote, was "enough to curdle one's blood."[49] Despite the horror of communal riots, Sahni made desperate attempts to mobilize peace activities by singing songs about Hindu-Muslim unity at street corners to collect crowds and then persuade them to keep the districts free of riots. In his autobiography, Sahni writes: "From morning till night, we would roam the entire city on our bicycles, taking our message to the people."[50] Nonetheless, in this state of communal disarray, it was difficult to collect actors and organize plays. The turmoil of the partition ultimately forced Sahni to relocate from Rawalpindi. With no room for

Hindus in Pakistan and having lost all his wealth and property, Sahni moved to Bombay, where he pursued a career in films.

Despite such upheavals, the IPTA continued to function as a politically committed theater. The documents and chronicles of the 1950s reveal the association's continuing efforts to intervene in the political process. The provincial IPTA squads continued staging plays on the themes of partition, on landlord problems, on workers' exploitation, and so forth at a time when the euphoria of independence brought along its own disappointments. Numerous dramas attacking the continuing power structures in postcolonial India were staged. For example, the Kerala stage presented *You Made Me a Communist,* a play on landlordism. Pannu Pal's play, *Chargesheet* (1948?), which urged the release of hundreds of communists who were thrown in jail without trial after the government ban on the Communist Party of India, was taken to working-class *bastis* (settlements) and remote villages of Bengal. Portraying the story of a man who becomes a victim of the Hindu-Muslim riots on the eve of the country's partition into India and Pakistan, K. A. Abbas's *Main Kaun Hoon? (Who Am I?,* 1947) was shown to different strata of people to save the country from religious bigotry and hatred. Ritwik Ghataka's *Dalil* (1952), which dealt with refugee problems after the crisis of the partition, was performed by the South drama squad in many different parts of the country. In 1948, Sahni wrote *Jadoo Ki Kursi (The Magical Chair),* a play, which, in his own words, "devastatingly lampooned Jawaharlal Nehru and his policies."[51]

Along with the IPTA's presentation of politically subversive material, one also discerns a shift toward classical "Indian" forms. This shift occurs from the IPTA's "peace-building" efforts after the 1940s in the wake of Hindu-Muslim discord emanating in the postpartition and post-Indo-Pakistan war of 1948, the problem in Kashmir, and the attempt to build a united nation to prevent the economic and political neocolonialism that threatened to creep in through the domination of British capital over India's economy as well as increasing U.S. interference, especially over the Kashmir issue.[52] At such a time IPTA members held on to an identifiable "Indianness," using the rhetoric of a lost "Indian" heritage to carve out an "Indian" identity. During its annual meetings, organizers emphasized the greatness of India's cultural heritage by invoking images of a national past whose glory had faded under the heel of a foreign power. While exploring the relationship between "peace and people's theatre," Anna Bhau Sathe, the IPTA's general secretary, posited in 1953 in *Unity,* the organization's official journal, that peace could be achieved through "our great dramatists, their dramas and immortal sayings" and evoked names of classical dramatists from the past such as Bhasha and Shudraka (200 B.C.) as exemplars for social change.[53] Abbas, too, called for peace through an invocation of the ancient Hindu texts such as the *Rigveda*, the *Yajurveda*, the *Upanishads*, and the *Mahabharata*, contending that, "in ancient Indian culture . . . in spite of wars and strife, friendship and brotherhood pervade the literature of the past."[54]

While the government endorsed the IPTA's effort to propagate its "Indian" heritage, it kept the IPTA's subversive character in check. Regular subjection to censorship in various regions was a major impediment to the IPTA's activities and succeeded, to a large degree, in preventing the IPTA plays from being taken to villages and towns. A number of performances were in fact disrupted by the police. The government also attempted to crush the movement through its entertainment tax policy. This policy was a major detriment for the IPTA, which was a nonprofit organization and often performed free of charge. On the other hand, the government patronage of the development of "Indian" arts and culture was provided to the Sangeet Nataka Academy, the Lalit Kala Academy, and others. "The various akademies [*sic*], the All-India Radio, the proposed Book Trusts, the institution of prizes and rewards — all these . . . [were] so worked [out] as not to give any scope for the thousands of worker-peasant artists and writers who look upon culture as the weapon of struggle for genuine people's democracy and lasting peace."[55]

At a time of nation building in the life of the newly independent nation, all cultural productions that appeared to be subversive or political were obliterated from state-controlled university curricula and various government-funded cultural organizations. It is no coincidence that at this juncture, the trends of New Criticism and modernism were taken to be ideally constituted for defining culture. Mainstream Indian critics such as Srinivasan Iyengar launched into a New Critical rhetoric of "an 'authentically Indian sensibility' " while "embracing a universalist metaphysic."[56] A combination of these factors led to the ultimate demise of the IPTA.

CONCLUSION

The IPTA was not an undifferentiated phenomenon. Its themes ranged from fascism and war to imperialism and exploitation, both British and Indian. It recognized the many layers of oppression that existed in society and sought to rectify the vexing wrongs committed against the marginalized classes. To effectively disseminate its messages to a geographically and linguistically diverse population and establish intimate links among the masses from various regions, the formalistic and linguistic concerns of its plays were constantly reconfigured. Such concerns imparted a rich significance to its political agenda. For instance, the translation of plays into different languages suggests a political action on the part of IPTA organizers. Through linguistic diversification, IPTA artists used the theater as a vehicle for awakening a spirit of protest among "the people" that would merge into a collective antifascist and anti-imperialist consciousness. Similarly, joint authorship of plays indicates a collective political undertaking on the part of the organizers. Keeping a theory of social realism as its central concern, which forged an interpretive relationship with the audience, IPTA organizers constantly experimented with an amalgamation of theater forms, both indigenous and Western. Borrowing from European theories of realism and epic theater and altering these theories according to the cultural traditions of the people, the space of the performance, and the time required to engage the attention of huge audiences often led to the production of one-act plays. The result was the emergence of a heterogeneous theater that was unique and innovative and acquired a multifaceted character. This heterogeneity of the theater became a strategic tool for enabling the IPTA to carry out its subversive attempts at interrogating existing power structures. Thus, the IPTA inaugurated an alternative model of cultural production that became a significant site of sociohistorical struggle on which the drama of colonial exploitation and domination was played out.

The multifaceted character of the IPTA enabled its organizers to counter the colonial authorities' repressive policies of censorship through dramatic formulas and spaces that tried to escape the reach of the censors and challenge the status quo. The accomplishments of the IPTA thus were crucial. It initiated the entry of the masses into active political life. It revived indigenous drama, which had suffered a great setback because of the valorization of European theaters and the imposition of censorship on native drama through the Dramatic Performances Censorship Act of 1876.

The IPTA also changed the structure and conception of theater in various parts of India. By mobilizing plays that were constructed according to the sociopolitical environment, the IPTA altered the use of theater from merely a means of entertainment to a forum for people's struggles. By performing for the rural and the nonliterate public instead of a limited upper-class audience, the IPTA made the political theater available to those who previously had little or no access to it. An important ramification of the process was that the plays provided exposure of political problems in the public space to those women whose lives were largely confined to the domestic sphere. However, while the IPTA provided exposure to women, dealt with the problems of female workers in public spaces such as factories and tea plantations, and sought women's involvement in the movement, it rarely staged the problems confronting women in the domestic sphere. This oversight emerged from its homogenization of all marginalized classes under the category of "the people." For instance, in *Zubeida* (1944), a play about the relief work done by a young Muslim girl during the 1944 cholera epidemic, its author K. A. Abbas provides no context about Zubeida's own difficulties in stepping out of the domestic space.[57] The cholera epidemic was largely a result of the famine in 1943; shortage of food and lack of clean water facilitated disease and death. This, combined with a shortage of medical supplies that were being channeled for the troops abroad, resulted in the epidemic. Affected by the funeral processions of the cholera casualties, Zubeida casts aside her *purdah* and moves out of the domestic space to a public one to volunteer for relief work.[58] However, like the people she tries to help, Zubeida too dies because of a scarcity of vaccine. Zubeida's role in the cholera epidemic is hardly insignificant, but is emblematic of two challenges: her stepping out of the home is a challenge to the male-dominated domestic space that can no longer keep her confined, and her efforts to save the cholera victims represent an act of intervention in the colonial policies that were responsible for the epidemic. While Abbas recognizes Zubeida's contribution, his construction of Zubeida is problematic. In focusing on her activism, Abbas mystifies the politics of religion and *purdah* in the private space from which she emerges. Moreover, Abbas confines Zubeida's activism to the role of a nurturer who tends to the cholera victims and sacrifices her own life to save them. Zubeida may step out of the domestic space to participate in the nationalist process but only in a desexualized and feminized role that Abbas conceived for her.[59] Such a portrayal becomes all the more stark in contrast to the "masculine" roles of the male activists in *Four Comrades*.[60] However, this gap has been redressed in recent years by women's theater groups such as the Theatre Union, which is the continuation of the women's collective Stree Sangharsh (Women's struggle). Through street theater along the lines of the IPTA, the group confronts women's problems such as the dowry murders, rape, self-immolation by widows, female foeticide, and so forth.[61]

The IPTA left a strong legacy for political theater groups in India.

Most of the contemporary theater groups draw on the IPTA's concept of a traveling theater for propagating political activism. These, among others, include the numerous theater groups in Calcutta, one of the largest centers of political theater activity in India; Karnataka's community theater Samudaya, formed by R. P. Prasanna in 1975 during the emergency to campaign against Indira Gandhi; the Association of the Rural Poor in Tamil Nadu, composed mainly of *dalits,* untouchable landless farmworkers; and the Cultural Caravans in Kerala.[62] The work carried on by these organizations amidst official and unofficial censorship and with practically no financial support from the state shows that as long as there is commitment, the theater will continue to force to the surface questions of exploitation and human rights violations.

NOTES

I am grateful to Barbara Harlow for her invaluable comments and suggestions. To Elizabeth Richmond-Garza for her discussions on the theoretical questions regarding drama and theater and W. B. Worthen, who helped me think through important issues about theater and performance, I am extremely grateful. Thanks to Shoba Vasudevan and Preet Aulakh, who were very generous with their time and suggestions when I was revising my paper. My thanks to Purnima Bose, Rachel Jennings, Louis Mendoza, Louis Merentes, and Hosam Aboul-Ela for critiquing earlier versions of the paper. I gratefully acknowledge my colleagues at the colloquium held at the Humanities Research Institute, UC Irvine, for the opportunity to discuss this paper. And finally thanks to David Lloyd and Lisa Lowe for their unflagging support.

1. Utpal Dutt, *Towards a Revolutionary Theatre* (Calcutta: M. C. Sarkar Sons, 1982), 19. Dutt joined the IPTA in 1950 and left the organization in 1951 after an ideological falling out with other members.

2. *Indian People's Theatre Association Bulletin,* no. 1 (July 1943), quoted in Sudhi Pradhan, ed., *Marxist Cultural Movements in India: Chronicles and Documents. 1936–47* (Calcutta: National Book Agency, 1979), 129.

3. Pradhan, *Marxist Cultural Movements in India 1936–47,* 129.

4. K. A. Abbas, "India's Anti-Fascist Theatre," in *Asia and the Americans* (December 1952): 711.

5. Ibid. The *jatra,* which literally means "to go in a procession," is a traveling theater popular in Bengal, Orissa, and Eastern Bihar. A typical *jatra* performance contains about sixty songs and lasts a couple of days. *Tamasha* is a popular theater of Maharashtra; the songs in a *tamasha* are accompanied by two drummers. *Burrakatha* is a popular folk narrative of Andhra Pradesh that depicts the lives of ordinary people in song and dance. The *burra* is a clay

instrument. See Balwant Gargi, *Folk Theatre of India* (Seattle: University of Washington Press, 1966).

6. Immanuel Wallerstein, "The Construction of Peoplehood: Racism, Nationalism, Ethnicity," in *Race, Nation, Class: Ambiguous Identities,* ed. Etienne Balibar and Immanuel Wallerstein, Balibar trans. by Chris Turner (London: Verso, 1991), 81. Wallerstein discusses this "problem of cohesion" in the context of South Africa.

7. According to Malini Bhattacharya, on one occasion at a Kisan Sabha conference, the Bengali IPTA troupe had to stop the performance because of a heavy storm and rain. The audience of around twenty thousand people waited for the rain to stop and the play was finally performed to an enthusiastic response.

8. Abbas, "India's Anti-Fascist Theatre," 711. It is alleged that the IPTA was a cultural wing of the Communist Party of India, was involved primarily with communist propaganda, and rigidly followed the dictates of the Communist Party. The chronicles and documents of the IPTA reveal that most members, such as the Kisan Union leaders and cultural and student fronts, had a leftist orientation and were immensely influenced by the Leninist brand of Marxism, the Revolution of 1917 having inspired them (Pradhan, *Marxist Cultural Movements in India 1936–47*). Therefore, they also endorsed the viewpoint of the Communist Party of India. The keynote of the IPTA program during the years 1942 to 1947 regarding Hindu-Muslim unity, release of Congress leaders from jail, and opposition to the Quit India movement followed the political line of the Party during that time (ibid., xiii–xiv). However, it must be specified that not all of its organizers were card-holding members of the Party: they were progressive intellectuals from all walks of life committed to the task of mobilizing a "people's" theater. The IPTA, thus, was not bound by the Party in any way.

9. Abbas, "India's Anti-Fascist Theatre," 711. The inspiration of the Progressive Writers' Union came from the antifascist cultural organizations in Europe, especially the International Association of Writers for the Defence of Culture against Fascism, which was supported by Romain Rolland, Maxim Gorky, Thomas Mann, and Andre Malraux among others. At its first conference the members of the PWA unanimously resolved the need for a progressive literature, defining progressive literature as that which "must deal with the basic problems of our existence today — the problems of hunger and poverty, social backwardness and political subjection" (quoted in Pradhan, *Marxist Cultural Movements 1936–47,* 21). In the same year, progressive Indian intellectuals such as Rabindranath Tagore, Sarat Chatterjee, Munshi Premchand (a great proponent of progressive socialist realism in his Hindi writings of this period), P. C. Roy, Jawaharlal Nehru, Nandlal Bose, and others sent a letter to the Second Congress of the International Writers' Association in London, declaring their open hostilities to war.

10. I have provided only those dates that are available.

11. Susie Tharu and K. Lalita, eds., introduction, in *Women Writing in India, 600 B.C. to the Present,* vol. 2, *The Twentieth Century* (New York: Feminist Press, 1993), 80–81.

12. In this paper I will discuss a few plays as examples of the IPTA's participation in the political process through cultural productions. I am grateful to the Humanities Research Center at the University of Texas at Austin for providing me access to the plays *Four Comrades* and *Roar China*. Most of the IPTA plays were created during discussions among members and then acted out extemporaneously. Therefore, most playscripts are not available. Some remained unpublished, and typed or handwritten copies were made available to provincial IPTA squads for a charge of one rupee for the paper and typing (Pradhan, *Marxist Cultural Movements in India, 1936–47*, 161); thus they are difficult to obtain. Other scripts, such as Balraj Sahni's *Jadoo Ki Kursi*, were destroyed. In his autobiography, Sahni admits that he tore up the only available copy of the play.

13. According to the "Provincial Reports, Bombay," one IPTA branch performed *Four Comrades* at a Kisan (farmers') rally of 20,000 peasants (Pradhan, *Marxist Cultural Movements in India 1936–47*, 148).

14. The Russian play was written in 1924 by Sergei Mikhailovich Tretiakov, an important leader of the "Left Front" movement in Soviet Literature. In 1924 Tretiakov went to China and taught at the National University of Peking. During his stay in China, on June 22, 1924, a dispute broke out between the British Navy and the native Chinese. Captain Whitehorn of the British Gunboat *Cockchafer* ordered two innocent Chinese put to death. The British captain received a decoration. Appalled by the British behavior, Tretiakov wrote a play based on the episode called *The Cockchafer*. The play was rejected by the Proletcult Theatre as well as the Theatre of the Revolution. In the meantime, French, American, and English imperialism continued to grow in China, and Tretiakov expanded the play to cover the methods of these aggressors in China and the consequent ill feeling among the Chinese working classes. On January 23, 1926, the play was "rechristened" *Roar China* and produced by Meyerhold's Theatre in Moscow. Later the play was produced in Berlin and elsewhere in Europe. In America, the Theatre Guild produced it on October 22, 1930. Because of its critical portrayal of the British Navy, the public staging of *Roar China* was not permitted in England. Later, in November 1931, the play was produced privately by Mr. F. Sladin-Smith of the Unnamed Society and was published with certain alterations, including the substitution of the British Navy by the French Navy. See H. W. L. Dana, introduction, in *Roar China*, by Sergei Mikhailovich Tretiakov, trans. F. Polianovska and Barbara Nixon (New York: International Publishers, n.d.), 3–5.

15. Sergei Mikhailovich Tretiakov, *Roar China* (Bombay: The Indian People's Theatre Association, Dramatics For National Defense, 1942?), 1.

16. Sumit Sarkar, *Modern India 1885–1947* (Delhi: Macmillan, 1983), 388. In 1942 Gandhi called for a nonviolent protest during the Quit India movement, but, as Gyanendra Pandey posits, the movement went well beyond the confines of what Gandhi had envisaged. See Gyanendra Pandey, *The Indian Nation in 1942* (Calcutta: Centre for Studies in Social Sciences, 1988).

17. These words were contained in the original draft of the Allahabad Work-

ing Committee Session of April 1942, which was finally removed upon Nehru's insistence. See Sarkar, *Modern India 1885–1947*, 390.

18. Tretiakov, *Roar China*, 9–10.

19. Ibid., 6.

20. Ibid., 13.

21. See Shahid Amin, "Gandhi as Mahatma: Gorakhpur District, Eastern UP, 1921–2," in *Subaltern Studies III: Writings on South Asian History and Society,* ed. Ranajit Guha (Delhi: Oxford University Press, 1984), 1. In his essay Amin explores the ways in which the idea of Gandhi as "Mahatma" was thought out and reworked in the popular imagination.

22. *Four Comrades* (Bombay: The Indian People's Theatre Association, National Dramatics for Defense, 1942?), 11.

23. Sarkar, *Modern India 1885–1947*, 392. For a detailed study on the causes of famines see Amartya K. Sen, *Poverty and Famines: An Essay on Entitlement and Deprivation* (Delhi: Oxford University Press, 1981). Arguing against the commonly held views that attribute famines to overpopulation and a scarcity of food, Sen posits that, among other things, people starve when their "entitlement" is not enough to buy the food necessary for sustenance.

24. Conventionally, European realism concentrated on reproducing the appearance of social reality to the minutest details. Through an "accurate" imitation of life, the realist writer attempted to create the illusion that the staged presentation reflected life as experienced by the spectator. Its purpose was to evoke empathy through identification with the action and induce forgetfulness on the part of the spectator, who became an unobserved listener through "an invisible fourth wall." To achieve this illusion of reality, the dramatic realist typically chose an ordinary person as protagonist and preferred the commonplace and the everyday to the rarer aspects of life. The characters lived through the same experiences and problems as those of the common people. Their speech was the colloquial idiom of everyday life, devoid of the mechanics of rhetorical speech. The play unfolded through a logical sequence of events. The rigors of realism thus involved, in addition to its subject matter, a special literary form that was to be a very mirror held up to real life. Although a lifelike reproduction invited the spectators' empathy and subsequent understanding, it also prevented their ability to act by inducing only passive consumption as invoked by the classical model.

In the 1930s, Brecht ruptured the illusionism of realism, introducing through his Epic Theatre a nonillusionistic apparatus that sought to destroy the verisimilitude of a realist performance to create a critical distance between the stage and the spectator. However, according to some critics, the Brechtian model was as elitist as the realist model that he dismissed. The nonillusionist drama that he proposed was too intellectualized and put pressure on the spectators to grasp the nuances of his plays' messages. IPTA artists often debated among themselves over the use of Brecht and Stanislavsky, who sought identification by eliciting a realist drama through an actor's transformation into the character that he or she played. Bijon Bhattacharyara did not particularly like the Brechtian model but was willing to try it so long as it was altered according to the cultural context of rural Bengal.

25. Malini Bhattacharya, "The IPTA in Bengal," *Journal of Arts and Ideas* 2 (January–March 1983), 9.

26. James Clifford, "On Ethnographic Allegory," in *Writing Culture: The Poetics and Politics of Ethnography,* ed. James Clifford and George E. Marcus (Berkeley: University of California Press, 1986), 98.

27. K. A. Abbas, *I Write As I Feel* (Bombay: Hind Kitabs, 1948), 31.

28. Sarkar, *Modern India 1885–1947,* 84.

29. Quoted in Pradhan, *Marxist Cultural Movements in India 1936–47,* 144; translation in Pradhan.

30. A *beedi* is a cigarette made by rolling tobacco in dry leaves.

31. Balwant Gargi, *Theatre in India* (New York: Theatre Arts Books, 1962), 188–189.

32. See Gauri Vishwanathan, *Masks of Conquest: Literary Studies and British Rule in India* (New York: Columbia University Press, 1989).

33. The classical Sanskritic tradition has been consciously set apart from the popular traditions, and Sanskrit dramas were valorized as exotic forms of art. One such example is Kalidasa's *Sakuntala,* which, upon being translated by William Jones, had been widely received in Europe with immense enthusiasm. Marking these diametrically opposed reactions to the two Indian traditions was a colonialist ideology. Treating the Sanskritic texts as exclusive and superior marked the British as a superior race who could decipher esoteric texts that were comparable to the Greek classics. Moreover, by appreciating the texts of the elite Brahmanic caste, the British sought to cement an alliance with a select class of Indians and to receive their consent and help for effective governance. Through such collaboration, British rulers wanted to educate these elites in their own traditions to produce what Macaulay called "a class of persons, Indian in blood and colour, but British in tastes, in opinions, in morals and in intellect," in other words, a class of people perfectly suited for facilitating the colonial administration of the country. See Thomas Babington Macaulay, "Minute on Indian Education," in *Selected Writings,* ed. John Clive (Chicago: University of Chicago Press, 1972), 249.

34. In *The Parlour and the Streets: Elite and Popular Culture in Nineteenth Century Calcutta* (Calcutta: Seagull Books, 1989), 4, Sumanta Banerji provides a detailed discussion of the development of elite and popular culture in nineteenth-century Calcutta. Banerji posits that the traditional folk culture forms in the nineteenth century "were objects of derision in the eyes of the 'Orientalists' as well as the 'rationalist' school of thought."

35. Rustom Bharucha, *Rehearsals of Revolution: The Political Theatre of Bengal* (Honolulu: University of Hawaii Press, 1983), 8.

36. It is an interesting irony that plays like those of Shakespeare, Ibsen, and Shaw, which were subversive within their own context, became "high" culture in the Indian context because of their association with the West.

37. Gargi, *Theatre in India.*

38. *Unity* (July 1952), quoted in Sudhi Pradhan, ed., *Marxist Cultural Movements in India: Chronicles and Documents. 1947–1958,* vol. 2 (Calcutta: Navana, 1982), 90, 92.

39. Hemani Bannerji, "Language and Liberation: A Study of Political Theatre in Bengal," *Ariel* 15 (1984): 131–144.

40. Home Department Proceedings, "Draft Bill to Empower the Government to Prohibit Certain Dramatic Performances" (Delhi: National Archives of India, March 1876).

41. Throughout the association's career, IPTA directors attempted to fight state censorship, pledging at every annual all-India conference to challenge the government on this front.

42. Quoted in Pradhan, *Marxist Cultural Movements in India,* vol. 2, 187.

43. The ban was ultimately revoked because of pressure from the public.

44. Quoted in Pradhan, *Marxist Cultural Movements in India,* vol. 2, 252.

45. Quoted in ibid., 188.

46. Bhattacharya, "The IPTA in Bengal," 14.

47. Ibid.

48. On 29 June 1946, Wavell estimated a deficit of 3 million tons, while imports from the United States remained uncertain, leading to a drastic cut in rations. See Sarkar, *Modern India 1885–1947,* 419.

49. Balraj Sahni, *Balraj Sahni: An Autobiography* (Delhi: Hind Pocket Books, 1979), 140–141.

50. Ibid., 141.

51. Ibid., 153–154.

52. In the report about the IPTA's all-India peace conference of 1952, Narahari Kaviraj vehemently stated, "Constant attempts are being made by certain powers to intensify their control over India. These intrigues are leading to certain new developments in the Indian situation — the most important being the increasing U.S. interference in the affairs of our country. In the economic sphere, due to the domination of British capital over our economy, the conditions in our country are as bad as they can be. The increasing integration of Indian and American economy through the Point Four programme, the World Bank Loan, the Food Loan and other private U.S. investments, signifies an additional burden upon our people" (quoted in Pradhan, *Marxist Cultural Movements in India,* vol. 2, 315.

53. Quoted in ibid., 176.

54. Quoted in ibid., 321. Abbas invoked several ancient texts, including those in Bengali, Hindi, Urdu, Telugu, Malayalam, Rajasthani, and Punjabi.

The glory of India's past to invoke nationalist sentiments was set in motion by the nineteenth-century Eurocentric reception in Europe of India's dramatic arts, such as Kalidasa's *Sakuntala.* William Jones's translations of *Sakuntala* has been widely distributed in Europe and had especially appealed to German Romantic sensibilities. Schiller, Wilhelm Von Humbolt, and Goethe praised *Sakuntala* for its "pastoral charm" and "lyric beauty." Marking this reception, says Sue-Ellen Case, was "a colonialist ideology . . . [hinging upon] the reception of Sanskrit in European studies and the studied promulgation of the English language and literature in colonial India" ("The Euro-Colonial Reception of Sanskrit Poetics," in *The Performance of Power: Theatrical Discourse and Politics,* ed. Sue-Ellen Case and Janelle Reinelt [Iowa City: University of Iowa Press, 1991], 112). In her analysis, Case limits her arguments to the Eurocentric constructions of Sanskrit drama and their ideological ramifications in the creation of stereotypes about Indian society. It is also important to note that Indian nationalists avidly seized upon the exoticized images of India's dramatic arts to reconstruct India's past glory and generate pride in that past. The glorification of the cultural achievements of the past Hindu era "set in motion by nineteenth century Orientalists, contributed to the awakening of a national self-consciousness among the . . . Hindu intelligentsia" (Banerji, *The Parlour and the Street,* 6). This pride in India's heritage became visible in Anna Bhau Sathe's praises for Kalidasa and *Sakuntala* when Sathe discussed the IPTA's role in creating peace for the nation, which he said was even hailed by "Goethe, the great German poet," who "danced with joy" upon reading *Sakuntala* (quoted in Pradhan, *Marxist Cultural Movements in India,* vol. 2).

55. Quoted in Sudhi Pradhan, *Marxist Cultural Movements in India: Chronicles and Documents. 1947–1964* (Calcutta: Mrs. Santi Pradhan, 1985), 486.

56. Tharu and Lalita, *Women Writing in India,* 92.

57. For a discussion on *Zubeida* see Bharucha, *Rehearsals of Revolution,* 41–42; Tharu and Lalita, *Women Writing in India,* 80–81; and Sahni, *Balraj Sahni: An Autobiography.*

58. Tharu and Lalita, *Women Writing in India,* 81.

59. Radha Kumar discusses the problems pertaining to the "nationalist feminist woman activist" during the freedom struggle, who, as Kumar posits, "was seen both as a symbol and a bulwark of women's emancipation: [but] the fact that the image of a woman activist which had been constructed in this period itself limited and restricted women was not questioned. Though activist women did not themselves dwell on this, clearly nationalists, revolutionary terrorists and communists saw a certain threat in women's activism, for each, in their different ways, tried to restrict it. Their chief desire seems to have been to somehow divest women of the sexuality associated with them; either through total desexualization as preached by Gandhi, or through domestication and subjugation, as for example, in the communists' preference for women who were married to male activists" (*The History of Doing: An Illustrated Account of Movements for Women's Rights and Feminism in India, 1800–1990* [London: Verso, 1993], 94).

60. In *Rehearsals of Revolution,* Rustom Bharucha posits that one historical importance of *Zubeida* lies in the fact that "many of the spectators . . . included women who had never seen a play in their lives" (42). While *Zubeida*'s action was an attempt to mobilize women's participation in the colonial insurgency, its sanctioning of women's roles as sacrificers sends a message of subjugation.

61. Formed in 1981 by Anuradha Kapoor, Maya Rao, and Rati Bartholomew, the group has made the problems of gender public and open for intervention. In

1981 Kapoor organized a street play on dowry deaths, which has been performed three hundred times since then. According to Kapoor in a personal interview with Eugene Van Erven, "performances of the dowry play regularly resulted in lengthy discussions in the audience, who often asked the performers where they should go for help." See Eugene Van Erven, *The Playful Revolution: Theatre and Liberation in Asia* (Bloomington: Indiana University Press, 1992), 118.

62. See ibid.

CHUNGMOO CHOI

The Discourse of Decolonization and
Popular Memory: South Korea

The crisis consists precisely in the fact that the old is dying and the new cannot be born; in this interregnum a great variety of morbid symptoms appear.
ANTONIO GRAMSCI[1]

I begin this essay by invoking Antonio Gramsci's image of an interregnum, a space of crisis, which is pregnant with morbid grotesquery. This
is the space from which I present the problems of "postcolonial" South
Korea. I do not purport simply to identify the predicament of South
Korea as such, although inevitably this issue will be discussed in order
to locate the problems I am planning to address. In this essay, I intend to
examine critically the Southern Korean discourse of discolonization
and offer an occasion to rethink its subversive strategies so that the new
can be born.

WHEN IS POSTCOLONIAL?—THE PERMANENCE
OF COLONIALISM IN SOUTH KOREA

When is postcolonial in South Korea? The official history written in
South Korea denies the legitimacy of this rhetorical question because
the physical absence/removal of Japanese colonial rule after 1945
defines South Korea as essentially postcolonial. However, assuming
South Korea to be postcolonial eludes the political, social, and economic realities of its people, which lie behind that celebrated sign *post*
of periodization, without considering the substantive specificity of
Korean histories. The actual landscape of the postcolonial space is a
contestatory one. This very contestation tests our sensibilities and demands that we rethink the "postcolonial" realities of the (ex-)colonies.
As I will attempt to illustrate throughout this essay, "postcolonial"
South Korea is a space lying between the empty signifier, *postcolonial,*
and the reality that it (mis)represents.

I do not intend here to echo Anne McClintock's and Ella Shohat's
recent critique of postcolonialism, in which they contend that the term

postcolonial does not correspond to the social and historical realities of many third world countries where imperial powers vibrantly exercise colonial and neocolonial practices.[2] We may extrapolate from the arguments of McClintock and Shohat that the term *postcolonialism* is impregnated with a universalizing character that privileges the subjective position of the Western imperial powers. That is, the term *postcolonial* does honor the colonial masters' de jure loss of sovereignty over their former colonies, while it disregards the deferred postcoloniality in many of these former colonies. Shohat actually points out that the term *postcolonial* is a diluted replacement of the term *third world* that once profferred revolutionary possibilities. While insisting that *postcolonial* is a politically vacuous term created in the increasingly depoliticized climate of U.S. academia, Shohat concludes with a rather predictable suggestion that we should consider historical, geopolitical, and cultural contexts.

I would like to take this debate further. In essence, what is at issue here is not the matter of rethinking or reinventing a term that may universally represent the realities of the "postcolonial" third world, but the necessity of the decolonization discourse in the true sense of the word so that the cause of this discomfort with the term itself can be made obsolete. As a contribution to this project I will offer a strategy that revises the old notion of decolonization that emphasizes the restoration of the political and ideological sovereignty of a nation. Locating the decolonization discourse in the arena of national sovereignty alone buries the intractable ambiguities of the postcolonial subject position with split loyalties, allowing a colonization of consciousness. By colonization of consciousness I mean the imposition by the dominant power of its own worldview, its own cultural norms and values, on the (colonized) people so that they are compelled to adopt this alien system of thought as their own and therefore disregard or disparage indigenous culture and identity.[3] Colonization of consciousness thus perpetuates cultural dependency and colonial subjectivity. I will argue that the strategy of the decolonization discourse in the largely "postcolonial" era requires a self-reflective examination of this ambiguity that deters decolonization from within, beyond the more palpable material conditions and hegemonic forces from without. In this light, the discourse of decolonization cannot safely rely on the self/other formula of the anticolonial discourse, although the two share a certain common property in their casual relationship. I suspect that JanMohamed's strategic formula of Manichaean struggle,[4] for instance, risks significant oversight of the constant slippage in the binary opposition of self/other, which the decolonization discourse attempts to overcome. Homi Bhabha's[5] notion of colonial mimicry may be more productive, in that it can be extended to that of mutual mimicry and thus offers an alternative view: the notion of ambivalence, which may ease the rigidity of the binarism. JanMohamed criticized Homi Bhabha's notion as positing the unity of the colonial subject that dissolves the conflictual relationship between the colonizer and the colonized. I remain sympathetic to JanMohamed's conviction in the critique of the colonial discourse insofar as the Manichaean struggle maintains the sharpness of colonial subjectivity to unseat the authority of colonial discourse. However, I find Bhabha's formulation quite accommodating, in that it opens up the possibility of self-reflective criticism by suggesting the possibility of mutual mimicry between the colonizer and the colonized beyond the inflexible rigidity of self and other. The self-reflective positionality rescues the colonized subject from the trap of being a victim, which often (and dangerously) slips into self-glorification. Such glorification of victimhood often engenders an effect of Manichaean theology founded on binarism. Moreover, holding the imperial powers responsible for (neo)colonization, one not only minimizes one's own decolonizing potential but may also fail to activate the bottled-up subversive energy. I shall develop this point later, in my conclusion.

It is against this backdrop that I will address the issues of colonization of consciousness and explore the epistemological landscape of postcoloniality in South Korea. The project to decolonize consciousness will inevitably interrogate the issue of historical consciousness or lack thereof, which, in complicated alliances with the material forces of imperialism, often causes internal displacement among a colonized people culturally, socially, and psychologically.

The point of departure is Korea's official historical narratives: of the liberation, the national partition,[6] and the subsequent disenfranchisement of a nongovernmental Korean subjective position from history. The dominant narrative of South Korean history long acknowledged liberation as a gift of the allied forces, especially of the United States, since Koreans were excluded in the liberation process itself. This narrative not only justified Korea's position as restrained by the sovereign power of the former Soviet Union and the United States on the issues of Korean partition, but also is responsible for admitting cold war ideology as the ruling ideology of both Koreas. Such a narrative has delegitimated the Koreans as valid agents of both nation building and the subsequent military and economic dependence on the cold war superpowers, although to a differing degree in the North than in the South. The transitive verbs *to liberate* and *to partition* presuppose a subject (or subjects), who is external to the action and yet administers it, and a passive receiver (the object) upon which such actions are performed. This differential positionality between subject and object may also extend to the performative consequences of the terms *national liberation* and *independence*. This very breach between the subject-object positions illustrates the historical circumstances of "postcolonial" Korea. Although the debate on this subject shifted to a discourse of the Korean contribution, crediting the relentless Independence Movement of the Koreans for winning U.S. recognition, which in turn granted the liberation of Korea,[7] it required a tragedy before the Koreans would revise their analytic framework, which had uncritically privileged the centrality of the West in the shaping of their own fate.

During the cold war era, this alienation or exteriorization of the South Koreans from their own history was reinforced and internalized in the name of liberty and protection from a North demonized by the cold war discourse of wilderness and of poverty.[8] For more than two decades after the national partition, South Korean schoolchildren visually depicted North Koreans literally as red-bodied demons with horns and long fingernails on their hairy, grabbing hands, as represented in anticommunist posters and widely distributed propaganda materials, such as *Friends of Liberty*, a lavishly printed magazine distributed free to book-hungry Koreans in the war-devastated South. Once the dizzying frenzy of propaganda subsided and the demonic image of the Northern brothers faded, the question that haunted South Koreans was whether their Northern relatives were starving (as they have repeatedly assumed without any verifiable evidence). Understandably, the discourse of poverty has been deployed by both the North and the South as an effective technique of disciplining its people. Korean Americans are now allowed to travel to North Korea. The messages of the North Korean citizens to their kin in the South, conveyed through their relatives from across the Pacific, often express satisfaction with their material comfort. As the discourse of poverty has created a sense of crisis and, proportionally, promoted material fetishism, it has effectively sustained the South Korean military and economic dependence on the United States.

The materials of indoctrination also instilled a false sense of prosperity and a fetishism for what was out of reach, and this in turn engendered a pathology of self-pity occasioned by the lack of material goods. I remember once, in my childhood, seeing a picture of a roller-skating Korean couple in ballet outfits featured in one of these magazines. Nothing could have been further from the reality of starving, war-torn South Korea. Yet the picture captured my imagination and kindled my envy. Soon American mass culture towered over Korea's desolate cultural landscape as South Korea became one of the most heavily armed fortresses of the vast American empire. To live in this state of internal displacement and external dependency is to live in a state of colonialism. This "postcolonial" colonialism is not simply an expansion of the borders of the capitalist superpowers into the devastated former colonies. It cannot be confined to the arena of economics that neocolonialism often connotes. It is a colonization of consciousness, which results in a broad range of cultural expression, values, and behavior and the production of knowledge in an environment of tremendous material and cultural disparity. These symptoms are, in a sense, a product at once of the politics of assimilation and of separatism: the reproduction of the contradictory colonial double discourse. As I will illustrate later, colonial double discourse has created for colonized people an illusion of living in the same social and cultural sphere as that of the metropolis, while it ruthlessly exercises a discriminatory politics of hierarchy. Under these circumstances a (post)colonized people continues to live at the edge of the metropolis. In this borderland, as Vicente Rafael put it, "(a colonized) people constantly recasts, even as it appropriates, identities and languages: those of its real or imagined ancestors as well as those imposed on it by the colonial state or imputed to it by other ethnic groups. With these efforts, it seeks a place in social hierarchy, even as it struggles to project alternative conditions for future empowerment."[9] The negotiation that Rafael observes may manifest itself crudely as a collaboration or as a more subtle cultural assimilation.

South Koreans have lived on the same edge of both colonial and (post)colonial borderlands. As the people of South Korea acquired a detailed sense of distinction through appropriating Western symbolic capital,[10] which South Koreans have neither the resources to produce nor the cultural taste to appreciate, they adopted Western cultural ancestry as their very own. This is to adopt the logic of modernization that privileges Western culture. For those who adopt such a worldview, the lack of material resources to produce it is tantamount to an admission of one's own cultural inferiority. In this subaltern climate, the "postcolonial" Korean elite distinguish themselves as members of the privileged class by meticulously acquiring Western, that is, U.S. culture. The educational policy of the U.S. military government (1945–1948)[11] institutionalized such a cultural dependence. It was based, it should be noted, not on liberalism but on the structure of the Japanese-style educational system, which was originally designed to implement obedience and complacency toward the colonial rulers. Throughout their school years, South Korean children learn that competence in English, the most powerful of the colonial languages, and a knowledge of world history, that is, Western civilization, are not only the signs of enlightenment but also their symbolic capital. In other words, (post)colonial South Koreans have continued to mimic Western hegemonic culture and have reproduced a colonial pathology of self-denigration and self-marginalization, which have long blinded the South Koreans from critically assessing their "liberator-benefactor" as a colonizing hegemon.

In the following I will illuminate the workings of colonial double-talk, using three metaphors: Raymond Williams's country and the city, Baudrillard's simulacrum, and Lévi-Strauss's critique of totemism. This is a strategy to replace the older monotonic decolonization discourse that failed to predict the tenacity of colonialism in the "postcolonial" era. The shortfalls of the older discourse, I believe, stem partially from its failure to interrogate the truth claim of the colonial discourse and its hidden agenda, and from the broad and deep-seated impact of colonialism upon the social and cultural landscape of the ex-colonies, especially the lasting colonization of consciousness. The metaphor of the country and the city is helpful for understanding the power relationship between the metropolis and the "postcolonial" colony. Raymond Williams, in *The Country and the City*,[12] maps the relationship between the country-colony and the city-metropolis as a system that perpetuates material disparity by calling attention to the differences of the two locations that are interconnected through the patriarchal power hierarchy. In this relationship, I am attempting to show that the metropolitan discourse lies external to the lives of the indigenous people, and the internal hegemonic discourse not only reproduces the discourse of the former colonial master but also transmits and, moreover, simultaneously reinforces the neocolonial metropolitan superpower. This is what I mean by colonial double-talk. This discontinuous interconnectedness between the metropolitan discourse and the internal(ized) hegemonic discourse is what (post)colonial discourse must interrogate.

But before I discuss this postcolonial reproduction of colonialism in the (post)colonies, I would like to consider Baudrillard's notion of simulacrum as another metaphor for colonialism, especially Japan's colonization of Korea and the further mimicry of this colonization by the military government of South Korea. Baudrillard explains simulacrum as the generation by models of a real without origin or reality. Baudrillard explains that "the simulacrum is never that [which] conceals the truth. Rather it is the truth which conceals that there is none. It is the map that precedes the territory. It is more real than real, hyperreal." Baudrillard proposes this notion of simulacrum to reveal that the hyperreal is what holds power and dominates modern culture, especially the culture of late capitalism. According to Baudrillard, the so-called real can easily be produced from "miniaturized units, from matrices, memory banks and command models. It is a form of pastiche that can be reproduced indefinitely and which needs not appear rational, since it is not measured against any idea or 'negative instance.'"[13]

This pastiche may be interrogated historically, of course, because it left its traces in the genealogy of imperial discourses. As modern history has witnessed, Western colonialism was morally justified by the legitimacy of the "scientific knowledge" on race and the linear evolution of civilization. This "scientific knowledge" stabilizes racial hierarchy and firmly establishes the self/other binary opposition. However, the Enlightenment narrative authorizes "scientific knowledge" as the universal truth. Given the authority of the universal truth claim, scientific knowledge is endowed with the power to "mark off" the Other and to justify colonial conquest in the name of the Enlightenment obligation. When the "scientific" discourse invests the Other in this way, it turns the Other into a totem. As Lévi-Strauss's study of totemism attests, totemism never existed as a social institution but as an explanatory principle in defense of the Western moral universe. The "science of man" in the service of the Enlightenment has simply been a scholarly construct to mark off alterity, and thus to reproduce the self/other binary opposition. This opposition, as Albert Memmi would insist, enables the objectification and even thingification of Other (un)humans, while the colonizers themselves shed the humanity that they inscribed on themselves and over which they had claimed a preemptive monopoly.

While the European colonial discourse claimed scientific truth for its views on race and human institutions, and thus legitimized the Enlightenment obligation toward the Other, Japanese imperialism reproduced the fictionality of the European colonial discourse. It was a pastiche of the European Enlightenment. Japanese imperialism simulated and reproduced this grand but empty narrative, in yet another form of colonialism, not with any Enlightenment pretense but through a pastiche of colonization. The Japanese annexation of Korea was unmitigated capitalist expansionism. The colonization of Korea bred an archaic sense of subjugation with terrorism and military discipline. This was the real face of colonialism under the thinly disguised mask of European Enlightenment, we must remember.

Replacing the Enlightenment project in their discourse of colonization, the Japanese in Korea grafted the language of the political economy of colonialism onto a language of body. The colonial technique of separating while at the same time connecting "the country and the city" was repeated here in the body politic. It was imperial Japan's double discourse of assimilation that constructed an illusion of "one-body" (*ittai* 一体), the bodily connection of Korea to metropolitan Japan. However, the assimilation of Korea under the banner of the "one-bodiment of [civilized] inner land [that is, Japan] and [the uncivilized, hinterland] Korea" (*Naisen ittai* 内鮮一体) was not really a democratic "one-bodiment" but an em-bodying of Korea into the national body of Japan, represented by the heavenly body of the Japanese emperor, the *kokutai* 國体 (literally, national body).[14] This embodying of Korea, however, simultaneously dis-membered the Korean people from the national body of Japan. Korea was embodied as a part of Japan's national body only to extract human and natural resources from the former so that it could satisfy the needs of metropolitan Japan as a capitalistic body — but never be nurtured with the fruits harvested through the body's accumulation of capital. Colonized Korea became the organs without a body, and Japan the body without organs.[15] Thus the colony as organs was dismembered from the body, under the schizophrenic reality of colonialism, the capitalistic machine operating in a dismembered yet interconnected relationship.

The grotesqueness of this type of interconnectedness is characteristic of imperialism: power flows only in one direction in a vain attempt to satisfy the insatiable desire of capitalism. The imperialist power structure is simulated and reproduced locally in the form of state capitalism, as exemplified in South Korea and its Southeast Asian neighbors. Today the colonial relationship has an added dimension; it represents the double subjugation of the formerly colonized third world countries. They carry the tenacious legacy of colonial experience and power relationships that govern postcolonial realities and the commanding presence of neocolonial power.

What is remarkable is that, beyond the violence that this empty sign allowed the colonizers to inflict upon the colonized, in the so-called postcolonial era, the political elite of this former Japanese colony have mimicked the same techniques of terror that the colonizers had used to subjugate Korea and reproduced it in the form of an authoritarianism, especially under the patronage of the cold war superpower. In fact, the late President Park Chung Hee and his cohorts had been trained at a Japanese military academy in Manchuria during the colonial period. Interestingly, according to a military source, Park Chung Hee compared himself to the young officers active in the cause of the Showa Restoration (1932), which had helped to accelerate prewar military fascism in Japan. As William Pietz writes in his article, "The 'Post-Colonialism' of Cold War Discourse,"[16] the cold war discourse itself was a reproduction of colonial discourse, based on the geopolitical binary opposition of East/West, good/evil, civilized/primitive, in its construction of the Soviet Union as a "mythical," "oriental," evil empire.

It must be Baudrillard's myopia that kept him from seeing the real political consequences of his lighthearted mockery of modernity. This playfulness is an avoidance of interrogating the pastiche that has permitted the indefinite reproduction of colonialism, and a refusal to measure this pastiche against negative instances.

South Koreans did not awaken to the fact of their own subaltern condition until the popular uprising in Kwangju in 1980 led to a massacre of up to two thousand people by the military, allegedly connived or authorized by the U.S. commander, who led the UN forces.[17] Frantz Fanon had already warned that simply transferring the colonial legacy into the hands of the natives might result in the mimicking of the colonial discourse by local bourgeois nationalists, because "the national bourgeoisie identifies itself with the Western bourgeoisie, from whom it has learnt its lessons."[18] From this we may infer that the people of the former colony might have assumed a false sense of security created by the hegemonized bourgeois nationalists. This is exactly what blinded South Koreans to the reality of their subaltern status.

A South Korean "postnational-partition" (*pundan sidae*)[19] writer, Pok Kŏu-il, has been critical of this blindness and its accompanying inertia, which can be seen especially in the comfortable assimilation of the Korean middle class in the colonial realities of present-day Korea. In his novel, *In Search of an Inscription: Keijō, Shōwa 62*[20] (Shōwa 62 [1987] refers to the reign of Hirohito, the late heavenly emperor of shining peace [*shōwa*], and Keijō was the Japanese name given to the city of Seoul during the colonial period), the author criticizes the collective Korean amnesia with regard to their cultural and ethnic identity in the face of a sustained and then suspended colonialism. The novel allegorizes South Korea's present condition by imaginatively stepping outside the official history. In his fictional emergent history, the author writes that Japan continues to rule Korea today; gone are the history and language of the colonized *Handōjin*, the peninsular people. *Handōjin* was a name the Japanese gave to the Koreans during the colonial period (1910–1945) in order to mark off Korea's distinct hinterland status; it was colonial double-talk for an imperial citizenry set off against the civilized inner land, or *Naichi*.[21] Ironically, the novel's protagonist, a totally assimilated middle-class poet who aspires to a Japanese readership, falls in love with a Japanese woman who happens to be a direct descendant of the daimyo of Satsuma, who had subjugated Okinawa. The novel's hero admires this woman's (unquestioned) glorious ancestry. However, because of his status, this assimilated peninsular man with a Japanese surname, Kinoshita, has to give her up to a U.S. representative of a multinational corporation. In the novel, the colonized Koreans, denied their history and culture and doubly subjugated by a colonial master and a neocolonial superpower, are subjected to exploitation and oppression.

Through this novel Pok Kŏu-il urges his readers to rethink radically the current South Korean situation from the perspective of the colonial subject and not to slide into the comfortable misconception that they are "postcolonial." He attributes South Koreans' confusion between the colonial and the postcolonial to a number of factors, including the elimination of leftist intellectuals, represented in the novel as critical historians, and the silencing of dissenting voices by the authoritarian political structure. The voiceless people of the novel, the language-deprived *Handōjin,* are today's South Koreans, the author maintains. The novel concludes with a prophetic ending. The protagonist, Kinoshita, who is awakened to Korea's colonial reality, takes a fugitive's journey to Shanghai, where the Korean Provisional Government (1919–1945) is engaged in its sole activity—compiling a Korean-language dictionary. The determination of this colonized subject to recuperate the lost language here is a determination to restore the lost voice, the discourse of decolonization.

Interestingly, Pok Kŏu-il opens a debate on the issue of writing as a political act by critically invoking the writer Yi Kwang-su and the playwright Pak Yŏng-hi, the infamous nationalists-turned-collaborators under Japanese colonial rule. The author, however, seems to credit revisionist history as the foremost catalyst in the awakening of a people's historical consciousness. The author's depiction of the division of intellectual labor in the novel parallels the scene in the 1970s and 1980s in South Korea, which saw a surging intellectual movement qua social movement.

COUNTERMEMORY AND THE
THEATER OF PROTEST

For the past decade or so, South Korean intellectuals have been actively engaged in—even as they have marveled at—the explosion of critical studies in a wide range of disciplines, the more active ones being history, literary criticism, and the social sciences. Much of this energy has been spent on debating the cause of the national partition and the impact of continuing foreign domination, which has nurtured the monster that is the political culture of South Korea. This activity has led to a shift in the prevailing analytic paradigm from the universalizing Western-master narrative to that of the third world, especially from the perspective of South Korea, whose decolonization has thus far been denied. While the national literature debate, cast in the framework of third world literature, paved the way to this critical rethinking in the 1970s, the immediate catalyst for this intellectual movement was the publication in 1979 of the first volume of what was to become a six-volume series, *Haebang chŏnhusaŭi insik* (Understanding pre- and postliberation history), at the deathbed of the nearly twenty-year-old Park Chung Hee regime (1961–1979). The 1980 massacre of the citizens of Kwangju who rose up against the subsequent military coup was a watershed event. As noted earlier, at issue was the fact that for the supreme command of the South Korean armed forces to order a military action such as the one that took place in Kwangju, the approval of the U.S. army commander was mandatory. South Koreans began to question the role of the United States in the massacre, especially when the U.S. commander had played a key role in anointing the orchestrator of the massacre, Chun Doo Hwan, to the South Korean presidency. To the Korean public, the United States' brusque military interests in South Korea above and beyond humanitarian concerns became all too transparent. Many South Koreans began reassessing the relationship between South Korea and the United States and concluded that their country was nothing more than a U.S. military fortress.

At this dramatic moment of historical clairvoyance, Bruce Cumings's monumental work, *The Origins of the Korean War*, was published in 1981. It administered a "fresh shock" to South Korean intellectuals, who had been groping for a language to define Korea's deferred postcoloniality, and opened a new door to the critical discourse of discolonization.[22] In *The Origins of the Korean War*, Cumings courageously challenged the dominant discourse and declared that Korea had been denied its liberation. He insisted that the removal of Japanese rule from Korea was an insignificant event that gave way to the U.S. domination of Korea. The "postcolonial" designation, then, is the faded signpost that marks this insignificant event in Korean history.

Throughout the 1980s an avalanche of critical studies ensued, many of which adopted Marxist or neo-Marxist methodologies, recasting the role of South Korea in the totality of the internationalization of capitalism and its complicated domestic manifestations. For instance, in the social sciences, a critique of the dependence of Korean scholarship on Parsonian sociology and its dominant modernization theories ignited a heated neo-Marxist debate on economic and social formation in the mid-1980s. The critique of these modernization theories is not simply directed to the fact that they have privileged "modernization" and capitalistic accumulation, and thus have set the agenda for many countries that are relegated to underdeveloped status. Critical sociologists argue that the U.S.-dependent social sciences were responsible for the South Korean military government's implementation of its aggressive modernization policy, in the form of state capitalism, at the cost of enormous social problems, including the widening of class gaps and furthering the proletarianization of the underprivileged class. However, the sudden torrent of Marxist analyses that arose as a consequence often ran off without seeping into the hardened terrain of a South Korea sterilized against communism. This may be attributable to the uncritical and indiscriminate application of classic Marxism or to the orthodox state doctrines of some socialist countries, especially North Korea, and this accounts for the diminution of the insurgency's persuasive power in a formidably capitalistic South Korea.

These intellectual developments evolved in tandem with a broadly cast popular movement, known as the *minjung* movement, which began in the wake of the popular April 19 Revolution in 1960 and developed into an anticolonial national unification movement by the end of the 1980s. Its proponents considered it an extension of Korea's long tradition of popular nationalist movements, from the 1894 Tonghak Peasant War and the 1919 March First Independence Movement to the April 19 Revolution, which toppled the U.S.-sponsored Syngman Rhee regime (1948–1960). For the past three decades this movement has embraced a considerable agenda. The antiauthoritarian democracy movement, the labor movement, and the national unification movement have been some of the more prominent features of this broadly cast movement. Although its leaders have included various political dissenters from all walks of life, it is students that have always been at the center as the most active agents. The South Korean government, actively collaborating with its neocolonial masters and their disguised program of hegemony, and with the cold war militarists, has brutally repressed any sign of the Left and sweepingly labeled every organized protest as an act of communist infiltration. Nevertheless, the *minjung* movement has constituted a site of collective resistance against the politics of terror and the larger hegemonizing forces that have nurtured that terror.

The *minjung* movement has been conducive to a radical rereading and recuperation of histories. Its discourse constantly crosses over the boundaries between politics and culture, and between the present and the imagined past, to suggest an alternative future, while invoking a deep-seated popular sentiment for resistance. Such a blurring of boundaries and issues has misled scholars by permitting them to glimpse only fragmented pictures of the overall movement. Those who have speculated that the popular movement is a form of class struggle between the capitalist state and opposition groups infused with the North Korean version of socialism (known as *Chuch'e sasang*) find a certain satisfaction. However, a classical Marxist interpretation does not seem to embrace many other aspects of the movement, especially the pervasive conflation of the reputed international goal of socialism[23] and a nationalism that strives to recuperate or imagine anew the Korean identity.

As an alternative to the materialistic confines of a Marxist analysis, I offer to recast the *minjung* movement within the purview of decolonization: the emancipatory struggle from a colonial past and a neocolonial present that denigrates, if it does not abnegate, the Korean identity. The *minjung* discourse in South Korea has been the major contending voice aspiring to disrupt and subvert the dominant language, the language of the state and, by extension, of the neocolonial forces. In its subversive struggle, the *minjung* discourse has deployed counterhegemonic emergent history in its discursive field. The alternative history or radical reinterpretation of history reaudits the silenced history of "the people."

Foucault has suggested that a countermemory, which may become visible only through the Nietzschean notion of genealogy hidden under the orthodox history, may be an option for an alternative discourse. The hushed-up, erased social memory, he suggests, would contest the validity of the official, canonized memory, the orthodox history. The people of South Korea, deprived of their voice for almost a century, have carefully kept their memories alive, in the form of chilling nightmares, hushed personal narratives, or memories invoked through shamanic visions of terror, nursing their *han* (literally, pent-up resentment) so that one day the spark will be ignited. It is no accident that the metaphor of fire has often found its way into the novels and short stories written in recent times. For instance, the novelist Cho Chŏngnae titled the first part of his multivolume novel *T'aebaek Sanmaek* (The T'aebaek Mountains) "The Hearth Fire of *Han*." This novel casts the Korean War and the partisan guerrilla movement in the purview of a peasant protest against the delay in instituting land reform in South Korea. This is an alternative view to the official interpretation that sees the resistance movement as a communist insurgency. In this light the novel is an attempt to narrate an alternative history as remembered not by the state but by the actual participants in historical events. Through this kind of rememorization, South Koreans have begun to rescue their history and have finally been able to situate South Korea in the context of the postwar capitalist world system. It is during this moment in Korean history that the main focus of the movement has begun to shift from the discussion of domestic issues, contained within the boundaries of an imposing cold war ideology, to imagining a national unification that could finally transcend ideological differences.

The subversive reconstruction of the past has also involved appropriating and even inventing popular culture. The new theater genre called *madang guk* (the people's theater) has been one of the most effective means to recapture dangerous memories. It is a powerful instrument that is used to politicize and mobilize a large segment of the population in South Korea. The theater is an effective medium for delivering the movement's propaganda messages, but not by way of raw slogans. Rather, it narrates the problematized realities of marginalized people within the framework of folk theater and shamanic ritual, and thus successfully attracts public attention. The term *madang* refers to a space where communal activities take place. The reinvested meaning of this space, however, invokes a utopian plentitude of the imagined nonperiodized prelapsarian past and alludes to the advent of a postcapitalist unity in which the division between production and consumption collapses. *Madang guk,* then, is seen as a site where this utopia is to materialize through the carnivalesque communal festival and through a collective struggle against the ruling bourgeoisie as the commoners of the pre-rupture period are imagined to have carried it out. In addition to reintroducing this idea of classic utopian socialism, the ideology of *madang guk* adds an important historical dimension to the movement, in that it constantly re-members the people's history or social memory as a part of discourse.

The dramaturgy and aesthetics of *madang guk* animate this countermemory. *Madang guk* reaches beyond the Aristotelian tradition in Western drama, which purports to create an illusion and separates the play from its audience, and even beyond Brechtian theater, in which the spectators are informed of the theater's double yet delegate analytic power to the actors. *Madang guk* rather posits itself as a rehearsal of revolution, as Augusto Boal has suggested.[24] It appropriates a shamanic ritual format so that ancient time, space, and characters can be freely exchanged with those of the present through the mechanism of ritual ecstasy. This technique not only creates the effects of allusion and allegory, but also reunites them at different moments in history. Here the linear-progressive narrative is disrupted in a manner of "magical realism," which Homi Bhabha recognizes as the language of the emergent postcolonial world.[25] In this supratemporal theater, the linear progression of the plot loses its illusionary power, and the division between the actors and the spectators disappears. In this framework the theater opens up a discursive field, and the everyday-life stories of the participants are woven into the intended scenario of the play. This assemblage of semifictional life histories of people, who are disenfranchised at the edge of a "miraculous" economic development, draws the contours of life in the third world today. The polysemous layers of metaphor invested in *madang guk* have enriched and elevated the popular movement from the pursuit of a legitimate form of government or legal rights for workers to the pursuit of a romantic revolution as well, and this has fostered in the movement a great staying power.

Discourse, as Bakhtin observes,[26] presupposes dialogical heteroglossia. By this he implies dialogic interaction in which the prestigious languages, such as the language of the privileged, try to extend their control, and the subordinated languages, such as the language of the deviant subcultures, try to avoid, negotiate, or subvert that control. Discourse, then, is an area of agonistic, linguistic combat to achieve the intention of the word deployed to stratify and to advertise the social positioning of the speakers. Bakhtin's recovery of linguistic heterogeneity extends beyond sociolinguistics into the realm of social dialectics. Dialogism, in this sense, not only relativizes the universal claim of being the norm but also rescues the people whose voice has been silenced due to their nonnormative "low" language, the language of the margin. As such, *madang guk* is a language that represents the life of the oppressed. Moreover, the theater is at once a representation of and a process for narrativizing a people's history. Its precapitalistic, rituallike open structure, as opposed to a capitalist, rigid, closed structure, allows constant invocation and adumbration of social memories and realities, a process that rescues silenced histories and offers possibilities for constructing an alternative history.

The Hawk of Changsan'got, by Hwang Sŏg-yong (now living in exile for having "illegally" visited North Korea), is framed as a shamanistic ritual and interrogates the neocolonial penetration of Korea by the capitalist superpowers and the collaboration of the Korean government. In this drama, foreign traders, symbolically described as Westerners and Japanese, are protected by corrupt Korean officials who are in pursuit of their own interests by trading goods that they have extorted from the peasants. The Japanese traders eventually demand as tribute the guardian spirit of the village, the Hawk of Changsan'got. This demand incites a peasant rebellion. In the end, the intruders shoot the Hawk and the rebels are persecuted. As this moment of danger, the villagers dance their communal dance and solidify their will to overcome the tragedy, a will to revolt. The present-day threat of capitalist penetration is allegorically projected into the remembered past, and thus this drama at once invokes and preserves the "dangerous memory" of the people. Furthermore, it seeks to achieve a subversive power for the oppressed.

Here *madang guk* attempts to reaudit the popular memory in order to dedoxify (borrowing Linda Hutcheon's shorthand)[27] the orthodox claim of the state, the mere machinery of an invisible Big Brother in the international capitalist patriarchy. This alternative process of historicization makes lucid the acute symptoms of Korea's neocolonial realities, which are shaped by today's world capitalist system, namely, the epic of economic growth which confers sole legitimacy to the power of the incumbent South Korean government.[28] The polyphonic history of the people as constructed in *madang guk* leads us beyond the ideological façade that masks human sentiment and behavior, and disturbs the celebrated epic of capitalism.

Not quite accidentally, one of the most controversial *madang guk* (controversial because it crosses the line between theater and ritual), *The Divination*, attempts just that: it recuperates the repressed social memory, challenging the myth of the benevolent U.S. liberators. *The Divination* reinterprets the U.S. involvement in the national partition, the Korean War, and the Kwangju massacre. It is presented in the form of a shamanic death ritual of the historically marginalized Chŏlla province (where the city of Kwangju is located), in which the genealogy of two families is invoked in the shaman's vision. In the drama, the two families — a Northern family who lost their daughter during the Korean War, when she was raped and killed by a U.S. soldier because of her Northern (communist) origin, and a Southern mother who has lost her son in the Kwangju massacre — marry the spirits of the two young people, and in so doing, they overcome not only differences created by a more than forty-year time span but a spatial and ideological division as well. This spirit marriage not only symbolizes national unification, but attempts to realize it through efficacy of the ritual. The play challenges the vested interests of superpowers that insist on maintaining the status quo of a partitioned nation.

The Divination thinks the unthought, not only to counter the hegemonic authority but to rescue the utopian vision of independence from the forces of colonization. It is an attempt to liberate Koreans from the psychology of the colonized, from self-pity and degradation — a condition that JanMohamed might refer to as a Manichaean struggle — to overcome the Korean subaltern reality. What lies in the way of decolonization? The bleeding wound of history that has not been healed and the stories of *han* that have been stifled. In *The Divination*, the marriage ceremony is halted due to a violent repulsion between the spirit dolls, and once again the shaman has to divine the cause of this violence. Through the shaman's vision, the long-suppressed tale of a resentful rape victim (a metaphor for a feminized nation dominated by a patriarchal militarism) is narrated, and a silenced history regains its voice. Reauditing the erased history here has a healing power, and the collective sharing of a silenced tragedy strengthens the communal solidarity. At this moment of revelation the present and the past are reconciled. This moment of ecstasy is also a moment of communitas in which the lonely soul of an oppressed individual unites with the subaltern collectivity, which energizes the will for a collective struggle.

In this *minjung* history, past is surrealistically grafted to present. The supratemporality of history, or magical realism in this strategic construction of history, becomes the very fountainhead of the popular imagination that inspires revolution and decolonization. This faculty of popular imagination may be what Walter Benjamin[29] envisioned in his thesis on the faculty of mimesis. With his typical utopian appeal, Benjamin attempts to rescue the "nonsensuous similarity," which may be understood as a "nonsensuous iconicity of the sign." Benjamin believes that language is far from being a mere system of signs, as has been conventionally thought. Drawing from the early forms of such occult practices as magic and astrology, Benjamin suggests the possibility of conferring on language the power to "read what was never written." This capacity of language, or shall we say hermeneutic urge, he calls mimetic faculty. This mimetic faculty may be mobilized to counter the endless reproduction of simulacrum and its hidden violence.

The discourse of decolonization, it is increasingly clear, is ever more relevant in the postcolonial era, simply because the pastiche of colonialism continues to be reproduced, especially in the present-day realities of many former colonies. However, and this is my point, in interrogating the *minjung* movement, those involved have not challenged the universalizing authority of Western discourse with counterhegemonic "negative instances" of their own in order to reveal the "reallessness" of the colonial discourse. Moreover, in the discourse of modernity itself, the moral bankruptcy of the colonizers (that is, the colonizers' self-destructive metamorphosis into, or their mimicry of, the very [un]human that they have dehumanized) has never been called to account. This is because *minjung* intellectuals have never questioned the absence of the real or the rational in the construction of a racial hierarchy. The truth, which conceals the fact that there is no "real" in the rationale justifying the colonization of the Other, shares the empty property of simulacrum. As the simulacrum reproduces, that is, while the absence of the real remains uninterrogated, colonial discourse will continue and colonialism will continue to be reproduced. The "postisms" — poststructuralism, deconstructionism, postmodernism — all of which seek to displace self-contained, seamless, transparent, "scientific" knowledge, cannot be completed without interrogating the discourse of colonization, but with the critique of mutual mimicry fully deployed.

THE PROBLEM OF REPRESENTATION

It is in this spirit of self-reflective criticism that I offer a critique of South Korea's *minjung* movement as a discourse of decolonization. While I totally endorse the *minjung* movement's critique of the imperialistic hegemony of the capitalist superpowers, I am suspicious of the movement's discourse strategy. I am especially uncomfortable with their mode of representation.

In their practice of magical realism, opposition intellectuals emerge as the authorized representatives of the disenfranchised people and as the prophets of utopia. The new society that they envision would advance only through the struggles of the people, and this would make the hitherto oppressed people subjects of history. In order to prepare (educate) people to assume a role in revolution, these intellectual representatives of *minjung* attempt to instill a new epistemology and raise historical consciousness. In other words, the agenda of the representatives of the people is to shape the people they are representing; this implies the process of othering, while simultaneously representing and constructing "the people."

In the alternative histories, whether they take the form of literary narratives or the conventional genre of historiography, peasants are often depicted as people who have risen up and emancipated their fellow sufferers from powerful rulers both within and without. In these heroic epics the people are re-membered into history as larger-than-life tragic heroes.

The alternative histories are, then, hagiographies of idealized people inverting and ideologizing the trope, *minjung,* the people. In this hagiography, what would ordinarily be a negative quality of *minjung* — because of the association with backwardness according to the rationalizing logic of modernization — is emblematized in the intellectual discourse of resistance. For instance, the characters in the *madang guk* speak almost exclusively the dialect of Korea's most exploited and marginalized region, the Chŏlla provinces. The Chŏlla dialect has long been a stigma that signified a speaker's debased status. In the discursive space of resistance, however, the people of Chŏlla province now have become allegorical icons.

Bourdieu argues that this emblematization of stigma or idealization of the underprivileged class exalts symbolic power at the cost of promoting class ethnocentrism, and this tends to disguise the effect of domination. Popular language, which, from the point of view of the dominant language, appears as uneducated and vulgar, forces its speakers to fall victim to the logic that leads stigmatized groups to claim the stigma as a sign representing their identity. Bourdieu further asks: "when the dominated quest for distinction leads the dominated to affirm what distinguishes them, is this resistance? Conversely, if the dominated appropriate for the purpose of dissolving what marks them, is this submission?"[30]

This paradoxical impasse, which is inscribed in the very logic of symbolic domination and resistance, calls the act of representation into question. To be more specific, how effective is the work of the spokesperson in liberating the subaltern from this contradiction? Or does the discourse, which seems to lie largely external to the people, serve the interest of the people or their representatives? Is not the consecration of the people as the ideal subject of history or the representative's claim on the preemptive ties with the people a way of constructing a metonymic link with the people so that the entire project of representation is in essence a strategy for self-serving self-consecration? In fact, the self-serving end of such representation becomes clearer when we recall that the delegates of the people are inscribing their ideology in the epistemology of the people whom they represent and are therefore constructing the group in the service of certain interests within the movement, granting that the *minjung* movement is not a single unified movement. Could this be a form of hegemony in the Gramscian sense or even a colonization of consciousness?

The workings of hegemony could be disguised in the structure of representation, especially in the act of self-abnegation, to embody the people that it represents. This ostentatious selflessness presupposes the moral superiority of the delegate. This is most often manifested in the institutionalization of religion, as Nietzsche pointed out in his *Antichrist* with regard to the embodiment of the representative in the Catholic ministry.[31]

As we reexamine the act of representation among opposition intellectuals in this light, we find a certain affinity in Korea's *minjung* movement. When the newly emerged left-wing journal *Sahoe P'yŏngnon* held a symposium in July 1991 to reassess the *minjung* movement, focusing on the issue of its decline, many concerned critics voiced two seemingly contradictory views. One argument was that the movement needs to establish its power base in real politics. Critics attributed the weakness of the movement to the fact that the leading actors of the movement are students whose transitional status frees them from real social responsibilities. At the same time, the absence of social responsibility is privileged to claim the moral superiority of the movement. The underlying implications is that responsibility-free students are less susceptible to corruption and moral contamination than the older generation. In other words, privileging the representatives relies on appropriating the social valorization of innocence and, by extension, of purity, which confers on them an almost religious claim. This valorization of purity engenders an oracle-like effect on the increasingly monolithic *minjung* discourse that is replete with stories of superhuman self-victimization, as shown by the series of self-immolations in the streets of South Korea in 1991. The symbolic power of the powerless thus cashes in on this vested social faith to seduce the masses into their romantic venture. In fact, the second line of criticism is directed at the romantic nature of the *minjung* movement and its failure to embrace a larger populace, a charge of exclusionism. A former student activist and currently a political analyst, Yi Sin-bŏm, summarized the latter view as follows:

The student movement in the 60s was couched in a revolutionary romanticism that attracted wide public support. However, the *minjung* movement, being forged during the struggle against the brutal oppression of the 70s and 80s, has become an exclusive one led by a handful of professional revolutionary groups. A student movement is energized when the older generation subscribes to this romanticism and acknowledges their patriotic motivation. Radical activism loses the supportive masses.[32]

Despite a vehement denial of the charges of romanticism or exclusionism by *minjung* intellectuals, criticism of the *minjung* movement has confirmed some of its problems, which both the public and scholars have long deferred to express in precise terms. Why the public felt compelled to hold back is the issue here, because the invisible power that silences the critical voice itself shows the symptoms of dominance, a lesson for liberal intellectuals to learn, especially when we think of the intractable colonial nature of romantic third worldism and the precarious nature of Western humanism, which Spivak aptly criticized in her influential essay, "Can the Subaltern Speak?"[33] There is no glory in suffering. Resistance or struggle has real-life consequences beyond intellectual imagination. How we read what is not written needs to involve these practical considerations.

NOTES

1. Antonio Gramsci, *Selections from the Prison Notebooks,* ed. and trans. Quintin Hoare and Geoffrey Nowell Smith (New York: International Publishers, 1971), 276.

2. Anne McClintock, "The Angel of Progress: Pitfalls of the Term 'Post-Colonialism,'" *Social Text* 31–32 (summer 1992): 84–98; Ella Shohat, "Notes on the 'Post-Colonial,'" *Social Text* 31–32 (summer 1992): 99–113. Curiously, Korea was not on the authors' extensive list of world-class former and present colonies. Presumably, Korea was not a European colony and thus is disqualified from being an entry in this Western self-critique of the universalizing theoretical framework. I hope this was a technical oversight. However, the fact that the authors consistently failed to recognize Korea as well as Taiwan, Manchuria, Okinawa, and the South Pacific islands as prominent former colonies of Japan may imply the lasting impact of privileging even the Western colonialism.

3. For a related discussion, see John Comaroff and Jean Comaroff, "The Colonization of Consciousness," in *Ethnography and the Historical Imagination* (Boulder, CO: Westview Press, 1992).

4. Abdul JanMohamed, "The Economy of Manichaean Allegory: The Function of Racial Difference in Colonial Literature," in *"Race," Writing and Difference,* ed. Henry Louis Gates Jr. (Chicago: University of Chicago Press, 1985).

5. Homi Bhabha, "Of Mimicry and Man: The Ambivalence of Colonial Discourse," *October* 28 (spring 1984): 125–133. See also Homi Bhabha, "The Other Question: The Stereotype and Colonial Discourse," *Screen* 24 (November–December 1983): 18–36.

6. Although the Korean term *pundan* does not differentiate between "partition" and "division," an increasing number of South Koreans use the word in its passive meaning to indicate that Korea was not divided by the will of the people but partitioned by external forces.

7. There has been a series of debates among historians and social scientists on this issue in both South and North Korea. Central to this debate is to determine whether the liberation was "given" by the United States or "achieved" by the Koreans. Bruce Cumings, in *The Origins of the Korean War* (Princeton: Princeton University Press, 1981), denies the liberation itself on the ground that the sovereignty of Korea has not been restored. For a comprehensive review of the discourse, see Yi Wan-bŏm, "Haebang 3 nyŏnsaŭi chaengjŏm" (Issues of debate on the history of the three years after the liberation), in *Haebang chŏnhusaŭi insik* (Understanding pre- and postliberation history), vol. 6, ed. Pak Myŏng-nim et al. (Seoul: Hangilsa, 1989).

8. For the discourse of wilderness see, for example, Rey Chow, "Violence in the Other Country: China as Crisis, Spectacle and Woman," in *Third World Women and the Politics of Feminism,* ed. Chandra T. Mohanty et al. (Bloomington: Indiana University Press, 1991). William Pietz discusses the demonization of the USSR as the evil empire in Western cold war discourse. See W. Pietz, "The 'Post-Colonialism' of Cold War Discourse," *Social Text* 19–20 (spring 1988): 55–75. I thank James Hevia for directing my attention to this article by Pietz.

9. Vicente L. Rafael, "Anticipating Nationhood: Collaboration and Rumor in the Japanese Occupation of Manila," *Diaspora* 1 (1991): 67.

10. Pierre Bourdieu's fine analyses of the socialized sense of hierarchization of taste, in his *Distinction* (Cambridge, MA: Harvard University Press, 1984), is most instructive here. Symbolic capital is, of course, what cashes into symbolic power based on the social sense of taste and the acquisition thereof.

11. For detailed discussions, see Chong Hak-chu, "Haebanghu Han'guk kyoyug'gŭi kujojŏk kaldŭng" (The structural tension in postliberation Korean education), in *Han'guk sahoeron* (Korean society), ed. Kim Chin-gyun and Cho Hŭi-yŏn (Seoul: Hanul, 1990); Han Chun-sang, "Migukŭi munhwa ch'imt'uwa Han'guk kyoyuk" (American cultural invasion and Korean education), in *Haebang chŏnhusaŭi insik* (Understanding pre- and postliberation history), vol. 3, ed. Pak Myŏng-nim et al. (Seoul: Hangilsa, 1987); Yi Kwang-ho, "Migunjŏn'gŭi kyoyukchŏngch'aek" (The education policy of the American military government), in *Haebang chŏnhusaŭi insik* (Understanding pre- and postliberation history), vol. 2, ed. Kang Man-gil et al. (Seoul: Hangilsa, 1985).

12. Raymond Williams, "The New Metropolis," in *The Country and the City* (Oxford: Oxford University Press, 1973).

13. Jean Baudrillard, *Simulations* (New York: Semiotext(e), 1983).

14. For the discussion of Japanese nationalism and its signifier, the "national body," i.e., the emperor's body, see Norma Field, *In the Realm of a Dying Emperor* (New York: Pantheon Books, 1991), 33–104.

15. I am borrowing this metaphor from Gilles Deleuze and Félix Guattari, *Anti-Oedipus: Capitalism and Schizophrenia,* trans. Robert Hurley, Mark Seem, and Helen R. Lane (Minneapolis: University of Minnesota Press, 1983).

16. Pietz, "The 'Post-Colonialism' of Cold War Discourse."

17. For a detailed account in the English language, see Donald Clark, "Bitter Friendship: Understanding Anti-Americanism in South Korea," in *Korea Briefing, 1991,* ed. Donald Clark (Boulder, CO: Westview Press, 1991), 147–167.

18. Frantz Fanon, "The Pitfalls of National Consciousness," in *The Wretched of the Earth,* trans. Constance Farrington (New York: Grove Weidenfeld, 1968), 153.

19. *Pundan sidae,* or the period of (national) partition, was a term first coined by a South Korean historian, Kang Man-gil, in the mid-1970s. Not only does this term invoke all the contradictions that have been created due to the national partition, it also indicates the absence of a Korean voice in international

affairs that marks postwar periodization, e.g., postindependence or postcolonial. Yet *postwar* is equally inadequate, since Koreans were only forced to participate in the war qua conscripts from the colony — including eleven-year-old elementary school girls who were drafted to serve Japanese imperial soldiers at the Pacific War fronts.

20. Pok Kŏu-il, *Pimyongul ch'ajasŏ: Keijō Showa 62* (Seoul: Munhakkwa Chisŏngsa, 1987).

21. These are the terms that defined Korea as Japan's naturalized exteriority. The colonizers referred to Japan itself as *Naichi,* or inner land. However, Korea was not conferred the privilege of being defined by a comparable cultural term but was simply referred to as a peninsula, an undefined other specifiable only in its natural geographical configuration. Japan's border is defined as "inner land" only in the context where Japan needs to differentiate itself not only from Korea, but also from Okinawa or Hokkaido, the ethnic (Korean, Okinawan, Ainu, respectively) and territorial margin of the phallocentric "Nippon," rather than "Nihon." The peninsula, in this sense, is not used to define Korea's exteriority but Japan's ethnocentrality. It is Japan's practice of self-identification by the image mirrored in the marginalized self/other. If we were to borrow the Lacanian notion of the dynamics of the imaginary, namely, a child's identification of self with the specular image of himself or herself in the mirror and the child's experience imbued with aggression toward this self/other, the colonial violence toward the Koreans and the Okinawans may be explainable.

22. By the time two unauthorized translations appeared in 1987, *The Origins* had been widely used as reading material in underground reading circles on university campuses in South Korea.

23. Shlomo Avineri argues that Marxism does not address the issue of nationalism evenhandedly. As a result, Avineri argues that the relationship between Marxism and nationalisms has been inconsistent. See Shlomo Avineri, "Marxism and Nationalism," *Journal of Contemporary History* 26, nos. 3–4 (1991): 637–657.

24. Augusto Boal, *The Theatre of the Oppressed,* trans. Charles A. and Maria-Odilia Lean-McBride (New York: Theatre Communications Group, 1985), 122.

25. Homi K. Bhabha, introduction, in *Nation and Narration,* ed. Homi Bhabha (New York: Routledge, 1990), 7.

26. M. M. Bakhtin, *The Dialogic Imagination,* trans. Caryl Emerson and Michael Holquist (Austin: University of Texas Press, 1981).

27. Linda Hutcheon, *The Politics of Postmodernism* (London: Routledge, 1989).

28. The South Korean government underplays the facts of its enormous trade imbalance. In 1990, the South Korean trade deficit with Japan alone exceeded $90 million, which was approximately 3.5 percent of Korea's GNP in 1990. The U.S. trade deficit, $420 million, was about 0.75 percent of the U.S. GNP.

29. Walter Benjamin, "On the Mimetic Faculty," in *Reflections* (New York: Harcourt Brace Jovanovich, 1978).

30. Pierre Bourdieu, "The Uses of the 'People,'" in *In Other Words* (Stanford: Stanford University Press, 1990), 155.

31. Pierre Bourdieu, "Delegation and Political Fetishism," *Thesis Eleven* 10–11 (1984–1985): 56–70; reprinted in *Language and Symbolic Power* (Cambridge, MA: Harvard University Press, 1991). I thank Ann Anagnost for directing me to this article.

32. *Hangyŏre sinmun*, June 1991.

33. Gayatri Spivak, "Can the Subaltern Speak?" in *Marxism and the Interpretation of Culture*, ed. Cary Nelson and L. Grossberg (Urbana: University of Illinois Press, 1988), 271–313.

MARTIN F. MANALANSAN IV

In the Shadows of Stonewall:
Examining Gay Transnational Politics and
the Diasporic Dilemma

In a world of collapsing borders, gay ideologies, practices, and images are tracing modernity's trajectories. Within this context, the globalization of the gay "movement" has proven to be problematic. This essay was written on the heels of and in the "heat" of the celebration of the twenty-fifth anniversary in June 1994 of the Stonewall Rebellion. While this event is decisive in figuring certain globalizing ideas and practices, an increasingly globalized view of Stonewall and of the gay and lesbian political movement have been prevalent for the past two decades. Media and popular consciousness have long taken for granted that gay and lesbian culture and politics have spread worldwide. Consider the following events or representations from the Stonewall anniversary:

— The "official" Stonewall '25 march held on June 26, 1994, started not in Greenwich Village or more specifically in the bar where it all started, the Stonewall Bar, but at the United Nations building. Initially, the organizing committee proposed two starting points for the march, the Stonewall site or the UN building in midtown Manhattan. When the city government would only give a permit for one starting site, the committee chose the UN because of its "global symbolism."

— Souvenirs and artifacts being sold to commemorate the Stonewall festivities included T-shirts with the name *Stonewall* set against a globe and a pink pin with the words "Come Out UN."

— The brochure for the Stonewall march included a preamble similar to the Universal Declaration of Human Rights. In this document, there is a call for the UN as an international governing body to promulgate the rights and well-being of gay, lesbian, and transgender peoples.

In this paper, I examine the conditions for cultural production, circulation, and reception of the "international" gay and lesbian movement. I problematize this inquiry by juxtaposing descriptions, readings, and analyses of this "internationalism" against texts and narratives by Filipino "gay" men living in the Philippines and in New York City. I am interested in the movement and travel of bodies and ideas within a circuit of exchange as well as the criss-crossing chains of disjunctions and syncretic engagements that are experienced and transformed by Filipino gay men. I focus on the various configurations of "Stonewall" as a moment of universal gay and lesbian liberation and as a construction of "liberation" itself.

In the first section, I examine the rhetoric of transnational[1] gay and lesbian politics by looking not only at the Stonewall march and its attendant cultural activities, but at the recent International Lesbian and Gay Association conference. A review of current scholarship on transnational processes and gay and lesbian studies suggests how contemporary "transnational" flows of gay and lesbian "culture" and politics raise the following questions:

— Who bestows legitimacy on the narration of Stonewall as the origin of gay and lesbian development? What does this narrative of origins engender? What practices and locations are subordinated by a privileging of Stonewall as origin?

— Does the search for "authentic" native or primordial "gay and lesbian" phenomena in the nonmetropolitan periphery impose a Eurocentric universalism on the variety of sexual practices that exist worldwide?

— What political idioms and maneuvers are deployed to establish, execute, and justify international credos of egalitarianism?

— What strategies exist to resist such appropriations and subordinations?

My essay begins from the premise that the globalization of gay and lesbian oppression obfuscates hierarchical relations between metropolitan centers and sub-urban peripheries. By privileging Western definitions of same-sex sexual practices, non-Western practices are marginalized and cast as "premodern" or unliberated. Practices that do not conform with Western narratives of the development of individual political subjects are dismissed as unliberated or coded as "homophobic." I suggest, in contrast, that we must conceive of "gay" practices as a broad category of analysis,[2] and as multiply determined by national culture, history, religion, class, and region, in and across various cultural and political locations and even within a single group. In this regard, Filipino gay men, whether immigrants to the United States or residents of the Philippines, offer examples of practices that invoke and strategically deploy multiple formations as they declare affinities and differences in response to global gay and lesbian agendas.

The second and third sections of the paper examine the configuration, translation, affirmation, and negation of the rhetoric of gay and lesbian oppression by Filipino gay men living in the Philippines and in

New York City. Drawing upon recent writings of Filipino gay writers and activists as well as reflections on a two-year ethnographic study of Filipino gay men in New York City, the second section specifically situates the notion of "gay liberation" within the existing cultural, political, and economic conditions of the Philippines today. The third section consists of excerpts from interviews with Filipino gay men living in New York City regarding Stonewall: the first narrative is by a Filipino gay man who was present at the actual rebellion and was arrested in the process; the second is taken from a conversation between two informants after the 1994 Stonewall celebrations. The final section is a reading of the themes and issues that have been presented.

WHOSE REBELLION? THE FABLE OF STONEWALL AND THE RHETORIC OF GLOBAL OPPRESSION AND LIBERATION OF GAYS AND LESBIANS

The official guide to the Stonewall festivities noted: "People will celebrate the rebellion that transformed the existing Homophile Movement into our contemporary, global, Lesbian, Gay and Transgender Rights Movement. Our goal is to mobilize the largest human rights march and rally the world has ever seen. We have victories to be proud of and injustices to protest. With pride, we celebrate our courage and accomplishments from around the world. We will hear how the struggle for human rights is being waged in different lands and cultures. We will recall/learn and teach our history. We see that we are fighting back and winning victories."[3] From this declaration, we may observe that the discourse about Stonewall has changed from localized descriptions of a series of police raids in a downtown Manhattan gay bar in 1969 into a revolutionary moment that originates liberation for gays and lesbians everywhere. These transformations have repercussions for defining and shaping the category *gay*.

Gay within this view of Stonewall is defined within a temporalized understanding of both sexuality and society. That is, *gay* gains meaning according to a developmental narrative that begins with an unliberated, "prepolitical" homosexual practice and that culminates in a liberated, "out," politicized, "modern," "gay" subjectivity. Such temporalized narratives about gayness are widespread and accepted by many "queer" publications as well.[4] For example, in an anthology of international gay and lesbian writing, Stephen Likosky discusses gay writing after Stonewall and describes Stonewall as an event where "gays, many of them Third World transvestites, took to the streets of New York to battle the police, who had raided the Stonewall Inn, a neighborhood bar."[5] In marking the periods before and after Stonewall, Likosky employs Barry Adam's distinctions between anthropological or historical homosexuality and "modern" homosexuality.[6] Anthropological/historical homosexuality is "characteristic of societies where homosexuality is obligatory and universally practiced such as those where sexual relations between old and younger males are part of the socialization process into manhood (e.g. in Melanesia, central Africa, Amazonia and western Egypt . . .)."[7] Modern homosexuality, on the other hand, is defined as follows:

— Homosexual relations have been able to escape the structure of the dominant heterosexual kinship system.
— Exclusive homosexuality, now possible for both partners, has become an alternative path to conventional family forms.
— Same-sex bonds have developed new forms without being structured around particular age or gender categories.
— People have come to discover each other and form large-scale social networks not only because of existing social relationships but also because of their homosexual interests.
— Homosexuality has come to be a social formation unto itself, characterized by self-awareness and group identity.

Gay in this instance, then, is meaningful within the context of the emergence of bourgeois civil society and the formation of the individual subject that really only occurs with capitalist and Western expansion. Categories of same-sex phenomena are placed within a Western-centered developmental teleology, with "gay" as its culminating stage. Other "nongay" forms or categories are constructed metaleptically, rendered "anterior," and transformed into archaeological artifacts that need only be reckoned with when excavating the roots of pan-cultural/ pan-global homosexuality. In other words, the "internationalizing" transnational gay and lesbian movement does not as yet contain a critique of its own universalizing categories; without an interrogation of its Eurocentric and bourgeois assumptions, this globalizing discourse risks duplicating an imperial gaze in relation to non-Western nonmetropolitan sexual practices and collectivities.

The Pink Book, a regular publication of the International Lesbian and Gay Association (ILGA), contains many similar rhetorics and assumptions.[8] The ILGA, based in Belgium with strong chapters in the United States, was formed to provide the organizational and (sometimes) financial resources to monitor, react to, and understand the political and social conditions of gays and lesbians worldwide. *The Pink Book* is a kind of status report of the "global picture," with in-depth essays detailing the issues and problems of particular nations and an abbreviated survey of the social and legal positions of gays and lesbians in various countries.

In the latest edition of this book, an essay by Tielman and Hammelburg "investigates" 202 countries, gathering data on 178 of them. In this survey the focus was on "(1) official attitudes and the law regarding homosexuality, (2) social attitudes to homosexuality, and (3) the gay and/or lesbian movements all over the world." Investigators found that the overall social and legal situations were "worst in Africa and best in Europe." The following entry on the Philippines is somewhat typical of many for other countries:

Philippines

Official Attitudes and the Law

Homosexual behavior between consenting adults is not mentioned in the law as being a criminal offense. Laws referring to "public morality" are used against gays and lesbians. The Philippines' immigration [authorities] has declared a "war against pedophiles," particularly in Manila. Foreigners are expected to be the first targets of the campaign. The government has banned the radical women's group, "Gabriela" on November 7, 1988, as part of the government counterinsurgency program, "for having possible ties to some underground leftists."

Society

Closeted homosexuality is tolerated, but "sex tourism" has a negative impact on the social position of homosexual men. A minority of the population is in favor of gay and lesbian rights.

The Gay and/or Lesbian Movement

A group exists called the Movement for Social Equality and Recognition of Homosexuals. In the AIDS Center, "The Library," many open gays are active.

The entries regularly employ words like *closet, homophobia, gay,* and *lesbian* without interrogating the Western assumptions embedded in each term, as if they were natural, given concepts that did not need to be contextualized within specific national histories. Apart from the light and caricaturish descriptions of social norms and attitudes, the survey boldly asserts a normative "gay" subject who is not dissimilar to the Euro-American modern political subject. Like the "straight" modern political subject, the "gay" subject moves from the "immature" concealment of his or her sexuality to the "mature" visibility of political participation in the public sphere. The assumption that practices that are not organized around visibility are "closeted" and the interpretation that lack of explicitly gay-identified people in the public arena signifies that a "homophobic" attitude is prevalent in the culture are not interrogated.

While there is some perfunctory discussion of cultural diversity, the tendency to deploy monolithic and universalist constructions of gayness and gay liberation in popular and scholarly literature is quite widespread and observable. For example, at one of the ILGA preconference sessions held in Manhattan after the Stonewall celebrations, where "people of color" issues were to be discussed, potential participants were limited to "people of color only." A number of delegates were puzzled about how they would categorize themselves. Although there may be some understanding among this group that gender and sexuality are socially constructed, it seems a difficult task to persuade the same people of the constructedness of race and nationality, and the imbrication of gender and sexuality within race and nationality. Efforts such as these to confront marginality within the "gay and lesbian world community" by fixing and reifying racial difference have led ILGA to create boundaries that actually promote more marginalization.

The time and place of the ILGA conference in New York City provided a kind of symbolic flag for the view that Stonewall is "ground zero" for all gay and lesbian efforts. Holding the conference in the United States also presented problems for potential participants, which the ILGA did not take into account. A number of delegates (including some twenty from the Philippines) were unable to attend because of financial or legal constraints; conference registration cost $300, and Filipino delegates were denied visitor visas by the U.S. embassy in Manila.

The ILGA, while attempting to host regional meetings in different parts of the world, has at the same time insisted on a universalized vision of how the politics and the future of all gay and lesbian political and cultural efforts should look. In the introduction to *The Pink Book*, the secretaries-general of ILGA write, "the increased visibility of lesbians, gay men and bisexuals, supported by a strong movement, has proved to be a successful *formula* for confronting and fighting homophobic tendencies in all types of society. Well organized groups in many countries have succeeded in at least partially improving *our* human rights."[9] The specular economy that measures political value in terms of visibility, profoundly rooted in epistemologies of revelation rooted in the European Enlightenment, is nowhere interrogated.

Within the context of transnational cultural, economic, and political exchanges, monolithic construction and prescriptions are, at the very least, doomed to failure. What do we really mean when we say *gay* in a world where hybridity and syncretism provide the grist for cultural production, distribution, and consumption? To what creative forms of engagement do people who live outside the gay-idyllic world of Europe resort in order to interrogate the discourses of "rights" and social acceptance? The next section is an attempt to respond to such questions by looking at the writings of three Filipino gay men living in the Philippines.

"GAY" LIBERATION: PHILIPPINE STYLE(S)

Homosexuality in the Philippines has long been seen by popular media and by many Filipinos to be a "nonissue." However, in recent years, with the ascendance of gay and lesbian studies in the West as well as the growth of the AIDS pandemic, cultural production around "gay" issues has increased tremendously in the Philippines. In this section, I consider the works of three Filipino writers, Tony Perez, Jomar Fleras, and J. Neil C. Garcia. They are the most vibrant writers about gay political issues in the Philippines today, and they also present various modes of engagement with the issues of "gay" identity and politics (qua liberation). Before I analyze these three writers' works, it is necessary to contextualize their ideas within Filipino tradition around the *bakla*.

The Bakla

Bakla is a Tagalog term used for particular types of men who engage in practices that encompass effeminacy, transvestism, and homosexuality. The *bakla* is conceptualized in terms of epicene characteristics.[10] On one hand, the *bakla* is stereotypically seen to exist in the vulgar public spaces of the carnival (*baklang karnabal*), the beauty parlor (*parlorista*), and the market place (*baklang palengke*). On the other, the *bakla* is also seen as the cross-dressing man with the female heart (*pusong babae*), searching for the real man and trying hard not to slip into vulgarity or dismal ugliness. These images form part of everyday discourse and sometimes find their way into the works of Filipino gay writers and activists.

Bakla as a form of selfhood is popularly seen as a lower-class phenomenon even among scholars. For example, Michael Tan equated *bakla* and "gay" with real class divisions. Creating a tripartite grouping of the subcultures of "men who have sex with men" or MSM,[11] he argues that the *parlorista* (signifying the stereotypical occupation of the male homosexual, which is that of a beautician or beauty parlor employee) or the stereotypical homosexual, is primarily found in low-income groups such as domestic servants, small market vendors, and waiters. The other two groups that compose this MSM constellation include the callboys or male sex workers (who are from the urban and rural poor), who oftentimes identify as "straight," and the "gays" who are from the higher-income groups.

Although Tan attempts to specify the *bakla* through terms like *parlorista,* it is unclear from his formulation how and if the complexity of practices that comprise the *bakla,* as selfhood, can exist across class lines. By lumping the *bakla* with the MSM population, he conflates the dynamics of self-fashioning not only in terms of sex object choice, but also with the act of same-sex physical encounters. While he recognizes the gender dimensions of the *bakla,* Tan's rigidly assigned class status to the *bakla* is itself a stereotypical view from a specific class position. I assume that he derives his categories from privileging the vantage point of educated, upper-class men who attended safe sex workshops in Manila.

In the next section, it will be clear that I do not correlate directly or consistently the identification of either *bakla* or gay with specific class positions. Rather, my data suggest that class is inflected with race, immigration status, and a range of other factors. Furthermore, I suggest that the *bakla* is an extravagant and complicated figure whose practices go beyond the strictures of transvestism, same-sex encounters, gossip, and vanity. Fenella Cannell's ethnographic study of a small Filipino rural community provides illuminating views on this point.[12] She suggests that the *bakla* is a master of transformation and mimicry. Focusing on the performative aspects of identity and self formation, Cannell emphasizes the mercurial aspects of the *bakla.* For example, the *bakla* from the rural poor is able to negotiate with "high-class" culture such as Hollywood icons and music through participation in beauty pageants and amateur shows, and may attempt to emulate the dress, visage, and manner of glamorous Tagalog and Hollywood female celebrities. In doing so, these men are able not only to negotiate with another culture or class, but, more importantly, they are able to make this culture — through successful imitation — their own. Significantly, Cannell asserts that the *bakla* is always careful not to slip into vulgarity. Therefore, class position and sexual and gender identities are more complicated than Michael Tan's static taxonomy of men who have sex with men.

Tony Perez's collection of short stories and poetry, *Cubao 1980* is sub-titled *The First Cry of the Gay Liberation Movement in the Philippines* (my translation from Tagalog).[13] The ideas in the book are crystallized in one of its poems, "Manipesto" (Manifesto), which is an injunction to transform the *bakla* into the "gay" man. In the poem, Perez provides a kind of call-to-arms to eradicate the stereotype of the *bakla* as a gossip, an unambitious, bitchy, and effeminate queen. He declares that unless the "illusion" is destroyed and the "mistake" corrected, there can never be any attainment of rights. Writing from a self-conscious "gay libera-tionist" perspective, Perez views *bakla* salvation as conditional and contingent upon an unquestioned set of modern Western values and qualities that Nicanor Tiongson, a Filipino cultural historian, empha-sizes in the book's foreword:

The *bakla* needs to accept:

1. That he was born biologically male and that he should stop feminizing his features or behavior
2. That "gay" [men] are not some cheap impersonator(s) in some carnival but are honorable laborers, soldiers, priests, professors, businessmen, and athletes
3. That the right partner for the *bakla* is another *bakla*, otherwise the relation-ship would be unequal
4. That the gay relationship will never be the same as a heterosexual relation-ship that has the blessings of church and society
5. That being *bakla* is not an illness that one can become cured of or that should be cured.[14]

Jomar Fleras's essay, "Reclaiming Our Historic Rights: Gays and Lesbians in the Philippines," extends Perez's argument into the "gay" history. Writing in the latest edition of the ILGA *Pink Book*, Fleras finds the rationale for gay and lesbian rights in male pre-Spanish religious shamans called *babaylan* who cross-dressed and reputedly indulged in same-sex practices. Significantly, *babaylan* occupied honored positions in the community. Fleras deploys the symbol of the once-dormant vol-cano, Mt. Pinatubo, figuring gay activism as an eruptive awakening from historical slumber and invisibility.

Fleras is not alone in this view (a gay group at the University of the Philippines is called Babaylan). While he links gays and the historically prior cross-dressing shamans in order to naturalize modern gay prac-tice, Fleras also echoes Perez's views by disparaging the cross-dressing practices and transgender behavior of some Filipino gay men, and asserting that these practices and behaviors are historical remnants or residues of a former "premodern" past: "While the Stonewall riots gave birth to gay liberation in the U.S., in the Philippines, homosexual men and women were still perpetuating the feudal stereotypes. Gay men portrayed themselves in the media as 'screaming queens' who did nothing but gossip, act silly and lust after men. . . . To legitimize their existence, homosexual men and women came out with the concept of gender dysporia [sic]: the gay man thought of himself as a woman trapped in a man's body while the lesbian envisioned herself with a trapped male soul that phallicized her."[15]

Fleras pathologizes the *bakla* and foretells the destruction of this "false" image. By asserting that gay liberation is gay men and lesbians "deconstructing and breaking away from the feudal stereotypes imposed upon them by society,"[16] he casts the *bakla* as "feudal," underdeveloped, and temporally prior to the "modern" gay. According to Fleras, with modernization, the future of the gay liberation movement in the Philippines is extremely bright. He notes, "Plans are even under way for a Gay Pride week, which will feature an international lesbian and gay film festival, a theater festival, mardi gras, and a symposium. Soon there will be a gay press. Gay men are now banding together to battle the spread of AIDS. . . . Gay and lesbian activism [in the Philippines] is in practical terms just starting. . . . Gay men and lesbian women will assert their personhood. They will fight and eventually win their historic rights as leaders and as healers."[17]

Fleras's nativist attempts to historicize the fight for gay and lesbian rights in the Philippines fall apart when he unconditionally takes the Western model of sexual object choice as characteristic of gay identity and repudiates the gender-based model of the *bakla*. Fleras falls into a kind of conceptual trap even as he tries to reveal the particularities of the Philippine experience of gays and lesbians. He does not interrogate the notion of visibility/invisibility and instead portrays the fight for rights in terms of public cultural practices such as parades, films, and books. He constructs a polarized dichotomy in which the *bakla* identity of the Philippine traditions is feudal and pathologically underdeveloped, while the gay identity of the international cultural network is "modern" and liberated. Like the ILGA constituency for which he writes, Fleras unwittingly prioritizes a Eurocentric model of liberation.

Of the three, Garcia is the only one who reflects on the exigencies of *bakla* culture vis-à-vis the emerging politicized gay culture. His essay appears in an anthology called *Ladlad* (Unfurling), which he coedited. In a close reading of a play by another Filipino author, Orlando Nadres, *Hangang Dito na Lamang at Maraming Salamat* (Up to this point and thank you very much), Garcia focuses on the two main characters, the seemingly masculine, respectable Fidel, and Julie, the screaming vulgar queen—the stereotypical *bakla*. He points out that the author has Fidel identify with Julie, and he demonstrates the startling realization that it is Julie who rises up from the chaotic world he lives in. Garcia writes, "Nadres then depicts the political and strategic desirability of using Julie for the gay movement, when he makes Julie emerge from the floor of Fidel's childish rage and frustration, in tatters yet brimming with pride. For this short and noble moment . . . [the play] is finally a celebration of gay resistance and pride, pure and simple."[18]

Garcia articulates the need to look beyond one monolithic construction of a "gay" community. He writes, "The urgency of forming a community that embraces all kinds of homosexuals—be they the selectively out Fidel or the unabashedly and uncompromisingly out Julie—is clear in *Ladlad*, where themes on *kabaklaan* [being *bakla*] intersect if not merge with the homoerotic self-avowals of those 'other gays' whose primary anguish concerns their desire and the difficulty of pursuing it to fulfillment."[19] Garcia's multivocal conception of a "gay" community is an attempt to nuance the types of practices that emerge from sites characterized by hybridity, sites in which local traditions, attitudes, and practices are historically fused with "outside" influences owing to colonialism and foreign capital. Instead of uncritically "transferring or buying the technology" of gay and lesbian politics from the outside, Garcia proposes a syncretic move: a notion of a multiply determined subject and a possibility of coalitions between different identities and political agendas.

However, what is missing is a critical examination of notions such as coming out, visibility, and the closet. What kind of conceptual space is the closet, such that it confines people who seem neither highly politicized nor self-reflexively "gay"? In the next section, I juxtapose the words of three Filipino gay immigrants living in the United States and examine how their resistance to the highly spectacular images of mainstream U.S. gay culture, particularly the story of Stonewall, represents a different kind of engagement from that of Perez, Fleras, and Garcia.

OPPOSITIONS AT THE SIDELINES:
THE WORDS/WORLDS OF DIASPORIC FILIPINO GAY MEN

The two extracts that follow are from ethnographic fieldwork on Filipino gay men in New York that I have been conducting for three years.

The first is from a life narrative interview with Mama Rene,[20] who participated in the riots at the Stonewall Inn. The other is from a conversation between two Filipino gay men, Rodel and Ron. In both texts, the meaning of Stonewall is translated and configured by the life narratives of these men.

I met Mama Rene in the summer of 1992, when I was told by my other Filipino gay men informants that he was one of the few remaining Filipinos who took part in the Stonewall Rebellion. As one of my informants told me, Mama Rene is one of the "pioneers" among Filipino gay men in New York. Mama Rene is an affable man of about fifty to sixty years (he refused to state his age). He emigrated to the United States in the mid-1960s to study at New York University. We talked for about two hours before he even mentioned being arrested in 1969. When I asked him to narrate that moment, Mama Rene nonchalantly said:

It was one of those nights. It was so hot. I was wearing white slacks — dungarees, I think you call them — and I was really sweating. I knew that there had been a police raid several nights before, but I didn't want to be cooped up in my apartment so I went there — to the Stonewall Bar. Anyway, I was standing there — trying to look masculine — it was the thing then. All of a sudden the lights went on and the police barged in. They told us that they were arresting everybody there — I don't know why — I guess I forgot why they were doing that. Of course it was harassment, but anyway. So . . . we were led out of the building to the streets. And you know what? There were lights, huge spotlights, and all these gay men clapping. I felt like a celebrity. The police took us in, booked us, and then we were released. We were supposed to appear a week later, I think to be arraigned or tried, but the charges were dropped.

When I asked him how he felt about being part of that historic event, Mama Rene just shrugged and said, "They say it is a historic event, I just thought it was funny. Do I feel like I made history? People always ask me that. I say no. I am a quiet man, just like how my mom raised me in the Philippines. With dignity."

Mama Rene rarely goes out to watch gay pride parades. He said, "Too many people and quite chaotic." He insisted that he was not an "activist" like most of the white gay men he knew. He had nothing to say to the public, nor was he particularly interested in doing so.

In their disengagement from the originary event of Stonewall, Ron's and Rodel's attitudes are not dissimilar from those of Mama Rene. Both Ron and Rodel emigrated in the early 1980s and are now in their thirties. We were comparing our plans for the following several weeks when the conversation turned to the Stonewall anniversary celebrations and took a curious turn. I moved to the backseat, a listener. The following is a transcription of what transpired. (I have translated the Tagalog words and phrases; the interchange was conducted in both English and Tagalog.)

Rodel: The march is on June 23. Are you going to watch or maybe join a float in drag?

Ron: Oh please, why would I do that? Besides, why do people do it? What do they [these gay men] have to prove?

Rodel: Yes, that is true. It is too much. All these drag queens in floats and macho muscle men wearing almost nothing. It is like the carnival.

Ron: Every year we have these celebrations—won't it stop?

Rodel: Hey, aren't you the one who likes to go around in drag?

Ron: It isn't the drag part that is awful, it is the spectacle. It is a different thing if I go to clubs and cruise in drag, but it is another thing to parade on Fifth Avenue in high heels—you lose your mystique, your mystery.

Rodel: That is so true. It would seem like you are a *baklang karnabal* [*bakla* of the carnival].

For some Filipino gay men, public spaces such as the "streets" (as in the Stonewall slogan, "Out of the bars and into the street") are not spaces of pride, but, to the contrary, are potential arenas of shame and degradation. These informants' views are not the result of homophobia, but are racialized and classed readings of the gay world. The kinds of exclusions and boundaries involved in the immigrant experience form the parameters for these ideas. The term *baklang karnabal* carries over meanings from Filipino traditions that illustrate the differences these three Filipino gay men perceive between American gays and themselves. For these men and some other Filipino gay men I have interviewed, American gay men practice the kind of spectacular and scandalous cross-dressing of the *bakla* in the carnival sideshows, unlike their own mode that attempts verisimilitude. In other words, these informants apprehend this public display of identity to be inappropriate, reminiscent of the kind of carnivalesque vulgarity of a particular type of *bakla*.

While class elements partially underlie these attitudes toward Stonewall, further conversation with these three informants indicate that class issues (they all come from different class backgrounds in the Philippines) are subordinated to the immigrant experience. For Ron and Rodel, the experience of coming to the United States to start a new life was both exciting and traumatic. When I asked Ron and Rodel about the symbolic meaning of Stonewall, Ron answered, "I am an ordinary *bakla*. I have no anger. I have no special joys. Other gay men have so much anguish. I came here to America to seek a new life. I have been successful. I don't have too much *drama*."[21]

Rodel's recuperation of the idiom *baklang karnabal* is not only an instance of his understanding of certain practices as vulgar and carnivalesque, it also implicitly suggests that there are different, multiple ways in which to perform "*bakla*ness." Ron differentiated himself from other gay men by calling himself an "ordinary *bakla*." In doing so, he unwittingly exposes a specific mode of *bakla* self-fashioning that resists and renounces the inelegant and churlish public performance of gay identity. Ron's words in fact exemplify the kinds of translations and transvaluations of the closet and the process of coming out by Filipino gay men.

Public visibility, canonized in the mainstream gay community, is questioned and held at bay by these men. In my conversations with many Filipino gay men, coming out, or, more properly, the public avowal of identity, is not necessary for their own self-fashioning. In a discussion group that involved members of Kambal sa Lusog, a Filipino gay and lesbian organization based in New York, several individuals expressed their concern about the usefulness of coming out narratives based on their experiences as immigrants or children of immigrants. One person in the group actually declared: "coming out" is a "foreign thing — totally American and not at all Filipino."

For my immigrant informants who self-identify as gay, narratives of the "closet" and "coming out" fragment and are subordinated in relation to the more highly fraught arena of the law and citizenship. I asked one informant whether he felt that coming out as a gay man was an important issue for him; he reminded me that until very recently to publicly declare oneself as a homosexual or as a gay man was a cause for the denial of entry visas, permanent residency, or citizenship. Until the late 1980s, U.S. immigration laws categorized homosexuality, together with membership in the Communist Party and being convicted of a crime, as grounds for barring individuals from entering the country. However, he went on to say, "When you are an illegal alien, you have other things to hide apart from being gay. It is actually the least of your problems." Another informant said that he would rather declare he was gay than say he was a Filipino, since he was here illegally. He said, "I had no qualms about acting like a queen, but I would lie and tell people I was Hawaiian since there would not be any questions about citizenship."

The closet and the process of coming out are not culturally constituted by Filipino gay men in the same way as the mainstream gay community. As one informant said, "I know who I am, and most people, including my family, know about me — without any declaration."

Filipino gay men argue that identities are not just proclaimed verbally, but are also "felt" (*pakiramdaman*) or intuited. The swardspeak term *ladlad ng kapa* (which literally means "unfurling the cape" and has been unproblematically translated as "coming out") belies how identity is something "worn" and not always "declared." It is this act of "wearing" identity that makes public arenas for gay identity articulation superfluous for many of my informants. This idea of identity is what spurred Ron to declare himself as one "ordinary *bakla*." This particular phrase is echoed by the opinions of several other informants about how their identities go against the simplistic movement from the private domain to the public realm implied by the ideas of the closet and coming out. One informant, Joe, encapsulated their opinions: "Here in America, people always talk about everything, including those things that you really don't need to or necessarily want to divulge . . . isn't it all obvious anyway? Talking is a luxury. A lot of us [Filipinos] don't have that luxury. Besides, I don't think we need it [talking about sexual identities]. When I see another *bakla,* he does not need to say anything. I don't have to say anything. Instantly, we know. Or, with my friends and family, they know . . . they have known way before my cape [*kapa*] ever unraveled or I mistakenly stepped all over it. I have been wearing it all my life!"

Informants who came here as immigrants considered narratives about success and "making it" in the United States to be more important than coming out. Here class and its translation in a diasporic setting is very telling. Many of my informants who came here illegally, but were well-educated and hailed from privileged backgrounds, were forced to take working-class or low-wage jobs such as janitors, sales clerks, and domestics. As one informant would say, "That is part of coming to America." This sublimation of class runs parallel with Americans' discomfort with notions of class and the rhetoric of equal opportunity. Many of these Filipinos imply that to survive in the United States, it is necessary, at least provisionally, to relegate class to the background. This does not mean, however, that class does not figure into their narratives. Rather, class loses its central location in identity articulation and is implicated and inflected by other important nodes of identity, such as race.

Race and racial difference, which is not a popular or highly visible discourse in the Philippines, acquired a greater importance for many of my informants once they had immigrated to the United States. While only a few of them reported direct racial discrimination, they recognized that not all gay spaces were open to them. Some informants told me of how they were ostracized in several gay establishments that catered to particular racial and class groupings. One informant said, "I may be a doctor, wear expensive clothes, but when I go to [a predominantly white, upper-class bar on the Upper East Side of Manhattan], I feel left out. Like I do not belong." Some reported being hounded out of predominantly white or black gay bars. Others have complained about how the gay media do not consistently have many images of "people who look like me." The crucial markers of difference among *bakla* in the Philippines do not readily cross the borders to the United States.

Amid the realization of racial tensions and differences, there have been attempts by Filipino gay men to create ties and establish affinities with other groups of gay men. Close affinities have been established with other Asian gay men. While racial stereotypes about the Chinese and Japanese and an aversion to being called "Asian" still exist among Filipinos, the situation in the gay community that lumps them into "Orientals" and ghettoizes them into "rice" bars has encouraged the creation of groups such as the Gay Asian Pacific Islander Men of New York (GAPIMNY). Hector, another informant, said, "I know we are very different from the other APIS [Asian and Pacific Islanders], but we're always placed in situations where we are together and, in fact, whether we like it or not, are oppressed together. Remember, we are the gooks, chinks, and brown-skinned fags — even other fags can't seem to stand us. So, I think that if we are to survive in the gay world, we need to connect with other Asians. I used to think, what for? Now, I realize there are a lot of things we can do if we band together."

Cross-dressing has provided a kind of anchor for the creation of affinities with other Asian men, Latinos, and African Americans.[22] One informant suggested that cross-dressing among "minorities" or "people of color" contrasts sharply with "white" notions of drag.[23] Vogueing or culture houses, which are composed predominantly of Latino and African American gays and lesbians, are notorious for excluding or being particularly unfriendly to Caucasians, but have in many cases been welcoming of Asians, specifically Filipinos.[24] I witnessed a competition where a Caucasian was dissed and booed while he/she was on the runway, while in the same category, a Filipino gay man who was a member of the house was wildly applauded. This Filipino voguer or house member rationalized the disparate reactions in this way: "We know all too well that there are very few places where people like us can really feel at home. I know that some of my Filipino friends think that associating with Latinos and African Americans is kinda tacky, but tell me, where can you find better cross-dressers than these guys? And where else can our skills as *bakla* be better appreciated than in those fabulous balls? White men are not really skilled. They are too big and too 'unreal.'"

The myth of Stonewall that founds U.S. gay politics is often incongruous with the forms and practices of the gay men in the Filipino diaspora who are my informants. For Mama Rene, his greatest achievement was eventually getting his green card and being legalized after almost fifteen years of living illegally in the United States. The identity politics of American gays therefore becomes just another new local "custom" for Filipino men, as they face racism and encounter the other vicissitudes of immigrant life.

The narratives of these diasporic Filipino gay men demonstrate that the closet is not a monolithic space, and that "coming out" or becoming publicly visible is not a uniform process that can be generalized across different national cultures. Filipino gay men in the diaspora have, to use their own rhetoric, a different *drama,* that is, a particular performance of coming out and identity articulation, that is emblematic of both their experiences of the gay community in the United States and of *bakla* culture. While Fenella Cannell argued that the *bakla* in a rural area of the Philippines negotiate their identities with images of the United States, I suggest that Filipino gay immigrants like Ron make sense of their existence in the United States by utilizing experiences in and symbolic practices from the Philippines. This particular performance, afforded by the diasporic experience, enables the contestation of long-held beliefs about the translation and transferal of modern gay technologies. For example, Mama Rene's refusal to valorize Stonewall displaces it as an originary event and contests the model of "coming out" for which Stonewall has become the emblem.

The writings of Filipino gay men in the Philippines represent various engagements with "gay culture" through "native" lenses. In these cases, the liberatory rhetoric often constructs a shift from *bakla* to gay in both political organizing and cultural production (gay film festivals, parades, and books). With the exception of one or two authors, these writers uncritically echo the modern global rhetoric of the international gay and lesbian movement. On the other hand, Filipino diasporic gay men reinterpret the *bakla* and articulate it in terms of being in excess of the modern gay subject. The words of Mama Rene, Ron, and Rodel rewrite the public, visible, and verbalized gay identity against the grain of the *bakla*. However, it must be noted that the comparison between gay writers in the Philippines and gay Filipinos in New York is a leap between genres. Nevertheless, both instances provide particular articulations and engagements with gay identity and gay political culture.

I have attempted to clarify and analyze the practices of gay transnational politics. Gay "technologies," in the Foucauldian sense, resurrect the images of "uneven development" and first world and third world economic relationships. However, by juxtaposing the globalizing rhetoric with which various individuals, agencies, and institutions speak of Stonewall and gay/lesbian identity against the multiple "localized" articulations of Filipino gay men in different sites, we find that implications and connections do not follow a single axis from center to periphery. As Arjun Appadurai has suggested, disjunctive lines and boundaries form as borders break down.[25] Focusing on global gay culture, Ken Plummer has warned against suggesting a convergence of homosexual lifestyles across the world, against "one true universal gayness." Plummer writes that each national and local culture brings its own richness, its own political strategies, its own uniqueness: "Along with globalization comes an intensification of the local. Indeed, with the process of globalization comes a tendency towards tribalism: a fundamentalism winning over difference, a politics that separates rather than unites."[26] Likewise, A. Ferguson advocates a view that promotes a sensitivity to the processes of self-determination of local and national movements within the global gay and lesbian movement.[27] However, Ferguson's dialectical approach suggests a kind of bifurcation of spaces and, as I have argued above, the articulations of *bakla* and gay involve diverse engagements from different locations. The local and national are inflected and implicated in manifold ways with each other and with the international/transnational on the level of the everyday and political mobilization.

In the shadows of Stonewall's history lie multiple engagements and negotiations. Conversations about globalizing tendencies of gay identity, politics, and culture are accompanied by disruptive local dialogues from people who speak from the margins. Such eruptions need to be heard. I conclude with a particular voice, of Ted Nierras, a young Filipino gay man educated in the United States, who articulates a strategy for Philippine gay politics:

Thus, our perspectives are always partial, always interested. When we say to straight people or more rarely, to Western gay people, "we are like you," we must also remember to add "only different." When we say "we are different," that our difference at the margin creates their sameness, already bifurcated into a violently oppressive hierarchy of gender at the straight Western center and replicated and transformed into another oppressive hierarchy of gender here. . . . We need yet to listen more carefully and more seriously to narratives of global and interconnected sexual and racial dominance and subordination, to narratives of our poor and unjustly inequitable national social reality, to narratives of the women in our society, whether they attempt to destroy or to affirm our "humanity." We need yet to speak our different desires, we need to speak our name.[28]

NOTES

An earlier version of this paper was presented at the sixth North American Conference on Lesbian, Gay and Bisexual Studies at the University of Iowa, 17–20 November 1994. The author would like to express appreciation to Lisa Lowe and David Lloyd for their comments. Special thanks to Victor Bascara and Chandan Reddy for their critical reading of earlier drafts.

1. The literature on diaspora and transnationalism indicates varied modes of dispersal and settlement as well as divergent ways of apprehending movement and travel of people and technologies; see the following contending views: Gillian Bottomley, *From Another Place: Migration and the Politics of Culture* (Melbourne: Cambridge University Press, 1992); Linda Basch, Nina Glick Schiller, and Cristina Szanton Blanc, *Nations Unbound: Transnational Projects, Postcolonial Predicaments and Deterritorialized Nation States* (New York: Gordon and Breach, 1994); James Clifford, "Traveling Cultures," in *Cultural Studies,* ed. L. Grossberg, C. Nelson, and P. Treichler (New York: Routledge, 1992), 96–116, and "Diasporas," *Cultural Anthropology* 9, no. 3 (1994): 302–338; Stuart Hall, "Cultural Identity and Diaspora," in *Identity: Community, Culture, Difference,* ed. J. Rutherford (London: Lawrence & Wishart, 1990), 222–237. In this paper, I have developed these two concepts in terms of syncretic dynamics (Kobena Mercer, "Diaspora Culture and the Dialogic Imagination," in *Blackframes: Critical Perspectives on Black Independent Cinema,* ed. M. Cham and C. Watkins [Cambridge, MA: MIT Press, 1988], 50–61) and creolizing dynamics (Ulf Hannerz, *Cultural Complexity: Studies in the Social Organization of Meaning* [New York: Columbia University Press, 1992].

2. See Chandra Talpade Mohanty, "Under Western Eyes: Feminist Scholarship and Colonial Discourses," *Feminist Review* 30 (1988): 65–88.

3. Stonewall 25 Committee, *New York Pride Guide* (New York: Pride Publishing, Inc., 1994), 19.

4. For a travelogue-type of "gay" journalism, see Neil Miller's *Out in the World: Gay and Lesbian Life from Buenos Aires to Bangkok* (New York: Random House, 1992), where he maintains that "the spread of Western notions of sexuality and relationships appeared inevitable," at the same time "the creation of a universal gay and lesbian identity, culture, and movement [was] difficult at best" (360).

5. Stephan Likosky, *Coming Out: An Anthology of International Gay and Lesbian Writing* (New York: Pantheon Books, 1992), xvi.

6. Likosky oversimplified Adam's argument. In the later chapters, Adam problematized the issues of the gay and lesbian movement in the 1980s by looking at political organizing in different parts of the world. However, by limiting his conception of the global conditions of the gay and lesbian movement to the establishment of organizations and acquisition of rights, Adam did not consider the various cultural engagements with gay and lesbian subjection. In the end, he implicitly presented a teleological view of the gay and lesbian movement.

7. Likosky, *Coming Out*, xvii.

8. A. Hendriks, R. Tielman, and E. van der Veen, eds., *The Third Pink Book: A Global View of Lesbian/Gay Liberation and Oppression* (Buffalo: Prometheus Books, 1993).

9. John Clark, Aart Hendriks, Lisa Power, Rob Tielman, and Evert van der Veen, introduction, in ibid., 17; emphases mine.

10. See Martin Manalansan, "Speaking of AIDS: Language and the Filipino Gay Experience in America," in *Discrepant Histories: Translocal Essays on Filipino Cultures,* ed. Vicente Rafael (Philadelphia: Temple University Press, 1995), 193–220, for an extended discussion on the social construction of the *bakla.*

11. Michael L. Tan, "From Bakla to Gay: Shifting Gender Identities and Sexual Behaviours in the Philippines," in *Conceiving Sexuality: Approaches to Sex Research in a Postmodern World,* ed. John Gagnon and Richard Parker (New York: Routledge, 1995). Men who have sex with men, or MSM, is an epidemiological category of a particular "risk group" that attempts to encompass various configurations of sexual identities.

12. Fenella Cannell, "The Power of Appearances: Beauty, Mimicry and Transformation in Bicol," in *Discrepant Histories: Translocal Essays on Filipino Cultures,* ed. Vicente Rafael (Philadelphia: Temple University Press, 1995).

13. Tony Perez, *Cubao 1980 at iba pang katha: Unang Sigaw ng Gay Liberation Movement sa Pilipinas* (Cubao 1980 and other works: The first cry of the Gay Liberation Movement in the Philippines). (Manila: Cacho Publishing House, 1992). Cubao is a commercial district in Quezon City which is part of metropolitan Manila and is known for (among other things) male hustlers who dot the area.

14. Ibid., xvii; translation mine.

15. Jomar Fleras, "Reclaiming Our Historic Rights: Gays and Lesbians in the Philippines," in *The Third Pink Book: A Global View of Lesbian/Gay Liberation and Oppression,* ed. A. Hendriks, R. Tielman, and E. van der Veen (Buffalo: Prometheus Books, 1993), 74.

16. Ibid., 76.

17. Ibid., 78. Danton Remoto, *Seduction and Solitude: Essays* (Manila: Anvil Press, 1995), chronicled the first Philippine Gay Pride March on 26 June 1994 amid what he termed "gay bashing in the local media" (183–199).

18. J. Neil C. Garcia, "Unfurling Lives: An Introduction," in *Ladlad: An Anthology of Philippine Gay Writings,* ed. J. N. C. Garcia and D. Remoto (Manila: Anvil Press, 1993), xvi.

19. Ibid., xviii.

20. All names of informants and other identifying situations and facts have been changed to protect their identities.

21. In Filipino gay argot, or swardspeak, *drama* can mean personhood, occupation, health, sexual role, sadness, fate, or plans.

22. According to reports from Asian AIDS Project staff members, transvestite sex workers in the Tenderloin District, which has a significant number of Filipino *bakla,* were exhibiting interesting cultural alignments that ran across racial and ethnic lines. Apparently, Latino and African American transvestite sex workers were utilizing Filipino swardspeak as coded speech to protect themselves in risky situations. For example, one report indicated that the sex workers would warn each other when the police were in the area by shouting "*Kagang*" (swardspeak for "police") to each other.

23. I discuss this issue of cross-dressing among Filipinos, other gay men of color, and white mainstream gay men in a manuscript on a religious pageant transformed and performed by Filipino gay men in Manhattan.

24. These informal groups are named after fashion labels or designers such as Mizrahi, Revlon, and Armani. They hold balls or competitions for cross-dressing individuals. In these balls, which are patterned after fashion shows, there are categories that promote the notion of "realness" or the attempt to look like the opposite sex.

25. Arjun Appadurai, "Global Ethnoscapes: Notes and Queries for a Transnational Anthropology," in *Recapturing Anthropology,* ed. R. Fox (Santa Fe: School of American Research Press, 1991). See also Inderpal Grewal and Caren Kaplan, eds., *Scattered Hegemonies: Postmodernity and Transnational Feminist Practices* (Minneapolis: University of Minnesota Press, 1994).

26. Ken Plummer, "Speaking Its Name: Inventing a Gay and Lesbian Studies," in *Modern Homosexualities: Fragments of Lesbian and Gay Experience,* ed. K. Plummer (London: Routledge, 1992), 17.

27. A. Ferguson, "Is There a Lesbian Culture?" in *Lesbian Philosophies and Cultures,* ed. J. Allen (Albany: State University of New York Press, 1990).

28. Eduardo R. Nierras, "This Risky Business of Desire: Theoretical Notes for and against Filipino Gay Male Identity Politics," in *Ladlad: An Anthology of Philippine Gay Writings,* ed. J. N. C. Garcia and D. Remoto (Manila: Anvil Press, 1994).

TANI E. BARLOW

Woman at the Close of the Maoist Era in the Polemics of Li Xiaojiang and Her Associates

This essay explores the complex debates on the question of women's subjectivity that emerged in post-Maoist China of the 1980s and early 1990s. It takes up both the ideological shifts that produced new, critical openings for alternatives to the Maoist revolutionary woman subject — *funü* — and the material and political constraints against which such alternatives perforce operated. In the course of the debates, two different concepts of womanhood came to the fore: *nüxing* (effectively, essential woman) and *nüren* (effectively, women or woman as a social category).

In the late 1970s, the Chinese Communist Party's Women's Federation (Fulian) began to document women's gains under communism, thereby reviving *funü*. Subsequently, the historians of women's history whom Fulian had empowered actually set into circulation a counter-identity to which they referred as *nüxing,* who should, they implied, supersede the older Maoist collectivity, *funü*. Finally, by the late 1980s, *nüren,* which I would define as an intermediate subjectivity within nonstatist Marxian discourse, emerges from these debates as the favored theoretical subject. *Nüren* scholars make the claim that the writing of universal women's history holds out great promise for creating a transnational theory and practice of women's liberation.

At its broadest, then, Chinese women's studies has forged a direction within the Chinese social sciences that has turned research toward the task of representing women in history. It seeks to relocate that history on an empirical, documentary, quasi-scientific ground that will ensure without question that women's experience is represented in scholarship. As an academic discipline, however, it is part of a larger debate over representation and scientific truth claims in post-Maoist China. It participates in dismantling state ideological categories and in the ongoing efforts of the intellectual community to establish a scientific discourse that takes "nature" (in the case of natural science) and "society" (in the case of social science) as its referents.

Elsewhere, I have discussed the ramifications of this genealogy of definitions of Chinese womanhood.[1] To focus this discussion, however, I will concentrate on the work of the post-Maoist feminist Li Xiaojiang, who, by virtue of her position in relation to the Party and the state, and of her theoretical interventions, has been one of the most influential theorists of women's practice and women's studies in contemporary China. This essay argues that Li Xiaojiang's theoretical feminism is part of a Beijing-centered dispute over how to rethink Chinese modernity and how to universalize its implications for world history. Definitively post-Maoist, though in a troubled, nuanced way, Li pioneered the now commonplace argument that alleges that Maoist policy successfully denaturalized women's bodies during the Great Proletarian Cultural Revolution (GPCR, 1966–76). Li's polemics and her pedagogic and bureaucratic outreach through the Chinese Women's Federation all affirm against this denaturalization the corporeal existence of an eth-nicized, nationalized, culturalized, and finally universalized modern Chinese female subject: *nüren*. She has advocated policies that would make women's studies a curricular designation in Chinese universities in order to institutionalize the theoretical subject of modern Chinese woman. In Chinese modernist discourse on women's liberation, how-ever, as in the vast majority of theoretical feminisms in the "interna-tional" or enlightened frame, affirmative female subjects are not easily stabilized because Woman is conventionally cast theoretically in terms of lack, as a deficient other of Man, for instance, or simply as a nascent, biophysical entity emerging "on the horizons of history" into social-political subjectivity, as Beijing Lacanians Dai Jinhua and Meng Yue argue.[2] The turn from Li Xiaojiang's critique of Maoism's alleged de-naturalization of woman to her affirmation of the embodied subject of Chinese women's liberation discourses embroiled Li in national dis-putes in the 1980s over modernization theory and practical politics. This paper describes the context and significance of some of those debates.

Also, the essay shows how Li Xiaojiang's various engagements shape her positions in contradictory ways. She continues to endorse the Chi-nese Communist Party's patently statist modernization agenda (so long as it does not abrogate what Li considers Nature's prior claims, she does not question the state's prerogative to exploit the bodies of its citizens), yet she is foremost in castigating a previous, Maoist state for forcing women's liberation onto an underdeveloped female population incapa-ble (in her view) of assuming the burden of subjectivity. She embraced the reenvisioning of Chinese Enlightenment proposed in the 1980s by the political philosopher Li Zehou, who has been described as a neo-Kantian, neo-Confucian, and anti-Maoist Marxist. Yet Li Xiaojiang's most important polemics of the last half of the 1980s nonetheless sys-tematically critiqued Li Zehou's postsocialist Marxism on the grounds that it made the theoretical subject of Chinese modernity male. Practically, Li Xiaojiang's concern with the bodies of women has led her to endorse Chinese state birth control programs and the emergent transnational capitalist investment in limiting China's rural population growth; she is a consistent ally of the Ford Foundation in China. Finally, Li's popular writing promotes a vision of Chinese modernization that depends on mobilizing women to do the work of consuming what production the new domestic markets makes available. This latter commitment has led Li to encourage the notion that ordinary women abandon public forms of social production and return to the domestic production of one-child families, sequestered in comfortable, emotionally interiorized, aesthetically appealing, nationalized personal space.

Li Xiaojiang's theoretical work amounts to nothing less than a Chinese feminist critique of Chinese modernity undertaken in conditions of rapid marketization with the thoroughly complicit objective of pioneering a commodified subjectivity for women organized around the duty and pleasures of consumption. Yet, paradoxically, this female subject of Chinese modernity rests historically, as Li herself has intimated, on the political, bureaucratic, and explicitly ideological category Woman (*funü*) established in the disavowed tradition of crude Maoism.[3] What distinguishes Li Xiaojiang's theoretical work from the feminisms of other Chinese theorists of the 1980s is her simultaneous disavowal and retention of the theoretical subject of Maoist woman. Li's work is significant in a final way that I cannot elaborate here, but will mention briefly at various points in this essay. She belongs to what is by now a century-old movement of intellectuals who, though they write in Chinese, have engaged global critique assuming that they are legitimate heirs of the European Enlightenment. Indeed, they argue, the Maoist Revolution qualifies them to speak with particular authority on the relation of theory and practice and on questions in Marxism generally. This is, at least in part, the politics of theory that led Jing Wang to declare that Chinese theoretical production is "overdetermined from within."[4] The grounds of those claims require discussion far beyond the parameters of this study.

The feminist polemics of Li Xiaojiang and her associates in the 1980s revolved around a sense of bodiliness that responded to the relative disembodiment of the Maoist *funü*. Bodiliness has been theorized and materialized in popular representations of women in the post-Mao era in remarkable ways. Not since the 1930s' dissemination of sexualized female bodies in advertising images has anything approaching contemporary levels of semiotic freight been attached to images of women's bared flesh. Bodily awareness has also shaped the consciousness of the activist intellectuals of the late 1980s, many of whom, like Li Xiaojiang, grew up during the Cultural Revolution. In a widely cited, significant essay entitled "Toward Womanhood" (*Zouxiang funü,* which appeared in 1990 in the journal *Nüxing/Ren*), Li described her memory of the moment she realized that she was more than just a human, that she was also female. This new consciousness arrived in the form of an embodied political trauma when, without warning, her first menstrual bleeding started just as Red Guard vigilantes seized her father and began interrogating him. The larger point, which she treated abstractly and impersonally in earlier, theoretical writing, defined her generation, men and women. And that was simply that while women may have benefited individually under the egalitarian Maoist order of merit, yet issues of sexual maturity, marriage, childbearing, and child care continued to rupture the illusion of human equality. Chinese women realized how the comfortable world of Maoist politics had obscured fundamental sexual difference and had robbed women of their innate sexuality. Sexual difference is basic, irrevocably physical. Female bodies may signify differently in different domains (art, leisure, medicine, everyday life). Essential difference, however, is grounded and foundational. It is the organic and scientifically apprehendable (i.e., the objective), material, sexual, and reproductive body of woman.[5]

CULTURAL FEVER

Li Xiaojiang began publishing critical essays toward the end of an interval of national intellectual ferment. The parameters and significance of this era's defining event, the 1984–85 Cultural Fever (*wenhua re*), as well as the more diffuse intellectual mood of cultural reflexivity (*wenhua fansi*) that suffused the decade, are still being evaluated. Imprecisely speaking, however, the late 1980s witnessed major scholarly and political movements that unfolded primarily among progressive Marxists and cultural intellectuals, enraged at the prodigal injustices and squandered hopes of the Maoist Cultural Revolution (1966–76), who hoped to return Chinese historical development to its "natural," teleological course, that is, toward parity with the modern West. They sought an ideological grid that would sustain the government's economic modernization policies. As is widely known, a characteristic of modern Chinese governmentality has been a close relation binding academic ideological work and actual governance. So, for instance, the heavily policed and contested touchstone of ideological work in Maoist politics, "Mao Zedong Thought," did, in reality, adjudicate relations of government policy to practical initiative, as well as working hard to limit the thinkable in explicitly cultural and popular arenas.[6] Elite intellectuals engaged in theoretical production during the late 1980s had every reason to think that they would govern the country eventually, so that the renegotiation of the terms of Chinese modernity in theory which they undertook was not a purely academic offensive. Li Zehou, Liu Zaifu, Jin Guantao, Gan Yang, Su Xiaokang, and the many others of the era set out to establish a benchmark sense of what pre-Maoist Chinese modernity had been, in order to theorize the relation of past and present in a discourse of post-Maoism, and thereby to enable current state policy formulation.[7]

To recuperate Chinese Marxism they detoured backward, skirting Maoism, to a prerevolutionary Chinese Marxism that had already assimilated and coproduced much Enlightened theory during the era 1890–1930. This return to the roots of Chinese Marxisms is well illustrated in Li Zehou, whose work I will discuss in a moment. But one of the other things that happened in the recovery of earlier, pre-Mao Chinese traditions of modern political philosophy was that the question of equivalence resurfaced. Stefan Tanaka has demonstrated, in the case of Japanese orientalism, that once the Enlightenment paradigm is accepted, the rules of play make it impossible to posit the simultaneous or coeval existence of progress in center and periphery, since Enlightenment historiography does not accommodate the other as an equal.[8] The strategy of Japanese orientalists, Tanaka shows, was to accumulate empirical scholarship that supported the existence of a realm called *toyo* (East Asia) that lay adjacent to the Western "Orient," but which was not the same as the Orient; *toyo*'s purpose was theoretical and strategic: to "take Japan out of the shadow of the West."[9] A different but strategically analogous move unfolded during the events in question here. Better educated in the historiography of revolutionary thought and the European Enlightenment than peers in the United States and Europe, many Chinese intellectuals argued that their actual experience of revolution gave them a distinct advantage in relation to interpreting historical reality. Because they had inherited two lines of revolutionary thought and action—the mistaken doctrines of the culturalist Mao Zedong and the truthful theories of fundamentalist Marxist economism—they had the theoretical and practical wherewithal to adjudicate claims about theory's viability (theory understood mimetically as the rational reflection of reality). The ultimate ground of this equivalence was modern science.[10]

Li Zehou

Because much of what Li Xiaojiang has to say about woman theory is a rewriting of Li Zehou's Marxist humanism, I will center most of my general review of Cultural Fever around the latter's positions. Li Zehou's preoccupations help clarify reasons why, in the circuit of East Asia cultural theory and consumer capital, there is so little interest shown in arguments rooted in epistemological questions of cultural incommensurability. This, in turn, helps clarify at least some of the aggressive positions that Li Xiaojiang has taken with regard to universal subjects of women in Marxist women's studies. Li Zehou's primary strategic move in theory was to measure Maoism's apostasy from Marxism. This he did in several ways. He rewrote Chinese Marxism's relation to Enlightenment, this time calling on Kant's vision of the centrality of the creative modern subject, an explicit critique of the Maoist diminution of the effectiveness of individual agents and its peculiarly voluntarist exalting of mass subjects (*qunzhong zhuti*). Yet Li also assaulted theoretical systems (Maoism, Frankfurt School, colonial discourse school) that, in his view, overvalorize culture or make culture an autonomous, discursive critical space of action, or that in any way loosen superstructural elements from their grounding in the mode of production. By these operations he intended to undercut the extreme voluntarism of late Maoism and expedite the reworking of Chinese Marxism into an ideology that could support national modernization. Modernization, the purposive transformation of the national social-economic base, would forestall future Cultural Revolutions because it could install, in a resolutely material sense, a public sphere that would ground Reason and empower creative individuals to make progress in terms that Li called "practices" (i.e., "material production and the practice of tool making").[11]

In the course of outlining his extremely influential critique, Li Zehou developed key terms that became so current as to be adopted by many people, including Li Xiaojiang. These include "cultural-psychological formation" (*wenhua xinli jiegou*), to describe the effect of the heavily coded superstructure grounded in the Chinese agricultural mode of production and its ability to forestall the autonomous development of capitalism in China; "sedimentation" (*jidian*), the process by which archaisms accumulate into the social unconscious of the people; "internalization" (*neihua*), a notion developed from Piaget's theories of affective and cognitive development to describe how subjectivity is circumscribed by cultural-psychological formations; "humanization" (*renhua*), the process by which human praxis acts on Nature through dialectical processes of sedimentation; and "imperial subject" (*zhuti*), the self-sufficient, activist, social subject available only in the process of modernization that transforms both substructure, the agricultural mode of production, and popular cultural-psychological formations at the ideological or superstructural levels.[12]

But, as Jing Wang has demonstrated, Li Zehou also recuperated into post-Mao Chinese Marxism key elements of the Confucian scholastic heritage. When Li Zehou retooled hoary textual strategies of the Confucian scholastic tradition, he in effect bolstered, at least for the duration of the Fever era, powers that accrue to theorizers. To take one of Jing Wang's examples, Li Zehou systematically eschewed binary difference in favor of reconcilable polarities on the neo-Confucian analogy of the "unity of Heaven and Man" (*tianren heyi*). This textual strategy provided Li a theoretical tool for abrogating incommensurability, since in neo-Confucian logics of unity, all differences (past and present, traditional and modern, East and West, male and female) are remediable, are in effect manageable, since differences interpenetrate and thus are simply moments on tangible continua. It almost goes without saying that Confucian poetics also privilege the Confucianists who undertake the hard textual and practical work of reconciling and remediation. In any case, this is not the place to review every inconsistency Jing Wang locates in Li Zehou's pro-modernization, instrumentalist, fundamentalist, Confucian Chinese Marxism. I adopt her point only to illustrate how the textual sophistication of Confucianized Marxism enabled several further moves.[13]

Li Zehou also pioneered a crucial modification of periodization of the modern Chinese historical record, as Liu Kang and Tang Xiaobing have shown. In Li's teleologies, the "thought revolution" of the first Chinese Enlightenment of the 1920s becomes the key moment in modern Chinese history, replacing Maoist historiography that had privileged popular peasant uprisings and the vanguard actions of the Chinese Communist Party's rural social revolution. The pivotal action in modern Chinese history, according to Li Zehou and his followers, was not class revolution, but the forging of humanist values in the May Fourth era (named for the scholarly, patriotic social movement against imperialism that initiated the social and intellectual transformations of the 1920s; it is also known as the Chinese Enlightenment or Chinese Renaissance). One further step took this line of reasoning from privileging consciousness to privileging thinkers. For complex reasons, including the internal pressures of a reinvented Confucian scholarly practice and normalized styles of Maoist heroism, the question of the subject (*zhuti*) of modernity eventually came to dominate theoretical work among intellectuals of all schools of thought in the late 1980s.[14] The effect was the popularization of a teleology that held that immanent efforts at enlightenment and modernization were acting upon a historical imperative: to make "a concerted and self-conscious effort to redefine the intellectual self as an autonomous, self-determining, self-regulating, and free subject."[15]

PRECONDITIONS OF THE THOUGHT OF LI XIAOJIANG

The conflict between economic efficiency and principles of fairness is concentrated on women's bodies. . . . But women's liberation has prerequisites; even if social conditions permitted a high level of material and cultural development, there must always be the subjective condition of women's conscious desire to develop, that is, the awakening of women's subjectivity. LI XIAOJIANG, 1994[16]

Li Xiaojiang commences from a dilemma that is perhaps not unfamiliar elsewhere: she confronts the fact that Chinese theoretical modernity (like homologous discourses elsewhere) is gendered, and that many Chinese cultural narratives of modernity rest on the immobilized body of an underdeveloped female subject burdened with illustrating the other side of masculinized universals of modernity, civility, and humanity. At the same time, she embraces the modernist argument and argues for the alleviation of inequality by raising the economic standing of women and stimulating in them subject formations that are equivalent to (though, of course, not the same as) the subjectivities that men already enjoy and have enjoyed historically since the bourgeois revolutions initiated by capital. Her own local recitation of familiar narratives of capitalist modernity maintains a hierarchical relation of woman to man, however, because Li's solution locates sexual difference extensively in corporeal difference.

But whatever its similarities, Li Xiaojiang's thinking does not desire to emulate or reproduce "Western feminism." Just as Li Zehou sees no incongruity in forwarding himself as the legitimate heir of European Enlightenment, Li Xiaojiang forecloses all possibility that the historical conventions of thinking about women's liberation in China, now a century old, might be derivative or secondary in any way. While she reads *The Second Sex* in Chinese translation and feels free to adopt some of its arguments, she does not consider Simone de Beauvoir to be her precursor; she does not discuss the status of Chinese women or

Chinese feminism in relation to Simone de Beauvoir; she is not concerned with fundamental or ontological gap between her own context and that of postwar France. This claim to *European* Enlightenment is linked equally to a belief in the legitimacy and primacy of the *Chinese* legacy of thinking about women's liberation *for Chinese women*. The grounds for this certainty in Li's thought is less cultural specificity than the organic, scientific, corporeal body that, in her view, all women share. History may make us superficially different, she argues, but our material bodies make us similar in the last analysis. The ideologically and scientifically correct appreciation of the centrality of the material body means that Chinese woman theory is at liberty to universalize its theoretical findings to all women should it choose to. This reasoning, in turn, permits Li Xiaojiang to assert the line between correct appreciations of the woman problem and "Western feminism," which has erred in recent years by overriding an ineradicable sexual divide.[17]

There are three factors conditioning Li Xiaojiang's critique of what she holds to be Li Zehou's masculinist representations of Chinese modernity. These are epistemological, psychodynamic, and institutional, and each bears on Li Xiaojiang's Enlightenment project. Let me address them one at a time, beginning with the question of epistemology.

An important critique of Maoist epistemology has pointed out that in Maoism mass political subjects emerged into policy because of the way Mao had turned Stalinism upside down. Maoism did not accept the economism of Stalin. Rather, Maoism privileged politics and formulated mass subjects on the basis of differentiated experiences of exploitation. "The determination of experience" in Maoism, this critique holds, "shifted from the workers' relationship with scientific technique, to the people's level of exploitation and degree of participation in struggle; it was no longer 'read off' the economic instance but rather off the political."[18] This is the heart of Mao's thesis of continuous revolution, since the experience of the exploited provided the basis on which political ideologies and actions were judged to be true or false and on which purposive action was plotted. But the point, evidenced in late 1980s Chinese cultural theory's preoccupation with the problem of subjectivity, is that Maoism was as rationalist as Stalinism in the sense that it, too, posited a knowing subject capable of envisioning totality when correctly positioned in relation to the political. The difference between Maoism and Stalinism, then, was that Stalin retained a Euro-Marxian individual knower intact, whereas Mao Zedong Thought substituted for this individual Bolshevik knower collective mass subjects like "the people," "the peasantry," "woman," and so on. These were precisely the mass subjects (*qunzhong zhuti*) that critical theorists in the late 1980s undertook to undo. Among those concerned with the woman problem, Li Xiaojiang and her associates, extensive critiques appeared arguing that the Maoist mass subject of Chinese womanhood, *funü*, did not properly represent existential reality and would have to be replaced institutionally and epistemologically.[19]

But modernization theory in the late 1980s sought to jettison the political and return the economic field to ontological priority. This is as true for an institutionally less powerful theoretician like Li Zehou as it was for very powerful politicians like Ye Jianying and Chen Yun, two major architects of the Deng Xiaoping economic restructuring policies of the 1980s and 1990s. Modernization theorists like Li Xiaojiang and Li Zehou shared with national planners the view that the more sophisticated the national productive forces and the more scientific the experience of the people generally, the better able the nation would be to grasp itself in thought and monitor its own progress into modernity. That is because Chinese thinkers, for the most part, given their institutional complicity with statist governmentality, had no reason to question the basic theoretical conventions of reform thinking. Inside and outside planning bureaucracies, theorists shared the assumption that theoretical work requires a ground or field of objective knowledge on top of which certain kinds of knowing subjects are established in theoretical work and practical experiments. Both Maoist and post-Mao versions of Chinese Marxism, in other words, retained a largely empiricist orientation.[20] And to make the point germane to the discussion of Li Xiaojiang's critique of masculinist modernization narratives, when theoreticians dismantled the elements of Maoism that had been most responsible for the brutality of the earlier regime, they left in place a range of assumptions about the relation of subject and object fields. While they shifted from the political to the allegedly economic ground of theory, they left intact the centrality of the knowing subject: the mechanisms of agency remained, though faith in the legitimacy of the specific agents or subjects in question was called into crisis.

In the case of polemics on woman, the Maoist epistemological status of subjects had underwritten the peculiar formation of a mass subject of woman, *funü*. As Li herself argued from time to time, the Maoist subject of woman has advantages. It allowed her to engage in the public sphere of revolutionary experience and in the bureaucracy on equal terms with men. It gave Chinese women the advantage of an already emancipated female citizenry to draw on in the struggle to modernize the economy and stimulate subject consciousness in somnolent peasants and workers. It was not that the collective mass subject "woman" was regrettable, in Li Xiaojiang's view, so much as that Maoist woman had no body; the ideologically construed *funü*'s body did not menstruate, give birth, feel sexual desire, or seek pleasure. If the positive features of *funü* were that it enabled individual women to achieve and affirmed the rights of women in positive terms, the negative features of the mass subject woman were that she could not pose her difference from man affirmatively. That was precisely because she was not different from man: she was the same, and that was the problem.

The second factor conditioning Li Xiaojiang's theoretical work is psychodynamic. Here the form that troubled post-Mao woman theory took shape in the specific texts and the general debate around Chinese women's literature in the 1980s. As Meng Yue and many other critics have pointed out, Chinese literature in the era from 1942 through the 1980s had worked in a peculiar fashion that did two things simultaneously: first, it disrupted what Meng states was the evolutionary, historical development of modern Chinese fiction that had, on the analogy of women's literature everywhere else, a "gendered eye"; second, Chinese literature had formed a vehicle, driven by statist ideologies, that made possible the paranoid collapse of all forms of the signification of difference into a recoding machine that did nothing but repeat the same topos over and over again, and that master-topos was the dominant position of the party-state over the people-nation.[21] However, early in the 1980s women writers began to publish who tended to focus on experiences of de-Maoicization endured by female protagonists. It is no coincidence that the work that Li Ziyun termed the first truly psychological fiction of the post-Maoist period was produced by a female author, veteran writer Zong Pu, and concerned the emotional disintegration of a female protagonist. For the first half of the 1980s, de-Maoicizing literature written by women dominated Chinese literary culture.

Thus, in the early to mid-1980s, just as Li Xiaojiang started to think about political remedies for institutionalized oppressions, major female literary figures like Zhang Jie were already writing simple sociological fictions about previously banned subjects that came to be classified as the "woman question," though in fact they raised general issues about the emotional pathologies born of the lack of personal life, sexual despair and the pain of sublimation, homosexual desire, the psychologies of people forbidden to love or, on the opposing hand, compelled to marry by the stifling force of social convention, and so on. Zhang Jie, Dai Qing, Zong Pu, Wang Anyi, and Zhu Lin pioneered the discussion of politics and personal life that predominated during the period that led up to the outbreak of Cultural Fever. Indeed, they continued to address questions — often in fiction and oral history — that in male-dominated academic circles were articulated in enlightened terms as the projects of theorizing subjectivity, modernity, nationalism, and so on. It was not a strictly policed division of gendered labor. Women theorists and male-authored literary texts explicitly negotiated questions of bad subject forms in the halting efforts at literary de-Maoicization in the early 1980s and found through these early writings that their own thinking had been deformed by a question that had lain submerged during the years of Maoist hegemony: the question of subjectivity outside the state-dominated political regime.[22]

But, and this is the third factor shaping Li Xiaojiang's woman theory, in the mid-1980s Li entered a forum that had already emerged in the immediate post-Mao era and that consisted of debate over how modern women would be represented scientifically (as opposed to politically or ideologically) and what role knowledge of women had in alleviating oppressions particular to their sex. I have already suggested that part of the critique of Maoist order was a repudiation of the merely political and an attempt to reground reason in reality, that is, in scientifically ascertainable, experimentally tangible, real conditions. As de-Maoicization proceeded, Li Xiaojiang, like many other educated, well-positioned, Party-educated intellectuals, aggressively pursued institutionally based change by launching criticism of the past record of government bureaucracy, and in Li's case, by establishing classes, pedagogical aids, critiques in simple language published in popular media, and finally in a book series that explicitly argued for the institutionalization of women's studies and woman as subject. During much of her initial work Li worked through a particular bureaucracy, the Women's Federation (*Fulian*), whose raison d'être was promoting the interests of *funü*. As I indicated above, the assumption always prevails in theoretical work among ranking Chinese intellectuals that their thought is assuredly capable of being translated into government policy. In the years that Li's theoretical writings circulated most widely, an overhaul of the government bodies that had previously policed official representations of women and femininity was undertaken. Once the economic reforms began to relink China's economy to transnational capitalism, corresponding social formations also began to shift, and with them the mission of government agencies in Chinese modernization policy.[23]

But the point I want to stress here as I move toward the explication of her thinking is that, while Li joined other feminist critics in voicing strong reservations about modernization policy's effects on women, she came to differ with most over the status of the subject of woman in theory. Nowhere in her work is there sustained commitment to the notion that femininity is defined in terms of "lack" or "absence." Rather, she addresses the lack of full subjectivity in Chinese women in terms of their feudal, semicolonial, and finally Maoist exclusion from historical agency. In doing so, she seeks to rest the emergence of modern Chinese women subjects in part on the ways in which the Maoist *funü* had transformed women's roles. Not only that, but, as we will see, Li aggressively pursued a certain subject formation in her scholarly writing and by virtue of the influence she and others in the women studies movement have increasingly brought to bear on government policy regarding women's lives. In her theoretical and practical work this affirmative female subject draws evidently from the social and political legacy of *funü*. In the next section I show how Li's position developed, starting with the means by which she mobilized an affirmative female subject of liberation and continuing on to the ways that this project dovetailed with government policy on consumption practices.

THE THOUGHT OF LI XIAOJIANG

In the mid-1980s networks of female scholars began linking up at the federal level all over China.[24] I first encountered Li Xiaojiang's name on essays that I read serially in a publication called *Women's Organizations and Activities: Published Press Materials Reader* (*Funü zuzhi yu hudong: yinshua baokan ziliao*), clippings of articles on various women-topics mined from the national press. Many of her articles that I discovered piece by piece in the reader have since appeared in book form; I am grateful that I read them unbound because the process of finding them among many other documents increased my sense of Li's range and passions. Her essays were usually the most provocative in contexts, although they were also difficult to follow because of their high theory vocabulary. In an essay titled "Why I Edit the Research on Women Series" (*Wo weishemma zhupian "Funü yanjiu congshu"*?), Li located the significant founding moments of her Enlightenment series publication project in her own first attempt to teach a course on women's literature and the first post-Mao Women's Research Conference held at Zhengzhou University (both in 1981) and in 1985 when exclusionary pressure on young female academics had become so acute that she and several friends initiated a scholarly discussion group at the Henan Provincial University. The experiences and meetings generated the desire to found a scholarly publication, which eventually became the Henan University Enlightenment Project series devoted to scholarship on women. The extraordinary takeoff phase of the Communist

Party market reforms occurred in 1986, and the ensuing surge of social pressure, including markets for a new, commercialized women's media, guaranteed success. Consequently, during the Cultural Fever, scholarship on women and Li Xiaojiang's Research on Women Series (*Funü yanjiu congshu*) were nearly synonymous, particularly to the nonspecialist reader, and most of the leading lights in woman theory, sex theory, and the critique of women's literature traditions published volumes in the series.[25]

The mission statement that prefaces each volume reiterates Li Xiaojiang's founding impulse, which was to establish a new discipline of women's studies through publication and to support the discipline with an academic scholarly field built on the foundation of Enlightenment scholarship.

Research on Women [*funü yanjiu*] is the consequence of the trend toward synthesis in the human sciences in the era following the sixties . . . and the trend toward scientific self-reflexivity [*kexue fansi zishen*]. Research on women can produce a new discipline—women's studies [*funüxue*]—that takes women as the subject of its special research, points out the customary elisions in the traditional humanities; research can also shape the sort of methodology that can examine human existence from the point of view of sexed beings [*you xing de ren de jiaodu*]. . . . Its charge: to use scientific research as its methodological base, human sciences as its background, to employ leading specialists to do research on women and to push for theoretical progress so that we can establish a respectable base for a national women's studies.

The people are in China, the books are in China. This "Series'" basic characteristics are all Chinese![26]

In 1988, when she wrote the mission statement, Li anticipated that the series would include twenty to twenty-five monographs on all aspects of the traditional sciences and humanities, including political science, law, economics, ethics, demographics, history, literature, aesthetics, psychology, sexology, the behavioral and social sciences, and philosophy. Encyclopaedic in the spirit of the European Enlightenment, it would disseminate scientific or truthful knowledge.[27]

Like Li Zehou, Li Xiaojiang raised the question of Enlightenment, but she began from a fundamentally different starting point. Her point of origin was the incommensurate relation of masculine and feminine. In other words, for Li Xiaojiang, sexual difference, what she termed the sexual gap (*xing gou*), was foundational. To approach the study of gender she needed to theorize a legitimate method that recognized the gendered subject(s) of modernity. She settled on women's studies, though, as she realized, certain problems attended her choice, and women's studies was itself simply a branch of the social or human sciences. Women's studies, Li noted, had emerged first in the United States and only then had spread to Europe, Canada, Japan, and the rest of the globe, where it had a salutary and transformative impact in humanist studies. The problem confronting Li and other Chinese women who sought to colloquialize women's studies in China was that, "in our nation," unlike other arenas globally, where women's studies had been integrated into customary humanism, "the scholarly and theoretical worlds" still have a tendency to "despise and discriminate against questions having to do with women," making it necessary to go to the extreme of "establishing a special scholarly emphasis."[28]

But despite this perception of specific Chinese hindrances to the development of women's studies, Li Xiaojiang recognized that women's studies must have for its principal object the study of women in China. "Why raise the issue of Chineseness [in this context]?" she asked rhetorically. "Because the first principle of the founding of the human sciences is the principle of nationalism [*minzuxing*]." Indeed, Li argued, "there is no such thing as abstract Humanity." Except for the primary difference of sex/gender (*xingbie chayi* or *xing gou*), nothing is more absolute in the thought of Li Xiaojiang than national origin.[29] The dialectic between the abstraction embedded in the very category "woman" and its specific national and/or local realizations is crucial to her thinking:

The starting point of research in a Marxist women's studies must be movement from the totality of Humanity [*renlei zhengti zhong*] into greater abstraction. Insofar as abstraction is concerned, it must be able to investigate woman as if it were one element of the totality of Humanity; at the same time woman must be seen as a special case in the social life of Humanity — one that contains all of the categories of totality, and from it this abstraction must determine the relative basis of its own Self. Only in this manner will it be possible for us to raise a scientific theory on the basis of the multiple totality of the Human Sciences to address the practicalities of the woman question and women's liberation.[30]

In spite of its national focus, Li founded her feminist Enlightenment project in the supposedly universal medium of social science theory, and most of the projected titles listed in the 1987 introduction to the series are basic texts in scholarly method and disciplinary regimes: *Funü jingjihuodong lun* (On the economic life of women), *Nüxing yü chouxiang kexue* (Women and the abstract sciences), *Guoji fudong liangbainian* (Two hundred years of the international women's movement), and so on. It social science foundation situated the Research on Women Series in the Cultural Fever, but, as I indicated above, Li's aim was a critique of modernization theory on the basis of the wedge of corporeal difference in the Real.

Li produced five volumes of her own in the late 1980s: *Funü yü jiazheng,* 1986 (Woman and domestic science), *Xiawa de tansuo,* 1988 (Eve's Exploration), *Nüren: yige youyuan meili de chuanshuo,* 1989 (Woman: A distant, beautiful legend), *Nüxing shenmei yishi tanwei,* 1989 (Inquiry into women's aesthetic consciousness), and *Xinggou,* 1989 (The sexual gap).[31] The first section of what is certainly her most famous collection, *Eve's Exploration,* is titled "The Oversight of Reason," for obvious reasons. In "Oversight," which performs a Chinese Marxist feminist ground clearing, Li is preoccupied with doing away with speculation about women under socialism. Marx and Engels, she argues, were more progressive than their contemporary utopian or bourgeois rights feminists since they did address the material origins of gender and class oppression and their critique did provide Chinese Communism a winning strategy. After 1949 the Chinese Communist Party (CCP) ran into trouble, however. Its woman theory failed to adapt; it made the women's liberation movement synonymous with proletarian emancipation, and it reinforced a move initiated by Chinese women themselves to abandon femininity and to adopt a strategy of "human first, female only after." Li seeks a revitalized woman theory and a revived, autonomous women's liberation movement that accommodates women's femininity and mobilizes a less flawed (*quehan*) female Subject that is more self-conscious (*ziwo yishi de*).

Li's target is not materialist forms of historiography generally, but actual Maoist state policies. In fact, she argues, Marxist women's work foundered during the GPCR because Maoism declared scientific (i.e., Stalinist) Marxism itself off-limits and refused to allow theorists to mobilize science for exploring new social phenomena or establishing fresh social truths. It also prevented "woman" from emerging into Marxism as an abstract category, which made it altogether too easy for the Gang of Four to disable work among women by banning the Women's Federation and undermining the potential of even the mass subject of woman. Now Chinese women must recover their femininity and Chinese Marxist woman theory must prove again that indeed "Marxism is an open philosophic system as well as a world view and stands at the apex of progress in terms of its starting point." The solution to the weaknesses of Chinese classical Marxism, insofar as the woman question is concerned, argued Li, would be to take up the Deng Xiaoping slogan "Seeking truth from facts" and simply declare on-limits the very areas that Maoism had tabooed: sexuality, the analytic divisibility of gender and class, and the global history of bourgeois feminisms. So, in fact, Li's willingness to engage with standard CCP historiography is as marked as her interest in the previously "off-limits" topics of feminism and establishing the analytic foundations for the subject she calls total or universal woman (*zhengge funü*) in this first essay, *nüren* elsewhere.[32]

When she enjoined Chinese Marxism to reconsider the woman question in theoretic work, Li had argued that "Woman theory essentially belongs to the human sciences."[33] In "The Sublime of Humanity" (*Renxing de shenghua*), her critique of Li Zehou's philosophic masculinism, she developed this point at great length. With that interest she placed herself within the camp of the Kantian-Marxists and particularly in that of Li Zehou's project to "spell out a Marxist practical philosophy, which would lay the philosophical foundation for a notion of subjectivity as the main conceptual framework with which to examine Chinese culture and history."[34] Indeed, much of Li Zehou's familiar vocabulary of subjectivity, the sublime, reflection, consciousness, sedimentation, interiorization, and so on appears without comment in Li Xiaojiang's volume. Marxism, she argued in dialogue with Li Zehou, indeed ought to reinvent itself in terms of the academic discourse of the human sciences, but neo-Marxism must surpass classical schemes by making sure that its subject, Humanity, is distinguished by sex: It is no longer acceptable that Man (*ren*) obscure the femininity of half of Humanity (*renlei*). Since the human sciences are broadly theoretical and since their subject, Humanity, is doubled, in the scholarly practices of the human sciences the representation of Woman is the measure of accuracy while the measure of a theory's viability is whether woman emerges in it as an abstract category. "In classical Marxist theory the position of woman is the same as other social problems, since in Karl Marx's time the woman question had not attained abstract theoretical status and become an aspect of the bourgeois social structure or even become the subject of historical examination," she argued. Theory or abstraction and scholarly representation or practice are inextricably linked: the woman question must be raised in both for the human sciences and neo-Marxism to fulfill their potential. As the movement to develop a Marxist human sciences must include the dual subject of Humanity, so all research and theorizing about woman must appreciate the degree to which representation is representation of Humanity and the progress of Humanity in historical development toward Enlightenment. This explains the apparent contradiction between *funü* and *nüren* in Li's work, and the dialectic she engages in considering the universality of Enlightenment through the particularity of the Chinese experience. The revolutionary subject of Maoism emphasizes and to some extent produces an equivalence between men and women. Effectively, then, Maoism produces a female subject akin to but historically beyond the point of Enlightenment feminisms. Its negation in turn by the fully gendered subject that emerges in post-Maoist theory (*nüren*) opens the space theoretically for a synthesis between the public, civic woman as political subject and the subjectivity of Woman in all her difference from male subjects. This possibility would realize the claim that the specific Chinese revolutionary experience not only continues the Enlightenment but raises it to greater levels of human/universal potentiality than are available to Western feminism. The actual probability of realizing such a synthesis under the economic and social conditions of Chinese modernity will be discussed further on.

In the first place, however, the theoretical project itself will prove to be difficult because "reflected in the academic domain is an indifference to theory on women which in actual fact is impeding the establishment of a systematized human science." That is to say, Li Zehou and the masculinists had quite unconsciously tainted their own advances by leaving out of their critique the central and explosive problem of gender. So "theoretical research" (*lilun yanjiu*) may indeed constitute "a kind of science," and may indeed be an expression of Reason. But none of the current theoretical exercises have undertaken to ensure that the enigma of woman is unraveled. Neither the theoretical world, which excludes women, nor the women's world, which does not deign to engage theory, have come to terms with the challenge posed by the human sciences on the one hand and the real-world progress of women's liberation on the other. Until now: "What is woman theory [*funü lilun*]? Plainly put, woman theory is the abstractions about woman made in philosophy. In practice, women's theoretic research can oppose two different objects, forming its own relatively independent theoretical category [*lilun fanchou*]. So far as women's liberation is concerned, practice itself constitutes the first concrete object of women's theoretic research."[35] In the history of the human sciences as in all other academic science, according to Li, truth is established step by step in an orderly progression: from simple to complex, from phenomenon to essence, from analysis to synthesis. To make the human sciences complete, a newly wrought truth about woman must interrupt the assumption that Humanity is male. Like all other human sciences, this truth must have a place in theory (i.e., as the abstract category of woman) and be a subject in history (i.e., the universal historical movement toward women's emancipation and thereby toward the true apotheosis of Humanity). Once Li Xiaojiang authorized woman theory in the human sciences, her next move was to plot out the field of knowledge

History of the Concept *Woman*	Marxist Woman Theory	History of Woman Theory
GynoHuman Science	Woman History	Woman Sociology
Concept of Humanity	History Social Progress	Sociological Frameworks
Research Origins	History of Woman's Life (foreign)	Structure of Woman
Sexual Science	History of Woman's Liberation (foreign)	Organizations of Woman
Female Anatomy	History of Progress Marriage and Family	Woman and Society
Female Physiology		Woman and Family
Female Psychology		Woman and Children

Female Aesthetics

The Framework of Aesthetics

Women's Literature

Female Arts[36]

that the forging of the abstract category of woman in philosophy made available (see table).

Li Xiaojiang elaborated this outline at great length, inviting Chinese scholars to draw liberally on international theorists like Simone de Beauvoir, Ellen Key, Betty Friedan, Alexandra Kollantai, and August Bebel, as well as Chinese research of the 1920s and 1930s on Chinese women, pioneered during the May Fourth Enlightenment. She also stated in diagrammatic, terse language where she thought research ought to head. To those who might object that this notion of women's studies is too heavily indebted to Western and specifically American prototypes, Li replied that "our women's studies [*funüxue*] is not a ready-made textbook copy of theirs," because it is taking shape within the historical context of Chinese discussion and Chinese concerns.[37] But also it has more potential than non-Chinese forms do for the simple reason that Chinese scholars and Chinese women have already experienced revolutionary change: though Chinese women's studies presently lags "twenty years behind Western nations," it exceeds, at least in potential, what non-Marxist and non-Chinese scholars are doing now because Chinese women's studies can begin with a subject already liberated in certain domains. Thus, despite the fact that the revolution fell short, the cumulative effect of liberatory legislation and experience is that Chinese women's studies is in a privileged position globally; nationally, its position is also redemptive because it can assume "new responsibility for those who would continue social progress today."[38]

To this point in her argument Li Xiaojiang had foregrounded a critique of the masculinism of Li Zehou–style Marxist humanism. But as soon as she began making affirmative arguments about the positivity of woman as a category in the privileged scholarly regime of Chinese women's studies, she encountered problems, since it is analytically more difficult to sustain affirmative accounts than to offer up a critique of the masculinist positions of others. Partly this is because she set in motion the logic of the Self and the Other. But also, when Li authorized the subjects "woman" and "China" she confronted multiplying questions of difference. One in particular that recurred for her was the question of whether, if the subject woman always emerged, even in the foundational human sciences, in nationalized form, how should one answer the universalizing question, What is a woman?

Li Xiaojiang's solution was, as we have seen, to embrace the absolute incommensurability of males and females. The virtue of this position is that it enabled her to unfold historical teleologies inside specific national modernities, with appropriate attention to the differences of each nation-state's experiences in global capitalism, yet mediated these historical differences through a trans- or supranational incommensurable gap of sexual difference. And it made possible the argument that Enlightenment shifted ground like mercury on an uneven surface; emerging in Europe, it had shifted eastward through Russia and finally, in the present, to post-Mao China. In one of her earliest major statements, "The Self-Comprehension of Woman," Li introduced the basic formula of the sexed, universal subject of *nüren,* reiterated and elaborated in many other essays.[39]

Nüren, she argued here, exists within historical evolutionary flows that govern the laws of development for all national formations and thus all peoples. Regardless of nationality, all women share a universal history and certain synchronized, historical stages through which their sex, *nüren,* must pass; specificities are secondary and advances in one region stand for advances for all women. But specific differences among women do exist and all women, regardless of nationality, will undergo those stages even if at different moments. The universal stages of the evolution of *nüren* are matriarchy, slavery, and liberation. The important point here is that *nüren*'s evolutionary path is dissimilar to that of men or *nanzi,* whose trajectory follows the more familiar Marxist sequence of matriarchy (the one stage the sexes share, though on terms of inequality), feudalism, and bourgeois dominance. This sex-historical, evolutionary difference (*chayi*) is both a positive and negative thing: it is positive in the sense that it corresponds to the physiological reality of sexual difference, but it is negative because in modernity Chinese women have yet to achieve full subjectivity and thus differ from Chinese men by virtue of their insufficiencies, their lack of cohesion, their presubjectivity.

The motor driving history is therefore not just class struggle à la Marx and Engels but, at an even more profoundly organic level, the immutable and natural sexual division of labor that began in the transition from matriarchy to patriarchal small families in the period of slavery and which modern history must both mediate and preserve. The claim is that, left to its own devices,[40] history can socialize nature and forward the slow, evolutionary development of equality. Or at least that is the implication of Li Xiaojiang's dialectic of nature and culture expressed in this passage: "Therefore, we can say about the starting point of human civilization that the social division of society into classes was absolutely natural. The social division of labor forces in fact maintained for a considerable time the natural division of human labor—what ensued historically was the socialization of appropriate natural divisions."[41] And this is where the implications of Li Xiaojiang's critique of Li Zehou begin to surface quite vividly. Because the natural divisions determined by procreation are normatively immutable, Li is forced to conclude, there have been eras when the forward progress of Humanity *required a historical degradation* to be visited on *nüren*. In the slave stage of history, for instance, men set about resolving the problems that history had set for them. They built a rich material and social existence. Li is very clear on this: Men created civilization and the marvels of social production are the product of men's work during the era that men enslaved women, that is, from the rise of patriarchy to the era of Enlightenment. The creativity of men rested upon a cruel but necessary devolution of women into "tools of existence" (*cunzhong de gonzhu*).

This leads Li to draw the obvious yet peculiar conclusion that "over the entire history of civilization, although men and women have lived together on this earth, they have experienced two totally different evolutions."

Man—[exists] in opposition to Nature [*ziran*]: in the struggle with Nature he gradually created an independent Subject consciousness [*zhuti yishi*]. It is Man that transforms nature and creates wealth under the pressure of this subject consciousness. In the process of the accumulation of wealth, men feel they have the capacity to withstand material changes. . . . Women—impeded by Nature, continue their own individual physiological destiny and the collective natural mission of humans as a collective whole, using their very dehumanization to reproduce humankind. In the development of civilization, the importance of woman is to be concretized in relation to man and in concert with other natural phenomena, to passively endure the great transformations of humanized Nature, and to endure forced alienation by men. Thus have these two obviously different tracks [*guidao*] deeply yet often invisibly and unconsciously inscribed the great "sex divide" [*xinggou*] into human life.[42]

It is not precisely clear in the end whether *nüren* is the feminine of the species or the missing, abstract feminine part of a Li Zehovian Humanity, since in crediting mankind with the development of civilization Li Xiaojiang undercut strategies for equality based on justice claims and reinforced such commonsensical nationalist arguments as that ameliorating the lot of women contributes to national wealth and power.

So historical development and justice for women are agonistically opposed to some degree, even at the level of the nation. Amelioration of women's suffering presupposes economic reform. Economic reform will make the pleasures of consumption available to women, who become conscious of their former reduction to bodiliness as *funü*. The next task for Chinese women must involve the stimulation of "the subjective condition of women's conscious desire to develop, that is, the awakening of women's subjectivity." The task of women's studies is to encourage Chinese women generally to ask themselves "Who am I?" and "What is *nüren* now?[43] The answer to the latter question we have already explored: *nüren* is a universal, evolutionary, anatomical, physiological, menstruating, and procreative body. In her popular writing, Li described the corporeality of woman's body in elaborate anatomical detail, beginning from the fetal matter's constitution in XX and XY chromosomal patterns, through birth and childhood (*yuerqi*), youth (*qingchunqi*), maturity (*chengshuqi*), transition (*gengnianqi*), and menopause (*jiejingqi*). All *nüren* are universally reducible in part to this body that signals its genuinely natural difference from man's body by flowing, changing, erupting, reproducing, and so on.

Li Xiaojiang strongly cautions those who evade the demands of this body and either fail to marry heterosexually or refuse pregnancy and childbirth. Women who do not use their bodies in sexual reproduction have, she argues, been misled into thinking that equality can be purchased at the expense of difference and have betrayed their physiological destiny as *nüren*. There are two noteworthy aspects to this construction of *nüren*'s body in this context. The first is the significance Li attaches to menstruation. You will recall that in her personal experience, menstruation was equated with political trauma. In her theoretical work, negotiating the difficulties of menstruation is the greatest danger *nüren* face and leads potentially to moral and developmental failures. Second, each biophysiological stage in Li's description of the anatomical specificities of *nüren* is related—foundationally related—to moral development in female subject formation. *Nüren* who successfully negotiate the dangers of the onset of menses and enter the period of psychosexual and reproductive maturity can, given their historical era, expect to achieve an "I" (*wo*) of some sort: be this a traditional, selfless I (*wangwo*), contemporary not-I (*feiwo*), or future Greater I (*dawo*) in which the *nüren* finally achieves what men have enjoyed since the beginning of the slave era, the prize of individuality or individual being, *renge*.[44]

This is the overtly physiological or corporeal heart of Li's critique of *funü* and Maoist woman policy generally. When the CCP ignored the body of *nüren*, it encouraged the socialization of women who had neither the individuality of men nor the femininity of women. They were, in Li's parlance, neither true *nüren* nor *nüxing* because they sought liberation only in a public realm and in ways that denied fundamental bodily differences. To resume their progress toward Enlightenment (and therefore their historical mission to move Humanity toward the end of history) women must achieve selfhood through the struggle to achieve the natural stages of their psychosexual maturation.[45] Awakening women's subjectivity is in part a matter of making women aware of the nature of their own physical being.

The problem women's studies must overcome is that women as subjects, in China particularly, are simply underdeveloped in comparison to men as subjects.[46] To illustrate her general thesis of female underdevelopment, Li argued a teleology complete with causal factors and elaborate, multistage temporalities. To each evolutionary stage of human history there belongs a corresponding "model" (matriarchy-*natural,* slave-*domestic,* liberation-*social*). Corresponding to each model is a form of female consciousness. Under the matriarchal formation, for instance, woman's consciousness took form as a spiritual, selfless love of mother for child. However, during the slave era woman's consciousness atrophied. Attendant thereupon, she lost all possibility of human agency, since without a consciousness will is not available. Woman presently confronts the problem of how to negotiate a transition from slave consciousness to consciousness of liberation. Lacking a sense of self, she is badly situated and, moreover, history is forever exceeding her own sense of agency. (Women's liberation, for instance, is not actually the invention of women at all. It is the product of a global industrialization that quite simply tore women out of their domestic sphere and placed them willy-nilly into the social sphere.)

The key issue for Li is not that liberation for women initially "just happened," or even that women should have been able to put the state's imposed liberations to better use, but rather that because of the differences in their separate historical evolutions, men and women confronted the present with very different resources for achieving subjectivity. Whereas men-in-history have always had a class nature and enjoyed subjectivity as masters or slaves, landlords or tenants, capitalists or workers, women, on the other hand, living an evolutionary course outside men's history, have stagnated for a thousand years because they were constitutionally unable to achieve "individual being" (*dulide renge*).[47] Women had no consciousness of their own individual subjectivity because they were confined within the natural-historical roles necessarily conferred upon them historically, the kinship roles (*jiaose*) of mother, sister, wife, and daughter. This has meant that women as a species entered the modern era inherently disadvantaged. During the European Enlightenment, while men achieved the necessary modern "self-consciousness as complete or essential Self" (*zuowei ren de zhengti zijue yishi*), women had to wait a full century before certain foremothers seized Enlightened Reason and established an abstract subject woman on women's behalf. How did this opportunity make itself available? History working through imperialism initiated the global women's liberation movement and thus imperialism laid the ground for the historical reconciliation of the sexes in the progress of Humanity.

Enlightenment for *nüren* requires self-recognition, and the process by which *nüren* comes into consciousness of herself for herself is precisely the liberationist project of women's studies. I underline this element of Li's argument because I think it significant that to this point in her writing career, she had simply assumed that women in industrial and postindustrial countries were successfully negotiating their own Enlightenment to the degree that they were no longer primarily burdened with a selfhood stitched together out of semifeudal "roles." Since the particular instantiation of *nüren* and the given consciousness or mind in question is always specific and concrete, it is necessary to turn to the consciousness of one instance of woman—Chinese woman—to proceed any further.

"Oriental woman" (*dongfang nüxing*) is a stereotype deployed in some of Li Xiaojiang's most Li Zehovian exposition. It represents her analysis of the consciousness possible for contemporary Chinese women and begins from an analysis of the "sedimentation" (*jidian*) of historical qualities that have historically led to Chinese women's present "disposition" (*qizhi*). The sedimented formation of the Oriental woman is the consequence of three lines of causality: the social structural (great feudal–great family system), economic foundational (the small peasant cultivator's self-reliance), and the ideological (Confucian, Daoist, and Buddhist), which through the vehicle of aesthetic consciousness produces the traditional elements contributing to the consciousness of Oriental woman: restraint (*kezhi*), steadfastness (*jianren*), reserve (*hanxu*), and dignity (*ningzhong*).[48] While women globally in the modern era are torn between desire to procreate and the need to work outside the home, Oriental women felt the contradiction most heavily because of semifeudal semicolonialism. Later, robbed by the Communist Party of her essential difference from men, yet bearing within her sedimented feudal remnants as the shards of a failed subjectivity, Oriental woman could not enter public life. The so-called liberation imposed on women during the GPCR reinforced rather than solved the problem, which is why equality without difference led Chinese women to despicable subject positions: lack of self on the one hand and loss of self on the other. In any case, Oriental woman currently possesses neither the powers of the old female roles under feudalism (*jiating jiaose*) nor a coherent subjectivity in postfeudal modernity. That— more than anything else—is the reason why women's studies is central to the reemancipation of Chinese women back into their psychoanatomical difference and thus central to China's progress as a whole.

The peculiar circumstances of the underdeveloped consciousness of Chinese woman led Li Xiaojiang to perhaps her most famous thesis of all, the notion of the double burden. The double burden in her thinking has two aspects. First, it means that, whereas in Europe women gave up feudal social formations and took on the contradictions of the modern era, in China women simply added modern roles (*jiaose*) to the feudal roles they already had inherited, doubling their alienation from personal being (*renge*). More commonly, the double burden refers to Li's belief that when the CCP prematurely "liberated" Chinese women by fiat, the result was that they engaged in social production while at the same time doing the necessary and essential work of domestic reproduction. To "awaken to self-consciousness," contemporary Chinese women must resolve the crushing contradiction of the double burden in their own particular fashion.[49] They may take advantage of the maternity leaves given Chinese women under law, or they may choose to retire completely from social production to focus on the domestic sphere. In any case, they will have to take some time off work to obey the central imperative of sexual difference, which is simply that women must procreate.

The resolution to the contradiction [procreating] women face is actually historical. We must clearly recognize that now, under the present conditions of our country, there exist restrictions on the progress of the economic standard of living and so we cannot simply give up women's responsibility for doing domestic labor; the responsibility of children is still something that women must undertake and the work of upholding family responsibilities must rest on the shoulders of women. The anxiety of dual roles is a heavy millstone around our necks, but it is one that we must continue to shoulder. *This is the price we must pay for the advancement of History and women.*[50]

The model of liberated Chinese womanhood under the current economic reforms is a repatriated, modern housewife.

Li Xiaojiang's analyses left an obvious lacuna: Where was the momentarily unreflexive (*feiwo*), passive, misdirected Chinese woman to turn for the kind of knowledge that would allow her to recognize herself as a biogenetic, humanized, and nationalized yet still wholly universal subject *nüren*? Certainly the women's studies materials that Li projects and the volumes her series produces do form part of the new archive. But not all women are well educated enough to find such academic work interesting and scientific work is not the only recourse women have when they set out to establish individual subjectivity. One of the obligations of the female leadership of the women's liberation movement had to be to provide material that would allow ordinary women to raise their own consciousness. And it is with this object in mind that Li pioneered popular writing and popular consciousness-raising within the framework of the Women's Federation. This made the project of Enlightenment in Culture Fever woman theory doubly complex. It had to establish the foundation of female subject formation but also required the dissemination of materials for nurturing subjectivity in ordinary Chinese women. In prosecuting this argument Li rekindled an argument that was as old as Chinese modernity, emerging directly out of the May Fourth archive: the question of personal being (*renge*) in women. If Chinese women are presently defined by their lack of personal being, then what is present within them that can stimulate desire to redress this fundamental lack?[51] How can one affirm the potential subject of Chinese woman while one defines the present subjects in terms of their lack of *renge*?

The volume *Woman: A Distant, Beautiful Legend* illustrates the double bind Li got caught up in. Dedicated to *nüren* everywhere, "no matter what their color, race, nationality, profession or age," the opening passages of the introduction reiterate in simple language many of the points Li had raised in more academic writing.[52] She particularly emphasizes the devastating effects male dominance (using the euphemisms "masculine consciousness" and "masculine will") have wrought on women: They are lost to the world and forgotten even by themselves; their centuries of enslavement have devastated their ability to act; women by and large are simply in thrall to fetters that bind them; they have lost sight of their track, and so on. Then the narrative takes a rhetorical stand:

What is the historical course of women [*nüren*] then? What if we search the historical classics and archives for her? Well, the consequence is this: *nüren* has no history! . . . It appears that *nüren* is a distant, beautiful legend. In this complex world of sacred and profane, dream and reality, one finds the marks of *nüren*'s existence and actions left behind in the realm of literature. Literature, it seems, is the mirror of the life of Humanity, reflecting for better or worse social reality. . . . This book [of mine] is written by a woman for other women to read. It is a paean to beauty, and the greatness of the feminine; it is a paean to love, the belief of women; it is a song to the children and to humanity; to the selflessness of women and peace, the strength of women. This book seeks to employ a great, boundless maternal humanism to usher women into the glory of History and to enlighten today's women into consciousness of Self. To be a person, a *nüren* requires that we locate an imperial subjectivity for women![53]

The contents of this book, dedicated to the affirmation of the recuperation of true, universal womanhood, knit together a secret history of woman from the subliminal world of myths and global literature. "You must still recognize that you are indeed a *nüren,* and you need to see clearly your female status [*nüxing shenfen*]," the narrative argues. "If you really want to understand yourself, then you must understand this first; *you are a woman.* Yet, woman, that category does not belong to you. Woman is sacred and she is the enigma wrapped in the shroud of a hundred thousand years. But if you really wish to grasp this you must begin with the recognition that you are woman!"[54] The subsequent three hundred pages stitch together Li's evidence. Starting with myths and stories about women in the ancient world of matriarchy (in the "west," the Queen of Sheba; in the "east," Xiwangmu the western matriarch, etc.), the narrative continues with stories about women in the era of slavery, when women's sphere was exclusively domestic, then follows the course of woman from the awakening in the European Enlightenment, through the Russian and Chinese Enlightenments to modern woman's struggles with modernity. The final section, "Woman," focuses on the liberation movements of the 1960s in the United States, relaying information in chatty, anecdotal style. The volume sets out to convince the reader that she should abandon the Maoist attempt to make Chinese women into Chinese men and admit that her historic mission as a universal historical subject of woman is, in descending order of importance, mother, creator of life, fighter for justice, and, in the familiar May Fourth metonymy of the nascent, modern Chinese woman, to embody the historical qualities of brave Sophia, the novelist Ding Ling's partly awakened, modern Chinese female subject, in the final historic step toward global women's liberation.[55]

CONCLUSION

Li Xiaojiang was not the only feminist active during the Cultural Fever. Quite the contrary. Her brief for women's studies was only one argument among what became in ensuing years a vaster, transnationally connected, general field of scholarship in China focused on women.[56] A huge variety of schemes for classifying the new study contended for institutional power; the United Nations Conference on Women held in Beijing in 1995 testifies to the activity of scholar-activists still developing institutional venues for scholarship on women and political initiative that call attention to the need for government regulation of slavery, wholesaling of brides, forced maternity, and other documented violations of basic human rights in the frontier atmosphere of Chinese capitalism. Some scholars have turned to the Chinese archives to find institutional precedents, while others have apprenticed themselves to the subdiscipline of women's studies in the U.S. academy.[57] My point, however, is that the rhetoric of Li Xiaojiang and her Enlightenment Press series always attracted its share of criticism. Particularly as the circuit inside of which Chinese feminisms travel is enlarged to include other developing nations and Japan, the reinvention of the Chinese Enlightenment may appear in retrospect to be a very particular moment in the history of thinking about Chinese women's liberation.

As the editors of the seven-hundred-page compendium, *Women's Theoretic Studies in China from 1981–1990* (*Zhongguo funü lilun yanjiu shinian*) argue in their introduction to work previously published in the journal *Women's Researches* (*Funü yanjiu*), theoretic studies (*lilun yanjiu*) differs from women's studies (*funüxue*) by virtue of the fact that theoretic studies are (1) politically practical, (2) constituted via more flexible and informal categories, and (3) methodically truly scientific.[58] Yu Yan, for instance, argues stoutly *against* the institutionalization of women's studies (classified as *nüxingxue*) on the ground that the anthropology of women (*nüxing renleixue*), with its established, scientific research methodology, is quite simply intellectually superior. The problem with the patched-together discipline of women's studies, Yu Yan points out, be it *funüxue* or *nüxingxue*, is simply that the category woman is so difficult to isolate and therefore the discipline can be said to have no definite theoretic subject: "Sure, among research disciplines we can ascertain the significance of woman [*nüxing*] in political science, economics, psychology, history and so on, but in the end we still do not understand what is woman [*nüxing*]? *Nüxing* [in a categoric sense] is not the *nüxing* of political science, is not the *nüxing* of economics, is not the *nüxing* of psychology, is not the *nüxing* of the arts. . . . What is 'the complete woman' [*wanzheng de nuxing*] then? This is a question that women's studies simply has no answer for at present."[59]

Chinese feminist readings of Lacanian psychoanalysis also made a point of criticizing the masculinism of cultural theory in the late 1980s and came to conclusions about the predicament of Chinese women in the post-Mao era that were implicitly critical of the positions Li Xiaojiang established.[60] The most enduring work has been the highly influential volume *Fuchu lishi dibiao: Xiandai funu wenxue yanjiu* (Woman on the horizon of history) by Meng Yue and Dai Jinhua, which Li published as part of the Enlightenment series in 1989.[61] The introduction to this general survey of Chinese women's fiction between 1917 and 1949 is a fifty-page, tightly argued reworking of the women's tradition in Chinese fiction through the critical psychology of Kristeva and Lacan. Meng and Dai focus on the texts of modern Chinese women's literature. These constitute a hidden historiography encoded in modern fiction that in criticism can reactivate the Lacanian imaginary against the repressive Maoist old order.[62] "Women are the blindspot of history," they argue. "The women's question is not a simple matter of gender relations or a question of gender equality, however, but rather it affects the entire way that we envision history and explain history."[63]

Historiography for Meng and Dai grafts Lacanian-Freudian rhetoric onto the familiar Marxian economic teleology to make an argument that is not radically different from that of Li Xiaojiang. The significant differences lie in the area of practice. Rather than espousing the sort of state politics that Li would invoke to legislate avenues to equality, the Chinese Lacanian project nurtured a female self in literary practice resting on a reassembled Chinese female literary tradition beginning with Ding Ling. It promised a Chinese language of the feminine that would make the sound of woman and in so doing double the subject of Chinese modernity. Obviously, Meng and Dai were writing outward, into the metropolitan theory circuit, and they deployed Western theorists like Lacan and Kristeva in ways that Li, with her Chinese-centered academic training and Maoist legacy, seems unwilling or unable to do.

The most significant challenge, however, is that despite Li's elaborate attempts to sexualize woman theory, figures like Li and organizations like the Women's Federation are steadily losing ground to popular media images that are not controllable in academic, theoretical, or even statist terms. Xiaoqun Xu has documented the ways that literary reportage (*baogao wenxue*), a privileged site of justice arguments in Li's heyday and an important literary form as early as the late 1930s, has given way to representations of sexuality and femininity in a popular genre now called journalistic literature (*jishi wenxue*). Scandal mags, generic street corner "case studies" that read like police blotter crime stories, soft-porn glossies, sex manuals, news journals, all routinely publish elaborate narratives about female sexual desire and deviance, questions of conscience about promiscuity and personal willfulness, the social problems that sexual incompatibility raises in conventional marriages, and so on. The overwhelming effect of this genre has been to naturalize the notion that women are defined almost completely by their sexual needs. As Xu's investigation suggests, desublimation of the sexual image in popular culture has also authorized sex journalists to police the perimeter of the discourse and discredit as "Western feminism" anything—including orthodox Maoism—that smacks of late 1980s justice arguments.[64] In other words, Li Xiaojiang's theoretical works have lost all transgressive power now that postsocialist transnationalism has alleviated for some the dreadful physical discomforts imposed during the Maoist era and underwritten the surge of pleasure that accompanies consumer capitalism. The Cultural Fever that made Li's arguments meaningful a decade ago has ended, and academic "theory," which in fact had always derived its social power from the very Maoist state oppression that it sought to skewer and disavow, has lost the field to more pleasurable, popular media. Advertising machines saturate the arena of representation in China, as they do in all NIC's within the Japan–East Asia capital flow.

But Li Xiaojiang did instigate a great debate. She disavowed the older political reading of Chinese women's liberation. She took a formless feeling that there should be more concerted knowledge about women and turned it into a battleground for women's studies. She fought to bring a semblance of scholarly order to enthusiasm through a long-term, academically respectable project that would emphasize the Chineseness of Chinese women's studies. Li's interest in qualifying Chinese women's studies as culturally Chinese can be read as her effort to localize *nüren* and make certain that Chinese women's studies inoculates itself against colonization by the larger, often either insensitive or indifferent North American women's studies establishment. In doing so, her writing really did address feminine experiences that had exceeded representation by the older Maoist grids and mass subjects. Li affirmed these common, private, female experiences and feelings in graphic bodily terms. She turned the body into the substructure and erected a complex superstructural argument about the possibilities and deficiencies of female subject forms, and in this affirmation she caught herself at the level of theoretical speculation in inescapable material contradictions. The pressure Li herself placed on Chinese women to return to domesticity and to make a career of domestic consumption was ironically completely coherent with the mass commodification of daily life that overwhelmed urban China in the 1990s. Extraordinarily unequal in its application, it glorifies the life of those consuming women who are able to turn to full-time domestic service; this is in itself significant, given the extraordinary inflation that has impoverished the very people who produced and consumed post-Mao Chinese Enlightened theory during the late 1980s, that is, social servants, the old professional class, teachers, and anyone still dependent on the state sector for a salary. Li Xiaojiang's theoretical work may, in retrospect, appear as nothing less than the ideological justification for a form of national womanhood that is handmaiden to economic boom and frontier capitalism. The polemics of Li and her associates in the late 1980s may turn out to be the end of a trajectory rather than a reenvisioning of Chinese Enlightenment. The structure of affirmation and its top-heavy baggage of cultural theory have vanished over the horizon. But what *has* emerged in its wake is not merely commodity fetishism, but the semi-official work of a transformed Women's Federation and the new internationally connected NGOs.

NOTES

To Donald Lowe I owe particular thanks for reading successive versions of this essay. The following also kindly contributed: David Lloyd gave the essay a final, elegant edit, Lisa Lowe and David Lloyd invited me to participate in their initial workshop, Jing Wang gave me access to her work on Li Zehou as I drafted the essay and subsequently offered important refinements, Wang Zheng ensured that I had books and reviewed the final draft, Inderpal Grewal suggested alternatives, and Lin Chun provided criticism and fellowship.

I regret that I was not always able to incorporate the good advice of these friends, but wish to reassure them that all liability for error remains exclusively with me.
1. See Tani Barlow, "Politics and Protocols of *Funü*: (Un)Making National Woman," in *Engendering China: Women, Culture and the State,* ed. Chris Gilmartin et al. (Cambridge, MA: Harvard University Press, 1994), 338–359.

2. See their highly influential book, Dai Jinhua and Meng Yue, *Fuchu lishi dibiao: Xiandai funü wenxue* (Floating on the horizon of history: Modern Chinese women's literature) (Hunan: Renmin chubanshe, 1989). Unless noted otherwise all translations are my own.

3. Much Chinese feminist theory throughout the 1980s may be similarly characterized, and far more nuanced scholarship is now widely available. I focus on Li Xiaojiang because she was an important pioneer and because her formulations evidence problems so vividly. Also, she had become a controversial player in the politics of Chinese feminism in the 1990s. For further detail on the debates in Chinese feminism in the 1980s, see Barlow, "(Un)Making National Woman."

4. See Jing Wang, *High Culture Fever: Politics, Aesthetics, and Ideology in Deng's China* (Berkeley: University of California Press, 1996). For an example of a still unapologetic heir of Enlightenment, see Wang Hui and his colleagues, who edit the scholarly journal *Xueren* (Scholar), an elite scholarly journal of primarily historical studies that are attempting to reestablish a localized or nationalist school of historiography of the twentieth century. Wang Hui's essay, "The Fate of Mr. Science in China," appears in T. E. Barlow, ed., *Formations of Colonial Modernity in East Asia* (Durham: Duke University Press, 1997).

5. See Li Xiaojiang, "Zouxiang nüren" (Toward womanhood), *Nüxing/Ren,* special issue 4, "Who Controls My Body" (1990), for the incident referred to above. For a recent reconsideration of the body question in feminist film theory, see Dai Jinhua, "Invisible Women: Contemporary Chinese Cinema and Women's Film," trans. Mayfair Yang, *positions* 3, no. 1 (1995). Also see Angela Zito and Tani E. Barlow, eds., *Body, Subject, and Power in China* (Chicago: University of Chicago Press, 1994), and Susan Brownell, *Training the Body for China: Sports in the Moral Order of the People's Republic* (Chicago: University of Chicago Press, 1995).

6. This intimate connection of thinking and government action sustained some intellectuals in relative emotional comfort throughout the Maoist era because the rewards for purposeful work are satisfying. Few critics have been willing to address this element of the tragedy of the Cultural Revolution, since it is so much simpler to either assume the victim position or keep one's thoughts to oneself.

7. Only now is sustained work appearing that charts the history of the various scholarly movements — humanism, neo-Confucianism, post-Mao Marxism, Enlightenment theodicy, the various modernisms and postmodernisms and pseudomodernisms, and so on — that fed the incredible cultural intensity of the last half of the 1980s. A chronology of these movements is charted in Jing Wang, *High Culture Fever,* but Wang advocates a strict construction of events; only 1985–86 and perhaps the 1988 discussion of the film series *Heshang* are properly "Cultural Fever" years. For my purpose, which is only to clarify the context that nurtured the resurgence of feminist discussion in the 1980s, I will adopt a relaxed use of the term. In doing so I am simply situating interrogation of woman in terms of its political economy at the end of the Mao era in the

intellectual and cultural ferment that accompanied the politics of economic reform.

The so-called Tiananmen Event of June 1989 and the subsequent burgeoning of a popular, commodified, capitalist culture has apparently ended the sorts of dense, theoretical, elite, and scholarly discussions to which the signifier "Cultural Fever" refers. However, it did not end the feminist discussion, broadly construed, that played its role as critic of late-1980s masculinist humanism. The contents and the causes of the still vital feminist theory project lie beyond the restricted focus of this essay.

8. Stefan Tanaka, *Japan's Orient: Rendering Pasts into History* (Berkeley: University of California Press, 1993).

9. Ibid., 49.

10. See Liu Kang, "Aesthetics and Chinese Marxism," *positions: east asia cultures critique* 3, no. 2 (fall 1995), special issue on "Marxist Scholarship."

11. Liu Kang, "Subjectivity, Marxism and Cultural Theory in China," in *Politics, Ideology and Literary Discourses in China: Theoretical Interventions and Cultural Critique,* ed. Liu Kang and Xiaobing Tang (Durham: Duke University Press, 1993), 34. Liu Kang points out that Li Zehou "insists on the determination of the material component and the secondary character of the psychological. . . . But his original and creative move is to place great emphasis on the constitutive character of 'practice,' defined as material production and the practice of tool making, rather than 'praxis,' which is used most frequently in Western Marxist writings to include theoretical and cultural productions."

12. See Lung-kee Sun, "Historians' Warp: Problems in Textualizing the Intellectual History of Modern China," *positions: east asia cultures critique* 2, no. 2 (fall 1994), for the argument that the agonistic psychodynamic subject of the U.S. psychologized historiography is distinctive: as distinctive as the social subject of socialized, modern, Chinese historiographic convention.

13. See Wang, *High Culture Fever,* for discussion of methods of Confucian reading practices.

14. Ibid., chap. " 'Who Am I?' Questions of Voluntarism in the Paradigm of Socialist Alienation," for a discussion of humanism in the era of the early 1980s.

15. This paragraph is indebted to Liu Kang, "Subjectivity, Marxism, and Cultural Theory in China," and the citation is from pp. 25–26.

16. Li Xiaojiang, "Economic Reform and the Awakening of Chinese Women's Collective Consciousness," in *Engendering China,* ed. Chris Gilmartin et al. (Cambridge, MA: Harvard University Press, 1994), 374–375.

17. This is a far more complex problem than I am making out here. However, my point in raising this commonplace is simply to suggest that the minority status of the colonial paradigm may bespeak a certain realism about China's place in the East Asian economic circuit. The People's Republic of China is a behemoth. It is not homologous with Taiwan, Hong Kong, Vietnam, or other past or future NICs simply because it will doubtless outstrip these capital-rich ministates. Its population and problems of governance unfold on a scale that is

simply monstrous by comparison. When Li Xiaojiang upholds the legitimacy and positivity of a nonderivative Chinese feminism there is in the claim a certain aggressive insistence that, given its extraordinary bulk, what happens in China is a positivity, if for no other reason than by virtue of the extent to which it will influence the world in the future.

18. Michael Dutton and Paul Healy, "Marxist Theory and Socialist Transition: The Construction of an Epistemological Relation," in *Chinese Marxism in Flux, 1978–84: Essays on Epistemology, Ideology and Political Economy*, ed. Bill Brugger (Armonk, NY: Sharpe, 1985), 38.

19. Barlow, "(Un)Making National Woman," 346–351.

20. Dutton and Healy, "Marxist Theory and Socialist Transition," 46. Both agree on "the real as the raw material, the starting point of knowledge production . . . [and] the subject abstracting the essence (the quintessential, the true) of the real object, eliminating all that is inessential (the coarse, the false), thus producing knowledge."

21. Meng Yue, "Female Images and National Myth," in *Gender Politics in Modern China*, ed. Tani Barlow (Durham: Duke University Press, 1993).

22. See Lingzhen Wang, "Retheorizing the Personal: Identity, Writing and Gender in Yu Luojin's Autobiographical Acts," *positions* 6, no. 1 (forthcoming).

23. This paragraph is adapted from my "(Un)Making National Woman," 344–345.

When Li Xiaojiang began to think about the linked questions of femininity and politics, the dominant subject of woman was still *funü*. This term named a national female subject in Maoist lexicon, and had come into official use as a mobilization category during the CCP's guerrilla war. *Funü* originated in propaganda affirmed in nationalist terms and iconography, the revolutionary female subjects of the Chinese nation standing against Japanese imperialism, the West, bourgeois feminisms of all kinds, and all degenerate oppressor classes. After 1949 the CCP, like Communist parties elsewhere, organized a state bureaucracy, the Women's Federation, for liberating women into wage labor. The Federation actively lay at the heart of the project of bureaucratizing female subjects and obviating the need for an autonomous women's movement. Anyway, subsequent Maoist woman theory maintained *funü* to be a state or bureaucratic subject, not merely a subcategory of the proletariat. In other words, rather than being definitionally other than the men of the working class, *funü* resembled an ethical norm. . . . In this way, bureaucratization of womanhood circumscribed possibilities for gendered identities and yet enabled political remediation of women's oppressions under state auspices, in a way unheard of outside the Communist world.

Other terms signifying modern female subject have circulated, too, though these have until recently played a subordinate, adjectival role as one aspect of CCP hegemony. *Nüxing*, a Japanese neologism introduced at the turn of the century, literally signifies "female sex," and apparently came into use when Darwinian philosophy appeared in Chinese translation. *Nüren* (literally "female person/s") accrued a less directly sexual connotation, but also grounded subjectivity in the sexed female body of modern science. Though it possesses a categorical ring, *nüren* also suggests the female equivalent of the European, humanist term *Ren* or *renlei,* meaning Mankind or Man. My main point in raising all these terms is that Chinese feminist thinking has shared with modernist discourses elsewhere a complex and internally divided subject woman/ women; I am not even considering here older, semifeudal syntax of gender that persisted into the Communist period.

My reason for tracing these terms and for reading them as subjectivities rather than simply as signs stems from interest in three recent problems: the question of the general crisis in feminist studies occasioned by historicization of the subject of woman, the question of extranational feminisms raised most prominently in postcolonial studies of transnational feminism, and the question of writing histories that represent the architechtonics of the event of modern feminism. I am suggesting . . . (1) that a means of reestablishing feminist practices across differences may be to historicize the subjects women as instances of the imbrication of universals at locales and (2) that these frequently simultaneous yet nonderivative surfacings of gender trouble are common enough to encourage responsible alliances.

Immediately after the Cultural Revolution intellectuals in China began a critique of communist woman policy just as the Women's Federation, decimated during the GPCR, received state authorization to rebuild its bureaucracy. Subsequently, critics within but mostly outside the Federation argued that Chinese women had never sought the liberation inflicted on them and that official feminism did not represent the needs or interests of women. Others argued that Maoist *funü* had no essential sexuality and thus could not accurately represent women, and, for the first time since the May Fourth movement, the question of naturally inscribed sex differences between women and men became an intense focus of debate. In the mid-eighties critics coined the neologism *xingbie* (literally "sex difference," from the Anglophone term "gender") to describe essential difference and used this occasion to recycle the repressive hypothesis of sexuality, inspired by the rediscovery of Freud in China and by the reopening of the literary archive of the 1920s and '30s. Criticism of the limitations and oppressions inflicted on Chinese women by the government coalesced around the question of whether the Women's Federation "truly represented" women or not. Post-Mao polemics against the national female subject ended the ability of *funü* to act as the uncontested, hegemonic signifier.

For an example of the essential sex difference problem see Li Xiaojiang's uncompromising argument that equality is an "insult to nature," in *Xinggou* (Sex gap) (Beijing: Sanlian shudian, 1989). A more equivocal restatement of the social mediation of sex difference appears in her recent short essay "Zongjian kuyue 'xinggou' zhi qiao" (Establish a bridge for overcoming the 'sex gap'), *Dongfang zazhi* 4 (1995): 14–16. Thanks to Dong Yue for bringing this latter essay to my attention. For Freudianism in the heritage of the May Fourth era, see Zhang Jingyuan, "Sigmund Freud and Modern Chinese Literature, 1919–1949" Ph.D. diss., Cornell University, 1989. University Microfilm Index.

24. I argue in "(Un)Making National Woman" that the non-Federation group has colonized the Federation. For less tendentious accounts, see Li Xiaojiang and Li Hui, "Women's Studies in China," *National Women Studies Association* 1, no. 3 (spring 1989): 458–460; Wan Shanping, "The Emergence of Women's Studies in China," *Women's Studies International Forum* 2, no. 5 (1988): 455–464; Qu Wen, "A Brief Account of the Current Status of Research on Women" (unpublished and undated report from the Women's Research Institute of the Women's Federation); and Wang Zheng, "Research on Women in Contemporary China—Problems and Promises," unpublished manuscript, 1993.

Since then the fields of women's studies seem to have retained their affiliations with state agencies but have sheltered non-Party scholars in academies and universities, as well as activists inside and outside China whose interests lie with nongovernmental organizations (NGOs). For NGO connections and a summary of events in the world of women's studies in 1993, see Liu Bohong, "1993: Funü yanjiu zouxiang" (1993: Toward women's studies) and "1994: Funü yanjiu qushi" (1994: Trends in women studies), both in *Funü yanjiu* (Beijing: Remindaxue shubao ziliao zongxin, 1994), 24–25.

25. I am thinking here of foundational work by Dai Jinhua, Meng Yue, Pan Suiming, Liu Bohong, and Li Xiaojiang herself. Often what appears in Anglophone discussions of Maoist "ungendering" or the Communist effort to stamp out gender difference during the Mao period is simply uncredited, derivative reassertion of notions first raised by these major theorists in the mid- and late 1980s. Some misattribution may be due to simple ignorance of the record, since in the early years of the movement academics, theorists, and popular writers had to publish their work in out-of-the-way venues to escape the attention of the censors. On the other hand, it could also stem from a confusion over the status of theoretical work; that is, feminist critique of humanism is read as mimetic, truthful representation of a homogeneous historical reality.

26. This "note to the series" appears in each volume of the publication.

27. Another integral part of the mission of universal knowledge is consciousness awakening. I will discuss this application of universal knowledge in a later section.

28. Li Xiaojiang, *Xiawa de tansuo* (Eve's explorations, hereafter cited as *Eve*) (Changsha: Henan renmin chubanshe, 1988), p. 8.

29. See ibid., 8. The hierarchy of differences is central to Li's notion of the universal female subject and the teleology of the emancipation of *nüren* in the movement of the bi-gendered world subject of humanity. So while the series incited discourse on the sexual subject, it has from its founding felt impelled to manage national difference within an unstable universalizing Chinese academic theory. This mediation is a constituting part of the field of women's scholarship, and differences of many kinds—local and global, Chinese and other, modern and feudal, national and international, man and woman—are endemic in Li's thought. See, for instance, the Zhengzhou University Women's Center collection, *Dangdai shijie nüchao yü nüxue* (Woman tide and women's studies) (Zhongzhoui: Henan renmin chubanshe, 1990), Du Fangqin's *Nüxing guan-*

nian de yanbian (Evolution of the female concept) (Zhengzhou: Henan renmin chubanshe, 1988), and Zheng Husheng's *Shanguhua Xia yü hunyin* (Ancient Chinese woman and marriage) (Zhengzhou: Henan renmin chubanshe, 1988).

30. Li, *Eve*, 87–88.

31. This exposition of her thinking draws heavily on the first three. I will not address the issues raised in *Inquiry into Women's Aesthetic Consciousness.*

32. Li Xiaojiang, "Longzhao zai nüjie de mituan" (The enigma veiled within the world of women), in *Eve*, 14–34.

33. Li, *Eve*, 25.

34. Kang, "Subjectivity, Marxism and Cultural Theory," 32. For Li's assertion that woman theory belongs in the human sciences, see *Eve*, 25, and "The Sublime," in *Eve*, 74–107.

35. Li, "Enigma," in *Eve*, 17–20.

36. Li, *Eve*, 89.

37. Ibid., 29.

38. Ibid., 98.

39. Li Xiaojiang, (The Self-Comprehension of Woman) *Nüzi yü jiazheng* (Women and domestic science) (Zhengzhou: Henan renmin chubanshe, 1986).

40. Untroubled, that is, by "unnatural" government policies such as those promulgated under the Gang of Four during the period of the ultraleft high tide.

41. Li, *Eve*, 40.

42. Ibid., 42.

43. The quote is: "Female self-consciousness [*nüxing ziwo yishi*] is like a woman who asks herself: 'what am I?' whereas female self-comprehension [*nüxing ziwo renshi*] is more like an exploration of the question '*what is woman [nüren]?*'" (Li, *Domestic Science*, 3; original emphasis).

44. Li Xiaojiang discusses the roots of this theoretical commitment in her important essay "Zouxiang *nüren*" (Towards woman), first published in the transnational journal *Nüxing/Ren* 4 (1990), 255–266.

45. Li, *Domestic Science*, 12–23.

46. Li Xiaojiang is by no means alone in this view. Also see Wang Zheng, trans. and ed., "Three Interviews: Wang Anyi, Zhu Lin, Dai Qing," in *Gender Politics in Modern China*, ed. Tani Barlow (Durham: Duke University Press, 1993).

47. Li, *Domestic Science*, 53.

48. Li, *Eve*, 135–157, "History — The Riddle of the Oriental Woman."

49. In the later definition she apparently was influenced by Betty Friedan.

50. Li, *Eve*, 133. Also see Li, *Domestic Science*, 27. Li attempts to balance what she calls woman's three great responsibilities against woman's three great pursuits. Women are responsible to husband, children, and work, but they desire or pursue, as a consequence of these responsibilities, sexual love, mother love, and self-love through relations with husband, child, and creative work. The woman who sacrifices work imperils self-love and threatens to undermine her pursuit of individual being.

51. I have developed the question of *renge* as a founding element of Chinese discourses of modernity in "Biology and Modernity," paper delivered at the Modernism Colloquium, University of California, Berkeley, Center for Chinese Studies, April 1993.

52. Li Xiaojiang, *Nüren: yige youyuan meili de chuanshuo* (Woman: A distant, beautiful legend) (Shanghai: Renmin chubanshe, 1989).

53. Ibid., 3–4.

54. Ibid., 3–5.

55. This is a reference to Ding Ling's "Miss Sophia's Diary," which Li Xiaojiang and many other feminist critiques have embraced as the quintessence of modern Chinese women's subjectivity. For a translation of the story in question, see Ding Ling, "Miss Sophia's Diary," trans. Tani Barlow in *I Myself Am a Woman,* ed. Tani Barlow (with Gary Bjorge) (Boston: Beacon Press, 1989).

56. As I will argue shortly, Li Xiaojiang's account of what constitutes *funüxue* is only one such possible definition.

57. See Li Min and Wang Fukang, who produced what they believe to be the first full-length study of women's studies in China. They express their belief that women's studies is an invention of U.S. academic pressures. See their *Zhongguo funüxue* (Chinese women's studies) (Nanchang: Jiangxi renmin chubanshe, 1985). Wang Zheng cites Sun Xiaomei, whose brief *The Basic Concepts of Funüxue* sounds like a scientized version of Li Xiaojiang's feminist critique of humanism. See Wang Zheng, "Research on Women in Contemporary China," *Journal of Women's History* (January 1997).

58. Xiung Yumei, Liu Ciaocong, Qu Wen, eds., *Zhongguo funü lilun yanjiu shinian* (Women's theoretic studies in China, 1981–1990) (Beijing: Zhongguo funü chubanshe, 1992), 1–5.

59. Yu Yan, "Nüxing renxue: jiangou yü zhanwang" (Women's anthropology: Establishment and future prospects), in ibid., 3.

60. For instance, a discussion of the deficiencies of Liu Zaifu's concept of the subject of humanism appears in Zhao Xiaoming and Wang Wei, "The Discourse of the 'Imperial Subject,' Its Blind Spots and Limitations: On the Scholarly Work of Liu Zaifu," in the popular scholarly journal *Dushu* (1989) 6.

61. A special issue of the elite scholarly journal *Beijing Wenxue* (Beijing literature) featured the pathbreaking feminist critiques of Dai Jinhua, Ji Hongzhen, Meng Yue, Zhang Jingyuan, and Zhang Guwu. To my knowledge this issue, no. 7, 1989, has never appeared as a collected book volume.

62. Dai and Meng, *Fuchu lishi dibiao.*

63. Ibid, 4.

64. Xiaoqun Xu, "The Discourse on Love, Marriage, and Sexuality in Post-Mao China; or, A Reading of the New Journalistic Literature on Women," *positions* 4, no. 2 (fall 1996), 381–414.

Abbas, K. A. *I Write As I Feel.* Bombay: Hind Kitabs, 1948.

———. "India's Anti-Fascist Theatre." *Asia and the Americans* (December 1952): 711–712.

Abdel Kader, Soha. *Egyptian Women in Changing Society 1899–1987.* Boulder: Lynn Reinner Publishers, 1988.

Abrams, Tevia. "Folk Theatre in Maharashtrian Social Development Programs." *Educational Theatre Journal* 27, no. 3 (October 1975): 395–407.

Abu-Lughod, Leila. *Veiled Sentiments: Honour and Poetry in a Bedouin Society.* Berkeley: University of California Press, 1986.

Acuna, Rodolfo. *Occupied America: A History of Chicanos.* New York: Harper, 1981.

Adam, Barry D. *The Rise of a Gay and Lesbian Movement.* Boston: Twayne, 1987.

Adams, Parveen, and Elizabeth Cowie, eds. *The Woman in Question.* Cambridge, MA: MIT Press, 1990.

Adorno, Theodor. *Negative Dialectics.* Trans. E. B. Ashton. New York: Seabury Press, 1973.

Agamben, Giorgio. *Infancy and History: Essays on the Destruction of Experience.* Trans. Liz Heron. London: Verso, 1993.

Agoncillo, Teodoro. "On the Rewriting of Philippine History." *Historical Bulletin* (Philippine Historical Association) 17 (1973): 178–187.

Agoncillo, Teodoro, and Oscar Alfonso. *History of the Filipino People.* Manila: University of the Philippines, 1960.

Ahmed, Leila. "Feminism and Feminist Movement in the Middle East." *Women's Studies International Forum* 5, no. 2 (1982): 153–168.

———. *Women and Gender in Islam: Historical Roots of a Modern Debate.* New Haven: Yale University Press, 1992.

Alarcón, Norma. "The Theoretical Subject(s) of 'This Bridge Called My Back' and Anglo-American Feminism." In *Making Face, Making Soul/ Haciendo Caras: Creative and Critical Perspectives by Women of Color,* ed. Gloria Anzaldúa. San Francisco: Aunt Lute, 1990.

Alexander, M. Jacqui, and Chandra Talpade Mohanty, eds. *Feminist Genealogies, Colonial Legacies, Democratic Futures.* New York: Routledge, 1997.

Allen, Ernest, Jr. "Waiting for Tojo: The Pro-Japan Vigil of Black Missourians." *Gateway Heritage* 15, no. 2 (fall 1994): 16–33.

Allen, Ernest V. "When Japan Was 'Champion of the Darker Races': Satokata Takahishi and the Flowering of Black Messianic Nationalism." *The Black Scholar* 24, no. 1 (1995): 29.

Allen, Robert. *Black Awakening in Capitalist America: An Analytic History.* Trenton, NJ: Africa World Press, 1990.

Alloula, Mallek. *The Colonial Harem.* Minneapolis: University of Minnesota Press, 1986.

Althusser, Louis. *Lenin and Philosophy and the Other Essays.* Trans. Ben Brewster. New York: Monthly Review Press, 1971.

Althusser, Louis, and Etienne Balibar. *Reading Capital.* London: Verso, 1979.

Amin, Samir. *Delinking.* Trans. Michael Wolfers. London: Zed Books, 1990.

Amin, Shahid. "Gandhi as Mahatma: Gorakhpur District, Eastern UP, 1921–2." In *Subaltern Studies III: Writings on South Asian History and Society,* ed. Ranajit Guha. Delhi: Oxford University Press, 1984.

Anderson, Benedict. "Cacique Democracy in the Philippines: Origins and Dreams." *New Left Review* 169 (May–June 1988): 3–33.

———. *Imagined Communities: Reflections on the Origin and Spread of Nationalism.* London: Verso, 1991.

Andors, Phyllis. "Women and Work in Shenzhen." *Bulletin of Concerned Asian Scholars* 20, no. 3 (1988): 22–41.

Appadurai, Arjun. "Global Ethnoscapes: Notes and Queries for a Transnational Anthropology." In *Recapturing Anthropology,* ed. R. Fox. Santa Fe: School of American Research Press, 1991.

Appelbaum, Richard P. "Multiculturalism and Flexibility: Some New Directions in Global Capitalism." In *Mapping Multiculturalism,* ed. Avery Gordon and Christopher Newfield. Minneapolis: University of Minnesota Press, 1996.

Appleby, Joyce, Lynn Hunt, and Margaret Jacob. *Telling the Truth about History.* New York: Norton, 1994.

Arocha, Jaime. "La Ensenada de Tumaco: Invisibilidad, Incertidumbre e Innovación." *América Negra* 1 (1991): 87–112.

Asad, Talal. *The Genealogy of Religion.* Baltimore: Johns Hopkins University Press, 1993.

Aseniero, George. "A Reflection on Developmentalism: From Development to Transformation." In *Development as Social Transformation: Reflections on the Global Problematique.* London: Hodder and Stoughton/UN, 1985.

Asian Immigrant Women's Advocates. *Immigrant Women Speak Out on Garment Industry Abuse: A Community Hearing Initiated by Asian Immigrant Women Advocates.* Oakland: Asian Immigrant Women's Advocates, 1 May 1993.

Asian Women United of California. *Making Waves: An Anthology of Writings by and about Asian American Women.* New York: Beacon, 1989.

Atkinson, James. *Customs and Manners of the Women of Persia and Their Domestic Superstitions.* New York: Burt Franklin, 1832.

Aulestia, Gorka. *Basque-English Dictionary.* Reno: University of Nevada Press, 1989.

Avineri, Shlomo. *Hegel's Theory of the Modern State.* London: Cambridge University Press, 1972.

———. "Marxism and Nationalism." *Journal of Contemporary History* 26, nos. 3–4 (1991): 637–657.

Bailey, Beth, and David Farber. *The First Strange Place: Race and Sex in World War II Hawaii.* Baltimore: Johns Hopkins University Press, 1992.

Baldwin, James. *The Fire Next Time.* New York: Dial, 1963.

Balibar, Etienne, and Immanuel Wallerstein. *Race, Nation, Class: Ambiguous Identities*. London: Verso, 1991.

Bakhtin, Mikhail M. *The Dialogic Imagination*. Trans. Caryl Emerson and Michael Holquist. Austin: University of Texas Press, 1981.

Bambach, Charles R. *Heidegger, Dilthey, and the Crisis of Historicism*. Ithaca: Cornell University Press, 1995.

Bamdad, Badr ol-Moluk. *From Darkness into Light: Women's Emancipation in Iran*. Trans. and ed. F. R. C. Bagley. Smithtown, NY: Exposition Press, 1977.

Bandarage, A. "Women and Capitalist Development in Sri Lanka, 1977–87." *Bulletin of Concerned Asian Scholars* 20 (1988): 57–81.

Banerji, Sumanta. *The Parlour and the Street: Elite and Popular Culture in Nineteenth Century Calcutta*. Calcutta: Seagull Books, 1989.

Bannerji, Hemani. "Language and Liberation: A Study of Political Theatre in Bengal." *Ariel* 15 (1984): 131–144.

Bantug, Jose P. *Bosquejo historico de la medicina Hispano-Filipina* (Unfinished historical sketch of Spanish-Filipino medicine). Madrid, 1952.

Bappa, S., and M. Etherton. "Third World Popular Theatre: Voices of the Oppressed." *Commonwealth* 25, no. 4 (1983): 126–130.

Baraka, Amiri [LeRoi Jones]. *Blues People*. New York: Random House, 1963.

Barbrook, Richard. A New Way of Talking: Community Radio in 1980s Britain. *Science as Culture* 1, no. 1 (1987): 81–129.

Barcones, Enrique Mateo. *Estudio para un Nosologia Filipina* (Towards a scientific classification of Philippine diseases). Madrid, Asilo de Huerfanos. 1895.

Barker, Francis. *The Culture of Violence: Essays on Tragedy and History*. Chicago: University of Chicago Press, 1993.

Barlow, Tani. "Biology and Modernity." Unpublished paper delivered at the Modernism Colloquium, University of California, Berkeley, Center for Chinese Studies, April 1993.

———. "Politics and Protocols of *Funü*: (Un)Making National Woman." In *Engendering China: Women, Culture and the State*. Ed. Chris Gilmartin et al. Cambridge, MA: Harvard University Press, 1994.

———, ed. *I Myself Am a Woman*. Trans. Tani Barlow with Gary Bjorge. Boston: Beacon Press, 1989.

Barrera, Marrio. *Race and Class in the Southwest*. Notre Dame: University of Notre Dame Press, 1979.

Basch, Linda, Nina Glick Schiller, and Cristina Szanton Blanc. *Nations Unbound: Transnational Projects, Postcolonial Predicaments and Deterritorialized Nation States*. New York: Gordon and Breach, 1994.

Bassets, Lluís, ed. *De las ondas rojas a las radios libres: Textos para la historia de la radio*. Barcelona: Editorial Gustavo Gili, 1981.

Basso, Keith. *Portraits of the Whiteman: Linguistic Play and Cultural Symbols among the Western Apache*. Cambridge: Cambridge University Press, 1979.

Baudrillard, Jean. *Simulations*. New York: Semiotext(e), 1983.

Bedawi, Jamal A. *The Muslim Woman's Dress According to the Qur'an and the Sunnah*. London: Ta-Ha Publishers, n.d.

Bello, Walden, D. Kinley, and E. Elinson. *Development Debacle: The World Bank in the Philippines.* San Francisco: Food First Publication, 1982.

Beneria, Lourdes, and Martha Roldan. *The Crossroads of Class and Gender: Industrial Homework, Subcontracting, and Household Dynamics in Mexico City.* Chicago: University of Chicago Press, 1987.

Benjamin, Walter. "Theses on the Philosophy of History." In *Illuminations,* ed. Hannah Arendt, trans. Harry Zohn. New York: Schocken, 1969.

——. *Reflections: Essays, Aphorisms, Autobiographical Writings.* Ed. Peter Demetz. Trans. Edmund Jephcott. New York: Harcourt Brace Jovanovich, 1978.

Beverley, John, and José Oviedo, eds. *The Postmodernism Debate in Latin America.* Special issue, *boundary 2,* 20, no. 3 (1993).

Bhabha, Homi K. "The Other Question: The Stereotype and Colonial Discourse." *Screen* 24 (November–December 1983): 18–36.

——. "Of Mimicry and Man: The Ambivalence of Colonial Discourse." *October* 28 (spring 1984): 125–133.

——. "Down among the Writers." *New Statesmen and Society* (28 July 1989): 38–39.

——, ed. *Nation and Narration.* New York: Routledge, 1990.

Bhadra, Gautam. "Four Rebels of Eighteen-Fifty-Seven." In *Selected Subaltern Studies,* ed. Ranajit Guha and Gayatri Spivak. New York: Oxford University Press, 1988.

Bharucha, Rustom. *Rehearsals of Revolution: The Political Theatre of Bengal.* Honolulu: University of Hawaii Press, 1983.

Bhattacharya, Malini. "The IPTA in Bengal." *Journal of Arts and Ideas* 2 (January–March 1983): 5–22.

Bhattachryara, Bijana. *Nabanna.* 1944. Reprint, Kalakata: Prama, 1984.

Birou, Alain, Paul-Marc Henry, and John Schlegel. *Toward a Redefinition of Development: Essays and Discussions on the Nature of Development in an International Perspective.* Paris: Development Center, OECD/Pergamon Press, 1977.

Blauner, Robert. *Racial Oppression in America.* New York: Harper, 1972.

Bloch, Marc. *The Historian's Craft.* 1954. Reprint, Manchester: Manchester University Press, 1984.

Boal, Augusto. *Theatre of the Oppressed.* London: Pluto Press, 1979.

Boggs, James. *The American Revolution: Pages from a Negro Worker's Notebook.* New York: Monthly Review Press, 1963.

Boland, Eavan. *A Kind of Scar: The Woman Poet in the National Tradition.* Dublin: Attic Press, 1989.

Bonacich, Edna. "Asians in the Los Angeles Garment Industry." In *New Asian Immigration in Los Angeles and Global Restructuring.* Philadelphia: Temple University Press, 1994.

Bottomley, Gillian. *From Another Place: Migration and the Politics of Culture.* Melbourne: Cambridge University Press, 1992.

Bourdieu, Pierre. *Distinction.* Cambridge, MA: Harvard University Press, 1984.

——. "The Uses of the 'People.'" In *In Other Words.* Stanford: Stanford University Press, 1990.

———. *Language and Symbolic Power*. Ed. John B. Thompson. Trans. Gino Raymond and Matthew Adamson. Cambridge, MA: Harvard University Press, 1991.

Braudel, Fernand. *On History*. Trans. Sarah Matthews. Chicago: University of Chicago Press, 1980.

Braverman, Harry. *Labor and Monopoly Capital: The Degradation of Work in the Late Twentieth Century*. New York: Monthly Review Press, 1974.

Brecht, Bertolt. *Brecht on Theatre*. Trans. John Willett. New York: Hill and Wang, 1986.

Breuilly, John. *Nationalism and the State*. New York: St. Martin's Press, 1982.

Browne, Nick. "Race: The Political Unconscious of American Film." *East-West Journal* 6, no. 1 (1992): 5–16.

Brownell, Susan. *Training the Body for China: Sports in the Moral Order of the People's Republic*. Chicago: University of Chicago Press, 1995.

Brunk, Samuel. "Zapata and the City Boys: In Search of a Piece of the Revolution." *Hispanic American Historical Review* 73, no. 1 (1993): 33–65.

Burawoy, Michael. "The Anthropology of Industrial Work." *Annual Review of Anthropology* 8 (1979): 231–266.

———. *The Politics of Production*. London: Verso, 1985.

Burke, Peter. *The Renaissance Sense of the Past*. London: Edward Arnold, 1970.

Butler, Judith. *Gender Trouble: Feminism and the Subversion of Identity*. New York: Routledge, 1990.

———. *Bodies That Matter: On the Discursive Limits of Sex*. New York: Routledge, 1993.

Cabral, Amílcar. *Unity and Struggle: Speeches and Writings of Amílcar Cabral*. Trans. Michael Wolfers. New York: Monthly Review Press, 1979.

Camagay, Maria Luisa. "Manila — A City in the Throes of Epidemics." *Historical Bulletin* 26 (1982): 105–108.

Cannell, Fenella. "The Power of Appearances: Beauty, Mimicry and Transformation in Bicol." In *Discrepant Histories: Translocal Essays on Filipino Cultures,* ed. Vicente Rafael. Philadelphia: Temple University Press, 1995.

Capeci, Dominic J., Jr. *Race Relations in Wartime Detroit: The Sojourner Truth Housing Controversy of 1942*. Philadelphia: Temple University Press, 1984.

Carr, E. H. *What Is History?* New York: Vintage, 1961.

Case, Sue-Ellen. "The Euro-Colonial Reception of Sanskrit Poetics." In *The Performance of Power: Theatrical Discourse and Politics,* ed. Sue-Ellen Case and Janelle Reinelt. Iowa City: University of Iowas Press, 1991.

Castañeda, Jorge G. *Utopia Unarmed: The Latin American Left after the Cold War*. New York: Vintage, 1993.

———. *Sorpresas te da la vida: México 1994*. Mexico City: Aguilar, 1994.

Central American Historical Institute. "Masaya Peasants Prompt Land Expropriations." *Update* 4, no. 23 (1985): 1–4.

———. "Agrarian Reform Undergoes Changes in Nicaragua." *Update* 5, no. 4 (1986): 1–6.

———. "Reactions to Agrarian Reform Modifications in Nicaragua." *Update* 5, no. 20 (1986): 1–4.

Centro de Investigacion y Estudios de la Reforma Agraria. "Estudio de Las Cooperativa de Produccion." Mimeograph. Managua, 1985.

——. "Propuesta de Trabajo para un Diagnostico de la Situacion del Movimiento Coperativo." Mimeograph. Managua, 1986.

——. *Cifras y Referencias Documentales.* Managua: CIERA, 1989.

Certeau, Michel de. "On the Oppositional Practices of Everyday Life." *Social Text* 3 (fall 1980): 3–43.

——. *The Practice of Everyday Life.* Berkeley: University of California Press, 1984.

Chakrabarty, Dipesh. *Rethinking Working-Class History: Bengal 1890–1940.* Princeton: Princeton University Press, 1989.

——. "Marx after Marxism." In *Marxism beyond Marxism,* ed. Saree Makdisi. New York: Routledge, 1996.

Chandra, Bipan. "Colonialism, Stages of Colonialism and the Colonial State." *Journal of Contemporary Asia* 10, no. 3 (1980): 272–285.

Chatterjee, Partha. "More on Modes of Power and the Peasantry." In *Selected Subaltern Studies,* ed. Ranajit Guha and Gayatri Spivak. New York: Oxford University Press, 1988.

——. "Their Own Words? An Essay for Edward Said." *Edward Said: A Critical Reader,* ed. Michael Sprinker. Oxford: Blackwell, 1992.

——. *National Thought and the Colonial World: A Derivative Discourse?* Minneapolis: University of Minnesota Press, 1993.

Cheval, Jean-Jacques. "Local Radio and Regional Languages in Southwestern France." In *Ethnic Minority Media: An International Perspective,* ed. Stephen H. Riggins. London: Sage, 1992.

Cho, Soon Kyong. "The Labor Process and Capital Mobility: The Limits of the New International Division of Labor." *Politics & Society* 14, no. 2 (1985): 185–222.

Chong Hak-chu. "Haebanghu Han'guk kyoyug'gŭi kojojŏk kaldŭng" (The structural tension in postliberation Korean education). In *Han'guk sahoeron* (Korean society), ed. Kim Chin-gyun and Cho Hŭi-yŏn. Seoul: Hanul, 1990.

Chow, Rey. "Violence in the Other Country: China as Crisis, Spectacle and Woman." In *Third World Women and the Politics of Feminism,* ed. Chandra Talpade Mohanty et al. Bloomington: Indiana University Press, 1991.

Clark, Donald. "Bitter Friendship: Understanding Anti-Americanism in South Korea." In *Korea Briefing, 1991,* ed. Donald Clark. Boulder, CO: Westview Press, 1991.

Clark, John, Aart Hendriks, Lisa Power, Rob Tielman, and Evert van der Veen. Introduction. In *The Third Pink Book: A Global View of Lesbian Gay Liberation and Oppression,* ed. A. Hendriks, R. Tielman, and E. van der Veen. Buffalo: Prometheus Books, 1993.

Clark, T. J. *The Absolute Bourgeois: Artists and Politics in France, 1848–1851.* London: Thames and Hudson, 1973.

Clifford, James. "On Ethnographic Allegory." In *Writing Culture: The Poetics and Politics of Ethnography,* ed. James Clifford and George E. Marcus. Berkeley: University of California Press, 1986.

——. "Traveling Cultures." In *Cultural Studies,* ed. Lawrence Grossberg, Cary Nelson, and Paul Treichler. New York: Routledge, 1992.

——. "Diasporas." *Cultural Anthropology* 9, no. 3 (1994): 302–338.

Cólas, Santiago. "Silence and Dialectics: Speculations on C. L. R. James and Latin America." In *Rethinking C. L. R. James,* ed. Grant Farred. Cambridge, MA: Basil Blackwell Publishers, forthcoming.

Colburn, Forrest D. *Post-Revolutionary Nicaragua.* Berkeley: University of California Press, 1986.

——, ed. *Everyday Forms of Peasant Resistance.* London: M. E. Sharpe, 1989.

Collier, George A., with Elizabeth Lowery Quaratiello. *Basta! Land and the Zapatista Rebellion in Chiapas.* Oakland, CA: Institute for Food and Development Policy, 1994.

Collingwood, R. G. *The Idea of History.* 1936. Reprint, London: Oxford University Press, 1976.

Collins, Joseph. *What Difference Can a Revolution Make?* New York: Grove Press, 1986.

Collins, Patricia Hill. *Black Feminist Thought.* Boston: Unwin Hyman, 1990.

Comaroff, Jean. *Body of Power, Spirit of Resistance.* Chicago: University of Chicago Press, 1986.

Comaroff, John, and Jean Comaroff. "The Colonization of Consciousness." In *Ethnography and the Historical Imagination.* Boulder, CO: Westview Press, 1992.

Committee for Asian Women. *Many Paths, One Goal: Organizing Women Workers in Asia.* Hong Kong: Committee for Asian Women, 1991.

Connolly, Clara. "Communalism: Obstacle to Social Change." *Women: A Cultural Review* 2, no. 3 (winter 1991): 214–215.

Conroy, Michael E., ed. *Nicaragua: Profiles of the Revolutionary Public Sector.* Boulder, Westview Press, 1987.

Consejo de Estado. *1979–1984 Principales Leyes Aprobadas por el Gobierno de Reconstruccion Nacional.* Managua: Consejo de Estado, 1985.

Constantino, Renato. *The Philippines: A Past Revisited.* Quezon City, 1975.

——. "Identity and Consciousness: The Philippine Experience." *Journal of Contemporary Asia* 6, no. 1 (1976): 5–29.

Constantino, Renato, and Letizia Constantino. *The Philippines: The Continuing Past.* Quezon City: Foundation for Nationalist Studies, 1978.

Cornell, Drucilla. *The Philosophy of the Limit.* New York: Routledge, 1992.

Crookes, Philip, and Patrick Vittet-Philippe. *Local Radio and Regional Development in Europe.* Manchester, England: European Institute for the Media, 1986.

Cruikshank, Bruce. *Samar: 1768–1898.* Manila: Historical Conservation Society, 1985.

Cuesta, Angel, O.A.R., *History of Negros.* Manila: Historical Conservation Society, 1980.

Cumings, Bruce. *The Origins of the Korean War.* Princeton: Princeton University Press, 1981.

Dahl, Gudrun, ed. *Green Arguments for Local Subsistance.* Stockholm: Stockholm University Press, 1993.

Dai Jinhua. "Invisible Women: Contemporary Chinese Cinema and Women's Film." Trans. Mayfair Yang. *positions* 3, no. 1 (1995): 255–280.

Dai Jinhua and Meng Yue. *Fuchu lishi dibiao: Xiandai funü wenxue* (Floating on the horizon of history: Modern Chinese women's literature). Hunan: Renmin chubanshe, 1989.

Dana, H. W. L. Introduction. In *Roar China*, by Sergei Mikhailovich Tretiakov. Trans. from Russian by F. Polianovska and Barbara Nixon. New York: International Publishers, n.d.

Daniels, Roger. *Concentration Camps USA: Japanese Americans and World War II.* New York: Holt, Rinehart, and Winston, 1971.

Das Gupta, Hemendranath. *The Indian Stage.* Vol. 4. Calcutta: M. K. Das Gupta, 1946.

Davies, Miranda. *Third World–Second Sex.* London: Zed Press, 1983.

Davis, Angela Y. *An Autobiography.* New York: Random House, 1974.

———. *Women, Race and Class.* New York: Random House, 1981.

———. *Women, Culture, and Politics.* New York: Random House, 1989.

Davis, Mike. "A Prison-Industrial Complex: Hell-Factories in the Field." *The Nation* 260, no. 7 (1995): 229–234.

Davis, Paul, and John Gribbin. *The Matter Myth: Beyond Chaos and Complexity.* Harmondsworth: Penguin, 1992.

Deere, Carmen D. "Agrarian Reform in the Transition." In *Transition and Development,* ed. Richard Fagen, Carmen D. Deere, and Jose L. Coraggio. New York: Monthly Review Press, 1986.

Deere, Carmen D., and Peter Marchetti. "The Worker-Peasant Alliance in the First Year of the Nicaraguan Agrarian Reform." *Latin American Perspectives* 8, no. 2 (1981): 40–73.

de Guzman, Domingo Castro. "Millenarianism and Revolution: A Critique of Reynaldo C. Ileto's *Pasyon and Revolution." Journal of Social History* (Institute of Social History, Polytechnic University of the Philippines) 3–4, 31–95.

de Jesus, Edilberto C. *The Tobacco Monopoly in the Philippines, 1766–1880.* Quezon City: Ateneo de Manila Press, 1989.

de Kruif, Paul. *The Microbe Hunters.* New York: Harcourt Brace, 1926.

de la Gironiere, Paul. *Adventures of a Frenchman in the Philippines.* 9th ed. Manila: Burke-Miailhe, 1972. Originally published in French in 1853.

De la Pena, Guillermo. *A Legacy of Promises: Agriculture, Politics and Ritual in the Morelos Highlands of Mexico.* Austin: University of Texas Press, 1981.

de Lauretis, Teresa. "Eccentric Subjects: Feminist Theory and Historical Consciousness." *Feminist Studies* 16, no. 1 (spring 1990): 115–150.

Deleuze, Gilles, and Félix Guattari. *Anti-Oedipus: Capitalism and Schizophrenia.* Trans. Robert Hurley, Mark Seem, and Helen R. Lane. Minneapolis: University of Minnesota Press, 1983.

———. *A Thousand Plateaus.* Trans. Brian Massumi. Minneapolis: University of Minnesota Press, 1987.

———. *Qué es la Filosofía?* Barcelona: Anagrama, 1993.

de Lima-Sison, Julieta. "Jose Maria Sison on the Mode of Production." *New Philippine Review* 1 (1984): 1–3.

Departmento Nacional de Planeación de Colombia. *Plan Pacífico: Una Estrategia de Desarrollo Sostenible para la Costa Pacífico de Colombia.* Bogotá: DNP, 1992.

Derrida, Jacques. *Specters of Marx: The State of the Debt, the Work of Mourning, and the New International.* Trans. Peggy Kamuf. New York: Routledge, 1995.

de Shon, George. "Medical Highlights of the Philippine-American War." *Bulletin of the American Historical Collection* 12 (1984): 69.

Ding Ling. "Miss Sophia's Diary." Trans. Tani Barlow. In *I Myself Am a Woman*, ed. Tani Barlow and Gary Bjorge. Boston: Beacon Press, 1989.

Douglas, Mary. *Purity and Danger: An Analysis of the Concepts of Pollution and Taboo.* Harmondsworth: Penguin, 1970.

Dower, John. *War without Mercy: Race and Power in the Pacific War.* New York: Pantheon, 1986.

Du, Fangqin. *Nüxing guannian de yanbian* (Evolution of the female concept). Zhongzhou: Henan renmin chubanshe, 1988.

Du Bois, W. E. B. *Dark Princess.* Jackson: Banner Books, University Press of Mississippi, 1995.

Dubos, Rene. *Mirage of Health: Utopias, Progress and Biological Change.* New York: Harper, 1959.

Dudziak, Mary L. "Desegregation as Cold War Imperative." In *Critical Race Theory*, ed. Richard Delgado. Philadelphia: Temple University Press, 1995.

Dunlop, R. H. W. *Service and Adventure with the Khakee Ressalah or, Meerut Volunteer Horse, during the Mutinies of 1857–58.* London: R. Bentley, 1858.

During, Simon. "Is Literature Dead or Has It Gone to the Movies?" *Age* (Melbourne) 19 June 1993.

Dutt, Utpal. "Theatre as a Weapon." *Drama Review* 15, no. 3 (spring 1971): 225–237.

———. *Towards a Revolutionary Theatre.* Calcutta: M. C. Sarkar & Sons, 1982.

Dutton, Michael, and Paul Healy. "Marxist Theory and Socialist Transition: The Construction of an Epistemological Relation." In *Chinese Marxism in Flux, 1978–84: Essays on Epistemology, Ideology and Political Economy*, ed. Bill Brugger. Armonk, NY: Sharpe, 1985.

Eaton, Richard Maxwell. *Sufis of Bijapur 1300–1700: Social Role of Sufis in Medieval India.* Princeton: Princeton University Press, 1978.

———. *The Rise of Islam and the Bengal Frontier, 1204–1760.* Berkeley: University of California Press, 1993.

Eberhardt, Isabelle. *The Passionate Nomad: The Diary of Isabelle Eberhardt.* Ed. and introduction by Rana Kabbani. London: Virago, 1987.

Ecumenical Institute for Labor Education and Research. *Manggagawa, Noon at Ngayon* (The worker, past and present). Manila: EILER, 1982.

Edwards, Jon R. "Slavery, the Slave Trade and the Economic Reorganization of Ethiopia." *African Economic History* 11 (1982): 3–14.

Eley, Geoff. "Nations, Publics, and Political Cultures: Placing Habermas in the Nineteenth Century." In *Habermas and the Public Sphere,* ed. Craig Calhoun. Cambridge, MA: MIT Press, 1992.

Elson, D., and R. Pearson. "The Subordination of Women and the Internationalization of Factory Production." In *Of Marriage and the Market,* ed. K. Young et al. London: CSE Books, 1981.

Engels, Friedrich. *The Condition of the Working Class in England.* Trans. W. O. Henderson and W. H. Chaloner. Stanford: Stanford University Press, 1968.

Enloe, Cynthia. *Bananas, Beaches, and Bases.* Berkeley: University of California Press, 1989.

Enriquez, Laura J., and Rose J. Spalding. "Banking Systems and Revolutionary Change." In *The Political Economy of Revolutionary Nicaragua,* ed. Rose J. Spalding. Boston: Allen and Unwin, 1987.

Escobar, Arturo. "Power and Visibility: The Invention of the Third World." Ph.D. diss., University of California, Berkeley, 1987.

———. "Imagining a Post-Development Era? Critical Thought, Development, and Social Movements." *Social Text* 31–32 (1992): 20–56.

———. *Encountering Development: The Making and Unmaking of the Third World.* Princeton: Princeton University Press, 1995.

———. "Constructing Nature: Elements for a Poststructuralist Political Ecology." In *Liberation Ecologies,* ed. R. Peet and M. Watts. London: Routledge, 1996.

———. "Viejas y nuevas formas de capital y los dilemas de la biodiversidad." In *Pacífico: Desarrollo o Diversidad?,* ed. Arturo Escobar and Alvaro Pedrosa. Bogotá: CEREC/ECOFONDO, 1996.

Escobar, Arturo, and Socia E. Alvarez, eds. *The Making of Social Movements in Latin America: Identity, Strategy, and Democracy.* Boulder, CO: Westview Press, 1992.

Escobar, Arturo, and Alvaro Pedrosa, eds. *Pacífico: Desarrollo o Diversidad? Estado, Capital y Movimientos Sociales en el Pacífico Colombiano.* Bogotá: CEREC/ECOFONDO, 1996.

Escobar, Edward. "The Dialectics of Repression: The Los Angeles Police Department and the Chicano Movement, 1968–1971." *Journal of American History* 74, no. 4 (March 1993): 1483–1504.

Espiritu, Yen Le. *Asian American Panethnicity.* Philadelphia: Temple University Press, 1992.

Esposito, John. *Islam: The Straight Path.* New York: Oxford University Press, 1988.

Essien-Udom, E. U. *Black Nationalism: A Search for Identity in America.* Chicago: University of Chicago Press, 1962.

Evanzz, Karl. *The Judas Factor: The Plot to Kill Malcolm X.* New York: Thunder's Mouth, 1992.

EZLN: Documentos y comunicados, 1 de enero/8 de agosto de 1994. Prologue by Ántonio García de León and chronicles by Carlos Monsiváis and Elena Poniatowska. Mexico City: Editorial Era, 1994.

Fagen, Richard, Carmen D. Deere, and Jose L. Coraggio, eds. *Transition and Development.* New York: Monthly Review Press, 1986.

Fanon, Frantz. *A Dying Colonialism*. Trans. Haakon Chevalier. New York: Grove Weidenfield, 1965.

———. *The Wretched of the Earth*. Trans. Constance Farrington. New York: Grove Press, 1968.

———. "Racism and Culture." In *Toward the African Revolution: Political Essays*. Trans. Haakon Chevalier. New York: Grove Press, 1988.

Farred, Grant, ed. *Rethinking C. L. R. James*. Cambridge, MA: Basil Blackwell Publishers, 1996.

Fawcett, J. T., S-E. Khoo, and P. C. Smith, eds. *Women in the Cities of Asia*. Boulder, CO: Westview, 1984.

Fellows, Mary Louise, and Sherene Razack. *The Race to Innocents: Relations among Women in Law and Feminism*. New York: New York University Press, 1996.

Ferguson, A. "Is There a Lesbian Culture?" In *Lesbian Philosophies and Cultures*, ed. J. Allen. Albany: State University of New York Press, 1990.

Ferguson, James. *The Anti-Politics Machine*. Cambridge: Cambridge University Press, 1990.

Fernandez-Kelly, Maria Patricia. *"For We Are Sold, I and My People": Women and Industry on Mexico's Frontier*. Albany: State University of New York Press, 1983.

Fernandez-Kelly, Maria Patricia, and A. Garcia. "Informalization at the Core: Hispanic Women, Home Work, and the Advanced Capitalist State." *The Informal Economy*, ed. A. Portes, M. Castells, and L. Benton. Baltimore: Johns Hopkins University Press, 1989.

Fernea, Elizabeth Warnock. *Guests of the Sheikh*. New York: Doubleday, 1965.

Ferrer, Ricardo. "On the Mode of Production in the Philippines: Some Old-Fashioned Questions." *New Philippine Review* 1 (1984).

Field, Norma. *In the Realm of a Dying Emperor*. New York: Pantheon, 1991.

Fischer, Humphrey J. *Ahmadiyah*. Oxford: Oxford University Press, 1963.

Fiske, John. *Reading the Popular*. Boston: Unwin Hyman, 1989.

Fitzgerald, Valpy. "National Economy in 1985: Transition in Progress." Unpublished mimeograph. Managua, 1985.

Fleras, Jomar. "Reclaiming Our Historic Rights: Gays and Lesbians in the Philippines." In *The Third Pink Book: A Global View of Lesbian Gay Liberation and Oppression*, ed. A. Hendriks et al. Buffalo: Prometheus Books, 1993.

Foucault, Michel. *Madness and Civilization: A History of Insanity in the Age of Reason*. Trans. Richard Howard. New York: Random House, 1965.

———. *The Birth of the Clinic: An Archaeology of Medical Perception*. Trans. A. M. Sheridan Smith. New York: Vintage, 1973.

———. "Nietzsche, Genealogy, History." In *Language, Counter-Memory, Practice: Selected Essays and Interviews by Michel Foucault*, ed. D. Bouchard. Ithaca: Cornell University Press, 1977.

———. *Discipline and Punish: The Birth of the Prison*. Trans. A. Sheridan. New York: Vintage, 1979.

———. *The History of Sexuality*. Vol. 1. Trans. R. Hurley. New York: Vintage, 1980.

———. *Power/Knowledge: Selected Interviews & Other Writings 1972–1977.* Ed. Colin Gordon. Trans. Colin Gordon et al. New York: Pantheon Books, 1980.

———. "What Is an Author?" In *The Foucault Reader,* ed. Paul Rabinow. New York: Pantheon, 1984.

———. "What Is Enlightenment?" In *The Foucault Reader,* ed. Paul Rabinow. New York: Pantheon, 1984.

———. "Governmentality." In *The Foucault Effect: Studies in Governmentality,* ed. Graham Burchell, Colin Gordon, and Peter Miller. London: Wheatsheaf, 1991.

Four Comrades. Bombay: The Indian People's Theatre Association, National Dramatics for Defence, 1942.

Franklin, John Hope. *From Slavery to Freedom: A History of Negro Americans.* 4th ed. New York: Knopf, 1974.

———. "Their War and Mine." *Journal of American History* (September 1990): 576–579.

Fraser, Nancy. *Unruly Practices.* Minneapolis: University of Minnesota Press, 1989.

———. "Rethinking the Public Sphere: A Contribution to the Critique of Actually Existing Democracy." In *The Phantom Public Sphere,* ed. Bruce Robbins. Minneapolis: University of Minnesota Press, 1993.

Frenkel, María Veronica. "The Evolution of Food and Agricultural Policies during Economic Crisis and War." In *Nicaragua: Profiles of the Revolutionary Public Sector,* ed. Michael E. Conroy. Boulder, CO: Westview Press, 1987.

Freud, Sigmund. "The Dissolution of the Oedipal Complex" (1924) and "Some Psychical Consequences of the Anatomical Distinction between the Sexes" (1925). In *On Sexuality: Three Essays on the Theory of Sexuality and Other Works,* ed. Angela Richards, trans. James Strachey. Harmondsworth: Penguin, 1977.

Froebel, F., J. Heinrichs, and O. Kreye, eds. *The New International Division of Labor.* Cambridge: Cambridge University Press, 1980.

Fujita, K. "Women Workers, State Policy, and the International Division of Labor: The Case of Silicon Island in Japan." *Bulletin of Concerned Asian Scholars* 20, no. 3 (1988): 42–53.

Fusco, Coco, and Guillermo Gómez-Peña. "New World Radio." In *Radio Rethink: Art, Sound and Transmission,* ed. Daina Augaitis and Dan Lander. Banff, Canada: Walter Phillips Gallery, 1994.

Gambino, Ferruccio. "Malcolm X, Laborer: From the Wilderness of the American Empire to Cultural Self-Identification." Paper presented at Colloque 1984 de L'Association Française d'Etudes Americaines Dourdan, 25–27 May 1984.

Garcia, J. Neil C. "Unfurling Lives: An Introduction." In *Ladlad: An Anthology of Philippine Gay Writings,* ed. J. N. C. Garcia and D. Remoto. Manila: Anvil Press, 1993.

García Canclini, Néstor. *Culturas Híbridas: Estrategias para Entrar y Salir de la Modernidad.* México: Grijalbo, 1990.

Gargi, Balwant. *Theatre in India.* New York: Theatre Arts Books, 1962.

———. *Folk Theatre of India.* Seattle: University of Washington Press, 1966.

Garvin, Thomas. *The Evolution of Irish Nationalist Politics.* Dublin: Gill and Macmillan, 1981.

Geertz, Clifford. *Peddlers and Princes.* Chicago: University of Chicago Press, 1962.

Gellner, Ernest. *Nations and Nationalism.* Ithaca: Cornell University Press, 1983.

Gelven, Michael. *A Commentary on Heidegger's "Being and Time."* DeKalb: Northern Illinois University Press, 1989.

Gibbons, Luke. "Identity without a Centre: Allegory, History and Irish Nationalism." *Cultural Studies* 6, no. 3 (October 1992): 358–375.

Gibson, Bill. "Structural Overview of the Nicaraguan Economy." In *The Political Economy of Revolutionary Nicaragua,* ed. Rose J. Spaulding. Boston: Allen and Unwin, 1987.

Gillespie, Michael Allen. *Hegel, Heidegger and the Ground of History.* Chicago: University of Chicago Press, 1984.

Gilroy, Paul. *There Ain't No Black in the Union Jack: The Cultural Politics of Race and Nation.* Chicago: University of Chicago Press, 1987.

———. *The Black Atlantic: Modernity and Double Consciousness.* Cambridge, MA: Harvard University Press, 1993.

Glenn, Evelyn Nakano. "Racial Ethnic Women's Labor: The Intersection of Race, Gender, and Class Oppression." *Review of Radical Political Economics* 17, no. 3 (1983): 86–109.

Global Environmental Facility/United Nations Development Program. *Conservación de la Biodiversidad del Chocó Biogeográfico: Proyecto Biopacífico.* Bogotá: DNP/Biopacífico, 1993.

Goffman, Erving. *Stigma: Notes on the Management of Spoiled Identity.* New York: Simon & Schuster, 1963.

Gorham, Deborah. *The Victorian Girl and the Feminine Ideal.* Bloomington: Indiana University Press, 1982.

Gossen, Gary H. "From Olmecs to Zapatistas: A Once and Future History of Souls." *American Anthropologist* 96 (1994): 553–570.

Gramsci, Antonio. *Selections from the Prison Notebooks.* Ed. and trans. Quintin Hoare and Geoffrey Nowell Smith. New York: International Publishers, 1971.

Greenberg, Cheryl. "Black and Jewish Responses to Japanese Internment." *Journal of American Ethnic History* 14, no. 2 (winter 1995): 3–37.

Greene, Robert Ewell. *Black Defenders of America, 1775–1973.* Chicago: Johnson Publishing, 1974.

Grewal, Inderpal, and Caren Kaplan, eds. *Scattered Hegemonies: Postmodernity and Transnational Feminist Practices.* Minneapolis: University of Minnesota Press, 1994.

Griffith, Beatrice. *American Me.* Cambridge, MA: Houghton Mifflin, 1948.

Grimshaw, Anna, ed. *The C. L. R. James Reader.* Cambridge, MA: Blackwell Publishers, 1992.

Gross, Joan, David McMurray, and Ted Swedenburg. "Rai, Rap and Ramadan Nights: Franco-Maghribi Cultural Identities." *Middle East Reports* 22, no. 5 (September–October 1992): 11–16.

Grossman, Rachel. "Women's Place in the Integrated Circuit." *Southeast Asia Chronicle* 66 (1979): 2–17.

Grueso, Libia. "Diagnósticos, Propuestas y Perspectivas de la Región del Chocó

Biogeográfico en Relación con la Conservación y Uso Sostenido de la Biodiversidad." Report presented to Proyecto Biopacífico, Bogotá, 1995.

Grueso, Libia, and Carlos Rosero. "El Proceso Organizativo de Comunidades Negras en el Pacífico Sur Colombiano." Unpublished manuscript, 1995.

Grueso, Libia, Carlos Rosero, and Arturo Escobar. "The Politics of Nature and the Black Movement of the Pacific Coast of Colombia." In *Cultures of Politics/Politics of Cultures: Revisioning Latin American Social Movements,* ed. Sonia E. Alvarez, Evelina Dagnino, and Arturo Escobar. Boulder, CO: Westview Press, forthcoming.

Guattari, Félix. "Las radios libres populares." In *De las ondas rojas a las radios libres,* ed. Lluís Bassets. Barcelona: Editorial Gustavo Gili, 1981.

———. "Millions and Millions of Potential Alices." In *Molecular Revolution.* Trans. Rosemary Sheed. London: Penguin, 1984.

Guerrero, Amado. "Specific Characteristics of Our People's War." In *Philippine Society and Revolution.* Manila: International Association of Filipino Patriots, 1979.

Guerrero, Milagros. "Luzon at War: Contradictions in Philippine Society." Ph.D. diss., University of Michigan, 1977.

Guha, Ranajit. *Elementary Forms of Peasant Insurgency.* Dehli: Oxford University Press, 1983.

———. "The Migrant's Time." Unpublished ms.

———, ed. *Subaltern Studies IV: Writings on South Asian History and Society.* New York: Oxford University Press, 1985.

Guha, Ranajit, and Gayatri Chakravorty Spivak, eds. *Selected Subaltern Studies.* New York: Oxford University Press, 1988.

Guillermoprieto, Alma. "The Shadow War." *New York Review of Books* 42, no. 4 (1995): 34–43.

Gupta, Akhil, and James Ferguson. "Beyond 'Culture': Space, Identity, and the Politics of Difference." *Cultural Anthropology* 7, no. 1 (February 1992): 6–22.

Gurr, Ted R. *Minorities at Risk: A Global View of Ethnopolitical Conflicts.* Washington, D.C.: U.S. Institute of Peace Press, 1993.

Gutiérrez, David. *Walls and Mirrors: Mexican Americans, Mexican Immigrants, and the Politics of Ethnicity.* Berkeley: University of California Press, 1995.

Haldane, J. B. S. *Everything Has a History.* London: Allen and Unwin, 1951.

Hall, Stuart. "Gramsci's Relevance for the Study of Race and Ethnicity." *Journal of Communications Inquiry* 10 (summer 1986): 5–27.

———. "Cultural Identity and Diaspora." In *Identity, Community, Culture, Difference,* ed. J. Rutherford. London: Lawrence & Wishart, 1990.

———. "Cultural Studies and Its Theoretical Legacies." In *Cultural Studies,* ed. Lawrence Grossberg, Carl Nelson, and Paula Treichler. New York: Routledge, 1992.

Han Chun-sang. "Migukŭi munhwa ch'imt'uwa Han'guk kyoyuk" (American cultural invasion and Korean education). In *Haebang chŏnhusaŭi insik* (Understanding pre- and postliberation history). Vol. 3, ed. Pak Myŏng-nim et al. Seoul: Hangilsa, 1987.

Hanatrakul, S. "Prostitution in Thailand." In *Development and Displacement: Women in Southeast Asia*, ed. G. Chandler, N. Sullivan, and J. Branson. Clayton, Australia: Monash University Papers on Southeast Asia, no. 18, 1988.

Hannerz, Ulf. *Cultural Complexity: Studies in the Social Organization of Meaning.* New York: Columbia University Press, 1992.

Hansen, Miriam. "Early Cinema, Late Cinema: Permutations of the Public Sphere." *Screen* 34, no. 3 (1993): 197–210.

———. "Unstable Mixtures, Dilated Spheres: Negt and Kluge's *The Public Sphere and Experience,* Twenty Years Later." *Public Culture* 5, no. 2 (1993): 179–212.

Haraway, Donna. "Situated Knowledges: The Science Question in Feminism and the Privilege of Partial Perspective." *Feminist Studies* 14, no. 3 (Fall 1988): 575–599.

———. *Simians, Cyborgs, and Women: The Reinvention of Nature.* New York: Routledge, 1991.

———. "The Promises of Monsters: A Regenerative Politics for Inappropriate/d Others." In *Cultural Studies,* ed. Lawrence Grossberg, Cary Nelson, and Paula Treichler. New York: Routledge, 1992.

Harlow, Barbara. *Resistance Literature.* Methuen: London, 1987.

Harris, Cheryl. "Whiteness as Property." *Harvard Law Review* 106, no. 8 (June 1993): 1707–1791.

Hartsock, Nancy. "The Feminist Standpoint: Toward a Specifically Feminist Historical Materialism." In *Money, Sex, and Power.* Boston: Northeastern University Press, 1985.

Harvey, David. *The Condition of Postmodernity: An Enquiry into the Origins of Cultural Change.* Oxford: Basil Blackwell, 1990.

Hase, Michiko. "Race, Status, and Culture in Trans-Pacific Perspective: African American Professionals in Japan." Paper presented at the annual meeting of the American Studies Association, Nashville, Tennessee, 28 October 1994.

Heidegger, Martin. *Being and Time.* Trans. John McQuarrie and Edward Robinson. Oxford: Blackwell, 1985.

Hellwig, David J. "Afro-American Reactions to the Japanese and the Anti-Japanese Movement, 1906–1924." *Phylon* 37, no. 1 (1977): 93–104.

Hendricks, A., R. Tielman, and E. van der Veen, eds. *The Third Pink Book: A Global View of Lesbian/Gay Liberation and Oppression.* Buffalo: Prometheus Books, 1993.

Henry, Michel. *Marx: A Philosophy of Human Reality.* Bloomington: Indiana University Press, 1983.

Hietala, Thomas R. "Muhammad Ali and the Age of Bare Knuckle Politics." In *Muhammad Ali: The People's Champ,* ed. Elliott J. Gorn. Urbana: University of Illinois Press, 1995.

Hill, Jane. "Hasta la vista, baby: Anglo-Spanish in the American Southwest." *Critique of Anthropology* 13, no. 2 (1993): 145–176.

Hill, Robert A., ed. *The Marcus Garvey and UNIA Papers.* Berkeley: University of California Press, 1983.

Hilton, Anthony. "How to Ruin Inter-Cultural Relations in One Evening." Unpublished manuscript. Montreal: Concordia University, Department of Psychology, 1993.

Himes, Chester B. "Zoot Riots Are Race Riots." *The Crisis* (July 1943): 200–222.

——. *If He Hollers Let Him Go.* New York: Thunder's Mouth Press, 1986.

——. *Lonely Crusade.* New York: Thunder's Mouth Press, 1986.

Ho, Laura, Catherine Powell, and Leti Volpp. "(Dis)Assembling Rights of Women Workers along the Global Assemblyline: Human Rights and the Garment Industry." *Harvard Civil Rights–Civil Liberties Law Review* 31, no. 2 (summer 1996): 383–414.

Hobart, Mark, ed. *An Anthropological Critique of Development.* London: Routledge, 1993.

Hobsbawm, Eric J. *Primitive Rebels: Studies in Archaic Forms of Social Movement in the 19th and 20th Centuries.* New York: Norton, 1959.

——. *Bandits.* 1969. Revised, New York: Delacorte, 1981.

——. *Nations and Nationalism Since 1780: Programme, Myth, Reality.* Cambridge: Cambridge University Press, 1990.

Holloway, Joseph E., ed. *Africanisms in American Culture.* Bloomington: Indiana University Press, 1991.

Hong, Kyungwon, and Mary Tong. "Aguirre v. AUG: A Case Study." In *Multinational Human Resource Management: Cases and Exercises,* ed. P. C. Smith. Tulsa, OK: Dame Publishing, forthcoming.

Hoodfar, Homa. "A Background to the Feminist Movement in Egypt." *Bulletin of Simone de Beauvoir Institute* 9, no. 2 (1989): 18–23.

——. "Feminist Anthropology and Critical Pedagogy: The Anthropology of Classrooms' Excluded Voices." *Canadian Journal of Education* 17, no. 3 (1992): 303–320.

——. "Return to the Veil: Personal Strategy and Public Participation in Egypt." In *Working Women: International Perspectives on Labour and Gender Ideology,* ed. Nanneke Redclift and M. Thea Sinclair. London: Routledge, 1991.

——. "Veiling as an Accommodating Strategy: Muslim Women in Canada." In preparation.

hooks, bell. *Ain't I a Woman: Black Women and Feminism.* Boston: South End Press, 1981.

——. *Talking Back: Thinking Feminist, Thinking Black.* Boston: South End Press, 1989.

——. "Talking Back." In *Out There: Marginalization and Contemporary Cultures,* ed. R. Ferguson, M. Gever, T. Minh-ha, and C. West. Cambridge, MA: MIT Press, 1990.

Horne, Gerald. *The Fire This Time: The Watts Uprising and the 1960s.* Charlottesville: University of Virginia Press, 1995.

Hossfeld, Karen J. " 'Their Logic Against Them': Contradictions in Sex, Race, and Class in the Silicon Valley." In *Women Workers and Global Restructuring,* ed. K. Ward. Ithaca: University ILR Press, 1990.

Hsiung, Ping-Chun. *Living Rooms as Factories: Class, Gender, and the Satellite Factory System in Taiwan.* Philadelphia: Temple University Press, 1995.

Hutcheon, Linda. *The Politics of Postmodernism.* London: Routledge, 1989.

Ileto, Reynaldo Clemeña. *Pasyon and Revolution: Popular Movements in the Philippines, 1840–1910.* Quezon City: Ateneo De Manila Press, 1979.

——. "Rizal and the Underside of Philippine History." In *Moral Order and Change: Essays in Southeast Asian Thought,* ed. D. Wyatt and A. Woodside. New Haven: Yale Southeast Asia Studies, 1982.

——. "Bonifacio, the Text, and the Social Scientist." *Philippine Sociological Review* 32 (1984): 19–29.

——. "Cholera and the Origins of the American Sanitary Order in the Philippines." In *Imperial Medicine and Indigenous Societies,* ed. David Arnold. Manchester: Manchester University Press, 1988.

Instituto Historico CentroAmerico. "The Right of the Poor to Defend Their Revolution." *Envio* 4, no. 36 (1984): 1–33.

——. "The Nicaraguan Peasantry Gives New Direction to Agrarian Reform." *Envio* 4, no. 51 (1985): 1–19.

Jackson, Charles. "Plight of Japanese Americans." *Militant* 10 March 1945. Reprinted in *Fighting Racism in World War II,* ed. C. L. R. James et al. New York: Monad Press, 1980.

Jaffe, Alexandra. "Obligation, Error, and Authenticity: Competing Cultural Principles in the Teaching of Corsican." *Journal of Linguistic Anthropology* 3, no. 1 (1993): 99–114.

James, C. L. R. " 'Civilising' the 'Blacks.' " *New Leader* (29 May 1936).

——. *Nkrumah and the Ghana Revolution.* London: Allison & Busby, 1977.

——. *Beyond a Boundary.* New York: Pantheon, 1983.

——. "C. L. R. James on Poland." *Cultural Correspondence* (winter 1983).

——. *The Black Jacobins: Toussaint L'Ouverture and the San Domingo Revolution.* 2d ed., revised. New York: Vintage Books, 1989.

Jameson, Fredric. *Postmodernism, or the Cultural Logic of Late Capitalism.* Durham: Duke University Press, 1991.

——. *The Geopolitical Aesthetic: Cinema and Space in the World System.* Bloomington: Indiana University Press, 1992.

——. "Postmodernism, or the Cultural Logic of Late Capitalism." *New Left Review,* no. 146 (July–August 1984): 53–92.

JanMohamed, Abdul. "The Economy of Manichaean Allegory: The Function of Racial Difference in Colonialist Literature." In *"Race," Writing and Difference,* ed. Henry Louis Gates. Chicago: University of Chicago Press, 1985.

Janzen, Daniel, and H. Hallwachs. *All Taxa Biodiversity Inventory.* Philadelphia: University of Pennsylvania Press, 1993.

Janzen, Daniel, H. Hallwachs, J. Jiménez, and R. Gómez. "The Role of the Parataxonomists, Inventory Managers and Taxonomists in Costa Rica's National Biodiversity Inventory." In *Biodiversity Prospecting,* by World Resources Institute. Oxford: Oxford University Press, 1993.

Jayawardena, Kumari. *Feminism and Nationalism in the Third World*. London: Zed Press, 1986.

Jeffords, Susan. *The Remasculinization of America: Gender and the Vietnam War*. Bloomington: Indiana University Press, 1989.

Joint Committee for Moro Concerns. *Ang Moro* (The Moro). Marawi: Joint Committee for Moro Concerns, 1985.

Jones, Jacqueline. *Labor of Love, Labor of Sorrow: Black Women, Work, and the Family from Slavery to the Present*. New York: Basic Books, 1985.

Joyce, James. *Ulysses*. New York: Random House, 1986.

Jun, Helen Heran. "Contingent Nationalisms in Korean and Korean American Women's Oppositional Struggles." *positions: east asia cultures critique* 5, no. 2 (fall 1997).

Kabbani, Rana. *Europe's Myths of the Orient*. Bloomington: Indiana University Press, 1986.

Kandiyoti, Deniz. "Identity and Its Discontents." In *Colonial Discourse and Post-Colonial Theory: A Reader*, ed. Patrick Williams and Laura Chrisman. New York: Columbia University Press, 1994.

Kang, Liu. "Subjectivity, Marxism and Cultural Theory in China." In *Politics, Ideology, and Literary Discourse in China: Theoretical Interventions and Cultural Critique*, ed. Liu Kang and Xiaobing Tang. Durham: Duke University Press, 1993.

———. "Aesthetics and Chinese Marxism." *positions: east asia cultures critique* 3, no. 2 (1995).

Kant, Immanuel. "Idea of a Universal History on a Cosmo-political Plan." In *Works*. Vol. 12. Trans. Thomas de Quincey. Edinburgh: Adam and Charles Black, 1862.

Kasmir, Sharryn. "The Myth of Mondragón: Cooperatives, Politics, and Working Class Life in a Basque Town." Ph.D. diss., City University of New York, 1993.

Keddie, Nikki R. *Religion and Rebellion in Iran: Tobacco Protest of 1891–92*. London: Frank Cass, 1966.

Keddie, Nikki R., and Beth Baron. *Women in Middle Eastern History: Shifting Boundaries in Sex and Gender*. New Haven: Yale University Press, 1991.

Keddie, Nikki R., and Lois Beck. *Women in the Muslim World*. Cambridge, MA: Harvard University Press, 1978.

Kelley, Robin D. G. *Hammer and Hoe*. Chapel Hill: University of North Carolina Press, 1991.

———. *Race Rebels: Culture, Politics, and the Black Working Class*. New York: Free Press, 1994.

———. Introduction. In *A History of Negro Revolt*, by C. L. R. James. Chicago: Charles H. Kerr, 1995.

Khazmadar, Cherif. "Tendencies and Prospects for Third World Theatre." *Drama Review* 17, no. 4 (1973): 33–35.

Kim, Min-Jung. "Moment of Danger: Continuities, Discontinuities between Korean Nationalism and Korean American Nationalism." *positions: east asia cultures critique* 5, no. 2 (fall 1997).

Kim, S. K. "Women Workers and the Birth of Labor Unions in Masan, Korea."

Paper presented at the annual meeting of the American Anthropological Association, Phoenix, Arizona, December 1988.

Kim, S. N. "Lamentations of the Dead: The Historical Imagery of Violence on Cheju Island, South Korea." *Journal of Ritual Studies* 3, no. 2 (1989): 251–271.

Kloppenburg, Jack. *First the Seed: The Political Economy of Plant Biotechnology, 1492–2000.* Cambridge: Cambridge University Press, 1988.

Knight, Alan. *The Mexican Revolution.* 2 vols. Cambridge: Cambridge University Press, 1986.

Kogawa, Tetsuo. "Free Radio in Japan." In *Cultures in Contention,* ed. Douglas Kahn and Diane Neumaier. Seattle: Real Comet Press, 1985.

Koo, Hagen, Stephen Haggard, and Frederic Deyo. "Labor and Development Strategy in East Asian NICS." *Items* 40, nos. 3–4 (1986): 64–68.

Kumamoto, Bob. "The Search for Spies: American Counterintelligence and the Japanese American Community, 1931–1942." *Amerasia Journal* 6, no. 2 (1979): 45–75.

Kumar, Kapil. "Rural Women in Oudh 1917–1947: Baba Ram Chandra and the Women's Question." In *Recasting Women: Essays in Indian Colonial History,* ed. Kumkkum Sangari and Sudesh Vaid. New Brunswick, NJ: Rutgers University Press, 1990.

Kumar, Radha. *The History of Doing: An Illustrated Account of Movements for Women's Rights and Feminism in India, 1800–1990.* London: Verso, 1993.

Kung, Lydia. *Factory Women in Taiwan.* Ann Arbor: University of Michigan Research Press, 1983.

Laclau, Ernesto. *Politics and Ideology in Marxist Theory.* London: New Left Books, 1977.

Landes, Joan. *Women and the Public Sphere in the Age of the French Revolution.* Ithaca: Cornell University Press, 1988.

Las Casas, Bartolomé de. *El Tratado de las "Doce Dudas."* In *Obras Completas,* vol. 11:2, ed. J. B. Lassegue. Madrid: Editorial Alianza, 1992.

Lazreg, M. "Feminism and Difference: The Perils of Writing as a Woman on Women in Algeria." *Feminist Studies* 14, no. 1 (1988): 81–107.

Lee, Benjamin. "Going Public." *Public Culture* 5, no. 2 (1993): 165–178.

Leonard, Kevin Allen. "'Is That What We Fought For?' Japanese Americans and Racism in California: The Impact of World War II." *Western Historical Quarterly* 21, no. 4 (November 1990): 463–482.

Lewis, Peter. "Community Radio: The Montreal Conference and After." *Media, Culture, and Society* 6 (1984): 137–150.

Li Min and Wang Fukang. *Zhongguo funäxue* (Chinese women's studies). Nanchang: Jiangxi renmin chubanshe, 1985.

Li Xioajiang. "The Self-Comprehension of Woman." In *Nüzi yü jiazheng* (Women and domestic science). Zhengshou: Henan renmin chubanshe, 1986.

———. *Xiawa de tansuo* (Eve's explorations). Changsha: Henan renmin chubanshe, 1988.

———. *Nüren: yige youyuan meili de chuanshuo* (Woman: A distant, beautiful legend). Shanghai: Renmin chubanshe, 1989.

——. *Xinggou* (Sex gap). Beijing: Sanlian shudian, 1989.

——. "Zouxiang *nüren*" (Toward womanhood). *Nüxingren* 4 (1990): 255–266.

——. "Economic Reform and the Awakening of Chinese Women's Collective Consciousness." In *Engendering China: Women, Culture and the State,* ed. Chris Gilmartin et al. Cambridge, MA: Harvard University Press, 1994.

——. "Zongjian kuyue 'xinghou' zhi qiao" (Establish a bridge for overcoming the 'sex gap'). *Doongfang zazhi* 4 (1995): 14–16.

Li Xiaojiang and Li Hui. "Women's Studies in China." *National Women's Studies Association* 1, no. 3 (spring 1989): 458–460.

Likosky, Stephan. *Coming Out: An Anthology of International Gay and Lesbian Writing.* New York: Pantheon Books, 1992.

Lim, Linda Y. C. *Women Workers in Multinational Corporations: The Case of the Electronics Industry in Malaysia and Singapore.* Ann Arbor: University of Michigan Women's Studies Program. Occasional Paper no. 9, 1978.

Lim, Linda Y. C., and E. F. Pang. "Technological Choice and Employment Creation: A Case of Three Multinational Enterprises in Singapore." In *The Pacific Challenge in International Business,* ed. W. C. Kim and P. K. Y. Young. Ann Arbor: University of Michigan Research Press, 1985.

Lin, V. "Productivity First: Japanese Management Methods in Singapore." *Bulletin of Concerned Asian Scholars* 16, no. 4 (1984): 12–25.

Lindenmeyer, Otto. *Black & Brave: The Black Soldier in America.* New York: McGraw-Hill, 1970.

Lipietz, Alain. "New Tendencies in the International Division of Labor: Regimes of Accumulation and Modes of Regulation." In *Production, Work, Territory: The Geographical Anatomy of Industrial Capitalism,* ed. A. Scott and M. Stroper. Boston: Allen and Unwin, 1986.

Lipsitz, George. *Dangerous Crossroads.* New York: Verso, 1994.

——. *Rainbow at Midnight: Labor and Culture in the 1940s.* Urbana: University of Illinois Press, 1994.

——. *A Life in the Struggle: Ivory Perry and the Culture of Opposition.* Philadelphia: Temple University Press, 1995.

Liu Bohong. "1993: Funü yanjiu zouxiang" (Toward women's studies). In *Funü yanjiu.* Beijing: Remindazue shubao ziliao zongzin, 423, 1994.1.

——. "1994: Funü yanjiu qushi" (Trends in women's studies). In *Funü yanjiu.* Beijing: Remindazue shubao ziliao zongzin, 423, 1994.1.

Lloyd, David. *Anomalous States: Irish Writing and the Post-Colonial Moment.* Durham: Duke University Press, 1993.

——. "Counterparts: *Dubliners,* Masculinity and Temperance Nationalism." In *Burning Down the House,* ed. Rosemary Marangoly George. Boulder, CO: Westview Press, 1997.

——. "Regarding Ireland in a Post-colonial Frame." In *Cultural Studies.* Forthcoming.

Loo, Chalsa. *Chinatown: Most Time, Hard Time.* New York: Praeger, 1991.

Loo, Chalsa, and Paul Ong. "Slaying Demons with a Sewing Needle: Feminist Issues for Chinatown's Women." In *Chinatown: Most Time, Hard Time,* by Chalsa Loo. New York: Praeger, 1991.

Lorde, Audre. "The Master's Tools Will Never Dismantle the Master's House." In *This Bridge Called My Back: Writings by Radical Women of Color,* ed. Cherríe Moraga and Gloria Anzaldúa. Watertown: Persephone Press, 1981.

Lorimer, Norman. "Philippine Communism — An Historical Overview." *Journal of Contemporary Asia* 7, no. 4 (1977): 462–485.

Louie, Miriam Ching. "Immigrant Asian Women in Bay Area Garment Sweatshops: 'After Sewing, Laundry, Cleaning and Cooking, I Have No Breath to Sing.'" *Amerasia Journal* 18 (1992): 14.

Lowe, Donald. *The Function of "China" in Marx, Lenin, and Mao.* Berkeley: University of California Press, 1966.

Lowe, Lisa. *Critical Terrains: British and French Orientalisms.* Ithaca: Cornell University Press, 1991.

———. *Immigrant Acts: On Asian American Cultural Politics.* Durham: Duke University Press, 1996.

Lowe, Lydia. "Paving the Way: Chinese Immigrant Workers and Community-Based Labor Organizing in Boston." *Amerasia Journal* 18, no. 1 (1992): 39–48.

Lucero, Rosario Cruz. "Negros Occidental, 1970–1986: The Fall of the Sugar Industry and the Rise of People's Theater." Ph.D. diss., University of the Philippines, 1990.

Luddy, Maria, and Cliona Murphy, eds. *Women Surviving: Studies in Irish Women's History in the 19th and 20th Centuries.* Dublin: Poolbeg, 1990.

Lugo, Alejandro. "Cultural Production and Reproduction in Ciudad Juarez, Mexico: Tropes at Play among Maquiladora Workers." *Cultural Anthropology* 5, no. 2 (1990): 173–196.

Lyotard, Jean-François. *The Postmodern Condition: A Report on Knowledge.* Trans. Geoff Bennington and Brian Massumi. Minneapolis: University of Minnesota Press, 1984.

Mabro, Judy. *Veiled Half-Truths: Western Travellers' Perceptions of Middle Eastern Women.* London: I. B. Tauris, 1991.

Macaulay, Thomas Babington. "Minute on Indian Education." In *Selected Writings,* ed. John Clive. Chicago: University of Chicago Press, 1972.

MacCurtain, Margaret, and Donncha O Corrain, eds. *Women in Irish Society: The Historical Dimension.* Westport, CT: Greenwood Press, 1979.

Mackinnon, Catharine. "Feminism, Marxism, Method, and the State: An Agenda for Theory." *Signs* 7 (1982): 515–544.

MacLeod, Arlene Elowe. *Accommodating Protest: Working Women and the New Veiling in Cairo.* New York: Columbia University Press, 1991.

Makõisi, Saree, et al., eds. *Marxism beyond Marxism.* New York: Routledge, 1996.

Malcolm, John. *Sketches of Persia from the Journals of a Traveler in the East.* London: J. Murray, 1949.

Malcolm X and Alex Haley. *The Autobiography of Malcolm X.* New York: Grove Press, 1965.

Manalansan, Martin. "Speaking of AIDS: Language and the Filipino Gay Experience in America." In *Discrepant Histories: Translocal Essays on Filipino Cultures,* ed. Vicente Rafael. Philadelphia: Temple University Press, 1995.

Mani, Lata. "Multiple Mediations: Feminist Scholarship in the Age of Multinational Reception." *Feminist Review* 35 (1990): 24–41.

Marcos, Ferdinand. *Outline: Tadhana, the History of the Filipino People.* Manila: Marcos Foundation, 1980.

———. "A Sense of National History." *Historical Bulletin* 26 (1982): 1–15.

———. *An Ideology for Filipinos.* Manila: Marcos Foundation, 1983.

Mariscal, George. "'Chale Con la Draft': Chicano Antiwar Writings." *Viet Nam Generation* 6, nos. 3–4 (1995): 126–131.

Markievicz, Constance. *Prison Letters.* With a biographical sketch by Esther Roper and preface by President De Valera. London: Longmans Green, 1934.

Martin, JoAnn. "Contesting Authenticity: Battles over the Representation of History in Morelos, Mexico." *Ethnohistory* 40, no. 3 (summer 1993): 438–465.

Martin, Tony. *Race First: The Ideological and Organizational Struggles of Marcus Garvey and the Universal Negro Improvement Association.* Westport, CT: Greenwood Press, 1976.

———. *The Pan-African Connection: From Slavery to Garvey and Beyond.* Dover, MA: Majority Press, 1983.

Marx, Karl. *Capital: A Critique of Political Economy.* Vol. 1. Ed. Friedrich Engels, trans. Samuel Moore and Edward Aveling. London: Lawrence and Wishart, 1954.

———. *Grundrisse: Foundations of the Critique of Political Economy.* Trans. Martin Nicolaus. Harmondsworth: Penguin, 1974.

Marx, Karl, and Friedrich Engels. *The Communist Manifesto.* Intro. A. J. P. Taylor. Harmondsworth: Penguin, 1967.

Mather, Celia. "Industrialization in the Tangerang Regency of West Java: Women Workers and the Islamic Patriarchy." *Bulletin of Concerned Asian Scholars* 15, no. 2 (1983): 2–17.

Mazon, Mauricio. *The Zoot-Suit Riots: The Psychology of Symbolic Annihilation.* Austin: University of Texas Press, 1984.

Mazumdar, Sucheta. "General Introduction: A Woman-Centered Perspective on Asian American History." In *Making Waves,* ed. Asian Women United of California. Boston: Beacon Press, 1989.

McCain, Thomas, and G. Ferrel Lowe. "Localism in Western European Radio Broadcasting: Untangling the Wireless." *Journal of Communication* 40, no. 1 (winter 1990): 86–101.

McClintock, Anne. "The Angel of Progress: Pitfalls of the Term 'Post-Colonialism.'" *Social Text* 31–32 (summer 1992): 84–98.

McCoy, Alfred. "Baylan: Animist Religion and Philippine Peasant Ideology." In *Moral Order and Change: Essays in Southeast Asian Thought,* ed. D. Wyatt and A. Woodside. New Haven: Yale Southeast Asia Studies, 1982.

McCoy, Alfred, and Ed de Jesus, eds. *Philippine Social History: Global Trade and Local Transformations.* Quezon City: Ateneo de Manila, 1982.

Medina, Isagani. *Cavite before the Revolution, 1571–1896*. Diliman: University of the Philippines, 1994.

Mehran, Golnar. "Ideology and Education in the Islamic Republic of Iran." *Compare* 20 (1990): 53–65.

Mehran, Golnar. "The Creation of the New Muslim Woman: Female Education in the Islamic Republic of Iran." *Convergence* 24, no. 4 (1991): 42–53.

Mehta, Deepak. "The Semiotics of Weaving: A Case Study." *Contributions of Indian Sociology* 26, no. 1 (January–June 1992): 77–113.

Menchú, Rigoberta, with Elisabeth Burgos-Debray. *Me llamo Rigoberta Menchú y así me nació la conciencia*. Mexico City: Siglo XXI, 1983.

Meng Yue. "Female Images and National Myth." In *Gender Politics in Modern China*, ed. Tani Barlow. Durham: Duke University Press, 1993.

Mercer, Kobena. "Diaspora Culture and the Dialogic Imagination." In *Blackframes: Critical Perspectives on Black Independent Cinema*, ed. M. Cham and C. Watkins. Cambridge, MA: MIT Press, 1988.

Mernissi, Fatima. *The Veil and the Male Elite: A Feminist Interpretation of Women's Rights in Islam*. New York: Addison-Wesley, 1991.

Meyerowitz, Joanne, ed. *Not June Cleaver: Women and Gender in Postwar America, 1945–1960*. Philadelphia: Temple University Press, 1994.

Mies, Maria. *Patriarchy and Accumulation on a World Scale: Women in the International Division of Labor*. London: Zed Press, 1986.

Milkman, Ruth. *Gender at Work: The Dynamics of Job Segregation by Sex during World War II*. Urbana: University of Illinois Press, 1987.

Miller, Neil. *Out in the World: Gay and Lesbian Life from Buenos Aires to Bangkok*. New York: Random House, 1992.

Millett, Kate. *Going to Iran*. New York: Coward, McCann, and Geoghegan, 1982.

Milton, Kay, ed. *Environmentalism: The View from Anthropology*. London: Routledge, 1993.

Ministerio de Planificacion Nacional. *Programa de Reactivacion Economica en Beneficio del Pueblo*. Managua: MIPLAN, 1980.

——. *Programa Economico de Austeridad y Eficiencia*. Managua: MIPLAN, 1981.

Mintz, Sydney. "The Rural Proletariat and the Problem of the Rural Proletarian Consciousness." In *Peasants and Proletarians*, ed. R. Cohen, P. Gutkind, and P. Brazier. New York: Monthly Review Press, 1974.

Mir-Hosseini, Ziba. *Marriage on Trial: A Study of Islamic Law*. London: I. B. Tauris, 1992.

Mitter, Swasti. *Common Fate, Common Bond: Women in the Global Economy*. London: Pluto, 1986.

Miyoshi, Masao. "A Borderless World? From Colonialism to Transnationalism and the Decline of the Nation-State." *Critical Inquiry* 19 (summer 1993): 726–751.

Moghadam, Val. "Women, Work, and Ideology in the Islamic Republic." *International Journal of Middle East Studies* 20 (1988): 221–243.

——. *Modernizing Women: Gender and Social Change in the Middle East*. Boulder, CO: Lynne Rienner Publishers, 1993.

Mohan, Rajeswari. "The Crisis of Femininity and Modernity in the Third World." *Genders* 19 (Fall 1994).

Mohanty, Chandra Talpade. "Feminist Encounters: Locating the Politics of Experience." *Copyright* 1 (1987): 30–44.

———. "Under Western Eyes: Feminist Scholarship and Colonial Discourse." *Feminist Review* 30 (1988): 65–88.

———. "Cartographies of Struggle." In *Third World Women and the Politics of Feminism,* ed. Chandra Talpade Mohanty, Ann Russo, and Lourdes Torres. Bloomington: Indiana University Press, 1991.

———. "Under Western Eyes: Feminist Scholarship and Colonial Discourses." In *Third World Women and the Politics of Feminism,* ed. Chandra Talpade Mohanty, Ann Russo, and Lourdes Torres. Bloomington: Indiana University Press, 1991.

———. "Feminist Encounters: Locating the Politics of Experience." In *Destabilizing Theory,* ed. Michelle Barrett and Anne Phillips. Stanford: Stanford University Press, 1992.

Mohanty, Chandra Talpade, Ann Russo, and Lourdes Torres, eds. *Third World Women and the Politics of Feminism.* Bloomington: Indiana University Press, 1991.

Moore, Henrietta. *Feminism and Anthropology.* Minneapolis: University of Minnesota Press, 1988.

Moraga, Cherríe, and Gloria Anzaldúa, eds. *This Bridge Called My Back: Writings by Radical Women of Color.* New York: Kitchen Table Press, 1981.

Mukherjee, Sushil. *The Story of the Calcutta Theaters: 1753–1980.* Calcutta: Bagchi, 1982.

Mulvey, Laura. "Myth, Narrative, and Historical Experience." *History Workshop,* no. 23 (spring 1987): 3–19.

Muñoz, Carlos. *Youth, Identity, Power: The Chicano Movement.* London: Verso, 1989.

Muto, I. "The Free Trade Zone and Mystique of Export-Oriented Industrialization." *AMPO: Japan-Asian Quarterly Review* 8.4–9.1–2 (1977): 9–32.

Nader, Laura. "Orientalism, Occidentalism and the Control of Women." *Cultural Dynamics* 2, no. 3 (1989): 323–355.

Nairn, Tom. *The Break-up of Britain: Crisis and Neo-Nationalism.* London: New Left Books, 1977.

Nalty, Bernard C. *Strength for the Fight: A History of Black Americans in the Military.* New York: Free Press, 1986.

Nash, June. *We Eat the Mines and the Mines Eat Us.* New York: Columbia University Press, 1983.

Nash, June, and Maria Patricia Fernandez-Kelly, eds. *Women, Men, and the International Division of Labor.* Albany, NY: State University of New York Press, 1983.

Nashat, Guity. Introduction. In *Women from Medieval to Modern Times in Islam,* by Wiebke Walther. New York: Markus Wiener, 1982.

———. "Women in the Ancient Middle East." In *Restoring Women to History: Teaching Packets for Women's History Courses on Africa, Asia, Latin America, the Caribbean, and the Middle East.* Bloomington, IN: Organization of American History, 1988.

Nee, Victor G., and Brett de Bary Nee. *Longtime Californ': A Documentary Study of an American Chinatown.* New York: Pantheon, 1972.

Negri, Antonio, and Michael Hardt. *Labor of Dionysus: Communism as Critique of the Capitalist and Socialist State-Form.* Minneapolis: University of Minnesota Press, 1994.

Negt, Oskar, and Alexander Kluge. *The Public Sphere and Experience.* Trans. Peter Labanyi, Jaime Daniel, and Assenka Oksiloff. Minneapolis: University of Minnesota Press, 1993.

Nelson, Dennis Denmark. "The Integration of the Negro into the United States Navy, 1776–1947." Master's thesis, Howard University, 1948.

Ng, Fae Myenne. *Bone.* New York: Hyperion, 1993.

Nierras, Eduardo R. "This Risky Business of Desire: Theoretical Notes for and against Filipino Gay Male Identity Politics." In *Ladlad: An Anthology of Philippine Gay Writings,* ed. J. N. C. Garcia and D. Remoto. Manila: Anvil Press, 1994.

Norman, Diana. *Terrible Beauty: A Life of Constance Markievicz.* Dublin: Poolbeg, 1991.

Ochoa, Maria, and Teresia Teaiwa, eds. "Enunciating Our Terms: Women of Color in Collaboration and Conflict." *Inscriptions* 7 (1994).

O'Connor, Martin. "On the Misadventures of Capitalist Nature." *Capitalism, Nature, Socialism* 4, no. 4 (1993): 7–34.

Odets, Clifford. *Waiting for Lefty.* In *Six Plays of Clifford Odets.* 1933. Reprint, New York: Random House, 1963.

Oh, Soon Joo. "The Living Conditions of Female Workers in Korea." *Korea Observer* 24, no. 2 (1983): 192–93.

Okihiro, Gary Y. *Cane Fires: The Anti-Japanese Movement in Hawaii, 1865–1945.* Philadelphia: Temple University Press, 1991.

Oliver, Melvin L., and Thomas M. Shapiro. *Black Wealth, White Wealth: A New Perspective on Racial Inequality.* New York: Routledge, 1995.

Omatsu, Glenn. "The 'Four Prisons' and the Movements of Liberation: Asian American Activism from the 1960s to the 1990s." In *State of Asian America: Activism and Resistance in the 1990s,* ed. Karin Aguilar-San Juan. Boston: South End Press, 1994.

Omi, Michael, and Howard Winant. *Racial Formation in the United States, from the 1960s to the 1990s.* New York: Routledge, 1994.

Ong, Aihwa. "Disassembling Gender in an Electronics Age. Review Article." *Feminist Studies* 13 (1987): 609–627.

———. *Spirits of Resistance and Capitalist Discipline: Factory Women in Malaysia.* Albany: State University of New York Press, 1987.

———. "Colonialism and Modernity: Feminist Re-presentations of Women in Non-Western Societies." *Inscriptions* 3–4 (1988): 79–93.

———. "The Production of Possession: Spirits and the Multinational Corporation in Malaysia." *American Ethnologist* 15 (1988): 28–42.

———. "Japanese Factories, Malay Workers: Class and Sexual Metaphors in Malaysia." In *Power and Difference: Gender in Island Southeast Asia,* ed. J. Atkinson and S. Errington. Stanford: Stanford University Press, 1990.

Ong, Paul, Edna Bonacich, and Lucie Cheng, eds. *New Asian Immigration in Los Angeles and Global Restructuring.* Philadelphia: Temple University Press, 1994.

Ormazabal, Sabino. "El movimiento juvenil vasca." Unpublished manuscript.

Padmore, George. *The Life and Struggles of Negro Toilers.* London: The RILU Magazine for the International Trade Union Committee of Negro Workers, 1931.

Pandey, Gyanendra. *The Indian Nation in 1942.* Calcutta: Centre for Studies in Social Sciences, 1988.

———. *The Construction of Communalism in Colonial North India.* Delhi: Oxford University Press, 1992.

Pandey, Sudhakar, et al., eds. *Studies in Contemporary Indian Drama.* Delhi: Indian Society for Commonwealth Studies, 1990.

Pani, Narendar. *Staging a Change.* Bangalore: Samudaya Prakashana, 1979.

Parish, Helen-Rand, and Harold E. Weidman. *Las Casas en México: Historia y obra desconocidas.* Mexico City: Fondo de Cultura Económica, 1992.

Pastner, C. M. "Englishmen in Arabia: Encounters with Middle Eastern Women." *Signs* 4, no. 2 (1978): 309–323.

Patajo-Legasto, Priscelina. "Philippine Contemporary Theater, 1946–1985: A Materialist Analysis." Ph.D. diss., University of the Philippines, 1988.

Patel, Pragna. "Alert for Action — Women Living under Muslim Laws, Dossiers 1–6." *Feminist Review* 37 (spring 1991): 95–102.

Payne, Charles M. *I've Got the Light of Freedom: The Organizing Tradition and the Mississippi Freedom Struggle.* Berkeley: University of California Press, 1995.

Pena, D. "Tortuosidad: Shopfloor Struggles of Female Maquiladora Workers." In *Women on the U.S.-Mexican Border,* ed. Vicky Ruiz and Susan Tiano. Boston: Allen & Unwin, 1987.

Perez, Tony. *Cubao 1980 at iba pang katha: Unang Sigaw ng Gay Liberation Movement sa Pilipinas* (Cubao 1980 and other works: The first cry of the gay liberation movement in the Philippines). Manila: Cacho Publishing House, 1992.

Phelan, John. *The Hispanization of the Philippines: Spanish Aims and Filipino Responses, 1565–1700.* Madison: University of Wisconsin, 1967.

Pietz, William. "The 'Post-Colonialism' of Cold War Discourse." *Social Text* 19–20 (spring 1988): 55–75.

Pinchbeck, I. *Women Workers and the Industrial Revolution, 1750–1850.* 1930. Reprint, London: Virago, 1981.

Pineda-Ofreneo, R. "Sub-contracting in Export-Oriented Industries: Impact on Filipino Working Women." In *Development and Displacement: Women in Southeast Asia,* ed. G. Chandler, N. Sullivan, and J. Branson. Clayton, Australia: Monash University Papers on Southeast Asia, no. 18, 1988.

Plummer, Brenda Gayle. *Rising Wind: Black Americans and U.S. Foreign Affairs, 1935–1960.* Chapel Hill: University of North Carolina Press, 1996.

Plummer, Ken. "Speaking Its Name: Inventing a Gay and Lesbian Studies." In *Modern Homosexualities: Fragments of Lesbian and Gay Experience,* ed. K. Plummer. London: Routledge, 1992.

Pocock, J. G. A. *The Ancient Constitution and the Feudal Law.* 1957. Reprint, Cambridge: Cambridge University Press, 1990.

Pok Kŏ-il. *Pimyongul ch'ajasŏ: Keijō Showa 62.* Seoul: Munhakkwa Chisŏngsa, 1987.

Poovey, Mary. *Uneven Developments: The Ideological Work of Gender in Mid-Victorian England.* London: Virago Press, 1989.

Portes, Alejandro, M. Castells, and L. Benton. *The Informal Economy.* Baltimore: Johns Hopkins University Press, 1989.

Pradhan, Sudhi, ed. *Marxist Cultural Movement in India: Chronicles and Documents. 1936–47.* Calcutta: National Book Agency, 1979.

——, ed. *Marxist Cultural Movement in India: Chronicles and Documents. 1947–1958.* Vol. 2. Calcutta: Navana, 1982.

——, ed. *Marxist Cultural Movement in India: Chronicles and Documents. 1947–1964.* Calcutta: Mrs Santi Pradhan, 1985.

Prakash, Gyan. *Bonded Histories: Genealogies of Labor Servitude in Colonial India.* Cambridge: Cambridge University Press, 1990.

Pred, Alan. "In Other Wor(l)ds: Fragmented and Integrated Observations on Gendered Languages, Gendered Spaces, and Local Transformations." *Antipode* 22, no. 1 (1990): 33–52.

Preston, P. W. *Theories of Development.* London: Routledge and Kegan Paul, 1982.

Qu Wen. "A Brief Account of the Current Status of Research on Women." Unpublished report, Women's Research Institute of the Women's Federation, n.d.

Rabasa, José. "Aesthetics of Colonial Violence: The Massacre of Acoma in Gaspar de Villagrá's *Historia de la nueva México.*" *College Literature* 20, no. 3 (1993): 96–114.

Rabasa, José. "Pre-Columbian Pasts and Indian Presents in Mexican History." In *Subaltern Studies in the Americas,* ed. Robert Carr, José Rabasa, and Javier Sanjinés. Special issue, *Dispositio/n* 46 (1994): 245–270.

——. " 'Porque soy Indio': Subjectivity in *La Florida del Inca.*" *Poetics Today* 16, no. 1 (1995): 79–108.

Rabasa, José, and Javier Sanjinés. "Introduction: The Politics of Subaltern Studies." In *Subaltern Studies in the Americas,* ed. Robert Carr, José Rabasa, and Javier Sanjinés. Special issue, *Dispositio/n* 46 (1994): v–xi.

Rabinow, Paul. "Artificiality and Enlightenment: From Sociobiology to Biosociality." In *Incorporations,* ed. J. Crary and S. Kwinter. New York: Zone Books, 1992.

Radhakrishnan, Radha. "Nationalism, Gender and the Narrative of Identity." In *Nationalisms and Sexualities,* ed. Andrew Parker et al. New York: Routledge, 1992.

Rafael, Vicente. "Anticipating Nationhood: Collaboration and Rumor in the Japanese Occupation of Manila." *Diaspora* 1 (1991): 67–87.

——. *Contracting Colonialism: Translation and Christian Conversion in Tagalog Society under Early Spanish Rule.* Durham: Duke University Press, 1993.

Raha, Kironmoy. *Bengali Theatre*. New Delhi: National Book Trust, 1978.

Rawick, George P. *From Sundown to Sunup*. Westport, CT: Greenwood Press, 1972.

Razack, Sherene. "What Is to Be Gained by Looking White People in the Eye? Culture, Race, and Gender in Cases of Sexual Violence." *Signs* 19, no. 4 (1994): 894–923.

Redclift, Nanneke, and M. Thea Sinclair, eds. *Working Women: International Perspectives on Labour and Gender Ideology*. London: Routledge, 1991.

Remoto, Danton. *Seduction and Solitude: Essays*. Manila: Anvil Press, 1995.

Richmond, Farley. "The Political Role of Theatre in India." *Educational Theatre Journal* (October 1973): 318–334.

———. *Indian Theatre: Traditions of Performance*. Honolulu: University of Hawaii Press, 1990.

Rivera, Temario, et al., eds. *Feudalism and Capitalism in the Philippines*. Quezon City: Foundation for Nationalist Studies, 1982.

Robinson, Cedric. *Black Marxism: The Making of the Black Radical Tradition*. London: Zed Books, 1982.

Robinson, Michael C., and Frank N. Schubert. "David Fagen: An Afro-American Rebel in the Philippines, 1899–1901." *Pacific Historical Review* 64, no. 1 (February 1975): 69–83.

Rofel, Lisa. "Hegemony and Productivity: Workers in Post-Mao China." In *Marxism and the Chinese Experience*, ed. A. Dirlik and M. Meisner. Armonk, NY: M. E. Sharpe, 1989.

Romero, César. *Marcos: ¿Un profesional de la esperanza?* Mexico City: Editorial Planeta, 1994.

Romero, Mary. *Maid in the U.S.A.* New York: Routledge, 1992.

Rosenberg, C. E. "Cholera in Nineteenth-Century Europe: A Tool for Social and Economic Analysis." *Comparative Studies in Society and History* 8 (1966).

Ross, John. *Rebellion from the Roots: Indian Uprising in Chiapas*. Monroe, ME: Common Courage Press, 1995.

Rostow, W. W. *Stages of Growth: A Non-Communist Manifesto*. Cambridge: Cambridge University Press, 1960.

Rubin, I. I. *Essays on Marx's Theory of Value*. Montreal: Black Rose Books, 1975.

Ruccio, David. F. "The State and Planning in Nicaragua." In *The Political Economy of Revolutionary Nicaragua*, ed. Rose J. Spaulding. Boston: Allen and Unwin, 1987.

Rugh, Andrea. *Reveal and Conceal: Dress in Contemporary Egypt*. Syracuse, NY: Syracuse University Press, 1986.

Ruiz, Vicki. *Cannery Women, Cannery Lives: Mexican Women, Unionization, and the California Food Processing Industry, 1930–1950*. Albuquerque: University of New Mexico, 1987.

Ruiz, Vicki, and Susan Tiano, eds. *Women on the U.S.-Mexican Border*. Boston: Allen & Unwin, 1987.

Sahgal, Gita. "Fundamentalism and the Multi-Culturalist Fallacy." In *Against the Grain: A Celebration of Struggle and Survival*, ed. Southall Black Sisters. Southall: Southall Black Sisters, 1990.

———. "Secular Spaces: The Experiences of Asian Women Organising." In *Refusing Holy Orders,* ed. Gita Sahgal and Nira Yuval-Davis. London: Virago, 1991.

Sahni, Balraj. *Balraj Sahni: An Autobiography.* Delhi: Hind Pocket Books, 1979.

Said, Edward. *Orientalism.* London: Routledge and Kegan Paul, 1978.

———. "Traveling Theory." In *The World, the Text and the Critic.* Cambridge, MA: Harvard University Press, 1983.

———. *Culture and Imperialism.* New York: Knopf, 1993.

Salaff, Janet. *Working Daughters of Hong Kong.* Cambridge: Cambridge University Press, 1981.

Saldaña, María Josefina. "The Discourse of Development and Narratives of Resistance." Ph.D. diss., Stanford University, 1993.

Sanasarian, Eliz. *The Women's Rights Movement in Iran.* New York: Praeger, 1982.

Sánchez de Friedemann, Nina. *Críele Críele Son.* Bogotá: Planeta, 1989.

Sandoval, Chela. "U.S. Third World Feminism: The Theory and Method of Oppositional Consciousness in the Postmodern World." *Genders* 10 (spring 1991): 1–24.

Sangari, Kumkum, and Sudesh Vaid, eds. *Recasting Women: Essays in Indian Colonial History.* New Brunswick, NJ: Rutgers University Press, 1990.

Sarkar, Sumit. *Modern India, 1885–1947.* Delhi: Macmillan, 1983.

Sassen-Koob, Saskia. "Notes on the Incorporation of Third World Women into Wage Labor through Immigration and Off-Shore Production." *International Migration Review* 13 (1984): 1144–1167.

Saulaiers, Alfred H. "State Trading Organization in Expansion." In *Nicaragua: Profiles of the Revolutionary Public Sector,* ed. Michael E. Conroy. Boulder, CO: Westview Press, 1987.

Scheper-Hughes, Nancy. "The Subversive Body: Illness and the Micropolitics of Resistance." In *Anthropology in the 1990s,* ed. R. Borowski. New York: McGraw Hill, 1991.

Schumacher, John, S. J. "The Propagandists' Reconstruction of the Philippine Past." In *Perceptions of the Past in Southeast Asia,* ed. A. Reid and D. Marr. Singapore: Heinemann, 1979.

Scott, James C. *Weapons of the Weak: Everyday Forms of Peasant Resistance.* New Haven: Yale University Press, 1985.

———. "Everyday Forms of Resistance." In *Everyday Forms of Peasant Resistance,* ed. Forrest D. Colburn. London: M. E. Sharpe, 1989.

Scott, William Henry. *Cracks in the Parchment Curtain.* Quezon City: New Day, 1982.

Seler, Eduard. "Wall Paintings of Mitla: A Mexican Picture Writing in Fresco." In *Eduard Seler: Collected Works in Mesoamerican Linguistics and Archaeology.* 4 vols. Trans. Charles P. Bowditch. Culver City, CA: Labrinthos, 1990–1993.

Sen, Amartya K. *Poverty and Famines: An Essay on Entitlement and Deprivation.* Delhi: Oxford University Press, 1981.

Sen, Dinesh Chandra. *History of Bengali Language and Literature.* Calcutta: University of Calcutta, 1911.

Sen, S. N. *Eighteen Fifty-Seven.* Foreword by Maulana Abul Kalam Azad. Delhi:

Publications Division, Ministry of Information and Broadcasting, Government of India, 1957.

Sen, Sukumar. *Bangala sahityer itihas* (in Bengali). Vol. 1. Calcutta: Ananda Publishers, 1978.

Shiva, Vandana. *Monocultures of the Mind: Perspectives on Biodiversity and Biotechnology.* London: Zed Books, 1993.

——, ed. *Close to Home: Women Reconnect Ecology, Health and Development Worldwide.* London: Zed Books, 1994.

Shohat, Ella. "Notes on the 'Post-Colonial.'" *Social Text* 31–32 (summer 1992): 99–113.

Silverstein, Ken, and Alexander Cockburn. "The Killers and the Killing." *The Nation* 260, no. 9 (1995): 306–311.

Siriporn, S. "In Pursuit of an Illusion: Thai Women in Europe." *Southeast Asia Chronicle* 96 (1985): 7–12.

Sivanandan, A. "All That Melts into Air Is Solid." *Race and Class* 31, no. 3 (January–March 1990): 1–30.

Smyth, Ailbhe. "States of Change: Reflections on Ireland in Several Uncertain Parts." *Feminist Review* 50 (Summer 1995), special issue, *The Irish Issue, the British Question,* 24–43.

Sommer, Doris. "Resisting the Heat: Menchú, Morrison, and Incompetent Readers." In *Cultures of U.S. Imperialism,* ed. Amy Kaplan and Donald E. Pease. Durham: Duke University Press, 1993.

Southall Black Sisters, ed. *Against the Grain: A Celebration of Struggle and Survival.* Southall: Southall Black Sisters, 1990.

Spalding, Rose J., ed. *The Political Economy of Revolutionary Nicaragua.* Boston: Allen and Unwin, 1987.

Spivak, Gayatri Chakravorty. "Can the Subaltern Speak?" In *Marxism and the Interpretation of Culture,* ed. Cary Nelson and Lawrence Grossberg. Urbana: University of Illinois, 1988.

——. "Subaltern Studies: Deconstructing Historiography." In *Selected Subaltern Studies,* ed. R. Guha and G. C. Spivak. New York: Oxford University Press, 1988.

——. "Politics of Translation." In *Outside in the Teaching Machine.* New York: Routledge, 1993.

——. "Supplementing Marx." In *Whither Marxism?: Global Crises in International Perspective,* ed. Bernd Magnus and Stephen Cullenberg. New York: Routledge, 1995.

Stallybass, Peter, and Allon White. *The Politics and Poetics of Transgression.* Ithaca: Cornell University Press, 1986.

Stonewall 25 Committee. *New York Pride Guide.* New York: Pride Publishing, Inc., 1994.

Strathern, Marilyn, ed. *Dealing with Inequality.* Cambridge: Cambridge University Press, 1987.

Stroper, M., and R. Walker. *The Capitalist Imperative: Territory, Technology, and Industrial Growth.* New York: Basic Blackwell, 1989.

Sturtevant, David. *Popular Uprisings in the Philippines, 1840–1940.* Ithaca: Cornell University Press, 1976.

Sullivan, R. J. *Exemplar of Americanism: The Philippine Career of Dean C. Worcester.* Ann Arbor: University of Michigan Press, 1991.

Sun, Lung-kee. "Historians' Warp: Problems in Textualizing the Intellectual History of Modern China." *positions* 2, no. 2 (1994): 356–381.

Sun, Soon Hua. "Women, Work, and Theology in Korea." *Journal of Feminist Studies in Religion* 3 (1987): 125–134.

Suratgar, Olive Hepburn. *I Sing in the Wilderness: An Intimate Account of Persia and Persians.* London: Edward Stanford, 1951.

Swann Committee. *Education for All.* Report of the Committee of Enquiry into the Education of Children of Ethnic Minority Groups. London: HMSO, 1985.

Tabari, Azar, and Nahid Yeganeh. *In the Shadows of Islam: The Women's Movement in Iran.* London: Zed Press, 1982.

Takezawa, Yasuko I. *Breaking the Silence: Redress and Japanese American Ethnicity.* Ithaca: Cornell University Press, 1995.

Tan, Michael L. "From Bakla to Gay: Shifting Gender Identities and Sexual Behaviors in the Philippines." In *Conceiving Sexuality: Approaches to Sex Research in a Postmodern World,* ed. John Gagnon and Richard Parker. New York: Routledge, 1995.

Tanaka, Stefan. *Japan's Orient: Rendering Pasts into History.* Berkeley: University of California Press, 1993.

Taussig, Michael. "Reification and the Consciousness of the Patient." *Social Science and Medicine* 14B (1980): 3–13.

———. *The Devil and Commodity Fetishism in South America.* Chapel Hill: University of North Carolina Press, 1984.

Tavakoli-Targhi, Mohammed. "The Exotic Europeans and the Reconstruction of Femininity in Iran." Paper presented at Middle East Studies Association of North America, 25th annual meeting, Georgetown University, Washington, DC, November 23–26, 1991.

Taylor, F. W. *Two Papers on Scientific Management.* London: Routledge and Sons, 1919.

Taylor, Quintard. "Blacks and Asians in a White City: Japanese Americans and African Americans in Seattle, 1890–1940." *Western Historical Quarterly* 23, no. 4 (November 1991): 401–430.

———. *The Forging of a Black Community: Seattle's Central District from 1870 through the Civil Rights Era.* Seattle: University of Washington Press, 1994.

Terray, Emmanuel. *Le Troisième Jour du Communisme.* Arles: Actes Sud, 1992.

Tharu, Susie, and K. Lalita, eds. Introduction. In *Women Writing in India: 600 B.C. to the Present.* Vol. 2. *The Twentieth Century.* New York: Feminist Press, 1993.

Thompson, E. P. *The Making of the English Working Class.* New York: Vintage, 1963.

———. "Time, Work Discipline, and Industrial Capitalism." *Past and Present* 38 (1967): 56–97.

———. "The Moral Economy of the English Crowd in the Eighteenth Century." *Past and Present* 50 (February 1971): 76–136.

Tiano, Susan. "Maquiladoras in Mexico: Integration or Exploitation?" In *Women on the U.S.-Mexican Border,* ed. Vicki Ruiz and Susan Tiano. Boston: Allen & Unwin, 1987.

Tielman, Rob, and Hans Hammelburg. "World Survey on the Social and Legal Position of Gays and Lesbians." In *The Third Pink Book: A Global View of Lesbian Gay Liberation and Oppression,* ed. A. Hendriks et al. Buffalo: Prometheus Books, 1993.

Tillion, Germaine. *The Republic of Cousin: Women's Oppression in Mediterranean Society.* French edition 1966. Printed in English, London: Al Saqi Books, 1983.

Torres-Reyes, Lulu. "Anticipating Hegemony: Brecht and the Philippines Today." *Makisa* 1, no. 1 (1st quarter 1989): 18–19.

Trejo Delarbre, Raúl, ed. *Chiapas: La Guerra de las Ideas.* Mexico City: Editorial Diana, 1994.

Tretiakov, Sergei Mikhailovich. *Roar China.* Bombay: The Indian People's Theatre Association, Dramatics for National Defence, 1942.

Troung, Thanh-Dam. *Sex, Money, and Morality: Prostitution and Tourism in Southeast Asia.* London: Zed Books, 1990.

Tsuchiya, T. "Introduction." *AMPO*: Japan-Asian Quarterly Review 8.4–9.1–2 (1977): 1–32.

Tucker, Judith E. *Women in Nineteenth-Century Egypt.* Cambridge: Cambridge University Press, 1986.

Urla, Jacqueline. "Cultural Politics in an Age of Statistics: Numbers, Nations and the Making of Basque Identity." *American Ethnologist* 20, no. 4 (1993): 818–843.

Urzúa, Camú, and Tótoro Taulis. *EZLN, el ejercito que salio de la silva.* México: Grupo Editorial Planeta, 1994.

Utting, Peter. "Domestic Supply and Food Shortages." In *The Political Economy of Revolutionary Nicaragua,* ed. Rose J. Spalding. Boston: Allen and Unwin, 1987.

Van Erven, Eugene. "Imagining a Post-Development Era? Critical Thought, Development and Social Movements." *Social Text* 31–32 (1992): 20–56.

———. *The Playful Revolution: Theatre and Liberation in Asia.* Bloomington: Indiana University Press, 1992.

Veneracion, Jaime. Review of Ferdinand Marcos's *Tadhana* in *Kasaysayan* 1 (University of the Philippines) (November 1977): 213–216.

Vera Herrera, Ramón. "Relojes japoneses." *Ojarasca* 44 (1995): 20–25.

Veyne, Paul. *Writing History: Essays on Epistemology.* Trans. Mina Moore-Rinvolucri. Middletown, CT: Wesleyan University Press, 1984.

Vilas, Carlos. *The Sandinista Revolution.* New York: Monthly Review Press, 1986.

Vincent, Joan. *Teso in Transformation.* Berkeley: University of California Press, 1982.

Viswanathan, Gauri. *Masks of Conquest: Literary Studies and British Rule in India.* New York: Columbia University Press, 1989.

Wade, Peter. *Blackness and Race Mixture: The Dynamics of Racial Identity in Colombia.* Baltimore: Johns Hopkins University Press, 1993.

Walker, Cheryl. "Feminist Criticism and the Author." *Critical Inquiry* 16 (spring 1990): 551–571.

Wallerstein, Immanuel. *The Modern World-System.* Vol. 1. New York: Academic Press, 1974.

——. "The Construction of Peoplehood: Racism, Nationalism, Ethnicity." In *Race, Nation, Class: Ambiguous Identities,* ed. Etienne Balibar and Immanuel Wallerstein. Trans. of Etienne Balibar by Chris Turner. London: Verso, 1991.

Waltz, Michael L. "The Indian People's Theatre Association: Its Development and Influences." *Journal of South Asian Literature* 13, nos. 1–4 (1977–1978): 31–37.

Wan Shanping. "The Emergence of Women's Studies in China." *Women's Studies International Forum* 2, no. 5 (1988): 455–464.

Wang Hui. "The Fate of Mr. Science in China." In *Formations of Colonial Modernity in East Asia,* ed. T. E. Barlow. Durham: Duke University Press, 1997.

Wang, Jing. *High Culture Fever: Politics, Aesthetics, and Ideology in Deng's China.* Berkeley: University of California Press, 1996.

Wang, Lingzhen. "Retheorizing the Personal: Identity, Writing and Gender in Xu Luojin's Autobiographical Acts." *positions* 6, no. 1, forthcoming.

Wang Zheng. "Research on Women in Contemporary China — Problems and Promises." Unpublished manuscript, 1993.

——, trans. and ed. "Three Interviews: Wang Anyi, Zhu Lin, Dai Qing." In *Gender Politics in Modern China,* ed. Tani Barlow. Durham: Duke University Press, 1993.

Ward, Margaret. *Maud Gonne: Ireland's Joan of Arc.* London: Pandora, 1990.

Warman, Arturo. *"We Came to Object": The Peasants of Morelos and the National State.* Trans. Stephen K. Ault. Baltimore: Johns Hopkins University Press, 1980.

Weber, Max. *The Protestant Ethic and the Spirit of Capitalism.* Trans. T. Parsons. New York: Charles Scribner & Sons, 1958.

Weeks, John. "The Mixed Economy in Nicaragua." In *The Political Economy of Nicaragua,* ed. Rose J. Spaulding. Boston: Allen and Unwin, 1987.

Weizsacker, Christine von. "Competing Notions of Biodiversity." In *Global Ecology,* ed. W. Sachs. London: Zed Books, 1993.

Westbrook, Robert B. " 'I Want a Girl Just Like the Girl That Married Harry James': American Women and the Problem of Political Obligation in World War II." *American Quarterly* 24, no. 4 (December 1990): 587–614.

Whelan, Kevin. "Come All Ye Blinkered Nationalists: A Post-Revisionist Agenda for Irish History." *Irish Reporter* 2 (2d quarter 1991): 24–26.

White, Walter, and Thurgood Marshall. *What Caused the Detroit Riot? An Analysis by Walter White and Thurgood Marshall.* New York: National Association for the Advancement of Colored People, 1943.

Whitten, Norman. *Black Frontiersmen: Afro-Hispanic Culture of Ecuador and Colombia.* Prospect Heights, IL: Waveland Press, 1986.

Wikan, Unni. *Behind the Veil in Arabia.* Chicago: University of Chicago Press, 1982.

Williams, Brackette F. *Stains on My Name, Blood in My Veins: Guyana and the Politics of Cultural Struggle.* Durham: Duke University Press, 1991.

Williams, Raymond. *The Country and the City.* Oxford: Oxford University Press, 1973.

———. *Marxism and Literature.* Oxford: Oxford University Press, 1977.

———. *Politics and Letters.* London: Verso, 1979.

Willis, Paul. *Learning to Labor: How Working Class Kids Get Working Class Jobs.* New York: Columbia University Press, 1977.

Wilson, Edward O. *The Diversity of Life.* New York: Norton, 1992.

Wolf, Diane L. *Factory Daughters: Gender, Household Dynamics, and Rural Industrialization in Java.* Berkeley: University of California Press, 1992.

Womack, John. *Zapata and the Mexican Revolution.* Harmondsworth: Penguin, 1972.

Wong, Diane Yen-Mei, and Dennis Hayashi. "Behind Unmarked Doors: Developments in the Garment Industry." In *Making Waves: An Anthology of Writings by and about Asian American Women,* ed. Asian Women United of California. New York: Beacon, 1989.

Woodhull, Winifred. "Unveiling Algeria." *Genders* 10 (1991): 112–131.

Worcester, Dean C. *History of Asiatic Cholera in the Philippines.* Manila: Bureau of Printing, 1909.

———. *The Philippines Past and Present.* New York: Macmillan, 1914.

World Resources Institute. *Biodiversity Prospecting.* Oxford: Oxford University Press, 1993.

World Resources Institute, World Conservation Union, United Nations Environmental Program. *Global Diversity Strategy.* Washington, DC: WRI/IUNC/UNEP, 1991.

Xiung Yumei, Liu Ciaocong, and Qu Wen, eds. *Zhongguo funü lilum yanjiu shinian* (Women's theoretic studies in China, 1981–1990). Beijing: Zhongguo funü chubanshe, 1992.

Xu Xiaoqun. "The Discourse on Love, Marriage, and Sexuality in Post-Mao China; or, A Reading of the New Journalistic Literature on Women." *positions* 4, no. 2 (1996): 381–414.

Yadav, Alok. "Nationalism and Contemporaneity: Political Economy of a Discourse." *Cultural Critique* 22 (winter 1993–94): 191–229.

Yi Kwang-ho. "Migunjŏn'gŭi kyoyukchŏngch'aek" (The education policy of the American military government). In *Haebang chŏnhusaŭi insik* (Understanding pre- and postliberation history). Vol. 2, ed. Kang Man-gil et al. Seoul: Hangilsa, 1985.

Yi Wan-bŏm. "Haebang 3 nyŏnsaŭi chaengjŏm" (Issues of debate on the history of the three years after the liberation). In *Haebang chŏnhusaŭi insik* (Understanding pre- and postliberation history). Vol. 6, ed. Pak Myong-nim et al. Seoul: Hangilsa, 1989.

Yinger, J. Milton. *A Minority Group in American Society.* New York: McGraw-Hill, 1965.

Young, G. "Gender Identification and Working-Class Solidarity among Maquila Workers in Cuidad Juarez: Stereotypes and Realities." In *Women on the U.S.-Mexican Border,* ed. Vicki Ruiz and Susan Tiano. Boston: Allen & Unwin, 1987.

Young, K., C. Wolkowitz, and R. McCullagh, eds. *Of Marriage and the Market.* London: CSE Books, 1981.

Yu Yan, "Nüseing renxue: jiangou yü zhanwang" (Women's anthropology: Establishment and future prospects). In *Zhongguo funü lilun yanjiu shinian* (Women's theoretic studies in China, 1981–1990), ed. Xiung Yumei, Liu Ciaocong, and Qu Wen. Beijing: Zhongguo funü chubanshe, 1992.

Yuval-Davis, Nira. "Women and Empowerment." In *Feminism and Psychology.* Boulder, CO: Sage, 1994.

Yuval-Davis, Nira, and Floya Anthias. *Women–Nation–State.* London: Macmillan, 1989.

Zhang Jingyuan. "Sigmund Freud and Modern Chinese Literature, 1919–1949." Ph.D. diss., Cornell University, University Microform Index, 1989.

Zhao Xiaoming and Wang Wei. "The Discourse of the 'Imperial Subject,' Its Blind Spots and Limitations: On the Scholarly Work of Liu Zaifu." *Dushu* 6 (1989): 00.

Zito, Angela, and Tani E. Barlow, eds. *Body, Subject and Power in China.* Chicago: University of Chicago Press, 1994.

Žižek, Slavoj. *The Sublime Object of Ideology.* London: Verso, 1989.

Zheng, Husheng. *Shanguhua Xia yü hunyin* (Ancient Chinese woman and marriage). Zhengzhou: Henan renmin chubanshe, 1988.

Zhongzhou University Women's Center, *Dangdai shijie nüchao yü nüxue* (Woman tide and women's studies). Zhongzhoe: Henan renmin chubanshe, 1990.

INDEX

Abbas, Khwaja Ahmed, 434, 446, 449, 450, 452

Abu-Jamal, Mumia, 303, 321

Abyssinia. *See* Ethiopia

Adam, Barry: *The Pink Book*, 488–90, 493

Adorno, Theodor, 189–90, 313–14

Africa(n), 4, 5, 174, 332, 343; diaspora, 218. *See also* North Africa; Pan-Africanism

African American(s), 5, 25, 324–48 passim; Black Panthers, 303, 305–7, 344; gays and lesbians, 500; middle classes, 303; movement, 303, 305–7, 310; Nation of Islam, 305, 329, 330, 333; National Association for the Advancement of Colored People, 336–38, 345; Southern Christian Leadership Conference, 332; Student Nonviolent Coordinating Committee, 306, 310, 332; women: 25, 304, 306, 308, 310–11, 316–18. *See also* Civil Rights movement (USA)

African-Carribean(s), 5, 227–45 passim; music, 285; women (in Britain), 5, 25, 376–79

Afro-Columbian(s), 5, 25, 204–5, 207, 209, 213–23

Agoncillo, Teodoro, 99–100, 104

Aguinaldo, Emilio, 118, 123, 185

Alexander, M. Jacqui, 317, 30 n.27

Algeria, 282. *See also* Fanon, Frantz

Althusser, Louis, 133, 190; *Reading Capital* (with Etienne Balibar), 14, 359–60

Anand, Mulk Raj, 445–46

Anderson, Benedict, 4, 173, 181, 287

Anglo-Irish War (1919–22), 183

Anzaldúa, Gloria, 309

Appadurai, Arjun, 502

Aristide, Jean Bertrand, 241–42, 244

Asad, Talal, 387

Asia, 20, 23, 24, 61–66, 67–71, 74, 80–2, 318, 358–59, 360, 363–64. *See also* China; Hong Kong; India; Japan; Malaysia; Philippines; Singapore; South Korea; Sri Lanka; Taiwan; Thailand; Vietnam

Asian Americans, 303, 327, 331, 340, 342–44, 354–70; immigrant workers, 25, 319–20, 354–70; movement, 303, 344; women, 310, 316, 317, 321. *See also* Civil Rights movement (USA)

Asian Immigrant Womens Advocates, AIWA (USA), 310, 317, 320, 354–56, 364–65

Asian Women's Health Organization (USA), 317

Bakhtin, Mikhail, 293, 475

Bakla, 491–500

Baldwin, James, 341

Balibar, Etienne, 7; *Reading Capital* (with Louis Althusser), 14, 359–60

Barthes, Roland, 422

Basque Nationalist Party (PVN), 287

Basque, language, 289–93; radio, 5, 282–88; region, 281–83, 290–91

Baudrillard, Jean, 466, 467, 469

Beneria, Lourdes, 65, 79

Bengal, 46, 47, 53, 433, 434, 438; language of, 37, 38, 46–47, 49; popular theatre of, 433–38; workers in, 16, 53–54. *See also* India

Haldane, J. B. S., 36

Hall, Stuart, 218, 227, 304

Haraway, Donna, 27 n.6, 201, 424

Harvey, David, 1, 68

Hawaii, 335, 338–39, 346

Hegel, Georg, 51, 312, 408

Heidegger, Martin, 49

Henry, Michel, 53

Himes, Chester, 335–36, 340, 345–46

History and Class Consciousness (Lukács), 314

Hitler, Adolf, 333–34, 337, 342, 435

Ho, Chi Minh, 329

Hobsbawm, Eric, 8, 115, 117, 173, 176, 178

Hong Kong, 65, 67, 71, 81, 354, 363; women workers in, 68, 69, 80

Hoover, J. Edgar, 305, 335

Hwang Sog-yong: *Hawk of Changsan'got,* 475

Ileto, Reynaldo, 188

Immigration and Nationality Act of 1965 (USA), 319, 361, 367

India, 5, 6, 35–52, 56, 106, 432–53 passim; Hindu-Muslim relations, 377, 448–49; feminism in, 381, 452. *See also* South Asia(n)

Indian People's Theatre Association, 11, 26, 432–53 passim

Indigenous movements. *See* Comité Clandestino Revolucionario Indigéna Comandancia General; Mexico; Native American(s)

Indonesia, 26, 209

International African Service Bureau, IASB (UK), 237, 240, 242–244

International Lesbian and Gay Association (ILGA), 486, 488, 490, 493

International Monetary Fund (IMF), 48, 62

Iran, 250, 251, 254, 257, 258–67, 272–73; women in, 250, 251, 257, 258–67, 272–73; women in Britain, 375, 386

Ireland (Irish), 11, 178, 183–84, 192; Anglo-Irish War, 183; British colonialism, 183–84; feminism in, 11, 183–84, 189; Free State, 184, 189; Marxist republican socialism, 183; nationalism, 178, 183–84, 192; Northern Ireland, 385; women in Britain, 5, 25, 375, 384–86, 393

Irish Women's Abortion Support Group, IWASG (UK), 385

Islam, 46–47, 75, 248, 251, 253–54, 258, 264, 272, 377, 382, 391; Bengali Islam, 45–47; constructions of Islam and Muslims, 248–50, 253, 254–57, 267, 382; Hindu-Muslim relations, 377, 448–49; Islamic nationalism, 174; Julahas, 43–44; Nation of Islam, 305, 329, 330, 333. *See also* Women, Muslim

Jackson, George, 307

James, C. L. R., 4, *The Black Jacobins,* 227–45

Jameson, Fredric, 1, 27 n.1–2, 60 n.25, 371 n.7

JanMohamed, Abdul, 462, 463, 476

Japan, 5, 64, 66, 229; colonialism in Korea, 461, 465–70; colonialism in Southeast Asia, 435–36, 438; "Great Co-Prosperity Sphere," 64; India, relations with, 433, 435–36, 438, 442; Japanese army, 25, 324, 326, 330, 331, 332, 342; occupation of Philippines, 125, 185; transnational corporations, 63, 64, 71, 72, 365; U.S. war with, 5, 327, 331, 342–43

Japanese Americans, 332, 336–41, 344; Alien Land Laws, 340–41; internment, 5, 338, 340; Japanese American Citizens League (JACL), 337. *See also* Asian Americans

Maoism (China), 12, 506–12, 514–18, 521, 523, 535; Maoism (Philippines. *See* Guerrero, Amado), Marxist republican socialism (Ireland), 188; national Marxism ("third world"), 3, 12, 14, 24, 104, 183, 185; neo-Marxism, 133, 471; Pan-Africanism, and, 228, 236–42; political praxis, 7, 11, 46, 133, 178, 360; Third International, 236, 239; Trotskyism, 236, 239; Western Marxism, 2–4, 12–16. *See also* Communist Party; Gramsci, Antonio; Marx, Karl

May Fourth Movement (China), 524, 531, 533

Mazzini, Giuseppe, 178

McClintock, Anne, 461, 462

Memmi, Albert, 467

Menchú, Rigoberta, 424

Meng Yue, 507, 516, 534

Mexican American(s), 331, 337–45. *See also* Chicano/a(s)

Mexico, 20, 21, 62, 64, 66, 67, 72, 79, 318–19, 320–21, 363, 365, 399–425 passim; Ciudad Juarez, 74, 75–76, 78–79; *indio(s)* (Indians), 399, 411–25; Mexican revolution, 409, 411, 413; Tijuana, 365; women workers, 75, 78, 82, 318–19, 361, 363, 365. *See also* U.S.-Mexico border

Middle East. *See* Iran, Egypt

Mies, Maria, 15, 22

Millet, Kate, 266–67

Mintz, Sydney, 77

Mitra, Shimbu, 434, 438

Mitter, Swasti, 15, 22

Mohanty, Chandra Talpade, 17, 30 n.27, 309, 356, 365

Monsiváis, Carlos, 399, 401, 404

Moraga, Cherríe, 309, 363, 371–72 n.11

Morrison, Toni, 308

Muhammad, Elijah, 300, 329, 333

Mulvey, Laura, 327

Muslim. *See* Islam

Mussolini, Benito, 435

Nairn, Tom, 173, 175, 176

Nash, June, 77

National Association for the Advancement of Colored People, NAACP (USA), 336–38, 345

National Coalition Against Domestic Violence (USA), 317

National Democratic Front, NDF (Philippines), 103, 104

Nationalism, 6–11, 16–17, 179–92; anticolonial, 6, 8–11, 24, 176–78; Basque, 281, 287, 296; Chinese, 520, 527; European, 8–10, 98, 177–78; Irish, 11, 183–84, 192; Indian, 436; Islamic, 174; national Marxism, 3, 12, 14, 104, 184–86; Philippines, 11, 99–105, 118, 123, 125, 184–88; and the state, 6, 7–8, 174, 188, 191

National Women's Studies Association (USA), 317

Native American(s), 303, 319; American Indian Movement, AIM (USA) 306; women, 316, 317

Native American Women's Health Project (USA), 317

Negri, Antonio, 403–4, 419

Negt, Oscar, 280

Nehru, Jawaharlal, 163

New People's Army, NPA (Philippines), 185

Newly Industrializing Countries (NICs), 67. *See also* Hong Kong, Singapore, South Korea, Taiwan

Newtonian Science, 36–39

Ng, Fae Myenne: *Bone,* 366–68

Nicaragua, 15, 24, 26, 132–66 passim

Nietzsche, Friedrich, 125, 473, 479

Nkrumah, Kwame, 229, 237, 242, 244–45

CONTRIBUTORS

TANI E. BARLOW is a historian of modern China who teaches in the Women's Studies Department at the University of Washington. She is editor and cotranslator with Gary Bjorge of *I Myself Am a Woman: Selected Writings of Ding Ling,* editor and contributor with Angela Zito of *Body, Subject and Power in China,* editor of *Gender Politics in Modern China: Writing and Feminism,* and editor and contributor to *Formations of Colonial Modernity in East Asia.* She is the editor of *positions: east asia cultures critique.*

NANDI BHATIA is Assistant Professor of English at the University of Western Ontario. She has published essays on colonialism and imperialism in Kipling's *Kim* and Jean Renoir's film, *The River,* and on twentieth-century Hindi literature. She is currently working on a book-length study of political theater in colonial and postcolonial India.

DIPESH CHAKRABARTY is a founding member of the Subaltern Studies collective and teaches South Asian studies in the Department of History at the University of Chicago. He is the author of *Rethinking Working-Class History: Bengal 1890–1940* and many pivotal essays on subaltern studies and postcoloniality that have appeared in *Representations, History Workshop, positions: east asia cultures critique,* and other journals.

CHUNGMOO CHOI teaches culture theories, colonialism and postcoloniality, feminism of color, and Korean literature at the University of California at Irvine. Her book, *Frost in May: Decolonization and Culture in South Korea* (Duke University Press), is forthcoming. She is also an editor of *Nationalism and Korean Women* (Routledge, forthcoming) and a special issue of *positions: east asia cultures critique* on politics and history of "comfort women."

CLARA CONNOLLY and PRAGNA PATEL are currently studying law at the University of Westminster in London. They continue to work with *Women Against Fundamentalism,* BM Box 2706, London WCI 3XX.

ANGELA DAVIS is Professor in the Board of Studies in the History of Consciousness at the University of California, Santa Cruz. Her articles and essays have appeared in numerous journals and anthologies, both scholarly and popular. She is the author of five books, including *Angela Davis: An Autobiography; Women, Race and Class;* and the forthcoming *Blues, Legacies, and Black Feminism: Gertrude "Ma" Rainey, Bessie Smith, and Billie Holiday.* Currently she is conducting research on incarcerated women and alternatives to imprisonment, which will be the subject of her next book.

ARTURO ESCOBAR was born and grew up in Colombia. His main areas of interest are the anthropology of development, social movements, and the environment. He has been doing research on the Pacific coast of Colombia since the early 1990s, focusing on the political strategies for cultural affirmation, biodiversity conservation, and alternative development advanced by the region's social movements. He is currently Associate Professor of Anthropology at the University of Massachusetts, Amherst, and is the author of *Encountering Development: The Making and Unmaking of the Third World*.

GRANT FARRED is Assistant Professor of English and Comparative Literature at the University of Michigan, Ann Arbor. He is editor of *Rethinking C. L. R. James* and has published in journals such as *Social Text, Genders,* and *Alphabet City*.

HOMA HOODFAR is Associate Professor in the Department of Sociology and Anthropology at Concordia University in Montreal. She received a Ph.D. in social anthropology at the University of Kent in Canterbury and has conducted extensive fieldwork in Cairo, Tehran, and Montreal. Her work has appeared in academic journals and grassroots activist magazines. Her most recent publications are *Between Marriage and the Market: Intimate Politics and Survival in Cairo* and *Development, Change, and Gender in Cairo,* edited with Diane Singerman.

REYNALDO C. ILETO is Reader in Asian History at the Australian National University. He is the author of *Pasyon and Revolution: Popular Movements in the Philippines, 1840–1910* and "Religion and Anticolonial Movements" in the *Cambridge History of Southeast Asia*. He is currently working on American colonial representations of the Philippines.

GEORGE LIPSITZ teaches in the Department of Ethnic Studies at the University of California, San Diego. He is the author of *Dangerous Crossroads, Rainbow at Midnight, Sidewalks of St. Louis, Time Passages,* and *A Life in the Struggle: Ivory Perry and the Culture of Opposition*. His current research concerns the racialization of space in U.S. cities since the 1970s.

DAVID LLOYD is Hartley Burr Alexander Chair in Humanities at Scripps College, Claremont. He is the author of *Nationalism and Minor Literature: James Clarence Mangan and the Emergence of Irish Cultural Nationalism* and *Anomalous States: Irish Writing and the Postcolonial Moment*. He coedited with Abdul JanMohamed *The Nature and Context of Minority Discourse*.

LISA LOWE is Professor of Comparative Literature at the University of California, San Diego. She is the author of *Critical Terrains: French and British Orientalisms* and *Immigrant Acts: On Asian American Cultural Politics* and coeditor with Elaine Kim of *New Formations, New Questions: Asian American Studies,* a special issue of *positions: east asian cultures critique*.

MARTIN F. MANALANSAN IV is an anthropologist who was born and raised in Manila, Philippines. He is presently Director of Education at the Asian and Pacific Islander Coalition of HIV/AIDS, Inc., and AIDS service agency in New York City. He has published articles in several anthologies and journals, including *positions: east asian cultures critique, Amerasia,* and *GLQ*. He is currently editing an anthology of ethnographic studies of Asian American communities and completing a manuscript entitled "Exhuming the Nation: Death, Gender and Diaspora in the Filipino Imaginary."

AIHWA ONG is Associate Professor of Anthropology at Berkeley. She is the author of *Spirits of Resistance and Capitalist Discipline* and coeditor of *Bewitching Women, Pious Men: Gender and Body Politics in Southeast Asia* and *Ungrounded Empires: The Cultural Politics of Modern Chinese Transnationalism.*

MARÍA JOSEFINA SALDAÑA-PORTILLO is Assistant Professor in the English Department at Brown University. She is currently working on a manuscript considering the intersection between the discourse of national development and the constructions of revolutionary subjectivity and change that emerged in response to post–WWII neocolonial relations in the United States, Nicaragua, Guatemala, and southern Mexico. She has recently published "Regarding Myself: Menchú's Autobiographical Renderings of the Authentic Other," in *Socialist Review* 94, nos. 1–2 (1995).

JOSÉ RABASA teaches in the Department of Romance Languages and Literatures at the University of Michigan. He is the author of *Inventing America: Spanish Historiography and the Formation of Eurocentricism* and editor with Javier Sanjinés and Robert Carr of *Subaltern Studies in the Americas,* a special issue of *Dispositio/n.*

JACQUELINE URLA is Associate Professor of Anthropology at the University of Massachusetts at Amherst. She is the author of several articles on Basque language politics and coeditor of *Deviant Bodies: Critical Perspectives on Difference in Science and Popular Culture,* and is currently finishing a book entitled *Being Basque, Speaking Basque: Language Revival and Cultural Politics in the Post-Franco Era.*

Library of Congress Cataloging-in-Publication Data

The politics of culture in the shadow of capital /

edited by Lisa Lowe and David Lloyd.

p. cm.

Includes bibliographical references and index.

ISBN 0-8223-2033-9 (cloth : alk. paper). — ISBN 0-8223-2046-0
(paper : alk. paper)

1. Capitalism — Developing countries. 2. Economic development.

3. Women — Developing countries — Social conditions. I. Lowe, Lisa.

II. Lloyd, David.

HC59.72.C3W67 1997

330.12'2 — dc21   97-8900